10e

SUPERVISORY MANAGEMENT

The Art of Inspiring,
Empowering and
Developing People

MOSLEY

MOSLEY

PIETRI

Cengage

Australia • Brazil • Canada • Mexico • Singapore • United Kingdom • United States

LLF Supervisory Management: The Art of Inspiring, Empowering, and Developing People, 10e

Donald C. Mosley., Jr., Donald C. Mosley, Sr., and Paul Pietri

Senior Vice President: Erin Joyner

Product Director: Bryan Gambrel

Project Manager: Julie Dierig

Content Developer: Kayci Wyatt, MPS

Product Assistant: Rhett Ransom

Marketing Manager: Emily McLellan

Project Management and Compostion: SPi Global

Sr. Art Director: Michelle Kunkler

Text Designer: Emily Friel, Integra Software Services Pvt. Ltd

Cover Designer: Tippy McIntosh

Cover Image: Lucian BOLCA/Shutterstock.com

Intellectual Property

    Analyst: Diane Garrity

    Project Manager: Sarah Shainwald

For product information and technology assistance, contact us at
Cengage Customer & Sales Support, 1-800-354-9706 or support.cengage.com.

For permission to use material from this text or product, submit all requests online at **www.copyright.com.**

Library of Congress Control Number: 2017957881

ISBN: 978-1-337-62295-0

Cengage
200 Pier 4 Boulevard
Boston, MA 02210
USA

Cengage is a leading provider of customized learning solutions with employees residing in nearly 40 different countries and sales in more than 125 countries around the world. Find your local representative at **www.cengage.com.**

To learn more about Cengage platforms and services, register or access your online learning solution, or purchase materials for your course, visit **www.cengage.com.**

Printed in the United States of America
5 6 7 8 9   27 26 25 24 23

This edition is dedicated to Emily, Meredith, and Caroline.

Brief Contents

Contents

PART 3   Leading   156

PART 5   Controlling   392

PART 6 Managing Human Resources and Diversity 452

Preface

The goal of this tenth edition of *Supervisory Management* continues to be that of preparing students to be effective supervisors and leaders. As in the prior edition, the common thread throughout this text is that supervision is working with people to inspire, empower, and develop them so that they become better and more effective in their working roles. Although coverage is provided of the management functions of planning, organizing, staffing, and controlling, the largest number of chapters is directly devoted to leading. Seven of the text's 16 chapters are leadership focused, including a chapter solely devoted to leadership, as well as chapters on communication; motivation; group development and team building; meetings and facilitation skills; coaching for higher performance; and managing conflict, stress, and time. These all are essential supervisory leadership tools.

As authors with strong real-world consulting backgrounds, almost all of our research and consulting has involved thousands of team leaders and supervisors in many for-profit and not-for-profit organizations, including service, manufacturing, governmental, and entrepreneurial firms. We have found some of the most exemplary, creative, and exciting practices of supervision and leadership in these environments. Many of the examples in this book, including interviews, examples, and cases, are taken from our interactions with leaders in real organizations. We pass these experiences on to you, continuing to appreciate Kurt Lewin's statement that "nothing is as practical as good theory."

Like the previous edition, the tenth edition, aligns closely with the federal government's report of the Secretary's Commission on Achieving Necessary Skills (SCANS) requirements for workplace competencies. Specifically, skill-building exercises will help students develop their abilities in five key areas: identifying, organizing, planning, and allocating resources; working with others; acquiring and evaluating information; understanding complex interrelationships; and working with a variety of technologies. Additionally, the text provides students with a three-part foundation of skills and personal qualities needed for job performance. Our text was the first supervisory text to use icons in the end-of-chapter Skill Builder exercises to identify the SCANS competencies and skills targeted for development. This edition strives to maintain a workplace context and a practical emphasis throughout.

What's New in the Tenth Edition

This edition reflects a number of changes intended to keep its skills focus timely, fast paced, and relevant to the action-oriented environments facing today's supervisors.

- *Broader examples of supervisory/organizational settings.* In this edition, we have sought to provide balanced coverage of supervisory practices in the service, manufacturing, and not-for-profit sectors, in large, medium, and smaller entrepreneurial firms. For example, the Chapter 2 opening preview highlights the challenges and successes of Strategic Wealth Specialists, a growing financial services firm, while Chapter 4 focuses on leading and supervising in a merchandising retail environment—Walmart. The end-of-chapter cases provide broader coverage ranging from entrepreneurial ventures to service businesses, such as those in Chapters 3, 7, 11, and 13. Students and those who are presently supervisors reading this book will appreciate that many more of the supervisory concepts presented apply to supervisors of all organizations.

- *Significant revisions and coverage of new topics.* The challenges that supervisors face in working in today's diverse, technology-driven, and continuously changing organizational environment are emphasized throughout the book. The chapters have been updated and content rewritten to include a number of new or significantly revised topics, including leadership, employee engagement, coaching and diversity, creativity, benefits of employee mentoring, legal issues, electronic communication technology, employee training, and control techniques. The chapters have been updated with new actual organizational examples and statistics.
- *Greater emphasis on skill development.* As in previous editions, chapter-ending Skill Builder exercises enable students to cultivate much-needed abilities for the workplace. Through the use of icons, instructors and students can see how each exercise correlates to the federal government's SCANS competencies. This system helps students effectively strategize a means to developing skills in each area and achieving competency in all five SCANS competencies.
- *Diversity coverage.* Throughout this book's chapters, emphasis is placed on the challenges supervisors and leaders face in managing a workforce that is increasingly diverse. Such diversity is included throughout the text, ranging from supervisory challenges in communicating with the growing number of Hispanic workers whose English-speaking skills are limited to issues that arise when dealing with a temporary workforce. In addition to traditional coverage of diversity issues ranging from gender to ethnicity and race, this edition also examines diversity issues posed by the different generations of workers—Traditionalists, Baby Boomers, Gen X, Gen Y, and the emerging Gen Z. Numerous examples and photos in each chapter reflect the diverse nature of the supervisor's work environment.
- *Continuing Emphasis on Ethics.* Although ethics is the central topic in Chapter 3 (Decision Making, Problem Solving, and Ethics), it is a key concept that is addressed as well throughout the book.

Features of the Book

We continue to strive to make the book reader-friendly. To facilitate understanding and retention of the material presented, each chapter contains these features:

- *Learning Objectives.* Each chapter begins with a statement of Learning Objectives. Icons identifying the Learning Objectives appear throughout the text material. The Chapter Review also is organized by Learning Objectives.
- *Opening Preview Case.* An Opening Preview Case sets the stage for each chapter by illustrating one or more major topics to be covered in the chapter. This piques students' interest in the chapter. Nine of the new edition's opening cases are either updated or new. Specifics from the opening case often are referred to within the chapter to reinforce key concepts discussed.
- *Key Terms and Phrases.* New terms and phrases are highlighted as each is introduced in a chapter. Marginal notes highlight definitions when they first appear in each chapter; the end of each chapter features an alphabetical listing of all key terms.
- *Text Enhancing Exhibits/Photos.* Numerous exhibits and photos add insights into the major concepts found in each chapter. They also give the text an inviting, reader-friendly appeal. We have added new exhibits to the tenth edition. Our goal is to inject these strategically so that they enhance, rather than fragment, the chapter's continuity. Exhibits may be informational, such as Exhibit 1-11: "Changing Views of the Supervisor's Job"; skills-oriented, such as Exhibit 7-7: "Ways to Apply Expectancy Theory"; or assessment-oriented, such as Exhibit 6-15: "Rate Your Listening Habits."

- *Stop and Think.* Stop and Think questions appear several times within each chapter, allowing students to test their understanding of concepts as they learn new material. This feature also helps improve students' study routines by serving as a simplified self-study guide. Some instructors report that they use Stop and Think questions as a basis for class discussion.
- *Chapter Review, and Questions for Review and Discussion.* The Chapter Review and the Questions for Review and Discussion encourage students to reflect upon what they have read in a way that will help them better understand and learn the material. Each Chapter Review highlights answers to the Learning Objectives identified at the beginning of each chapter.
- *Skill Builder Exercises.* Skill Builder Exercises appear at the end of each chapter; each relates to the federal SCANS requirements followed by many schools. The eighth edition was the first supervisory textbook to use SCANS icons to help teachers and students easily identify the competencies targeted by each Skill Builder Exercise and ensure that students are developing skills in all five key areas. The tenth edition continues this practice.
- *Cases.* Cases located at the end of each chapter can be used to synthesize the chapter concepts and stimulate the practice of supervision. Of the book's 16 chapters, several new cases are provided in this edition.

Instructional Resources
Ancillary Material

- *Instructor's Manual.* The *Instructor's Manual* streamlines course preparation with its presentation of chapter outlines, teaching suggestions, and lecture notes correlated with the PowerPoint slides, as well as solutions to all end-of-chapter questions, Skill Builder exercises, and case questions.
- *Test Bank.* The Supervisory Management test bank is composed of multiple-choice, true/false, and essay questions. When used with the Cognero software provided on the instructor Web site, test preparation is a cinch. Instructors can add or edit questions, instructions, and answers, and can select questions by previewing them on the screen and selecting them randomly or by number. All questions have been correlated to the text's Learning Objectives to ensure students meet the course criteria.
- *PowerPoint slides.* A comprehensive set of PowerPoint slides assists instructors in the presentation of the chapter material and enables students to synthesize key concepts.

Acknowledgments

We appreciate the efforts of our publishing team at Cengage Learning, which is one of the best in the industry. From editors to sales reps, they have all been supportive and responsive to our needs and concerns. Individuals whom we would like to especially thank include Scott Person, Julie Dierig, Kayci Wyatt, Sangeetha Vijay, and Katherine Caudill.

About the Authors

DONALD (Don) C. MOSLEY JR. Don C. Mosley Jr. is Executive Director of the Melton Center for Entrepreneurship and Innovation in the Mitchell College of Business at the University of South Alabama. He received his Ph.D. in Business Administration from Mississippi State University, his Master of Business Administration from the University of South Alabama, and his Bachelor of Arts from Millsaps College.

Don first began consulting with the Synergistic Group in 1995 and has served as trainer/consultant to a variety of organizations in the private and public sectors. He has designed and implemented programs for organizations such as USA Health Systems, Baykeeper, Airbus, the City of Fairhope, the U.S. Army Corps of Engineers, the Federal Emergency Management Agency, Johnstone, Adams Law Firm, Kemira Water Solutions, Parsons Brinckerhoff, Providence Hospital, Thompson Engineering, the U.S. Navy, and the Retirement Systems of Alabama tower project.

Don teaches Management Theory and Practice, Organizational Behavior, and High Performance Organizations at the undergraduate level, as well as the doctoral seminar in Organizational Behavior. He has published in such journals as *Educational and Psychological Measurement, Journal of Applied Social Psychology, Journal of Business Research, Journal of Managerial Issues,* and *Organization Development Journal.* Don is a member of the Academy of Management Association and Southern Management Association.

Don thanks his colleague Paul, wife Emily, and daughters Meredith and Caroline for their encouragement and support.

PAUL PIETRI Paul Pietri is Emeritus Professor of Management in the Mitchell College of Business at the University of South Alabama. With extensive background as a trainer/consultant to private and public sector organizations, he has designed, administered, and conducted training at the supervisory level for organizations in 36 states and Canada, including Toshiba USA, International Paper Company, Bowater Carolina, Shell, Dupont, and the U.S. Departments of Agriculture, Labor, and Defense. Paul was one of seven U.S. representatives selected by the Center of International Studies to participate in a São Paulo, Brazil, conference designed to help Brazilian industry develop its first-line supervisors. He also helped design the curriculum for the series "Supervisory Communication," produced by Mississippi Public Television.

He has international teaching experience, having taught in Germany and France. His most meaningful consulting experience was an extended involvement to help a major U.S. manufacturer shift its culture. Over a six-year period, he logged 2,000 training hours with all managers and supervisors in the 1,500-employee firm, helping them accept and learn the new skills of empowering, developing, coaching, and facilitating.

Paul's writings reflect his training and design experiences and have appeared in such publications as *Training, Organization Development Journal, Industrial Management, Journal of Business Communication, MSU Business Topics, Annual Handbook for Consultants,* and others. He enjoys continuing to teach students in the Mitchell College of Business and supervisors and managers in training programs throughout the south.

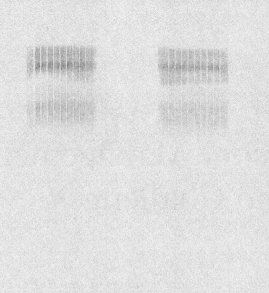

1
Supervisory Management Roles and Challenges

LEARNING OBJECTIVES

After reading and studying this chapter, you should be able to:

1. Explain why management is needed in all organizations.

2. Describe the different levels of management.

3. Discuss what managers do.

4. Explain the basic skills required for effective management.

5. Explain where supervisors come from.

6. Clarify the different relationships supervisory managers have with others.

7. Discuss the emerging position of supervisory managers.

8. Discuss some trends challenging supervisors.

Supervisors are linking pins who are members of, and link or lock together, independent groups within an organization.

—Rensis Likert

Ariel Skelley/DigitalVision/Getty Images

Many supervisors in positions like Jackie Schultz's face the common challenge of achieving results through the efforts of others.

Preview

JACKIE SCHULTZ, PANERA BREAD SUPERVISOR With sales volume of more than $5 billion, 100,000 associates, and 2,040 bakery-cafes, Panera Bread continues to outperform in the casual dining industry. With its mission statement "A loaf under every arm," CEO/owner Ronald Shaich states that the centerpiece of Panera's vision is the highest quality experience for its customers—quality ingredients, quality preparation, quality presentation, and quality service. Let's take a closer look within one of its stores to see how it happens.

Jackie Schultz joined Panera in one of its Southeast stores as an associate (as Panera employees are called) while a high school senior. A quick learner, she cross-trained for multiple associate jobs (Panera has nine areas of certification) and, within six months, was named an associate trainer. A year later, she was promoted to shift supervisor and training specialist. Her supervisory role is the focus of this case.

As one of three supervisor/managers who report to the overall store manager (Exhibit 1-1), Jackie has prime responsibility for the associates' delivery of Panera quality to the restaurant floor. Associates in Jackie's store are a diverse group: The 21 employees are mostly under 25, with the youngest being 17 and the oldest nearly 50. Thirteen of the

EXHIBIT 1-1

Partial Organization Chart for Panera Bread

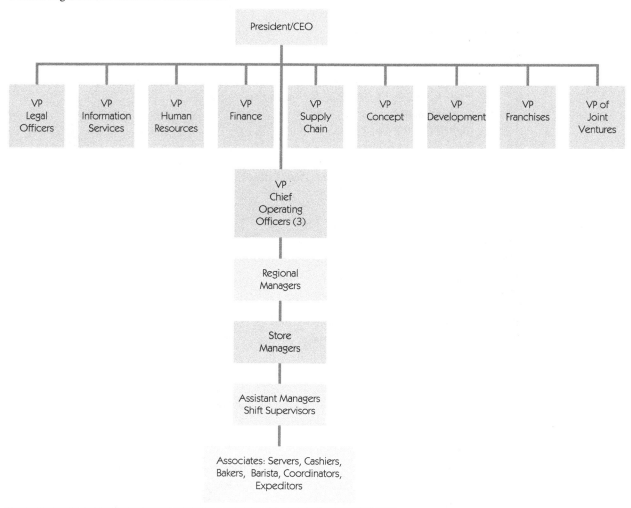

21 employees are females, 13 are white, seven are African American, and one is Asian. Twenty associates work full time (25 or more hours), one works part time, seven attend college, all are high school graduates or equivalent, and three are parents.

As a supervisor, the core of Jackie's daily job is making sure Panera's commitment to quality is reflected in her associates' job performance. To control quality, Panera has standardized procedures for all important store activities. Its stores have consistent procedures for baking, food/beverage displays, customer greeting, order taking, cashiering, handling food, preparation and placement of food on a tray, kitchen and store sanitation, cleanliness, and others. Name an activity that is related to quality within the store, and Panera has an in-place procedure to achieve it.

> *Our associates are well trained and highly motivated in keeping up their performance. The challenge comes when we're shorthanded or really busy. We often have large groups come in—tennis players participating in national/regional tournaments at local courts, or*

sometimes we get a busload of tourists or a high school group, such as cheerleaders. That's when our quality is tested. I will be right in there with my associates, on the line myself as needed, having someone redo a customer's order, clean a spill in the dining area, or bus a table. Regardless of how busy the store is, it's important for our customer's experience to be great. Greeting with a smile and making the connection is what we're about. We want to provide an everyday oasis for all of our customers.

Schultz wears a number of hats during the typical day, which is characterized by many different activities and multitasking—coordinating, communicating with, and encouraging associates; pitching in and helping on the line as needed; visiting customers; handling phone calls; meeting with a supplier or a corporate visitor; and meeting with her own general manager. Some store manager meetings may be formal, regarding such topics as new Panera policies to be relayed to associates or discussing food costs, new products, or profitability. Schultz may initiate a meeting with her own manager to get a question answered, to nominate an associate for special recognition, or to mention problems or concerns. She also spends time in her training role, encouraging and helping associates cross-train for certification in different associate jobs, as this is one objective that upper management has for each store. The certification system is completed by associates online, in the store. "I encourage my associates to be certified in as many areas as they can, as it helps them understand the whole store concept, which makes them more valuable, and, in fact, earns them more money." Jackie's certification in all nine store areas enhances her own credibility as a supervisor.

Recognition plays an important part in associates' buy-in to the Panera concept. There are formal recognition forms, such as a hat pin for reaching certification, formal "Wow" recognition by the store manager for special performance, and recognition with gift certificates at the three or four meetings attended by all employees, called "Bread Bashes." Schultz believes strongly in giving praise and recognition on her shift, especially when she sees someone doing something special.

I'm really big on verbal praise. It might be a "Thank you for helping that couple," to praise for an associate who without being asked brings an elderly couple's food to their table, or a "Wow, I loved the way your bakery display is so clean, organized, and has a waterfall effect." Recognition is especially important for new associates. I'm glad that I was an associate before I went into management. I know where they're coming from, what they appreciate, and how different everyone is. For example, I understand associates' different learning styles, such as visual, auditory, and hands-on. Visual learners can pick things up from a computer screen or out of a book of drawings and illustrations. To others you may be able to explain it, and they'll get it. Others learn best by actually doing it. It's important for a supervisor to clue into their preferences.

Looking back at how her management style has changed over the past four years, Jackie feels that she was perhaps too "soft" when she first assumed the supervisor role at age 18, and that being that young was a disadvantage. She recalls discussing with her dad the fact that associates seemed to test her authority quickly following her promotion to supervisor. He said, "Jackie, you're the youngest, you've not been there long, you're a female, you're 4'10", and you also happen to be half Asian. What do you expect?" Now she feels at ease in her role, enjoys leading others, and has no trouble being assertive as called for, as when discussing an associate's tardiness or failure to follow a procedure or even when having to give a written reprimand. Her biggest assets are her communication skills, sensitivity to others, and technical expertise.

Jackie sums up her supervisory role as similar to that of a coach/facilitator in helping associates perform at their best. Many associates have developed a special relationship with repeat customers. She states, "We've had customers send cards or gifts for special occasions to our associates, like when they've graduated, gotten married, or had a baby. Our store is a special place."[1]

This case illustrates well the many aspects of a supervisor's job and some of the major challenges that supervisors face. Note that

1. Jackie performs a broad set of duties, ranging from scheduling work, to assigning tasks, coordinating workflow, monitoring performance, training, providing recognition, and disciplining when necessary.
2. She interfaces with people from multiple groups, including her associates, fellow supervisors, manager, corporate personnel, suppliers, and customers.
3. She uses a variety of skills, including her interpersonal skills, computer expertise, and technical skills/understanding of the primary tasks performed by associates.

Jackie faces a common challenge of supervisors—obtaining results through others. In a sense, her effectiveness is determined by how successful her personnel are. One way of looking at the supervisor's job, then, is to think of it in terms of "helping your people be as good as they can be." This preview case indicates some of the many factors that affect the work of supervisors and managers at all organizational levels, such as the need for excellent communication skills, the use of technology, and recognition of workforce diversity. At no time has the job of supervision been recognized as being so important. Likewise, at no time has it been more challenging. In reading this material, you will be introduced in more depth to the roles and challenges of being a supervisor.

The Need for Management

Whenever a group of people work together in a structured situation to achieve a common objective, they form an **organization**. The organization may be a student group, a business firm, a religious group, a governmental institution, a military unit, a sports team, or a similar group. The main objective of such organizations is to produce a product or provide a service. Other organizational objectives may be to provide satisfaction to members, employment and benefits to workers, a product to the public, and/or a return to the owners of the business (usually in the form of a profit). To reach these objectives, management must perform three basic organizational activities: (1) **operations**, or producing the product or service; (2) **marketing**, or selling and distributing the product; and (3) **financing**, or providing and using funds. These activities must be performed in almost all organizations, be they large corporations or small entrepreneur shops, whether they operate for profit or not for profit.

What Is Management?

Organizations are the means by which people get things done. People can accomplish more working together than they can achieve alone, but to combine and coordinate the efforts of the members of the organization, the process of management is required. Without management, people in the group would go off and try to reach the organization's objectives independently of other group members. If small organizations lacked management, the members' efforts would be wasted. If management were absent in larger, more complex organizations, objectives would not be reached and chaos would result. In summary, *managers are needed in all types of organizations.*

Management can be defined as the process of working with and through people to achieve objectives by means of effective decision making and coordination of available resources. The basic resources of any organization are **human resources**, which are the

---

organization

A group of people working together in a structured situation for a common objective.

operations

Producing an organization's product or service.

marketing

Selling and distributing an organization's product or service.

1. Explain why management is needed in all organizations.

financing

Providing or using funds to produce and distribute an organization's product or service.

management

Working with people to achieve objectives by effective decision making and coordination of available resources.

human resources

The people an organization requires for operations.

EXHIBIT 1-2

How Management Combines the Organization's Resources into a Productive System

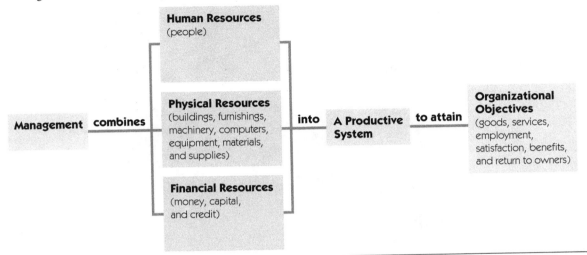

---

physical resources

Items an organization requires for operations.

financial resources

The money, capital, and credit an organization requires for operations.

people involved; **physical resources**, which include buildings, furnishings, machinery, computers, equipment, materials, and supplies; and **financial resources**, such as money, capital, and credit. Exhibit 1-2 shows *the vital task of management: combining resources and activities into a productive system to attain organizational objectives*.

Consider this situation:

Pete Bolton, entrepreneur, operates a one-person shoe repair shop. Pete performs all the necessary activities, including repairing shoes, serving customers, ordering equipment and supplies, maintaining equipment, keeping records, paying bills, and borrowing money. He does it all. Would you say that Pete is performing management?

Our position is that he is not. On the one hand, he certainly employs *physical* and *financial resources*. On the other hand, while he does interact with customers, they are not an employed resource because they do not perform work. The only *human resource* that Pete utilizes is himself. Now consider a new scenario for Pete:

Business is so good that Pete leases the adjacent office and removes the wall, creating five times more floor space for the shop. He hires four employees: Three perform shoe repairs and one is a counter clerk/repairer. Whereas in the first situation he was a doer, performing all activities himself, in the second situation Pete must manage, guide, and direct others who perform tasks. The skills required for Pete to perform successfully in the new situation differ markedly from those required in the first. Pete must now perform "management."

This simple example explains why many individuals perform successfully in nonmanagement positions such as entrepreneurs, technicians, operators, and professionals but often fail when placed in positions of supervision. The material you are reading will help you succeed in the second situation!

Levels of Management

2. Describe the different levels of management.

Except in very small organizations, the different levels of management are usually based on the amount of responsibility and authority required to perform the job. Individuals at higher levels of the organization have more authority and responsibility than those at

Supervisors help their employees learn, grow, and develop so that company objectives can be reached.

authority

Given the right to act in a specified manner in order to reach organizational objectives; the right to tell others how to act to reach objectives.

responsibility

Occurs when key tasks associated with a particular job are specified. The obligation of an employee to accept a manager's delegated authority.

top management

Responsible for the entire or a major segment of the organization.

middle management

Responsible for a substantial part of the organization.

lower levels. **Authority** is the right to tell others to act or not act in order to reach objectives. **Responsibility** is the obligation that is created when an employee accepts a manager's delegated authority.

Large organizations usually have at least three levels of management, plus a level of operative employees. These levels are generally referred to as (1) *top management*, (2) *middle management*, and (3) *supervisory management*. In large organizations, there may be multiple levels of top and middle management.

STOP AND THINK

In the chapter preview, for example, note that five levels of management exist at Panera Bread. The president/CEO and vice president levels comprise top management, the regional managers and store managers comprise middle management, and supervisors comprise the supervisory management level.

Exhibit 1-3 shows that authority and responsibility increase as one moves from the nonmanagerial level into the managerial ranks and then into the higher managerial levels. The titles and designations listed are only a few of those actually used in organizations.

Although the duties and responsibilities of the various management levels vary from one organization to another, they can be summarized as follows. **Top management** is responsible for the overall operations of the entire organization or oversees a major segment of the organization or a basic organizational activity. **Middle management** is responsible for a substantial part of the organization (perhaps a program, project, division, plant, store, or department).

EXHIBIT 1-3

How Management Authority and Responsibility Increase at Higher Levels

supervisory management

Controls operations of smaller organizational units.

Finally, **supervisory management** has control over the operations of a smaller organizational unit (such as a production line, operating unit, office, or laboratory). Managers in this last group, such as Jackie Schultz of Panera Bread (see chapter preview), are in charge of nonmanagerial or rank-and-file employees, and are the managers with whom most employees interact.

Our focus is primarily upon the first level of managers, who may be called *supervisory managers* or simply *supervisors*. This group is the organization's primary link with most of its employees. A recent Gallup study found managers are responsible for "at least 70% of the variance in employee engagement."[2] Another study of 17,000 federal agency employees concluded that "frontline supervisors" are important determinants of federal agency performance: "they are key figures in building and sustaining an organization culture that promotes high performance and they influence many factors of agency performance and effectiveness."[3] In some organizations, the term "team leader" may be used interchangeably with "first-line supervisor." In other organizations, it refers to a position quite different from that of a supervisor. For example, in organizations that use self-directed work teams, the work team itself performs many functions considered "supervisory" or "managerial," such as planning, scheduling, and evaluating its own work, and assigning tasks to members. "The team leader of such a group is a working team member who facilitates the team's effectiveness by encouraging members, helping resolve problems, scheduling and leading team meetings, serving as the team's spokesperson with other organizational groups, and so on. Although these types of team leaders lack the formal authority of a traditional supervisor, their roles are similar in many ways."[4]

What Do Managers Do?

It is now time to see what managers do that makes them so necessary to an organization's success. We first examine the functions managers perform, and then look at some roles managers play. Note at this point that not all managers spend the same amount of time performing each management function or playing each role.

3. *Discuss what managers do.*

managerial functions
_____

Broad classification of activities that all managers perform.

planning
_____

Selecting future courses of action and deciding how to achieve the desired results.

Functions Performed by Managers

Managerial functions are the broad classification of activities that all managers perform. There is no single, generally accepted classification of these functions, but we believe that five separate but interrelated basic functions must be performed by any manager at any level in any organization. Successful managers perform these functions effectively; unsuccessful ones do not. The functions are

1. Planning
2. Organizing
3. Staffing
4. Leading
5. Controlling

As shown in Exhibit 1-4, these functions reflect a broad range of activities.

Planning   Planning involves selecting goals and future courses of action and deciding how to achieve the desired results. It also encompasses gathering and analyzing information to make these decisions. Through planning, the manager establishes goals and objectives and determines methods of attaining them. All other basic managerial functions depend on planning because it is unlikely that they will be successfully carried out without sound and continuous planning.

Organizing   Deciding what activities are needed to reach goals and objectives, deciding who is to perform what task, dividing human resources into work groups, and assigning

EXHIBIT 1-4
The Management Functions in Action

PRIMARY FUNCTION	EXAMPLES
Planning	Determining resources needed Setting daily, weekly, monthly performance objectives Developing work schedules Anticipating and preparing for problems before they occur
Organizing	Making sure members understand roles and responsibilities Deciding who is best suited to perform a given task Assigning tasks to team members Coordinating members' activities
Staffing	Interviewing and selecting potential employees Securing needed training to upgrade members' skills Helping employees grow and develop through coaching, job rotation, broadening of assignments
Leading	Communicating relevant information to members Coaching, encouraging, supporting members Praising, recognizing, rewarding for work well done Building employee acceptance of change
Controlling	Observing and monitoring employee performance Ensuring employee compliance with standards, procedures, rules Identifying and resolving crises, problems that occur Following up to ensure implementation of decisions

organizing

Deciding what activities are needed to reach goals and dividing human resources into work groups to achieve them.

staffing

Recruiting, training, promoting, and rewarding people to do the organization's work.

leading

Guiding, influencing, and motivating employees in the performance of their duties and responsibilities.

controlling

Comparing actual performance with planned action and taking corrective action if needed.

roles

Parts played by managers in the performance of their functions.

each group to a manager are tasks that make up the **organizing** function. Another aspect of organizing is bringing together the physical, financial, and human resources needed to achieve the organization's objectives.

Staffing The process of recruiting, selecting, training, developing, promoting, and paying and rewarding people to do the organization's work is called **staffing**. This basic function is sometimes regarded as a part of the organizing function, but we think it is important enough to be considered separately.

Leading The **leading** function involves guiding, influencing, and motivating employees in the performance of their duties and responsibilities. It consists of coaching and empowering employees, facilitating their activities, communicating ideas and instructions, and motivating employees to perform their work efficiently. Typically, middle managers and supervisory managers spend a larger proportion of their time in leading—that is, "working with their people directly"—than do top managers.

Controlling The **controlling** function involves comparing actual performance with planned standards and taking corrective action, if needed, to ensure that objectives are achieved. Control can be achieved only by setting up standards of performance, checking to see whether they have been achieved, and then doing what is necessary to bring actual performance in line with planned performance. This function must be executed successfully to ensure that the other management functions are effectively performed.

How the Functions Are Related

Although the five management functions must be performed by managers in all types of organizations and at all management levels, they may be performed in different ways and given different emphasis by various managers. One or more functions may be stressed over another at a particular level. For example, planning is done most often by top management, and leading and controlling are common among supervisory managers. Yet the functions are interrelated, interactive, and interdependent, as shown in Exhibit 1-5. Although they may be performed in any order, the functions tend to be performed in the sequence indicated by the numbers in the exhibit.

Roles Played by Managers

The preceding discussion of the management functions might lead you to believe that the manager's job is orderly, well organized, systematic, and harmonious, but this is just not so. In performing these functions, managers engage in a great many varied, disorganized, fragmented, and often unrelated activities. These activities may last for a very short time or may extend over a longer period.

In carrying out these activities, managers play **roles** as if they were actors, and these roles change rapidly and frequently. A landmark management study identifies 10 roles, grouped as follows: (1) interpersonal roles, (2) informational roles, and (3) decision-making roles.[5] Exhibit 1-6 shows how each might be carried out by a supervisor like Jackie Schultz (chapter preview).

Like managerial functions, these roles are given varying degrees of emphasis by managers in different organizations and at different levels in the same organization. Managers vary in how they interpret the roles, the time they devote to them, and the importance they assign to them. With training and experience, supervisors can learn to perform these duties effectively.

EXHIBIT 1-5

How the Management Functions Are Related

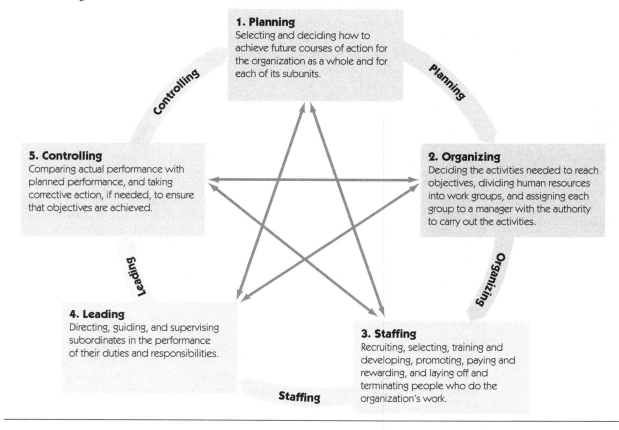

1. Planning
Selecting and deciding how to achieve future courses of action for the organization as a whole and for each of its subunits.

2. Organizing
Deciding the activities needed to reach objectives, dividing human resources into work groups, and assigning each group to a manager with the authority to carry out the activities.

3. Staffing
Recruiting, selecting, training and developing, promoting, paying and rewarding, and laying off and terminating people who do the organization's work.

4. Leading
Directing, guiding, and supervising subordinates in the performance of their duties and responsibilities.

5. Controlling
Comparing actual performance with planned performance, and taking corrective action, if needed, to ensure that objectives are achieved.

Skills Required for Effective Management

4. *Explain the basic skills required for effective management.*

You may be wondering at this point what basic skills managers need to perform the managerial functions and play the managerial roles most effectively. Although many skills are needed, a few of the most common ones are as follows:

1. Conceptual skills
2. Human relations skills
3. Administrative skills
4. Technical skills

The relative importance of these skills varies according to the type of industry in which managers work, the organization to which they belong, their level in the managerial ranks, the job being performed, and the employees being managed. Exhibit 1-7 shows an estimate of the relative importance of these skills at different management levels.

Conceptual Skills

conceptual skills

Mental ability to become aware of and identify relationships among different pieces of information.

Conceptual skills involve the ability to acquire, analyze, and interpret information in a logical manner. All managers need to understand the environments in which they operate, as well as the effects of changes in those environments on their organization. In other

EXHIBIT 1-6

Roles Played by Managers

ROLE	WHAT IS INVOLVED	EXAMPLES
INTERPERSONAL ROLES		
Figurehead	Representing the unit as its symbolic head.	Greeting department visitors; attending meetings and ceremonies; representing company on community boards.
Leader	Helping personnel reach organizational and personal goals.	Motivating, encouraging, supporting associates; providing feedback about performance; building morale.
Liaison	Maintaining relationships between the unit and outsiders.	Meeting with departmental heads, supervisors, suppliers, and customers.
INFORMATIONAL ROLES		
Monitor	Seeking out useful information that is especially relevant for the unit/organization.	Attending professional meetings; learning about forthcoming changes.
Disseminator	Providing relevant information to appropriate organization members.	Routing reports and information to employees and others; copying departmental head on memos sent to employees.
Spokesperson	Representing employees to supervisors and vice versa; representing the unit to others.	Representing the department at weekly meetings; speaking out against changes that adversely affect employees.
DECISION-MAKING ROLES		
Entrepreneur	Tackling problems; seeking changes to improve unit.	Introducing new equipment; encouraging improved methods; promoting innovation by employees; taking risks.
Disturbance handler	Responding to crises/problems that arise.	Resolving employee conflicts; soothing employees' resistance to change.
Resource allocator	Allocating the unit's resources.	Preparing a budget; deciding which associates receive new equipment, which are offered overtime work.
Negotiator	Negotiating differences with employees, managers, and outsiders.	Negotiating with a difficult customer; bargaining for favorable terms with employees, other departments, own department head, and others; getting better terms from a supplier.

Source: "Roles Played by Managers" adapted from *The Nature of Managerial Work* by Henry Mintzberg. Copyright © 1973 by Henry Mintzberg. Reprinted by permission of Henry Mintzberg.

STOP AND THINK

Which roles are being performed when Jackie Schultz of Panera Bread (see chapter preview) performs each of the following tasks?

1. Visits a competitor store, Atlanta Bread Company, to observe its operations.
2. Reconciles a situation with a customer who is unhappy with his meal/service.
3. Meets with store manager to voice her and her associates' disapproval of a new policy regarding overtime pay.
4. Compliments an associate for special service to a customer.

HISTORICAL INSIGHT

Taylor's "Scientific Management" and Fayol's "Management Principles"

Historically, evidence of early management practice is easy to find. It was required to organize and build the Roman Empire and other civilizations. China's Great Wall, Egypt's pyramids, and other massive architectural feats stand today as concrete examples of successful management. The same can be said of the great amount of planning and organization required in building massive, effective organizations, including governments, religious institutions, and armies.

Early approaches to managing consisted primarily of trial and error. Businesses were small, entrepreneurial ventures with personal oversight by owners or foremen, each of whom achieved efficiency in his or her own most effective way. In the mid-1800s, the advent of the factory system changed that approach. Inventions of machinery and tools caused production to shift from "made by hand" to "made by machine" and enabled mass production. In the United States, the expansion of transportation (railroads) and communications (telegraph, telephone, and postal systems), the

development of Western frontiers, and the building of mechanized plants created larger organizations and the need for more systematic management. It was during this changing of the organizational landscape toward larger organizations in both the United States and Europe that two key figures, American Frederick W. Taylor (1856–1915) and Frenchman Henri Fayol (1841–1925), began careers that would lead them to be considered major pioneers in management. Both were engineers, but their careers focused on two distinct management areas: Taylor at the operating level, Fayol at the executive level.

Taylor and Scientific Management. Taylor's business career took him through positions of physical laborer, foreman, head engineer, and private consultant until his death in 1915 at age 59. It was during his work at Midvale Steel, a large Philadelphia foundry, and later at Bethlehem Steel that he began to research ways to improve efficiency. Operating in a production

Taylor and Fayol were pioneers in the study of management in early 20th-century mass production work environments like this 1917 Detroit aircraft factory.

environment with few substantiated "rules of thumb," Taylor systematically conducted numerous experiments involving efficiency. These included time study; determining physical weight loads that workers could efficiently handle during a day; efficiencies of equipment, such as optimum shovel head size; and many others. His theme was that through proper work methods, workers could produce more work while earning higher pay, benefiting both employers and workers. Taylor's systematic approach was called "Scientific Management," and through papers presented at professional meetings and word of successful applications, his system gained much recognition. He was elected head of the prestigious American Society of Mechanical Engineers, became a consultant, taught courses at Harvard, and traveled extensively, presenting his new gospel of efficiency. He spawned a number of other "efficiency" associates who themselves gained national popularity, including Carl Barth (inventor of the slide rule), Frank Gilbreth (motion study), and Henry Gantt (production charts).

Taylor's books, *Shop Management* and *Principles of Scientific Management*, laid the groundwork for his system. His "Scientific Management" distinctly shaped management practice during the critical period when American industry was shifting from smaller, manager-owner firms to larger-scale operations. Ford Motor Company, for example, used Taylor's ideas in building its Highland Park, Michigan, plant, which opened in 1910.

Fayol and Management Principles. Like Taylor, Frenchman Henri Fayol began his career in technical work when, following his graduation as a mining engineer, he joined a large iron mining/foundry operation, Commentary-Fourchambault, in 1860. Earning a reputation for developing ways to fight underground fires, Fayol was promoted to several management positions and, in 1888, was named managing director, today's equivalent of CEO. When he took over, the company was in severe financial straits and its key mineral/ore deposits severely depleted. Fayol succeeded in turning the company's fortunes around. It was during his long experience as a top manager of a full-scale, fully integrated enterprise of 9,000 employees that Fayol developed his ideas about management. Unlike Taylor's operational focus, Fayol built a theory of management from the perspective of an executive. He felt that management was sufficiently important that it should be studied and theories developed; then, this being done, it could be taught and studied in universities. The body of management theory he developed included "principles" of management, including principles for planning, organizing, staffing, and controlling. He felt that all managers in all organizations must perform certain basic management functions, very similar to the functions just presented in this chapter.

Like Taylor, Fayol was a writer and paper presenter at meetings. His major work, *General and Industrial Management*, was published in 1916, nine years before his death in 1925. Unfortunately, it was not until the 1940s that an English translation of his book would lead to proper recognition of his work in the United States. Many of Fayol's ideas form the framework for contemporary management theory, most notably those dealing with the planning and organizing functions.

Sources: Frederick W. Taylor, *The Principles of Scientific Management* (New York and London: Harper and Brothers, 1911); Henri Fayol, General and Industrial Management, trans. Constance Storrs (New York: Pitman, 1949; originally published in French, 1916); Daniel Wren, The Evolution of Management Thought, 3rd ed. (New York: John Wiley and Sons, 1987), especially Chapters 7, 11, and 12, which discuss Taylor, and Chapter 10, which discusses Fayol.

words, managers should be able to "see the big picture." Top managers particularly need strong conceptual skills because changes affecting the organization tend to be more important at their level than at other managerial levels. About one-third of their time is spent using conceptual skills.

Human Relations Skills

human relations skills

Understanding other people and interacting effectively.

Human relations skills consist of the abilities to understand other people and to interact effectively with them. These skills are most needed in performing the leading function because they involve communicating with, motivating, leading, coaching, empowering, and facilitating employees, as well as relating to other people. These skills are important in dealing not only with individuals, but also with people in groups and even with relationships among groups. These skills are important to managers at all levels, but especially to supervisory managers, who spend almost one-half of their time using human relations skills.

EXHIBIT 1-7

The Relative Importance of Managerial Skills at Different Managerial Levels

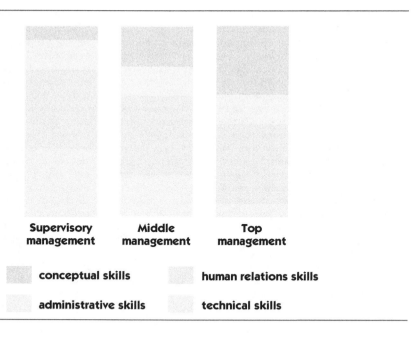

Supervisory management   **Middle management**   **Top management**

conceptual skills   human relations skills

administrative skills   technical skills

Recall that Jackie Schultz (chapter preview) considered her human relations skills to be one of her biggest strengths as a supervisor.

Administrative Skills

administrative skills

Establishing and following procedures to process paperwork in an orderly manner.

Administrative skills are the skills that permit managers to use their other skills effectively in performing the managerial functions. These skills include the ability to establish and follow policies and procedures and to process paperwork in an orderly manner. By lending *coordination*, *order*, and *movement* to tasks, administrative skills underlie the ability some people have to "make things happen" and "get things done." These skills are very similar to those possessed by good students, who are well organized and get things done efficiently.

Technical Skills

technical skills

Understanding and being able to supervise effectively specific processes required.

Technical skills include understanding and being able to supervise effectively the specific processes, practices, or techniques required to perform specific duties. Technical skills are more important for supervisors than for top managers because supervisors are closer to the actual work being performed. They must often tell—or even show—employees how to perform a job, as well as know when it is done properly.

A head nurse in a hospital, for example, must have some degree of technical understanding of proper equipment use, nursing procedures, medication, chart maintenance, and other important aspects of a nurse's job. We are not saying that the head nurse or any other supervisor must necessarily be a technical expert, but that a supervisor needs a basic understanding of the work being done to perform the managerial functions and roles effectively.

The four skills we have just discussed form the basis for a wide variety of important management actions. For example, effective time management requires *conceptual* and *administrative* skills to prioritize activities and efficiently dispose of required paperwork; being an effective trainer requires the *technical* skills or an understanding of the subject matter and the *human relations* skills of being sensitive and able to communicate

Supervisors often use both their human relations and their technical skills in discussions with employees.

emotional intelligence (EI)

The capacity to recognize and accurately perceive one's own and others' emotions, to understand the significance of these emotions, and to influence one's actions based on this analysis; an assortment of skills and characteristics that influence a person's ability to succeed as a leader.

effectively with a trainee; political know-how requires *conceptual* and *human relations* skills to identify the potential implications of actions and to build strategic relationships.

More recently, the concept of *emotional intelligence* has become a popular way to view a specialized skill set involving people's emotions. It involves use of both conceptual and human relations skills. **Emotional intelligence, or EI** as it is often referred to, is the capacity to recognize and accurately perceive one's own and others' emotions, to understand the significance of these emotions, and to influence one's actions based on this analysis. Examples of emotional intelligence might be controlling one's anger when under duress, reading an employee's facial expressions and body language as expressions of disappointment or anger, or perhaps ending a team meeting because of diminished energy/interest by participants. Studies of emotional intelligence have linked it with leadership success. You will learn more about emotional intelligence in Chapter 6.[6]

In summary, effective supervisory management requires all of the skills—conceptual, human relations, administrative, and technical. The appropriate mix, however, depends on the level of management and the circumstances surrounding the managerial situation.

STOP AND THINK

Which of the four skills are reflected when a supervisor performs these tasks?

1. Prepares a to-do list for next week.
2. Completes paperwork required for an employee to attend a training seminar.
3. Conducts a weekly performance review meeting with a new employee.
4. Completes her unit's daily performance report.

The Transition: Where Supervisors Come From

5. *Explain where supervisors come from.*

Each year, several hundred thousand nonmanagers become supervisors or managers. Skilled operators or technicians become supervisors, teachers become principals, ministers become pastors, nurses become head nurses, and salespeople become sales managers. Most of these positions are filled by current employees.

Internal promotions make sense for at least three reasons. First, an inside candidate understands the organization and its culture. In addition, if promoted within the same department, he or she will know the tasks required, the personnel, fellow supervisors, and likely the new boss. Second, management has firsthand knowledge of the employee's record of accomplishment and can use this as a predictor of success. Third, to promote someone internally serves as a reward and as an incentive for those employees who have an interest in management and demonstrate management potential.

Unfortunately, organizations commonly make two crucial mistakes when selecting supervisors. One is to automatically select the best present performer. Although the best performer may have excellent technical skills, as you saw earlier, other skills, especially human relations skills, are also important.[7] Frequently, outstanding technical performers have unreasonably high expectations or little patience with nonproducers. Moreover, they may find it difficult to let go of their old positions, at which they were so good. Instead, they continue to perform their unit's operating work, neglecting the supervisory responsibilities of their position.

One of the authors was scheduled to interview a maintenance supervisor of a large paper manufacturer. His assistant informed the author that he was running late for the interview because of an equipment breakdown. An hour or so later he entered the office, sleeves rolled up, with grease covering his hands. "Sorry about missing the appointment; I'll be right with you after I wash up," he said. The author learned from this supervisor's crew that for this supervisor, almost every breakdown was a "major one." He micromanaged, insisted on being notified of every development, and continually took over his technicians' jobs, especially the most challenging ones. His crew members had little opportunity for skill development and little initiative. As one stated, "Our best work is done when he [the supervisor] is out of the plant, like on vacation." Note in Exhibit 1-8 that micromanagement/failure to delegate is one of the primary reasons supervisors/managers fail.

Another crucial mistake made by organizations stems from inadequately preparing the employee to assume a supervisory position. Unfortunately, it is common to hear a supervisor say that the transition to supervisor went like this: "When I left work on Friday, I was a lab technician. With absolutely no training or warning, on Monday morning I learned I was a lab supervisor." Ideally, an organization should take great care when identifying potential candidates for supervisory positions and, once candidates are chosen, should help new supervisors make the transition. Before a permanent position is assigned, promising potential supervisors can be identified, assessed, and trained. Thus, such candidates may fill in as temporary supervisors when the supervisor is absent because of illness or vacation or may occupy a "lead" position that actually entails some supervisory responsibility. Fortunately, organizations are doing a much better job nowadays of identifying people with supervisory potential and preparing them through appropriate training to help them make a successful transition.

Supervisory Relationships

6. *Clarify the different relationships supervisory managers have with others.*

If we are to understand the role of supervisory managers in organizations, we must look at some of the relationships they have with different individuals and groups. For example, supervisors are legally a part of management and interact upward with other members of management. However, they are often not accepted as peers by those managers, who come from outside the organization—usually with more education—and have higher social

EXHIBIT 1-8
Why Supervisors and
Managers Fail

There are many reasons why supervisors and managers fail to be effective. Formal research about manager failure has focused on "derailment," referring to managers selected by their organizations for a rapid advancement but who don't make the grade. Typically, it is people issues, such as items 1 and 2 below, that bring them down. In our own experiences in conducting manager/supervisor training workshops, we typically ask attendees to identify bosses they've had who have been ineffective. The list below shows common reasons given.

Ten Reasons Supervisors/Managers Fail

1. Insensitive to others; dominating, intimidating, bullying style.
2. Feeling of superiority; arrogant, cold, indifferent to employees.
3. Unwilling to listen.
4. Unable to get people to work as a team.
5. Betrayal of team's trust—deceptive, untruthful, manipulative.
6. Micromanagement; failure to delegate.
7. Out for self; overly political, not sharing credit, pushing one's own career.
8. Too nonassertive; hands-off; won't address performance problems/issues.
9. Lack of technical skill/understanding.
10. Boss-related issues; unable to get along, overdependence, unwilling to disagree.

Sources: Also see Robert D. Ramsey, "The Most Important Skills for Today's Supervisors," *Supervision*, November 2007, pp. 3–6; Chuck Williams, *Management* (Mason, OH: Thomson South-Western, 2008), pp. 14–15; E. Van Velsor and J. Brittain, "Why Executives Derail: Perspectives across Time and Cultures," *Academy of Management Executive*, November 1995, pp. 62–72.

status and position. Before their promotion, supervisors typically worked as peers with those they now supervise.

The three major types of relationships that supervisors have, as shown in Exhibit 1-9, are (1) personal, (2) organizational, and (3) external. These comprise the supervisor's **relationships network**, the major individuals and groups with whom the supervisor interacts.[8]

**relationships
network**

The major individuals
and groups with
whom the supervisor
interacts.

Personal Relationships

At one time, it was believed that managers and employees left their personal problems at home when they entered the workplace. We now recognize that people bring their problems—as well as their pleasures—to their jobs. Supervisors' relationships with their families and their friends determine their attitudes and frame of mind as they perform managerial duties. Their attitudes, in turn, influence the relationships they have with other people, both inside and outside the organization.

Organizational Relationships

Within the organization, supervisory managers have varied and often conflicting relationships with several organizational entities. As shown in Exhibit 1-10, these are the supervisor's employees, the supervisor's peer group supervisors, the union steward (if the company is unionized), and the supervisor's managers.

Supervisor-to-Employee Relationships   Supervisory managers must relate to their own employees and to people from other units who perform some type of service for them. As Exhibit 1-10 illustrates, a manager-to-employee relationship exists where the supervisor facilitates and directs nonmanagerial personnel.

Relationships with Peer Supervisors and Union Steward   There are essentially two sets of horizontal relationships: those with other supervisory managers and those with the union steward or other representative(s) of the employees. Supervisors need the feeling of support and reinforcement that comes from associating with other supervisors who are considered their equals or peers. Yet the relationship can result in competition or even conflict if they seek to be promoted to the same job at the next higher level.

EXHIBIT 1-9

The Supervisor's Network of Relationships

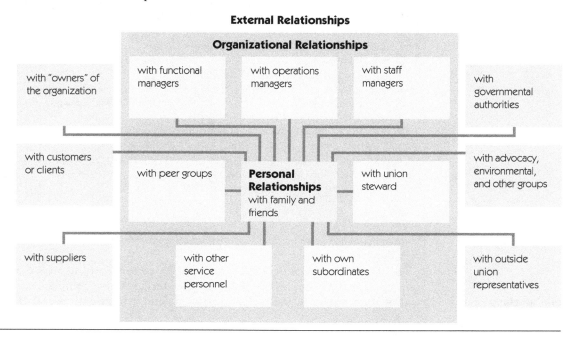

EXHIBIT 1-10

The Flow of Supervisors' Organizational Relationships

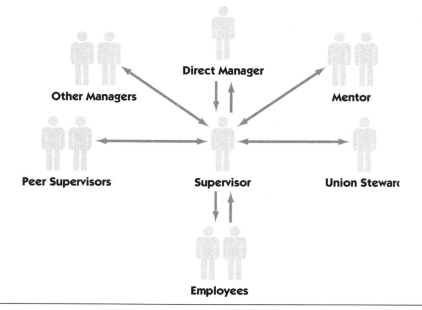

union steward

A union member elected by other members to represent their interests in relations with management.

In a unionized organization, employees select a **union steward** to represent them in their dealings with management. Although the steward is a supervisor's peer—legally, if not organizationally—he or she does represent the supervisor's employees. Therefore, the association between the supervisor and the union steward may be competitive or even combative. This association provides supervisors with a challenge but also can be frustrating. For example, a supervisor will probably attempt to motivate employees to improve productivity, whereas a union steward may encourage them to maintain the status quo for fear that their jobs will be eliminated.

Supervisor-to-Manager Relationships Supervisors have a *reverse* manager-to-employee relationship with their immediate manager. As a result of downsizing, reengineering, empowering, and similar new managerial approaches, this relationship is being upgraded. In addition to a supervisor's direct manager, staff managers in other departments, such as legal and research, also may tell supervisors what to do. Functional executives, such as the controller and the human resource manager, also may interact with supervisors in handling certain activities. Often, supervisors have an upper manager who serves as **mentor** and acts as advocate, teacher, and advice giver.

mentor

An experienced manager who acts as an advocate and teacher for a younger, less-experienced manager.

External Relationships Supervisory managers also must deal with people outside the organization. Some of the people who must be served or catered to are the owners of the business, customers or clients, suppliers, higher-level union representatives, governmental authorities, and leaders of environmental and advocacy groups. These relationships can be quite difficult and frustrating for supervisors, who represent their organizations but usually do not have the authority to make decisions and enforce them.

The Emerging Position of Supervisory Managers

7. Discuss the emerging position of supervisory managers.

Peter Drucker, world-renowned management consultant, author, and academic, correctly predicted over 30 years ago that important changes in the role of supervisors would occur as a result of organizations' quest for improved quality. He noted that top management, of necessity, would conclude that the commitment and involvement of rank-and-file employees in improving quality would make them central in leading the quality charge. The result would be greater authority or empowerment for rank-and-file employees to make key decisions on their own, including such things as planning, determining the resources needed to perform their jobs best, and interfacing directly with people who affect their job, such as customers, suppliers, and service department personnel. Under this scheme, Drucker reasoned, the supervisory role would shift. No longer would supervisors effectively manage by fear and the pressure of "my way or the highway" management. Instead, they would assume supportive, facilitating roles as leaders, teachers, and coaches.

Several other trends have fueled the shift in supervisory roles that Drucker predicted. One is the trend toward leaner organizations with fewer levels of management. Another is organizations' present commitment to helping employees at all levels grow and develop. The resulting shift in the role of supervisory managers looks like that shown in Exhibit 1-11.

STOP AND THINK

Does Jackie Schultz's style as a supervisor (see chapter preview) fit the traditional or emerging view of the supervisor's job?

EXHIBIT 1-11
Changing Views of
Supervisor's Job

TRADITIONAL VIEW OF SUPERVISOR'S JOB	EMERGING VIEW OF SUPERVISOR'S JOB
Supervisor-focused work unit	Team-focused work unit
Dominant role	Supportive role
Technical skills emphasis	Facilitation skills emphasis
Seeking stability	Encouraging change
Telling, selling skills	Listening skills
Personal responsibility for results	Shared responsibility for results
Personal problem solving	Team problem solving
Narrow, vertical communication	Broader, horizontal, external communication
Fear, pressure used to motivate employees	Pride, recognition, growth used to motivate employees
Autocratic decision style	Participative decision style

No matter what type of role supervisors play, their goals are the same—getting out production, maintaining quality, holding down costs, maintaining high morale, and otherwise serving as management's representative while also acting as a spokesperson for employees. Although the knowledge and skills required today to perform most supervisory jobs have greatly increased from, say, 35 years ago, the central objective has remained the same—to obtain quality and quantity production while maintaining good human relationships.

A study of supervisors in two plants within the same company illustrates this point.[9] One plant followed traditional organizing practices: The supervisor had authority to supervise, to determine working conditions, to plan the work and schedule it, and to control it. In the other plant, "team advisors" were used instead of supervisors, with the focus being on facilitation rather than traditional direction of the work teams. As it turned out, "exceptional" and "average" supervisors at both plants, whether they were called supervisors or team advisors, exhibited characteristic behaviors.

"Exceptional" supervisors

1. Were competent, caring, and committed both to getting the job done and to supporting their employees.
2. Pushed for high quality, provided clear direction, and motivated employees with timely, accurate feedback.
3. Willingly shared information with personnel, even if the system didn't require it.
4. Were committed to teamwork and employee participation in the department's decisions.
5. Shared skills and knowledge willingly and saw their role as one of coach rather than driver.
6. Understood what was involved beyond their own units, from the broader perspectives of the plant.
7. Took the initiative in implementing changes and new approaches.

Supervisors considered only "average" in the two differently organized plants also exhibited similar behaviors. These supervisors

1. Set narrowly defined goals and had more specific performance standards.
2. Were less attuned to the plant's overall goals and focused more narrowly on their own unit.

3. Provided less information or feedback about performance to their work groups.
4. Were less flexible, less innovative, and less willing to change.
5. Maintained tighter controls and were uncomfortable practicing participative management.

Note that the "exceptional" supervisors exhibited behaviors that were more consistent with the emerging view of the supervisor's job (Exhibit 1-11).

Some Current Trends Challenging Supervisors

8. *Discuss some trends challenging supervisors.*

As shown earlier, today's supervisors must be prepared to adjust to the many current trends that will challenge their best performance. Among the more significant of these trends are (1) dealing with a more diverse workforce, (2) emphasizing team performance, (3) coping with exploding technology, (4) adjusting to occupational and industry shifts, (5) meeting global challenges, (6) improving quality and productivity, (7) improving ethical behavior, and (8) responding to crises.

Dealing with a More Diverse Workforce

diversity

Refers to the wide range of distinguishing employee characteristics, such as sex, age, race, ethnic origin, and other factors.

Diversity refers to the wide range of characteristics that distinguish employees, such as sex, age, race, ethnic origin, and other factors. At no time in history has the U.S. workforce been so diverse, and this trend is expected to continue. Comments here focus only on broad trends regarding gender, race, ethnicity, and age.

According to the U.S. Department of Labor, in 2014, males represented 53 percent of all U.S. workers. However, the shifting U.S. population calls for decreasing numbers of males. Hispanic employment will grow substantially and is projected to represent 80 percent of the total growth in the labor force through 2050. Asian employment over that same period is expected to double in size, adding 9 million workers, and African-American employment will increase by 6.4 million. Overall, women will account for 47 percent of the total

David Joel/The Image Bank/Getty Images

More diverse work groups are becoming the norm in today's organizations.

workforce by 2024.[10] Although men and women are entering the workforce at about the same rate, men, who have been in the workforce longer, are retiring at a faster rate. Thus, like racial and ethnic minorities, women will continue to occupy many types of jobs and positions that were previously the domain of men, including supervisory and management positions.

glass ceiling

Invisible barrier that limits women from advancing in an organization.

Providing opportunities for women is particularly challenging, as there appears to be a **glass ceiling** in many organizations. These ceilings are considered invisible barriers that limit the advancement of women into higher levels of the organization. Thus, supervisors will be expected to design programs to attract and develop women and minority employees and to provide them with a full range of opportunities for growth and development, the same as they do for all other employees.

Along with changes in gender, race, and ethnicity, the workforce is aging, as is the rest of the U.S. population. Those in the 55-or-older age group made up 19.5 percent of the 2010 workforce, but their number will increase and comprise 25.2 percent by 2020. In addition to an aging workforce, one of the biggest potential challenges for today's supervisors is managing so many different generations, each with different needs, motives, and styles. For example, Baby Boomers born between 1946 and 1964 are driven and competitive, and live to work; whereas Gen X individuals, born between 1965 and 1977, are independent, skeptical, and effective relationship builders. On the other hand, Gen Y or Millenials born after 1977 are technologically savvy, prefer a work-life balance, and enjoy working in teams. Gen Z, with their own unique characteristics, are the next generation to enter the workforce. Anecdotal evidence based on one author's training and development experiences suggests that supervisors are increasingly finding their ability to blend so many different generations into a well-functioning unit is one of their greatest challenges.[11] Being able to effectively manage such diverse individuals requires greater supervisory skills than was the case with the more homogeneous work groups of past decades.

Emphasizing Team Performance

empowerment

Granting employees authority to make key decisions within their enlarged areas of responsibility.

As organizations seek to equip employees to function on their own, less direct supervision is required. This **empowerment** results in supervisors increasingly working with work groups or teams. These teams make suggestions for improvements in activities to make things run smoothly and to accomplish goals effectively.

When supervisors work with these teams, their roles are changed. No longer are they "bosses"; instead, they become leaders, facilitators, or **team advisors**, who share responsibility with the team for maintaining cost, quality, and prompt and effective delivery of products. Therefore, supervisors must provide further training to their teams to manage the production process more effectively.

team advisors

Share responsibility with team for cost, quality, and prompt delivery of products.

Coping with Exploding Technology

Most working Americans now earn their living by creating, processing, utilizing, and distributing information, and the technology revolution shows no sign of slowing. As innovations in technology have displaced thousands of workers who used different skills, new opportunities are opening up for those who have the required education, training, and temperament. Conversely, employees with outdated skills are being replaced in the workplace.

Information technologies continue to revolutionize how organizations function, affecting how tasks are performed, customers served, and people supervised.

Jackie Schultz (chapter preview) uses the Panera Bread intranet daily to access menu and product information, view her store's performance, and help train her associates. Panera's corporate software system can help forecast the number of customers based on historical data and even local weather forecasts. She uses e-mail and text messaging to communicate with her own manager and corporate personnel, in addition to associates and suppliers.

The primary effect of exploding technology on supervisors will be the need to keep personally abreast of changes that can potentially improve effectiveness, improve training of employees, and overcome employees' resistance to change. Change brings with it uncertainty, and because most people resist that which is uncertain, overcoming employee resistance to technological change becomes an increasing part of the supervisor's job.

Adjusting to Occupational and Industry Shifts

reinventing

Organizations dramatically changing such elements as their size, organizational structure, and markets.

The previously mentioned technological advancements, along with cultural and marketing changes, have resulted in shifts in occupation and industry mixes. First, emphasis on the traditional industries has declined, with a concurrent shift toward more people-related activities such as services and marketing. Along with these shifts, many organizations have been **reinventing** themselves, dramatically changing their size, organizational structure, and markets. Many of the large companies also have been **reengineering** their activities. A common reengineering approach is to ask, "If we blew this place up and started over, what would we do differently to improve cost, quality, service, or speed? What should we eliminate? What can we do that would make things easier for our customers?" Not only are manufacturing companies reengineering, but so are many service companies, such as Best Buy and Taco Bell. These and other activities resulted in another trend, called **downsizing**, in which an organization strives to become leaner and more efficient by reducing its workforce and consolidating departments and work groups.

reengineering

"It means starting over. . . . It means asking and answering this question: If I were creating this company today, given what I know and given current technology, what would it look like?" Rethinking and redesigning processes to improve dramatically cost, quality, service, and speed.

During the recession that began in 2008, downsizing became necessary as organizations adapted to the resulting decreased demand for services and products. However, organizations also downsize to become more efficient. Results often include eliminating 10 to 20 percent—or more—of a company's jobs, especially at the management level. This means that frontline workers—and their supervisors—must handle more diverse tasks, think more creatively, and assume more responsibility. On the downside, those same people must work harder and therefore are under more pressure.

In an effort by organizations to avoid health care expenses and other costs associated with maintaining a large workforce, and to aid in transitions during downsizing, temporary workers have been in much demand.[12] However, with the economic recovery under way, temporary employment figures may level off or decline as economic confidence rises.[13] Even so, supervisors face numerous challenges when integrating temporaries into their teams of permanent employees, who often view temporaries as obstructing their own overtime, commissions, or higher pay. Temporaries, knowing their assignment is only for a few days, weeks, or months, typically know little about the organization and often show little inclination to be included as team members.

downsizing

Eliminating unnecessary levels of management; striving to become leaner and more efficient by reducing the workforce and consolidating departments and work groups.

Meeting Continued Global Challenges

As business activities have become more global, those interested in supervisory management need to understand that they may have to operate in a one-world market. In fact, we estimate that up to one-half of all college graduates will work in some type of international activities in the future. Although we usually think of product exports as autos, movies, or computers, exports of financial information and other services are growing even faster.

A result of the global challenge is the large number of U.S. businesses, such as Magnavox, Wilson Sporting Goods, Uniroyal, and others, that are foreign owned. This changing ownership may lead to differing cultures and management styles, especially at supervisory levels. U.S. production facilities also have moved to Mexico, China, and other countries where low wages and high productivity lead to a competitive advantage. When supervisors move to those areas to supervise local workers, or when a foreign company acquires a domestic company, supervisors must learn to adapt to cultural differences and find ways to adjust to nontraditional styles.

Improving Quality and Productivity

No organizational theme has run deeper in the past decade than has the search for improved quality and productivity. Global competition has been the primary force behind this interest. The view of quality being embraced today reflects a comprehensive organizational approach to customer satisfaction through continuous improvement in organizational processes.[14] Almost all major firms, similar to that of Panera Bread (chapter preview), have adopted some form of quality management focus that addresses not only such processes as product design and manufacturing, but also marketing, purchasing, human resource management, and others. The supervisor, as management's direct link with employees, plays an important role in an organization's quality initiatives. It is the supervisor who is challenged to find ways to gain employee commitment to high-quality performance.

Equally important as achieving better quality is achieving improved productivity, which is a measurement of the amount of input needed to generate a given amount of output. Because productivity is the basic measurement of the efficiency of people and processes, it becomes a challenge for supervisors to improve through having people work better and smarter.

Improving Ethical Behavior

The downfall of major organizations, such as Enron, Arthur Andersen, Tyco, WorldCom, HealthSouth, Bernard L. Madoff Investment Securities, Daewoo, Lehman Brothers, AIG, and Countrywide, has dramatically called attention to the issue of organization ethics. Although the problems in these companies resulted primarily from the behaviors of upper-level managers, the vulnerability of organizations to ethical misdeeds was clearly exposed. The result is that organizations have raised the "ethics" bar for all employees and management levels—including supervisors—for a wide range of issues, not just financial ones.

AP Images/Richard Vogel

Many U.S. production facilities have relocated to other countries. This trend will likely extend into the foreseeable future and will continue to have an effect on management ideologies and style.

These include accuracy and truthfulness in reporting results, reporting employee discrimination and sexual harassment, responsibility for supporting employee development, and due vigilance in reporting what can be viewed as unethical requests and behavior by others.

In this environment, supervisors will likely continue to face **ethical dilemmas** in which they are not sure of the correct action in a given situation involving themselves or their employees.[15]

ethical dilemmas

Situations in which the supervisor is not certain of the correct behavior.

Responding to Crises

Dealing with crises—events that have a major negative or potentially negative impact on entire organizations or on individual managers or supervisors—has always been part of managerial life. Recently, however, the scope of such events has been dramatically increasing. As the first management interface with operating employees, supervisors are particularly challenged to maintain production and morale during such times.

One such crisis was the collapse of the U.S. and global credit markets in 2008 and the economic recession that followed. Major corporations were humbled, including Citibank, Merrill Lynch, Lehman Brothers, General Motors, Chrysler, Circuit City, and many others, large and small. Consider the impact on employees of the auto companies, their suppliers, and their dealerships—uncertainty as to which brands, plants, and dealerships would remain viable. Downsizings have occurred throughout many large industries and organizations, such as PepsiCo, Dow Chemical, Boeing, GE, and Disney, as well as smaller organizations. However, crises also take other forms, such as mergers and acquisitions, illegal mismanagement, and even acts of terrorism or natural disasters. The World Trade Center attacks of September 11, 2001, resulted in the indirect or direct loss of 55,000 jobs. Hurricane Katrina, which hit Louisiana, Mississippi, and Alabama in 2005, negatively affected 145,000 businesses and 2.5 million employees.[16]

Add to these extraordinary crises those associated with technological outages, equipment breakdowns, job accidents, incidents of workplace violence, and sudden loss of key suppliers/customers, and one can view the supervisor's role as increasingly one of addressing workplace crises.

Final Note: The Supervisor and Leading

In the pre-1990 years, managers who were adept at planning, organizing, staffing, and controlling—and not so effective in leading—could function effectively. Unlike the relatively stable environment then, today's management challenges make effective "leading" essential. Managers and supervisors must do more with fewer personnel, integrate more diverse team members, ask personnel to reach increasingly higher performance levels, and continuously implement change. No longer do they rely on authority as the primary means to achieve these goals, but on influence and persuasion. In short, their leadership is being tested at much higher levels than ever before, and the results have not been satisfactory, according to many critics of U.S. business, who say, "We need more leaders and fewer managers." What they really mean, given the new, dynamic environment, is that we need managers at all levels who are better at performing leadership.

As highlighted in the opening case with Jackie Schultz, supervisory leadership is essential to Panera Bread's success. One recent study conducted by *Stock Advisor*, in which they asked their investing members to rate Panera Bread based on the purchase experience and the quality of the food, found that 90 percent of respondents categorized their experience as "very good" or "amazing," while 70 percent selected "very good." In an effort to enhance the customer experience, Panera Bread has invested over $120 million in an initiative called Panera 2.0 that provides customers with digital ordering and customization options. Enhanced digital technologies in the kitchen ensure the customized orders are accurate, improving operational efficiencies. Customers can skip the lines and go directly to a "fast lane" kiosk to pick up their order. Panera 2.0 is improving the customer experience, resulting in increased satisfaction. With Panera projected to continue to grow over the next 10 to 12 years, supervisory leadership will continue to be a key indicator of its overall success.[17]

Note the title of this book: *Supervisory Management: The Art of Inspiring, Empowering, and Developing People.* While coverage is provided of the other four management functions—planning, organizing, staffing, and controlling—the largest number of chapters are devoted to leading. These include a chapter on leadership itself as well as chapters on communicating, motivating, coaching, resolving conflict, implementing change, and managing teams, all of which are essential leadership tools.

Chapter Review

1. *Explain why management is needed in all organizations.*

Management is needed whenever people form organizations. An organization is a group of people in a structured situation with a common purpose. People form organizations because they realize they can achieve more by working together than they can alone.

Management is the process of working through people to achieve objectives by making effective decisions and by coordinating the development and use of scarce human, financial, and physical resources.

2. *Describe the different levels of management.*

Large organizations usually have at least three levels of management. Top management oversees the overall operations—or a major segment of the organization or one of the basic organizational activities; middle management is responsible for a smaller part, such as a division or department; and supervisory management controls a smaller organizational unit.

3. *Discuss what managers do.*

Managers at all levels do essentially the same things, but to different degrees. First, they perform the same functions—namely, planning, organizing, staffing, leading, and controlling. In performing these functions, managers engage in many varied and often unrelated activities that require them to play different roles. In playing interpersonal roles, a manager may act as a figurehead, a leader, or a liaison between different groups. Informational roles include acting as a monitor, disseminator, and/or spokesperson. Finally, decision-making roles require the manager to be an entrepreneur, a disturbance handler, a resource allocator, and/or a negotiator.

4. *Explain the basic skills required for effective management.*

Effective managers need various skills to perform their functions and play their roles. Conceptual skills are needed in acquiring, interpreting, and analyzing information in a logical manner. Human relations skills involve understanding other people and interacting effectively with them. Administrative skills provide the ability to get things done by using other skills effectively. Technical skills consist of understanding and being able to supervise the processes, practices, or techniques required for specific jobs in the organization.

5. *Explain where supervisors come from.*

By far most supervisory positions are filled through internal promotion. This has several advantages. Insiders understand the organization and its culture, and when promoted within their own department, the tasks, personnel, and other supervisors are familiar as well. Managers know something about the potential supervisor's capabilities through his or her record of accomplishment. In addition, internal promotion serves as a reward and incentive for present employees who desire to move up. Organizations can help to ensure a successful transition to supervision by identifying, assessing, and training potential supervisors and observing how they perform in temporary supervisory assignments.

6. *Clarify the different relationships supervisory managers have with others.*
Supervisory managers are involved in at least three sets of relationships. First, they have personal relationships with their families and friends. Second, they have sometimes conflicting organizational relationships with lower-level employees, fellow supervisors, and higher levels of management. Third, they have external relationships with outsiders, such as business owners, customers or clients, suppliers, union representatives, governmental authorities, and leaders of environmental and advocacy groups.

7. *Discuss the emerging position of supervisory managers.*
The role of supervisory managers has drastically changed during the past 25 years. In the traditional role, supervisors had strong technical expertise, had much authority over employees, and were key problem solvers. Pressure was often the tool used to motivate employees. The emerging role of supervisors has resulted from organizational trends toward greater organizational emphasis on quality, empowerment of employees, downsizing of management ranks, and commitment to employees' growth and development. These trends have given employees authority to plan their own work, to determine the resources they need, and to resolve job problems themselves. While still responsible for achieving results, supervisors have shifted toward leading, facilitating, and supporting employees, in contrast to the dominant, authority-laden traditional role.

8. *Discuss some trends challenging supervisors.*
As the supervisory position grows in importance, it is becoming more complex because of many trends that are challenging supervisors' abilities to perform their jobs. The more important trends challenge supervisors to (1) deal with a more diverse workforce, (2) emphasize team performance, (3) cope with exploding technology, (4) adjust to occupational and industry shifts, (5) meet global challenges, (6) improve quality and productivity, (7) improve ethical behavior, and (8) respond to crises.

Key Terms

organization, p. 6
operations, p. 6
marketing, p. 6
financing, p. 6
management, p. 6
human resources, p. 6
physical resources, p. 7
financial resources, p. 7
authority, p. 8
responsibility, p. 8
top management, p. 8
middle management, p. 8

supervisory management, p. 9
managerial functions, p. 10
planning, p. 10
organizing, p. 11
staffing, p. 11
leading, p. 11
controlling, p. 11
roles, p. 11
conceptual skills, p. 12
human relations skills, p. 15
administrative skills, p. 16
technical skills, p. 16

emotional intelligence (EI), p. 17
relationships network, p. 19
union steward, p. 21
mentor, p. 21
diversity, p. 23
glass ceiling, p. 24
empowerment, p. 24
team advisors, p. 24
reinventing, p. 25
reengineering, p. 25
downsizing, p. 25
ethical dilemmas, p. 27

Discussion Questions

1. Why do people form organizations?
2. Identify the five functions every manager must perform and briefly explain each.
3. Why is management needed in organizations?
4. What are the three levels of management found in most large organizations? Describe each, giving its responsibilities.
5. Identify the four skills that managers need. Can someone be weak in one of these skill areas and still function effectively as a supervisor? Explain.
6. How are most supervisory positions filled? Explain why this is so.
7. What are the three types of supervisory relationships? Explain.
8. Identify each of the trends challenging today's supervisors and explain how each affects supervisors.
9. What are some reasons why "leading" is such a critical skill for supervisors and managers today?

Skill Builder 1.1

Interpersonal Skill

Information

Technology

Analysis of Supervisor/Management Job Descriptions

The purpose of this exercise is to have you view some actual job descriptions for supervisory/management positions as listed by real organizations.

Instructions:

1. Think about a supervisory/management position that interests you. The position must be a first-line supervisor/manager position of your choice. In addition, you may include the type of industry in your search, such as banking supervisor, nursing supervisor, recreation manager, hotel maintenance supervisor, etc.
2. Visit Monster.com at http://www.monster.com.
3. Type the name of the supervisory/management position in the "Search Jobs" box. You may leave blank the "U.S. Locations" box, which will result in a nationwide search. Clicking "Search" will likely result in numerous listings, depending on how general or specific your "Search Job" supervisory/management listing was.
4. Scroll the listings, viewing job titles and the names of the organizations for which there are position vacancies. Find a position/organization that looks of interest, and click the job title. You will then find the company's job description for the position.
5. Select and print out job descriptions for three different organizations, noting the differences in responsibilities, duties, and requirements. What conclusions about supervision/management and the organizations can be drawn from these?
6. Write a report, one-half to one page in length, to your instructor, commenting on the differences noted. Include printouts of the three job listings.
7. Be prepared to discuss your results in class, individually or in teams, as determined by your instructor.

Skill Builder 1.2

Interpersonal Skill

The Personal Interest Inventory

Directions:

Each of the following questions is worth a total of 3 points. For each question, assign more points to the response you prefer and fewer points, in order of preference, to the others. For example, if one response receives 3 points, the other two must receive 0; if one receives 2 points, then the others must receive 1 and 0; or each may receive 1 point. Enter your scores in the Score Matrix.

Information

1. Which activity interests you most?
   _____ a. Working with your hands
   _____ b. Working with people
   _____ c. Reading books
2. Which skills would you invest time in learning?
   _____ a. Research and writing
   _____ b. Organizing and leading
   _____ c. Crafts and art
3. Which job activities would you enjoy most?
   _____ a. Counseling and coaching
   _____ b. Building and doing
   _____ c. Thinking and planning
4. Which trait is most characteristic of you?
   _____ a. Helper
   _____ b. Doer
   _____ c. Scholar
5. Which would you most enjoy doing?
   _____ a. Talking with people
   _____ b. Writing a book
   _____ c. Building a house
6. How do you prefer to use your spare time?
   _____ a. Outdoor projects
   _____ b. Social activities
   _____ c. Thinking
7. Which of these traits is most important to you?
   _____ a. Physical coordination
   _____ b. Ability to deal with people
   _____ c. Mental ability
8. Which jobs most reflect your interests?
   _____ a. Teacher, social worker, counselor
   _____ b. Engineer, surveyor, craftsman
   _____ c. Researcher, historian, author
9. Which ability is your strongest?
   _____ a. Communication skills
   _____ b. Creative thinking
   _____ c. Physical skills

10. Which tasks do you perform best?
    _____ a. Operating and maintaining
    _____ b. Communicating and motivating
    _____ c. Developing and planning
11. Which occupation interests you most?
    _____ a. Pilot
    _____ b. Judge
    _____ c. Politician
12. Which of the following is most interesting to you?
    _____ a. Helping others
    _____ b. Thinking things through
    _____ c. Using your hands
13. Which skills could you learn with the least effort?
    _____ a. Leading and negotiating
    _____ b. Artwork and handicrafts
    _____ c. Language and theoretical reasoning
14. What tasks appeal to you most?
    _____ a. Developing new theories
    _____ b. Helping people with problems
    _____ c. Developing a skill
15. What assignment appeals to you most?
    _____ a. Working with ideas
    _____ b. Working with people
    _____ c. Working with things
16. Which is your greatest attribute?
    _____ a. Creativity
    _____ b. Competence
    _____ c. Sensitivity
17. For which occupation do you have a natural talent?
    _____ a. Counselor
    _____ b. Builder
    _____ c. Scientist
18. Which subject interests you most?
    _____ a. Practical arts
    _____ b. Philosophy
    _____ c. Human relations

19. To which group would you prefer to belong?

    ____ **a.** Scientific society

    ____ **b.** Outdoor group

    ____ **c.** Social club

20. How do you like to work?

    ____ **a.** In a group, discussing and recommending solutions

    ____ **b.** Alone, using ideas and theories

    ____ **c.** Alone, using tools and materials

SCORE MATRIX

QUESTION	THINGS	PEOPLE	IDEAS
1.	a.	b.	c.
2.	c.	b.	a.
3.	b.	a.	c.
4.	b.	a.	c.
5.	b.	c.	a.
6.	a.	b.	c.
7.	a.	b.	c.
8.	b.	a.	c.
9.	b.	c.	a.
10.	a.	b.	c.
11.	a.	c.	b.
12.	b.	c.	a.
13.	b.	a.	c.
14.	c.	b.	a.
15.	c.	b.	a.
16.	c.	a.	b.
17.	b.	a.	c.
18.	a.	c.	b.
19.	b.	c.	a.
20.	c.	a.	b.
	TOTAL	TOTAL	TOTAL

Instructions: The Personal Interest Inventory should give you some insight into the strengths you would bring to a management position. If you enjoy an activity, it is likely to be something that you do well. The three areas shown in the Score Matrix—things, people, and ideas—correspond to the following skills, which managers must use in doing their job:

Things: Technical skills
People: Human relations skills
Ideas: Conceptual skills

1. After scoring your inventory, break into groups of three to five and discuss your profiles. To what extent are they similar? Different? Are any of the areas dominant in the group? Underrepresented? Discuss.

2. Generalize about the kinds of supervisory jobs that might call for

   a. High technical skill

   b. High human relations skill

   c. High conceptual skill

3. Are your answers on this inventory consistent with the type of management job that you have in mind? If there are inconsistencies, what do they mean?

Source: Based on an exercise designed by Billie Stockton, Anita Bullock, and Anne Locke, Northern Kentucky University, 1981.

Skill Builder 1.3

Interpersonal
Skill

Information

Effective and Ineffective Supervisors

Instructions:

1. Think of all the supervisors for whom you've ever worked—part time or full time. If you have not worked for a supervisor, consider some of your teachers or perhaps a coach.

2. Select two—one who was most effective and one who was least effective—and list the behaviors of each.

3. In groups of three to five classmates, share your lists and discuss. Were there common behaviors? Select a spokesperson to present your discussion results to the class.

Skill Builder 1.4

Information

Do You Have the Makings to Become a Great Supervisor?

Based on what you learned from the exercise about effective supervisors, do you believe that you have the makings of a great supervisor? Do you have the desire to become a great supervisor? Assuming that you do, what are your strengths and weaknesses that would assist or hinder you in becoming a successful supervisor? Brainstorm and create a separate list for each.

Reflect on your lists and prioritize your top three strengths and top three weaknesses. How did you come to possess each one? How can you ensure that you will be able to maintain your strengths as you work on completing this course/your degree? Be specific. If you were to select one weakness to work on improving this term, which one would it be, and what specifically can you do to make strides in this area? The last aspect of your improvement plan should include a self-evaluation at the end of this term to assess your progress in this area.

CASE 1.1

COACH X: EFFECTIVE HOSPITAL ADMINISTRATOR*

Assume that you are a member of the search committee that is evaluating applicants for the position of administrator of a 300-bed, community-owned hospital in your city. In examining the applicants' resumes, you note that most have had experience in health care settings, many having previous experiences as administrators or assistant administrators.

One application, however, is quite different. It is from one of the most successful college football coaches in the country, someone we will call X. Being a sports fan, you have seen this person many times on national television as his teams have consistently placed in the top 10 NCAA ratings. He has won five national championships in the past 15 years. His school leads major colleges in athlete graduation rates; throughout his 30-year coaching career, his programs have not been charged with a single NCAA violation. He has won the national coach-of-year title four times. He has mentored countless assistant coaches, who themselves have become successful. His former players have been among the NFL's biggest stars. He has charisma and is a gifted motivational speaker. No one is more highly respected in the profession. Serving also as athletic director during the past five years, he oversees a $57 million budget and 400 employees, and the university's athletic department is one of the most profitable in the country. His university's sports teams annually win the award given to the university having

the best overall team performance across all sports. He has served with distinction as head of the National Association of College Coaches and is often selected to represent his peer coaches on significant NCAA issues. Presidents Bush and Obama have named him to important presidential commissions. He often has been courted by Democrats and Republicans as an easily winnable gubernatorial or U.S. Senate candidate. Why is he interested in the position of head administrator of the hospital? In his application, he states that it was always his ambition to change careers by age 55. While acknowledging his lack of experience in the health care field other than through hospital stays with family, players, and friends, he would love the challenge of hospital management.

Instructions:

1. Respond to the following question: Would X be someone whom you would consider as a viable potential candidate for the hospital administrator position, despite his limited technical expertise? _____ Yes _____ No Why?
2. Suppose that the position being sought was that of supervisor of the hospital's computer technology department. Would your answer be the same? Why?
3. In groups of four to six, discuss your answers, and be prepared to report highlights of your discussion to the overall class.

---

*Any association of Coach X as presented in this case with a real person or persons is coincidental.

Notes

1. Since our initial interview with Jackie Schultz in 2009, her career with Panera has continued to advance. In 2012, she was promoted to training manager for Panera store locations in a two-state area, a position she held at the time of our most recent interview. Additionally, since joining Panera part time as a high school senior in 2004, she has completed both undergraduate and graduate degrees. Sources: Management bio. (n.d.), https://www.panerabread.com/en-us/company/about-panera/management-bios.html; Interviews with Jackie Schultz by Paul Pietri, January 16, 2013, and May 28, 2009. For more information about Panera, see B. Kowitt, "Founder's Bold Gamble on Panera," *Fortune*, August 2012, pp. 9–21; C. Hajim, "Not by Bread Alone," *Fortune*, July 2006, p. 126.

2. "State of the American Manager: Analytics and Advice for Leaders," Gallup (n.d.), http://www.gallup.com/services/182216/state-american-manager-report.aspx.

3. G. A. Brewer, "In the Eye of the Storm: Frontline Supervisors and Federal Agency Performance," Journal of Public Administration Research and Theory 15, no. 4 (2005), p. 519.

4. For more information about team leaders' roles in self-directed teams, see P. R. Scholtes, B. L. Joiner, and B. J. Streibel, The Team Hand-book, 3rd ed. (Madison, WI: Oriel, Inc., 2003), Chapter 2, pp. 2–3.

5. H. Mintzberg, "The Manager's Job: Folklore and Fact," Harvard Business Review, 1975, pp. 489–561.

6. Pamela S. Lewis, Stephen H. Goodman, Patricia M. Fandt, and Joseph F. Mitshlisch, *Management* (Mason, OH: Thomson/South Western, 2007), p. 334.

7. See Rene Cordero, George F. Farris, and Nancy DiThomasco, "Supervisors in R&D Laboratories: Using Technical, People, and Administrative Skills Effectively," *IEEE Transactions of Engineering Management* 51, February 2004, pp. 19–30. The authors studied more than 2,000 technical professionals and found that for them to have a "stimulating" work environment, it was more important for their supervisors to possess people and administrative skills rather than technical skills. As the authors stated, "This appears a reversal from the traditional assumption that technical skills are the most important qualifications for promoting technical professionals into supervision."

8. Tiziano Casciaro and Migues Sousa Lobo, "Competent Jerks, Lovable Fools, and the Formation of Social Networks," *Harvard Business Review* 83, June 2005, pp. 92–100.

9. Janice Klein and Pamela Posey, "Good Supervisors Are Good Supervisors—Anywhere," *Harvard Business Review* 64, November–December 1986, pp. 125–128.

10. M. Toossi, "Projections of the Labor Force to 2050: A Visual Essay," *Monthly Labor Review*, 2012 (Bureau of Labor Statistics Publication), https://www.bls.gov/emp/ep_pub_labor_force.htm; M. Toossi, "Labor Force Projections to 2020: A More Slowly Growing Workforce," *Monthly Labor Review*, 2012 (Bureau of Labor Statistics Publication), http://www.bls.gov/opub/mlr/2012/01/art3full.pdf; Bureau of Labor Statistics, "Table 10: Civilian Labor Force by Age, Sex, Race, and Hispanic Origin: 1996–2006–2016," http://www.bls.gov/news.release/ecopro.t10.htm.

11. Toossi, "Projections of the Labor Force to 2050"; Toossi, "Labor Force Projections to 2020"; Bureau of Labor Statistics, "Table 10 "; "How to Manage Different Generations," *Lessons in Leadership* (n.d.), http://guides.wsj.com/management/managing-your-people/how-to-manage-different-generations/; K. Higginbottom, "The Challenges of Managing a Multi-generational Workforce," *Forbes*, March 2016, https://www.forbes.com/sites/karenhigginbottom/2016/03/17/the-challenges-of-managing-a-multi-generational-workforce/#7d6aca187d6a.

12. See K. Dill, "Even Post-recession, Demand for Temporary Employees Remains High," *Forbes*, August 2014, https://www.forbes.com/sites/kathryndill/2014/08/26/even-post-recession-demand-for-temporary-employees-remains-high/#6e5bc29b6e5b.

13. Anna-Louise Jackson and Anthony Feld, "Healing U.S. Labor Market Means Fewer Temporary Jobs," *Bloomberg*, November 8, 2012, http://www.bloomberg.com/news/2012-11-09/healing-u-s-labor-market-means-fewer-temporaryjobs.html.

14. James W. Dean and James R. Evans, *Total Quality*, 2nd ed. (Cincinnati, OH: South-Western College Publishing, 2000), p. 13.

15. Bruce Drake, Mark Meckler, and Debra Stevens, "Traditional Ethics: Responsibilities of Supervisors for Supporting Employee Development," *Journal of Business Ethics*, June 2, 2002, pp. 141–155.

16. Nancy Hatch Woodward, "Lessons Learned from the Gulf Coast Can Help You Manage Employee Communication in the Aftermath of the Unthinkable," *HR Magazine* 50, December 2005, pp. 52–57.

17. See B. Withers, "Panera Bread's Tech Obsession Is Paying off," *The Motley Fool*, March 2017, https://www.fool.com/investing/2017/03/20/panera-breads-tech-obsession-is-paying-off.aspx?source=isesitlnk0000001&mrr=0.10; J. Mueller, "Channel Check: Panera Bread," *Motley Fool Stock Advisor*, May 2013, pp. 1–10.

2
Fundamentals of Planning

If you don't know where you're going, any road will get you there.
—Author Unknown

After you have made up your mind just what you are going to do, it is a good time to do it.
—Josh Billings

PR Image Factory/Shutterstock.com

Effective planning is critical to personal and professional success, whether you are dealing with a short-term project or the long-term objectives of an organization like Strategic Wealth Specialists, featured in the chapter preview.

Preview

STRATEGIC WEALTH SPECIALISTS—CARESSE FINCHER Now that you have seen some of the roles played by supervisors and some of the challenges they face, it is time for you to see how they play these roles and meet these challenges.

Caresse Fincher is a managing director with Strategic Wealth Specialists, a distributor of Guardian Life Insurance Company. Several years ago, the business previously known as Adams and Associates underwent a transformation when the original general agent and owner, Mr. Adams, decided to retire. Because a succession plan did not exist, Guardian Life took over the firm during the transition and brought in a new general agent and owner. At that time, the firm was made up of a single office with a new general agent, two financial advisors, and Caresse Fincher, who was hired as the recruiting director responsible for hiring new advisors. Before long, a new vision was developed, which was to recruit and grow the business and operate multiple offices. This translated into targeting 10 offices in 10 cities in Mississippi, Alabama, and the Florida panhandle by 2019. To achieve this strategic goal, Strategic Wealth Specialists had to reorganize. The general agent would be responsible for the entire firm and provide the necessary leadership for it to achieve its vision. The two financial advisors and Caresse became managing directors at the next level with three areas of responsibility: (1) maintain a book of clients to work with, (2) grow the business by recruiting new financial representatives, and (3) work jointly as a team and mentor new members. The third level was comprised of financial representatives who would become managing directors over time.

According to Caresse, leadership and day-to-day management were and still are important as the business grows. Leadership is critical because it helps everyone keep the end (vision) in mind. Strategic Wealth Specialists has weekly leadership meetings on Monday to ensure the vision and mission are articulated to and in front of the team. They work backward from the vision to the operational level so everyone knows what needs to be done month to month, week to week, and day to day to reach the vision. Planning is all about writing down goals and keeping lists, lists with daily action steps to achieve the goals. In order to translate the vision to the operational level, the firm has its members write a one-page business plan and a one-page personal plan. The purpose of the plans is to consider the "why": Why are you at Strategic Wealth Specialists? What do you want to gain from this association? What do you have to do to obtain those things? What do you have to do weekly? Day-to-day? What are the metrics that need to be tracked? The personal plan is a very important piece in the overall system. To the extent the business plan helps to achieve the personal plan, the financial representatives will be internally motivated and accountable. This is a continuous process of development.

Caresses shares, "I am the coach for my team, but unlike sports coaches that stand on the sidelines, my job is to be on the field with my team members helping to pave the way for them to score." Successful representatives are goal and list oriented. They have a roadmap in front of them every day and they have the support they need. The financial representatives submit a weekly report detailing their progress towards their goals. Caresse notes, "As a manager, you inspect what you expect." The weekly reports hold everyone accountable. The financial representatives are held accountable for making progress towards their goals and the managing directors are held accountable for coaching and providing feedback, which is validating for both.[1]

Many managers see themselves as being strictly "fire fighters"—handling first this problem, next another, and then another. As the chapter preview illustrates, managers in all types of organizations and at all levels must become more proficient at planning—perhaps the most neglected function of management at all levels.

Planning involves selecting future courses of action for your organization and deciding how to achieve the desired results. This chapter builds on that definition. We focus on the first of the management functions—planning—and show that much planning must precede effective empowerment of employees and achievement of improved quality.

Some Important Points about Planning

1. *Discuss some of the more important points about planning.*

Suppose you and a group of friends decide to take a weekend camping trip. Effective planning requires answers to the following kinds of questions: What constraints impact the group, such as the distance you can travel or the funds you have available? What activities most interest the group, such as hiking, boating, fishing, or mountain biking? What camping sites are available to choose from, and which activities are offered at each? What supplies and equipment will be needed, and does the group have the means to obtain them? Only after questions such as these are answered can you do more effective planning. Then your group can decide when and where to go, what time to leave, and who will bring what, and perhaps even schedule your planned activities. Your plan also should anticipate future contingencies such as weather and occupancy of sites. Should rain be forecast, might you postpone the trip to a later date? If not, might you bring rain gear or have games available for indoor use? Might you reserve a site in advance or, if not, have a nearby backup site in mind?

As you can see, the trip's effectiveness depends greatly on the quality of planning that you and your group put into it. Supervisory planning works much the same way. Supervisors do planning—both routine and detailed—as an ongoing part of their jobs. This may include plans for scheduling work, developing and living within budgets, making job assignments, and so on. They also must plan for major events that happen infrequently, such as when a department manager of a major department store plans for an annual inventory count or when a pizza store manager knows a week in advance that he or she must deliver 300 freshly baked pizzas to a convention of 600 people.

EXHIBIT 2-1

The Three Planning Steps

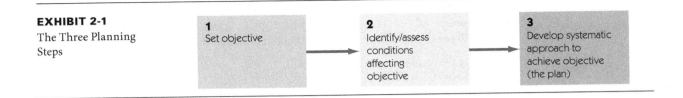

Basic Steps Involved in Planning

2. Explain the steps involved in planning.

Planning means deciding what will be done in the future; in other words, planning is forward looking. A manager must have a lot of discipline to set aside the time needed to solve current problems and plan for the future. As you can see, much planning is intellectual—a "between the ears" activity that involves hard work. Effective managers must use conceptual, human relations, administrative, and technical skills. Planning is normally an example of a conceptual skill, but it also requires other skills, especially to get the plans adopted and implemented.

Planning covers a wide variety of activities, from simple to complex, and from short to long term. In all cases, however, the three basic planning steps are as follows:

1. Setting an objective or goal.
2. Identifying and assessing present and future conditions affecting the objective.
3. Developing a systematic approach to achieve the objective (the *plan*).

These are shown in Exhibit 2-1.

Three additional steps also must be taken to achieve effectively the objective or goal established in step 1, although they are not exactly planning steps. These include the following:

4. Implementing the plan (organizing, leading, staffing).
5. Monitoring the plan's implementation (controlling).
6. Evaluating the plan's effectiveness (controlling).

These last three steps illustrate how closely planning is related to the other managerial functions, especially controlling.

The *first step in planning—setting an objective or goal*—addresses the issue of what one hopes to achieve. Notice in the chapter preview that the strategic planning process involved identifying the organization's vision and working backward to develop individual business and personal plans to strategically map to the vision.

The *second planning step—identifying and assessing present and future conditions affecting the objective*—recognizes important variables that can influence objectives. In the camping trip example given earlier, these would include such factors as equipment needed, weather, and site availability. Because planning involves the future, certain assumptions about the future must be made.

The *third step of planning is developing a systematic approach to achieve the objective.* This third step becomes the *plan*. It addresses such issues as the how, when, who, and where of the plan. The plan's complexity and importance are major factors in determining how formal and detailed this final step must be. For example, a plan to build a new 200-bed–wing expansion for a hospital would be much more formal and detailed than a plan to shut down a paper-making machine for routine maintenance. Many daily plans are routine, however, and are carried about in supervisors' heads rather than being committed to paper.

Planning Is Most Closely Related to Controlling

Of the managerial functions, planning is probably most closely related to controlling. As you will see in more detail in a later chapter, the steps in controlling are as follows:

1. Setting performance goals, or norms.
2. Measuring performance.
3. Comparing performance with goals.
4. Analyzing results.
5. Taking corrective action as needed.

Note carefully the first step in the preceding list. It involves planning!

Many Managers Tend to Neglect Planning

Poor planning results in disorganized and uncoordinated activities, thus wasting time, labor, and money, but because thinking is often more difficult than doing, many managers— including supervisors—tend to slight planning. It is very tempting to forgo thinking about the future in order to get busy performing a task or solving present work problems. Thus, it is not unusual for a supervisor to spend the day fighting one "fire" after another—seemingly never catching up. The result is frequently unsatisfactory. Consider the following example:

> *Henrietta Green, one of my supervisors, had a hectic schedule and was about to be driven up a wall. She said, "Today I had three no-shows because of the weather, and my department is absolutely swamped. I'm pitching in myself, but I've also got to conduct a tour for some of our home office staff personnel after lunch. I'm supposed to meet with our industrial relations people on a case that goes to arbitration next week. To cap it off, Barbara Brown is asking for a transfer out of the department and wants to talk about it today. She and two of the other workers can't get along. This afternoon, I've got to have some important figures ready for the cost accounting department. On top of all this, I'm supposed to supervise my 19 people, three of whom are new hires who are just being broken in. What a day! But recently, they all seem to be like this."*

Is it any wonder that this supervisor forgoes planning when her typical daily schedule is so demanding. Ironically, many of the short-run crises that confront supervisors could be greatly eased by proper planning. As shown in Exhibit 2-2, when a supervisor devotes too little time to planning, short-run problems are likely to result, including impossible deadlines, unforeseen obstacles, crises, and crash programs. These problems preoccupy the supervisor, leaving little time to devote to planning—and the cycle goes on and on!

EXHIBIT 2-2
The Nonplanner's
Cycle

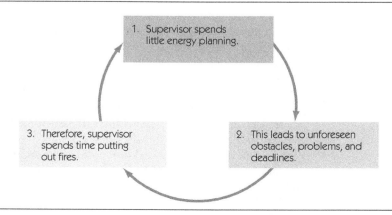

Contingency Planning Anticipates Problems

contingency planning

Thinking in advance about possible problems or changes that might arise and having anticipated solutions available.

It is important for supervisors to build flexibility into their plans by preparing contingency plans. **Contingency planning** means having anticipated solutions in advance for problems or changes that may arise and being prepared to deal with them smoothly when they do arise.

You might think of contingency planning as the responses to the "What if . . . ?" questions that describe serious events. Thus, contingency planning separates effective managers from ineffective ones. Proper anticipation of a problem may prevent it from happening. If you are to be a good contingency planner, you will need to ask yourself the following questions and find answers to them:

1. What might happen that could cause problems within my area of responsibility?
2. What can I do to prevent these events from happening?
3. If these events do occur, what can I do to minimize their effect?
4. Have similar situations occurred in the past? If so, how were they handled?

Assume you are a department supervisor of a major retail store chain, and sales in your store are down 10 percent from last year due to the poor economy in your area. What options do you have to reduce costs and improve your department's numbers? While you cannot directly control the local economy, you can choose how to respond to the downturn. You could lay off personnel, reduce staff hours across the board, or put a hold on the internship program with the local college—all of which are valid contingency options.

Or imagine you are the store manager of a local shoe retailer and your supplier of girls' Oxford saddle shoes just went out of business. How would you respond? What could you have done to prevent this supply disruption and loss of sales? You might have begun offloading some of your orders to another supplier to begin developing a relationship with a secondary source. Conducting business with two suppliers rather than putting all your eggs in one basket with one supplier has the advantage of providing you with contingencies should supply issues arise. However, every contingency will have different impacts, so remember to consider the long-term effects when deciding on the most appropriate courses of action. For instance, if you choose to add an additional supplier, doing business with two rather than just one might result in an initial cost increase because you are buying smaller quantities from both suppliers. Yet, the incremental cost increase may be worth the potential loss of sales and customers because other suppliers' manufacturing schedules would likely be full. You could offset some of this initial cost increase by developing a plan to grow this segment of your business over the next 12 to 24 months to increase the quantities purchased from both suppliers.

scenario planning

Anticipating alternative future situations and developing courses of action for each alternative.

A variation of contingency planning is **scenario planning**, which involves anticipating alternative future situations and developing courses of action for each alternative. Scenario planning has a long-term focus and is typically associated with planning at upper levels within organizations. Front-line managers are becoming more involved with this type of planning, with the continuing emphasis on utilizing collective or participatory management approaches. Thus, scenario planning is a necessary tool for most managers today.[2] Consider municipal managers in the public sector. The public sector has to deal with expectations that are different from those in the private sector. A municipality must aim to accommodate and assist all citizens, which involves proactively developing an emergency response plan for the worst scenario imaginable and devising alternative options based on that position.[3]

Many municipalities use disaster planning control tools similar to a yes/no command flow chart when planning for future critical incident scenarios. Once a possible scenario has been identified, such as a gunman on the loose in the city's hospital or at one of its schools, the disaster planning command center is used to establish responsibilities, devise reporting relationships, identify assigned areas, preset critical contact information, and allocate vehicles for transportation. Next, critical incident drills are performed to simulate a gunman on the loose.[4]

3. *Explain how planning differs at top, middle, and supervisory management levels.*

strategic planning

Has longer time horizons, affects the entire organization, and deals with its interface to its external environment.

mission

Defines the purpose the organization serves and identifies its services, products, and customers.

objectives

The purposes, goals, and desired results for the organization and its parts.

strategies

The activities by which the organization adapts to its environment to achieve its objectives.

operational planning

Consists of intermediate- and short-term planning.

Planning Differs at Different Management Levels

Management planning differs according to the level of management at which it occurs, as shown in Exhibit 2-3. Top managers like the general agent at Strategic Wealth Specialists in the opening case are more involved in **strategic planning**, which has longer time horizons, affects the entire organization, and deals with the organization's interaction with its external environment. Strategic plans include the following:

1. The **mission**, which defines the fundamental purpose the organization attempts to serve and identifies its services, products, and customers.
2. The overall **objectives** that drive the organization, such as profitability, customer satisfaction, employee relationships, environmental protection, or other critically important ends to be sought.
3. **Strategies**, the activities by which the organization adapts to the important factors that comprise its external environment, including consumers; customers; suppliers; competitors; and social, political, economic, and technological conditions.

Middle- and supervisory-level managers like Caresse Fincher and the other managing directors at Strategic Wealth Specialists are more concerned with operational planning. **Operational planning** consists of intermediate- and short-term planning that facilitates achievement of the long-term strategic plans set at higher levels. As shown in Exhibit 2-3, these plans operationalize the plans made at higher levels and are much narrower in scope and much shorter term than those formed at higher levels. As one supervisor related:

Planning? Sure, I spend time planning. But most of my department's goals, objectives, and schedules are handed down to me from above. My planning is more along these lines: How can I get better performance from my work group members? How can I cut down turnover and absenteeism? Given my group's workload for the week, or for the day, what's the best way to attack it? Whom should I assign to various jobs?

Take last week, for example. Four of my people were out—two sick and two on vacation—and I had to do a lot of planning in order to figure out who'd work where and when. Things seemed to go a lot more smoothly because I'd put in some time anticipating the problems. I've learned to plan on having a few people out "sick" on the opening day of hunting season!

As you can see, all managers need to plan, regardless of their position in the hierarchy. Although planning at the supervisory level generally is less complex and involves less uncertainty than planning at higher levels, it is still crucial that such planning be done effectively.

EXHIBIT 2-3
Planning at Three Management Levels

LEVEL	PLANNING PERIODS	WHAT IS PLANNED
Top managers	Strategic long-term, intermediate-range plans of 1–5 or more years	Growth rate Competitive strategies New products Capital investments
Middle managers	Intermediate- and short-range plans of 1 month to 1 year	How to improve scheduling and coordination How to exercise better control at lower levels
Supervisors	Short-range plans of 1 day, 1 week, 1–6 months	How to accomplish performance objectives How to implement new policies, work methods, and work assignments How to increase efficiency (in costs, quality, etc.) Employee and supervisor vacations

---

STOP AND THINK

What are some other examples of events for which supervisory managers must plan?

Importance of Setting Objectives

Objectives are crucial to effective planning. As one of the opening quotations in this chapter implied, only if you first know where you are heading can you effectively plan to get there.

What Are Objectives?

As previously stated, objectives are the goals that provide the desired purposes and results for an organization and its parts. Plans are aimed at achieving objectives. They answer the question "What do I want to accomplish?"

Is there a difference between an *objective* and a *goal*? Management experts disagree on this matter. Some say that goals are broad and nonspecific, whereas objectives are narrow and specific. Others reverse the distinction just given. Still others do not distinguish between the two. Because the terms *goal* and *objective* are often used interchangeably, we will treat them as synonyms in this book.

Objectives Serve as a Stimulus for Motivation and Effort

If you follow organized sports, you know that athletes frequently have objectives they try to achieve. For example, baseball players may strive to hit .300; basketball players may attempt to average 20 points; and football quarterbacks seek to average 50 percent pass completions. A weekend golfer may step up to the first tee with an 85 in mind. A Friday-night league bowler may shoot for an average of 150. Just as athletes are motivated by goals or objectives, so are people in the world of work.

> *Union Pacific railway equipped their locomotives with GPS tracking systems to evaluate their fuel efficiency. Every train engineer seeks to hit specific fuel efficiency goals set by the company. The cost savings are shared with those that achieve the highest fuel efficiency ratings! This approach to setting goals helps Union Pacific motivate its train engineers while also lowering its costs to be more competitive.*[5]

In summary, objectives provide a stimulus for effort; they give people something to strive for. If the train engineers had no set goals—if they simply planned to go out and do their best to conserve fuel—they would have no benchmark for determining whether they were doing well or poorly.

4. *Explain how the hierarchy of objectives works.*

hierarchy of objectives

A network with broad goals at the top level of the organization and narrower goals for individual divisions, departments, or employees.

Hierarchy of Objectives

In any organization, objectives are first needed at the top management level. Once top management has determined broad objectives or goals, other levels of the organization, including supervisory management, reflect these in objectives or goals of their own, thus creating a **hierarchy of objectives**. Exhibit 2-4 presents a hypothetical hierarchy of objectives for a firm, Computronix.

Computronix's overall organizational objectives are increased profits, improved market share, new product introductions, and cost effectiveness, as well as others not mentioned. Note how one of these, the cost-effectiveness objective, is reflected at progressively lower

EXHIBIT 2-4
Hierarchy of Objectives for Computronix

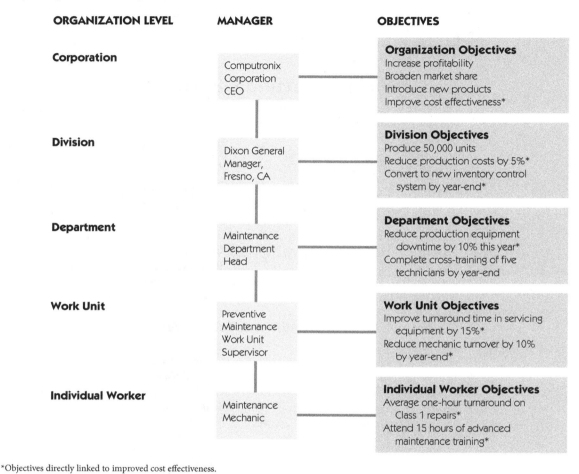

ORGANIZATION LEVEL	MANAGER	OBJECTIVES
Corporation	Computronix Corporation CEO	**Organization Objectives** Increase profitability Broaden market share Introduce new products Improve cost effectiveness*
Division	Dixon General Manager, Fresno, CA	**Division Objectives** Produce 50,000 units Reduce production costs by 5%* Convert to new inventory control system by year-end*
Department	Maintenance Department Head	**Department Objectives** Reduce production equipment downtime by 10% this year* Complete cross-training of five technicians by year-end
Work Unit	Preventive Maintenance Work Unit Supervisor	**Work Unit Objectives** Improve turnaround time in servicing equipment by 15%* Reduce mechanic turnover by 10% by year-end*
Individual Worker	Maintenance Mechanic	**Individual Worker Objectives** Average one-hour turnaround on Class 1 repairs* Attend 15 hours of advanced maintenance training*

*Objectives directly linked to improved cost effectiveness.

organizational levels. At the division level, the Computronix's Dixon Division general manager's objectives address cost effectiveness by seeking a 5 percent reduction in production costs and implementing a new inventory control system. The Dixon Division maintenance department reflects the plant's 5 percent production cost reduction through the objectives of reduction of equipment downtime, and the work unit objectives reflect the maintenance department head's objectives, and so on down the line. The diagram in Exhibit 2-4, though simplified, shows how the individual worker can be linked to top corporate levels through objective setting.

Unified Planning through Objectives

A major advantage of organizational objectives is that they give managers at lower levels guidance in developing their own operational plans and coordinating their own activities. Ideally, top management's objectives should give tactical plans at lower levels unity of

unified planning

Coordinating departments to ensure harmony rather than conflict or competition.

purpose. **Unified planning** means ensuring that plans at all organizational levels are in harmony, rather than at cross-purposes, with one another. Unified planning is especially important where coordination is required among departments or work units. Many supervisors are extremely dependent on other departments in accomplishing their own objectives. Continuing with our hypothetical example in Exhibit 2-4, a lack of unified planning at Computronix's Dixon Division has led to difficulties!

> *"This is ridiculous! They are trying to cut me down," stormed Juan Fernandez, supervisor of the processing department at the Dixon Division. The division was under the gun to reach its monthly production quota, and Fernandez's department absorbed a lot of the pressure. Fernandez continued: "If we don't process quota, the division doesn't make quota. It's as simple as that. But those jerks in maintenance are killing me. Last week, they were supposed to shut me down for PM [preventive maintenance]. But what happened? Absolutely nothing! They couldn't get to me because they were caught short-handed. You tell me why they had to send three of their technicians to a training school last week. I built my whole departmental schedule around last week being slack. They knew I was scheduled for PM last week. There's no way they're shutting me down for even 1 minute during the next 3 weeks."*

Dixon has a problem here! Fernandez doesn't want to shut down for maintenance, but he risks some downtime later if his equipment doesn't receive the proper preventive maintenance. The lack of unified planning at lower levels may cost Dixon its objectives. It has already strained the relationships among personnel in the plant.

STOP AND THINK

What action would you take now if you were Juan Fernandez? What should be done to prevent this type of situation in the future?

As you will see shortly, other types of plans also may be established to aid in unified planning at lower levels. These other types of plans—policies, procedures, and rules—are more specific than objectives and spell out the methods used at lower levels.

Guidelines for Setting Objectives

5. *Discuss some important guidelines in setting objectives.*

Objectives set out for employees what they must do to make their performance acceptable. Because all supervisors should set objectives in their departments, the following guidelines should prove helpful to managers at all levels.

1. *Select key performance areas for objectives.* Because objectives focus attention and effort, the more important areas will suffer if there are too many objectives. Instead of having 15 objectives, select four or five key areas of performance, such as quality, quantity, customer relations, and cost controls, that really count!
2. *Be specific, if possible.* The objective "to have good quality" probably means different things to you and to your employees. "To produce parts with a 99 percent acceptance rate by the quality control inspector" is more specific, and it gives the worker a tangible measure of progress.

3. *Set challenging objectives.* Objectives should not be set so low that they can be met through "average" effort. Instead, they should require some stretching, but they should not be so difficult to achieve that an employee is discouraged from attempting to achieve them.

4. *Keep objective area in balance.* Effort expended in one performance area frequently affects another. The quality of work required influences the quantity of work, and the quantity of work may affect employee safety. Therefore, objectives may be needed in each of these areas to balance them properly.

5. *Objectives should be measurable.* If you want to determine whether employees are achieving objectives, there should be some way of measuring the extent to which those objectives are being attained.

6. *Involve employees in setting objectives.* What do employees consider the key performance areas of their job? What do they think is a challenging but fair objective in a given area? When possible, ask these questions. There are times, however, especially during periods of financial difficulties and other crises, when it is not feasible or desirable to involve employees in objective setting.

7. *Follow up.* Once objectives have been set, supervisors tend to let up. Frequently, only the supervisor knows the results of a worker's performance. Discuss progress with employees. Sharing results and discussing employees' progress will improve their commitment and demonstrate your own. Remember Caresse Fincher's words in the opening case, "Managers inspect what they expect."

STOP AND THINK

Note the quality objective in guideline 2: "to produce parts with a 99 percent acceptance rate by the quality control inspector." Do you see any problems with making this the only objective? Explain.

Types of Plans

6. Differentiate the various kinds of standing and single-use plans.

Once objectives have been set to determine *what* needs to be accomplished, plans can be developed to outline *how* the objectives can be attained. These plans fall into two categories: *standing plans* and *single-use plans*.

Standing Plans

standing plans or repeat-use plans

Plans that are used repeatedly over a period of time.

Standing plans or repeat-use plans are those that are used repeatedly over a period of time. The three most popular types of standing plans are *policies, rules,* and *procedures*.

policy

Provides consistency among decision makers.

Policies   A **policy** is a guide to decision making—a sort of boundary on a supervisor's freedom of action. That is, it is a way to provide consistency among decision makers. For example, suppose that an *objective* of Computronix is "to operate our divisions so as to achieve high safety." Note that this objective tells the "what." A *policy* for achieving this objective at the various divisions could be that "all flammable substances will be stored and handled in a manner consistent with federal, state, and local regulations." Another policy might be: "Each division shall emphasize safety performance of employees through a well-designed promotional campaign." Within the Dixon Division of Computronix, an overall policy established by the general manager might be: "Each operating department shall hold safety meetings at least once every three months to encourage adherence to rules and solicit employee safety suggestions." Other examples of policies are shown in Exhibit 2-5.

EXHIBIT 2-5
Examples of Policies

Compensation policy: "This company shall establish and maintain wages on a level comparable to those paid for comparable positions in other firms in the community."

Overtime policy: "Supervisors shall offer overtime opportunities first to the most senior employees in the department."

Grievance policy: "Each employee shall have an opportunity for due process in all disciplinary matters."

Purchasing policy: "Where feasible, several sources of supply shall be utilized so as not to be solely dependent on one supplier."

Supervisory policy: "Managers shall periodically hold group meetings with employees for the purposes of discussing objectives, explaining new developments that may affect employees, responding to questions, and, in general, encouraging more effective and accurate communications within the organization."

Supervisory managers fit into the policy picture in two key ways. First, they play an important part in implementing organizational policies that have been established by higher management. Second, they create policies within their departments as guides for their own work groups. Here are some examples:

1. *Absence notification.* "Employees who will be absent should notify their supervisor in advance, assuming this is feasible."
2. *Decision making.* "Employees are encouraged to make decisions on their own within their area of responsibility."

STOP AND THINK

What are some other examples of supervisory policies? Can you think of any examples of policies established by the teacher of this course?

Policies established by upper-level managers should be put into writing because they must be enforced at operating levels by supervisors. Also, they often form the basis for legal proceedings against the organization and its management. Supervisory policies like the ones just mentioned, however, may be communicated orally. Some policies may be unwritten, implied, or based on past practices because "that's the way things actually happen."

It was Mary Hicks's first week on the job. Her supervisor, Clara Sanchez, had been very helpful in showing her the ropes. Each day, Mary had shown up for work a few minutes before starting time—just to make sure she was on time. She noticed, however, that at least a third of the employees drifted in 5 to 10 minutes late. This was true not only in her department, but also in others throughout the building. On asking one of her coworkers about this, she was told, "Yeah, they don't get really upset about 5 or 10 minutes, just so it's not the same person all the time."

The preceding example describes a practice that has become so widespread that supervisors may treat it as a policy. Supervisors must keep in mind that action or even inaction may be thought of as policy by employees and serve as a guide to their behavior.

rule

A policy that is invariably enforced. Rules are inflexible requirements and are much stronger than guidelines. It is important for supervisors to know when they can be flexible in promoting the objectives of their company and when they have to enforce rules.

Policies are relatively permanent but should not be set in stone. Circumstances change, and management must from time to time reexamine the appropriateness of its policies.

Rules   Like policies, rules provide guidance. But a **rule** is stronger than a policy in that the guidance given by a rule is final and definite. Rules are inflexible and *must* be obeyed, under threat of punishment. If you work in an organization that has the rule "No smoking on the premises," you cannot smoke, and that is that. Note the difference between a policy and a rule as shown in the following examples:

1. *Policy*: "Employees who violate the no-smoking rule are *subject to discharge*."
2. *Rule*: "Employees who violate the no-smoking rule are *automatically discharged*."

Exactostock/SuperStock

Rules are inflexible requirements and are much stronger than guidelines. It is important for supervisors to know when they can be flexible in promoting the objectives of their company and when they have to enforce rules.

Why distinguish between rules and policies, especially when the distinction is sometimes a fine one? First, as a supervisor, you must know when you do not have flexibility. Second, too many rules can result in over-management. Taking too much discretion away from the employees leads them to say, "Well, let me look in the rule book and see what I'm supposed to do."

STOP AND THINK

What are some examples of rules that you can think of? Can a supervisor establish his or her own rules? Give an example.

Although rules have an important place in organizations, their overuse can lead to problems. When there are too many rules, supervisors lose their individualism and may use the rules as crutches. Or they may offer weak, apologetic reasons when they enforce the rules. For example, consider the following dialogue:

Supervisor: "Catherine, I'm sorry to have to write you up for punching in three minutes late."

Catherine: "But you know I was actually here 10 minutes early and just forgot to punch in. I was at my desk all the time. I can't afford to get laid off half a day for being written up."

Supervisor: "Sorry, Catherine. It doesn't seem fair to me, either, but I've got to stick by the rulebook. A rule's a rule."

procedure

Steps to be performed when a particular course of action is taken.

Procedures   The need for procedures arises when an organization or a department requires a high degree of consistency in activities that occur frequently. Procedures are established to avoid "reinventing the wheel" and to ensure that an effective sequence is followed. A **procedure** outlines the steps to be performed when a particular course of action is taken. Organizations have procedures for obtaining leaves of absence, ordering parts through central purchasing, taking weekly inventory, processing an employee's grievance, and so on.

STOP AND THINK

Can you think of a procedure for a regular activity that takes place in each of the following organizations: airline, hospital, retail store, college? Procedures used in driving a car? Preparing a payroll?

---

single-use plans

Developed to accomplish a specific purpose and then discarded after use.

program

A large-scale plan composed of a mix of objectives, policies, rules, and projects.

Single-Use Plans

Single-use plans are developed to accomplish a specific purpose and are then discarded. Unlike policies, rules, and procedures, single-use plans detail courses of action that won't be performed on a repetitive basis. Examples of single-use plans are programs, projects, budgets, and schedules. These plans are more numerous and diversified than standing plans.

Programs   We hear and read about programs daily—such as your city's pollution control program and a voter registration program. A **program** is a large-scale plan that involves a mix of objectives, policies, rules, and smaller projects. A program outlines the specific steps to be taken to achieve its objectives and the time, money, and human resources required to complete it. It is essentially a set of single-use plans carried out over a period of time. Other examples of programs are as follows:

1. A tourism marketing program undertaken by your state.
2. A research program undertaken by drug producer Pfizer to develop vaccines for major diseases, such as AIDS and Parkinson's.

project

A distinct part of a program.

budget

A forecast of expected financial performance over time.

7. *Apply scheduling techniques.*

schedule

A plan of activities to be performed and their timing.

gantt chart

Identifies work stages and scheduled completion dates.

Projects   A **project** is a distinct, smaller part of a program. For example, a state's tourism program involves many projects, such as selecting a tourism committee, benchmarking several states with outstanding tourism programs, promoting public attractions, and upgrading the welcome centers that greet transit visitors on interstate highways. Each project has its own objectives and becomes the responsibility of personnel assigned to oversee it.

Budgets   Most individuals, families, or organizations use some form of budgeting. A well-planned budget serves as both a planning and a controlling tool. Simply stated, a **budget** is a forecast of expected financial performance over a period of time. A departmental budget covers such items as supplies, equipment, scrap, overtime, and personnel payroll.

Schedules   A **schedule** is a plan showing activities to be performed and their timing. Scheduling techniques range from a simple note or appointment book used to schedule your day to sophisticated schedules for such major challenges as building a new plant or launching a space shuttle. Two scheduling approaches with which you should be familiar are the Gantt chart and the critical path method.

The **Gantt chart** is a visual progress report that identifies work stages or activities on a vertical axis and scheduled completion dates horizontally. It is named after its developer, Henry Gantt, a management consultant who introduced the basic idea in the early 1900s. Since then, Gantt charts have been used extensively as a planning tool. Exhibit 2-6 illustrates a simplified Gantt chart. Note the specific activities that proceed from contract negotiation to job start-up and the scheduled times for each. Also note that one activity, long

EXHIBIT 2-6
Example of Gantt Chart Showing Activities Needed in Production Start-Up

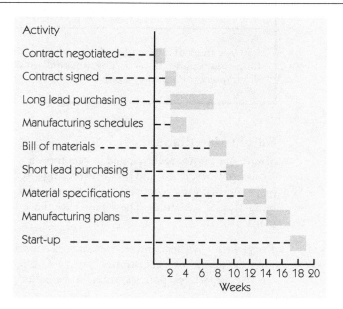

lead purchasing, can be carried on simultaneously with development of a manufacturing schedule. In actual practice, Gantt charts may include movable strips of plastic to represent bars, with different colors to indicate scheduled and actual progress. At a glance, a manager or supervisor can see whether a project is on time, ahead of schedule, or behind schedule. While the Gantt chart is helpful as a planning tool, it does not show directly how the various activities involved in a job depend on one another. It is in showing such dependencies of activities that the critical path method can be helpful.

critical path method

A management scheduling tool that identifies the activities needed to complete a task or project, specifies the time each activity will take, and shows the relationships among the network of activities to determine the total completion time of the task or project.

The **critical path method** is a management scheduling tool that identifies the activities needed to complete a task or project, specifies the time each activity will take, and shows the relationships among the network of activities to determine the total completion time of the task or project. The supervisor first lists each activity, then the order of completion, and finally the time each will take. The supervisor diagrams the total process including all activities using appropriate software or manually for simple projects. The critical path method is used on highly complex, one-time projects, such as building a skyscraper or completing the prototype of a new jet aircraft. However, its principles are relevant for many supervisors, especially in planning and scheduling various aspects of their jobs.

Let's examine the critical path method as it applies at the supervisory level. Suppose that you are a maintenance supervisor and your department has to overhaul an important machine. You have determined that the following activities must be done to complete the job:

A. Remove the machine from its foundation.
B. Haul the machine to the repair shop.
C. Dismantle the machine.
D. Order and receive new replacement parts from the manufacturer.
E. Repair the machine.
F. Test-run the machine.
G. Build a new machine foundation.
H. Move the repaired machine to the factory floor.
I. Secure the machine to the new foundation.

Now, assume that you are asked to estimate when the machine can be ready for use again. The network of events and activities involved in your analysis is shown in Exhibit 2-7. The numbered squares represent events at which the different activities to complete the job *begin* and are *completed*. For example, Event 2 marks the completion of Activity A and the beginning of Activities B and G. The lines represent the activities to be performed. The hours represent your estimate of how long each activity will take to complete based on your experience or on information supplied by others.

critical path

The series of activities that comprise the longest route, in terms of time, to complete the job.

Note that the estimated completion time for the job is 62 hours. This total time is obtained by adding the hours necessary to complete the series of activities that comprise the *longest* route, in terms of time, to complete the job. This route is called the **critical path**. The series of activities on the critical path include A, B, C, D, E, F, H, and I. These are the

EXHIBIT 2-7
Critical Path for Completing Machine Overhaul

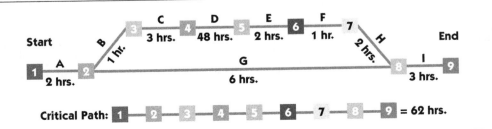

activities that determine the completion time for the job. Activity G is not a critical step in the network because it can be begun and completed independently of Activities B through I and is not included on the critical path.

A major advantage of the critical path method, even for simple problems, is that they graphically display the dependent parts of a total job. The supervisor thus has a better grasp of the total job to be completed.

STOP AND THINK

Suppose that it takes you four hours rather than the two hours estimated to repair the machine (Activity E) as shown in Exhibit 2-7. Will this cause your project to be completed later than planned?

Chapter Review

1. *Discuss some of the more important points about planning.*

Supervisors do planning as an ongoing part of their jobs. They must include planning for scheduling work, developing and living within budgets, and making job assignments.

2. *Explain the steps involved in planning.*

Planning is deciding what will be done in the future. The three planning steps are (1) setting an objective or goal, (2) identifying and assessing present and future conditions affecting the goal, and (3) developing a systematic approach to achieving the goal. Properly done, planning helps managers accomplish the four other management functions of organizing, leading, staffing, and controlling. Of these functions, planning is most closely linked to controlling. Because it is a difficult and time-consuming process, many supervisors tend to neglect planning. Instead of planning, they scurry about solving one problem, then another, seemingly too busy to plan anything. Effective planning anticipates many problems so that they are more easily handled when they occur. Contingency planning is thinking about anticipated problems in advance and having potential solutions available.

3. *Explain how planning differs at top, middle, and supervisory management levels.*

Planning differs for top-, middle-, and first-level management. Top managers spend a greater proportion of their time developing strategic long-term and intermediate-range plans of one to five or more years. Strategic plans include the organization's mission, objectives, and strategies and interfacing with its external environment. Middle-level and supervisory managers perform operational planning—intermediate-range and short-range plans of one year to one day—that operationalize strategic plans.

4. *Explain how the hierarchy of objectives works.*

Objectives are crucial to effective planning. Once established, objectives provide a stimulus for individual effort. The objectives set at one management level reflect the objectives of the next higher operational level. This network of objectives is called a hierarchy of objectives. Objectives permit unified planning and coordination at lower management levels.

5. *Discuss some important guidelines in setting objectives.*

Among the guidelines for setting objectives are (1) setting them in only selected, key performance areas; (2) making them specific; (3) making them challenging rather than easy; (4) balancing them properly, as may be the case with volume and quality; (5) stating them in measurable terms; (6) involving employees in setting them; and (7) following up on results.

6. *Differentiate the various kinds of standing and single-use plans.*

After objectives have been established, plans can be developed throughout the organization. Standing, or repeat-use, plans direct action that deals with recurring situations. They include policies, rules, and procedures. A policy is a guide to individual decision making. Policies allow some flexibility, whereas rules are final and definite as to what action must be taken. A procedure outlines the steps that should be taken to complete a given action, such as applying for vacation leave or processing a grievance. Single-use plans are one-time plans that are discarded on completion. Examples of these are programs, projects, budgets, and schedules.

7. *Apply scheduling techniques.*

Two important types of schedules are Gantt charts and the critical path method, each of which provides a visual display of activities to be performed and the time frames involved.

Key Terms

contingency planning, p. 41
scenario planning, p. 41
strategic planning, p. 42
mission, p. 42
objectives, p. 42
strategies, p. 42
operational planning, p. 42
hierarchy of objectives, p. 43

unified planning, p. 45
standing plans or repeat-use
 plans, p. 46
policy, p. 46
rule, p. 48
procedure, p. 49
single-use plans, p. 49
program, p. 49

project, p. 50
budget, p. 50
schedule, p. 50
gantt chart, p. 50
critical path method, p. 51
critical path, p. 51

Discussion Questions

1. What are the three basic steps in planning? Why do supervisors tend to slight the planning function?
2. How does planning differ among top, intermediate, and supervisory management levels?
3. What are some guidelines for setting objectives?
4. What is meant by a hierarchy of objectives? Explain.
5. What is the difference among a policy, a rule, and a procedure?
6. What is a Gantt chart? How does it differ from the critical path method?
7. What is contingency planning? Explain.
8. Distinguish between objectives and strategies.

Skill Builder 2.1

Resources

Testing Your Planning Skills (Group Activity)

The general manager (GM) of the Marshall Biscuit Division of Lancaster Colony Corporation has just named you as chairperson of the first annual blood drive, to be conducted at the plant site. A strong believer in the company's participation in community affairs and himself a member of the local Red Cross board of directors, the GM has committed

Interpersonal
Skill

the division's employees to the blood drive. Your committee will set the exact dates for the drive, which is to be held in three or four months. As chairperson, you have been assigned a team of four other company employees to plan and implement the project. All members are highly respected, competent people, representing a true cross-section of the employees: One is a production worker who is responsible for operating the ovens; another, an engineer, represents the professional segment; the human resources manager represents the management group; and a payroll clerk represents the administrative office group. The GM was given your name by your boss, who expressed confidence in your ability to lead a successful donor campaign at the plant. At 27, you are the youngest person on the committee and anxious to do a good job. You have called the first committee meeting, which you have advertised as a "preliminary planning meeting," to identify key factors that must be planned for if the committee is to meet its objective of having a successful blood drive at Marshall Biscuit.

Instructions:

1. Make a list of what you consider the key planning issues to be identified by the committee at this initial planning meeting.

2. Of the items on your list, which two or three do you believe are the most crucial? Why?

3. Identify major problems that could prevent accomplishment of your objective. What contingency planning could be done to avert them or minimize their impact?

4. To help in your preparation for the planning meeting, identify 6 to 10 steps that you feel will be needed to achieve a successful blood drive. These steps might be such things as:

   a. Determine a date.

   b. Identify a location.

   c. Secure commitment from Red Cross.

   Perform a critical path analysis and draw a chart that shows the sequence and relationship of the activities identified. (You need not be concerned with the length of time needed for each activity.)

5. Compare your responses to questions 1, 2, 3, and 4 with those of other students. To what extent do they agree with you?

Skill Builder 2.2

Resources

Interpersonal
Skill

Information

Determining Priorities: Put Savings First

Prior to the global economic downturn, the savings rate in the United States was precariously low, even negative at times. However, personal savings is a key means of ensuring a stable future for you and your family. Take a moment to test your personal planning skills with the following personal budgeting activity.

Instructions:

Step 1: For one month, track your personal income and expenses using a pocket-sized notebook and pen or a personal electronic device. Regardless of how small the purchase price is, be sure to track ALL expenditures for one month. Record all items and break them into categories. For example, your income may possibly be categorized as follows: money earned waiting tables, monthly student loan income, and money provided by family. Some common expense categories would include rent, car insurance, and gas.

Step 2: Analyze your monthly habits to determine where your money is going. Do you have money left over at the end of the month, spend all that you make, or finance your current lifestyle with unsecured debt (credit cards)? Begin to think about ways to reduce your expenses or increase income stream(s).

Step 3: Set a savings goal for yourself; remember to use the goal-setting principles you learned about in this chapter to guide your efforts. For example, you want to be realistic about what you can achieve, and if you are not currently a saver, look for discretionary expenses you could eliminate to free up even small amounts. For example, just finding an extra $30 per month equals $360 per year. As you become a savvy saver, you can create a more challenging goal.

Step 4: Think about alternative ways to achieve your goal. Pick one that will work for you and stick to it! One suggestion is to visit various financial planning Web sites, such as http://www.suzeorman.com/, to benchmark plans that have worked for others. One strategy shared by some financial advisors, including Suze Orman, is to have your local bank or credit union electronically transfer your savings goal each month from your checking to your savings account. This strategy ensures that you pay yourself first, and in most cases, if you don't see the money in your account, you won't miss it!

Skill Builder 2.3

Estimate the Completion of a Maintenance Project

Recall that the critical path method is a management scheduling tool that identifies the activities needed to complete a task or project, specifies the time each activity will take, and shows the relationships among the network of activities to determine the total completion time of the task or project. Let's examine the critical path method as it applies to a maintenance project. Suppose that you are a maintenance supervisor and your department has to overhaul a piece of equipment. You have determined that the following activities must be completed in the following order and each will take a specific number of days to complete (see table below).

MAINTENANCE PROJECT		
ACTIVITY	IMMEDIATE PREDECESSOR (ORDER OF ACTIVITIES)	TIME TO COMPLETE ACTIVITY IN DAYS
A	None	7
B	A	2
C	A	4
D	B, C	5
E	D	2
F	D	4
G	F, E	5

Estimate how long it will take you to finish this maintenance project. Remember, the estimated completion time is obtained by adding the hours necessary to complete the series of activities that comprise the *longest* route, in terms of time, to complete the job.

CASE 2-1

ISLAND SHADES:

Terry Allen has an idea for a new business. She would like to start a retail operation that would provide high-quality eyewear to discriminating consumers. The business, Island Shades, would use a focused differentiation strategy, catering to middle- and upper-income individuals ranging in age from 16 to 50 years. These customers would range from avid outdoors people to birdwatchers to Sunday drivers. She envisions carrying high-end sunglasses (Gucci, Prada, Oakley, Ray Ban, Costa Del Mar, etc.) and custom-prescription sunglasses. She will stock a wide assortment of styles and a variety of colors.

Although Terry will stock some affordable options in each product category, the bulk of her inventory will be priced at $100 or greater. She estimates that she will need to invest $75,000 to $95,000 in inventory to begin her business and ensure she has the variety and quality her discerning customers will expect. She estimates that her monthly sales will start at $15,000 and fluctuate depending on the seasonal peaks and valleys. For instance, the first, second, and fourth quarters of the year will be much more lucrative than the third quarter due to ski season, summer activities, and the holiday season. Terry expects to average $35,000 per month in sales over this time period. Currently, she is also planning to pay a consultant to develop an interactive Web site enabling customers to purchase merchandise online. The initial quote for the up-front cost for development is $4,000, with an ongoing annual fee of $300.

Terry believes that the perfect location for this retail store is in the Palacio, an upscale and trendy shopping village just off a major interstate highway in a mid-sized city with a population of 295,000 (the population for the greater metropolitan statistical area is 500,000). Palacio is centrally located within the city and easily accessible from several high-end neighborhoods. One key factor in choosing this location is that other upscale retail shops and restaurants currently operate at Palacio that attract the desired target market. Terry believes that she will need around 2,000–2,500 square feet. Terry recently checked with a local leasing agent and found out the following information:

A 2,400-square-foot corner unit is open.
The rent is $3,300 per month. (Taxes and insurance charges are included.)
The build-out cost is $16.00 per square foot.
The lease term is 3 to 5 years with several different renewal options.

Terry wants a comfortable friendly atmosphere that is alluring without being stuffy. The quote she received for the build-out cost would enable her to accomplish this objective. It includes displays, but furniture and accessories would be additional. Terry estimates that these features would run an additional $5,500. Space is available now and going quickly. Even though it is August, she would like to get started and sign a lease agreement.

Terry is quite aware that she will be working long hours at the beginning. She plans to be open Monday through Saturday from 10:00 A.M. to 7:00 P.M. These hours will allow her to operate when potential customers are eating lunch and dinner and browsing at Williams Sonoma, Anne Taylor, Adventure Outdoors, and so on. Based on these hours of operation, Terry believes she needs two to three part-time employees who would rotate shifts. She is planning on tapping the local high schools and universities to recruit quality part-time employees. Based on the data she has gathered, she expects to pay between $8 and $10 an hour. Because she is relying on part-time employees, there would be no need to pay benefits such as medical and dental.

CASE QUESTIONS

Answer the following questions:

1. Analyze Terry's goal and plan based on the concepts you learned in this chapter. Are there additional key performance areas that Terry could identify for action? Is her goal realistic?
2. Do you agree with Terry's view that Island Shades will be successful? Why or why not?
3. Would you recommend any changes or modifications to her goal or plan? Discuss.
4. Present a summary of your analysis and recommendations to the class.

Notes

1. Interview with Caresse Fincher with Strategic Wealth Specialists, May 2017.
2. M. Gene, "Contingency Planning Essentials," *Industrial Engineer*, July 2003, p. 24.
3. Interview with James Gillespie by Don Mosley Jr., May 2006.
4. Interviews with Chris Browning, Jennifer Fidler, James Gillespie, Dan McCrory, and Steve Seay by Don Mosley Jr., May 2006.
5. M. Gunther, "Union Pacific: Building America," *Fortune*, July 5, 2010, pp. 120–124.

3
Decision Making, Problem Solving, and Ethics

LEARNING OBJECTIVES

After reading and studying this chapter, you should be able to:

1. Explain the role of decision making in the supervisor's job.

2. Discuss why supervisors need to make so many decisions.

3. Define decision making and identify at least four elements involved.

4. Discuss how decisions are made.

5. Name some factors to keep in mind when making decisions.

6. Decide whether to use the individual approach or the group approach when making decisions.

7. Discuss some ways of improving decision making.

8. Explain the role of ethics in the organization's and supervisor's decision making.

It is management's public responsibility to make whatever is genuinely in the public good become the enterprise's own self-interest.
—Peter F. Drucker

Ethics is a code of values which guide our choices and actions and determine the purpose and course of our lives.
—Ayn Rand

All the analyst really requires for the solution to a problem is: first, the painstaking assembly of all the phenomena; second, exhaustive patience; and third, the ability to comprehend the whole problem with afresh and unbiased imagination.
—Ellery Queen

dotshock/Shutterstock.com

Every business leader, such as Jeff Mackin with Teklinks, has to take care with making decisions to maintain the organization's success.

Preview

TEKLINKS, INC.—JEFF MACKIN Jeff Mackin is Director of Enterprise Sales for Teklinks, Inc., an integrated information technologies (IT) solutions provider. Throughout his career, Jeff has worked for a number of different companies (Oracle, SSI Group, Gorrie-Regan, McAleer Solutions, and ADP) in a variety of roles including regional director, vice president, and CEO. In his current position, he manages a team responsible for developing client relationships and providing IT solutions. Jeff and his team make important decisions that impact the company. According to Jeff, "there are two primary schools of thought (direct and collective) on how to approach making decisions." One is a direct approach that is leader led in which the leader believes one alternative is best. The challenge is to build support for the decision within the team, department, or organization. The real key to gaining support is trust. The follower(s) need to trust and believe the leader has their best interest in mind when deciding what to do.

On the other hand, collective decision making involves some level of participation, whether the leader asks for input and decides or together everyone reaches a consensus. The challenge with the collective approach is someone ultimately has to be responsible for guiding or facilitating the group. Jeff believes it is important for the facilitator to keep a few things in mind. First, the group needs to agree on the end goal up-front and they need to stay focused on it throughout the process. Write it on the board or project it on the screen. Next, the group must have a deadline for the decision to keep them on point. Now, the group is ready to focus on the task and one way to start is by going around the room and allowing each person a designated amount of time to share his or her thoughts (later in the chapter, other group-processing techniques are presented). During this process, the facilitator uses a variety of techniques to keep the group focused, including asking the right questions, summarizing information, and helping transition to the next stage in the decision-making process.

Jeff prefers the direct approach. He is naturally achievement oriented and when leading a group, he has a fierce resolve to accomplish the vision and mission. A direct approach allows for quick, decisive action. When Jeff was the CEO of McAleer Solutions, he used the direct approach and the end goal was to grow the business. He was able to build support within the company and keep his team focused, such that the company grew over 300 percent in 12 months and over 700 percent in three years. But during a weekly meeting, a young lady on his team said, "I love your style, you are a go-getter, we are doing well, and everybody is happy. But the world needs workhorses as well as racehorses. You have to have people who are plowing the fields." In other words, Jeff and the company had been so focused on growth they had lost sight of what it took to run the business internally. He admits, he learned a valuable lesson that day. Her input changed the way they did business. As this example illustrates, it takes time and practice to learn how to effectively supervise, lead, and facilitate group decision making.[1]

As you can see from the opening case, decision making is an important and ongoing process occurring at all levels within an organization. In many cases, the supervisory role in high-tech companies such as Facebook, Google, and Apple is to provide team leadership. When supervisors work with highly skilled, empowered teams, their roles are to facilitate, coach, and advise members so the team can accomplish its mission. We will discuss the subject of decision making in considerable detail throughout this chapter. Decisions must be made about people, processes, and priorities, to name just a few issues!

Role of Decision Making in Supervisory Management

1. *Explain the role of decision making in the supervisor's job.*

Managers must make decisions whenever they perform any of the five management functions—planning, organizing, staffing, controlling, and leading. Without decision making, the entire management system would cease to exist. For example, in *planning*, the supervisor must decide which objectives to seek, which policies to establish, and what rules to institute. In *organizing*, choices must be made as to who gets what authority and how duties and responsibilities are grouped. In *staffing*, decisions must be made concerning employee selection, placement, training, and development; performance appraisal; compensation; and health and safety. In *controlling*, if actual performance does not conform to planned performance, decisions must be made about how best to bring them together. The function of *leading* entails deciding how best to communicate with and motivate employees.

The decisions that managers make often must be made quickly—and frequently with little information, or even conflicting information. Then, those decisions must be carried out to achieve the department's objectives!

Decision Making: The Heart of Supervisory Management

Decision making is central to the supervisor's job. Supervisors must continually decide what is to be done; who is to do it; and how, when, and where it is to be done. As we will show throughout the chapter, although these decisions may be discussed separately, they are interrelated. One decision is affected by, and builds on, previous ones. For example, what your department produces determines what types of production facilities are needed. Decisions about production, in turn, influence the types of employees needed and the training and compensation they should receive. All of these decisions affect the amount of resources budgeted for the department.

Why Supervisors Need to Make So Many Decisions

2. Discuss why supervisors need to make so many decisions.

Supervisory managers—even more than managers at other levels—are involved in directing employees' behavior toward achieving the organization's goals, as well as those of the employees themselves. Supervisors must make more decisions more frequently—and often more quickly—than other managers because they're operating on a production-oriented, day-by-day, person-to-person basis. These decisions involve a variety of activities, as the following example illustrates.

Wilma Malone, nursing supervisor at Alquippa Medical Center, had been at work for only three hours, but she had already made several major decisions. For example, she had

1. *Signed up to attend a one-day course on time management, to be offered the following week;*
2. *Assigned performance ratings to five of her new nurses on their performance appraisal forms;*
3. *Approved vacation requests for two nurses in her department;*
4. *Referred to the floor physician, a patient's request to be taken off a prescribed medication;*
5. *Resolved a dispute between one of the nurses and a floor orderly;*
6. *Selected Jane Moore to serve as her replacement when she was to take her vacation in three weeks; and*
7. *Requisitioned supplies needed by her department.*

In addition, she made a handful of other minor decisions. The young trainee assigned to Malone said, "Are you always this busy, or is it just because it's Monday morning?" Malone replied, "It's all a normal part of a supervisor's job."

Employees look to their supervisors for more direction, assistance, guidance, and protection than do subordinates of managers at higher levels. Also, in general, supervisors spend more time socializing with others in the organization because they have more employees than other managers. All of these activities require decision making.

span of management

The number of immediate employees a manager can supervise effectively.

One basic truism of management is that the lower the level of management, the greater the **span of management**, which is the number of immediate employees a manager can supervise effectively. Therefore, supervisors make decisions that affect not only their own behavior, but also that of many other people.

What Is Decision Making?

3. Define decision making and identify at least four elements involved.

It is now time to define decision making, discuss its characteristics, look at some selected types of decisions, and consider some differences between decision making and problem solving.

Decision Making Defined

Have you known people who couldn't ever make up their minds? They might say, "I really don't know what to do. If I do this, such and such will happen. If I do that, then something else might happen." They just can't make decisions.

The word *decide* comes from a Latin word meaning "to cut off." When you make a decision, you first consider a matter causing you some uncertainty, debate, or dispute, and then make a choice or judgment that more or less results in a definite conclusion. You cut off further deliberation on the matter. Thus, **decision making** is the conscious consideration and selection of a course of action from among two or more available alternatives in order to produce a desired result.

Elements Involved in Decision Making

There are several facts you should know about decision making. The most important ones are (1) a decision may not be needed, (2) decisions involve the future, (3) the process is a conscious one, and (4) there must be more than one alternative solution.

A Decision May Not Be Needed   A wise decision maker begins by asking, "Is a decision needed?" It may seem strange to include this question in a discussion of decision making, but it is important. In many supervisory situations, no decision is needed, and decision making would be in vain. If a given event is inevitable or if higher management is going to act in a certain way regardless of the supervisor's wishes, then making a decision is a waste of time. Some things cannot be changed regardless of the supervisor's wishes or actions.

Decisions Involve the Future   Surely you have heard others say, "If only I had done this, then that wouldn't have happened." They assume that if they had made a different decision, it would have resulted in a happy marriage, a rapid promotion, or a killing in the stock market. It is said that hindsight is 20/20, but the supervisor's world is no place for Monday-morning quarterbacking. Rather, it's a place to prepare for today or tomorrow. Because a supervisor's decision making is oriented toward the future, it always contains an element of uncertainty. The goal is to make the best decision at a specific time given the information available.

Decision Making Is a Conscious Process   Decision making involves a conscious process of selection. No decisions are needed about breathing or digestion because these are unconscious, reflexive actions. In making a decision, the individual consciously

EXHIBIT 3-1
Decision-Making
Process

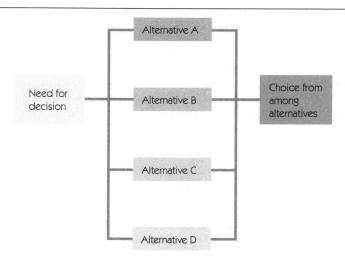

(1) becomes aware of a want that needs to be satisfied, (2) seeks relevant behavioral alternatives, and (3) evaluates them as a basis of choice, as shown in Exhibit 3-1.

Decision Making Involves More Than One Alternative   As indicated earlier, for a true decision to be made, there must be two or more available alternatives to choose from, including the possibility of doing nothing. Frequently, there are only two choices, as in a "yes or no" or "to do or not to do" situation. The decision to do nothing is sometimes the worst decision.

Most decision situations involve several alternatives with varying expected outcomes. You may not be aware of some of the alternatives and may not have decision authority over others. For other alternatives, you must estimate expected outcomes. You then evaluate each outcome in terms of its desirability. Sometimes there are no desirable alternatives. In such cases, you have to decide between two undesirable ones.

STOP AND THINK

Consider a recent decision you made. How many alternatives did you consider?

Types of Decisions to Be Made

Although there are many ways of classifying decisions, we will discuss only one at this point—namely, categorizing decisions as either programmed or nonprogrammed.

programmed decisions

Routine and repetitive decisions.

Programmed decisions are those that are routine and repetitive. Because such decisions tend to be similar and must be made frequently, supervisors usually establish a systematic way of handling them. Here are some examples of this type of decision:

1. How to handle an employee who reports to work late or is absent without permission.
2. How to schedule work, shifts, vacations, and other time variations.
3. How to determine which employees need training and what type of training should be given to them.
4. How frequently to do maintenance servicing of machinery and equipment.

The effective supervisor handles these decisions in a systematic way and may even set up a decision framework, including guidelines such as policies, procedures, or rules to be followed.

nonprogrammed decisions

Decisions that occur infrequently and require a different response each time.

Nonprogrammed decisions are those that occur infrequently. Because different variables are involved, requiring a separate and different response each time, establishing a systematic way of dealing with such decisions is difficult. Some examples of unprogrammed supervisory decisions include the following:

1. Whether to buy an important piece of machinery or equipment, especially an expensive, complex piece.
2. How to react to a union representative who says that a grievance will be filed if you give a written reprimand to a certain worker for a work-related violation of safety rules.
3. How to handle a severe accident or explosion.
4. Whom to promote to a supervisory position.

opportunity

A chance for development or advancement.

How Decision Making and Problem Solving Relate

In one of his educational films, Joe Batten, a well-known management consultant, has a manager say, "We have no problems here, just opportunities. Each problem should be considered an opportunity." Although we don't necessarily agree with that conclusion, it does give us a chance to show how decision making and problem solving are related. An **opportunity** is a set of circumstances that provides a chance to improve a situation or help reach a goal. A **problem** is an existing unsatisfactory situation causing anxiety or distress that must be addressed.

problem

An existing unsatisfactory situation causing anxiety or distress.

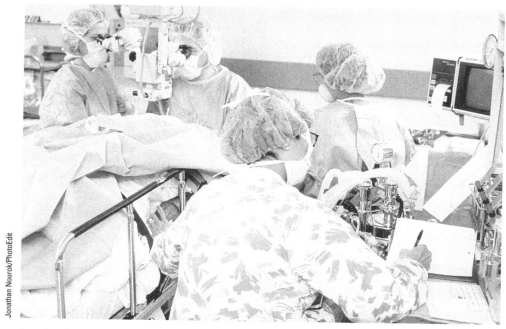

Imaging the numerous decisions required of a nurse working in a supervisory position in a hospital helps us understand what decision making is, the types of decisions that must be made in a workday, and how decision making and problem solving relate to one another.

Effective supervisors must be able to identify problems and their cause(s), to analyze complex and involved situations, and to solve problems by removing their cause(s). However, placing too much emphasis on problems can prevent one from identifying opportunities. After all, solving a problem only eliminates or neutralizes a negative situation. Progress or advancement comes from seeking and identifying opportunities; recognizing the emotions, needs, and motivations of the people involved; and analyzing ways of satisfying them. Here are some examples of "opportunity" decision making at the supervisory level:

1. Replacing a piece of equipment that, although it is still functioning well, can be upgraded to increase efficiency.
2. Improving an already-effective preventive maintenance system.
3. Cross-training employees to broaden their skills and raise morale.
4. Creating a new position for a highly skilled technician who has recently left the employ of a competitor.
5. Instituting the most innovative new processes and techniques.

STOP AND THINK

What other examples of "opportunity" decision making can you think of?

How to Make Decisions

4. Discuss how decisions are made.

Exhibit 3-2 shows that the decision-making process involves six basic steps. We have already mentioned most of them.

Step 1: Define the Idea or Problem

Peter Drucker once stated that a decision is only as good as the correct definition of the problem. In other words, the right cure for the wrong problem is just as bad as the wrong cure for the right problem. However, it is not always easy to know what the problem is or which opportunity is the best one to seek. When you have a fever, it is only a symptom of the true problem—an infection or other disorder. Likewise, as a supervisor, you remember that low morale, high turnover, many complaints or grievances, waste, and declining sales are not the real problem. They are only symptoms of the real problem.

If the decision to be made involves solving a problem, its cause, or the factors that are creating it, must be determined. Without identifying the cause (or causes), it is difficult to solve the problem because you may be treating its symptom rather than the root cause(s). Exhibit 3-3 highlights some action steps that can be taken to identify the source of elusive problems.

EXHIBIT 3-2

Steps in Decision Making

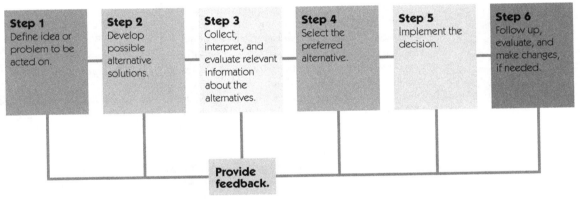

EXHIBIT 3-3

How to Identify the Source of Elusive Problems

Every supervisor, manager, and foreman has experienced it. Something's wrong—but you can't quite put your finger on it. Something doesn't feel right. But what is it?

Supervisors are, first and foremost, "fixers." If something is not clicking in your factory, shop, office, department, or division, it's your job to find out why and get things back on track. That's why there is a little bit of detective in every effective supervisor.

Following are 10 action steps many successful managers take to identify the exact source and origin of elusive problems in the workplace. They may help you root out problems, sooner rather than later, as well:

1. *Ask. Some managers think they have to know or come up with all the answers.* They're wrong. Even though you are the "boss," you don't have to detect and dissect every problem all by yourself. It's OK to ask others (e.g., colleagues, employees, customers). There are lots of ways to inquire about problems and solutions. Hold brainstorming sessions. Conduct individual interviews. Initiate question-driven interdisciplinary dialogues and discussions. Don't be afraid to try a variety of approaches.

2. *Let someone else do the asking.* Employees won't always tell their supervisors bad news—even if it is true. They may not want to upset the boss, betray confidences or be viewed as an informant. In some toxic organizational cultures, "whistle-blower" is looked down on as "stool pigeon," which translates to "traitor." What often works best is to bring in a respected third party to pick employees' brains and ask around about what's not working.

(Continued)

EXHIBIT 3-3
Continued

Workers may open up more to an objective outsider than to their own supervisor. This approach succeeds only if the outsider has universal credibility and is trusted by all parties involved. Widely respected former managers, union representatives, retirees, or outside third parties with a reputation for integrity are the best choices.

3. *Check out rumors.* Rumors are usually just gossip—part venting and part entertaining. But sometimes, rumors are more. Rumors can be symptoms of a problem. Clues to a problem. Or the problem itself. In any case, it's worth tracing down ugly or dangerous rumors to their source and determining their credibility.

4. *Pay attention to veteran employees.* Novices and newcomers are seldom the source of serious problems within the organization. They are not usually allowed enough latitude to do significant damage. Besides, they are normally under close scrutiny to see if they are going to work out.

5. *Test the communication systems.* More organizational problems are caused by poor communication, miscommunication, or lack of communication than by any other source. That's why any supervisory sleuthing to uncover an internal problem should include a communications audit.
   The questions to ask include:

   - Are employees at all levels getting the information they need?
   - Is the information accurate and consistent?
   - Are employees receiving needed information in a timely manner?

   The easiest, quickest, and best way to resolve, eliminate, or prevent internal problems is to make sure that all operations are completely transparent. This requires open, accurate, and complete information flowing freely in all directions

6. *Revisit policies and procedures.* The legendary comic strip hero Pogo once proclaimed, "We have met the enemy and he is us." He could have been talking about overorganized organizations (particularly business organizations) that become so obsessed with their own rules, regulations, and rituals that these trappings take on a life of their own—actually displacing or replacing the organization's core mission and purpose. Sound familiar?

7. *Reexamine expectations.* What you expect is what you get. Right? Not always. Expectations can be stepping stones—or stumbling blocks. When expectations, goals, quotas, or targets are unreasonably high, workers eventually get frustrated. Often, they just give up and start going through the motions. Conversely, if expectations are too low, there is no challenge. Workers quickly get bored and inattentive, which leads to sloppy work—and mistakes. It is only when expectations stretch employees, but remain reachable, that they promote continuous growth and drive peak performance.

8. *Review the reward system.* Reward symbols (bonuses, perks, gifts, prizes, and recognition awards) are designed to honor the best and challenge the rest. But it doesn't always work that way. If you reward the wrong workers or distribute the wrong rewards in the wrong way, the system can backfire. The result is likely to be disappointment, jealousy, and resentment, rather than motivation, incentive, and challenge. When the reward system is the problem, the solution may be as simple as asking three employees what rewards are most appropriate and appreciated and allowing workers to help choose the most worthy recipients.

9. *Reevaluate vendors.* Vendors are part of the extended family of your organization and a vital factor in its success or failure. A new vendor who is unfamiliar with your operation or a current vendor who lowers quality measures or standards or changes delivery or maintenance systems can send ripples of readjustment throughout your organization. As a supervisor, it's your job to track down the source of the problem wherever it is.

10. *Look to the competition.* Occasionally, what appears to be an internal problem is really a different kind of trouble altogether. If your organization is slipping behind, it may not mean you are doing something wrong. It may just be that the competition is doing something "righter." When you are doing everything as well as ever and still are losing ground, the competition is flat-out beating you. It's time to discover what your competitors are doing differently and figure out a way to equal or surpass their success.

(Continued)

The 10 steps above provide a systematic checklist for defining and finding the source of problems in the workplace. But what if you exhaust the list and still haven't discovered what's wrong? If your staff, team, or crew is still having a problem and you can't find the source by looking inside and outside the organization, what's left? Where else can you look?—In the mirror. Remember Pogo?

Look at your own leadership. Is your attitude, management style, planning, execution, or follow-through falling short? If you are the problem, you have to be the solution. How? Change, quit, or wait to be ousted. It's that simple.

All good supervisors have to be problem solvers. In business, as in the medical model, the basis for any solution (cure) is an accurate diagnosis. To succeed as a problem solver, you have to learn to be a good diagnostician. The first rule is don't guess or rush to judgment. Be methodical and thorough. Take your time in identifying what's wrong. Misdiagnosis in management—as in the medical profession—is the first step to malpractice. And there is no malpractice insurance for supervisors.

Source: Adapted from Ramsey, Robert D. "How to Identify the Source of Elusive Problems." *Supervision* 70.1 (Jan 2009): 10(4). Academic OneFile. Gale. University of South Alabama (AVL). 7 July 2009. Reprinted by permission of National Research Bureau.

Step 2: Develop Alternatives

The second step is to develop alternative ways of solving the problem or taking advantage of the opportunity. **Alternatives** are possible courses of action that can satisfy a need or solve a problem. Several choices are usually available if you are able to identify and develop them. However, supervisors may jump on the first feasible alternative without carefully considering other options. Brainstorming and nominal grouping, discussed later in the chapter, are good techniques to use to generate a full set of alternatives. Because it is easier to choose from a few alternatives than from many, it is good to reduce the number at some point by creating a "short list." Also, be aware that, if choices are limited, they may include only undesirable ones.

This is the stage in which you decide whether you should make the choice or channel it to some other person who has the authority or expertise to make it. If you decide that it is your "call," one choice is to do nothing, hoping that the problem will go away or solve itself in time. You must be careful, though, that this doesn't become an excuse for not making a difficult choice. If it does, you may get a reputation for being indecisive—the "kiss of death" to many promising supervisory careers.

Step 3: Collect, Interpret, and Evaluate Information about Each Alternative

Usually there are many sources from which to gather information affecting a decision. Sometimes standing orders, policies, procedures, and rules provide relevant information. In fact, these documents already may have made the decision for you—or at least may indicate how you should decide. Other sources of information include your own experience, company records and reports, discussion with the people directly and indirectly involved, and personal observations.

Perhaps you've heard the saying, "Tell me what you want to prove, and I'll get you the data to prove it." The effective evaluation of alternatives involves looking *objectively* at the pros and cons of each one. Choices can be evaluated in many ways. The information can be written down on a type of balance sheet, as shown in Exhibit 3-4, with the reasons for each alternative on one side and the reasons against it on the other. Or a process of elimination can be used in which the undesirable (or less desirable) choices are dropped.

alternatives

Possible courses of action that can satisfy a need or solve a problem.

5. *Name some factors to keep in mind when making decisions.*

EXHIBIT 3-4
Evaluating
Alternatives

Step 4: Select the Preferred Alternative

Finally, you reach the point where you must make a choice. You look at your conclusions from step 3 and then logically and rationally pick the alternative you think is most desirable for all concerned from objective, ethical, and practical points of view.

Selecting the preferred alternative involves cost/benefit analysis and risk analysis. Using the technique of **cost/benefit analysis**, you estimate what each alternative will cost in terms of human, physical, and financial resources. Then you estimate the expected benefits. Finally, you compare the two estimates. You choose the one with the greatest payoff, where the ratio of benefits to cost is most favorable.

cost/benefit analysis

Estimating and comparing the costs and benefits of alternatives.

STOP AND THINK

Based on the information in the opening case, do you think the potential rewards associated with balancing growth and internal processing outweigh the potential risks of growing less rapidly?

---

risk

The possibility of defeat, disadvantage, injury, or loss.

Analysis of risk is inherent in decision making. **Risk** is the possibility of defeat, disadvantage, injury, or loss. Prudent decision makers try to minimize risk by effectively forecasting outcomes and considering all variables.

Step 5: Implement the Decision

Effective decision making doesn't stop when you choose from among alternatives. The decision must be put into operation. For example, you might need to obtain and allocate some equipment and supplies. Or you might need to develop methods and procedures. Or you might have to select, train, or even terminate some employees. This is a difficult part of decision making because you must face and deal with people who may not like your choice. Many good supervisory decisions are ineffective because of the way they're implemented.

Step 6: Follow Up, Evaluate, and Make Changes—If Needed

This last step in the decision-making process involves exercising management's control function. It determines whether the implementation of the decision is proceeding smoothly and achieving the desired results. If not, and the decision can be changed or modified, it should be. If it can't be changed, then you must live with it and try to make it succeed.

Approaches to Decision Making and Problem Solving

6. *Decide whether to use the individual approach or the group approach when making decisions.*

Two approaches that are particularly useful in both decision making and problem solving are the Myers–Briggs Type Indicator and the Vroom–Yetton model. The Myers–Briggs Type Indicator is the better known and is used throughout the world.

The Myers–Briggs Type Indicator

Myers–Briggs Type Indicator® (MBTI®)

Helps identify an individual's personal style related to decision making and problem solving.

The 126-item **Myers–Briggs Type Indicator® (MBTI®)** helps to identify an individual's personal style.[2] Although it measures eight dichotomies of personality types, we will concern ourselves with only the four internal dimensions: (1) sensing versus (2) intuition and (3) thinking versus (4) feeling. These four are directly related to decision making and problem solving. (The Myers–Briggs concept is based on the work of scholar–physician Carl Gustav Jung, born in Switzerland and a contemporary of Sigmund Freud. Isabel Myers and her mother, Katherine Briggs, further refined and added to the basic theory.)

According to Myers and Briggs, people who rely primarily on *sensing*, or becoming aware of things through the five senses, tend to be patient, practical, and realistic. Those who rely primarily on *intuition* tend to be impatient, idea and theory oriented, and creative. Although everyone uses both ways of perceiving, Myers and Briggs indicate that at an early age, we develop a preference for one method over the other. Therefore, we tend to use our favorite approach and slight the one we enjoy less. Thus, people develop a set of traits based on whether they prefer sensing or intuition, as shown in the top half of Exhibit 3-5.

People who trust and prefer *thinking*, or using a rational, logical process to come to impersonal conclusions, are quite skillful in dealing with matters that require logic, objectivity, and careful examination of facts. On the other hand, those who trust and prefer *feeling*, or using innate processes that take into account one's own and others' values and beliefs, tend to be adept at working with other people and successful in applying skills in interpersonal and human relations. Such people are normally tactful and appreciative and have the ability to empathize with other people's problems and feelings. The bottom half of Exhibit 3-5 compares thinking and feeling types.

Although experience and growth opportunities can help develop weaker dichotomies, most people have two developed dimensions. The ideal is to maintain a balance by developing capability in all four. This is especially important for decision making because all four dichotomies can be valuable in the decision-making method described earlier.

Sensing, which helps in developing and facing facts as well as being realistic about the nature of the problem or opportunity, is helpful in step 1, recognizing a problem or opportunity. *Intuition*, on the other hand, is used in areas where creativity is needed to see possibilities and develop opportunities. It is therefore helpful in step 2, developing alternative courses of action.

Because *thinking* is impersonal and logically considers the consequences of cause and effect, it is helpful in step 3, evaluating the alternatives. *Feeling* comes into play when it is necessary to consider the values and ethics of others and the impact of the final decision on them. This provides sensitivity in selecting the preferred alternative and implementing it.

EXHIBIT 3-5

Characteristics of
Different Personality
Types

HOW DO YOU PREFER TO TAKE IN INFORMATION? THE S–N DICHOTOMY	
SENSING	INTUITION
People who prefer Sensing like to take in information that is real and tangible—what is actually happening. They are observant about the specifics of what is going on around them and are especially attuned to practical realities.	People who prefer Intuition like to take in information by seeing the big picture, focusing on the relationships and connections between facts. They want to grasp patterns and are especially attuned to seeing new possibilities.
Characteristics associated with people who prefer Sensing:	*Characteristics associated with people who prefer Intuition:*
• Oriented to present realities • Factual and concrete • Focus on what is real and actual • Observe and remember specifics • Build carefully and thoroughly toward conclusions • Understand ideas and theories through practical applications • Trust experience	• Oriented to future possibilities • Imaginative and verbally creative • Focus on the patterns and meanings in data • Remember specifics when they relate to a pattern • Move quickly to conclusions, follow hunches • Want to clarify ideas and theories before putting them into practice • Trust inspiration

HOW DO YOU MAKE DECISIONS? THE T–F DICHOTOMY	
THINKING	FEELING
People who prefer to use Thinking in decision making like to look at the logical consequences of a choice or action. They want to mentally remove themselves from the situation to examine the pros and cons objectively. They are energized by critiquing and analyzing to identify what's wrong with something so they can solve the problem. Their goal is to find a standard or principle that will apply in all similar situations.	People who prefer to use Feeling in decision making like to consider what is important to them and to others involved. They mentally place themselves into the situation to identify with everyone so they can make decisions based on their values about honoring people. They are energized by appreciating and supporting others and look for qualities to praise. Their goal is to create harmony and treat each person as a unique individual.
Characteristics associated with people who prefer Thinking:	*Characteristics associated with people who prefer Feeling:*
• Analytical • Use cause-and-effect reasoning • Solve problems with logic • Strive for an objective standard of truth • Reasonable • Can be "tough-minded" • Fair—want everyone treated equally	• Empathetic • Guided by personal values • Assess impacts of decisions on people • Strive for harmony and positive interactions • Compassionate • May appear "tenderhearted" • Fair—want everyone treated as an individual

Note: While the names of some of the MBTI® preferences are familiar words, the MBTI® meaning of the preferences is somewhat different from everyday use. Remember:

- "Extrovert" does not mean "talkative" or "loud."
- "Introvert" does not mean "shy" or "inhibited."
- "Feeling" does not mean "emotional."
- "Judging" does not mean "judgmental."
- "Perceiving" does not mean "perceptive."

Source: Reproduced by special permission of the publishers, Consulting Psychologists Press, Inc., Palo Alto, CA 94303, from *Introduction to Type*, by Isabel Briggs Myers. Copyright 1980 by Consulting Psychologists Press, Inc. All rights reserved. Further reproduction is prohibited without the publisher's consent.

STOP AND THINK

Reflect on the chapter preview. What type of MBTI decision style do you think Jeff Mackin possesses? Why?

Ideally, as a result of new experiences such as working in a team or being coached through training, we can develop balance and function effectively in all dichotomies. Although she is retired now, a bank officer who developed such balance while we were consulting with her bank is profiled next.

A Well-Balanced Myers–Briggs Profile

Linda Dean Fucci was secretary/treasurer at Auburn National Bank in Auburn, Alabama. Her duties included investment portfolio management, shareholder relations, asset liability management, strategic planning, accounting procedures, budgeting, tax planning, and control. Based on good performance, her duties were expanded to include the departments of data processing, marketing, and electronic services. Ultimately her good work efforts led to her promotion to senior vice president of the bank's holding company.

Linda had always had a strong work ethic. She graduated from Southern Union Junior College with a grade point average (GPA) of 4.0, and went on to complete flight training to the level of commercial pilot and flight instructor. Linda has always regretted not completing a Bachelor of Science degree in business, but this lack was not a barrier to her career achievement. For example, she graduated from Louisiana State University's Graduate School of Banking of the South—one of the premier schools in the country for bankers on a fast career track—with a GPA of 2.73 (out of 3.0). In a graduating class of 353 bankers, she not only ranked ninth in academic achievements but also was elected as class president. The Alabama Senate passed a resolution of commendation for that achievement. Her previous bank president, William Walker, singled her out in a speech at a state banking meeting as the best chief financial officer at the time of any bank in the state.

Linda's decision-making style is intuitive-thinking. Although these two dimensions are her strongest, she is quite flexible. Through experience and effort, she developed the sensing and feeling sides as well. In a confidential employee survey evaluating the effectiveness of the top-level Auburn National Bank officers, Linda received an excellent rating. Under the heading of "Additional Comments," one of the employees made this observation: "Linda is a great officer of the bank, representing us in a highly professional manner. She is a great manager and leader, earning a high degree of respect from her employees. She is my mentor. When I grow up, I want to be just like her."

Asked to describe her management philosophy and core values, Linda responded with the following impromptu remarks:

Maybe because I came up through the ranks, I can remember what it was like to be at all different levels. I can remember being unsure of myself and how different reactions made me feel. I try not to reprimand when people make mistakes but to understand and teach. I try never to make them feel "stupid." I do not think that people make errors intentionally.... I think that people need to feel important. Sometimes all it takes is a title. I do not like to call people "clerks." Doesn't "funds management assistant" sound better than "clerk"?

I try to provide my employees with as much knowledge as I can. I sincerely believe that shared knowledge is increased power. The more people in my department know, then the better they do their jobs and the better I, my department, and the whole organization look.

I don't think anything makes me feel better than to teach someone something and then see them excel at putting it to use.

Once my employees have learned enough to progress to a given level, I try to leave them alone to get their jobs done. I know they will make some mistakes, but I also think they will learn more this way.

I try to give lots and lots of credit. Whenever I am praised for something done in my department, if others had a hand in it, I give them credit. On the other hand, I try not to pass on the blame. We deal with that back in the department.

I try always to be honest with the employees in my department.

I guess it all comes down to treating others the way I want to be treated; putting myself in their place and feeling how they feel; sensing what is difficult for them to say, to do, and trying to make it easier.

I believe in participative management. I have seen it work in our institution. People are experts in different areas, and the pooling of that expertise creates an exceptional organization. People work harder for a plan they have had a part in than a plan simply dictated to them.

Source: Discussions and correspondence with Linda Dean Fucci.

Carl Jung saw type development as a lifelong, never-ending process. People grow and develop problem-solving and decision-making processes if they have the ability to learn from experience. In our profile of Linda Fucci (intuitive-thinking), we saw an example of development of the sensing and feeling dimensions. As a result, she has the ability to use the appropriate dimension at the appropriate time, thus gaining good balance and wholeness in problem solving and decision making.

The Vroom–Yetton Model

Vroom–Yetton model

Provides guidelines on the extent to which subordinates are involved in decision making or problem solving.

The **Vroom–Yetton model** provides guidelines on the extent to which subordinates are involved in decision making or problem solving.[3] This involvement may run the gamut from consensus decision making by a natural or self-managing work team, a committee, or an ad hoc task force to the manager making the decision with minimal or no involvement of others. The assistance of subordinates may occur at any of the decision-making steps.

The extent of employee involvement is a contingency call based on the situation, the quality of information available to the decision making, the importance of subordinates' acceptance of the decision, and the time to make the decision.

Participation   Exhibit 3-6 defines five alternative participation styles, as developed by Vroom and Yetton. There are two autocratic approaches (A and B), two consultative approaches (C and D), and one group consensus approach (E). These five approaches represent the varying degrees of participation by others a manager uses in decision making.

Appropriate Style   A manager can use a decision tree in determining which approach to use. One example of such a tree is shown in Exhibit 3-7. The questions shown at the top help the decision maker determine the characteristics of a given decision situation.

To use the model for a particular situation, you start at the left-hand side of the tree and work toward the right. When you encounter a box, answer the corresponding question and proceed to the next appropriate box. The decision style designation you finally reach will suggest which of the participation styles from Exhibit 3-6 you should probably use.

There are other parts of Vroom and Yetton's theory that are too detailed to present here. This classic model has been the subject of much attention and is being tested and evaluated by many management researchers.[4]

EXHIBIT 3-6

Managers' Participation Styles for Making Decisions

PARTICIPATION STYLE	DESCRIPTION
A	You solve the problem or make the decision yourself, using the information available to you at the present time.
B	You obtain any necessary information from subordinates, then decide on a solution to the problem yourself.
C	You share the problem with the relevant subordinates individually, getting their ideas and suggestions without bringing them together as a group. Then *you* make the decision.
D	You share the problem with your subordinates in a group meeting, in which you obtain their ideas and suggestions. Then you make the decision.
E	You share the problem with your subordinates as a group. Together you generate and evaluate alternatives and attempt to reach agreement (consensus) on a solution. You can provide the group with information or ideas, but you do not try to press them to adopt "your" solution, and you are willing to accept and implement any solution that has the support of the entire group.

Note: A & B = autocratic, C & D = consultative, E = group consensus.

Source: Figure 9.3 from *Leadership and Decision-Making*, by Victor H. Vroom and Philip W. Yetton, © 1973. Reprinted by permission of the University of Pittsburgh Press.

EXHIBIT 3-7

Decision Tree, Governing Group Problems

1. Is there a quality requirement such that one solution is likely to be more rational than another?
2. Do you have sufficient information to make a high-quality decision?
3. Is the problem structured?
4. Is acceptance of decision by subordinates critical to implementation?
5. Is it reasonably certain that your subordinates would accept the decision if you were to make it by yourself?
6. Do subordinates share the organizational goals to be obtained in solving this problem?
7. Is conflict among subordinately likely in preferred solution?

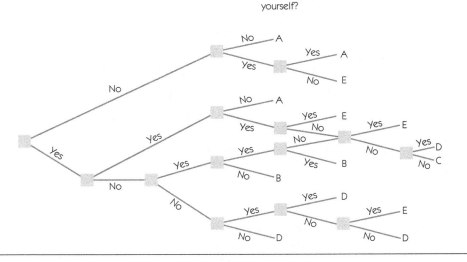

Two cases at the end of this chapter will give you an opportunity to put the model to use. Although a model such as the one just discussed can help in selecting the best decision-making method, a manager's personal style also has a major impact on the method chosen. (Exhibit 3-8 shows how to use the model in making the decision on a student banquet date.)

EXHIBIT 3-8

The Vroom–Yetton Model: Which Decision Style to Use

Decision Problem

As president of the Student Management Club at State University, you must make a decision concerning a date for the annual student banquet.

Q1   Is there a quality requirement such that one solution is likely to be more rational than another?

Ans   Yes. One solution is likely to be more rational because there are various dates that will be unsatisfactory because of competing activities.

Q2   Do you have sufficient information to make a high-quality decision?

Ans   No. You may have certain information on competing dates for some officially scheduled university activities, but there may be some other kinds of activities going on that you are unaware of.

Q3   Is the problem structured?

Ans   Yes. Selection of a given date for a banquet to be held within the next month is a well-structured decision problem.

Q4   Is acceptance of the decision by your subordinates critical to implementation?

Ans   Yes. If the subordinates (and others) don't show up, the banquet is a failure.

Q5   Is it reasonably certain that the decision would be accepted by your subordinates if you were to make it by yourself?

Ans   No. You might accidentally select a date that would not be suitable to your subordinates. For example, the day you select could be one on which subordinates have a major exam or term papers due the following day.

Q6   Do members share the view that the banquet date is important?

Ans   Yes. Members have shown good attendance at meetings and consider the banquet the highlight of the year. Awards are presented, next year's officers are announced, and so on.

Optimum Decision Style

As president, you should share the problem with members as a group, with the group generating and evaluating alternatives, and should attempt to arrive at a consensus decision.

Creative Problem Solving

More organizations and individual managers are involving subordinates in decision making and problem solving, particularly using styles similar to D and E in the Vroom–Yetton model. As a senior technician and union leader in a paper mill told one of the authors, "Management used to tell us what to do; now they ask us." One of the primary reasons for this trend is the concept of synergy.

The Concept of Synergy and Some Processes of Creative Problem Solving

7. *Discuss some ways of improving decision making.*

synergy

The whole is greater than the sum of the parts.

creativity

Creativity is the process of developing something unique or original.

Synergy means that the whole is greater than the sum of the parts. This concept is especially applicable in the use of teams and ad hoc task forces in problem solving. Assume that an ad hoc task force of five persons is presented with a complex problem that has an impact on the entire organization. If the team reaches a synergistic solution to the complex problem, then mathematically, synergy can be defined as $1 + 1 + 1 + 1 + 1 = $ more than 5.

Increasingly, this type of synergy is being achieved by teams throughout the world.

Developing Creativity

Creativity is the process of developing something unique or original. Scientists generalize that the right hemisphere of the brain captures our intuitive impulses. If we think of ourselves as problem solvers/decision makers, the right side of the brain generates ideas and is where imagination originates. Right-hemispheric functions are frequent catalysts for solution alternatives.

Alternatively, the brain's left hemisphere functions in logical, analytical, and linear ways, allowing the decision maker to evaluate his or her intuitive, imaginative alternatives. This is where judgment enters into the process. Although the brain has a multifunctional capacity, the decision maker may allow his or her preferred brain functioning to dominate and can allow left-side evaluation and analysis to encroach on right-brain intuitive ideas prematurely.

To gain the maximum benefit from ad hoc task forces, quality circles, self-managing work teams, or any problem-solving effort, the brain's left-hemisphere functions must be restrained initially. The key to doing so is to make use of the concept of deferred judgment. This is the idea behind brainstorming, and the secret is to develop right-hemispheric skills and to use them appropriately. After the ideas are generated, it is helpful to use analytical brain functions to evaluate and judge which insights are good, cost-effective, and so forth. Using right-hemisphere functions as thought generators and following them with left-brained functions results in powerfully effective "whole-brained" creativity. Three techniques that are very useful in the idea-generation process are brainstorming, the Crawford Slip technique, and the nominal grouping technique.

Brainstorming

brainstorming

Freely thinking of ideas without evaluating the ideas as they are generated.

One of the most effective techniques in creative problem solving is brainstorming. **Brainstorming** refers to a group of individuals responding to a question such as "How can we improve communication?" without evaluating the ideas as they are generated. The ideas are offered and recorded, no matter how silly they may appear and without regard to the rank of individuals or the value of any idea. Sorting out the value of respective ideas comes later. Larry Hirschhorn, management consultant and writer, has suggested four excellent guidelines when using this powerful technique:

1. The group favors quantity over quality.
2. Team members refrain from judging anyone's contributions; they can ask questions later, in the evaluation part.
3. Team members avoid censoring.
4. Pride of authority is minimized; team members should feel free to offer variants and build on one another's ideas.[5]

Brainstorming is especially useful in developing alternatives during step 2 of the decision-making or problem-solving process. In most cases in creative problem solving, the team will draw from a number of alternatives in putting together the action plan. In addition to identifying possible solutions, brainstorming also is useful in these dimensions of creative problem solving:

- *Defining all possible problems*
- *Redefining problems*
- *Determining all possible causes for a problem*
- *Listing all possible actions for implementing the chosen solution*

Unfortunately, based on the observations of the authors, formally appointed committees and management meetings with subordinates rarely use brainstorming in their deliberation. For example, a faculty committee spent the allotted time for a meeting (two hours) debating the pros and cons of the second idea presented. On the other hand, ad hoc task forces and problem-solving teams tend to use brainstorming in a more creative and effective manner.

STOP AND THINK

Why do you think formal committees or bosses meeting with their subordinates seldom use brainstorming in problem-solving endeavors?

Crawford Slip technique

Makes use of two elements that are important in achieving creativity—fluency and flexibility.

fluency

The ability to let ideas flow out of your head like water over a waterfall.

flexibility

The ability to use free association to generate or classify ideas in categories.

Crawford Slip Technique

The **Crawford Slip technique** was developed by Professor C.C. Crawford at the University of Southern California. It makes use of two elements that are important in achieving creativity—fluency and flexibility. **Fluency** is the ability to let ideas flow out of your head like water over a waterfall, and **flexibility** is the ability to use free association to generate or classify ideas in categories. Materials needed are a number of 3″ × 5″ scratch pads and a number of empty boxes distributed among the participants. The process starts by telling participants that they are about to engage in a new type of problem solving that will generate 50 to 100 new ideas.

For example, this technique was used with the top management of Baldor Electric Company, a very successful company listed on the New York Stock Exchange. Unfortunately, one of the large motors it produced was losing money. The following series of steps was initiated to deal with the problem.[6]

1. Participants were asked not to pause to evaluate ideas and not to generate such thoughts as "We've tried this before."
2. Every participant was given a 3″ × 5″ scratch pad.
3. In this technique, the leader presents a problem in how-to form. In the case of Baldor Electric, the problem presented was, "How can we reduce costs on our 300 series motors without affecting quality?"
4. Each person would write down as many answers to the problem as time would permit. After an idea was written on a slip, it was placed in the idea bank (box) anonymously.
5. After 10 minutes, the idea boxes were collected and task forces established. In the case of Baldor, there were three task forces. Idea slips were distributed to them like cards dealt from a deck.
6. Each task force was charged with arranging the ideas in categories, using judgment (left side of the brain) to throw out weak ideas, and then developing the good ideas and presenting recommendations to the larger group.

The CEO of the company then judged what ideas were most relevant to solving the problem and decided to implement them. Please note that although there was considerable participation in the process, *one person made the final decision.* In many instances, this is a desirable approach in using participative management.

Nominal Grouping Technique

nominal grouping technique (NGT)

A structured group technique for generating ideas through round-robin individual responses, group sharing without criticism, and written balloting.

The **nominal grouping technique (NGT)** also makes use of brainstorming, and we have found the technique to be very effective in developing creativity and generating useful information. Nominal grouping is a structured group technique for generating ideas through round-robin individual responses, group sharing without criticism, and written balloting. The authors have found it to be exceptionally beneficial to use nominal grouping in working with organizations. Exhibit 3-9 identifies the steps in nominal grouping when it is used in this manner. The following example illustrates the steps in the process.

The authors were asked to participate in a management development program for a branch plant of a corporation headquartered in our home state. The plant, located in another state, was struggling to achieve a break-even point, and the executive vice president hired us to conduct management training sessions. The authors were rotating training sessions, and the report after the first session was that the "canned management training was similar to placing a Band-Aid on a festering boil." During the break, the employees complained about issues and problems, the training program did not directly address. A consultation with the executive vice president resulted in a change in strategy for the next session.

Using the nominal grouping process, the 25 participants (supervisors, managers, and staff personnel) were asked to respond to two questions:

1. What are the strengths of the plant?
2. What are the problems preventing this plant from reaching its potential effectiveness?

Twelve strengths were generated, and 55 problems were initially identified. Through nominal voting, the top five problems were prioritized, task forces from the participants were formed, and action plans were developed to solve the plant's more pressing problems.

STOP AND THINK

Because in this process, only five problems were addressed, speculate on what happened to the majority of the other problems.

If your answer was, "They dissipated," you are correct.

Developing and implementing the action plans were catalysts in shifting the plant from a low performer to a high performer within a year.

Becoming Creative

Part of being creative is changing your perspective. For some, this may mean getting in touch with your intuitive side. To do so, try not to think logically about a situation, but rather, think about the possibilities. Don't worry about following rules; just have fun. If you have a narrowly focused job, step back and look at the big picture—think holistically.

For others, becoming creative may be as simple as doing something different: Go a different way to work; read a political blog or watch a news program that contains information that is completely opposite of your political views; spend time playing and having fun; try a different restaurant or bar; go to an event with the purpose of making new friends; or spend time with family.

EXHIBIT 3-9

Steps in Nominal Grouping

Divide into groups of six or nine persons.

Without interaction, list the strengths you feel are associated with Question 1, and then list the problems for Question 2.   (Time: 6 minutes.)

Select a recorder.

1. The recorder asks each member, one at a time, to read from his or her card one strength associated with Question 1. *Example*: What are the strengths of this plant?
2. The recorder writes each strength exactly as it is read.
3. Those having the same strength should raise hands. The recorder checkmarks each strength once for each person raising a hand.
4. When all Question 1 strengths are recorded, the procedure is repeated for Question 2 problems. *Example*: What are the problems preventing this plant from reaching its potential effectiveness?

Discuss the two lists. Clarify, defend, elaborate, or add other items as needed.   (Time: 5 minutes.)

Without interaction, each member lists on an index card the *five* items he or she considers most important with reference to Question 1; do the same for Question 2.

The recorder collects and records the votes.

The 2012 movie *Argo* illustrates how spending time with family can help a person think creatively. In the early part of the movie, CIA operative Tony Mendez, played by Ben Affleck, is trying to figure out how to rescue six U.S. diplomats from Tehran, Iran, during the 1979 Iran hostage crisis. Several options are being considered, but none seem to be viable. It is only when Mendez removes himself from the situation and goes home to spend time with his family that he is able to make the creative leap that leads to a viable rescue plan.

Ethical Considerations Play a Part

8. *Explain the role of ethics in the organization's and supervisor's decision making.*

Supervisors must be particularly concerned with ethical considerations when making decisions and solving problems. They should have a true concern for the well-being of others, both inside and outside the organization. Therefore, supervisors should not only obey all laws and conform to the ethical codes of practice established by their employer and society, but also have a personal set of ethical principles that guide their actions. However, the difficult question is, what is and what isn't ethical?

ethics

The standards used to judge the "rightness" or the "wrongness" of one person's behavior toward others.

Ethics are the standards used to judge the "rightness" or "wrongness" of one person's behavior toward others. As this concept of ethical behavior is the individual's personal *ethic*, it is the highest and most rigid level of behavior. The next highest level is adhering to professional and organizational *codes of ethics*, which are statements of what is and isn't acceptable behavior. The lowest level is the *legal level*, where we are all expected to adhere to the "law of the land."

Making a profit with no regard for the repercussions of operating methods can be disastrous. Ethical operations will take into account many factors including the impact on the overall economic well-being of the local community and the community at large. The reputation of a fine organization and its financial standing can be soiled quickly by operating in an unethical manner.

For example, Arthur Andersen, who headed one of the most respected accounting firms in the world, was a zealous supporter of high standards in the accounting industry. A stickler for honesty, he argued that an accountant's responsibility was to investors, not to the clients' management.

During the early years, it is reported that Arthur Andersen was approached by an executive from a local rail utility to sign off on accounts containing flawed accounting or else face the loss of a major client. Arthur Andersen refused in no uncertain terms, replying that he would not sign the accounts "for all the money in America."

For many years, Arthur Andersen's motto was "Think straight, talk straight." There is no doubt that Arthur Anderson was one of the most respected accounting firms in the world. This organization was built on being trustworthy. Its accounting expertise was highly valued. At the same time, it demonstrated high ethical standards and integrity that was beyond reproach. For decades, its accomplishments were rock solid.

Unfortunately, a huge lapse in ethical judgment by key management personnel regarding Enron erased the company's entire reputation. Its history of a highly prized reputation in professional accounting was damaged forever. Today, it is no longer a viable accounting firm.

Scandals involving Arthur Anderson and Enron are examples of ethically challenged organizations. Both of these companies were great at one time. Sadly, they stumbled along the way to success. They misplaced their ethics, with devastating results.[7]

Even after passage of the Sarbanes–Oxley Act, a response to the Enron debacle, media stories abound of mismanagement, fraud, and deceit (e.g., Bernie Madoff and Mark Bloom). So what is the best approach to ensure ethical decision making in organizations today? That is the focus of the next section.

STOP AND THINK

Consider the numerous media stories highlighting unethical business behaviors. Which one in your opinion is the most troublesome? Why?

Ethical Organizations

ethical organizations

Organizations composed of three pillars: ethical individuals, ethical leaders, and sound structures and systems.

Why is the topic of ethics so important for business managers to consider? To answer this question, business professors Marc Orlitzky, Frank Schmidt, and Sara Rynes looked at 52 studies on corporate social responsibility over a 30-year period. They found that well-run, profitable businesses also boasted solid social and environmental records.[8] In short, it makes economic sense! So how does a company manage ethics and social responsibility to differentiate itself from its competitors? Exhibit 3-10 shows that **ethical organizations** are composed of three pillars: ethical individuals, ethical leadership, and sound structures and systems.

EXHIBIT 3-10

The Three Pillars of Ethical Organizations

Source: Adapted from Linda Klebe Trevino, Laura Pincus Hartman, and Michael Brown, "Moral Person and Moral Manager," *California Management Review* 42, no. 4 (Summer 2000), pp. 128–142. Copyright © 2000, by The Regents of the University of California. Reprinted by permission of The Regents.

Ethical Individuals   Ethical individuals are honest and act with integrity. Ethical people can be trusted by others and can be relied upon to make the "right" choice, even in very challenging circumstances. To illustrate, consider the strength of Sherron Watkins's character, the person responsible for blowing the whistle on the aforementioned Enron and Arthur Anderson.

Were Sherron Watkins's actions worth the fallout? Since then, as one of America's most famous whistle-blowers, she has argued in published articles and speeches that her actions were not only justifiable, but ultimately beneficial. Watkins insisted that businesses must be judged on more than just the profits they create, and that "we need to reward the good, ethical ones." Although many people were hurt by her actions, she feels vindicated that her insistence on morality in business has lessened the chance that corruption will be rewarded.[9]

Managers may not be faced with the type of ethical dilemma Sherron Watkins had to deal with on a daily basis, but ethical issues do arise in the workplace. What separates people like Sherron from the rest of the pack is a firm belief in treating others fairly, with respect, and with dignity. Sometimes it is as simple as following the Golden Rule, treating others as you would like to be treated. However, as the collapse of Enron shows, simply hiring ethical individuals such as Sherron is not enough—it is only part of the solution. Leadership is at the core of initiating a vision of ethical behavior and setting the tone for what is and is not considered appropriate behavior.

Ethical Leadership   Look at Exhibit 3-10 again—this particular pillar is at the center of the ethical organization for a reason. Leaders guide the way; they are the visible face of the organization to internal as well as external stakeholders. As such, they are role models for others. This is especially true for supervisors. Your employees observe how you communicate with others, handle interpersonal conflict, and appraise others' actions, and even see some actions of which you are unaware! For example, if you openly communicate with your employees about ethics and important values, they will, over time, develop a sense of trust and a certain level of respect for you. If you act swiftly to deal with unethical behavior, this sends a direct message regarding what will and will not be tolerated. As a result, your employees' behaviors will become more consistent with the expectations that you have set. Consider the following story about Dan Amos.

Dan Amos, CEO of Aflac, joined the company in 1973. During his tenure, the company has grown into an international powerhouse in the insurance industry. Amos inherited a company that was founded on ethical principles, like many of the World's Most Ethical Companies. "This company was founded with the premise that if you take care of your employees, they will take care of the company. This principle has proven true for more than 50 years as Aflac has grown from a small family business to a Fortune 500 company," says Amos. One of the aspects that helps the company continue to thrive is Amos' transparent leadership. "As a public company there is a responsibility to tell people what is happening regardless of whether the news is particularly good or bad," Amos admits. "At Aflac, it is our custom to tell the people what we are doing and why we are doing it to limit any surprises in the future. As a publicly traded company, our actions impact the lives of shareholders and because they own our company, they have a right to know what lies ahead." This isn't just rhetoric—Amos can regularly be heard around the office telling employees, "Bad news does not improve with age." Amos notes that Aflac's ethics program isn't just intended for upper levels of management. Rather, an ethical culture is taught from the top down.[10]

STOP AND THINK

Visit Gallup's Web site at http://www.gallup.com/poll/1654/honesty-ethics-professions.aspx to view the poll results of how respondents rated the honest and ethical standards of people in a variety of professions. How did your profession rate? If the poll were administered today, do you believe any of the professions would be ranked differently? Why?

Structures and Systems   In addition to having ethical individuals and leaders, it is important that corporations create and sustain cultures that support ethical behavior. Developing a values statement or code of ethics is a good starting point, but to ensure this document has teeth, it is necessary to appoint a chief ethics officer to chair an ethics committee responsible for conducting ethics training and developing whistle-blowing mechanisms, such that the true spirit of the ethics document permeates throughout the entire organization.

Creating an ethical corporate culture is not easy. *Ethisphere* publishes a list of the world's most ethical companies each year. They utilize expert professors, government officials, lawyers, and organizational leaders to identify the initial pool of organizational candidates and develop and apply ethical criteria to generate a short list of potential winners. The winners of the World's Most Ethical Companies Awards are truly ethical leaders in their industries. (You may visit http://ethisphere.com to view winners for previous years or the current candidates.)

> *Each of these companies will have materially higher scores versus their competitors. They are the companies who force other companies to follow their leadership or fall behind. These are the companies who use ethical leadership as a profit driver. And each of these companies embody [sic] the true spirit of Ethispheres credo, "Good. Smart. Business. Profit."*[11]

External monitoring by watchdog groups is certainly a behavioral influence on organizations, but better internal monitoring is likely the key determinant of organizational change. As little as a decade ago, U.S. companies had few people to inspect thousands of manufacturing sites. Their superficial audits "didn't get at the root causes of problems," says Auret Van Heerden, executive director of the nonprofit Fair Labor Association.

> *Today, Van Heerden says, more corporations are strengthening their monitoring and teaching suppliers how to better run their plants and manage workers…. Nike (a 2010 Ethisphere Award Winner) is a seasoned veteran of audits. In the 1990s, the company was a favorite target of activists because of foreign sweatshops run by its suppliers.*

> *Now Nike inspects many of its 1,000 suppliers' factories worldwide. It grades them from A to D and warns poorly run sites to improve or get dropped.*[12]

Xerox (another 2013 Ethisphere Award Winner) has developed and implemented structures and systems to ensure honest, ethical interaction with another key stakeholder group—its employees.

Speaking with David Frishkorn, Director of Business Ethics & Compliance at Xerox, reveals a unique approach that Xerox employs in their ethics program. Many companies will place a strong emphasis on tone from the top, and stop there. Frishkorn prefers a different approach. "When everyone focuses on tone from the top, you can have somebody standing there, yelling and shouting, but if they're not respected, or if the message isn't properly received, or if the environment is one that is contrary to what the words from the top are, it's not going to be effective," says Frishkorn. "The real test of the tone from the top is that it's received well and that the employees commit to the program." To that end, Frishkorn says that Xerox helps employees get involved in the ethics program through a basic monthly survey that asks simple questions such as, "Do you think it's an ethical environment?," "Do you know about the helpline?," and "Would you call the helpline?" These fundamental questions help the compliance team get an accurate reading of the corporate environment. "There is ample opportunity and space in that survey for people to write in comments, and that's where we actually get a lot of the 'good' data," Frishkorn says. "So when something monumental happens that is either good or bad from the employees' perspective, relative to the ethics at Xerox, we can pick up on that pretty quick in the write-in comments."[13]

STOP AND THINK

Think of your own organization or, if you are not currently employed, a past employer or your school. Evaluate how ethical your organization is using the three pillars just described. Does your employer give equal weight to developing and sustaining all three pillars?

● Chapter Review

1. *Explain the role of decision making in the supervisor's job.*
This chapter focused on managerial decision making, which is the conscious selection of a course of action from among available alternatives to produce a given result. All employees, but especially managers, must make decisions.

2. *Discuss why supervisors need to make so many decisions.*
Programmed decisions are routine and repetitive and enable management to develop a systemic way to make them. Unprogrammed decisions occur relatively infrequently, and a separate decision must be undertaken each time.

3. *Define decision making and identify at least four elements involved.*
The five steps in managerial decision making are (1) recognizing a problem or opportunity, (2) developing alternative courses of action, (3) evaluating the advantages and disadvantages of the alternatives, (4) selecting a preferred alternative and implementing it, and (5) evaluating the decision results.

4. *Discuss how decisions are made.*

The decision-making method used also is influenced by the decision maker's personal problem-solving type or style. According to the Myers–Briggs Type Indicator, individuals have two ways of perceiving information and two ways of evaluating it. The four combinations of sensing-thinking, intuitive-thinking, sensing-feeling, and intuitive-feeling have a definite influence on problem solving and decision making. Ideally, a balance will be developed using all four dimensions in decision making.

5. *Name some factors to keep in mind when making decisions.*

To what extent should a manager involve others in the decision-making process? The Vroom–Yetton model helps answer the question by examining the key characteristics of given decision situations and identifying various decision-making styles. A particular decision style can be selected based on answers to questions about the characteristics of the given situation. Some techniques for involving others in creative problem solving are brainstorming, the Crawford Slip technique, and the nominal grouping technique.

6. *Decide whether to use the individual approach or the group approach when making decisions.*

The more effective supervisors use ethical value judgments in making decisions. Ethics are the standards used to judge the "rightness" or "wrongness" of actions or decisions when dealing with other people or organizations. Ethical value judgments have a wide range of consequences involving the decision maker, employees, stockholders, and the community in general, and, therefore, as much consideration should be given to people and their problems as to economical and financial factors.

7. *Discuss some ways of improving decision making.*

Decision making can be improved by individuals working together to achieve synergy. Brainstorming, the Crawford Slip, and the nominal grouping techniques are tools supervisors can use to enhance creativity and achieve synergy during the decision-making process. Getting in touch with one's intuitive side or changing perspectives can aid in enhancing one's creativity.

8. *Explain the role of ethics in the organization's and supervisor's decision making.*

Ethical organizations are composed of three pillars: ethical individuals, ethical leaders, and ethical structures and systems. Although ethical leadership is at the center of a well-grounded organization, a lack of one or more of these key elements makes an organization vulnerable to unethical tendencies and practices.

Supervisors must be particularly concerned with ethical considerations when making decisions and solving problems. They should have a true concern for the well-being of others, both inside and outside the organization. Therefore, supervisors not only should obey all laws and conform to the ethical codes of practice established by their employer and society, but also have a personal set of ethical principles that guide their actions.

Key Terms

span of management, p. 61
decision making, p. 62
programmed decisions, p. 63
nonprogrammed decisions, p. 63
opportunity, p. 63
problem, p. 63
alternatives, p. 67
cost/benefit analysis, p. 68

risk, p. 68
Myers–Briggs Type Indicator®
  (MBTI®), p. 69
Vroom–Yetton model, p. 72
synergy, p. 74
creativity, p. 74
brainstorming, p. 75
Crawford Slip technique, p. 76

fluency, p. 76
flexibility, p. 76
nominal grouping technique
  (NGT), p. 76
ethics, p. 78
ethical organizations, p. 79

Discussion Questions

1. Peter Drucker states that a big decision-making error supervisors frequently make is failing to get a handle on a problem. Often, managers plunge in prematurely. Why do you think many managers make this common mistake?

2. Discuss the following statement: It's better for a manager to try to carry out a poor decision for the sake of worker confidence. You can't build worker confidence by continually admitting the poor decisions you make.

3. What are the pros and cons of decisions made by groups such as committees and task forces as compared to decisions made by one person?

4. Is it possible for someone to be a good decision maker but a poor supervisor? Explain.

5. One supervisor says that she finds procrastination to be a big help in her decision making. Do you agree or disagree? Why?

6. Is it possible to operate as an ethical organization without one or more of the three pillars? Discuss.

Skill Builder 3.1

Resources

Information

Coast Guard Cutter Decision Problem

You are the captain of a 210-foot medium-endurance Coast Guard cutter, with a crew of nine officers and 65 enlisted personnel. Your mission is general at-sea law enforcement and search and rescue. At 2:00 this morning, while en route to your home port after a routine two-week patrol, you received word from the New York Rescue Coordination Center that a small plane had ditched 70 miles offshore. You obtained all the available information concerning the location of the crash, informed your crew of the mission, and set a new course at maximum speed heading for the scene to commence a search for survivors and wreckage.

You have now been searching for 20 hours. Your search operation has been increasingly impaired by rough seas, and there is evidence of a severe storm building to the southwest. The atmospherics associated with the deteriorating weather have made communications with the New York Rescue Coordination Center impossible. A decision must be made shortly about whether to abandon the search and place your vessel on a northeasterly course to ride out the storm—thereby protecting the vessel and your crew, but relegating any possible survivors to almost certain death from exposure—or to continue a potentially futile search and incur the risks it would entail.

Systems

Instructions:
You have contacted the weather bureau for up-to-date information concerning the severity and duration of the storm. While your crew members are extremely conscientious about their responsibility, you believe that they would be divided on the decision of leaving or staying.

Review the decision processes in this chapter in Exhibit 3-6 and decide which comes closest to what you would do if you were the captain in this situation. Circle your choice:

A B C D E

Source: Victor H. Vroom and Arthur G. Jago, *New Leadership: Managing Participation in Organizations*, 1st edition, © 1988. Reprinted by Permission of Pearson Education, Inc., Upper Saddle River, NJ.

Skill Builder 3.2

Resources

Information

Systems

New Machines Decision Problem
You are the manufacturing manager in a large electronics plant. The company's management has always been searching for ways of increasing efficiency. They have recently installed new machines and put in a new, simplified work system, but to the surprise of everyone, including yourself, the expected increase in productivity was not realized. In fact, production has begun to drop, quality has fallen off, and the number of employee separations has risen.

You do not believe that there is anything wrong with the machines. You have had reports from other companies that are using them, and the reports confirm this opinion. You also have had representatives from the firm that built the machines go over them, and they report that the machines are operating at peak efficiency.

You suspect that some parts of the new work system may be responsible for the change, but this view is not widely shared among your immediate subordinates—four first-level supervisors, each in charge of a section, and your supply manager. The drop in production has been variously attributed to poor training of the operators, lack of an adequate system of financial incentives, and poor morale. Clearly, this is an issue about which there is considerable depth of feeling within individuals and potential disagreement among your subordinates.

This morning you received a phone call from your division manager. He had just received your production figures for the last six months and was calling to express his concern. He indicated that the problem was yours to solve in any way that you thought best, but that he would like to know within a week what steps you plan to take.

You share your division manager's concern about the falling productivity and know that your people are also concerned. The problem is to decide what steps to take.

Instructions:
Review the decision processes in this chapter in Exhibit 3-6 and decide which comes closest to what you would do if you were the manager in the above situation. Circle your choice:

A B C D E

Source: Case IV from *Leadership and Decision-Making*, by Victor H. Vroom and Philip W. Yetton, © 1973. Reprinted by permission of the University of Pittsburgh Press.

Skill Builder 3.3

Information

Technology

Identifying Your Problem-Solving Style

Instructions:
Indicate the response that comes closest to how you usually feel or act. If you really cannot choose, two answers being an absolute toss-up, leave that question unanswered. There are no correct or incorrect answers.

1. Which are you more careful about,
   a. what people's rights are or
   b. how people feel?

2. Which phrase do you feel best describes you,
   a. having common sense or
   b. having vision?

3. Are you more likely to be impressed by
   a. principles or
   b. emotions?

4. Which phrase best describes your preference as to how to get a job done,
   a. using techniques that have proved effective in past situations or
   b. experimenting with new and different approaches?

5. In making decisions, which is more important to you,
   a. standards or
   b. feelings?

6. Which do you think is worse,
   a. not having a clear grasp of details or
   b. not having a clear grasp of the big picture?

7. Do your friends see you as basically more
   a. hardheaded or
   b. warmhearted?

8. Are you basically more interested in
   a. data or
   b. ideas?

9. If another person says something that is incorrect, which would you normally do,
   a. point out the error or
   b. ignore it?

10. Which kind of person would you prefer as a roommate,
    a. someone who's very practical, with both feet on the ground, or
    b. someone who's always having new ideas?

11. Are you best described as
    a. drawing conclusions in a logical, objective way or
    b. drawing conclusions based on feelings or emotions?

12. In making decisions, are you more likely to decide based on
    a. the real facts and data or
    b. your hunches?

13. As a student, would you prefer taking
    a. fact-oriented courses or
    b. theory-oriented courses?

14. Which do you feel is the greater error,
    a. to be too sympathetic or
    b. to be too firm?

15. Assume that a party contains two rooms of people, and in each room are the same types of people. Which room would you be drawn to,
    a. a room with sensible people or
    b. a room with imaginative people?

16. Which of the following terms best describes you:
    a. objective or
    b. compassionate?

17. Which do you value more highly,
    a. a strong sense of reality or
    b. a strong imagination?

18. Which role has the greater appeal to you,
    a. being a judge or
    b. being a peacemaker?

19. In which of these activities have you more interest:
    a. production or
    b. design?

20. Would you describe yourself as
    a. more firm than merciful or
    b. more merciful than firm?

Score Sheet Instructions:

Record your answers to each question in the appropriate box. Then add the total number of checks in each column. If you have an equal number of points for Sensor and Intuitor, circle the Intuitor; if an equal number of points for Thinker and Feeler, circle the Feeler.

	A	B		A	B
2	_____	_____	1	_____	_____
4	_____	_____	3	_____	_____
6	_____	_____	5	_____	_____
8	_____	_____	7	_____	_____
10	_____	_____	9	_____	_____
12	_____	_____	11	_____	_____
14	_____	_____	14	_____	_____
15	_____	_____	16	_____	_____
17	_____	_____	18	_____	_____
19	_____	_____	20	_____	_____
TOTAL	_____	_____	TOTAL	_____	_____
	SENSOR	INTUITOR		THINKER	FEELER

The Keirsey Temperament Sorter is very similar to the MBTI® in terms of question content, terminology, and personality types. To find out your complete personality type (using all four dimensions), you may visit http://www.keirsey.com/ to complete a multi-question instrument and receive a preview of your complete personality profile online. Simply proceed to http://www.keirsey.com/sorter/register.aspx to register and complete the online instrument.

Skill Builder 3.4

Resources

Interpersonal Skill

Information

Technology

The $100,000 Investment Decision

Assume that a wealthy entrepreneur has provided a $2 million fund for the management department at your school to be used in improving students' decision-making skills. The department has decided to use this course as the vehicle for student development in decision making.

Divide the class into teams of five to seven students. Each team is given $100,000 to invest for a period of five years. At the end of that period, a member of each team will have six months to liquidate the team's investment(s).

The $100,000 principal, along with 50 percent of profits, will be returned to the management department. The remaining 50 percent will be divided among team members. The department will cover any loss of principal up to $75,000. Each team's assignment is as follows:

1. Following the steps of the decision-making process, reach a decision about what your investment(s) will be. Write out your reasoning for each step in the decision-making process and turn in the report to your instructor.
2. Prepare a 10-minute PowerPoint presentation and discuss with the rest of the class why your decision will reap the best return in five years.

At the end of the exercise, class members will vote on which team seems to have made the best investment decision(s).

Skill Builder 3.5

Resources

Information

Systems

Prospect Theory

Prospect theory is one framework for decision making that focuses on how people evaluate potential losses and gains. Prospect theory was put forth by Tversky and Kahneman to understand framing effects, or the idea that how you frame a problem will influence what decision you arrive at. Let us apply prospect theory with the two scenarios. Read the first scenario and answer the question before looking at the second scenario.

Scenario 1

Imagine that the United States is preparing for the outbreak of an unusual Asian disease, which is expected to kill 600 people. Two alternative programs to combat the disease have been proposed. Assume that the exact scientific estimates of the consequences of the programs are as follows.

   Program A: If Program A is adopted, 200 people will be saved.
   Program B: If Program B is adopted, there is 1/3 probability that 600 people will be saved and 2/3 probability that no people will be saved.
   Which of the two programs would you favor?

Scenario 2

Now, imagine that you are given a new situation and the same setup applies: the United States is preparing for the outbreak of an unusual Asian disease, which is expected to kill 600 people. Two alternative programs to combat the disease have been proposed. Assume that the exact scientific estimates of the consequences of the programs are as follows.

   Program C: If Program C is adopted, 400 people will die.
   Program D: If Program D is adopted there is 1/3 probability that nobody will die and 2/3 probability that 600 people will die.
   Now, which of the two programs would you favor?

Source: Daniel Kahneman and Amos Tversky, "Prospect Theory: An Analysis of Decision Under Risk," *Econometrica* 47 (1979), pp. 263–292.

Supervisor Creativity—Supportive Behavior Assessment 3.1

Supervisor Assessment Exercise 3.1: Supervisor Creativity—Supportive Behavior
For each of the following questions, using a six-point Likert scale ranging from "never" (1) to "always" (6), select the answer that best describes how frequently your supervisor is engaged in the following behaviors.
   My functional manager/supervisor

1.	attempted to get materials I needed to do my job.	—
2.	worked persistently to secure resources I needed to be innovative in my work.	—
3.	served as a good role model for creativity.	—
4.	provided valued rewards for my creative work.	—
5.	publicly recognized my innovation efforts.	—
6.	encouraged me to set innovation goals.	—
7.	praised my creative work.	—
8.	"stood up" for my innovative efforts.	—
9.	praised my creative work.	—

10.	took pride in my work and accomplishments.	—
11.	bolstered my confidence in my creative potential.	—
12.	encouraged me to collaborate with others in my work.	—
13.	stressed the importance of idea sharing among colleagues.	—
14.	actively sought work interaction with outside members.	—
15.	tried to obtain work-related information necessary for my job.	—
16.	encouraged me to communicate openly with people in other departments.	—

Scoring and Interpretation

The high score on this instrument is a 96 ($6 \times 16 = 96$). The low score is a 16 ($1 \times 16 = 16$). The midpoint is 56.

Sum up your total points. A score of 76 or higher suggests superior creativity and supportive behavior skills. A score of 56–76 indicates above-average creativity and supportive behavior skills. A score below 56 suggests that there is room for improvement.

Source: Adapted from Pamela Tierney and Steven M. Farmer, "The Pygmalion Process and Employee Creativity," *Journal of Management* 30 (June 2004), pp. 413–432. Copyright © 2004 by Sage Publications. Reprinted by permission of Sage Publications.

CASE 3-1

WHEN YOUR PERSONALITY AND JOB DON'T MATCH—TIME FOR A CHANGE:

Cynde Greer began working for a well-known federal agency as soon as she graduated from high school. Not unlike many young people first starting out, her decision was based on the hourly pay and good benefits. But after working there for a very short period of time, she realized she didn't really like the job or the organization. The environment was very bureaucratic, stifling, and unfair. Cynde said, "My manager would give me work to do, and because of my work ethic, I would do the job to the best of my ability. After a while, my manager was giving me more work than the others, and I asked why. The manager said, 'I know you will do it and do it right.' So right then I knew if you show any drive, initiative, and know-how, you are NOT going to be promoted! They promote the people that can't get along with others and don't do the work!"

Without a college degree, she didn't think she could find a better job, so she continued to work at the federal agency. Over time, the negative environment really wore on Cynde's mental state. As she describes, "It is hard to work somewhere for 18 years where the only

type of feedback you get is negative. We were never complimented on our work or told we were doing a good job." Finally, the last straw was when her manager came to her and told her that of her two days off each week, she would have to give up Fridays. That was the turning point. Although she only needed to put in two more years of service to be eligible for early retirement, she knew she was too angry and stressed out to make it. So she quit.

As a member of a dual-income family, she started looking for another job. One day on the radio, she heard an advertisement for massage therapy school. She had always enjoyed getting a massage and pampering herself, so she decided to apply. Cynde was accepted and immediately knew she had made the right decision. Cynde said, "It just felt right! The day I gave my first massage, I got such positive feedback. I had not had that in my previous job. Helping others has always been important to me, and with massage therapy, you can see the transformation—the help you are providing people is apparent immediately. I thrived on the positive feedback."

Although Cynde truly felt her career move was the right decision, she and her husband, John, had to figure out if they could financially handle the $10,000 or so initial investment (including the cost of school) necessary to get Cynde started as a massage therapist after graduation. Based on their calculations, Cynde would have positive cash flows within the first year of operation that would enable her to effectively manage the debt she would incur. John's best estimate on break-even was about eight years. This estimate included the assumption of additional investments (e.g., continuing education units [CEUs], equipment). They decided to go for it!

Three main types of legitimate massage therapy exist. The first type is somewhat "spiritual" in the sense that the body's aura and energy are emphasized. The second type is focused on recreational massage or "spa therapy," which is often experienced at resorts. The third type is medical or health related. Cynde wanted her business mission to be the latter, helping people with pain management. She rented a 325-square-foot facility for $300 per month. Cynde did the painting, decorating, and Web site herself to keep her costs down. She initially tried joining business associations and various advertising strategies but soon realized the best way to get dependable customers was simple word of mouth.

After three years in business, Cynde is doing well. She charges $65 per hour with rate differentials for more or less time. Financially, she is making double what most therapists make. Her clientele is composed of individuals 35 years of age and older, with 85 percent being women and 50 percent being recurring customers. The business flows are somewhat seasonal—Christmas and spring are the most active periods. From January to May, her schedule is quite full, with summer being the slowest period. Cynde believes she has done better than most, even during economic downturns, because of her mission. People with pain don't take breaks. Her services are always in demand—so much so that in addition to her clients, she is now teaching classes at the massage therapy school! Her massage classes include Swedish, spa, sports, chair, and special populations (e.g., pregnancy), as well as courses in business management and laws/licensing. In addition, she sublets her facility off and on to another therapist when she is not using it. Even though the sublet brings in additional revenues, it is not a dependable arrangement.

At this point, Cynde is faced with another decision to make. What to do next? She has identified four possible alternatives.

1. Implement a stability strategy and continue operating just as she is currently.
2. Grow the business through independent contractors. She has spoken to her landlord and believes she can get the space next door, which is between 1,000 and 1,200 square feet. While the rent is negotiable, Cynde believes she may be able to negotiate a rate between $700 and $1,000 per month. The space is already set up for dividers, so she could conceivably put two to four other therapists in the space in separate areas. In addition to a bathroom, it has an area for a washer and dryer, which would enable Cynde to launder on site the sheets, blankets, and towels used by her clients. Cynde would rent each space for $600, which would include the use of her established business name, the space, utilities, and washing/drying services. Each therapist would handle all of his or her own customers, including appointments, billing, supplies, etc.
3. Grow the business by hiring employees. Assuming she could get the space next door under the same terms and conditions described in alternative 2, Cynde would hire one to two massage therapists, rather than using independent contractors. The employee could be paid $15 per hour to be on site for six to eight hours five days a week and could earn tips from clients. Because she is now teaching at the massage school, Cynde believes she will be in a position to offer an opportunity to the best graduates.
4. Diversify the business by becoming a full-service salon. This alternative would require moving to a different, larger, and more visible business location. The facility would need two separate entrances—one for massage therapy services and one for traditional salon services. Her daughter is thinking about cosmetology school, and this would be an opportunity for Cynde and her daughter to work together, with her daughter ultimately having something tangible as a career alternative. The full-service salon would provide hair styling, manicures, pedicures, a variety of massages (e.g., health, sports, spa), and personal care products. The salon would employ full-time employees as well as utilize independent contractors.

CASE QUESTIONS

1. What type of MBTI® decision style do you think Cynde has? Explain.
2. Based on your answer to question 1, what are Cynde's strengths and blind spots when making important decisions?
3. Help Cynde with steps 3 and 4 of the decision process (e.g., see Exhibit 3-2) by gathering information from the library and the Internet, visiting and interviewing similar types of businesses locally, and so on. Using this information and what you have learned from this chapter, how would you advise Cynde to proceed? Discuss.

Source: Prepared by Don C. Mosley Jr. and Charles Warren, Mitchell College of Business, University of South Alabama, Mobile, AL.

CASE 3-2

DEPARTMENTAL CHANGES: DEALING WITH DIFFERENT PERSONALITIES

James is a technician who works for a solvent and recycling company. He is task oriented and enjoys his job because it is structured and orderly. He is able to do his work by himself at a steady pace without interruption. James has received favorable performance reviews from Bill, his supervisor. Bill's ratings were based on several factors. First, James's ability to get things done and stay on schedule is important because it impacts product delivery schedules. Second, James can be counted on to honor commitments and follow through. Third, he works well within the department's chain-of-command structure.

Based on this information, what type of MBTI® style does James possess? Why?

Given your answer, consider the following scenario.

Bill's (James' supervisor) MBTI® style is ENFP (extraverted, intuitive, feeling, and perceptive). As such, he is enthusiastic, insightful, innovative, versatile, and tireless in pursuit of new possibilities. Bill sees an opportunity to reengineer the work processes in his department to make them more efficient and effective. The changes will be rather substantial. Currently, individuals perform separate jobs and the work is coordinated so it moves from one stage to the next until completion. Bill believes that reorganizing the workflow around employee teams with team leads will enable the department to be able to take on new projects alongside serving the needs of existing customers. Each employee will be cross-trained so he or she understands the complete work process and can assist where needed. The team leads will coordinate and schedule work activities. This will free up Bill to explore new solvents that his department could develop to expand the company's product lines.

While Bill sees the change as an opportunity, he understands that not all of his employees will. Bill also understands that in order to gain his employees' support, he must be able to communicate his thoughts and plans in such a way that they see and buy into the vision.

TASK:

Jeff Mackin, who was highlighted in the chapter's opening case, believes one of the biggest paradigm shifts for him as a manager was when he realized the importance of knowing others' personalities in order to communicate more effectively with them.

Your task is to put yourself in Bill's position. How do you communicate with James, whose personality profile is quite different, such that he will accept and be willing to go along with the departmental changes? Write up a detailed communication plan that anticipates James's thoughts, feelings, and actions. Now, pair up with someone in class and role play this communication scenario.

Notes

1. Interview with Jeff Mackin by Don Mosley Jr., May 2017.
2. Isabel Briggs Myers and Mary H. McCaulley, *Manual: A Guide to the Development and Use of the Myers–Briggs Type Indicator* (Palo Alto, CA: Consulting Psychologists Press, 1990).
3. Victor H. Vroom and Arthur H. Jago, *The New Leadership: Managing Participation in Organizations* (Englewood Cliffs, NJ: Prentice Hall, 1988).
4. T. L. Stanley, "Ethical Decision Making in Tough Times," *Supervision* 70.3, March 2009, p. 3. Academic OneFile. Gale. University of South Alabama (AVL). July 7, 2009.
5. See Mortimer R Feinberg and Aaron L. Wenstein, "How Do You Know When to Rely on Your Intuition?" *The Wall Street Journal*, June 21, 1982, p. 16.
6. Prepared by Julia Allen, from various sources, including "Persons of the Year," *Time*, December 30, 2002/January 6, 2003, pp. 30–31.
7. Ethisphere, "2008 World's Most Ethical Companies," retrieved on July 9, 2009 from http://ethisphere.com/wme2008/.
8. Marc Orlitzky, Frank L. Schmidt, and Sara L. Rynes, "Corporate Social and Financial Performance: A Meta-Analysis," *Organization Studies* 24, 2003, pp. 403–441
9. Andrew Caffrey, "FBI Takes Up Heavy Load of Corporate Fraud Probes," *The Boston Globe*, May 6, 2003, p. Al.
10. Ethisphere, "WME Honorees," retrieved on July 29, 2013 from http://m1.ethisphere.com/wme2013/index.html.
11. Ibid.
12. Ibid.
13. Ibid.

4
Fundamentals of Organizing

LEARNING OBJECTIVES

After reading and studying this chapter, you should be able to:

1. Understand the stages of organization growth.

2. Identify the advantages and disadvantages of the functional, product, and matrix departmentalization approaches.

3. Explain the principles of unity of command and span of control.

4. Describe the difference between line and staff.

5. Understand how to avoid excessive conflict between line and staff.

6. Explain the three types of authority found in organizations.

7. Distinguish between centralization and decentralization.

8. Discuss the benefits and costs of downsizing.

9. Explain the four types of contemporary organizational approaches.

10. Understand the relationship between management philosophy, strategy, and newer forms of organization.

The only things that evolve by themselves in an organization are disorder, friction, and malperformance.

—Peter Drucker

Betty LaRue/Alamy Stock Photo

In today's rapidly changing business environments, successful companies, like Walmart, periodically reorganize to increase customer satisfaction and retention.

Preview

WALMART'S EVOLUTION Walmart grew from a regional chain of discount stores to the top spot on Fortune's list of the top 500 largest U.S. companies (as of this writing) conducting business globally under a variety of corporate brands including Walmart's Supercenter, Sam's Club, and Neighborhood Market. Along the way, they continuously reorganized and adapted their structure and culture to remain competitive without losing sight of their mission.

In 2004, however, Walmart executives realized they had a problem. Between 2 percent and 8 percent of their customers no longer shopped with them, resulting in a significant drop in same-store sales. The reason? An image that had been eroding for some time due to a number of issues, including the negative economic impact of driving mom-and-pop stores out of business in smaller communities. People don't want low prices to come at the expense of other hard-working people. In addition, shoppers were alienated by crowded aisles, slow checkouts, less-than-friendly staff, and tired-looking servicescapes. Walmart executives knew they had to take action and the sooner the better.

Walmart attacked on two fronts. First, they beefed up their public relations staff by setting up quick response teams to field calls, handle concerns, and respond to the negative stories. Next, Eduardo Castro-Wright, Vice Chairman of Walmart, set out to completely overhaul U.S. stores by de-cluttering aisles; creating cleaner, friendlier servicescapes; and speeding up checkouts. Because customers spend an average of only 21 minutes in a store, Eduardo's mission was to make it easy for customers to buy more, thus increasing same-store sales.

Walmart aggressively transformed its stores as well as its brand. Based on consumers' preferences and buying habits, store layouts were redesigned. Milk, a high-volume product, was placed in the back of the stores in clear view of the entrances so consumers had to walk by a large selection of eye-catching products. New bold colors, skylights, wider aisles, and revamped floors improved store-level aesthetics. In-store risers providing excess inventory were eliminated (reduced in-store inventories by 10–15 percent), forcing managers to facilitate better product management to reduce costs. The transformation was a success. Today, Walmart stores provide customers a better shopping experience with fewer inventory and fewer staff, but same-store sales are higher than ever.

With more than 4,000 stores opening each year in the United States, Walmart goes to great lengths to ensure these structural and cultural changes are showcased in their new stores. Shawnalyn Conners, who worked for Walmart since she was 19 years old, through hard work, perseverance, and continuous learning, received her first opportunity at the age of 31 to manage a Supercenter in 2009 in Weaverville, NC. She introduced "the company's next generation of store design and customer experience in the area." Being a Supercenter manager is challenging. With approximately 176,000 square feet under one roof—the equivalent of three football fields—and average annual revenues of $70 million a year, her job is equivalent to the CEO of a small publicly traded company! Even more challenging, Shawnalyn faced her maiden voyage as the sole person responsible for implementing the next-generation store design and customer experience in Weaverville.

Shawnalyn was up to the challenge. She worked 12-plus-hour days to ensure a flawless design and layout, hire the right type of associates for about 350 jobs, and effectively train and indoctrinate the new associates in the "Walmart way." Associates are front-line strategists providing customers with service that exceeds their expectations. As such, they are taught the connections between service, safety, and the bottom line. When associates begin to think as "owners," the organization's structure flattens and they feel empowered to make a real difference.[1]

As you can see from the opening case, *organizing* is one of the key functions of any manager or supervisor. In this chapter, we present concepts, principles, and a frame of reference for understanding this function. Many first-level managers understand organization only from a narrow vantage point—their immediate department or perhaps one or two levels above them. We believe it is equally important to see and understand the organization from a much broader standpoint. The more completely supervisors understand the big picture, the better equipped they are to work effectively as key members of the management team. Consequently, organizing is presented from a broad, overall perspective in this chapter. Failure to understand the organizing function from a broader viewpoint can lead to the following problems:

1. Excessive violation of the unity of command principle.
2. Failure to develop additional departments or work groups when needed.
3. Unclear and improper assignment of duties and responsibilities to new employees.

4. Ineffective use of organizational units and inadequate development of human resources because of improper decentralization of authority.

5. Excessive and unhealthy conflicts between departments and between line supervisors and staff personnel.

The Four Stages in Growth of an Organization

1. *Understand the stages of organization growth.*

To see the organizing function of management in operation, let us study the growth and development of John Moody's hypothetical manufacturing business throughout the chapter. Usually, a business organization grows in four stages. Stage 1 is the one-person organization, stage 2 is the organization with assistants added, stage 3 is the line organization, and stage 4 is the line-and-staff organization. Not all organizations go through all of these stages. Many skip the first stage and go directly to stage 2. For clarity's sake, however, we'll discuss each stage.

Stage 1: The One-Person Organization

Our story begins in a Midwestern city of 175,000. Our main character is John Moody, 29, a high-school graduate and veteran, who has been working in a large paper mill on the outskirts of the city since his discharge from the service. John held the same semiskilled job at the operative level since he started at the mill. His wife's relatives believe he is a lazy person with a low IQ who will never amount to much. Actually, John is quite an intelligent person, but his basic satisfaction in life comes from the challenge of building and creating things in his garage workshop. Although he assumes he will never get rich, he feels his take-home pay is sufficient to take care of the necessities of life and to support his hobbies. Even though his job at the mill is not very challenging, he gets all the challenge he needs from tinkering around in his workshop. Unfortunately, the country began to slide into an economic recession, which adversely affects the paper industry. Several mill employees, including John, are laid off because of excessive inventory buildup. John signs up for unemployment compensation and decides to spend time building a new boat trailer in his garage. He puts a lot of thought and effort into the task. The result is an excellent trailer—such a fine one that several of his friends talk him into building trailers for them for 20 percent more than his expenses. Even at this price, his boat trailer sells for less than those sold in local stores. Before long, so many requests come in that John finds himself spending all his time in his garage. At this point, John decides to work full time building boat trailers as long as he can make a living doing so.

We see John Moody's business is in the first stage of organizational growth—that is, a one-person operation (Exhibit 4-1). This means John alone performs the four basic activities common to all manufacturing operations: administering, financing, producing, and selling.

EXHIBIT 4-1
John Moody's One-Person Organization

John Moody
Owner and Operator

Administration
Finance
Production
Sales

Stage 2: The Organization with Employees

After 3 months, so many orders come in that John Moody cannot fill them. In the past few years, the federal government built a number of dams near John's town, creating four new lakes in the region. Fishing has been good, and there is a large demand for boats and boat trailers. John now makes more money per day than when he was with the mill. To keep pace with the orders, he hires Ray Martin, a former army buddy, to help build the trailers. For a small monthly salary, John also hires his wife, Nancy, to keep the books and handle the financial details. Before the month is out, Ray has mastered his job so well that he and John produce more boat trailers than they have orders for. At this point, John and Ray start thinking about hiring someone as a salesperson. Ray's brother, Paul, just graduated from college with a major in marketing. After hearing about John's business from John and Ray, Paul decides it has possibilities. With the assurance of an opportunity to buy into the business in the future, Paul starts to work for John as a salesperson.

Exhibit 4-2 shows that John Moody had to hire three employees to help carry out the three primary activities of his business. This stage is a critical one; over 50 percent of new businesses fail in their first year of operation from lack of capital, ineffective management, or both.

Paul Martin proves to be an excellent salesperson, and the business continues to grow. To keep up with the increasing volume of orders, John hires additional people. Also, the business moves to a larger building. As Exhibit 4-3 shows, after two years, John has 16 people working for him. His net income is such that Nancy quits working, but John finds himself so busy he cannot enjoy his higher income. More important, he feels he is losing control of the business. The increased costs per trailer support this belief.

EXHIBIT 4-2
John Moody Hires Employees

John Moody
Owner and Manager

Nancy Moody
Finance

Ray Martin
Production

Paul Martin
Sales

EXHIBIT 4-3
John Moody's Organization after Two Years

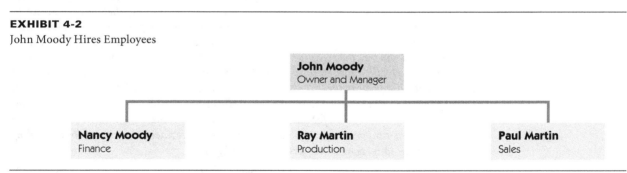

John Moody
Owner and Manager

Finance

Production

Sales

STOP AND THINK

Before reading further, look at the organization chart in Exhibit 4-3. Can you explain why John Moody is losing control of his business?

In desperation, John Moody asks the Martin brothers for advice about his problem. Paul Martin recalls that in one of his college courses, the instructor talked about the management principle of span of control. This principle holds that there is a limit to the number of people a manager can supervise effectively. In Paul's opinion, the solution is to select managers for the areas of office administration/finance, production, and sales.

Paul's solution seems so simple John wonders why he didn't think of it himself. He places Beth Fields—his best accountant—in charge of office administration and finance, Ray Martin in charge of production, and Paul Martin in charge of sales.

Stage 3: The Line Organization

Exhibit 4-4 shows that John Moody selected a manager for each of the three major departments, and his span of control has been reduced from 16 to three employees. Beth Fields is responsible for one employee, Ray Martin for nine employees, and Paul Martin for three employees. In effect, John Moody's business is now structured as a **line organization**. This means each person in the organization has clearly defined responsibilities and reports to an immediate supervisor.

There are two advantages to having a line organization at an early stage of a business organization's growth:

line organization

An organization concerned with the primary functions of the firm—in this case, production, sales, and office administration/finance.

1. Quick, decisive action on problems is possible because authority is centralized—it is in the hands of John Moody and his three managers.
2. Lines of responsibility and authority are clearly defined. Everyone knows what his or her job and obligations are. Thus, evasion of responsibility is minimized and accountability is maximized.

EXHIBIT 4-4

The Span of Control in John Moody's Line Organization

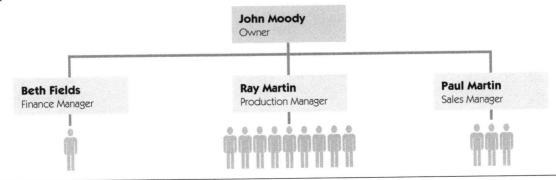

As a result of the line organization and the capabilities of each manager, the unit cost of making each boat trailer is lowered. Under the leadership of sales manager Paul Martin, the business expands its sales territory to cover most of the states in the Midwest. As sales increase, production also increases. New people are added in both sales and production. The line organization develops to accommodate the increased growth. Keeping in mind the principle of span of control, John Moody adds new sections in production and sales whenever the volume of business justifies the new additions. Also, he now finds time to concentrate more on tasks such as developing plans for the future, coordinating the work of the three departments, and supervising his managers.

After 10 years, John Moody's business employs over 200 people. During this period, John promoted Ray Martin to be in charge of five production department heads. Exhibit 4-5 shows this move created an additional level of management in the production department. The department heads, in turn, are responsible for four production supervisors. Each production supervisor is responsible for 10 production workers. Similarly, John made Paul Martin sales manager in charge of three regional sales managers, each of whom supervises eight salespersons.

Stage 4: The Line-and-Staff Organization

Unfortunately, increasing sales require John Moody's business to add more people to meet production quotas, so the profit on each unit produced declines. Finally, Beth Fields, the head of finance, reports to John that each $1.00 in sales costs $1.10. In other words, a boat trailer the business sells for $300 costs $330 to manufacture. Although the business is now financially sound, John is aware that with the way things are going, it will not take long for the business to go bankrupt. He decides to call in a reputable management consultant.

EXHIBIT 4-5
John Moody's Line Organization after 10 Years

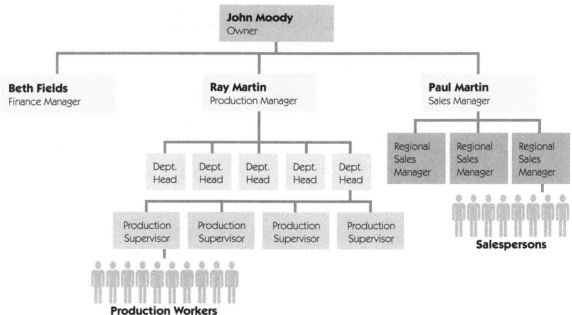

STOP AND THINK

Before reading the consultant's recommendations, decide what you think is the primary problem or problems causing manufacturing costs to increase in John Moody's business. The management consultant interviews managers from different levels in the company. After several days of investigation, the consultant makes the following report to John Moody:

line-and-staff organization

An organization structure in which staff positions are added to serve the basic line departments and help them accomplish the organization objectives more effectively.

My investigation reveals that you made a mistake that many companies make: You are operating purely as a line organization, whereas at your stage of growth, you need to adopt a **line-and-staff organization.** *This means you need to hire several staff experts to perform some of the activities your line managers presently do. As it now stands, your organizational structure tends to overload your managers. They are, in effect, wearing too many hats. More specifically, I found evidence of the following three types of inefficiency:*

1. *Your supervisors are doing their own hiring, firing, and disciplining. Consequently, you have no uniform way of screening, selecting, promoting, and disciplining employees. Moreover, a number of the supervisors are hiring friends and relatives for their departments, and other employees believe favoritism is rampant throughout the company.*
2. *Several department heads independently purchase materials and supplies for their departments. This duplication of effort causes excessive space and dollars to be tied up in raw materials inventory. In addition, this practice opened the door for waste and pilferage of supplies and materials.*
3. *Your department heads and supervisors are involved in method and layout studies, maintenance and repair work, scheduling and dispatching, and, to cap it off, quality control—all in addition to their primary jobs of supervising the work and motivating their employees. The old proverb "a jack of all trades is master of none" is certainly borne out by the situation I find in your plant.*

My primary recommendation, therefore, is that you hire a human resources specialist to screen and select new employees, a production control manager to do all the purchasing and inventory control, and an industrial engineering manager to do method and layout studies and the like. (Their relationship to the organization is shown in Exhibit 4-6.) By adding these three staff specialists, you give your department heads and supervisors a chance to concentrate on their primary job of overseeing production and motivating their employees. Equally important, you should receive immediate benefits and cost savings by eliminating inefficiencies and installing improved ways of operating.

STOP AND THINK

What adjustments will the supervisors need to make to accommodate the consultant's recommended changes? Do you think these changes will help or hinder the supervisor in the job of motivating and managing his or her crew?

The consultant went on to report that in the future, the company might want to consider diversifying by adding product lines that require similar skills and if the company's rate of growth continues, additional line and staff personnel will be needed.

EXHIBIT 4-6
John Moody's Line-and-Staff Organization

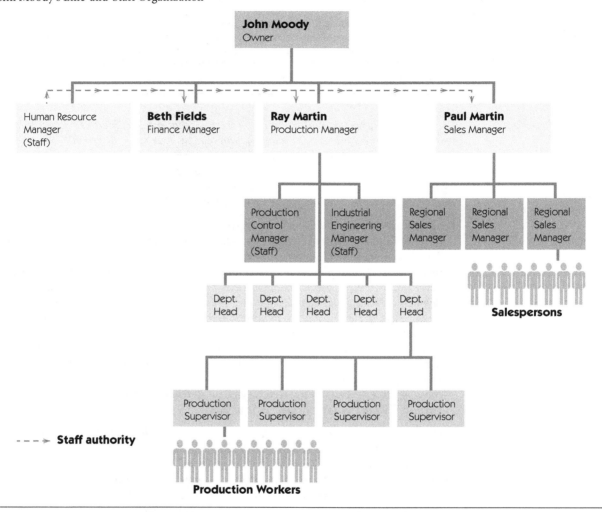

John Moody accepted the consultant's recommendations, and his line-and-staff organization went on to achieve not only record sales, but also record profits and growth. Ultimately, any growing business needs to pass into this fourth stage. Unfortunately, many do not, and some suffer the consequences of decline and bankruptcy.

In reality, companies grow at different rates, and most reach stage 4 and need staff support before reaching over 200 in size. However, our hypothetical example is presented so the differences at each stage are clearly illustrated.

2. Identify the advantages and disadvantages of the functional, product, and matrix departmentalization approaches.

departmentalization

The organizational process of determining how activities are to be grouped.

Departmentalization

The process of determining how activities are to be grouped is called **departmentalization**. There are many ways these activities may be organized. For example, types of departmentalization include organizing by function, product, service, process, territory, customer, and matrix. Note that most organizations use a combination of these forms; that is, most organizations use more than one of these approaches in their groupings. However, most organizations use a functional approach at the top and other approaches at lower levels. Because three of these forms are more complex and used extensively, we provide elaboration for functional, product, and matrix departmentalization.

Functional Departmentalization

functional departmentalization

A form of departmentalization that groups together common functions or similar activities to form an organizational unit.

Functional departmentalization groups common functions or similar activities to form an organizational unit. Thus, all individuals performing similar functions are grouped, such as sales personnel, accounting personnel, nurses, computer programmers, and so on. Exhibit 4-7 shows how functional departmentalization would be used at the top management level in dividing the three major business functions—production, sales, and finance.

Advantages of Functional Approach   The primary advantages of the functional approach are that it maintains the power and prestige of the major functions, creates efficiency through the principles of specialization, centralizes the organization's expertise, and permits tighter top-management control of the functions. For example, having all library-related activities on a college campus reporting to a common "library director" permits unified library policy to be carried out.

This approach also minimizes costly duplications of personnel and equipment. Having all computers and computer personnel in one department is less expensive than allowing several departments to have and supervise their own computer equipment and personnel.

Disadvantages of Functional Approach   There are also many disadvantages to a functional approach. Some of these are that responsibility for total performance rests only at the top, and because each manager oversees only a narrow function, the training of managers to take over the top position is limited. Organizations attempt to remedy this by transferring managers so they become "rounded," with experience in several functions. Coordination between and among functions becomes complex and more difficult as the organization grows in size and scope. Finally, individuals identify with their narrow functional responsibilities, causing subgroup loyalties, identification, and tunnel vision.

Product or Service Departmentalization

product departmentalization

A form of departmentalization that groups together all the functions associated with a single product line.

At some point, the problems of coordination under a functional approach become extremely complex and cumbersome, especially when rapid, timely decisions must be made. The functional approach is slow and cumbersome because there is no single manager accountable for all the given activities, so considerable coordination and communication are required before decisions can be reached. Consequently, some products or services that top management feels have the most potential may not receive the attention they deserve, and no one person is accountable for the performance of a given product or service line. What can be done to resolve this dilemma? One solution for many organizations is to shift to smaller, more natural, semiautonomous mini-organizations built around specific products, each with its own functional capabilities. This is known as **product departmentalization**, that

EXHIBIT 4-7
Functional Departmentalization at the Top Management Level

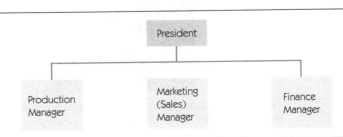

all the functions associated with a single product line are grouped. In service organizations, all the functions associated with a single service are grouped together. Exhibit 4-8 is an example of product departmentalization.

EXHIBIT 4-8

Example of Product Departmentalization

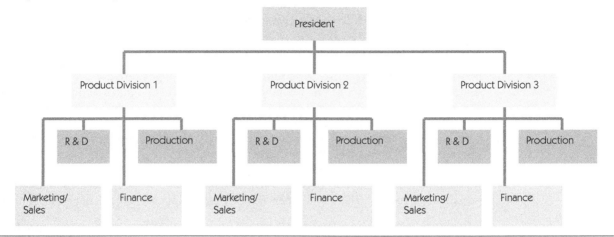

Types of departmentalization can vary widely according to the activities being grouped. Sales organizations, for example, often structure groups according to territories.

Some of the advantages of product or service departmentalization are that attention can be directed toward specific product lines or services, coordination of functions at the product division level is improved, and profit responsibility can be better placed. In addition, it is easier for the organization to obtain or develop several executives who have broad managerial experience in running a total entity. Walmart, previewed in the chapter's opening case, utilizes this form of departmentalization, such that its business services consist of the Supercenter, Sam's Club, Neighborhood Market, and International units. As you saw in the preview case, this type of departmentalization enabled the Supercenter group to transform itself to better meet customers' needs while also increasing efficiencies.

Some of the disadvantages of product departmentalization are it requires more personnel and material resources, it may cause unnecessary duplication of resources and equipment, and top management assumes a greater burden of establishing effective coordination and control. Top management must use staff support to create and oversee policies that guide and limit the range of actions taken by its divisions.

Matrix Departmentalization

matrix departmentalization

A hybrid type of departmentalization in which personnel from several specialties are brought together to complete limited-life tasks.

Matrix departmentalization is a hybrid of departmentalization in which personnel from several specialties are brought together to complete limited-life tasks. It usually evolves from one or more of the other types of departmentalization and is used in response to demands for unique blends of skill from different specialties in the organization. The matrix structure is used in conjunction with other types of departmentalization. Say, for example, a company had to complete a project requiring close, integrated work between and among numerous functional specialties. The project could be designing a weapons system or building a prototype for a supersonic aircraft. The traditional approaches to organization we discussed do not easily provide for the flexibility to handle such complex assignments that involve expertise from numerous functional areas of the organization. As shown in Exhibit 4-9, a project manager is given line authority over the team members during the life of the project.

The matrix organization provides a hierarchy that responds quickly to changes in technology. Hence, it is typically found in technically oriented organizations, such as Boeing, General Dynamics, NASA, and GE, in which scientists, engineers, or technical specialists work on sophisticated projects or programs. It is also used by companies with complex construction projects. Under this system, team members' functional departments maintain personnel files, supervise administrative details, and assemble performance reports while their members are on assignment.

Computer Programs and Systems, Inc. (CPSI), is an integrated health care information technology and solutions firm. One of its strategic business units uses a form of matrix departmentalization with teams to provide fully integrated health care delivery systems to rural and community hospitals. For instance, once a hospital is on board, teams of specialists assist the client with training of their personnel on using the new system. One team assists those on the business side of the hospital, while another team helps the clinical groups. Once the project is completed, the teams are disbanded and members return to the corporate office to assist with virtual troubleshooting and await their next project assignment. At that point in time, employees no longer report to a project manager, but rather to their corporate manager.[2]

Advantages of the Matrix Approach One advantage of the matrix approach is it permits open communication and coordination of activities among the relevant functional specialists. Another advantage is its flexibility enables the organization to respond rapidly to change. This response to change is the result of a self-imposed and professional desire

EXHIBIT 4-9

Example of Matrix
Departmentalization

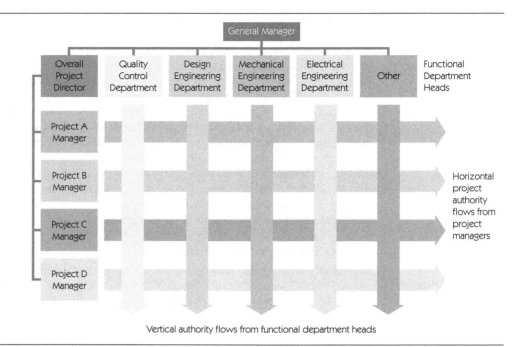

Vertical authority flows from functional department heads

to respond—not a response to a hierarchically managed change effort. The use of this approach is essential in technologically oriented industries.

Disadvantages of the Matrix Approach   One disadvantage of matrix departmentalization relates to the lack of clarity and coordination in assigned roles. Conflict may occur when the requirements of the project team result in decisions contrary to the philosophy and viewpoint of the home office. For example, a project team might want the authority to make most decisions on-site, while the home office wants tight control. Another possible source of conflict is the assignment of team members to more than one project; someone must determine how to allocate such team members' time on each project. Such situations require facilitators, who intervene to resolve clashes resulting from conflicting priorities.

Jean Johnson was a professor of management at Mid-Atlantic University.

For the past year, she taught in the management department and worked half-time on an interdisciplinary project to improve the university's information technologies. For the life of the project, she had two bosses—the project director and the chairman of the management department.

Until recently, this dual reporting had not caused any problem, but within the last month, the chairman of the management department put increasing pressure on Jean to teach an additional course for the fall term. A professor had resigned suddenly, leaving the department shorthanded. The dilemma was that the information technologies study was nearing completion and required a major commitment of time and effort from all project members.

In a matrix structure, who decides on the members' advancement and promotion? Moreover, who assigns them to their next projects? Normally, the functional department head makes these decisions, based in part on reports received from project managers for whom the persons have worked. But functional specialists are often caught in the middle of disputes and torn between loyalties to project managers and to their functional department heads.

Finally, there are disadvantages relating to the temporary nature of assignments under this form of departmentalization. Psychologically, employees may never feel they have "roots" while drifting from one project to another—perhaps an unrelated—project. Moreover, the close personal ties formed while working on a project team may be severed at the project's completion, in which case an individual's reassignment requires establishing a new set of working relationships with strangers.

Special Managerial Abilities Required Because of the complexities of the matrix approach, managers should have special abilities to be successful. They should be adept at teamwork and coordination and also have facilitation skills.

Two Important Organizing Principles

3. *Explain the principles of unity of command and span of control.*

Two important principles involved in the organizing function were illustrated in the case of John Moody's organizations. These are unity of command and span of control (or span of management). Let us now discuss these principles in detail.

Unity of Command

unity of command principle

States that everyone should report to and be accountable to only one boss.

The **unity of command principle** states that everyone in an organization should report to and be accountable to only one boss for the performance of a given activity. This supervisor should be responsible for evaluating performance, passing down orders and information, and developing employees to become better employees in the organization. It is to this person employees should turn for help in carrying out their duties and should communicate any deviations, either positive or negative, in implementing their duties. In sum, the supervisor is only responsible for motivating his or her employees to achieve effective results and taking action when employees deviate from planned performance.

Adherence to the unity of command principle is important for five reasons:

1. It prevents duplication and conflict when orders and instructions are passed down.
2. It decreases confusion and "passing the buck" because everyone—including managers—is accountable to only one person for a given assignment.
3. It provides a basis whereby a supervisor and his or her employees learn about each other's strengths and weaknesses.
4. It provides an opportunity for a supervisor and employees to develop supportive relationships and realize their individual and group potential in achieving organizational objectives.
5. It promotes higher morale than is generally found in organizations that do not follow the unity of command principle.

Unfortunately, some managers only give lip service to this principle, although their organization chart seems to reflect it. One of the authors of this book worked with a branch plant of a large company to tailor a management development program. Among other things, this author examined the leadership styles practiced by key managers and their effect on employees. To determine those leadership styles, the author interviewed managers at all levels. The results showed the plant manager, though unusually capable and generally effective, made one mistake with his employee managers: He violated the unity of command principle by periodically conducting inspections throughout the plant and making on-the-spot suggestions to operative employees. Often, he made these suggestions when the employees' supervisor was not present. As a result, operative employees followed instructions that their immediate supervisors were unaware of. Moreover, employees would stop working on their assigned duties to carry out the instructions of the plant manager. This practice caused a problem for supervisors, as illustrated by Exhibit 4-10.

As a result of this one error, a serious morale problem developed. Many of the plant manager's otherwise effective managerial practices were undermined. When this situation

Following the unity of command principle, the supervisor is solely responsible for motivating his or her employees to achieve company goals.

EXHIBIT 4-10
Violating the Unity of Command Principle

was called to his attention, he was quite surprised. It seems he slipped into this habit without being fully aware of its long-range consequences. When this manager began passing his suggestions and instructions through lower-level managers, morale improved.

Although employees should have only one supervisor, they may, of course, have relationships with many people. For example, in a line-and-staff organization, line supervisors and department heads have many contacts with staff personnel. These contacts are necessary so both line and staff personnel can accomplish their duties. Later in this chapter, we explain how these relationships can be developed without violating the unity of command principle. The important thing to remember is this: If a conflict results from a staff request and a line manager's command, the employee should have a single manager to turn to for clarification or a final decision.

Span of Control

Before World War II, experts maintained the span of control should be three to eight people, depending on the level of management. In those days, one of the first things an organizational consultant examined when a company had problems was the span of control at various levels. Today, the three-to-eight-people limit is no longer accepted as universally applicable. This is why we state the **span of control principle** simply as follows: There is a limit to the number of people a person can manage effectively. Just as your arms can span a limited number of feet and inches, your mental reach can only span a limited number of the problems, situations, and relationships that make up the activities of management.

span of control principle

States there is a limit to the number of people a person can supervise effectively.

Narrower Span of Control at the Top   One thing we can say without qualification: The greater the number of managers in an organization, the fewer people they should have reporting directly to them. There are at least three reasons for relating span of control to management level:

1. Top-level managers must solve a variety of different, nonrecurring problems. Much mental concentration is required to solve such problems.
2. Middle managers must spend much of their time doing long-range planning, working with outside interest groups, and coordinating the various activities of the organization. They cannot afford to be tied down by the excessive burden of supervision created when a large number of people report directly to them.
3. First-level managers, by contrast, tend to be concerned with more clearly defined areas of operation. Although they are responsible for a certain amount of coordination with other departments, most of their direct contacts are with their immediate employees. Hence, they are able to supervise more people than higher-level managers.

Different Approaches to a Supervisor's Span of Control   Exhibit 4-11 depicts three different approaches to a supervisor's span of control, leading to quite different jobs for supervisors A, B, and C. Can we say one of these approaches is best? No, because the correct size of a supervisor's span of control depends on a number of circumstances, as shown in Exhibit 4-12.

Companies following a policy of a narrow span of control are often hampered in achieving effective results. If an organization of a thousand people rigidly adheres to a span of between three and seven, this tall, narrow organizational structure (with many, many management levels) faces some disadvantages. Numerous supervisory managers are required, resulting in higher payroll costs. Communication passes up and down through many levels, increasing the possibility of distortion. Over-supervision restricts decision making by employees and limits their opportunities to achieve their full potential. On the other hand, an advantage of tight control is the work can be closely directed, so the company can hire relatively less-skilled people.

EXHIBIT 4-11

Narrow, Wide, and
Very Wide Spans of
Control

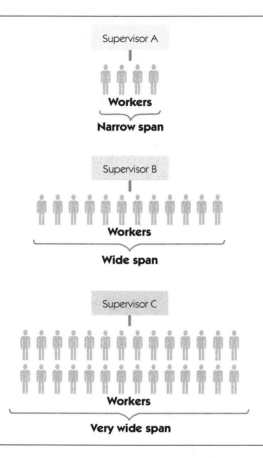

EXHIBIT 4-12

Factors Contributing
to a Narrow or Wide
Span of Control

FACTOR	NARROW SPAN INDICATED	WIDE SPAN INDICATED
How physically close are the people performing the work?	Dispersed, perhaps even in different geographical locations.	Very close, perhaps all in one physical work area in a building.
How complex is the work?	Very complex, such as development of a manned space station that will orbit the earth.	Rather routine and simple, such as an assembly-line operation.
How much supervision is required?	A great deal. So many problems arise that the supervisor needs to exercise close control.	Little. Workers are well trained and able to make normal job decisions easily.
How much nonsupervisory work is required of the supervisor?	Much. The supervisor spends much time planning, coordinating, and performing nonsupervisory tasks.	Little. Not much planning and coordination are required of the supervisor. The supervisor spends most of his or her time supervising employees.
How much organizational assistance is furnished to the supervisor?	Much. The supervisor may do his or her own recruiting, training, and controlling.	Much. The supervisor may be aided by a training department, quality control department, etc.

Tendency toward Wider Spans of Control   Over the years, many companies tended to broaden their span of control at all levels. There are at least four reasons for this trend:

1. Higher educational attainment, management and supervisory development programs, vocational and technical training, and increased knowledge generally on the part of the labor force improved the abilities and capacities of both managers and employees. The greater the supervisor's capacity, the more people he or she can supervise.
2. Research indicates that in many situations, general supervision is more effective than close supervision. A supervisor practicing general supervision delegates authority and supervises by results, whereas a supervisor practicing close supervision provides detailed instructions and often does the same type of work as the workers he or she supervises.
3. New developments in management permitted businesses to broaden their span of control and supervise by results, without losing control. For example, using enhanced technologies, an organization can process information more quickly and develop more efficient information-reporting systems.
4. Finally—and sometimes this is the primary reason—wider spans of control save the company money.

Relationships between Line and Staff

4. *Describe the difference between line and staff.*

line personnel

Carry out the primary activities of a business.

staff personnel

Have the expertise to assist line people and aid top management.

Line personnel carry out the primary activities of a business, such as producing or selling products and/or services. **Staff personnel**, on the other hand, use their expertise to assist the line people and aid top management in various areas of business activities. Line departments, therefore, are like a mainstream. Staff departments are like the tributaries serving and assisting the mainstream, although they should not be thought of as being secondary to the line departments. Both line and staff people are important.

STOP AND THINK

Of the various jobs you've held, which were "line" and which were "staff"?

Once a business reaches the fourth stage of growth and is no longer a small organization, it becomes more complex and difficult to coordinate. A line and staff structure that places competent specialists in certain positions—such as human resources management, legal and governmental departments, research and development, and public relations—helps eliminate confusion, duplication, and inefficiency. However, a growing organization must be continually alert to the pitfalls and potential trouble spots.

Conflicts between Line and Staff

One common problem in most large organizations is excessive conflict between line and staff personnel and between different departments. Differences in viewpoint between people and departments are natural, inevitable, and healthy, but excessive conflict disrupts an entire organization. As shown in Exhibit 4-13, many line and staff contacts are normal.

There are many reasons excessive conflict develops between line and staff personnel within an organization. Here are specific reasons for this type of conflict.

- *Staff personnel give direct orders to line personnel.*
- *Good human relations are not practiced in dealings between line and staff personnel.*

EXHIBIT 4-13
Line and Staff
Contacts

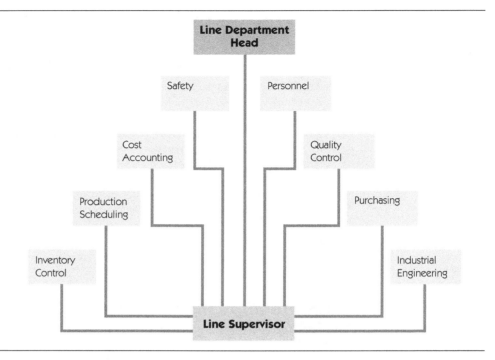

- *Overlapping authority and responsibility confuse both line and staff personnel.*
- *Line people believe staff people are not knowledgeable about conditions at the operating level.*
- *Staff people, because of their expertise, attempt to influence line decisions against line managers' wishes.*
- *Top management misuses staff personnel or fails to use them properly.*
- *Each department views the organization from a narrow viewpoint instead of looking at the organization as a whole.*

STOP AND THINK

Before reading further, decide what you think might be done to decrease or eliminate the reasons for conflict between line and staff personnel.

---

5. *Understand how to avoid excessive conflict between line and staff.*

6. *Explain the three types of authority found in organizations.*

advisory authority

Authority of most staff departments to serve and advise line departments.

How to Avoid Excessive Line-Staff Conflict: Delineating Authority

Although conflict between line and staff people is not likely to be eliminated, a major way to avoid it is to ensure people clearly understand the authority/responsibility relationships between individuals and departments. There are three types of authority: advisory, line, and functional.

Advisory Authority   The primary responsibility of most staff departments is to serve and advise the line departments. This type of authority is called **advisory authority** or the authority of ideas. However, some staff people may be so zealous in their efforts to sell their ideas to line personnel they, in effect, hand out orders. If the line supervisor permits this to occur frequently, the unity of command begins here to break down.

line authority

Power to directly command or exact performance from others.

functional authority

A staff person's limited line authority over a given function.

Line Authority   The second type of authority, **line authority**, is the power to directly command or exact performance from others. Having this power to command does not mean you elicit effective performance simply by giving out orders. It does mean, however, you are directly responsible for the results of a certain department or group of workers. Line authority is not restricted to line personnel. The head of a staff department has line authority over the employees in his or her department.

Functional Authority   The third type of authority, **functional authority**, is usually a restricted kind of line authority. It gives a staff person a type of limited line authority over a given function, such as safety or quality, regardless of where that function is found in the organization. For example, a staff safety specialist may have functional authority to insist that line managers follow standard safety procedures in their departments. The staff safety specialist may have top management's blessing to dictate to lower-level line managers exactly what they must and must not do concerning any matter that falls within the realm of safety. A quality control inspector may tell a line worker certain parts need to be reworked. A human resources specialist may say to a line supervisor the latter cannot fire a certain employee. A cost accountant may notify line departments certain cost information must be furnished weekly, and so on.

Ed Young/AgStock Images

Behind-the-scenes functions of research (accounting, quality control, and safety) are found in many companies. What kind of authority would a staff person have working in this environment?

STOP AND THINK

Can you think of some other common examples of functional authority?

Are you thinking functional authority seems to violate the unity of command principle? It does! For this reason, it is important all individuals clearly understand what functional authority is. Top-line managers have the major responsibility for defining the nature of functional authority. Moreover, it is important for line personnel to exercise their right to appeal to higher management levels when they have disagreements with staff personnel. Functional authority is necessary, but it can be dangerous if it is granted indiscriminately. Normally, it is given only to a staff area having a great deal of expertise and the staff expert's advice would be followed anyway.

Another way to avoid excessive conflict between line and staff people is to have effective communication between people and between departments. Key managers overseeing both line and staff people improve the communication process by periodically bringing line and staff people together to discuss problems that cut across departmental lines. This example may inspire lower-level managers to do the same thing with their key employees. Thus, the danger of seeing only part of the picture is minimized.

Decentralization versus Centralization

7. *Distinguish between centralization and decentralization.*

The concept of decentralization is closely related to the concept of delegation. Briefly, delegation is the process by which managers allocate duties and authority downward to the people who report to them and assign responsibility for how authority is used.

An example of delegation occurred when John Moody called in assistants to help him do a better job than he could do alone. He assigned his assistants duties in finance, production, and sales.

decentralization

The extent to which authority is delegated from one unit of the organization to another.

Both delegation and decentralization are concerned with giving authority to someone at a lower level. **Decentralization** is the broader concept, as the extent to which authority is delegated from one level or one unit of the organization to another. In a decentralized organization, middle and lower levels of management make broader, more important decisions about their units. In a centralized organization, upper management makes most of the important decisions that concern all levels or units within the organization.

Factors Affecting Decentralization

No organization is completely centralized or decentralized. Decentralization is a relative concept and depends on a number of factors, including the following:

1. *Top-management philosophy.* Some top managers have a need for tight control. They put together a strong central staff and want to make the most important decisions themselves. Others believe in strong delegation and push decisions to the lowest levels of their organization.
2. *History of the organization's growth.* Organizations grown by merging with other companies or acquiring them tend to be decentralized. Those that have grown on their own tend to be centralized.
3. *Geographic location(s).* Organizations spread out, with units in different cities or regions, tend to be decentralized so lower-level managers can make decisions that fit their territory or circumstances.

4. *Quality of managers.* If an organization has many well-qualified, well-trained managers, it will likely be decentralized. If it has few, top management will centralize and make the most important decisions.

5. *Availability of controls.* If top management has an effective control system—good, timely information about performance at lower levels—the organization tends to be decentralized. Without a good flow of control information for monitoring results, it tends to be centralized.

6. *The economy.* Generally, there is a tendency toward more centralization during poor economic times, such as a recession, and more decentralization during good economic times.

7. *Mergers, acquisitions, and joint ventures.* Unfortunately, many mergers, acquisitions, and joint ventures fail to achieve expected synergies and positive outcomes because they do not effectively plan and implement an early strategy to integrate different organizational cultures; evaluate old ways of operating; and, when appropriate, develop new ways of functioning. Certainly, not dealing with decentralization versus centralization can have a negative impact on the organization and its managers and supervisors.

8. *The external business environment.* Generally, in relatively certain or stable business environments, there is a tendency toward more centralization because the focus tends to be internally on improving efficiencies of operations. In dynamic, turbulent business environments, more decentralization occurs because rapidly responding and adjusting to environmental stimuli is most important. With product life cycles in some tech industries of less than 12 months, organizational flexibility and rapid response are critical for survival.

STOP AND THINK

In your opinion, which factors are most significant in determining whether an organization is centralized or decentralized? Why?

The degree to which an organization is decentralized has a direct effect on the number of levels within the organization. The trend in the United States is toward reducing the number of levels of management and decentralizing.

Downsizing

8. *Discuss the benefits and costs of downsizing.*

downsizing

Eliminating unnecessary levels of management; striving to become leaner and more efficient by reducing the workforce and consolidating departments and work groups.

In their book *In Search of Excellence,* Thomas Peters and Robert Waterman noted one of the attributes of excellent companies is a simple organizational structure with a lean top-level staff. Management theorist Peter Drucker predicted by the second decade of the 21st century, a typical large business would have half the levels of management and one-third the managers of its late 20th century counterpart.[3] Drucker's forecast is coming true throughout the United States and elsewhere around the globe. **Downsizing** is the process of eliminating unnecessary levels of management and employees, thus reducing the number of staff personnel and supervisors.

Benefits of Downsizing

One of the major benefits of downsizing is the tremendous cost reductions that occur almost immediately. Perhaps even more important are the improvements that take place in the way the organization is managed. Turnaround time in decision making is speeded up, and communication usually improves in all directions. Moreover, the organization becomes more responsive to customers and provides faster product delivery. Downsizing also removes the tendency for each level to justify its existence by close supervision and frequently asking for reports and data from lower levels. Without excessive interference and stifling of creativity at lower levels, line managers have more opportunity to develop and use their authority to make decisions affecting the bottom line. In the final analysis, all of these things translate into higher profits. These concepts are illustrated next.

> *A. T. Kearney analyzed management layers among both highly successful companies and others whose performance was not above average in their industry. The 15 not-so-successful companies typically had at least four more organizational layers than the 26 successful ones. Interviews confirmed that more layers in the organization inhibit productivity because the decision-making process is slower and the chances are greater that opportunities will be lost.*[4]

Costs of Downsizing

Downsizing has some costs that can wreck the prospect of higher profits if the process is not accomplished ethically and efficiently. Some companies downsize so rapidly and prune staff and middle management so much they lose control. In addition, some companies are insensitive in the way they go about downsizing, telling a number of loyal, effective managers they are no longer needed. A heavy-handed approach can lead to morale problems with remaining employees for years to come. Some other potential disadvantages are increased workloads, diminished chances of promotion, and threatened job security for those remaining.

Perhaps the greatest costs are the least known—the social costs. Research shows when employees lose their jobs because of downsizing, domestic problems increase. Fifteen percent lost their homes, despite an increase in the number of hours their spouses worked. Moreover, the suicide rate for laid-off workers is 30 times the national average.[5] Because of these costs, downsizing can never be painless, but thoughtful planning can minimize the pain.

Impact on Remaining Supervisors and Managers

Remaining managers and supervisors must adapt to fuzzier lines of authority and develop skills in team building. In tall, narrow structures, middle managers and supervisors are accustomed to carrying out orders, and suddenly they must operate differently. As a first-line supervisor in an International Paper Company mill told one of the authors: "They used to tell us what to do; now they ask us." With the increasing emphasis on quality and service management, a supervisor has to function more as a coach, a facilitator, an expediter, and a team developer.

STOP AND THINK

Because of the numerous internal and external environmental factors, downsizing has become a "preferred" course of action for many organizations. Is downsizing an ethical business practice? Why or why not?

Ways to Get Beyond Downsizing

Without question, downsizing has a negative impact on employee morale, but a recent study found companies that were more considerate of "employees' morale and welfare" during the process experienced fewer productivity problems.[6] Thus, it is important to look at

reengineering

"It means starting over... It means asking and answering this question: If I were creating this company today, given what I know and given current technology, what would it look like?" Rethinking and redesigning processes to improve dramatically cost, quality, service, and speed.

downsizing not as an end in itself but as a means to an end. The way to get back to health is to focus on the remaining employees by developing a strategy of support for survivors and a strategic plan for growth and development for the organization.

However, it is important not to go back to a traditional management and organizational design based on principles of command, control, and compartmentalization.[7] This danger can be negated by (1) developing effective work teams and (2) using a process called *reengineering.*

Reengineering is a reaction to the way many organizations perform work using the traditional methods of command, control, and compartmentalization. In a world of rapid change, firms that focus on the division or specialization of labor with a resulting fragmentation of work end up with vertical structures built on narrow pieces of a process. Consequently, decisions are slow, and people look upward to their department heads and bosses for answers, rather than looking horizontally to internal and external customers to solve problems and get answers.[8]

When Michael Hammer and James Champy, two of the world's leading experts on reengineering, were asked for a quick definition, they gave this answer: "It means starting over... It means asking and answering this question: If I were recreating this company today, given what I know and given current technology, what would it look like?"[9] Their more formal definition of reengineering is "the fundamental rethinking and radical redesign of business processes to achieve dramatic improvements in critical, contemporary measures of performance such as cost, quality, service, and speed."[10]

Reengineering can be very expensive, and so firms should not use it for everything. If you have an unprofitable business, it may be better to close it, or, if quality is a problem,

Jacobs Stock Photography/Photographer's Choice/Getty Images

After a layoff or restructuring, supervisors may find themselves functioning as coaches to help boost morale and restore a cooperative team atmosphere among the surviving employees.

focus on improving the quality rather than starting over. The general guideline is to save reengineering for big challenges that really matter, such as new product development or customer service. Although by one estimate, 50 percent of reengineering efforts fail to achieve the goals set for them, when it is done properly, reengineering has a big payoff. For example, Union Carbide used reengineering to save $400 million in three years.[11]

As Hammer and Champy have documented, the following types of changes occur when a company successfully reengineers business processes:

- *Work units change from functional departments to process teams.*
- *Jobs change from simple tasks to multidimensional work.*
- *Roles change from controlled to empowered.*
- *Job preparation changes from preparation to education.*
- *Focus of compensation shifts from activity to results.*
- *Advancement criteria change from performance to ability.*
- *Values change from protective to productive.*
- *Managers change from supervisors to coaches.*
- *Organizational structure changes from hierarchical to flat.*
- *Executives change from scorekeepers to leaders.*

Contemporary Organizational Perspectives
The Inverted Pyramid

9. *Explain the four types of contemporary organizational approaches.*

inverted pyramid

A structure widest at the top and narrowing as it funnels down.

The creation of the **inverted pyramid** has been attributed to Nordstrom, a specialty retailer. This type of structure is flat with few levels and employs a bottom-up management philosophy. The sales and sales support personnel, who are in direct contact with the customer, make the key decisions. The chart portrays "helping hands" symbolizing all other levels are there to help and support the sales personnel to better serve and satisfy the customer. Exhibit 4-14 shows Nordstrom's inverted pyramid and the helping-hand concept.[12] More companies have adopted flatter, customer-centric structures in order to respond to today's continuously changing business environments.

EXHIBIT 4-14
Nordstorm's Inverted Pyramid

Source: Based on description found in Robert Spector and Patrick D. McCarthy, *The Nordstrom Way: The Inside Story of America's #1 Customer Service Company* (New York: Wiley, 1996).

The Wagon Wheel

wagon wheel

An organization form with a hub, a series of spokes radiating from the hub, and the outer rim.

Management consultant and author Nancy Austin points out the **wagon wheel** is even more unorthodox than the inverted pyramid. In her words, "There are usually three main parts to these innovative formats: the hub of the wheel; a series of spokes, which radiate from the hub; and, finally, the outer rim. Customers are at the center. Whether you call the hub 'customers' or 'customer satisfaction,' customers show up inside the chart! Next come the spokes—business functions (finance, marketing, engineering) or teams (new-product development, customer satisfaction, suppliers). Keeping it all together on the outer rim— where the rubber meets the road—are the chief executive and the board, who are placed there to make sure everybody has at his or her fingertips everything needed to serve customers. Here, too, managers are coaches and supporters, not naysayers and devil's advocates. The stubborn 'Us vs. Them' antagonism spawned by the old hierarchical mentality begins to even out a bit."[13]

Team Structures

team structure

Utilizes permanent and temporary cross-functional teams to improve horizontal coordination and cooperation.

Team structure utilizes permanent and temporary cross-functional teams to improve horizontal coordination and cooperation. Exhibit 4-15 provides an example of the team structure. Teams provide speed and flexibility to meet the challenges associated with increasingly dynamic business environments. Take, for example, a retail store such as Family Dollar. Each employee is hired to perform a particular task, such a stocking, running the register, or managing the store, but as Vernon Mason, an assistant manager with Family Dollar, shares, "We cross-train all of our employees so they can perform a variety of jobs on an as-needed basis. When the truck arrives and we're pressed for time to get the stock out, we need everyone on board and able to do the task that needs to be done right then."[14] Teams provide supervisors the opportunity to use the diverse talents of each member to achieve effective outcomes.

Network Structures

network structure

Sometimes referred to as a modular structure; includes a central business unit, or "hub," linked to a network of external suppliers and contractors.

As Exhibit 4-16 illustrates, a **network structure**, sometimes referred to as a modular structure, includes a central business unit or "hub" linked to a network of external suppliers and contractors. With technology, such as the Internet, companies operate efficiently and effectively with a virtual network by focusing only on those core activities they do quite well. Many companies, such as Apple, Ashley Furniture, and Nike, outsource noncore business activities to reduce costs, speed production, use outside expertise, or some combination thereof.

EXHIBIT 4-15
Example of Team-Based Structures

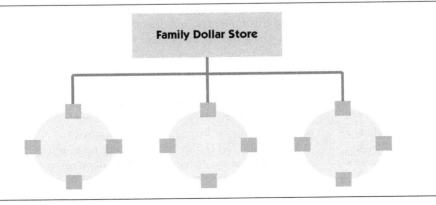

EXHIBIT 4-16
Example of a Virtual
Network

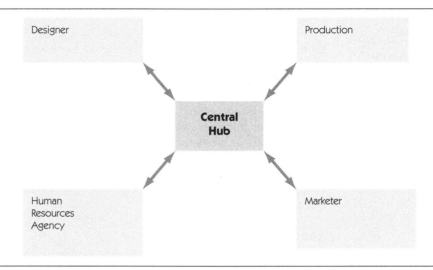

Designer

Production

Central Hub

Human Resources Agency

Marketer

Stop and Think

Is it possible to integrate the contemporary organizational structures with the more traditional (functional, product, and matrix forms) ones? Explain.

---

10. *Understand the relationship between management philosophy, strategy, and newer forms of organization.*

cost leadership strategy

Attempts to lower costs below those of competitors by focusing on creating efficiencies within organizational systems.

differentiation strategy

Used by managers to gain a competitive advantage through goods and/or services that are clearly unique or different from those of the competition.

Management Philosophy, Strategy, and Organization

Earlier in the chapter, we discussed the impact management philosophy has on the organization. Management philosophy is particularly significant when we discuss the newer forms of organizations, involving more decentralization, empowerment, team development, quality improvement, and networking. In a world of rapid change and global competition, more and more firms are shifting to increased decentralization, team development, and empowerment.

Strategy and Structure: The Fit Perspective

Competitive Strategies   Michael Porter identified that managers in organizations use a variety of competitive strategies to be effective. Two important ones are the cost leadership and differentiation competitive strategies. A **cost leadership strategy** attempts to lower costs below those of competitors by focusing on creating efficiencies within organizational systems. Walmart is an example of an organization following a cost leadership strategy. It became the cost leader in the retail arena through the use of technology to create a virtual inventory system, which effectively lowered its cost structure below those of its competitors. By creating efficiencies in inventory management, they single-handedly redefined profitability for every other retailer in the industry. Currently, Walmart uses radiofrequency identification (RFID) technology, tagging products to create additional efficiencies and improve inventory, distribution, customer management, and theft management practices.

A **differentiation strategy** is used by managers to gain a competitive advantage through goods and/or services that are clearly unique or different from those of the competition. Companies such as Harley Davidson, Apple, Publix, and Samsung successfully employed

HISTORICAL INSIGHT

Internal Systems Model

During the 1960s and 1970s, Dr. Rensis Likert and his team of researchers and consultants at the University of Michigan's Institute for Social Research Survey Research Center made tremendous contributions to management theory and practice. Likert's two best-known books, *New Patterns of Management* and *The Human Organization*, are considered management classics, and, in the opinion of the authors, many of the concepts are quite valid today.[15]

One concept especially relevant to this chapter is the researchers' conclusion that two causal variables affecting both intervening variables and results are (1)

EXHIBIT 4-17

Internal Systems Model

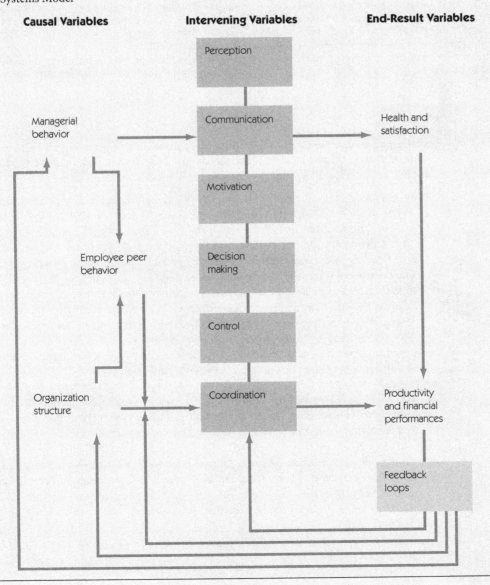

management philosophy and leadership behavior and (2) organization structure. It follows that if, over time, an organization has difficulties, they can be traced back to the causal variables where improvements and perhaps changes need to be made.

Exhibit 4-17 shows the *internal systems model* developed by Likert. The model groups the dimensions of a company's human organization into three broad categories of variables: *causal, intervening*, and *end result*.

1. *Causal variables.* Causal variables determine the course of developments within an organization and the results achieved by the organization. They include only those independent variables that can be altered or changed by the organization and its management. Causal variables include the structure of the organization, and management's policies; decision, business, and leadership strategies; skills; and behavior.

2. *Intervening variables.* Intervening variables reflect the internal state and health of the organization. They include the loyalties, attitudes, motivations, performance goals, and perceptions of organization members and their capacities for effective interaction, communication, and decision making.

3. *End-result variables.* End-result variables are dependent variables that reflect the achievements of the organization, such as productivity, costs, scrap loss, and earnings.

You can see causal variables affect intervening variables and intervening variables, in turn, affect the end results. Thus, an organization running into such difficulties as declining sales and profits or high turnover and absenteeism can usually trace the problem to deficiencies in variables of this sort: organizational structure or top management's policies, decisions, and leadership philosophies, strategies, and behavior.

a differentiation strategy such that consumers are willing to pay a higher price to purchase their products and services. As illustrated below, Marriot's brand, the Ritz-Carlton, uses a quality and service differentiation strategy to achieve success.

In 1995, Marriott International bought a 49 percent interest in the Ritz-Carlton Hotel Corporation for $200 million in cash and assumed debt. In 1998, Marriott bought the rest, and under Marriott's leadership, the high standard of excellence was continued. "Ritz-Carlton maintains a database on the preferences of nearly one million of its customers, detailing their likes, dislikes, family and personal interests, preferred credit card, etc. Each employee is responsible for identifying and recording guest preferences. The goal is to customize service and thereby create a lasting relationship with the customer."[16] Horst Schulze, the Ritz-Carlton's past president, is credited with catalyzing the chain's reputation for quality and service. In regard to the awards received during his tenure, Schulze stated, "We are not resting on the momentary glory or satisfaction of these awards. . . It is our intention to not only serve you with genuine care and comfort, but to fulfill all your needs in our hotels and give you complete service excellence all of the time."

"Today every employee, from housekeeper to server to manager, is committed to the ultimate dream and vision. . . . 100 percent guest satisfaction." The tailored features of the Ritz-Carlton's focus on quality, service, and guest satisfaction include

1. *In the 2-day orientation program for new employees, the training manager emphasizes that, "you serve but you are not servants"; rather, "you are ladies and gentlemen serving ladies and gentlemen."*
2. *In addition to the orientation program, 100 additional hours of training are provided to employees.*
3. *When processes are improved or reengineered in one hotel, the information and concepts are shared with all hotels.*

4. *Every worker is empowered to spend up to $2,000 to fix any problem a guest encounters.*

Patrick Mene, director of quality, reported employees do not abuse this privilege: "When you treat people responsibly, they act responsibly." Are employees achieving the goal of 100 percent guest satisfaction? In the eyes of one customer, they are. "They not only treat us like a king when we hold our top-level meetings in their hotels, but we just never get any complaints," said Wayne Stetson, the Staff Vice President of the Convention and Meetings Division of the National Association of Home Builders in Washington, D.C.[17] The Ritz-Carlton is a hotel that created a culture where the employees practice their credo. As they say in the business world, "they walk their talk."

Structure Fits Strategy   Exhibit 4-18 shows why it is important for an organization's structure to "fit" its strategy. The cost leadership strategy attempts to lower costs below those of competitors by focusing on creating efficiencies within organizational systems. As such, a centralized, vertical structure that focuses employee efforts internally is best suited to ensure stable operations. The characteristics associated with a vertical, functional structure are clear lines of authority, centralized decision making, and a focus on rules and procedures. In contrast, the differentiation strategy attempts to gain a competitive advantage through goods and/or services that are clearly unique or different from those of the competition. Innovation, flexibility, and responsiveness are keys to ensure this strategy is successful. Therefore, a horizontal structure that facilitates employee cooperation and coordination is the best fit. Other characteristics of a decentralized organization include decentralized decision making, informal interactions, and adaptive response.

STOP AND THINK

Do you agree that it is important for the firm's structure to fit its strategy? Why or why not? Would you expect Apple and United Parcel Service (UPS) to operate with similar or dissimilar strategies and structures? Explain.

EXHIBIT 4-18
Organizational Strategy and Structure: A Fit Perspective

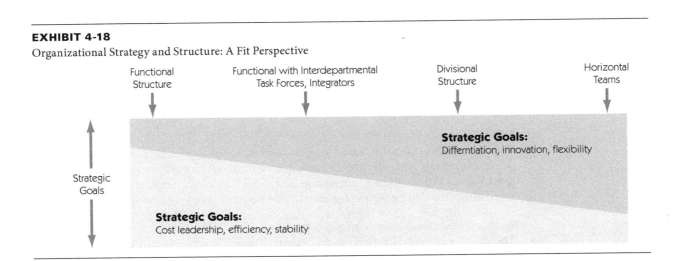

● **Chapter Review**

1. *Understand the stages of organization growth.*
This chapter focused on concepts that give supervisory managers a better understanding of their organization. A continuing case illustrated several phases of organization growth, from a one-person organization to a line-and-staff organization. It is important for a growing company to evolve from a line organization to a line-and-staff organization. This evolution allows the company to take advantage of specialization in such areas as human resources, quality control, purchasing, maintenance, scheduling, and safety. It also allows line managers and supervisors to concentrate on supervising and motivating their employees.

2. *Identify the advantages and disadvantages of the functional, product, and matrix departmentalization approaches.*
The span of control principle emphasizes there is a limit to the number of people a person can effectively manage. As one moves down the organization chart from top management to supervisory management levels, the span of control should increase. The reasons for tying span of control to management level are (1) top management requires the freedom to solve a variety of different, nonrecurring problems; (2) higher-level managers must spend much of their time doing long-range planning, working with outside interest groups, and coordinating the various activities of the business; and (3) supervisory managers tend to be concerned with more clearly defined areas of operation.

3. *Explain the principles of unity of command and span of control.*
Two important management principles for organizations are unity of command and span of control. Following the unity of command principle is important because it prevents duplication and conflict when orders and instructions are passed down. It also decreases confusion and "passing the buck" and provides a basis for managers and their employees to develop a better understanding of what they expect of each other. Finally, it promotes higher morale than is found in organizations that excessively violate the unity of command principle.

4. *Describe the difference between line and staff.*
Although both line and staff personnel are important, their duties differ. Line personnel carry out the primary activities of a business, such as producing or selling products and/or services. Staff personnel use their expertise to assist the line people and aid top management in various business activities.

5. *Understand how to avoid excessive conflict between line and staff.*
A line-and-staff organization sometimes leads to excessive conflict between line and staff departments. Conflict can be minimized by ensuring people understand the authority/responsibility relationships between individuals and departments.

6. *Explain the three types of authority found in organizations.*
The three types of authority found in organizations are advisory authority (common in staff departments), line authority (direct command authority over employees), and functional authority (limited line authority in a narrow area of specialization). Another way to avoid excessive conflict is to have effective communication between people and between departments.

7. *Distinguish between centralization and decentralization.*
The concept of centralization versus decentralization is important in understanding organizations. Some factors that influence the extent of centralization or decentralization are top management's philosophy, the history of the organization's growth, its geographic

location(s), the quality of managers, and the availability of controls. Computer technology increased the ability of higher management to shift in either direction. The trend, however, seems to be in the direction of decentralization.

8. *Discuss the benefits and costs of downsizing.*
Many organizations are currently being streamlined by downsizing, or by reducing the number of administrative levels. Although rapid downsizing can get out of control and there is unavoidable cost to the staff and supervisors who are laid off, the benefits to the organization in the form of cost reduction, faster decision making, and improved communication outweigh the costs. As a result of downsizing, supervisors often have more authority and responsibility, on the one hand, but they also are called on to act more as leaders, coaches, facilitators, and team developers.

9. *Explain the four types of contemporary organizational approaches.*
The four types of contemporary organizational approaches include the inverted pyramid, wagon wheel, teams, and network structures. In an inverted pyramid, first-line supervisors are empowered to address issues in a timely manner and make important decisions. With the wagon wheel, the customer is the focal point, emphasizing customer services. The team structure highlights the benefits of individuals cooperating and collaborating together in order to achieve synergistic outcomes. The network structure uses technologies to create and maintain virtual relationships. While each of the contemporary options has unique qualities, all of them enable managers to be responsive and flexible when adapting to changing environmental conditions.

10. *Understand the relationship between management philosophy, strategy, and newer forms of organization.*
The newer forms of organization being developed, the inverted pyramid and the wagon wheel, emphasize the role and importance of the customer and empowerment of employees who are close to the customer. Creative leadership is particularly valuable in developing innovative forms as a result of growth and new challenges.

Key Terms

line organization, p. 99
line-and-staff organization, p. 101
departmentalization, p. 102
functional departmentalization,
     p. 103
product departmentalization,
     p. 103
matrix departmentalization, p. 105

unity of command principle, p. 107
span of control principle, p. 109
line personnel, p. 111
staff personnel, p. 111
advisory authority, p. 112
line authority, p. 113
functional authority, p. 113
decentralization, p. 114

downsizing, p. 115
reengineering, p. 117
inverted pyramid, p. 118
wagon wheel, p. 119
team structure, p. 119
network structure, p. 119
cost leadership strategy, p. 120
differentiation strategy, p. 120

Discussion Questions

1. Outline the four stages of organizational growth, and relate them to an organization with which you are familiar.

2. What two important management principles affect the successful operation of a growing organization? Do you think John Moody's difficulties could have been avoided if he understood these principles? Discuss the advantages and disadvantages of functional, matrix, and product departmentalization.

3. What is the relationship between levels of management and span of control? Explain the advantages and disadvantages.

4. Distinguish between line and staff functions. Are they always easily identified in various types of business enterprises? Justify the existence of both line and staff departments.

5. What conflicts may arise between line and staff personnel? What reasons can you give for these problems? How does effective communication ease the conflict?

6. What are the three types of authority? Do they all exist in all four stages of functional growth?

7. What are some factors that favor centralization or decentralization?

8. How can a company minimize the negative effects of downsizing?

9. What are the potential benefits and potential drawbacks of reengineering?

10. What contemporary organization form would be the easiest to implement in a traditional functional organization?

11. Discuss the relationship between management philosophy, strategy, and forms of organization. If you were the owner/manager of 10 convenience stores in the same city, what type of strategy and structure would you use? If you were the owner/manager of 10 Certified Public Accountant (CPA) offices in various cities, what type of strategy and structure would you use?

Skill Builder 4.1

Resources

Information

Systems

YDL (You Deserve Luxury) Corporation

YDL Corporation designs and builds luxury, high-end yachts and mobile coaches. The company's niche market is wealthy individuals who can afford to pay millions to travel in style. Many of YDL's clients are famous celebrities, such as singers, actors/actresses, and royal families. The company's mission is as follows:

We are an international design and production firm intent on creating the highest quality yachts and mobile coaches for discerning clients. We work in partnership with our key stakeholders to deliver a high-end product tailored to meet our customers' needs. Thus, we recognize the importance of and emphasize building solid relationships with our customers, employees, and suppliers alike. Our promise is to deliver quality, on time.

YDL continues to grow even when other businesses' sales are declining. YDL's core competencies are quality and service, and it prides itself on its ability to adapt to customer and market changes. It employs between 125 and 150 total employees, depending on order levels. YDL's administrative and production facilities are located in California.

Answer the following questions:

1. What type of business strategy do you think YDL is pursuing? Explain.

2. What form of departmentalization (organizational structure) do you believe YDL utilizes? Why?

Skill Builder 4.2

Resources

Reducing Costs in an Accounting Firm (Group Activity)

Divide the class into groups of five to seven students, each group representing the managing partners of an accounting firm. Discuss the following situation and report to the class on what your group's plan is, and how you would communicate it to employees.

There are 30 employees in your organization and for the past year sales and profits have been down. In fact, for the past six months, the firm has operated at a loss.

Interpersonal Skill

Two months ago, a larger accounting firm acquired your firm in a friendly takeover. Its philosophy is to treat your smaller organization as a semiautonomous division of the accounting company, providing only general guidance and managing by results.

Systems

The accounting company CEO asked your group, the managing partners, to develop a plan to reduce costs. It is important to note 90 percent of your budget goes to salaries. The accounting company CEO also wants to know how you will communicate the plan to employees.

Source: The Synergistic Group, consulting files, 6 Schwaemmle Drive, Mobile, AL 36608.

Interpersonal Skill

Skill Builder 4.3

Information

Google's Organizational Structure (Group Activity)

Google experienced dramatic growth in a relatively short period of time, moving from an entrepreneurial venture to a publicly traded company seemingly overnight. All the reports and stories about the internal operations in the media suggest Google is a loosely structured network of creative energy. Form teams of three to five students. Your assignment is to conduct Internet research to uncover Google's true form of departmentalization (organizational structure). Each team's assignment is to prepare a brief report of its findings to present to the rest of the class.

Technology

CASE 4-1

JOHN MOODY: THE NEXT STAGE OF GROWTH:

When we last heard from John (see Exhibit 4-6), his organization was in a mature stage of organizational development. His business had grown from a single entrepreneur to a large, vertical, line-and-staff organization. The consultant John hired reported the possibility in the future of considering diversifying by adding product lines that require similar skills. Another possibility is to diversify by starting or acquiring unrelated businesses to reduce exposure to market and economic fluctuations.

PERFORM THE FOLLOWING TASKS

1. Using the information about John's company in the chapter, particularly the organizational chart in Exhibit 4-6, and considering the possibility of adding product lines or diversifying in unrelated ways, consider John's next stage of growth. What possibilities make sense and will they change the company's strategy and structure?
2. Prepare a report to include your recommends regarding what should be done to continue to grow this business. You should include an organizational chart in your report reflecting your recommendations.

Notes

1. M. Weitzner (Executive Senior Producer) (2009, September 10) *The New Age of Walmart* (Television Broadcast), viewed on CNBC on April 17, 2013, at 3:00 P.M. (Englewood Cliffs, N.J.: CNBC World); "Weaverville Welcomes Economic Boost from New Walmart," June 18, 2009, http://business.newsmvp.com/index.php?/topic/3352-weaverville-welcomes-economic-boost-from-new-walmart/.

2. CPSI Web Site, retrieved January 30, 2012 from http://www.cpsinet.com/corporate. Text originally published in D. Mosley Jr., W. Gillis, and R. Churchman, *Management for the 21st Century* (Dubuque, IA: Great River Technologies, 2013).

3. Thomas Peters and Robert Waterman, *In Search of Excellence: Lessons from America's Best-Run Companies*. New York : Harper & Row, c1982, 1982.

4. Ronald Henkoff, "Getting Beyond Downsizing," Fortune, January 10, 1994, p. 58.

5. Wayne F. Cascio, "Downsizing: What Do We Know? What Have We Learned?," *Academy of Management Executive* 2, no. 1 (February 1993), p. 95.

6. Roderick D. Iverson and Christopher D. Zatzick. "The Effects of Downsizing on Labor Productivity: The Value of Showing Consideration for Employees' Morale and Welfare in High-Performance Work Systems." *Human Resource Management* (Wiley), no. 1, 2011, p. 29. EBSCOhost, libproxy.usouthal.edu/login?url=http://search.ebscohost.com/login.aspx?direct=true&db=edsgea&AN=edsgcl.249577851&site=eds-live.

7. Phillip R. Nienstedt, "Effective Downsizing Management Structures," *Human Resources Planning* 12, 1989, p. 156.

8. R. L. Bunning, "The Dynamics of Downsizing," *Personnel Journal* 69 (September 1990), p. 70.

9. This section adapted from Michael Hammer and James Champy, *Reengineering the Corporation* (New York: Harper Business, 1993).

10. Ibid., p. 31.

11. Ibid., p. 32.

12. Frank Ostroff, *The Horizontal Organization* (New York: Oxford University Press, 1999), pp. 22–24.

13. Nancy K. Austin, "Reorganizing the Organization Chart," *Working Woman*, September 1993, p. 24.

14. Interviews and discussions with Vernon Mason, Assistant Manager with Family Dollar, by Don C. Mosley Jr., June and July 2009.

15. Rensis Likert, *New Patterns of Management* (New York: McGraw-Hill, 1961); Rensis Likert, *The Human Organization* (New York: McGraw-Hill, 1967).

16. George Benson, "Why the Ritz Is the Ritz," *Georgia Trend* 15 (August 2000), p. 99.

17. Excerpts from handout from the Ritz-Carlton, Island of Maui, Hawaii; Edwin McDowell, "Ritz-Carlton Keys to Good Service," *New York Times*, March 31, 1993, pp. C1–C3; Portrait: The Ritz-Carlton Hotel Company; interviews and discussions with Lenny Litz, General Manager, and staff of Ritz-Carlton, Maui; discussion with Sue Musselman, assistant to the Vice President of Quality, Ritz-Carlton Hotel Company, Atlanta, GA, and Mark Memmot, by Donald C. Mosley Sr., June 1994; "The Quality Quest," *USA Today*, June 28, 1993, p. 2B.

5
Delegating Authority and Empowering Employees

The greatest challenge in life is to be who you are and to become what you are capable of becoming.

—Robert Louis Stevenson

The second greatest challenge is to assist and empower other people to become what they are capable of becoming.

—Donald C. Mosley Sr.

Kinga/Shutterstock.com

In empowered organizations, teams thrive when leaders delegate some authority and people are able to learn from each other.

Preview

VALVE CORPORATION, SEI INVESTMENTS, AND SUN HYDRAULICS—
EMPOWER HUMAN CAPITAL Many companies have embraced empower-
ment, creating decentralized structures as a means to enhance their flexibility,
responsiveness, and competitiveness in the 21st century. However, the amount or
level of empowerment—the degree to which employees are encouraged to make key
decisions within their enlarged areas of responsibilities—varies widely. Examples
of companies that have achieved successes by implementing empowering strategies
include The Valve Corporation, SEI Investments, and Sun Hydraulics.

The Valve Corporation is a privately held video gaming company founded by former
Microsoft employees Gabe Newell and Mike Harrington in 1996 in Bellevue, Washington.
Valve is completely decentralized to take advantage of employees' creativity and innovative talents. Although the founders aspire to achieve greatness, they understand failure
is a natural part of the process. They believe that giving people freedom liberates them
to utilize their talents in creative ways. Instead of a manager telling staff members what
and when to do something, the staff decide what projects and teams to work on. Team
management is about facilitating and coaching rather than directing. This process of
self-selection results in strong employee–project fit, motivation, and professional decision
making. Valve's commitment to empowering employees is so pervasive the handbook for
new employees is subtitled "A fearless adventure in knowing what to do when no one's
there telling you what to do." With the widely successful games Half-Life and Portal, and
an ever-growing library of gaming technologies, Valve has achieved incredible success.[1]

Another company that has created a strong culture of empowerment is SEI. SEI provides asset management, investment processing, and investment operations solutions to
institutions, banks, investment advisors and managers, and families with high net worth.
Under the direction of founder and CEO Alfred West, SEI has grown from humble begin-
nings in 1968 to managing and administering $495 billion in global assets today. During

the early years, the company moved locations multiple times, but in 1996, SEI needed its own corporate headquarters and campus.

Innovation and creativity are at the core of SEI's culture, so creating a work environment that fostered these foundational elements while also supporting the pursuit of new opportunities, responses to industry and general environmental threats, and strategic change was of paramount importance. With a blank canvas, West and SEI, set out to design and build such a corporate space. Today, newly hired employees are given a desk and chair, on wheels, along with a phone and a computer, and provided with a "starting" location. Upon arriving at their "starting" locations, they push aside other desks and chairs to make room. There are tons of windows and open space, but no offices, cubicles, secretaries, or traditional barriers separating employees and managers. In fact, a new employee might select the spot next to the CEO!

SEI's open structure design reflects specific cultural elements: egalitarianism, empowerment, transparency, flexibility, teamwork, and interaction. To SEI, ideas are more important than hierarchy, and when employees begin acting as owners, they become intellectually productive. While the executive team sets the vision and strategy, as in most other companies, employees are empowered to create, join teams, and change locations to work on different projects when they want. Communication improves exponentially without barriers, and managers are able to better monitor the energy and vibe within a team or the company as a whole and make necessary changes quickly to sustain functional interaction. The one constant in business today is change, and SEI's corporate design embraces change and does away with complacency. The ultimate purpose in creating this type of environment was to enhance creativity and innovation, resulting in competitive advantages.[2]

Sun Hydraulics is a manufacturer of hydraulic manifolds and valves. It operates plants around the world, employing more than 700 people. Similar to SEI and Valve, Sun Hydraulics utilizes a flat organization structure to empower employees to ensure operations are efficient and effective. While the company's approach is similar to those of SEI and Valve, its mission and scope are different. According to Sun Hydraulics' Web site, "Our workplace is as distinctive as our products, and provides just as many advantages. We have no job titles, no hierarchy, no formal job descriptions, organizational charts or departments. We have open offices, promoting open communication. This environment encourages innovation and helps develop a spirit of entrepreneurship throughout the organization. The result is a workforce inspired to satisfy every customer, no matter the challenge." This philosophy obviously works with sales of approximately $200 million a year, and the stock price up 950 percent over the last 10 years.[3]

Empowering a workforce through decentralization is not only an effective strategy in privately held high-tech companies or publicly traded high-end finance firms in which creativity and innovation are keys to survival, it also works quite well in traditional manufacturing environments, as evidenced by Sun Hydraulics's success. So, are Valve, SEI, and Sun Hydraulics business anomalies or are they pace setters, establishing trends for the future? Time will tell, but one thing is fairly certain: The 21st century business environments will continue morphing dynamically at warp speed!

authority

Given the right to act in a specified manner in order to reach organizational objectives; the right to tell others how to act to reach objectives.

Concepts and Definitions

As you are probably already aware, not all companies embrace empowerment and delegate to the extent of those companies we have chosen to preview, but we wanted to give you a sense of some cutting-edge organizational cultures. A number of organizations have leaders that are intelligent and well educated, yet they do not practice true empowerment. There are many reasons this is so, and we will explore some of them later in the chapter. The authors are convinced that mastering the art of delegation and empowerment is essential

responsibilities

Occurs when key tasks associated with a particular job are specified. The obligation of an employee to accept a manager's delegated authority.

job descriptions

Provide information to employees about the important job-related tasks.

accountability

The obligation that is created when an employee accepts the leader's delegation of authority.

delegation of authority

The process by which leaders distribute and entrust activities and related authority to other people in an organization. The three key aspects of organization are (1) granting authority, (2) assigning duties and responsibilities, (3) requiring accountability.

to a leader's growth, development, and effectiveness, ultimately translating into team and/or organizational success. Consequently, we want to start with concepts and definitions to ensure we understand the process of delegation and empowerment.

Role of Delegation

Delegation is the process by which leaders distribute and entrust activities and related authority to other people in an organization. The three key aspects of delegation are (1) granting authority, (2) assigning duties and responsibilities, and (3) requiring accountability.

- *Authority* is the right to do something. When authority is delegated, an individual or team is given the power or right to act in a specified manner in order to reach organizational objectives. For example, a department chair at a university is given the authority to recruit faculty members to fill vacant positions without the president of the university having to interview each candidate to make a final decision.
- *Assigning duties and* **responsibilities** occurs when key tasks associated with a particular job are specified. In mid- to large-size organizations, **job descriptions** provide information to employees about the important job-related tasks. Due to the dynamic nature of business today, managers may assign nontraditional duties and responsibilities. For example, production employees in a southeastern furniture manufacturing plant are given the responsibility of projecting a positive image of the company both on the job and in the community. Because the plant competes for most of its production personnel from the surrounding rural area with other manufacturers, a positive corporate image is a key differentiating factor.
- *Accountability* is the obligation that is created when an employee accepts the leader's **delegation of authority**. Accountability flows upward, such that the delegatee is responsible to the next higher level of management to effectively carry out the assigned duties and responsibilities.

Decentralization

Although closely related to the concept of delegation of authority, decentralization is the broader concept, in that it refers to the extent to which authority is delegated from one level or unit of the organization to another, rather than from one individual to another.

The Role of Authority

Because authority is constantly being used, its nature and role should be well understood. As mentioned earlier, authority is the *right* to do something or to tell someone else to do it to reach organizational objectives. If no one in an organization had authority, employees could come to work and leave when they wanted, and they could carry out their assignments in any way they wanted, rather than in the way prescribed by higher authority. Without a system of authority, an organization could not function. The following are some examples of higher authority in action.

The PIC—person in charge—at one of Jimmy John's Gourmet Sandwich locations is responsible for overseeing the store during its hours of operation. The PIC's authority comes from the store manager or owner. A police officer gives a motorist a ticket for driving 45 mph in a 30-mph zone. The officer's authority derives from the city council.

The department manager at Macy's assigned the work shifts for her personnel during the Christmas holidays. Her authority was delegated by the store manager.

Bambu Productions/Iconica/Getty Images

Delegating allows employees an opportunity to learn by doing. It also allows the supervisor to perform other tasks, and it improves control. As a result, more work gets accomplished!

In each of these examples, the individual exercised the right to exert authority over others. That authority came with the position and resulted from delegation by a higher-level manager.

Sources of Authority

There are two contradictory views regarding the source of a manager's authority: the formal theory and the acceptance theory.

formal theory of authority

Authority exists because someone was granted it.

Formal Authority View   According to the **formal theory of authority**, authority is conferred; authority exists because someone was granted it. This view traces the origin of authority upward to its ultimate source, which for business organizations is the owners or stockholders. The head nurse in a hospital has authority granted by the nursing director, who has been granted authority by the hospital board, which has been granted authority by the stockholders (if a private hospital) or the public (if a public hospital). The formal theory is consistent with the definition of authority we presented in the previous section.

STOP AND THINK

You may be reading the material in this book because it has been assigned by an instructor. What is the source of the instructor's authority to make such an assignment, to give exams, and to assign a grade in the course?

---

acceptance theory of authority

A manager's authority originates only when it has been accepted by the group or individual over whom it is being exercised.

Acceptance of Authority View The **acceptance theory of authority** disputes the idea that authority can be conferred. Acceptance theorists (chiefly behaviorists) believe that a manager's authority originates only when it has been accepted by the group or individual over whom it is being exercised. Chester Barnard stated this position. He wrote, "If a directive communication is accepted by one to whom it is addressed, the authority for him is confirmed or established."[4] Thus, acceptance of the directive becomes the basis of action. Disobedience of such a communication by an employee is a denial of its authority for him or her. Therefore, under this definition, the decision about whether an order has authority lies with the person to whom it is addressed and does not reside in "persons of authority" or those who issue those orders, as implied in this example:

Jan was a manager in a large publishing company that had initiated a participative management by objectives process. Jan's immediate supervisor asked her to set objectives for her area and develop a one-year plan to accomplish those objectives. Jan consulted her employees and developed what she perceived as difficult but attainable objectives.

When her boss reviewed the objectives, he discovered he disagreed and revised them drastically. He then called Jan in and dictated that she accept the altered objectives. Jan responded that the objectives would be impossible for her staff to achieve and she could not agree to them in good conscience. At this point, Jan refused to accept her boss's authority, and, although her boss eventually capitulated, it caused some future difficulties in their relationship.[5]

STOP AND THINK

Do you agree with Jan's position in this example? Why or why not? Assuming that Jan was correct in feeling that the revised objectives would be impossible to attain, how might she have handled the situation differently?

We have defined authority in line with the position taken by the formal theorists—that authority is a right a manager has been formally granted by the organization. As we will shortly point out, though, the acceptance theorists seem to confuse authority with power or leadership, which involves the ability of a manager to influence employees to accept his or her authority.

The behaviorists, however, do make the point that *to be effective*, managers are certainly very dependent on acceptance by others of their authority.

A female supervisor in a traditionally male role may find her power tested by her subordinates.

The Role of Power

4. Understand the role of power and why it is a great motivator.

The leader's possession of authority is not always sufficient in itself to assure that subordinates will respond as the leader desires. In such cases, a leader must use some other approach, as the following example illustrates.

> *Mary Fleming was named supervisor of the Number 2 paper machine at the northern mill of a large national company.[6] She was the first female supervisor to be named to such a traditionally male position. The position carried much authority with it, but Mary was intelligent enough to realize that her authority alone would not get her workers to accept her and meet performance standards.*

> *Several of the employees tested her immediately by taking extended work breaks and making some snide remarks within her hearing about the department's "skirt supervisor." Mary ignored this behavior the first few days and felt that the worst thing she could do was to overreact and come on too strong. But the resistance persisted. Mary had a meeting with Carl White and Pete Antheim, the two senior members of the department, and asked for their advice about handling the situation. White and Antheim seemed flattered by being consulted and told Mary they'd handle the situation. The problems never recurred, and six months after the incident, Mary's group was highly supportive of her leadership, and the "female department head" issue had been forgotten.*

power

The ability to influence individuals, groups, events, and decisions.

We will now study this example with an eye toward the authority–power combinations illustrated in Exhibit 5-1. Mary used a leadership strategy that played a key role in getting her into quadrant 3, where she had both authority and power. **Power** is the ability to influence individuals, groups, events, and decisions, and is closely related to leadership. In an earlier example in this chapter—where Jan refused to accept impossible objectives dictated by her boss—we see an example of quadrant 2 in operation. Jan's boss had considerable

EXHIBIT 5-1
Authority–Power
Combination

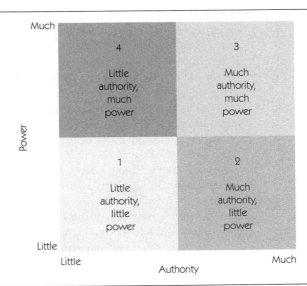

authority but little power to influence Jan to accept his edict. In other cases, staff personnel have little authority but much power to influence line managers (quadrant 4).

The belief of Sir Dahlberg Acton that "power tends to corrupt, and absolute power corrupts absolutely" is widespread in today's culture. In recent years, however, there has been an increasing awareness that power is not necessarily all bad—that the use of power may be essential for the effective accomplishment of individual, organizational, and social goals. Interest in power also has been generated by David McClelland's research showing that a high need for power is an important characteristic of successful managers.

How Power Is Obtained

As shown by J.R.P. French Jr. and Bertram Raven in one of the earliest—and still most useful—studies, power can be obtained from many sources.[7] Six of these sources have been translated into types of power, classified as follows:

1. **Reward power** arises from the number of positive rewards (money, protection, etc.) that a leader is perceived as controlling. As a supervisor, you may have the ability to determine your employees' bonuses, time off, schedules, and/or level of feedback, so the more options available, the more significant your reward power. But even if you possess relatively little formal reward power (pay, promotion, etc.), don't underestimate the power of informal rewards such as verbal praise and quality feedback.

2. **Coercive power** results from people's perceived expectation that punishment (being fired, reprimanded, etc.) will follow if they do not comply with the orders of a leader. Coercive power can be a necessary and effective means of influence, when used appropriately, but overreliance on this source of power can actually be detrimental and result in a leader's total power diminishing over time.

3. **Legitimate power** develops from internalized values that dictate that a leader has an inherent right to influence subordinates. According to this view, one has an obligation to accept that influence simply because a person is designated as a boss or leader.

4. **Control-of-information power** derives from the possession of knowledge that others do not have. Some people exercise this type of power by either giving or withholding needed information.

5. **Referent power** is based on people's identification with a leader and what that "leader" stands for or symbolizes. Personal charisma, charm, courage, and other traits are important factors in the exercise of referent power. However, noncharismatic individuals can garner similar respect in other ways. You have probably been a part of an athletic team, student club, or work group in which one person commanded the respect of the others through his or her actions—willing to start early and stay late, putting the needs of the whole above his or her own, persevering and demonstrating a tremendous work ethic. Leadership by example is another way to earn referent power.

6. **Expert power** results from a leader's expertise or knowledge in an area in which that leader wants to influence others. For example, a supervisor may possess the knowledge of how to effectively schedule a complex project using the critical path method, and people are willing to listen and follow directions because they know the supervisor has achieved successes on similar projects. Or the supervisor may have expertise operating a specific machine, and the employees may want to learn how to operate the machine so they can develop in their jobs.

Do not infer from this discussion that a given leader draws upon all of these types of power. Rather, leaders find their own sources of strength from many of these types. We can say that more effective leaders draw more on referent power and expert power, and practice more open communication in information sharing.

How Power Can Be Used

Some leaders believe that if a manager has power and shares it with others (delegates it), it is diminished. Actually, the best way to expand power is to share it, for power can grow, in part, by being shared. Sharing power is different from giving it or throwing it away—delegation does not mean abdication.

Effective leaders have a high need for power, but that need is directed toward the benefit of the organization as a whole. In addition, the need for power is stronger than the need to be liked by others. Thus, as a leader you must be willing to play the influence game in a controlled way. This does not imply that you need to be authoritarian in action. On the contrary, it appears that power-motivated leaders make their subordinates feel stronger rather than weaker. A true authoritarian would have the reverse effect, making people feel weak or powerless.

5. *Explain the role of empowerment and indicate ways to increase empowerment.*

empowerment

Granting employees authority to make key decisions within their enlarged areas of responsibility.

The Role of Empowerment

Empowerment essentially is the granting of authority to employees to make key decisions within their enlarged areas of responsibility. The driving idea of empowerment is that individuals closest to the work and to customers should make the decisions. It may be easiest to think of empowerment as a continuum with one end representing low levels of empowerment and the opposite end reflecting high levels, such that it is not a matter of whether a manager or company practices empowerment or not, but rather the degree to which employees are empowered. The companies in the chapter's opening case represent highly empowered organizations. It takes vision, time, and effort to develop this type of culture and sustain it over time, but through effective delegation, coaching, and mentoring, managers can develop the capability and confidence to make decisions and work in enlarged areas of responsibility. In fact, as you will learn in the motivation chapter, the younger generation, Gen Y, thrives in this type of culture.

STOP AND THINK

Reflecting on the companies discussed in the opening case, what are the keys to successfully empowering employees by implementing a decentralized approach? Are there specific organizational and work characteristics more suitable for operating with such a high degree of empowerment? Can you think of other types of companies that might benefit from using this approach?

These companies have one thing (among others) in common: They all place a high priority on recruiting and selecting the right people. They seek to hire individuals who possess some or all of the following characteristics:

- Highly competent with the proper mix of knowledge, skills, and abilities.
- Confident and willing to make important decisions.
- Comfortable working in teams.
- Effective problem solvers.

Not everyone suitably fits with a highly empowered culture. Some people simply want a job and others need more direction or external influence typically found in less decentralized, empowered environments. So for these three companies, choosing the right people is key to operating and sustaining a culture of empowerment.

In the following sections, we will discuss why leaders fail to delegate and the other challenges associated with empowering employees.

Why Leaders Fail to Delegate

6. Understand why some leaders are reluctant to delegate and why employees may not welcome delegation.

Many good and intelligent people have difficulty delegating authority when in leadership positions, particularly in the early stages of their careers. Our culture has a major influence on why this occurs so frequently.

In the formative years, success in school and in summer jobs depended primarily on the individual's efforts. Achievement and success did not come from inspiring, developing, and working with other people. Grades were determined primarily by hard work and self-discipline. Moreover, those who went to college had a high need for achievement and usually chose difficult majors. The majority who chose fields such as accounting, finance, and banking usually had a keen sense of responsibility, were very conscientious, and were good with details. A survey of bank leaders attending the Louisiana State University Banking School indicated that most of the participants had personality types that incorporated these qualities. One class of 65 bankers completed a home-study problem of identifying their primary weakness that needed improvement to increase their effectiveness as a bank leader. They also were asked to develop and implement an action plan to turn the weakness into a strength. The weakness that appeared most frequently in the banking class was inability to delegate effectively. The action plan to improve delegation by a vice president of lending is found in Exhibit 5-2.

STOP AND THINK

How many people do you know who are guided by the adage "if you want it done right, do it yourself"? Are you one of them? If you are a leader, what negative consequences does this mind-set have on effective delegation and employee empowerment?

EXHIBIT 5-2

Action Plan of James McKenney, Vice President of Lending

i. Statement of my objective

To greatly improve my efficiency and effectiveness in carrying out the delegation process with the leading officers reporting to me.

ii. Analysis of the problem or objective

A. At the banking school when we discussed the 16 problem styles (Myers–Briggs profiles and analysis), I discovered that the characteristics of my type could lead to being a very effective leader if a few potential blind spots can be overcome. It seems that those who are sensing/thinking types (as I am) are so conscientious that our attitude is "If you want it done right, do it yourself." This statement definitely applies to me.

B. When I was recently promoted to this position, the president of the bank gave me a number of positive reasons for my promotion. He also cautioned me that with my increased responsibilities, I could expect to get involved in activities as previously, but he wanted me to focus on developing the skills and knowledge of our loan officers and improve bottom-line results.

C. I realize that most of my life I earned good grades in high school and college because of individual effort. This carried over to my work habits as a loan officer, but I now realize that to be a successful supervisor, I need to develop my team and make use of coaching and empowerment.

iii. Development of alternative solutions

A. Start having biweekly meetings for one hour after banking hours.

1. At our first meeting we will jointly develop objectives that enhance and reinforce the bank's financial goal.

2. At our subsequent meetings we will review our progress and discuss any problem loans.

B. Set up a participative individual management-by-objectives program. This plan will allow individual bank officers to set performance objectives that support our lending division's objectives. During this process I will play the role of coach and mentor, and after the initial meeting, set up performance review sessions with each officer every six months or as needed.

C. Once every six months at our biweekly meeting we will conduct a brainstorming session to identify our strengths and any problems, issues, or missed opportunities we need to address.

D. I will explore educational opportunities available for our officers, including scheduling several officers for our state banking school or the Banking School of the South.

iv. Final action plan

I have begun implementing all of the alternative ideas (A, B, C, and D in Section III). Prior to sending this to you, I met with our president and CEO and discussed the ideas. He was most enthusiastic and supportive and is presenting the concept to our executive committee for possible implementation in all divisions of our bank.

Source: This example is based on the experiences of Don Mosley when he served as a coordinator and instructor for the management and leadership segment of the Banking School of the South at Louisiana State University. The name is fictional to ensure no embarrassment to the actual banker.

The late industrialist Andrew Carnegie once said, "When a man realizes he can get others in to help him do something better than he can do it alone, he has taken a big step in his life." The following are some other reasons why many leaders have difficulty delegating:

- Many leaders like to control but feel that when they delegate, they surrender some of their power and authority. One study found that managers tended to assign higher evaluations of work quality to their employees when the managers themselves were more involved in the production.[8] Because empowerment dilutes work supervision, many managers may make inaccurate evaluations of their workers' abilities, skills, and output.

- Some leaders do not delegate because of a lack of trust in others.
- Closely related to the above point, because leaders are being held accountable for results, they don't delegate out of fear employees will make mistakes. One research study found that a key determinant of managerial delegation was the strength of the manager–subordinate relationship. Managers delegated more to employees whom they perceived to be competent, who shared their task goals, and who had longer tenure.[9]
- Others do not delegate because they are insecure and are afraid that their employees will do so well that they will be recognized and promoted ahead of the leader.
- A legitimate reason why some leaders don't delegate is they correctly assess that employees need more training, coaching, and experience in certain assignments.

Why Employees May Not Welcome Delegation

Of course, there are also reasons why employees may not welcome delegation:

1. **Ambiguous or Unclear Duties and Responsibilities.** When delegating authority, the manager must clearly communicate to the employee the employee's duties and responsibilities, the need for and importance of the assignment, and why the employee was selected. In one case, the plant had been downsized so drastically that workers were being assigned responsibilities and duties that middle managers had previously performed. In this type of environment, change occurs rapidly, so there is always the chance that newly delegated responsibilities and duties will be poorly communicated, which can lead to negative outcomes.

2. **Fear of Failure.** Even if assignments are communicated so individuals understand what comprises their new duties, other problems may arise. Many managers misdiagnose the job maturity level of their employees and assign them tasks that are too difficult. This mistake may result in the employee being unfairly criticized during his or her performance review or perhaps even fired. A company that one of the authors worked with in a consulting capacity had a national presence and was growing rapidly; it promoted internally as a means of filling newly created positions and motivating its existing employees. One individual was promoted to manager of his work department because he had excelled as an operational-level employee and possessed the technical expertise that was needed. However, he had not had an opportunity to develop other skills needed in the new management position, such as team building, communication, conflict management, and leadership skills. His inability to employ a diverse skill set with his employees ultimately led to his being replaced as head of the work department.

3. **Increased Stress.** Finally, increased delegation can mean increased stress on employees. Even when effective communication and appropriate training are provided, employees still may resist delegation and empowerment. Management efforts to downsize or restructure the organization to be more competitive can lead to employee role overload. During the 1990s, the following comments seemed quite common: "They call it empowerment and say we get a chance to be a real part of this organization. I call it doing more work for the same amount of money." Some employees prefer not to be empowered. As Hackman and Oldham's Job Characteristics Model points out, the level of participation an individual is comfortable with is not just dependent on effective job design, communication, and training. Meaningful participation also depends on that person's need for growth and development. Managers must assess an employee's job maturity level and need for growth when selecting an employee for delegation.[10]

Facing Adaptive Challenges

7. Know how to face adaptive challenges.

Ronald A. Heifetz's book *Leadership Without Easy Answers* is an innovative and creative contribution to leadership.[11] In this book and in a follow-up article in the *Harvard Business Review* by Heifetz and Donald Laurie, a concept of adaptive challenges and work is presented. In their words:

> *To stay alive, Jack Pritchard had to change his life. Triple bypass surgery and medication could help, the heart surgeon told him, but no technical fix could release Pritchard from his own responsibility for changing the habits of a lifetime. He had to stop smoking, improve his diet, get some exercise, and take time to relax, remembering to breathe more deeply each day. Pritchard's doctor could provide sustaining technical expertise and take supportive action, but only Pritchard could adapt his ingrained habits to improve his long-term health. The doctor faced the leadership task of mobilizing the patient to make critical behavioral changes; Jack Pritchard faced the adaptive work of figuring out which specific changes to make and how to incorporate them into his daily life.*

> *Companies today face challenges similar to the ones confronting Pritchard and his doctor. They face adaptive challenges. Changes in societies, markets, customers, competition, and technology around the globe are forcing organizations to clarify their values, develop new strategies, and learn new ways of operation. Often the toughest task for leaders in effecting change is mobilizing people throughout the organization to do adaptive work.*

> *Adaptive work is required when our deeply held beliefs are challenged, when the values that made us successful become less relevant, and when legitimate yet competing perspectives emerge. We see adaptive challenges every day at every level of the workplace—when companies restructure or reengineer, develop or implement strategy, or merge businesses. We see adaptive challenges when marketing has difficulty working with operations, when cross-functional teams don't work well, or when senior executives complain, "We don't seem to be able to execute effectively." Adaptive problems are often systemic problems with no ready answers.*

> *. . . But the locus of responsibility for problem solving when a company faces an adaptive challenge must shift to its people. Solutions to adaptive challenges reside not in the executive suite, but in the collective intelligence of employees at all levels, who need to use one another as resources, often across boundaries, and learn their way to those solutions.*[12]

Reframing and Training   Reframing and training is one way to face adaptive challenges at work. It helps organizations and individuals to change values and behaviors and to identify new approaches and strategies. The essence of **reframing** is examining the "situation from multiple vantage points to develop a holistic picture. Effective leaders change lenses when they don't make sense or aren't working."[13] Leadership training and development have a major impact in getting leaders/managers to change. In the final analysis, the motivation to change and improve effectiveness in delegation and empowerment rests with the individual—both leader and follower.

reframing
_____

Examining the situation from multiple vantage points to develop a holistic picture.

Achieving Effective Delegation and Empowerment

8. Indicate ways to achieve effective delegation and discuss the roles of various parties in achieving effective delegation.

When the authors conduct workshops regarding leadership, team building, and partnering, we start by asking participants, "What is the most effective way you learn that produces the most insight, growth, and development?" Although we have received different answers, a core group of people always respond by saying that experience and, especially, mistakes are

Increased delegation can sometimes overwhelm employees

the best learning tools. We then ask, "What is the implication of saying, 'We know of people who have had one year of experience 20 times?'" Usually, someone correctly assesses that although those individuals have experience, they really haven't learned from that experience. Thus, the key to learning from experience, including both successes and failures, is to go through a disciplined reflection on that experience.

experiential learning

Using an integrated process of experiencing, identifying, analyzing, and generalizing to gain insights in learning.

Exhibit 5-3 shows the **experiential learning** model and highlights the importance of using feedback to gain insights in learning from experience. The use of this model, particularly in a coaching or mentoring environment, is very helpful for achieving successful delegation, empowerment, and results.

Coaching and Teaching

Two of the most significant ways of empowering and developing people are coaching and teaching. This area is so significant to the leadership process that we have an additional chapter covering the topic, so at this point, we will only introduce the process.

There are many different ways to coach and teach. The forthcoming story describes a way that may have been the catalyst for Dwight D. Eisenhower's becoming General of the Army and President of the United States. As a student at West Point, Eisenhower excelled as a football player until a football injury ended his career. After a bout with despondency, he regrouped and directed his energies to becoming a head cheerleader. During this period, he was not known for excelling in his studies and graduated in the middle of his class.

Most of his initial assignments after graduation involved coaching the football team; from all reports, he was a good coach. Fortunately, he was then assigned to Panama and reported to General Fox Conner, a graduate of West Point, who saw great leadership potential in young Eisenhower. In World War I, Conner had served as General Pershing's operations officer in France and was considered one of the smartest men in the army.

After the war, in 1922, Conner took command of the 20th Infantry Brigade in the Panama Canal Zone. He requested that Eisenhower be assigned to his command as executive

EXHIBIT 5-3

The Experiential Learning Model

Do = Experience:
The employee does something that results in a success or a mistake.

Experience

Grow = Generalize:
They draw conclusions and attempt to discover principles that would help in future situations.

Generalize

Identify

Look = Identify:
The supervisor and employee together identify what happened.

Analyze

Think = Analyze:
Together they analyze what factors were involved in causing the success or failure.

officer; Conner's old boss, U.S. Army Chief of Staff John Pershing, granted the request. Conner was a great teacher and coach for Eisenhower, and because their duties were light, they spent a lot of time in a teacher/coach/student relationship.

Conner insisted that Eisenhower read serious military literature and forced the younger man to think about what he was reading by asking probing questions. Eisenhower read memoirs of Civil War generals, then discussed with Conner the decisions Grant, Sherman, and others had made. What would have happened had they done this or that differently? What were the alternatives? Eisenhower was anxious to please, so anxious that he read *Clausewitz on War* three times—a difficult enough task to complete even once and made more difficult by Conner's insistent questioning about the implications of Clausewitz's ideas.

Conner and Eisenhower also discussed the future. Conner insisted there would be another war in 20 years or less, that it would be a world war, that America would fight with allies, and that Eisenhower had better prepare himself for it. He advised Eisenhower to try for an assignment under Colonel George C. Marshall, who had been with Conner on Pershing's staff. Marshall, Conner insisted, "knows more about the techniques of arranging allied commands than any man I know. He is nothing short of genius." Indeed, Conner's highest praise was "Eisenhower, you handled that just the way Marshall would have done."[14]

Many years after Eisenhower was identified as a world class leader, he stated that his three years under Conner were "a sort of graduate school in military affairs. . . . In a lifetime of association with great and good men, he is the one figure to whom I owe an incalculable debt." In fact, Eisenhower has stated frequently that Conner influenced him more than anyone else he ever served under.[15]

In the fall of 1924, Eisenhower was transferred back to Ft. Meade to coach football. He was greatly disappointed because he had his heart set on attending the infantry school; however, the Chief of Infantry turned down his request without discussion. The infantry school was a prerequisite for the Command and General Staff School (C & GSS) at

Ft. Leavenworth, Kansas, and only the best and brightest of officers were selected to attend. Finally, Conner used his influence with the war department to get Eisenhower to the C & GSS. Even then, the infantry command tried to discourage him. An aide to the Chief of Infantry wrote advising Eisenhower to stay away from C & GSS because "you will probably fail," in which case the failure would make him useless as an infantry officer.[16] Eisenhower then wrote to Conner expressing some self-doubts and asking his advice on how to prepare himself. In his reply, Conner said, "you may not know it, but because of your 3 years' work in Panama, you are far better trained and ready for Leavenworth than anybody I know."[17]

Conner was right. Eisenhower persevered, and through hard work, diligent study, and the development of a good mind, he finished number one out of a class of 275 of the best young officers in the Army.

STOP AND THINK

Do you agree or disagree on the importance of coaching and teaching in the empowerment and development of individuals? If you agree, identify, and reflect on who influenced you the most in the role of coach, teacher, and mentor. Specifically, share with someone else how you were influenced.

Benefits of Delegation

9. Recognize the benefits of delegation.

- **Employee Development.** Through delegation, employees can learn from their experiences. When managers enable their employees to succeed and/or make mistakes on their own, a valuable learning opportunity is created. The manager can assist the individual in analyzing the situation and evaluating the reasons for the success or failure, so the employee can grow from the experience.
- **Improved Control.** Contributing to the benefit of employee development, managers who delegate effectively emphasize results, not specific actions, and provide feedback when appropriate.
- **Improved Time Management.** Leaders who choose not to share their power may find they are so consumed with "putting out fires" that they have very little time to devote to truly important or long-term tasks. Conversely, managers who effectively delegate tasks to their subordinates have more time to spend on planning and trouble shooting.
- **Enhanced Power.** When employees are empowered, the environment created results in more people being knowledgeable and concerned about the organization's objectives. This concern leads to a sense of responsibility or ownership in the work itself.

Seven Habits of Unsuccessful Executives

We want to conclude this chapter with some interesting insights from leadership theorist Sydney Finkelstein, Professor of Management at the Tuck School at Dartmouth College. He wrote an article, "7 Habits of Spectacularly Unsuccessful Executives." Two of the seven habits are directly related to the concepts covered in this chapter, and others are indirectly related. The seven habits are as follows:

1. They see themselves and companies as dominating their environment.
2. They identify so completely with the company that there is no clear boundary between their personal interests and the corporation's interests.
3. They think they have all the answers.

4. They ruthlessly eliminate anyone who isn't 100 percent behind them.

5. They are consummate spokespersons obsessed with the company image.

6. They underestimate obstacles.

7. They stubbornly rely on what worked for them in the past.[18]

STOP AND THINK

Which two habits are directly related to the concepts in this chapter? Why?

Finkelstein goes on to say, "Most of the great destroyers of value are people of unusual intelligence and talent. . . . Nearly all of the leaders who preside over major business failures exhibit four or five of these habits."[19]

In our chapter review, we discuss the two habits most directly related to concepts in this chapter and how they relate to all leaders, not just to high-level executives.

● Chapter Review

1. *Recognize the importance of delegation.*
The delegation process is a partnering process between a supervisor and employees, bosses, and colleagues. Experiential learning is an important part of delegation, allowing employees to grow and develop by "learning through experience." Effective delegation is essential to performing the supervisory management job successfully. In addition to developing people, delegation (1) allows the supervisor to do other things, (2) accomplishes more work, and (3) improves control.

2. *Explain what is involved in the delegation process, including authority, responsibility, and accountability.*
The process of delegation has three aspects: granting authority, assigning responsibility, and holding people accountable for results. Because accountability is essential to maintaining effective control over results, a person who delegates an assignment should not be able to escape accountability for poor results. Controls to ensure effective delegation can include personal observation by the delegator, periodic reports by the delegate, and statistical reports concerning output, costs, and grievances.

3. *Understand the role of authority.*
Authority is the *right* to do something or to tell someone else to do it, to reach organizational objectives. If no one had authority, employees could do just what they liked in no prescribed manner; they could come and go as they pleased. Without a system of authority, an organization could not function.

4. *Understand the role of power and why it is a great motivator.*
Power is the ability to influence individuals, groups, events, and decisions, and is closely related to leadership. Power can be used for good or evil by leaders. Successful leaders have (1) the ability to influence others and (2) a greater need for power than for being liked or needing to do tasks alone. They also believe that to expand power, they need to share it with other members of the organization through delegation and empowerment.

5. *Explain the role of empowerment and indicate ways to increase empowerment.*
The driving role of empowerment is that individuals closest to the work and to the customers should make the decisions. When implemented properly, empowerment becomes an important way to improve organizational performance. Coaching and teaching are important in carrying out successful empowerment. Also critical to the process is sharing information with everyone and, where appropriate, using self-directed work teams.

6. *Understand why some leaders are reluctant to delegate and why employees may not welcome delegation.*
Despite the benefits of effective delegations, some supervisors fail to do so for a variety of reasons. For example, because of his or her accountability to a manager, a supervisor may closely monitor or even perform an employee's work. Also, many leaders or supervisors like control and do not want to surrender their power and authority. On the other hand, many employees do not welcome delegation. They may feel the duties and responsibilities are not clearly communicated; they may not understand the importance of the assignment or why they were selected. Also, there is the *fear of failure* factor. Other problems may arise that the employee is not prepared to solve, leading to an employee being unfairly criticized. With more responsibility frequently comes *increased stress* to get the job done correctly. Therefore, some employees may still resist delegation and empowerment.

7. *Know how to face adaptive challenges.*
Reframing and training, related to the concept of coaching and teaching, is one way to face adaptive challenges at work. It helps organizations and individuals to change values and behaviors and to identify new approaches and strategies.

8. *Indicate ways to achieve effective delegation and discuss the roles of various parties in achieving effective delegation.*
One of the solutions to ineffective delegation is to emphasize management training and development. However, effective delegation also requires knowing when to delegate, understanding how the delegation process operates, and taking the time to train employees. Although higher management should be supportive and supervisors should delegate clearly, it is the responsibility of employees to function on their own and turn to their supervisors for help when there is a *major* problem.

9. *Recognize the benefits of delegation.*
The first of four benefits is *employee development*. The manager can assist the individual in analyzing the situation and evaluating the reasons for the success or failure, so the employee can grow from the experience. The second benefit is *improved control*. Managers who delegate effectively emphasize results, not specific actions, and provide feedback when it is appropriate. *Improved time management* is the third benefit. Rather than leaders having their time consumed with "putting out fires," they can effectively delegate tasks to their subordinates and have more time for planning and trouble shooting. And finally, the fourth benefit is *enhanced power*. When employees are empowered, an environment is created resulting in more people being knowledgeable and concerned about the organization's objectives, which in turn leads to a sense of responsibility.

Key Terms

authority, p. 133
responsibility, p. 133
job descriptions, p. 133
accountability, p. 133

delegation of authority, p. 133
formal theory of authority, p. 134
acceptance theory of authority,
     p. 135

power, p. 136
empowerment, p. 138
reframing, p. 142
experiential learning, p. 143

Discussion Questions

1. Discuss four reasons why delegation is important.
2. Describe the process of delegation.
3. Explain the interrelationships among authority, responsibility, and accountability.
4. Why do some supervisors fail to delegate effectively? If this situation were a common problem in an organization, what could be done to increase supervisors' skills in delegating effectively?
5. What are the roles played in effective delegation?
6. In what way or ways can higher management affect the delegation process?
7. In what way or ways can employees affect the delegation process?
8. Do you think Commander Abrashoff's approach and philosophy would be successful in the private sector? Why or why not?
9. Do you agree or disagree with McClelland that power is the great motivator? Support your position.
10. How does a firm set boundaries to create autonomy and empowerment?

Skill Builder 5.1

Information

Delegating Tasks to Subordinates

For each of the following questions, select the answer that best describes your approach to delegating tasks to subordinates. Remember to respond as you *have* behaved or *would* behave, not as you think you *should* behave. If you have no managerial experience, answer the questions assuming you are a manager.

When delegating to a subordinate, I:

		USUALLY	SOMETIMES	SELDOM
1.	Explain exactly how the task should be accomplished.			
2.	Specify the end results I expect.			
3.	Feel that I lose control.			
4.	Expect that I'll end up doing the task over again myself.			
5.	Only delegate routine or simple tasks.			
6.	Clarify to subordinates the limits of their authority.			
7.	Establish progress report dates with the subordinate.			
8.	Inform all who will be affected that delegation has occurred.			

Scoring Key and Interpretation

For questions 2, 6, 7, and 8, give yourself 3 points for *Usually*, 2 points for *Sometimes*, and 1 point for *Seldom*.

For questions 1, 3, 4, and 5, give yourself 3 points for *Seldom*, 2 points for *Sometimes*, and 1 point for *Usually*.

Sum up your total points. A score of 20 or higher suggests superior delegation skills. A score of 15 to 19 indicates that you have room for improvement. A score below 15 suggests that your approach to delegation needs substantial improvement.

Source: Stephen P. Robbins and Phillip L. Hunsaker, *Training in Interpersonal Skills*, 3rd ed., p. 181, © 2003. Reproduced by permission of Pearson Education, Inc., Upper Saddle River, New Jersey.

Skill Builder 5.2

Information

Do You Delegate as Much as You Can?

By assigning duties in a more efficient way, delegating not only can create greater overall productivity but also can reduce overload and burnout of managers. To learn whether you are a good delegator, answer "yes" or "no" to each of the following questions:

_____ Do you often work overtime?

_____ Do you take work home evenings and weekends?

_____ Is your unfinished work increasing?

_____ Are daily operations so time-consuming that you have little time left for planning?

_____ Do you keep control of all the details needed to do a job?

_____ Do you frequently have to postpone long-range projects?

_____ Are you distracted by constant emergencies?

_____ Do you lack confidence in your subordinates' abilities to shoulder more responsibility?

_____ Do you find yourself irritable and complaining when the work of your group doesn't live up to expectations?

_____ Do conflict, friction, and loss of morale characterize the atmosphere of your work group?

_____ Do your subordinates defer all decisions to you?

_____ Do you instruct your subordinates to perform certain activities, rather than accomplish certain goals?

_____ Do you feel that you are abdicating your role as a manager if you ask for your subordinates' assistance?

_____ Have subordinates stopped presenting their ideas to you?

_____ Do operations slow down much when you're away?

_____ Do you believe that your status and the salary you earn automatically mean that you have to be overworked?

If nine or more of your answers are affirmative, it's likely that you're not delegating enough. If so, identify the negatives, and work on eliminating them. Here are the most common reasons for not delegating:

- Lack of patience. (It takes longer to explain it than to do it myself.)
- Insecurity. (I'm so eager to prove myself that I refuse to delegate.)
- Inflexibility. (I'm convinced that nothing can be done properly unless I do it myself.)
- Inadequacy. (I'm afraid of being shown up.)
- Occupational hobby. (I'm so attached to some aspect of the job that I just don't want to give it up.)

Source: From "Do You Delegate as Much as You Can?," in *Nation's Business*. Originally published July 1996. Reprinted by permission. uschamber.com, September 2009. Copyright © 1996, U.S. Chamber of Commerce.

Skill Builder 5.3

Resources

Delegating Simulation

Problem:

Mary Manager has taken a deep look at herself and her department and has decided she must delegate more to her employees for the following reasons: (1) She has consistently worked more than 40 hours a week for several years. (2) The pressure of trying to get everything done has put her on edge with some of the staff. (3) She has not been

(Continued)

**Interpersonal
Skill**

Information

Systems

sleeping well because of worry. Last night she spent three hours formulating a list of responsibilities she might delegate to her five employees. The list is as follows:

A. A weekly report that takes 50 minutes to prepare. This report could easily be delegated to Roberto, but it would reveal certain departmental figures that have not been revealed to employees in the past. There is nothing secret about the data, but Mary feels she might lose control if everybody knows what goes on.

B. A weekly fun job that Mary has always enjoyed. Kaylee would love to do the job (she would probably do it better than Mary), but Mary wants to keep it because it keeps her closer to her employees and facilitates communication. This job usually takes about an hour.

C. A very routine weekly stock or supply room count that takes an hour and a half. Mary has delegated this job before, but she always winds up taking it back because the grumbling from the employee disturbs her more than doing the job herself. Besides, sometimes the count is wrong and she ends up doing the job herself anyway.

D. A very short (15-minute) meeting every day at 4:00 P.M. to exchange information with her staff. Mary has refused to delegate this because she fears losing power/ respect with her employees. Terrance would be able to facilitate the meeting effectively and not be overloaded.

E. A daily (10-minute) delivery job of a special report to top management. Mary has kept this to do herself because it gives her a chance to have a cup of coffee and she can play a little politics with middle and top management executives.

F. A special routine meeting each month that many managers already delegate to an employee. It would be excellent training for Meredith to have this assignment. Mary has kept it to herself, however, because she is afraid that something will happen at the meeting that she won't know about.

Instructions:
Indicate which one is the most critical activity for Manager Mary to delegate, the next most critical activity, and so on. Next, assemble into teams of five to six members and try to reach a consensus regarding a team list of priorities to present to the class.

Individual Rankings
A. A weekly report _____
B. A weekly fun job _____
C. A very routine weekly stock or supply room count _____
D. A very short daily meeting _____
E. A daily delivery job _____
F. A special routine meeting each month _____

Rationale: _____
_____

Team Rankings
A. A weekly report _____
B. A weekly fun job _____
C. A very routine weekly stock or supply room count _____
D. A very short daily meeting _____
E. A daily delivery job _____
F. A special routine meeting each month _____

Rationale: _____
_____

Source: Adapted from Elwood N. Chapman, *Supervisor's Survival Kit*, 2nd ed. (Science Research Association, Inc., 1975), pp. 108–109.

Skill Builder 5.4

Resources

Interpersonal Skill

Information

Systems

Developing a Delegation Action Plan

The purpose of this exercise is to have you think of an actual delegation back on the job or at school. Identify at least one activity that you presently perform that would be a potential candidate for delegation to one or more of your team members.

A. Activity

_____

_____

_____

_____

B. What are the potential benefits of delegating this activity to one or more of your team members?

_____

_____

_____

_____

C. What are the potential obstacles to delegating this activity?

_____

_____

_____

_____

D. Develop a plan using the multistep delegation process you learned about in this chapter for putting the delegation in place. Your plan might address such things as to whom you will delegate the authority, how you will communicate the delegation, what information your delegate will need to perform the activity, whether others need to be informed, and your strategy for overcoming the obstacle and control/feedback mechanisms to assure the delegation is carried out effectively.

_____

_____

_____

_____

_____

_____

_____

_____

Pair up with another student in the class and role play the delegation meeting. Your partner will play the role of the employee. Be sure to put yourselves "mentally" in the actual setting with your partner providing realistic responses to your request(s). When you finish the role play, your partner should provide you with feedback regarding the strengths and weaknesses of your action plan to improve the actual meeting. Afterward, you and your partner should swap roles and go through the same process.

CASE 5-1

JOYCE WHEAT'S PROBLEM:

Joyce Wheat was quite pleased when she graduated from Florida Atlantic University with a degree in health care management. While pursuing her degree, she had been employed by a regional retirement community management company as an environmental services employee. She was a very efficient worker and had been promised an opportunity to move into management upon completion of her degree. After graduation, Joyce entered the rapidly growing company's management training program. From there, she was placed in a much busier facility in Jacksonville as an assistant manager. As an achievement-oriented person, Joyce saw this as the first step toward her long-range goal of becoming an environmental services manager and eventually holding the title of regional manager.

In her position as assistant manager, things went well. Wheat was familiar with all operations, and she practiced close supervision, stayed on top of things, and really stressed high production and friendly service. Approximately one year later, she was promoted to manager at another busier location that was one of the top five most efficient and profitable locations within the company. In fact, the previous manager had been promoted to regional manager and was Wheat's boss.

At this stage of her career, Joyce was well ahead of schedule in her long-range program of becoming a regional manager. She had anticipated spending a minimum of two to three years as an assistant before having an opportunity to advance to manager, but the company was growing so rapidly that new managers were in demand. Her next career objective of becoming a regional manager seemed well within reach because the industry and company were growing at a rapid rate.

Joyce surmised that what had worked for her as an assistant manager also would work for her as a manager. She was not really concerned that the assistant manager and five supervisors who would be reporting to her were older and more experienced. After all, results were what counted. At her first meeting, she stressed her high expectations and set as an objective "to increase productivity by 10 percent in three months." The yearly objective was to be 20 percent. Joyce expected "excellent" ratings for all her staff by the residents. She indicated that she believed strongly in the management principle of follow-up. Not only would she be closely following up on their work, but she also would expect them to do the same with their employees.

Two months later, overall productivity at her facility was down by 7 percent, and staff ratings had dropped to average. Wheat was beginning to worry. It seemed that the more she stressed excellence, increased productivity, and efficiency and tried to follow delegated assignments closely, the more resistance she encountered. Although the resistance was not open, it was definitely present. In fact, she sensed hostility even from the night shift, a group with which she had always been close.

At the end of three months, productivity was down by 10 percent, and staff evaluations were the worst they had ever been.

INSTRUCTIONS

Meet in groups of six or seven people. Make a diagnosis of what the problem is, and identify the critical issues involved. What are the main reasons that this problem exists within organizations? Select one member of your team to present what the team thinks Wheat's boss should do. After all teams have presented, the class should vote on which approach offers the best solution.

CASE 5-2

THE AUTOCRATIC MANAGER:

The plant manager of a paper mill has contacted your consulting firm to help diagnose why production has dropped in the last 18 months. Moreover, he wants a proposal from your firm on what can be done to turn things around. The partial organization chart indicates that there are seven levels of management and the mill employs 410 people.

This mill is a key one in a company that has many mills located throughout the country. The manufacturing process goes through several stages before turning out finished products. The mill employs a relatively large number of engineers, and most managers have an engineering background. The mill is unionized.

The plant manager has four years to go to retirement and wants to leave the firm with a reputation as a "manager who achieves effective results." He is a dynamic individual and has tended to use either an autocratic or a benevolent autocratic approach in managing. He took over the mill six years ago when production was low and a permissive management climate existed. He immediately shifted to a more autocratic management system, and for four years, production was high.

He is convinced that the reason for the current problem is that people at the foreman and supervisory level are not doing their jobs effectively. He thinks the solution is to develop detailed job descriptions for these positions and initiate a supervisor management development program that will teach the supervisors to get more work out of the unionized employees.

You suggest that interviews be conducted at different levels before making a diagnosis and developing a recommended plan of action. Below are the results of interviews discussing the question, "What problems are preventing this mill from reaching its potential effectiveness?"

RESULTS OF TOP MANAGEMENT INTERVIEWS

a. The problem is that we must get commitment from supervisors to management's higher performance expectations.

b. The greatest concern is abdication of responsibility by supervisors. They fail to insist on top performance, and they tend to let employees do what they want. Once we get hourly people under control, we will see an improvement and increased production.

RESULTS OF MIDDLE MANAGEMENT INTERVIEWS

a. Overmanagement from the top level to the supervisory level and undermanagement from the supervisory level down.

b. Too many levels of management.

c. Bypassing of middle management to supervise employees directly.

d. Dictatorial system of management in mill.

e. Supervisors and foremen oversupervised.

f. Foremen not given enough authority.

g. Fault-finding atmosphere in mill.

h. Employees will not accept foreman's job.

i. Up and down communication problems.

RESULTS OF INTERVIEWS WITH FOREMEN

a. Inability to make decisions because authority is not delegated or is taken away.

b. If you do make a decision, you don't get backing from your bosses. Example: Night supervisors have the ability to make 90 percent of the decisions the dayshift supervisors are required to consult someone else about.

c. Too much pressure and threats from above.

d. Constant criticism when we have equipment or people problems, but no praise when we run above standard.

e. Low morale and poor attitudes. People cover their tracks and have the attitude that "it's everyone's problem but mine."

f. Communication problems, especially with higher management.

INSTRUCTIONS

1. Why do you think the autocratic approach worked effectively for four years in this situation?

2. Diagnose the problems and/or issues facing this mill.

3a. Develop a PowerPoint presentation and present your consulting team's set of recommendations to the class.

3b. Develop a set of recommendations that you or your consulting team will present to the mill manager. Include suggestions regarding his leadership style. (Role play the presentation, keeping in mind that the manager is paying your consulting fee.)

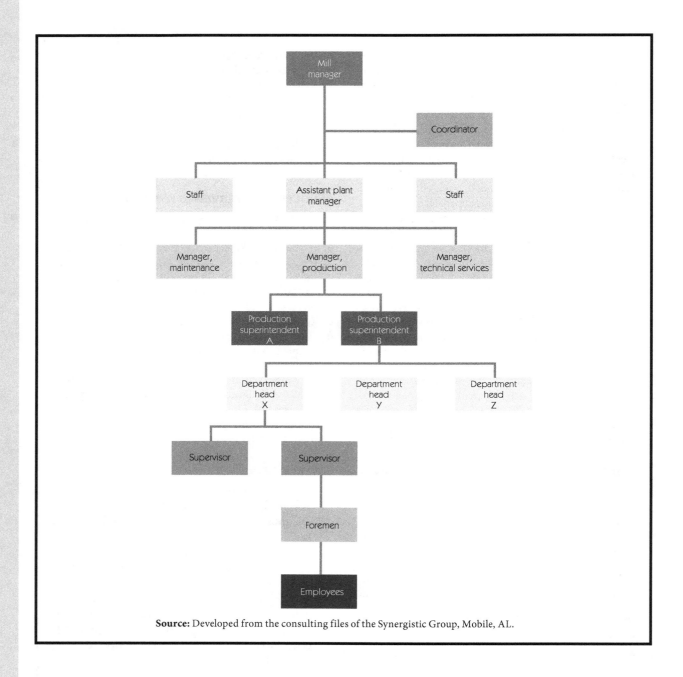

Source: Developed from the consulting files of the Synergistic Group, Mobile, AL.

Notes

1. Steve Denning, "A Glimpse at a Workplace of the Future: Valve," *Forbes.com*, April 27, 2012, http://www.forbes.com/sites/stevedenning/2012/04/27/aglimpse-at-a-workplace-of-the-future-valve/.

2. Alfred P. West Jr., and Yoram Wind, "Putting the Organization on Wheels: Workplace Design at SEI," *California Management Review* 49, no. 2 (Winter 2007), pp. 138–153; *About SEI*, http://www.seic.com/enUS/about.htm (retrieved May 10, 2013).

3. Steve Denning, "Another Workplace of the Future: Sun Hydraulics," *Forbes.com*, April 30, 2012, http://www.forbes.com/sites/stevedenning/2012/04/30/another-workplace-of-the-future-sun-hydraulics/; Kevin Meyer, "No Titles Except 'Plant' Manager," *Evolving Excellence: Thoughts on Lean Enterprising Leadership*, January 25, 2008, http://www.evolvingexcellence.com/blog/2008/01/no-titles-excep.html; *Welcome to Sun*, http://www.sunhydraulics.com/cmsnet/aboutus.aspx?lang_id=1 (retrieved May 10, 2013).

4. Chester Barnard, *The Functions of the Executive* (Cambridge, MA: Harvard University Press, 1938).

5. Personal experience as related to one of the authors.

6. Personal experience as related to one of the authors.

7. J. R. P. French Jr. and Bertram Raven, "The Bases of Social Power," *Studies in Social Power*, ed. D. Cartwright (Ann Arbor, MI: Institute for Social Research, 1959).

8. Jeffrey Pfeffer, Robert B. Cialdini, Benjamin Hanna, and Kathleen Knopoff, "Faith in Supervision and the Self-Enhancement Bias: Two Psychological Reasons Why Managers Don't Empower Workers," *Basic and Applied Social Psychology* 20 (1998), pp. 313–321.

9. Gary Yuki and Ping Ping Fu, "Determinants of Delegation and Consultation by Managers," *Journal of Organizational Behavior* 20 (1999), pp. 219–212.

10. J. Richard Hackman and Greg Oldham, "Development of the Job Diagnostic Survey," *Journal of Applied Psychology* 60 (1975), pp. 159–170.

11. Ronald A. Heifetz, *Leadership Without Easy Answers* (Cambridge, MA: Belknap Press of Harvard University Press, 1994).

12. Ronald A. Heifetz and Donald L. Laurie, "The Work of Leadership," *Harvard Business Review*, January-February 1997, p. 124.

13. *Partnering: The Central Artery/Tunnel Manual* (Boston: Massachusetts Highway Department, 1993), p. 2.

14. Stephen E. Ambrose, *Eisenhower: Soldier and President* (New York: Simon and Schuster, 1990), pp. 39–40.

15. Stephen E. Ambrose, *Eisenhower: Soldier, General of the Army*, President-Elect, 1890–1952 (New York: Simon and Schuster, 1983), p. 77.

16. Ibid., p. 78.

17. Ibid., p. 79.

18. Sidney Finkelstein, "7 Habits of Spectacularly Unsuccessful Executives," *Fast Company*, July 2003, pp. 86–89.

19. Ibid., p. 86.

6
Communication

Everyone has an invisible sign hanging around their neck saying "Make me feel important."

—Mary Kay Ash

When it comes to communication, my rule of thumb is it's not what you tell 'em but what they hear.

—Red Auerbach

Too many people think they are wonderful with people because they have the ability to speak well. What they fail to realize is that being wonderful with people means being able to listen well.

—Peter Drucker

Mark Agnor/Shutterstock.com

Alan X's company, highlighted in the opening preview, has undergone many changes, but good internal communication skills have helped pave the way for employees to adjust to the changes.

Preview

ALAN X: LEADER AND COMMUNICATOR As management training consultants, the authors continually work with managers who are exceptionally effective in leading their teams. One we observed over a period of years was Alan X (not his real name), a paper machine superintendent for a 1,000-plus-employee newsprint producer. Alan was hired from a competing firm known for its innovative management structure and practices. In past years, Alan's new company had been highly centralized, its employees joking that the company approach to managing employees was "Just leave your brains at the gate before you punch in, and do as you're told once you're here." The new CEO, however, was determined to change this approach in an effort to upgrade employee motivation and commitment. Alan, who was to head the primary operating department of 300 paper machine employees, was to be a key early player in the attempt to change the culture. He indeed made a significant early impact.

His first major change was directed toward assuring that his personnel better understood the big picture of their jobs. Learning that most had never set foot inside a newspaper publishing facility, he arranged with one of the company's large customers—a nearby newspaper publisher—for tours by his foremen and team members. His team boarded buses at the company mill and traveled 30 miles to the publisher's site. Here they were oriented by publishing managers about the newsprint industry, the pressures to control costs, the steps in the printing process, and, of course, the importance of high-quality newsprint. Alan's personnel visited the pressroom, observed it in action, and talked with pressroom operators and quality inspectors. They observed in use the actual paper that they themselves had produced only weeks earlier. This included some rolls rejected for poor quality (ink smearing, color bleeding, poor page separation). What a revelation! For Alan's group, the visit had a profound effect in painting the "big picture" of how their work strongly impacted the end user. When corporate learned of the success of Alan's action, visits to nearby newspapers were planned for employees at other company manufacturing sites.

Another early step Alan took was for him, his foremen, and his employees to develop an overall departmental mission statement, as none existed. Following a number of give-and-take meetings among his personnel, a finalized statement was produced: "Our department will be the #1 producer of the highest quality newsprint in the industry, while meeting our safety, cost, and productivity goals."

When approved by Alan's own boss, the statement was printed on a large banner and hung in the work area.

Alan also moved to improve performance feedback. On a large bulletin board, he began a daily posting of the crew's performance. It reflected key performance areas from the mission statement, including tonnage, grade (quality), downtime, costs, safety performance, absences, and others. Moreover, results showed comparisons for daily, weekly, monthly, and yearly goals.

Alan used team meetings in several ways. Meeting weekly with his foremen and staff to communicate and receive downward and upward information, he often brought in outside participants from departments that impacted his own, such as maintenance, quality, sales, safety, human resources, and even outsiders such as suppliers and customers. Additionally, he often assigned problem-solving groups to present their reports on topics such as cost cutting, overtime allocation, or training needs. Alan encouraged his foremen to implement regular team meetings with their own work groups.

Following the first year, Alan engaged the human resource department to survey his foremen and their employees about how they perceived his leadership. Results were distributed and discussed openly at team meetings. Following this, Alan had similar surveys conducted among each of his foremen's teams, with his expectation that foremen would then follow up with their own teams to discuss results.

Alan had other skills and traits that contributed to his effective performance as a manager, including his strong technical expertise, his planning skills, and his ability to manage his time effectively. But his leadership and communication skills, in particular, were exceptional.

Source: Personal experience of Paul Pietri.

Communication is a critically important managerial skill. A typical workday finds supervisors assigning jobs, discussing coordination efforts with people from other departments, having discussions with their own bosses, attending meetings, listening to and counseling employees—the list could go on and on. Studies of managers and supervisors show that they spend 70 to 80 percent or more of their time directly communicating with others in meetings, on the phone, online, or informally while walking around. Consider the management functions of planning, organizing, leading, and controlling—communication is essential in performing these. Moreover, the emerging supervisor role of teacher, leader, and coach depends heavily on effective communication. Studies of managers and supervisors, like Alan X, reinforce how important communication skill is in performing their jobs successfully.[1]

What Is Communication?

Many supervisors think that communication is just a matter of "telling it like it is." When communication breakdowns occur, they are more likely to place the blame on others rather than themselves. Supervisors with such attitudes fail to recognize the

1. *Describe the five components of the communication process model.*

downside of this narrow view of their communication responsibilities. To really understand a supervisor's role in communication, let us first learn about the basic communication process.

Communication Process Model

communication process

Model of the five components of communication and their relationships.

Rather than defining communication in words, we will use a model that illustrates the **communication process** (see Exhibit 6-1). The five elements of the model are (1) message encoding, (2) the channel, (3) message decoding, (4) feedback, and (5) noise.

The Sender Encodes the Message

sender

Originates and sends a message.

Encoding is the process by which a **sender** converts ideas into symbols, such as words or gestures that are capable of communicating. Each day, supervisors such as Alan X (see chapter preview) send hundreds of encoded **messages** to their employees, managers, other supervisors, personnel from other departments, and people outside the organization. These messages consist not only of spoken and written words, but also nonverbal messages such as tone of voice, appearance, placing a watch on a desk and smiling or frowning, or showing up on time—or late—for an important meeting.

messages

Words and/or nonverbal expressions that transmit meaning.

The Channel   The **channel** is the means used to pass the message. Channels include face-to-face communication, the phone, written forms (such as e-mails, memos, reports, or newsletters), and group meetings. Note in the chapter preview that Alan X placed much importance on team meetings as a communication vehicle with his foremen. A sender's choice of channel is often very important.

channel

The means used to pass a message.

> *One supervisor related how after his maintenance crew had completed an important machine repair, the plant manager chewed him out for taking too long to complete the job. "I didn't mind getting chewed out as much as I minded the way he did it," said the supervisor. "He did it by e-mail, and copied the whole plant."*

The Receiver Decodes the Message

receiver

The ultimate destination of the sender's message.

Decoding is the process by which a **receiver** converts an idea(s) into the communication symbol(s) encoded by the sender. Just as a sender's skill at encoding is important to effective communication, so also is the receiver's skill in decoding the sent message. Receivers give meaning to a message based on such factors as their interpretation of words, familiarity with the subject matter, perception of the sender's intent, ability to listen, and the meaning they attribute to the sender's nonverbal signals.

EXHIBIT 6-1
Communication
Process Model

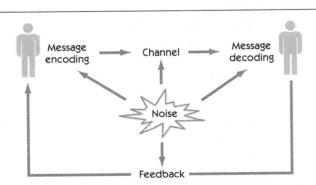

EXHIBIT 6-2
Communication Feedback

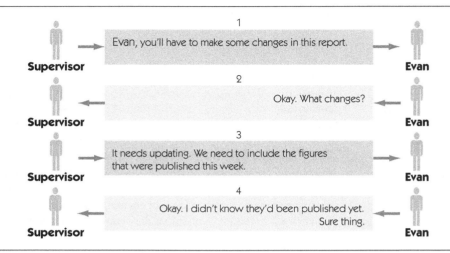

Feedback

feedback

The response that a communicator receives.

The message that we send in response to someone else's communication is called **feedback**. An advantage of the face-to-face communication channel is its immediate feedback and the number of feedback cycles allowed. Note in Exhibit 6-2 the information exchanged between the supervisor and Evan in just a matter of seconds, with each assuming the role of encoding, decoding, and providing feedback. Most importantly, a supervisor's decision about the feedback needed to achieve the communication goal determines the appropriateness of the communication channel used, be it a one-to-one meeting; a larger group meeting; a voicemail, e-mail, or text message; or a handwritten note.

Noise

E-mail

Refers to messages and documents created, transmitted, and usually read entirely on a computer.

Noise consists of the potential barriers to effective communication in each phase of the communication process model. An example of noise at the "encoding" stage might be a supervisor's choice of words. Suppose your boss told you by voicemail that he or she just talked with an important customer and that you need to follow up with the customer "*right away*." Does *right away* mean now, immediately after you hear the voice message? Or does it mean that you can do it several hours later? The nonspecific use of language is but one form of noise. Later in the chapter, you will learn more about "noise" when we discuss communication barriers.

2. *Explain the forms of electronic communication technology.*

Electronic Communication Technology

Communication practices at the supervisory level are being greatly impacted by advancements in electronic communication technology. Just as computer fluency has become an essential employee requirement in many jobs, it also has become a prerequisite for more supervisory positions. Increasingly, supervisors use electronically linked computer networks within their organization (intranets) and external to their organization (the Internet) to access and transfer information, and, importantly, to communicate through e-mail. **E-mail** refers to messages and documents created, transmitted, and usually read on a computer (see Exhibit 6-3).

EXHIBIT 6-3
E-mail Tips

Here are some tips to help make your e-mail more effective.

1. Use e-mail only for relatively simple, clear-cut messages. Don't use it when questions or information need discussion or clarification, or when the subject is sensitive or emotional.
2. Use a descriptive subject line.
3. Use short lines and short paragraphs, especially the first and last paragraphs.
4. For routine and positive messages, be direct, getting to the point in the first or second sentence.
5. For a message that contains emotional content, an indirect approach may be best, with some information leading up to the message. However, reconsider whether e-mail is the appropriate medium.
6. Avoid full caps for your text—it is the equivalent of shouting.
7. Treat an e-mail as a permanent record. It can be intentionally or mistakenly forwarded to others, and about 40 percent of companies monitor employees' e-mails. Be careful of what you write!

Sources: Marie Flatley and Kathryn Rentz, *Business Communication* (New York: McGraw-Hill/Irwin, 2010), pp. 30–33; Scott Ober, *Contemporary Business Communication* (Boston, MA: Houghton Mifflin Company, 2009), pp. 58–92.

Sharon Olds, sales supervisor for AutoFin, a large auto leasing company, uses electronic communication extensively, sending and receiving more than 50 e-mails daily. We've all heard on our phones a voice say, "This call may be monitored for quality. . . ." Monitoring calls by her 12 associates is how Sharon spends a major part of her day, listening to associates contact customers by phone to sell extended leases, vehicles, and extended warranties. Although her office is relatively close to the associates' cubicles, e-mail allows her to be spontaneous, reduces time involved in walking to see if someone is available, and enables easy record keeping. She uses e-mail to pass on to her team members information about policy and procedure, but she also uses it to recognize individual and group performance. Sharon also uses other electronic technology, such as PowerPoint software, when making presentations to associates or her own boss, and has used instant messaging and text messaging as part of a problem-solving team whose members worked at different locations.

instant message (IM)

Use of intranet or Internet technology that allows people to receive messages in real time.

text message (TM)

A written message sent by cell phone and that typically uses abbreviations.

An **instant message (IM)** uses intranet or Internet technology that allows people to receive messages in real time. It is similar to a phone conversation but in writing. It can include a group of people who type individual messages seen by everyone in the "chat room." A **text message (TM)** is a written message sent by cell phone; it typically uses abbreviations to be concise and save space, such as "cu2mor" ("see you tomorrow") or "?4u" ("I've a question for you"). Advances in voice communication technology also have considerably affected supervisory communication. Regardless of location, cellular phones enable a supervisor to keep in touch with employees and others. Digital pagers accomplish the same. Voicemail enables supervisors to leave and hear recorded voice messages. Teleconferences enable communication with people in different locations simultaneously; videoconferences provide the additional benefit of visual communication.

Amanda Phillips, sales manager for ADT, the large national home and business security system company, supervises salespeople who work a several-state area and reside in different locations. Her major daily means of communication with them is by e-mail and cell phone. A weekly team meeting is attended physically by some members; others participate through a remote cell phone conference call.[2]

EXHIBIT 6-4
How Nonverbal Communication Impacts Verbal Communication

Several important ways that nonverbal messages impact verbal communications are as follows:

1. **Repeating/Complementing.** Examples: pointing while giving directions; yawning while saying you're worn out; smiling while saying, "Nice job getting this out on time."
2. **Contradicting.** Examples: acting nervous and fidgeting when you say you're under control; yawning when you say you're interested; avoiding eye contact when saying, "Your job is safe."
3. **Substituting.** Examples: a raised hand substitutes for "I have a question"; the index finger pointed indicates "Over there"; a head shake says, "No"; a head nod says, "Yes."
4. **Emphasizing.** Examples: pounding a table when stating a disagreement; gritting your teeth when saying you're angry; raising your voice to make an important point.

Can you add some other examples to each of these?

---

3. Explain the different ways in which nonverbal communications influence supervisory communication.

voice signals

Signals sent by placing emphasis on certain words, pauses, or the tone of voice used.

body signals

Nonverbal signals communicated by body action.

facial signals

Nonverbal messages sent by facial expression.

object signals

Nonverbal messages sent by physical objects.

space signals

Nonverbal messages sent based on physical distance between people.

time signals

Nonverbal messages sent by time actions.

touching signals

Nonverbal messages sent by body contact.

Importance of Nonverbal Messages

Nonverbal messages are a rich communication source. Studies show that only about 10 percent of emotional meaning is communicated verbally; the other 90 percent is communicated nonverbally.[3] In other words, your impression of someone's emotions, such as anger, happiness, or fear, is formed more strongly from that person's tone of voice, facial expression, or other nonverbal means than from the words the person uses. Exhibit 6-4 shows some of the important relationships between verbal and nonverbal messages.

Note that supervisors must be careful that their verbal and nonverbal signals are consistent and do not give an impression not intended. Moreover, being sensitive to and observing the nonverbal messages sent by others is also quite important.

Nonverbal signals fall into seven categories:

1. **Voice signals** Emphasis on certain words, pauses, or tone of voice. For example, can you say, "Nice job, Evans," in such a way that it's actually a putdown?
2. **Body signals** Slumped posture, clenched fist, or the act of kicking a piece of equipment.
3. **Facial signals** Smile, frown, raised eyebrow, smirk, or degree of eye contact.
4. **Object signals** Office furniture, such as desks or chairs, plus carpet, plaques and awards on the wall, or clothing or jewelry worn.
5. **Space signals** Huddling close, being distant, or sitting beside someone.
6. **Time signals** Being on time, being available, or saving time. An interview was scheduled for a potential medical school intern at Johns Hopkins Hospital. The interview was scheduled for 11:00 A.M., but transportation was affected by a severe snowstorm. The student arrived at 1:00 P.M. for the interview, feeling his lateness would surely be acceptable. He was told, "What if a patient was in a life-and-death situation and you were on call and did not come in?" He was not given an interview.[4]
7. **Touching signals** Shaking hands, sympathetic pat on the back, or touching someone to gain attention.

STOP AND THINK

Steve Jobs, co-founder and former CEO of Apple Computers, often dressed very casually at work. He frequently wore jeans; a coat and tie were exceptions rather than standard attire. Jobs explained this as his personal style. Apple's current CEO, Tim Cook, wears casual clothes similar to what Jobs used to wear. In what ways does a manager's attire communicate?

Flows of Communication

4. *Identify the three basic flows of formal communication in an organization.*

To put the supervisor's communication role in perspective, we need to examine the flows of communication in an entire organization. Here we will look at communication *within* the organization, rather than with outside groups such as customers, suppliers, or government agencies. Exhibit 6-5 shows that formal communication flows in several directions: (1) downward, (2) upward, and (3) laterally or diagonally. A fourth flow is the flow of informal communication, commonly known as the **grapevine**.

grapevine

Informal flow of communication in organizations.

The Vertical Flows: Downward and Upward Communication

downward communication

Flows that originate with supervisors and are passed down to employees.

Downward communication originates with managers and supervisors and passes down to employees. Tremendous amounts of communication constantly flow in this direction. Examples of downward communication include announcements of goals and objectives, policies, decisions, procedures, job assignments, and general information.

> *A study of 336 organizations showed that up to two-thirds of their employees do not understand or even know their organization's mission and strategies. About 30 percent of the organizations indicated that this information was only available to their upper management.[5] Another showed that only 51 percent believe that downward messages are candid and accurate.[6] A more recent study found that only 29 percent of employees working for companies with "clearly articulated public strategies" were able to identify their company's strategy.[7]*

Studies show that employees consistently rate their direct supervisor as their preferred choice of communication channel. A recent study showed that nurses' perceptions of their supervisors' communication effectiveness affected the nurses' productivity, turnover, and overall nursing effectiveness.[8] Take a few seconds to examine the list shown in Exhibit 6-6 before reading further. Do any items on this list strike you as being more crucial than others? "Knowing where you stand" is often listed by employees as their single most important need.

upward communication

Communication that flows from lower to upper organizational levels.

Upward communication flows from lower to upper organizational levels. It may consist of progress reports on a job; requests for help or clarification; communication about employees' concerns, attitudes, and feelings; or ideas and suggestions for improvements on the job.

EXHIBIT 6-5
Flow of Formal Communication in an Organization

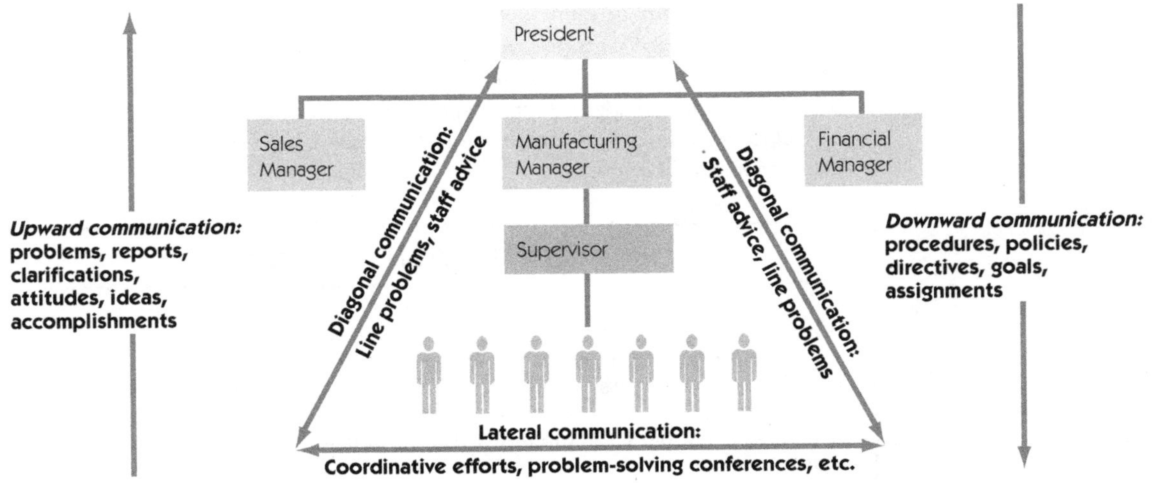

EXHIBIT 6-6

Communications
Employees Like to
Receive from Their
Supervisor

Role clarifications. What's expected of you, how much authority and responsibility you have, and your job assignments.

Performance feedback. How you're doing in your job, your supervisor's evaluation of your performance.

Praise and recognition. A supervisor's commendations on a job well done, compliments about you in the presence of third parties, spoken and written expressions of appreciation.

Constructive criticism and feedback. Tactful criticism that demonstrates interest and implies a personal and professional concern on the part of the supervisor.

Demonstration of interest. Communications reflecting interest in your professional growth and development, efforts to work with you to do a better job, and giving you undivided attention during conversation (as opposed to lack of eye contact or partial attention).

Requests for information or assistance. Asking your opinion and advice, and consulting with you about relevant matters on the job.

Information that
 a. Makes you feel important because you're "in the know."
 b. Pertains to your department's progress, to other work team members, to plans for the department, and to contemplated changes.
 c. Pertains to aspects of the overall organization, such as sales, forecasts, objectives, outlook for the future, and general internal changes of which the supervisor is aware.
 d. Pertains to promotions, merit increases, desirable job assignments, and favors that can be granted by the supervisor.

Unfortunately, many supervisors do not seek these forms of upward communication, especially progress reports, from their employees. Neither do they obtain information about their employees' true attitudes, feelings, or suggestions for improvements. Japanese managers have a much better reputation than American managers for being receptive to workers' needs and opinions, especially in the area of job improvements. In one year, for instance, Toyota implemented more than 60,000 new ideas that were received from workers at its five U.S. manufacturing plants.

In addition to requesting oral or written progress reports, other means of encouraging upward communication from employees include suggestion systems, an open-door policy, attitude and morale surveys, group or individual meetings at which employees are encouraged to speak up, and hotlines where employees can anonymously solicit answers to questions or report unethical practices.

One manager who we know holds a weekly meeting of his work group to review work progress, discuss job changes, and resolve problems. When issues are being discussed, he often makes sure that he gets others' opinions before giving his own. As he states, "I know personally that if this group knows how I feel about something, most will tell me what I want to hear. Some will come right out and ask what I think, as if once I tell them, the discussion should be over."

STOP AND THINK

Dramatic changes are taking place to make the workforce much more diverse, including increasing percentages of foreign workers and of U.S. workers of African American, Hispanic, Asian, and Native American descent. In what ways do these changes affect the *downward communication* flow from manager/supervisor to work team members and the *upward communication flow* from team members to manager/supervisor?

5. *Explain the managerial communication style grid.*

Managerial Communication Style Grid   Now that you have a good understanding of the vertical communication flows, you can better understand each supervisor's communication relationship with his or her team members. As shown in Exhibit 6-7, The Managerial Communication Style Grid, a supervisor's basic communications with team members consist of disclosing information (downward communication) and receiving information from them (upward communication). A supervisor can be considered high as an information discloser and high as an information receiver (box 4), high in one but not the other (boxes 2 and 3), or low in both (box 1).

When you work for a high discloser, you hear frequently about performance expectations, standards, your boss's likes and dislikes, where you stand, and the goings-on in the organization.[9] Low disclosers communicate less frequently and openly about such matters.

High information-receiving supervisors are accessible and maintain an environment that encourages feedback from employees. They are apt to spend much of their time listening to employees' discussions about performance progress, problems being experienced, and ideas and feelings about organizational and personal issues. In contrast, low information-receiving supervisors are less accessible and tend to create a less encouraging upward-communication environment.

What would you like your own boss's style to be? In our workshops and seminars, about 90 percent of managers and supervisors state a strong preference in working for a high discloser, high receiver (box 4). When seminar participants are told they must choose their boss's style as being either high disclosing, low receiving (box 3) or low disclosing, high receiving (box 2), most choose box 3 (high disclosing, low receiving). This reflects the importance managers place in knowing clearly their boss's performance expectations and his or her evaluation of their performance. To determine where you fall on the grid, see Exhibit 6-7.

EXHIBIT 6-7
The Managerial Communication Style Grid

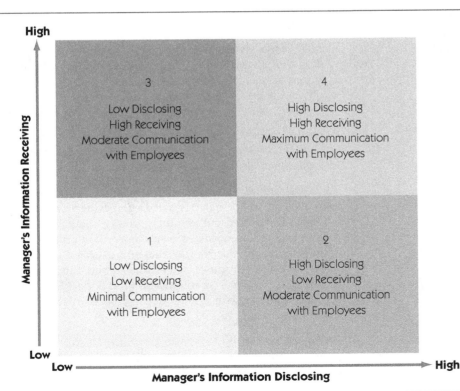

Lateral–Diagonal Flows

Lateral–diagonal communication takes place between individuals in the same department or different departments. This form of communication has become more important in the past 25 years for several reasons. First, organizations have become greatly specialized. Members of staff departments such as purchasing, human resources, cost accounting, maintenance, and others interact regularly with line personnel. This may be to provide services, coordinate, advise, and sometimes actually give directives.

In the chapter preview, note that Alan X's meetings often included personnel from maintenance, quality, sales, safety, training, human resources, and other departments. Because they work in different departments, they are very much "in the know" about a number of company matters long before the formal company communication channels carry them.

A second reason is the increased use of teams. Cross-functional, problem-solving teams composed of personnel from different departments have become an increasingly necessary approach to address problems that cut across organizational lines. One form of employee empowerment is the use of self-managed or autonomous work teams *within* departments. These teams often meet as a group on a daily basis and are highly dependent on communications among their members as they budget, schedule, and assign jobs, and control the quality of their *own* work.

Informal Communication

The upward, downward, and lateral–diagonal communication flows that we have just presented are examples of formal communication. **Informal communication** is that which exists separately from the formal, established communication system. Some examples of informal communication are given below. Each example represents a social network channel that you will not find listed in the company's organization chart. Yet, informal contacts such as these are a way of life and can be a valuable communication source for supervisors.

Lisa, Diane, Fred, and Roberto carpool because they all work for the same company and live about 35 miles away. Their driving time is usually spent talking about their departments, people who work at the company, and other job-related matters. Because they all work in different departments, they are very much "in the know" about a number of company matters long before the formal company communication channels carry them.

Branch manager Juan Vasquez had an important request of his General Manager for additional resources. Before approaching her, however, he sought advice from a fellow branch manager as to the best strategy.

The Grapevine   The best-known informal communication method is the grapevine, also called the *rumor mill*. It is called a grapevine because, like the plant it is named after, it is tangled and twisted and seemingly grows without direction. Yet some surveys have found the grapevine to be employees' major source of information about their company.[10] Because of the Internet and electronic media, information can move quickly along the grapevine.[11] In one study, 88 percent of supervisors surveyed indicated they knew grapevine activity increases when formal communication is lacking.[12] Moreover, it has been found to be surprisingly accurate, with studies showing that more than 75 percent of grapevine information is correct.[13]

Purposes Served by Informal Communication   Informal communication accomplishes a number of purposes. Among these are (1) providing a source of information not ordinarily available, (2) reducing the effects of monotony, and (3) satisfying personal needs

Mary Kate Denny/PhotoEdit

Coworkers having lunch together is a common setting for informal communication.

such as the need for relationships or status. Some people, in fact, take great pride in their unofficial knowledge of company matters.

Living with Informal Communication   Effective supervisors realize that informal communication serves important purposes. A supervisor must be aware that, unless employees are informed through formal channels, the informal channels will take up the slack. Keeping employees well informed is the best way to manage the grapevine, although it can never be eliminated. It will tend to be especially active when employees are concerned about job security or status.

Put yourself in the shoes of Bob Griem, production manager of *The Boston Herald* in the mid-2000s. Imagine the grapevine activity and uncertainty among the 300 production employees and their supervisors when the paper's circulation plummeted and not one, but several downsizings were carried out over a period of years. Ultimately, the downsizings were not effective enough to save the paper and the entire production function was outsourced.

Rather than feeding a destructive grapevine, Bob addressed each downsizing—even the final one for his department—in the same way. "I made a decision to communicate in a forthright, open, timely, and honest manner about what was coming and what I knew," he said. "It was always along the lines of 'Here's our situation, so we need to figure out what will work best.'"[14]

6. *Identify and explain how organizational, interpersonal, and language barriers affect supervisory communication.*

Barriers to Effective Supervisory Communication

Now that you understand the communication process, let's explore some typical communication barriers that a supervisor faces on the job. These barriers may be organizational, interpersonal, or language related.

Organizational Barriers

Three types of organizational barriers to communication are (1) layers of hierarchy, (2) authority and status, and (3) specialization and its related jargon.

Layers of Hierarchy   Have you ever asked someone to give a message to a third person and found that the third person received a message totally different from the one you sent? The same thing occurs in organizations. When a message goes up or down the organization, it passes through a number of "substations" at each layer. Each layer can add to, take from, qualify, or completely change the original message! At higher levels of management, messages are usually broad and general. At lower levels, these broad messages must be put into terms that are more specific. That's frequently the fly in the ointment, especially when lower and top levels have a gap of understanding between them.

Exhibit 6-8 illustrates this effect. Loss of information accuracy does not only occur as messages pass downward; losses that are even more serious occur in upward communication. Poor performance, grievances, and issues at lower levels may not be accurately conveyed. The stops along the way are subject to different interpretations, addition or elimination of parts of the message, or, often, discontinuation of the intended flow. In 1986, the space shuttle *Challenger* disaster resulted in the death of seven astronauts and a severe setback for NASA's space program because upper officials who made the launch decision had not received from lower levels their grave concerns about the shuttle's safety.[15] The same can be said about the large information gap among Federal Emergency Management Agency (FEMA) field representatives, FEMA top management, and the White House during the aftermath of Hurricane Katrina in 2005. When Hurricane Sandy ravaged the East Coast in 2012, FEMA, while far from perfect, was much more streamlined in its communication through the government hierarchy.[16]

Authority and Status   The very fact that one person is a boss over others creates a barrier to free and open communication.

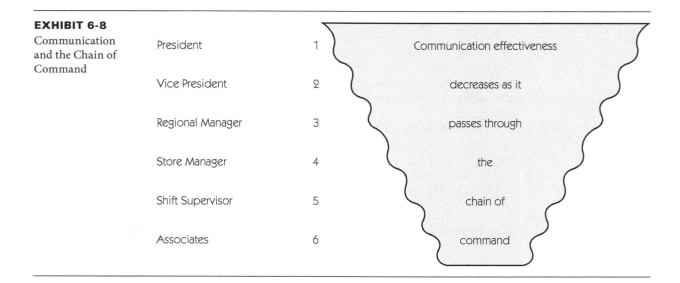

EXHIBIT 6-8

Communication and the Chain of Command

President	1
Vice President	2
Regional Manager	3
Store Manager	4
Shift Supervisor	5
Associates	6

Communication effectiveness decreases as it passes through the chain of command

STOP AND THINK

Recall your feelings, as a student in elementary or high school, when you were told to report to the principal's office. Even if you had done nothing wrong, you were probably still very anxious and defensive about the visit.

Conference room patter among the construction superintendents was loose and jovial. Some made negative remarks about the major agenda item, which was to push for early completion of the project on which they were assigned. One person joked about another being the one to tell the boss that everyone felt the present schedule wouldn't be met, much less an advanced one. However, when the Operations Vice President walked in, the mood shifted dramatically. The vice president did most of the talking in presenting the accelerated schedule. When he asked whether everyone bought into it, the superintendents' silence implied that they had.

The above scenario happens throughout all levels of management everywhere. Because managers exercise power over employees' performance evaluations, rewards and penalties, and favorable and unfavorable distribution of resources and job assignments, employees will not be so likely to give them unwelcome information or information that makes them look bad. In the earlier *Challenger* example, several announced launches had been postponed, adding to the pressures on lower-level managers not to disappoint their bosses. Accordingly, there is a built-in tendency for information about problems being experienced, employee frustrations, and disagreements to not be communicated openly and accurately.

Specialization and Its Related Jargon   The *principle of specialization* states that employees are more efficient when each performs just one task or only certain aspects of a task. For example, accountants do accounting work, salespeople sell, industrial engineers prepare efficiency studies, and safety specialists see to it that working conditions are safe.

Today's increased specialization, however, also creates problems. Specialists have their own technical language or jargon, interests, and narrow view of the organization. Many special terms used by accountants, computer technology personnel, marketing specialists, and other groups are foreign to people in other departments. This can severely hamper communication.

Interpersonal and Language Barriers

Even if the three organizational barriers just discussed did not exist, a supervisor's communication can still be distorted by interpersonal and language-related problems. Three important barriers are differing perceptions, language-related factors, and linguistic styles.

perception

How one selects, organizes, and gives meaning to his or her world.

Differing Perceptions   **Perception** is the process by which we select, organize, and give meaning to our world. All of us have a special way of filtering things around us based on our culture, needs, moods, biases, expectations, experiences, and so on.

Thus, a major barrier to communication results from the increasingly diverse workforce. Broad differences in age, race, sex, education, nationality, and other factors result in quite different interpretations of what is seen and heard, and they often result in different styles of communicating. This poses a much stronger communication challenge to supervisors than if all team members had similar backgrounds and shared similar characteristics with their supervisor.

One factor limiting perception is a person's inability to grasp the whole of a situation at a given time. Greater attention is paid to some aspects of the situation, while some receive none at all. Those that do come into focus usually serve some immediate purpose. A person's needs, moods, cultural and social influences, and attitudes all come together to determine which things are important and what they mean.

Take a factory accident, for example. The following persons might "see" the accident quite differently: a supervisor, who just lost a valuable worker; a safety manager, whose safety record is blemished and who will have to conduct an investigation; a fellow worker, who is the injured worker's best friend; a company nurse who attends to the injured worker; and a human resources manager, who worries about the worker's compensation claim and finding a replacement. Depending on with whom you communicated, might each have a different perspective of the accident?

stereotyping

The tendency to put similar things in the same categories to make them easier to deal with.

When we go about interpreting things around us, we have a tendency to put similar things in the same category, to make them easier to handle. This tendency is called **stereotyping**.[17] Stereotyping poses a formidable communication challenge, given the increasing diversity of employees. There are strong negative stereotypes for various nationalities, races, religions, sexes, occupations, and other groups in our society. As a supervisor, you must be aware that your and your employees' attitudes, biases, and prejudices—both positive and negative—strongly influence communications with others.

Language-Related Factors

A primary communication barrier is posed by the lack of a common primary language. More than 47 million Americans (almost 20 percent of the U.S. population) age 5 years or older speak a language other than English at home. Spanish is the dominant second language spoken in the United States, with Chinese being next. The influx of immigrants from Mexico, many of whom speak little or no English, has led many organizations to offer classes in both English and Spanish to increase communication effectiveness.[18] Marriott offers classes in English not only to its Hispanic employees, but also to the employees' families.[19]

In the Pacific Northwest, Hispanics comprise more than 60 percent of firefighting crews employed by private contractors. During a raging wildfire in southern Oregon, leaders of a fire crew got word to evacuate immediately a fire line that was being dug. The problem, however, was that all crew firefighters digging the line in the area were Hispanic, and none understood the instructions given in English. After much shouting and arm waving, someone was found to translate the message into Spanish and the crew was successfully evacuated.[20]

No one knows the specific number of U.S. workers having limited or no English skills, but estimates show that there may be as many as 10 million illegal Hispanic immigrants, making this total number significant. Throughout the United States, they are employed in many smaller entrepreneurial organizations in agriculture, trades, manufacturing, service, and not-for-profit sectors. Managers and supervisors with English- and Spanish-speaking skills are a hot commodity in many parts of the country, as are human resource personnel who are capable of conducting bilingual hiring, testing, orienting, training, and safety sessions. Sometimes managers themselves take the initiative to address the language barrier. Because most of his 50 employees are Hispanic, Bruce Frye, owner of Fresno, California-based Frye Roofing, went back to school to learn Spanish.[21]

Rick Wilking/Reuters

Growing diversity in the United States results in differing linguistic styles that can be barriers for successful communication. Supervisors need to be aware of these differences to manage their employees effectively.

Even when people speak the same language, language is still a major communication barrier. The fact that people interpret words differently can be traced to a lack of precision in the use of language.

Suppose as you and a nursing supervisor colleague are talking, one of your nurses passes by and you say to your colleague, "That's Judy Snead; she's a really good nurse." What does "good" mean to you? It might mean that Judy is a sympathetic listener who spends a lot of time talking with patients and being cheerful and friendly. To your fellow supervisor, a "good" nurse may be one who is knowledgeable and competent and goes about her or his work without trying to make much conversation.

Misinterpretation of the word "empty" by maintenance personnel led to 50 to 60 oxygen canisters labeled "empty" being shipped in the cargo hold of ValuJet Flight 592 en route to Atlanta from Miami on May 11, 1996. Unfortunately, the "empty" canisters were still highly volatile. They were routinely packed in cardboard boxes and stored in the plane's cargo hold without required safety measures. The canisters ignited in flight, causing the plane to crash in the Florida Everglades, killing 110 crewmembers and passengers. Subsequent investigations resulted in grounded ValuJet flights, adverse publicity, and severe financial repercussions for ValuJet, and a fine of $2 million for Sabretech, the airline maintenance firm responsible for shipping the canisters.[22]

Supervisors often use imprecise language when more precise language is necessary. Suppose a supervisor tells an employee, "You must improve on your absenteeism, as it has been excessive. Otherwise, you'll be disciplined." What does "improve on your absenteeism" and "excessive" mean? What "discipline" does the supervisor have in mind?

STOP AND THINK

How many times out of 100 possibilities would each of the following frequencies mean if an event happened?
Often ____ Seldom ____ Every Now and Then ____ Usually ____ Rarely ____
Compare your answers with someone else's. What's the message here about language?

Another language barrier is that words have multiple meanings and not all people have the same level of language skill, as exemplified in Exhibit 6-9. Many terms familiar to a veteran employee, for example, may be over the heads of a new crop of employees going through an orientation program. In some cases, people even try to "snow" others by using terms they know the others will not understand!

Linguistic Styles　Linguistic styles greatly reflect the continuing diversity in the United States and the ways employees communicate at work. Linguistic style refers to typical patterns in our speech, including such factors as volume, speed, and pauses; being direct or indirect; asking questions; and using body language with speech. Differences in linguistic styles are important communication barriers, especially among different cultures, where the styles vary greatly. For example, Asian workers tend to communicate very formally and show much respect toward their bosses by speaking softly.[23] They also use lengthy pauses to assess what is said. Americans, on the other hand, often forgo formality and view pauses as signs of uncertainty or insecurity. Brazilians and Saudis favor closer physical speaking distances than do Americans. An American supervisor may find a Brazilian employee's desire for a close speaking distance aggressive, when, in fact, for the employee, it is a normal physical distance. Another cultural linguistic style difference involves eye contact.

Several years ago, Barbara Walters interviewed Libyan leader Colonel Muammar al-Gaddafi for a national U.S. television audience. She was reportedly taken aback because during the interview he refused to look directly at her as he spoke. Walters considered this insulting, as if the intent was to demean her. Her reaction was attributable to differences in linguistic style of the two cultures. In al-Gaddafi's culture, not looking directly at her was a sign of respect.

Linguistic style also may vary among subcultures. Among some Native Americans, a child's continued eye contact with an adult is a sign of disrespect. Important differences

---

EXHIBIT 6-9

Multiple Interpretations of Words

FIX the machine to its foundation. (anchor)
FIX that nitpicking cost accountant. (give just due)
FIX the cash register. (repair)
FIXING to go to the storeroom. (getting ready to)
FIX our position regarding overtime policy. (establish)
FIX you up with that young engineer. (arrange a date)
A banquet with all the FIXIN'S. (special effects, side dishes)
FIX things up with the salespeople. (make amends, patch up a quarrel)
If we don't make quota, we're in a FIX. (a pickle, a bad position)
FIX the game (pay off someone to affect the outcome, rig it)
FIX your hair before seeing the boss. (arrange, make orderly)
FIX the department meal on Friday. (cook, prepare)
FIX the company's mascot dog. (neuter)

EXHIBIT 6-10

Linguistic Styles of
Men and Women

A number of popular books about the different linguistic styles of men and women have been written in recent years. Among them are Deborah Tannen's *You Just Don't Understand: Women and Men in Conversation* and John Grey's *Men Are from Mars, Women Are from Venus*. Some of their ideas, greatly simplified, are shown here.

	WOMEN	MEN
Object of talk	Establish rapport, make connections, negotiate inclusive relationships	Preserve independence, maintain status, exhibit skill and knowledge
Listening behavior	Attentive, steady eye contact; remain stationary; nod head	Less attentive, sporadic eye contact; move around
Pauses	Frequent pauses, giving chance for others to take turns	Infrequent pauses; interrupt each other to take turns
Small talk	Personal disclosure	Impersonal topics
Focus	Details first, pulled together at end	Big picture
Gestures	Small, confined	Expansive
Method	Questions; apologies; "we" statements; hesitant, indirect, soft speech	Assertions; "I" statements; clear, loud, take-charge speech

Source: From Mary Ellen Guffey. *Business Communication: Process & Product*, 5th ed. © 2006 South-Western, a part of Cengage Learning, Inc. Reproduced by permission. www.cengage.com/permissions.

exist between linguistic styles of American males and females, as shown in Exhibit 6-10. American males may find swearing and racy joke telling acceptable among themselves, but females often find this offensive. Furthermore, women's linguistic styles tend to be more indirect, expressive, and polite, whereas men's styles are more direct and assertive. Women view conversation as a means for establishing a "connection" and intimacy with others; men see conversation as a negotiation through which they seek to establish or maintain status and independence.[24] However, a recent study examining a traditionally female occupation—nursing—suggests this distinction may not always be true. Men were found to actively use a "feminine" relational style within their group. The linguistic style utilized may depend on the context to some degree.[25]

Improving Supervisory Communications

7. *Identify five specific actions supervisors can take to improve their communications.*

As we've indicated, communication is too critical to your success as a supervisor to be left to chance. Improving your skills in communication will help you accomplish your "task" and "people" goals. Some specific things you can do are (1) set the proper climate with your employees, (2) plan your communication, (3) use repetition to reinforce key ideas, (4) encourage the use of feedback, and (5) become a better listener.

Set the Proper Communication Climate

A supervisor doesn't communicate in a vacuum. Communications take place within the entire supervisor–employee or supervisor–group relationship. A supervisor and his or her workers each brings a store of experiences, expectations, and attitudes to the communication event. These mental pictures strongly influence the meaning each person assigns to the messages sent and received. Thus, the setting is very important for good communication.

What type of setting best contributes to effective communication? We believe that two important factors are (1) mutual trust between the supervisor and employees and (2) a minimum of status barriers.

Establish Mutual Trust   Trust helps communication in two ways. First, if an employee trusts you, he or she is more willing to communicate honestly and openly. Second, if employees trust you, they are less likely to distort your motives and make negative assumptions about your communications. If you fight for your employees' interests by bargaining with higher management, if you discipline fairly and consistently, and if you respect your employees' abilities, you are more likely to be trusted by them. You'll be considered a source of help in reaching their goals.

Minimize Status Barriers   Status barriers consist of those factors that call attention to the fact that the supervisor ranks higher than his or her employees. Status barriers may be such things as dress, formality, and office arrangement. Generally, the best communication occurs in a setting where people are relaxed and comfortable and status differences are reduced. For example, the way a supervisor arranges his or her office furniture has much to do with establishing a relaxed setting. Being seated across from a supervisor's desk is more formal than being able to sit at right angles or side by side.

> *One supervisor says he likes to discuss certain sensitive matters away from his own turf to make an employee feel more comfortable and less nervous. By design, supervisors may communicate in the employee's work area or in a neutral situation such as over a cup of coffee or lunch.*

> *President of Honda of America, Shoichiro Irimajiri, wore no tie and ate in the company cafeteria. On the front of his white overalls, which were just like those everyone else in the plant wore, was his nickname, "IRI." He had no private office but worked at a desk in the same work area as the 100 others in his white-collar work group. This represented a distinct effort to diminish the status differences between him and all other employees.*

Plan for Effective Communication

How many times have you completely blown a communication situation by not being prepared for it? After it's over, you think, "Now why didn't I say this?" or "I never should have said such and such."

Anticipate Situations   If you are a supervisor, many of your contacts will occur without much warning and may not allow much planning. Yet you can anticipate a number of situations. However, many situations allow time for planning in advance. You can give thought to the following situations before they occur:

1. Praising employees (see Exhibit 6-11).
2. Giving employees their performance evaluations.
3. Disciplining employees and making work corrections.
4. Delegating authority for a job and communicating job assignments and instructions.
5. Selling an idea to your boss or employees.

If you understand how complex good communications are, you will be more aware of the existing barriers and try to minimize their effects. To be understood by your team members, you must put yourself in their shoes and try to see things from their viewpoint.

EXHIBIT 6-11
Praising by E-mail

Earlier in this chapter, we mentioned that AutoFin supervisor Sharon Olds spent much of her day monitoring phone call performance of her 12 associates as they contacted leasing customers by phone. The following e-mail reflects how Sharon planned her message before sending it.

> Date: Tuesday, Nov. 7, 2010 2:44 P.M.
> From: Sharon Olds
> To: Angie@xxxxxxxx.com
> Subject: Great Job!
> Angie, great job working with that Miami customer. He was one tough sell. The way you listened effectively and patiently overcame his objections about price sounded like it came directly from our teaching manual. In fact, I'd like to bring it up at our team meeting on Friday if ok with you.
> Super work!
> Sharon
> cc: jhendrix@xxxxxxxx.com

Note Sharon's effective use of the subject line ("Great Job!"), the personalized praise reinforcing her effectively overcoming the customer's objections, and emphatic use of praise at the close ("Super work!"). The exclamations convey the supervisor's positive, enthusiastic tone. Using an e-mail might also have served as part of the plan by allowing her to copy her own boss, further reinforcing to Angie Sharon's appreciation for good work.

information richness

Amount of verbal and nonverbal information that a channel carries.

Select the Proper Channel Part of communication planning involves determining the appropriate communication channel or medium that will be used to convey the message. As mentioned earlier, common options include a personal or group meeting, a phone call, a memo or letter, an e-mail, or an electronic conference.

Generally, supervisors and managers prefer face-to-face communication because that channel is high in **information richness**—the amount of verbal and nonverbal information that a communication channel carries. As shown in Exhibit 6-12,

Dana White/PhotoEdit

One-on-one, face-to-face communication is the richest channel available to supervisors and managers.

EXHIBIT 6-12
Communication
Channel Richness

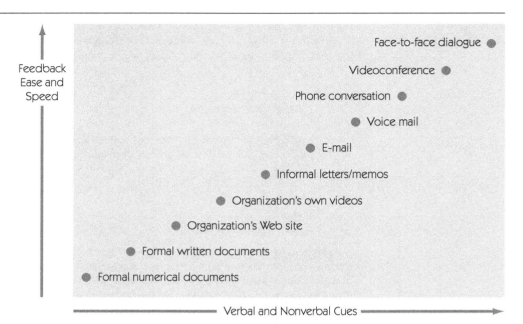

Source: Adapted from Don Hellriegel, John W. Slocum Jr., and Richard W. Woodman. *Organizational Behavior*, 10th ed. © 2004 South-Western, a part of Cengage Learning, Inc. Reproduced by permission. www.cengage.com/permissions.

face-to-face communication is the richest channel because it enables nonverbal messages and offers spontaneous feedback. The one-on-one, face-to-face setting is the richest communication form, followed by small-group meetings and phone messages. Phone messages have no visual contact but still enable nonverbal information to be passed through tone of voice, inflection, pauses, and volume. A voicemail message, however, loses much potential information richness because it lacks the opportunity for immediate feedback.

Lower information richness channels include the written communication forms: e-mails, memos, and letters. These channels lack nonverbal communication, and they do not provide a direct opportunity for spontaneous feedback. They are useful for delivering straightforward messages and presenting impersonal information, such as data, routine policy, and announcements, especially when a permanent record is useful. While the e-mail message of praise sent by Sharon Olds to her associate is very appropriate, written messages are clearly less suited when the content deals with complex or emotional issues or when clarification of the writer's intent is necessary to interpret properly a message's meaning. The e-mail message sent to 400 company managers by Neal Patterson, CEO of Cerner, a 3,000-employee software company, had a devastating effect. Some excerpts:

We are getting less than 40 hours of work from a large number of our KC-based EMPLOYEES. The parking lot is sparsely used at 8:00 A.M. likewise at 5:00 P.M. As managers you either do not know what your EMPLOYEES are doing or YOU do not CARE. You have created expectations on the work effort which allowed this to happen inside Cerner, creating a very unhealthy environment. In either case, you have a problem and you will fix it or

I will replace you. NEVER in my career have I allowed a team that worked for me to think they had a 40-hour job. I have allowed YOU to create a culture that is permitting this. NO LONGER. . . .

You have allowed this to get to this state and you will fix it or I will replace you . . . You have 2 weeks. Tick Tock.[26]

Patterson's message was leaked throughout the company intranet and then found its way to the Internet. Its harsh tone shocked thousands of employees and outside readers, especially financial analysts and investors. Within three days, the company stock dropped more than 25 percent. Patterson later apologized to all, wishing he had never hit the "Send" button, but the damage had been done. The message to supervisors and managers is this: Be careful in choosing your message channel. In Patterson's case, an e-mail sent to all employees was not the appropriate choice, especially given its angry, sarcastic tone.

If you must communicate a personal, sensitive message where empathy and listening are required, such as one involving discipline, transfer, promotion, or performance coaching, face-to-face communication is likely called for. On the other hand, if the message is straightforward or routine, involves much data or detail, or must serve as a record, then written communication is called for. A very important message may even call for both written and spoken channels to be jointly used.

Consider the Receiver's Frame of Reference   Earlier we discussed how each of us has unique filters that influence the way we interpret the world around us. Obviously, the better attuned you are to your subordinates' and others' patterns of evaluation, the more effective your communications to and from them will be. Effective communication, then, requires you to step into the shoes of others and visualize situations from their perspective.

A supervisor must frequently ask questions like these:

1. How is this person *like* me?
2. How is this person *different* from me?
3. How is this person *similar* to other employees?
4. How is this person *different* from other employees?
5. How will this person react if I say such and such?

Given increased organizational diversity, these questions are especially important. You don't find the answers to these questions by reading employees' biographical data from personnel files. The only way to discover employees' different motives, needs, attitudes, and ways of interpreting things is to interact with them directly, be sensitive to these differences, and use effective feedback and listening techniques.

Reinforce Key Ideas through Repetition

Let's begin this section with a simple experiment. Say aloud the following sequence of numbers: 84, 97, 62, 58, 84, 73, 32, 45, 84. Now glance away from the numbers and repeat as many as you can. It's a good bet that one of the numbers that made an impression on you was written more than once.

Repeating a message plays an important part in communicating effectively. This is especially true when certain parts of a message may be more important than others. Repetition, or redundancy, improves the reader's recall and reduces the chance that incorrect assumptions will be made by the receiver. For example, you might state a complicated message in several ways, using examples, illustrations, or comparisons. You also can say the same thing several times, but in different words. Here, for instance, is how a supervisor might communicate an instruction to an employee.

> *Danny, we just got a telephone order for a 42-by-36-inch fireplace screen in our KL–17 series. I know you haven't done one up like it since last year, when that customer in Idaho gave us so much trouble. That's the same style a different customer wants, with black and gold trim as shown in this catalog clipping. And you heard me right: He wants it 42 inches high by 36 inches wide. We don't get many like that—higher than wide, I know. (Hands Danny the written specifications for the screen.) Can you get it out in the next week?*

Note how the supervisor used a past example and a catalog to clarify the style of the fireplace screen and how the supervisor repeated the required measurements, even though he also provided written specs.

Encourage the Use of Feedback

8. *Show how a supervisor can use feedback to improve communication.*

Two ways a supervisor can encourage employees to provide feedback are to (1) create a relaxed environment and (2) take the initiative.

Create a Relaxed Environment   Earlier in this section, we discussed the importance of establishing a favorable setting for communication. Having a relaxed setting is especially important in obtaining feedback from an employee. As a supervisor, you certainly should not look down on employees for asking questions or for openly stating their opinions, suggestions, or feelings on a subject. A defensive attitude on your part discourages feedback. As you've learned about channel richness, how you communicate also determines, to a large extent, the amount of feedback you will receive, with face-to-face communication being the richest medium.

> *In ancient times, an Asian king hated to hear bad news. Whenever a courier reported bad news or an unfortunate event to the king, the king became furious and had the courier beheaded. After three couriers bit the dust, the king began hearing only good news! The moral here for supervisors is that they must be receptive to all information, both good and bad, from their employees, or they, too, will be surrounded by a smokescreen.*

Take the Initiative   Although the type of communication used and the setting for the communication are important in determining what feedback is obtained, a supervisor still must take the initiative in getting responses from the work group. For example, after giving a job assignment, you might ask, "Do you have any questions?" or "Did I leave anything out?" An even better approach would be to say, "To make sure I've gotten my message across, how about repeating it to me?" Frequently this approach produces a number of clarifications that someone might otherwise be unwilling to request for fear of looking stupid. You must be careful, however, not to use a patronizing tone of voice or to put too much of the burden of understanding on the employee. Remember—effective communication is a two-way street. Finally, you can set the stage for further feedback with a comment such as, "If anything comes up later or if you have some questions, just let me know." A participative leadership style relies heavily on good two-way communication, which is a form of feedback. When a supervisor allows team members to make decisions or to express opinions, their responses are a form of feedback. This style helps a supervisor better understand the team members' thinking.

Feedback also can help you learn how to send messages better in the future. When you discover that your initial message wasn't clear or that your use of persuasion was not effective, you can refine future messages. A summary of tips about feedback appears in Exhibit 6-13.

EXHIBIT 6-13

Tips about Feedback

- Generally, feedback is better where there is a trusting relationship among people. If a person doesn't trust you, he or she is not likely to level with you or share feelings very readily. As a result, you are told only what you want to hear instead of what you *should* hear. For example, the person may say, "Yes, sir, things are going okay on the Anders job," when, in reality, there is a lack of progress or some severe problem. Or the person may say, "I certainly agree with you, boss," when, in reality, the person doesn't agree with you at all but doesn't want to upset you or risk being chewed out.
- Some people give feedback readily, but others need some encouragement. Examples of the latter type are people who are timid, quiet, or insecure or have learned that "it's best to keep your mouth shut around here." *Asking* such people for their ideas, suggestions, or feelings may elicit feedback. For example, you can say, "Dale, how will this new policy affect your group?" or "What do you think about . . .?"
- Complimenting people for providing feedback reinforces their willingness to *continue* providing feedback. When you say, "I appreciate your honesty in discussing this" or "Thanks, Joan, for raising some issues that need to be clarified," you are encouraging the other party to give feedback in the future.
- When you are giving instructions, it is a good habit to ask the listener if he or she has any questions. For example, you can ask, "Is this clear, Tom? Do you have any questions?" Some supervisors end their instructions with "Now, Tom, let's see if we're together on this. In your own words, run by me what it seems I've just said." If the instructions are given over the phone, you can say, "Okay, Tom, read back to me those seven dates I just gave you so we can make sure we're together on this."
- When you have potentially negative feedback to give, it is helpful to begin by saying, "Sarah, may I offer a suggestion about . . .?" or "May I give you my impression of . . .?" or "Can I share my feelings about . . .?" This approach is less pushy, and the message will be received with less defensiveness than if you bluntly blurt out the negative information.
- Nonverbal signals and body language offer a wide variety of feedback. Frowns, nervous fidgeting, nods of the head, and other facial expressions and body movements give us a lot of information. Frequently, however, we overlook these signals completely because we are not looking at the other person or because we are absorbed in our own thoughts and messages.

Become a Better Listener

It has been said that Mother Nature blessed human beings with two ears and only one mouth as a not-so-subtle hint that, unfortunately, we often ignore. One of Dr. Stephen Covey's *Seven Habits of Highly Effective People* is "Seek first to understand, then to be understood."[27] Studies of managers show that, on average, they spend a larger percentage of their workday (about 60 percent) on listening than in the other communication forms—speaking, writing, or reading.[28] Yet, of the four basic communication skills—reading, writing, speaking, and listening—most adults have had limited, if any, listening training. Test your listening skills by completing Exhibit 6-14.

STOP AND THINK

If the three persons listed below were asked to rate your listening skills, which would rate you highest? Which would rate you lowest? Why?

a. *spouse or significant other* _____
b. *boss* _____
c. *best friend* _____

EXHIBIT 6-14

Rate Your Listening Habits

As a listener, how frequently do you engage in the following listening behaviors? Place a check in the appropriate column, and determine your rating based on the scale at the bottom of the page.

LISTENING HABIT	VERY SELDOM 10	8	6	4	ALMOST ALWAYS 2
1. Faking attention, pretending to be interested when you're really not.	_____	_____	_____	_____	_____
2. Being passive—not asking questions or trying to obtain clarifications, even when you don't understand.	_____	_____	_____	_____	_____
3. Listening mainly to what a speaker says rather than his or her feelings.	_____	_____	_____	_____	_____
4. Allowing yourself to be distracted too easily.	_____	_____	_____	_____	_____
5. Not being aware of the speaker's facial expressions and nonverbal behavior.	_____	_____	_____	_____	_____
6. Tuning out material that is complex or contrary to your own opinion.	_____	_____	_____	_____	_____
7. Drawing conclusions, having your mind made up before hearing the speaker's full line of reasoning.	_____	_____	_____	_____	_____
8. Allowing yourself to daydream or wander mentally.	_____	_____	_____	_____	_____
9. Feeling restless, impatient, eager to end the conversation.	_____	_____	_____	_____	_____
10. Interrupting the speaker, taking over the conversation to get in your own side of things.	_____	_____	_____	_____	_____

YOUR TOTAL SCORE:	
90–100	Superior
80–89	Very good
70–79	Good
60–69	Average
50–59	Below average
0–49	Far below average

active listening

A listening technique for understanding others and encouraging open feedback.

9. *Define and illustrate active listening skills.*

attending skills

A wide range of actions taken by a listener that facilitate the speaker's freedom of expression, such as eye contact, nods of the head, and eliminationg of distractions.

reflective statement

The listener repeats, in a summarizing way, what the speaker has just said.

Active Listening Techniques   A particular listening technique that is essential for good listening is called **active listening** (also known as *feeling listening, reflective listening, and nondirective listening*). Active listening is a technique for understanding others and encouraging open feedback from them. It requires strong listening commitment, and essentially states, "I am 100 percent interested in what you have to say." It is used by psychologists, psychiatrists, counselors, and others when it is especially important to understand how someone feels and thinks. We think that active listening is of great value to supervisors as a method for understanding employees and for encouraging more open feedback.

Attending skills are an essential part of active listening. They include a wide range of actions that a listener takes to facilitate the speaker's freedom of expression. These include such things as the supervisor's choice of setting (office or another area), elimination of distractions, eye contact, and demonstrations of interest in what the speaker says through facial expressions, leaning forward, head nods, and vocalizations such as "I see" and "uh-huh."

At a training session, one of the authors asked managers to identify situations when they attended especially well or poorly. One supervisor shared that she was in her office when a relatively new employee asked to speak with her. "I stood, greeting her, and gestured to the seat across from my desk. As I sat, I noted that she glanced at my opened office door as if to say, 'I don't feel comfortable with that open door.' So I got up and closed the door. Turns out she did have some very personal concerns about her work that I needed to hear about. I thought afterward that had I not gotten up and closed that door, I likely wouldn't have heard all she had to say."

The **reflective statement** is a form of active listening in which you repeat the gist of the sender's message as you understand it.

Suppose a team member, Joan Chavez, tells her supervisor about a problem.

Joan: "I have a little problem. It's about Klaric, our new guy. You asked me to help him transition into the team, but people have asked, 'Where'd we dig this guy up?' He has no clue about fitting in, and the others seem to resent him for that. While he's technically okay, he doesn't seem to care about being part of the team."

An effective reflective statement summarizes what the supervisor feels is the intended meaning of Joan's statement.

Supervisor: "So while he's competent, you feel that he's not making much progress fitting in as a team member."

This statement tosses the communication ball to Joan to clarify her statement if needed or to elaborate. A reflective statement may also go beyond the speaker's words and reflect for the speaker's feelings as demonstrated by Joan's body language, facial expression, and tone of voice.

Supervisor: "So it seems that you're pretty frustrated about his not fitting in."

Note that Joan has not stated in *words* that she is frustrated, yet her nonverbal actions and tone of voice may strongly suggest it to the supervisor. Assume that Joan further elaborates.

Joan: "Well, the thing that gets me most, I guess, is that I don't know how I could have messed up in evaluating him."

Now the supervisor has gained further insight into what Chavez really meant by her original statement.

Other Listening Fundamentals   *In addition to attending skills and reflective statements*, a number of other important techniques can help your listening effectiveness. These are presented in Exhibit 6-15. As you can see, good listening is hard work. But it is an essential tool for the supervisor!

EXHIBIT 6-15

Tips for Better
Listening

- Be empathetic. Try to put yourself in the speaker's shoes.
- Try to avoid doing most of the talking yourself. Give the other person an opportunity to speak.
- Don't interrupt. Let the person finish speaking before you respond.
- Listen with an open mind. Don't let your preconceived notions or biases prevent your listening fully to the other person.
- Avoid losing your temper or showing signs of being upset by what the speaker states.
- Act interested in what the other person says. Don't doodle, write, or work on something else. Give the employee your full attention.
- Ask questions. As long as the questions aren't considered nosy or brash, this will help keep you interested and encourage the employee to give more details.
- Listen with your eyes as well as your ears to the other party's facial expressions and body language.
- After an important conversation or meeting, jot down notes to yourself about the main points discussed.

Chapter Review

1. *Describe the five components of the communication process model.*
Supervisors spend anywhere from 70 to 80 percent of their time in some form of communication. The communication process consists of five parts: message encoding, a channel, message decoding, feedback, and noise.

2. *Explain the forms of electronic communication technology.*
Among the new forms of electronic communication that are impacting communication at the supervisory level are e-mail, instant messages, text messages, mobile phones, digital pagers, voicemail, teleconferencing, and videoconferencing.

3. *Explain the different ways in which nonverbal communications influence supervisory communication.*
"Meaning" lies in people rather than in words, and nonverbal messages communicate our emotions more strongly than words. Six categories of nonverbal communication signals are voice, body, object, space, time, and touching.

4. *Identify the three basic flows of formal communication in an organization.*
In any organization, there is a tremendous volume of formal communication that flows in three directions: downward, upward, and laterally or diagonally. Downward communication includes announcements of goals, objectives, policies, decisions, procedures, job assignments, and general information. Upward communication consists of progress reports from employees; their requests for assistance; communication about their attitudes, feelings, and concerns; and ideas and suggestions for job improvement. Lateral–diagonal communication occurs among persons within a department or in different departments. It typically involves contacts between line and staff members and among team members in natural, cross-functional, and self-managed teams.

5. *Explain the managerial communication style grid.*
The managerial communication style grid reflects supervisors' behaviors toward disclosing information and receiving information. Supervisors who are high disclosers are active downward communicators to their employees. Supervisors who are high information receivers are open, accessible, and receptive to upward communication from their employees.

6. *Identify and explain how organizational, interpersonal, and language barriers affect supervisory communication.*

A number of organizational, interpersonal, and language barriers can hamper a supervisor's effectiveness in communication. Organizational barriers include the levels of hierarchy through which a message must pass, the authority and status of managers, and the jargon of specialized departments. Interpersonal and language barriers include people's differing perceptions, the general imprecision of language, and different linguistic styles.

7. *Identify five specific actions supervisors can take to improve their communications.*

There are several ways to improve supervisory communication. First, a supervisor should establish the proper setting when communicating with employees. The proper setting is a climate where the trust level is high, the supervisor is viewed as a source of help, and status barriers are minimized. Second, a supervisor should plan his or her communication. This involves determining in advance a communication strategy and channel choice that will enable the supervisor's communication objective to be reached. Third, a supervisor must consider the receiver's frame of reference. This requires looking at things from the receiver's view, which can be difficult. Fourth, a supervisor should use repetition to reinforce key ideas. Finally, a supervisor should encourage and induce feedback and become a better listener.

8. *Show how a supervisor can use feedback to improve communication.*

Two ways in which a supervisor can encourage employees to provide feedback are by (1) creating a relaxed communication environment and (2) taking the initiative to encourage feedback from others. A favorable feedback environment makes team members feel comfortable and relaxed and encourages open expression of their true feelings. Supervisors can take the feedback initiative by asking questions and creating situations that encourage or require their employees to communicate.

9. *Define and illustrate active listening skills.*

Active listening, known also as *feeling listening, reflective listening,* or *nondirective listening,* is a method of encouraging feedback from others. Two forms of active listening are attending and reflective statements. Attending behaviors include a wide range of actions a listener can take to encourage a speaker to communicate. They include such things as creating a distraction-free environment, making eye contact, and showing interest in what the speaker states. Reflective statements restate back to the speaker a summary of what the listener has heard the speaker express.

Key Terms

communication process model, p. 159
sender, p. 159
messages, p. 159
channel, p. 159
receiver, p. 159
feedback, p. 160
e-mail, p. 160
instant message (IM), p. 161
text message (TM), p. 161

voice signals, p. 162
body signals, p. 162
facial signals, p. 162
object signals, p. 162
space signals, p. 162
time signals, p. 162
touching signals, p. 162
grapevine, p. 163
downward communication, p. 163
upward communication, p. 163

lateral–diagonal communication, p. 166
informal communication, p. 166
perception, p. 169
stereotyping, p. 170
information richness, p. 175
active listening, p. 181
attending skills, p. 181
reflective statement, p. 181

Discussion Questions

1. What are the five components of the basic communication process model? Define each. Identify some of the important forms of electronic communication discussed in the text.
2. Explain the six different ways in which nonverbal signals influence supervisory communication.
3. Identify the three major flows of communication in an organization.
4. Explain the managerial communication style grid. What are some purposes served by informal communication?
5. What are some examples of linguistic style communication differences that you have experienced? Explain.
6. How does planning aid communication effectiveness? Can you give a personal example?
7. Explain how a supervisor can use feedback to improve communication.
8. Define and give an example of active listening.

Skill Builder 6.1

Information

Interpersonal Skill

Communication Effectiveness Exercise

For this exercise, two-person teams will be used. One will be the supervisor, the other the subordinate.

1. The subordinate will turn his or her chair so that his or her back faces the supervisor.
2. The supervisor will draw on a sheet of paper a designated design (the master) which is to consist of five geometric figures.
   a. The only figures allowed in the master design are circles, rectangles, and triangles.
   b. The master design must include at least one circle, one rectangle, and one triangle. For example, the master design could include two circles, one rectangle, and two triangles.
   c. All figures used in the master design must touch one or more of the other four figures at only a single point.
   d. The supervisor may create his or her own design or your instructor may provide an identical design for all supervisors.
3. The supervisor's objective is to give verbal instructions to the subordinate such that he or she will draw the master design accurately. Note that only a spoken message by the supervisor is allowed.
4. The supervisor should not receive feedback from the subordinate during the exercise. This means the subordinate may not speak, such as interrupting to say, "Slow down," "OK, I'm following you," or "Speak louder." Nor should the subordinate respond nonverbally, as in holding a cupping an ear as a signal to the supervisor to speak more loudly, or raising a hand that means "Slow down."
5. After the supervisor completes the message, the parties turn their chairs face to face, and examine the results of their communication.
6. Respond to the following discussion points:
   a. What might account for differences in the two parties' designs?
   b. What might the supervisor have done differently to assure better understanding?

Skill Builder 6.2

Information

Systems

Interpersonal Skill

Choosing the Appropriate Communication Channel

Sharon Olds, AutoFin Leasing Supervisor, mentioned earlier in the chapter, supervises 12 associates who spend their day contacting and communicating with customers by phone to sell extended leases, new leases, direct ownership of vehicles, or extended warranties. Associates work in their separate cubicles, each having a sophisticated phone/computer/monitor display system at their desk,

Instructions: Put yourself in Sharon's shoes while reading each of the situations below.

a. For each situation, identify what you feel is the most appropriate communication channel, and explain why.

b. For each situation, identify what you feel is the least appropriate communication channel, and explain why.

c. Within teams of 3–5 classmates, compare your answers.

Situations

1. You need to notify all of your associates that your regular Monday 8:00 A.M. team meeting must be changed to Tuesday at 8:00 A.M. next week.
2. Yesterday, an associate submitted a written request for a week's vacation time to be taken during the week of March 14–18. However, you learned that new, upgraded software will be installed during the week the vacation was requested. Because of typical issues with such an install, your department must be at full-personnel strength on those days. Communicate this to your associate.
3. Express appreciation to one of your members for working overtime yesterday to resolve a customer's problem.
4. Remind each of your employees that the company blood drive is being held tomorrow.
5. Earlier in the day you attended a meeting and were briefed on the company's new health plan coverage. It was announced that under the new changes, beginning next month there will be a 15 percent monthly increase in costs to all employees. You are asked by your own boss to announce the plan and explain changes to your associates.
6. Ask one of your team members to mentor and help train an upcoming new hire.
7. You have just finished monitoring an abruptly ended customer call initiated by a recently hired associate. As sometimes happens, the customer was particularly rude, and slammed down the phone during the conversation. Hearing the dead line, the associate responded, "Adios to you, too, *#%$." Communicate to the associate that his behavior violates company protocol, even though the customer was no longer on the line.
8. Inform your most senior associate that you just learned about an upcoming opening for a "Lead Associate" position in another department. The associate has expressed interest to you in such a position.
9. Convey to your associates the results of last week's departmental production figures.

Skill Builder 6.3

Information

Interpersonal Skill

Listening Skills Practice

For this exercise, three-person teams will be used. One person will be the sender, another the listener, and the third the observer.

1. The sender speaks to the listener for 30 to 45 seconds on one of the following subjects:
   a. How I most like to spend my spare time
   b. What I plan to be doing five years from now
   c. What I most like about my job, school, or life (select one)
   d. The type of person I best get along with
   e. What I think the ideal job would be and why
   f. Other topics selected by speaker
2. The listener responds, making a statement that reflects accurately the main ideas communicated by the sender.
3. The observer gives his or her critique of the listener's reflective statement and the listener's nonverbal behavior while listening.
4. Sender, listener, and observer jointly discuss steps 1, 2, and 3.
5. The three parties rotate roles and repeat steps 1, 2, 3, and 4. This should be done until each party has served at least once in each role.

Skill Builder 6.4

Information

Interpersonal Skill

Technology

Using Repetition as a Communication Tool Information

This exercise is a study of the use of repetition as a communication tool.

Instructions:

1. Go to http://www.usconstitution.net/dream.html and download the text of Dr. Martin Luther King's famous "I Have a Dream" speech.
2. Print a copy of the speech.
3. Drop to paragraph 11, which begins "I say to you my friends . . ."
4. Read the rest of Dr. King's speech, and write a short analysis of his strategic use of repetition.
5. Bring your analysis to class and be prepared to discuss it with your classmates.

Skill Builder 6.5

One-Way Communication Activity

For this exercise, two-person teams will be used. Please position your chairs so that your backs are together and you are not able to see each other. One person will be the sender (e.g., the student on the left) and the other the listener (e.g., the student on the right). The sender and listener should each have a piece of paper and pencil or pen. The listener may not talk during the exercise.

1. The listener will close his or her eyes while the teacher writes a message on the board. The sender will copy the message on his or her paper. Once all senders have copied the message, the teacher erases the message on the board and announces the amount of time the teams have to complete the activity.

2. The sender communicates the message to the listener without looking at the listener or showing the message during the activity. The listener is to copy the message on his or her sheet of paper. The listener may not talk, ask for clarification, or look at the sender during the activity.
3. Once the activity is complete, the teacher asks the team members to share their messages and assess their encoding and decoding processes with each other.
4. Use the communication process model in Exhibit 6-1 to debrief the activity with the class. It is important to get feedback from senders and listeners and to evaluate why some teams were successful in communicating the message while others were not.
5. The two parties may rotate roles and repeat steps 1, 2, 3, and 4.

CASE 6-1

ROOM 406:*

It was 4:56 P.M. on the surgical floor of Collins Memorial Hospital. Nurse Rhoda Fleming, an efficient head nurse with 15 years of experience, was in charge of the floor that afternoon. As is the case in many hospitals, she had responsibility for several patients herself as well as assuming supervisory responsibilities over other floor nurses. Making a final room check of her own patients prior to the arrival of her 5:00 P.M. relief, in Room 406 she found that Mr. Henry Youstra, who had undergone surgery the week before and not done well, had died. She pulled the sheet over the face of the body and made a mental note to tell her relief to empty the room for a new patient, bed space being especially important at this time in the hospital.

After finishing her check, she returned to the floor desk. The evening shift supervisor, Anne Simmons, had already arrived and was waiting at the desk.

"Hi, Anne. 406 just died, so that room's all set to go again. Too bad. We can certainly use the space, though."

"That's for sure. Has 411 had her shot yet? Dr. Alpers really climbed on me yesterday about it. You know how he is."

"No, not yet. You'd better do that right away."

"Does the office know that 406 is ready?"

"No, you'll need to call them after you get things taken care of."

Nurse Supervisor Fleming then left, and Simmons gave 411 her shot and went about other duties,

dropping in on her own patients, and chatting with nurses on the shift.

At 5:45 P.M. she called the office and told them that room 406 was ready for occupancy, though she had not checked the room herself. She was told that a patient would be moved from recovery and would ultimately occupy 406.

Visitors' hours began at 7:00 P.M. at the hospital. As she had been doing three times daily throughout the week, as the fourth-floor elevator doors opened, Mrs. Henry Youstra walked out and went down the hall to visit her husband.

At 8:00 P.M., the end of visiting hours, Nurse Supervisor Simmons checked each of her assigned patient rooms to see that visitors had left. In room 406 she found Mrs. Youstra dead on the floor beside the bed containing her husband's body.

CASE QUESTIONS

1. Explain how "noise" impeded accurate communication between Shift Supervisors Fleming and Simmons in this incident.
2. What barriers to communication existed in the situation?
3. How might this miscommunication have been avoided?

*Adapted from William V. Haney, *Communication Patterns and Incidents* (Homewood, IL: Richard D. Irwin, 1960), pp. 71–72.

Notes

1. Richard L. Daft, *Management*, 10th ed. (Mason, OH: Thomson/South-Western, 2012), p. 482.
2. Interview with Amanda Phillips by Paul Pietri, May 18, 2006.
3. Don Hellriegel and John W. Slocum, Jr., *Organizational Behavior*, 11th ed. (Mason, OH: Thompson/South-Western, 2007), p. 339.
4. "Ten Killer Job Search Mistakes," *National Business Employment Weekly*, Winter—Spring 1995, p. 5.
5. "Why Am I Here? Cosmic Question Gets Frequently Asked at Work," *Training* 43 (April 2006), p. 13.
6. Jerald Greenberg, *Behavior in Organizations*, 10th ed. (Saddle River, NJ: Prentice-Hall, 2010), p. 309.
7. "When CEOs Talk Strategy, Is Anyone Listening?," *Harvard Business Review* 91, no. 6 (June 2013), p. 28.
8. Yvonne Brunetto and Rod Farr-Wharton, "Importance of Effective Organizational Relationships for Nurses: A Social Capital Perspective," *International Journal of Human Resource Development* 6 (July 18, 2006), pp. 232–236.
9. One study showed the circumstances in which high-disclosing supervisors are especially valued by team members. Employees whose jobs involve working with people outside the organization in unstructured, often ambiguous circumstances and who were physically remotely located from their supervisor (such as salespeople and customer service workers) rated as "most supportive" those supervisors considered to be "high disclosers." See Mark C. Johite and Dale F. Dohan, "Supervisory Communication Practice and Boundary Spanner Role Ambiguity," *Journal of Managerial Issues* 13 (Spring 2001), pp. 87–103.
10. Carol Kinsey Goman, "What Leaders Don't Know about the Rumor Mill," *Forbes*, November 30, 2013, https://www.forbes.com/sites/carolkinseygoman/2013/11/30/what-leaders-dont-know-about-the-rumor-mill/#677fc70d7b74.
11. Michael Hitt, J. Stewart Black, and Lyman W. Porter, *Management*, 3rd ed. (Upper Saddle River, NJ: Prentice-Hall, 2012), p. 310.
12. Goman, "What Leaders Don't Know about the Rumor Mill.,"
13. See Lisa A. Burke and Jessica M. Wise, "The Effective Care, Handling, and Pruning of the Office Grapevine," *Business Horizons* 71 (May–June 2003), pp. 71–76.
14. Interview with Bob Griem by Paul Pietri, November 2009.
15. Jeff Forest, "The Space Shuttle Challenger Disaster," http://www.dssresources.com/cases/spaceshuttlechallenger/index.html; also Paul Singer, "Brown's Flood of Criticism," *National Journal* 38 (March 3, 2006), pp. 2–5.
16. Brian Naylor, "Lessons from Katrina Boost FEMA's Sandy Response," *NPR.org* (November 3, 2012), http://www.npr.org/2012/11/03/164224394/lessons-from-katrina-boost-femas-sandy-response
17. J. Vaes and P. Paladino, "The Uniquely Human Content of Stereotypes," *Group Processes and Intergroup Relations* 13, no. 1 (2009), pp. 23–39.
18. Margery Weinstein, "Extreme Makeover: Training Edition," *Training* 46 (March 2009), p. 20; Charlotte Huff, "Powering Up a Hispanic Workforce," *Workforce Management* 88 (May 2009), pp. 25–29.
19. See http://Latinastyle.com/ls50/ls50-top-thirteencompanies-2011.php.
20. "Language Barriers in Fire-fighting: Rising Number of Hispanics Fight Western Wild Fires," *The South Bend Tribune*, August 31, 2003, p. A6.
21. Mark Hinrichs, "Como Se Dice? Break Down the Language Barrier between You and Your Employees," *Entrepreneur* 33 (December 2005), pp. 113–114.
22. Donald Fishman, "ValueJet Flt 592: Crisis Communication Theory Blended and Extended," *Communication Quarterly* 47 (Fall 1999), pp. 345–356.
23. Eric Eisenbert and H. Lloyd Goodall Jr., *Organizational Communication*, 4th ed. (Boston: Beford/St Martin's, 2004), p. 261.
24. Deborah Tannen, "Language, Sex, and Power: Women and Men in the Workplace," *Training and Development*, September 1997, pp. 34–40.

25. Joanne McDowell, "Masculinity and Non-Traditional Occupations: Men's Talk in Women's Work," *Gender, Work and Organization* 22, no. 3 (May 2015), pp. 273–391

26. Edward Wong, "A Stinging Office Memo Boomerangs," *The New York Times*, April 5, 2001, p. C1.

27. Stephen R. Covey, *The Seven Habits of Highly Effective People* (New York: Simon and Schuster, 1990), pp. 34–40.

28. Mary Ellen Guffey, *Business Communication: Process and Product*, 6th ed. (Mason, OH: South-Western Cengage Learning, 2008), p. 50.

7
Motivation

Give me enough medals and I'll win you any war.

—Napoleon Bonaparte

Journalist: "Your Eminence, the Vatican is such a huge place. About how many people work here?"
Pope: "About half, my son."

—Anonymous

CTK/Alamy Stock Photo

Todd Kletz's passion for his people has led to One Hour Heating and Air becoming an industry leader.

Preview

ONE HOUR HEATING AND AIR CONDITIONING—TODD KLETZ, The heating, ventilation, and air-conditioning (HVAC) industry is projected to grow over the next five to 10 years with the air-conditioning market climbing to $167 billion by 2024. While demand in the industry will be strong, employment numbers are projected to decline by "over 138,000 employees by 2022." Baby boomers are exiting the workforce, creating a shortage of skilled labor. Couple this fact with other forms of turnover and businesses are facing real challenges.

Employee turnover significantly impacts a business's ability to operate efficiently and serve its customers. It takes resources to hire, onboard, and train new employees. When employee numbers are low, supervisors shoulder a disproportionate amount of the work, taking them away from other areas such as managing sales and customers. Other negative outcomes include payment of overtime, loss of focus on safety, and lower morale. HVAC companies must be proactive and address these challenges. Let us take a look at Todd Kletz and One Hour Heating and Air Conditioning, one of the industry's top performers.

Todd Kletz is the owner of One Hour Heating and Air Conditioning, a heating and air-conditioning business located in Virginia Beach, VA, that has been family owned for 38 years. The company's mission is to provide "our heating and air conditioning customers with timely and exceptional service." In 2004, the company, formerly known as Classic Air, joined One Hour Heating and Air Conditioning to expand its service area. By 2016, it had over $14 million in sales and employed over 70 employees. It takes pride in delivering quality service to its customers, and it guarantees "punctual service, quality installation and repair work that gets done right the first time." As a result, it has received wide recognition, including "Top New Franchise" from *Entrepreneurship Magazine* for being an exceptional organization, committed to growth and service; "Best Place To Work"—*The Refrigeration News*; and "Small Business of the Year"—Hampton Roads Chamber of Commerce. It also has maintained an "A+ Rating" with the Better Business Bureau since 2008." So what is One Hour's secret? Simple: Its employees are motivated, committed to the company's mission, and choose to stay for the long term.

"One Hour changes peoples' lives," says Jay Jordan, field supervisor. "You can come here with nothing and go from living with your parents to buying a home and getting your first car." The reason is Todd Kletz's passion for people—employees and customers. "We put people before profit," said Jordan. "Todd truly cares about our performance and I really respect that about him." Kletz wants each employee to grow personally and professionally. On average, employees spend 130 hours being trained each year so they have the knowledge and skills to do their jobs to the best of their abilities. The managers hold daily meetings to direct and coach employees to ensure they are making progress toward their goals. Kletz believes, it is important for employees to find the "right" job so they can develop into leaders in that area as the company grows. Kletz's passion extends to his employees. According to Jordan, "We have a job to do and we get it done no matter the circumstances. We truly work to achieve 100% customer satisfaction."

One Hour Heating and Air Conditioning faces challenges too, but its family-oriented culture differentiates it from others in the industry. Alisha Lawrence, client care manager, describes a situation when her husband was transferred out of town. She was devastated. "It's a rare thing to find a job you enjoy—one that makes you excited about your future. When I told Todd, he said, 'Let's look at this; maybe you can work remotely.' Now, I work from home and come into the office for one week out of every month. He went above and beyond for me to be a productive member of the team, even though the position didn't fit the company mold."

Kletz treats his employees more like coworkers than employees because he believes they are in it together. The company has ongoing contests to ensure they are rewarded for their efforts. Sometimes the focus is on service call performance and prizes include money and gift cards. Or during the company's busy time in the summer, the person taking the least amount of time off wins a 55-inch flat screen TV. "Every summer I can earn a free week of vacation time by working hard during our busiest season," Jordan says. "Todd's always reinventing ways to make people happy."

It isn't by accident that One Hour Heating and Air Conditioning has become a top performer in its industry.[1]

Motivation: Some Fundamentals of Understanding Human Behavior

motivation

Willingness to work to achieve the organization's objectives.

The chapter preview demonstrates that understanding and motivating employees is the core of effective supervision. Perhaps you've heard people say no one can motivate someone else. What they mean is **motivation** comes from within. It is the result of a person's individual perceptions, needs, and goals. We define motivation as the willingness of individuals and groups, as influenced by various needs and perceptions, to strive toward a goal. Enlightened managers and supervisors like Todd Kletz attempt to integrate the needs and goals of individuals with the needs and goals of the organization.

EXHIBIT 7-1
Determining
Employee Engagement

The Gallup Poll is the most widely used measure of employee engagement, having been administered to over a million employees and more than 80,000 work units. Referred to as "Q12," the 12-question survey resulted from hundreds of focus groups and thousands of employee interviews. The 12 questions shown below are scored on a scale of 1 to 5, depending on a responder's weak or strong agreement. According to Gallup, there is a strong correlation between a high score and superior job performance. Note the important role one's supervisor plays in determining how each question would be answered:

1. Do you know what is expected of you?
2. Do you have the materials and equipment you need to do your work right?
3. At work, do you have the opportunity to do what you do best every day?
4. In the last seven days, have you received recognition or praise for doing good work?
5. Does your supervisor, or someone at work, seem to care about you as a person?
6. Is there someone at work who encourages your development?
7. At work, do your opinions seem to count?
8. Does the mission/purpose of your company make you feel your job is important?
9. Are your associates (fellow employees) committed to doing quality work? Do you have a best friend at work?
10. In the last six months, has someone at work talked to you about your progress?
11. In the last year, have you had opportunities to learn and grow?

Source: "The Relationship Between Engagement at Work and Organizational Outcomes, 2012 Q12® Item-Level Meta-Analysis," Gallup (online), February 2013, 14. Retrieved on July 8, 2013 from http://www.gallup.com/strategicconsulting/126806/Q12-Meta-Analysis.aspx.

The quest for high quality and quantity of work, safety, cost effectiveness, compliance with company policies and procedures, and punctuality are important issues supervisors face each day. For example, the cost of absenteeism is approximately $660 per employee, or about $25,000 annually for small companies and more than $10 million for larger organizations.[2] A global study of 85,000 employees in 18 countries across four continents showed only 14 percent considered themselves "highly engaged"—that is, they felt involved and enthusiastic about their work (Exhibit 7-1). The most engaged workers were found in Mexico, Brazil, the United States, and Belgium, in that order. Countries where workers reported the least engagement were Japan and Italy. Although U.S. employees rank among the most engaged workers, there is still much room for improvement. A recent Gallup Poll of U.S. workers found that only 32 percent were engaged in their jobs, 50.8 percent were only "moderately engaged," and 17.2 percent considered themselves "actively disengaged" such that their companies might be better off when they call in sick.[3]

In our management seminars, supervisors and managers are asked to anonymously rate on a scale from 1 (lowest) to 10 (highest), the motivational level of employees whom they supervise. The anonymous ratings are collected and written on a flip chart or board. Only rarely do scores higher than 8 appear; the average tends to be in the 5 to 6 range. When asked why ratings tend to be so mediocre, participants respond with comments such as "People today just don't seem to care as much," or "Some employees just want their paycheck and will do just enough to get by," or "There's no pride or commitment to their work." A survey of 250 executives found nearly one-third cited motivating employees as their biggest people challenge, outdistancing finding qualified staff, "training, retaining staff, and resolving staff conflict."[4]

Few social scientists would deny people often act emotionally, but many would dispute most people behave irrationally and unpredictably. They would argue if more people understood the *why* of human behavior, other people's behavior would seem more rational and predictable. Why don't more people have pride in their work? Why do they just do enough to get by? Why are others outstanding performers? The answer often lies in their motivation.

HISTORICAL INSIGHT

The Hawthorne Studies

You may already be familiar with Frederick Taylor's "scientific management" approach, emphasizing efficient employee work methods as the basis for achieving higher performance. In the late 1920s and early 1930s, other researchers discovered the importance played by employees' psychological attitudes toward their work.

The Hawthorne Studies were conducted at the Hawthorne Plant of Western Electric, a Chicago plant of 30,000 employees that was the manufacturing arm of giant AT&T. The studies began in 1924 as an experiment to determine whether increases in lighting affected worker productivity. Researchers studied two groups of workers, one called the research group, the other called the control group. In the research group, lighting levels were increased in stages over a period of months. In the control group, lighting levels remained the same. Researchers were confused to note productivity increased steadily throughout the study period for the research group, but also increased for the control group where no lighting changes had been made! Perplexed, the researchers introduced a new lighting variable in the research group; they reduced lighting to levels below those at which the experiment began. They were again stumped by a continued productivity increase. Baffled, the researchers regrouped. What was going on here to cause the higher performance?

Further research conducted at Hawthorne yielded some answers. In another study, six 15- and 16-year-old girls agreed to participate in the research and were put to work producing relay assemblies, a telephone component. The work area was separated from other plant areas to enable researchers to observe the employees and keep detailed records. For 2½ years, a series of changes in the girls' working conditions were introduced, including shorter workdays and workweeks, periodic rest breaks, free lunches and snacks, and changes in starting and quitting times. And, perhaps you have guessed the results. Throughout the entire 2½ years, their output increased from 2,400 to 3,000 relays weekly per worker. Moreover, their attendance and morale also increased steadily.

What do you think was causing these improvements? Subsequent experiments and an extensive interview program with workers throughout the plant attributed the improvements to psychological factors within the experimental groups. By being singled out to participate in the experiments, the workers selected felt "special" and important, causing them to operate under motivational conditions quite unlike other Hawthorne workers. Management directed attention toward them, and their results became more meaningful. An important result of the Hawthorne Studies was the discovery of a powerful motivational force that ushered in the beginning of the human relations era of management.[5]

Levels of Motivation

1. *Identify the three levels of employee motivation.*

Broadly, when we say someone is or is not motivated to engage in a certain behavior, we refer to three distinct, but often related, levels, as shown in Exhibit 7-2.[6] One level is the direction in which the individual behaves. Does an employee behave in desirable ways?

Let's take a look at an associate at AutoFin, an automobile and truck financing and leasing company. Does the associate

- *Spend 90 percent of his or her time on the phone with customers?*
- *Key into his or her computer the result of each contact as it occurs, as instructed by management?*
- *Attempt to sell a warranty agreement to each customer who extends the lease or purchases the vehicle outright?*
- *Cooperate with other associates by providing them with needed information about customer contacts they may have shared?*

A second motivation level relates to *how hard* the individual works to perform the behavior(s). An employee may be aware of the need for the behavior, but how much energy and effort does he or she exert to perform it properly?

EXHIBIT 7-2

The Three Levels of Motivation

Employee Motivation =	Direction of Behavior Or What Behavior(s) Employee Chooses To Perform	+	Level of Effort Or How Much Energy Employee Puts into a Behavior	+	Level of Persistence Or How Hard Employee Will Pursue Behavior When Faced with Obstacles

A welder at Inland Marine's Yard 2, John knows he should secure his safety harness when he works at heights three feet or more above ground, as this company safety requirement is regularly discussed at weekly safety meetings held by his supervisor. However, because he is experienced, John feels this requirement is often a nuisance, so he usually "forgets." He'd rather put his energy into welding, which is what he is paid to do, he says. As John's supervisor states, John just isn't motivated to be conscientious or exert effort in following established safety rules.

For many supervisors, it is this second motivational level—getting employees to put effort into what they do—that provides the biggest challenge. Retail department store managers often complain salespeople don't put energy into keeping their areas neat and orderly. A restaurant manager keeps watch, making sure bartenders don't spend too much time talking with friends or customers they've developed a relationship with while overlooking the beverage needs of others. A branch bank manager laments a teller may not try hard to make eye contact with customers, smile, call the customer by name, or attempt to cross-sell a certificate of deposit or loan.

The third and final motivational level reflects an employee's *persistence*. In the face of adversity, obstacles, or roadblocks, how hard does an employee keep trying? Some employees may be highly motivated when conditions are favorable, but what happens in the face of adversity or roadblocks? When an employee isn't feeling well in the morning, will she call in absent? If she shows up, will she still persevere and perform the job well? If her equipment acts up, will she be motivated to find a makeshift way to get the work done?

Frito-Lay is filled with tales of salespeople going to extraordinary efforts to meet their customers' needs. These include braving the fiercest of weather to ensure their daily contacts with stores they serve, or going to great lengths to help a store clean up after a hurricane or fire. Letters about such acts pour into Dallas headquarters.[7]

Intrinsic and Extrinsic Motivation

intrinsic motivation

Behavior an individual produces because of the pleasant experiences associated with the behavior itself.

Intrinsic motivation is a behavior an individual produces because of the pleasant experiences associated with the behavior itself. Employees who are intrinsically motivated feel satisfaction in performing their work. This satisfaction may come from any of several factors, including enjoying the actual work done, the feeling of accomplishment, meeting the challenges, and so on.

Anne Marie Bains has strong intrinsic motivation in her work as a pharmaceutical sales representative. She enjoys traveling and the freedom of planning her calls. But the highlight is the actual time she spends communicating with health care professionals—getting to know them on a professional basis, gaining their confidence, and sharing with them information about her company's products.

extrinsic motivation

Behavior performed not for its own sake, but for the consequences associated with it. The consequences can include pay, benefits, job security, and working conditions.

By contrast, **extrinsic motivation** is performed not for its own sake, but rather for the consequences associated with it. The consequences can include such factors as the pay, benefits, job security, or working conditions.

As loan collector for a local bank, Ben Harrison dislikes "putting the squeeze" on people, as he calls it. But because his job brings in money for the bank, he feels secure, can earn a nice bonus by reaching collection goals, and has excellent benefits, and the bank is located only a few minutes from his home.

Ben is extrinsically motivated. It's not what he does in his job that he finds satisfying, but the indirect factors of pay, benefits, and working conditions.

The Motivation—Performance Link

2. *Explain the relationship between performance and motivation.*

Many supervisors mistakenly assume performance is directly related to an employee's level of motivation. Initially, one might conclude the more highly motivated an employee is, the higher that employee's performance will be. This is not necessarily the case. Unquestionably, direction of behavior, level of effort, and persistence affect an employee's performance. However, the motivation-performance link is just not that simple. As shown in Exhibit 7-3, in addition to an individual's motivation, personal abilities and skills and level of organizational support also influence performance.

It is possible an employee with low motivation may indeed outperform a more highly motivated but less-skilled employee. New employees in particular often have strong motivation, but their performance will not be as good as that of more experienced personnel. Also, an employee's performance depends largely on what we call "organizational support." We all are familiar with sports examples of highly motivated players whose "performance" is below par, despite excellent skills and strong motivation.

Consider the National Football League (NFL) quarterback who made all-pro but this season has three rookie offensive linemen and no pass protection, the outstanding pass receiver who is handicapped this year by a rookie quarterback, or the pitcher whose infield leads the majors in errors. It works similarly in nonsports organizations. The level of organizational support, such as quality physical and financial resources with which to work, timely assistance, and upper management support, also strongly influence an individual's performance.

We conclude this discussion by stating that, *things being equal, employees who are more highly motivated will have higher performance.* However, things are seldom truly equal, which challenges the supervisor's diagnostic skills when examining the true cause of a performance-related problem.

Since the 1960s, much research has been done on the behavior of people at work. Some significant theories have been developed that are important to anyone in a position of leadership who wants to avoid unnecessary friction arising from human relationships in an organization. For a person of action, such as a supervisor who has to work with and through people, an understanding of motivation theory is essential. Kurt Lewin, famous

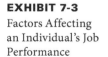

EXHIBIT 7-3
Factors Affecting
an Individual's Job
Performance

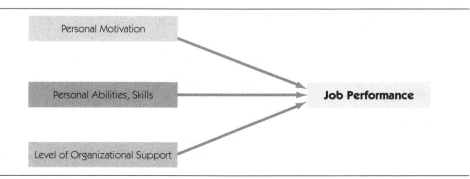

for his work in the study of groups, once said there is nothing so practical as good theory. The remainder of this chapter focuses on the important theories of motivation, with emphasis on their application to effective supervision.

Maslow's Hierarchy of Needs Theory

3. *Understand and explain Maslow's hierarchy of needs theory and the principle underlying his theory.*

One theory particularly significant and practical was developed by psychologist Abraham H. Maslow and is known as the hierarchy of needs. Of all motivation theories, it is probably the one best known by managers. The key conclusion drawn from Maslow's theory is that people try to satisfy different needs through work.[8]

Principles Underlying the Theory

hierarchy of needs

Arrangement of people's needs in a hierarchy, or ranking of importance.

physiological or biological needs

The need for food, water, air, and other physical necessities.

safety or security needs

The need for protection from danger, threat, or deprivation.

The two principles underlying Maslow's **hierarchy of needs** theory are (1) people's needs can be arranged in a hierarchy, or ranking of importance, and (2) once a need has been satisfied, it no longer serves as a primary motivator of behavior. To understand the significance of these principles to Maslow's theory, let us examine the hierarchy of needs shown in Exhibit 7-4.

Physiological or Biological Needs   At the lowest level, but of primary importance when they are not met, are our **physiological or biological needs**. "Man does not live by bread alone," says the Bible, but anything else is less important when there is no bread. Unless the circumstances are unusual, the need we have for love, status, or recognition is inoperative when our stomach has been empty for some time. When we eat regularly and adequately, we cease to regard hunger as an important motivator. The same is true of other physiological needs, such as those for air, water, rest, exercise, shelter, and protection from the elements.

Safety or Security Needs   When our physiological needs have been reasonably well satisfied, **safety or security needs** become important. We want to be protected from danger, threat, or deprivation. When we feel threatened or dependent, our greatest need is for protection or security. Most employees are in a dependent relationship at work, so they may regard their safety needs as being important. Clune Construction, a Chicago and Los Angeles interior construction firm that is listed as a "Best Place to Work," addressed the security/safety needs of its 200 employees when it guaranteed there would be no layoffs despite the economic recession.[9] Arbitrary or autocratic management actions such as

EXHIBIT 7-4
Maslow's Hierarchy of Needs

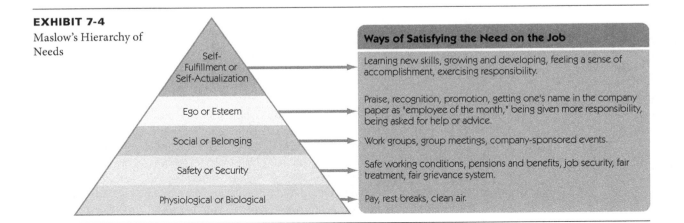

favoritism, discrimination, or the unpredictable application of policies can be a powerful threat to the safety of any employee at any level

social or belonging needs

The need for belonging, acceptance by colleagues, friendship, and love.

Social or Belonging Needs   **Social or belonging needs** include the need for belonging, association, acceptance by colleagues, and friendship and love. Although most supervisors know these needs exist, many assume—wrongly—they represent a threat to the organization. Fearing group hostility to its own objectives, management may go to considerable lengths to control and direct human efforts in ways detrimental to cohesive work groups.

When employees' social needs as well as their safety needs are not met, they may behave in ways that tend to defeat organizational objectives by becoming resistant, antagonistic, and uncooperative. While it is quite common for employees in many industries to be concerned about their pay, benefits, and supervisory relations, the following story about one of the author's consulting experiences may surprise you.

A Fortune 500 company hired consultants to conduct supervisory training for first and second-line managers at one of its plants. Over the course of the two-and-a-half days, it became apparent to the consultants the supervisors were quite concerned about the company's decision to cancel the annual company picnic in which employees and their families looked forward to participating. The event included a BBQ cook-off, dessert-judging contest, and the annual softball game.

The activities usually started early Friday with teams of employees setting up smokers to begin their time-honored tradition of competitive BBQ cooking. Teams went all out planning their cooking strategies and designing their smokers, making them more elaborate each year. The teams rotated shifts and cooked until Saturday mid-morning, about the time the dessert-judging contest concluded. Good fun was had and the winners of both events were awarded t-shirts and trophies. With the judging completed, the company-wide picnic commenced with everyone getting a chance to sample the winners' delights. The event ended with the much-anticipated softball game, where employees displayed their skills and the winners got to brag for a whole year.

The supervisors understood the company was cost conscious, but the amount of money spent on electricity, security, downtime, and port-o-lets paled in comparison to reduction in employee productivity that resulted from the decision to cancel the annual picnic. They could not understand why upper management couldn't see the problem and look elsewhere for cost savings. Or better yet, ask front-line employees to share process improvement ideas!

ego or esteem needs

The need for selfconfidence, independence, appreciation, and status.

Ego or Esteem Needs   Above the social needs are the **ego or esteem needs**. These needs are of two types: (1) those relating to one's self-esteem, such as the need for self-confidence, independence, achievement, competence, and knowledge, and (2) those relating to one's reputation, such as the need for status, recognition, appreciation, and respect from one's colleagues.

During World War I, General Douglas MacArthur, a 38-year-old brigadier general, had recently been named commander of a battlefield brigade in Europe. On the eve of a major battle in France, he met with the battalion commander. In an effort to inspire the men, MacArthur asked that when the signal was given to start the charge, the commander, a major, be the first one out to lead the charge, in front of his men. MacArthur said, "If you do this, your battalion will follow you, and you will earn the Distinguished Service Cross, and I will see that you get it." MacArthur then paused, looked at the major for several long moments, and said, "I see that you are going to do it. You have it now." With that, MacArthur removed from his own uniform his Distinguished Service Medal and pinned it on the major's uniform. The following day, proudly wearing his as yet unearned Distinguished Service Cross, the major was the first to lead the charge, his troops behind him, and they achieved their battlefield objective.[10]

Unlike the lower-level needs, ego needs are rarely fully satisfied because once they become important, people always seek more satisfaction of such needs. A few years ago, the typical organization offered few opportunities for lower-level employees to satisfy their ego needs. However, well-managed and innovative companies are doing a better job in this regard today.

self-fulfillment or self-actualization needs

The need concerned with realizing one's potential, selfdevelopment, and creativity.

Southwest Airlines is continuously ranked as one of the best U.S. companies to work for. Employees frequently use descriptions of their employment as, "Working here is truly an unbelievable experience. They treat you with respect . . . empower you . . . use your ideas to solve problems . . . they encourage you to be yourself."[11] *Still, the conventional method of organizing work, particularly in mass-production industries, gives little consideration to these aspects of motivation.*

Self-Fulfillment or Self-Actualization Needs   At the top of Maslow's hierarchy are the **self-fulfillment or self-actualization needs**. These needs lead one to seek realization of one's own potential, to develop oneself, and to be creative.

iStock.com/iofoto

Fun activities often arise out of the work environment that help employees meet their own social or belonging needs.

John B., age 64, is about three years from taking company retirement. He enjoys wood-working and has become quite good at it, his bowls and carved figures having won several awards at art fairs. John is one of the most knowledgeable technical service representatives in the company, but he continually turns down overtime work on weekends. "The extra money just isn't worth it to me anymore," he says. "I'd much rather spend my time working in my shop or showing my work at an arts and crafts show." Recently, John was asked on short notice to be flown over a weekend to a customer location to help resolve a difficult problem the site could not resolve. He accepted. As he stated, "It wasn't the money, it was the fact that nobody else could resolve it and I looked forward to the challenge."

It seems clear the quality of work life in most organizations provides only limited opportunities to achieve self-fulfillment/actualization needs, especially at lower organizational levels. When higher-level needs are not satisfied, employees compensate by trying to further satisfy lower-level needs. The needs for self-fulfillment may remain dormant.

STOP AND THINK

Reflect on the examples of motivation described in this chapter's preview. Which need-levels of employees are reflected in each of these?

Qualifying the Theory

Maslow's theory is a relative rather than an absolute explanation of human behavior. You should be aware of the following four important qualifiers to his theory:

1. The needs hierarchy is based on U.S. cultural values. Though the five needs are universal, the sequence of the hierarchy may differ, depending on the culture. Cultures such as those in Chile, Venezuela, and Japan value job security and lifelong employment much more strongly than achievement-oriented, individualistic cultures such as the United States and Great Britain.
2. The priorities of some individuals may differ. For example, an artist may practically starve while trying to achieve self-actualization through the creation of a great work of art.
3. Needs on one level of the hierarchy do not have to be completely satisfied before needs on the next level become important.
4. Unlike the lower levels, the two highest levels of needs can rarely be fully satisfied. There are always new challenges and opportunities for growth, recognition, and achievement. As the following description illustrates, a person may remain in the same job position for years and still find a great deal of challenge and motivation in his or her work.

Bob Buschka, a computer programmer for a large bank in a Midwestern state, held his position for 20 years, turning down several promotions. He is considered one of the top programmers in banking in the area. The bank sends him to various schools to keep him growing and developing on the job. "We know what a gem he is," says his boss, "and we give him lots of room to operate—special key projects, training and developing new programmers, and keeping up with the new applications to our industry."

Herzberg's Theory

dissatisfier or hygiene factors

Factors employees said most affected them negatively or dissatisfied them about their job, including low pay, low benefits, and unfavorable working conditions.

satisfier or motivator factors

Factors employees said turned them on about their job, such as recognition, advancement, achievement, challenging work, and being one's own boss.

In the 1960s, a researcher named Frederick Herzberg conducted in-depth interviews with 200 engineers and accountants from 11 different firms in the Pittsburgh, Pennsylvania, area.[12] Those interviewed were asked to recall an event or series of related events that made them feel unusually good and unusually bad about their work and how much the event(s) affected their performance and morale. Prior to Herzberg's study, a common assumption was factors such as money, job security, and working conditions were all strong positive motivators and pretty much worked the same way: If these things were not satisfied at work, people would be negatively motivated; if they were satisfied, people would be positively motivated. Herzberg's findings disproved this assumption and helped us better differentiate among various motivational factors.

Dissatisfiers and Motivators

Herzberg found two different lists emerged, one for factors making the engineers and accountants feel unusually good and the other factors that made them feel unusually bad. What people said most affected them negatively, or dissatisfied them (called **dissatisfier or hygiene factors**) about their jobs, were things such as low pay, low benefits, unfavorable working conditions, poor job security, and poor company policy/administration. The things that turned them on (called **satisfier or motivator factors**) tended to be recognition, advancement, achievement, challenging work, being one's own boss, and the work itself (see Exhibit 7-5).

A survey of 372 managers reinforced Herzberg's theory because 76 percent said personal achievement and job enjoyment motivated them the most, in contrast to only 30 percent who cited financial rewards.[13] Note the satisfier/motivator factors are found at the highest levels of Maslow's hierarchy, whereas the dissatisfier/hygiene factors are at the lower levels.

STOP AND THINK

Try to answer Herzberg's survey questions yourself. Think about a particular job you have held in the past or presently hold. If you haven't had a job, think of your schoolwork.

1. What specific incident or event (singular or recurring) gave you the most satisfaction?
2. What caused the most dissatisfaction?

Herzberg reasoned the dissatisfier factors are what people take for granted about their jobs, so their presence is not particularly stimulating. For example, consider an employee who said the most dissatisfying thing about his job was the work area was too hot. Assume the company addressed this issue and installed a cooling system throughout the plant. Six months later, would this employee be likely to say one of the most satisfying things about the job was the cool plant? Not likely.

Conversely, factors that cause *strong dissatisfaction* do not tend to be such things as the lack of responsibility or challenge in a job or absence of recognition. If a company seeks to eliminate dissatisfaction, it must address factors including wages, working conditions, and security. Note that supervisors often have greater ability to influence motivator factors such as recognition, assigning challenging jobs, and empowering employees than they

EXHIBIT 7-5

Herzberg's Satisfier/
Motivator and Dissat-
isfier/Hygiene Factors

SATISFIER/MOTIVATOR FACTORS	
+ Recognition	"The boss says I've done a good job."
+ Advancement	"I was promoted to team leader."
+ Challenging work	"I solved a really tough job problem."
+ Being one's own boss	"I was given a free hand to do my job."
+ Work itself	"I got to design the new system."
DISSATISFIER/HYGIENE FACTORS	
– Pay	"I'm not paid fairly for what I do."
– Benefits	"This company doesn't pay tuition or medical benefits."
– Working conditions	"It's so hot in the plant it's often unbearable."
– Job security	"With the seasonal work, I never know for sure if I'll have a job."
– Company policy/administration	"We have so much red tape to go through."

do hygiene factors of pay, benefits, working conditions, job security, and company policy. A recent study of the Irish health sector examined it from Herzberg's perspective. It found health sector managers have limited control over employees' pay, job security, and work load, much of this being determined by the "system." Although managers have a greater degree of control over motivational factors of achievement, recognition, and responsibility, the study concluded managers were not effectively using these motivational tools.[14]

Link to Intrinsic and Extrinsic Motivation

Earlier in the chapter, we discussed the subject of intrinsic and extrinsic motivation. The factors associated with positive motivation were intrinsic to the job, whereas those causing job dissatisfaction were extrinsic to it. When people felt good about their jobs, it was usually because something happened that showed they were doing their work particularly well or were becoming more expert in their professions. In other words, good feelings were keyed to the specific tasks they performed, rather than to extrinsic factors such as money, security, or working conditions. Conversely, when they felt bad, it was usually because something happened to make them feel they were being treated unfairly.

The crux of Herzberg's theory is dissatisfiers and satisfiers are each important in their own way. Dissatisfier factors, such as good pay, benefits, working conditions, and job security, must first be addressed by management as a motivational base to prevent employee dissatisfaction. Once dissatisfaction is removed, management gets more "bang for its motivational effort" by focusing on employees' opportunities for responsibility, recognition, advancement, and challenge in their jobs.

Walter Vaux was a young chemical engineer toiling in the lab when his boss walked in. "You're doing a wonderful job," he remembers the supervisor saying. "I'm so glad you're part of the department." It was just a few words, but the input was such a valuable motivator that Vaux, now retired, still talks of the lesson he learned—it takes more than cash. "Many other bosses have just taken my contributions for granted and felt that their response was more money. The real motivator was genuinely realizing my successes and telling me so."[15]

Qualifying Herzberg's Theory

Herzberg's results have been replicated in other studies involving nonprofessionals, such as food-service workers, assembly-line workers, and others. However, you should bear in mind some important qualifications to Herzberg's theory:

1. Money *can* be a motivating factor, especially when it is tied to recognition and achievement.
2. For some people, especially professionals, the absence of motivating factors such as recognition, advancement, and challenge can constitute dissatisfaction.
3. Critics contend a built-in bias of Herzberg's findings is when asked about something positive on the job, a person is biased toward mentioning something in which his or her behavior is the focal point, such as a feeling of achievement, meeting a job challenge, and so on. Conversely, when asked about dissatisfiers, a person is likely to mention extrinsic factors over which he or she has no control, such as pay or working conditions.

Despite these qualifications, we feel Herzberg's theory is valuable as a general guide to understanding behavior at work. It also helps set the stage to understand better job design theory, discussed later in this chapter.

Other Motivation Theories

5. *Understand and explain expectancy theory.*

This section explores other motivation theories with which you should be familiar. These include expectancy, goal-setting, equity, reinforcement, and job design theories.

Expectancy Theory

expectancy theory

Views an individual's motivation as a conscious effort involving the expectancy a reward will be given for a good result.

The theories of Maslow and Herzberg focus primarily on the individual and his or her needs as dominant employee motivation factors. **Expectancy theory** is more dynamic. It views an individual's motivation as a more conscious effort involving the interplay of three variables: (1) expectancy that effort leads to a given performance result, (2) probability of reward(s) associated with the performance result, and (3) the value of the reward to the individual.[16] Expectancy theory states most work behavior can be explained by the fact employees determine in advance what their behavior may accomplish and the value they place on alternative possible accomplishments or outcomes. Some writers termed this a "payoff" or "What's in it for me?" view of behavior. Developed by Victor Vroom of the University of Michigan, expectancy theory is illustrated in Exhibit 7-6.

Let us take a look at how expectancy theory operates. Suppose Maria's boss says, "If you are able to complete the project by Monday, Maria, I'll recommend you for a promotion to supervisor. I realize it means you will be putting in some heavy work without pay, but

EXHIBIT 7-6
Expectancy Theory

Motivation = Expectancy that increased effort leads to a given performance level ([1]Effort → Performance link) × Probability a performance level leads to a given reward ([2]Performance → Reward link) × [3]Value attached to reward

Or

Effort → Performance → Outcome (Value)

[1]E → P Link   [2]P → O ([3]Value) Link

Motivating employees through rewards is one aspect of expectancy theory.

think about it and let me know your answer." There are three important factors involved. As shown in Exhibit 7-6, one is the Effort → Performance relationship—Maria's expectancy that if she puts in the extra effort, she can realistically complete the project by Monday. The second factor is the Performance → Reward relationship—the likelihood if she does complete the project by Monday, Maria will actually be promoted to supervisor. In other words, does Maria's supervisor really have the influence to get her the promotion? The final factor is the value Maria places on being promoted to supervisor. Suppose the last thing in the world she wants is the responsibility and pressure of being a supervisor! In expectancy theory, then, the three factors—the Effort → Performance link, the Performance → Reward link, and the value of the reward—all interface to determine someone's motivation.

Note the perceptual process plays a critical role in maximizing employee motivation, according to expectancy theory:

1. Employees must perceive they have a good chance of achieving the targeted performance level.
2. Employees must perceive if they do reach the performance level, they will actually receive the reward.
3. Employees must perceive the reward to be something valued.

The authors are familiar with one Chicago manufacturer that used tickets to cultural and social events as rewards for a program that tried to improve daily attendance among its hourly workforce. The program had little impact. As one manager stated, rewards with a more targeted appeal, such as free dinners at Chicago restaurants or tickets to professional sporting events, would have been stronger motivators. Often, however, employees may not grasp the reward potential of assignments given by their supervisors. American Express managers are taught to "label and link" when delegating or giving assignments. This means telling why the assignment is important to the individual receiving the assignment.[17]

Supervisors can do a number of things to apply the principles of expectancy theory (see Exhibit 7-7): (1) they can train and coach employees to reach desired performance

EXHIBIT 7-7	1. Hire people who have adequate skill levels.
Ways to Apply Expectancy Theory	2. Set clear, recognizable, performance goals.
	3. Make sure employees know what is expected.
	4. Continually stress employee training and skill development.
	5. Use performance feedback and coaching to help employees gain skills.
	6. Have employees share knowledge and expertise with others.
	7. Give employees special jobs or assignments that stretch their abilities.
	8. Celebrate performance successes.
	9. Reward performance achievement.
	10. Develop trust in your commitments by others; do not overpromise rewards.
	11. Emphasize multiple rewards such as praise and recognition, being assigned desired work, receiving special training, and attending a conference.
	12. Determine what different individuals value as rewards (financial, social, being in the know, learning a new skill, etc.) and help make these happen.

EXHIBIT 7-8	Raises and bonuses
Manager's List of Potential Rewards	Social functions
	Outings
	A night on the town
	A nice meal or lunch courtesy of the manager
	Lunch as a group that the manager buys
	Dinner
	Day off or time off
	Picnics for teams
	Tickets to sports, special events
	Direct oral praise to individual, one to one
	Direct praise to individual in presence of others
	Direct praise/recognition at group events
	Peer recognition
	Letters of recognition to file or place where customers can see them
	Passing on customer compliments and commendations in voice mail or in writing
	Written praise
	Certificates and plaques
	Shirts, phones, pins, hats, cups, jackets, and so on, all with the name of the company on them
	Opportunity to attend conference, special training course
	A parking space
	Additional responsibilities
	Personal call or visit from CEO or senior executive
	New furnishings or equipment
	Being assigned more favorable jobs
	Allowing people to bid on projects/tasks they prefer

Source: Reprinted from Peter Meyer. "Can You Give Good, Inexpensive Rewards? Some Real-Life Answers," November–December 1994, pp. 84–85. Copyright © 1994, Reprinted with permission from Elsevier.

levels (the Effort → Performance link); (2) they can deliver on their commitments (the Performance → Reward link); and (3) they can reward performance in ways meaningful to employees (the reward). Exhibit 7-8 illustrates a wide range of rewards managers can provide, many of which are cost-free.

Here are some ways Sharon Olds, sales supervisor at Autofin, an automobile and truck financing and leasing company, uses expectancy theory:

Each of Sharon Olds' sales associates has a sales goal to book 35 monthly customers to a new lease contract or purchase of their present vehicle. At that point, a financial incentive kicks in. Sharon works especially hard on the Effort → Performance aspect of expectancy theory by building associates' confidence that if they work hard, they will actually achieve the 35 customer rate and higher.

Among the tools Sharon employs are continuous sales training of her associates, publicizing achievement levels and success stories, and performance feedback and coaching. "I do my best to make them feel they have the right stuff and my support to succeed. It is especially important for new associates to know if they work hard each day, they will achieve the necessary successes with customers. My full-timers have done it before and know they can get there, so my job is more one of encouraging them and rallying them."

Sharon also works hard to reinforce the rewards received by top performers. She knows the financial incentive is an important reward for most, but for others, it is the fact they achieved a high level of success. "That's why I like to make it a big deal when someone gets there, like e-mailing everyone in sight about it," she says. "For many, that is as satisfying or more satisfying than the extra money."

STOP AND THINK

Can you think of other rewards not listed in Exhibit 7-8 that would be motivating? Which ones have value for you? Identify your top five rewards. Interpret your top five based on Maslow and Herzberg's theories.

---

6. *Explain how supervisors can use goal-setting theory to motivate employees.*

goal-setting theory

Theory that task goals, properly set and managed, can be an important employee motivator.

Goal-Setting Theory

Task goals, in the form of clear and desirable performance targets, form the basis of Edwin Locke's **goal-setting theory** of motivation.[18] Goals are important not only in the planning process, but also as an important motivational factor. Locke's basic premise is that task goals can be highly motivating—if they are properly set and if they are well managed. Performance goals clarify the expectations between a supervisor and an employee and between coworkers and subunits in an organization. They also establish a frame of reference for task feedback and provide a foundation for self-management. In these and related ways, Locke believes goal setting is of primary importance in enhancing individual motivation and job performance and has spent much research since the 1970s substantiating that theory.

Listed here are the major ways that a supervisor can use goal setting as a motivational tool:

1. Set specific goals. Specific, concrete goals consistently lead to better performance than general ones, such as "do your best," or no goals at all.
2. Set challenging but reasonably difficult goals. Be careful, though, not to set unrealistic goals employees feel they have little chance of reaching. Several years ago, one professional football team posted in the dressing room the following offensive team goals: "Never allow our quarterback to be sacked; always score when inside the red zone (opponent's 20-yard line); never give up a fumble." Because they were unattainable, these goals were likely perceived as meaningless by the team's offensive players.

3. Ensure timely feedback to employees about goal achievement. This may be easier in certain situations, such as sales or production work, than in others.
4. Where practical, strengthen employees' commitment by allowing them to participate in goal setting. A key step in MBO (Management by Objectives) is involving employees in establishing their own key performance goals.
5. When multiple goals are established, make sure employees understand their priorities. For example, is meeting a quality goal more important than meeting a quantity goal or cost-effectiveness goal?
6. Reinforce goal accomplishment. When people reach or exceed goals, ensure timely rewards and recognition.

T. Paul Bulmahn, Chairman of ATP Oil and Gas, a 55-employee, Houston, Texas, offshore development company, wanted his company to grow, so he tried something he had not done before. At the company Christmas luncheon, he gave his employees a special challenge: triple daily production by the end of the year and boost the reserve replacement rate by 200 percent and everyone would go to Sweden and get new Volvo 760s. No kidding!

While it would surely be a challenge, employees committed to the task. However, the progress they made through the fall took a turn for the worse when hurricanes devastated the company's Gulf of Mexico operations. So Bulmahn extended the time frame another quarter. And darn if they didn't put forth a Herculean effort and achieve their goals!

Employees were ecstatic. Thirty-nine of the 55 employees with their spouse or a friend flew to Sweden with Bulmahn and selected Volvos; the others opted instead for a cash payment of $25,000. Bulmahn stated that he issued the challenge because the company had reached a point where it needed to move forward. Achieving the challenging goal of tripling production in a little over a year has put ATP in another league, he said. And doing it without an acquisition was unheard of.[19]

Equity Theory

7. *Define equity theory.*

equity theory

Theory that when people perceive themselves in situations of inequity or unfairness, they are motivated to act in ways to change their circumstances.

Employee motivation also can be viewed in terms of how fairly or "equitably" an employee feels he or she is rewarded as compared to others. **Equity theory** states that when people find themselves in situations of inequity or unfairness, they are motivated to act in ways to change their circumstances.

Two factors determine whether a person is in an equitable situation. One is the inputs, such as the skill, education, experience, and motivation an employee brings to the job situation. The second consists of the rewards a person receives for performance, including pay, advancement, recognition, or desirable job assignments. Think of equity theory, then, as an input/output comparison that responds to this question: Given what I bring to a job as compared to what others bring, are the rewards I receive fair as compared to theirs? If you asked this question of yourself and answered no, according to equity theory, you would likely act to reduce the inequity in several ways. Four options follow:

1. You can try to *increase your reward level* by making a case with your supervisor or relevant others, appealing to higher management, or filing a grievance;
2. You can *decrease your input level* by putting in less job effort, taking longer breaks, or being less cooperative;
3. You can *rationalize the inequity* exists for valid reasons. For instance, in some industries, such as technology and health care, consumer demand has been so great compared to the supply of eligible workers able to make the product or provide the service that starting salaries have been significantly higher from one year to the next; or
4. If you cannot restore equity in your present job, you can *leave the situation* by asking for a transfer or seeking a position with another employer.

Equity theory typically addresses broad, overall organizational issues such as salary and benefits, working conditions, and advancement. However, equity theory is quite relevant to individual supervisors. First, some supervisors may be in a position to influence employee pay and promotion when supervisors feel these are inequitable. Second, supervisors can provide rewards through job assignments, assignment of newer resources, and recognition. In these and other situations, the message is clear: Employees must feel rewards are equitably distributed; otherwise, they will be motivated to reduce the inequity.

Reinforcement Theory

Reinforcement theory uses rewards and punishments that follow a person's behavior as a way to shape that individual's future behavior.

Based on the law of effect, it holds that behaviors meeting with pleasant consequences tend to be repeated, whereas behaviors with unpleasant consequences tend not to be repeated. To the extent supervisors have a degree of control over the reward and discipline system for employees, they have some control over the law of effect. Suppose a worker's attendance has been spotty recently. Reinforcement theory can work in two ways: (1) You can positively reinforce (praise, reward) workers' favorable behavior (showing up on time), thereby encouraging them to repeat it, or (2) you can *discourage* the workers' unfavorable behavior through punishment (scolding, writing a disciplinary warning, assigning nondesirable work duties), thereby encouraging them not to repeat it.

Advocates of reinforcement theory argue strongly that positive reinforcement often is more effective than punishment in getting people to behave in desired ways.

Take, for example, an employee who is punished for not treating a customer well. When the employee is called on the carpet, she might not necessarily know what specifically she must do to improve. Moreover, she might not be in a situation where she feels like listening, even if told. She might respond by associating "customer" and "punishment" and try to avoid customers altogether.

If, on the other hand, when the employee does something right, the supervisor says, "I couldn't help but notice how patient and understanding you were in helping that customer work out her refund; I wanted to compliment you," then we are likely to get an employee out looking for customers to treat well. The specific behaviors (patience, understanding) lead to rewards that satisfy a person's need to enhance his or her self-image.[20]

Organizations and supervisors have a wide range of potential reinforcers available, as listed earlier in Exhibit 7-8. In addition to the more obvious raises and bonuses, a wide range of nonfinancial rewards was included. Eileen Rogers of Allegra Print and Imaging Company in Scottsdale, Arizona, keeps a supply of $2 bills on hand. Whenever a client expresses satisfaction with an employee's behavior, Rogers gives the employee a $2 bill and delivers a compliment in front of the entire team. Many post the bills near their desks, and one star employee is close to wallpapering her area with them.[21]

Most organizational "award" systems are based on management's recognition of employee performance. However, a system wherein customers, clients, and fellow workers recognize employees can be a powerful reinforcement tool. At American Equity Underwriters (AEU), a subsidiary of Charlotte-based AmWINS Group, a "WOW" board posts messages from clients who praise individual AEU employees for special efforts.

Unfortunately, one of the most effective and least used tools is the simple "thank you," according to Malcolm Baldrige Award examiner and management consultant Kevin

8. *Define and explain reinforcement theory.*

reinforcement theory

Based on the law of effect, holds that behaviors meeting with pleasant consequences tend to be repeated, whereas behaviors with unpleasant consequences tend not to be repeated, and rewards and punishments are used as a way to shape the individual.

McManus. He encourages supervisors to do a Thank You Assessment (TYA) of their own behavior by asking employees to count the number of times they hear a sincere "thank you" or "I appreciate that" from the supervisor in a given time period. As McManus states:

> *Failing to use this simple tool sends a powerful message to people, just as effectively using it does. . . . We spend lots of money trying to learn better ways to motivate people through the use of gift certificates, plaques, and tickets to sporting events given out to only a select group of people. At the same time, we fail to say "thank you" to each of our people every day in a manner that means something to them. . . . Saying "thank you" is free and it is a form of recognition that can be distributed at any time.*[22]

One recent survey showed 75 percent of employees felt praise from the boss was the strongest motivator they receive. An independent study conducted by management search firms wanted to find out why upper-level managers left their jobs. The leading reason, given by 34 percent of respondents, was "limited praise/recognition," compared to only 25 percent who said "compensation."[23] Indeed, when praise is properly used, it is one of the most effective reinforcers a supervisor has.

Motivating through Job Design: The Job Characteristics Model

9. *Explain the job characteristics model.*

job characteristics model

Approach to job design that focuses on five core job elements leading to intrinsic motivation and then positive work outcomes.

Job design can be used to explain why some supervisors and managers face a more daunting task in motivating employees than others. How a job is designed refers to the number, kind, and variety of tasks individual workers perform to complete their individual job. The **job characteristics model** of job design is composed of five core job elements leading to intrinsic employee motivation and other positive work outcomes.[24]

The five important structural characteristics of a job's design, according to the job characteristics model, are

1. Skill variety: Extent to which the job requires a worker to use a broad range of skills and talents to perform the job successfully.
2. Task identity: Extent to which the job requires a worker to complete a whole, identifiable piece of work.
3. Task significance: Extent to which the job substantially impacts the work or lives of others.
4. Autonomy: Extent to which the job entails substantial freedom and decision making in carrying it out.
5. Feedback: Extent to which the job itself provides information about whether it is performed successfully.

To understand the model, examine Exhibit 7-9. The left side (column 1) of the model lists the five core characteristics. The middle column (column 2) shows the important psychological states enabled by the five characteristics. Note the first three characteristics—the job's skill variety, identity, and significance—combine to create *meaningful work*. Autonomy enables a *feeling of responsibility*, and feedback enables *knowledge of a job's results*. On the far right, column 3 shows how each of the three psychological states (column 2) leads to high motivation, high-quality performance, high job satisfaction, and low absenteeism/turnover.

Direct praise is one way to reward employee performance.

EXHIBIT 7-9

Job Characteristics Model

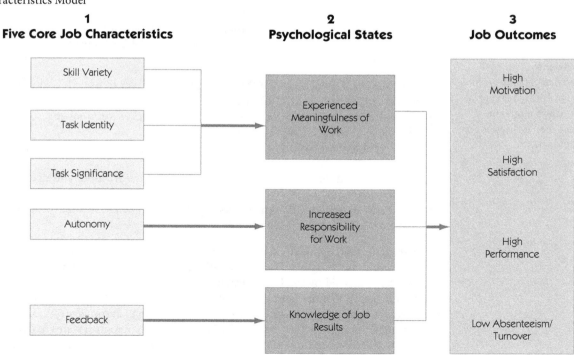

Source: Adapted from J. R. Hackman, "Work Design," in J. R. Hackman and J. L. Suttle, eds., *Improving Life at Work* (Goodyear Publishing, 1977), p. 159. Reprinted with permission.

To help understand the five characteristics, let's assume you work the first window of a two-window drive through at a local McDonald's.[25] We'll take each of the five characteristics in sequence:

1. Variety: low. You greet the customer, punch in the order on a computer screen, and collect the customer's money. You repeat a few standard phrases such as "Welcome to McDonald's. May I take your order? Drive to the next window please."
2. Task identity: low. Others cook the food, prepare the order, and hand the customer the completed order.
3. Task significance: low. There's not a lot riding on the tasks you perform.
4. Autonomy: low. You must use a standardized greeting; you can't give someone a free item because they were patient; and procedures dictate things such as your appearance, dress, and how you relay the order to the kitchen, use the cash register, and so on.
5. Feedback: some. From customer interaction, the number of cars in the drive through, how long it takes you to process them, and whether your register balances at the end of the shift, you do have some idea of how you're doing. Importantly, though, you don't know if you took and recorded orders correctly because this is determined at the next window!

Given the low scores on these five characteristics, we can conclude a worker who performs on window #1 at McDonald's will not experience high motivation or job satisfaction.

So, why do organizations make supervisors' jobs of motivating employees all the more difficult by having employees perform boring, nonchallenging tasks? The answer lies in the costs associated with change. These include the need to recruit more qualified personnel, increased costs of employee training, and possibly increased compensation. Moreover, not all employees will necessarily accept increased responsibility, especially if they haven't exercised it for extensive employment periods. Presence of a union contract also may be a discourager.

However, individual supervisors should note they can take some actions on their own to increase employee perceptions of the importance of their work. One of the authors observed this at a large newsprint producer that was plagued with poor quality. A new paper machine superintendent, learning that his personnel had never seen a newspaper produced, chartered buses, and arranged tours of a nearby major newspaper customer. The visitors received an on-site tour, interfacing with the newspaper's press room personnel, learning of the importance of high-grade newsprint in the printing process, and even viewing some newsprint pulled because of poor quality. This had a major impact on the perceived significance of their jobs.

The Different Generations: Some Insights for Motivation

10. *Explain how generational differences affect motivation.*

A generational looking glass can be a valuable tool in learning how people differ in the attitudes they bring to work and what they value. Generation members share certain commonalities of thinking and behavior. Shared economic conditions, world events, pop culture, social experiences, education, and parenting give each generation its own persona. Although a generational perspective may not give you a complete picture of a given individual, it can certainly be helpful. Exhibit 7-10 highlights differences among the generations.

With the entry of Generation "Y" (Gen Y) employees—those born since 1981—into the working world, the workforce for the first time contains four generations.[26]

EXHIBIT 7-10

Characteristics of Different Generations

	TRADITIONALISTS (PRE-1945)	BABY BOOMERS (1945-1964)	GENERATION X (1965-1980)	GENERATION Y (1981-1999)
AGE IN 2017→	AGE 73+	AGE 53-72	AGE 37-52	AGE 18-36
Formative Events	Great Depression World Wars	Post war prosperity	Globalization Downsizing Tech boom	Networking 9-11 World terrorism Internet
Qualities	Loyal Self-sacrificing	Competitive Optimistic	Independent Individualistic Entrepreneurial Lack loyalty	Diverse Skilled Demanding Sophisticated
Assets	Wisdom Experience Persistence	Social skills	Tech skills Educated	Multitasking Work ethic Technologically savvy
Lack	Technology skills	Technology skills	Social skills	Direction Focus Interpersonal skills
Value	Family Patriotism	Material success Free expression Equity	Skill more than title Work-life balance	Patriotism Family Respect
Style	Directive Take charge Do what's right	Respect authority Micromanage Proactive Work hard	Skeptical Reluctant to network Outcome focused Bend rules as needed	Plunge right in Negotiate Blend work/play Measure own success
Strategies for Managing	Respect their experience Value their loyalty Use their knowledge/ experience to help others	Give important role Value their contributions Show respect Minimize conflict	Provide autonomy Give quick feedbacks Update their tech skills Give credit for results Coach	Train/upgrade Assign meaningful work Use in teams Promote positive, open environment Mentor

Source: Adapted from Susan P. Eisner, "Managing Generation Y," *SAM Advanced Management Journal, Autumn,* 2005, v. 70, pp. 4–13; Suzanne M. Crampton and John W. Hodge, "Generation Y: Unchartered Territory," *Journal of Business & Economics Research,* April, 2009, 7 (4), pp. 1–6.

traditionalists

Workforce generation born before 1945.

Baby Boomers

Workforce generation born between 1945 and 1964.

Traditionalists: born before 1945 (10 percent of workforce). Children of the Depression and World War, they were typically raised in a home with a stay-at-home parent. Imbued with strong family values, traditionalists themselves had a parent stay at home to raise their own children. Loyal and self-sacrificing, they value hard work, get satisfaction from a job well done, and tend to stay with a company a long time.

Baby Boomers: born between 1945 and 1964 (45 percent of workforce). Raised in a period of prosperity in the 1950s and 1960s, baby boomers are the largest generation in history. They were the center of their parents' lives, likely having a stay-at-home parent. They are socially skilled, ambitious, and driven to succeed, which for them is often measured materialistically. They believe in growth, change, and expansion. Boomers grew up to want the best for themselves and their families and seek it through hard work and long hours. They, too, show loyalty toward employers and often have a "live to work" reference frame. They dislike authoritarianism and laziness; having paid their dues through hard work and loyalty, they feel particularly dismayed in today's era of downsizing and reengineering.

Generation Xers

Workforce generation born between 1965 and 1980.

Generation Xers: born between 1965 and 1980 (30 percent of workforce). Children of the workaholic Baby Boomers, Generation Xers did not see as much of their parents as earlier generations. In many cases, both of their parents worked; a tripling divorce rate also meant approximately half were raised in a one-parent home. Generation Xers learned to function on their own, being highly independent, self-reliant, and individualistic. This generation loves freedom and room to grow. Growing up, they heard their parents' laments about layoffs, downsizing, and managers who didn't treat their parents well. They view the employment relationship as one based on service for dollars paid, rather than loyalty, even if it means frequent employer changes. Generation Xers do not believe in paying their dues to achieve success; to them, success means following the opportunity. Although they possess strong technical skills, they lack the social skills of their parents' generations, not being particularly adroit at networking. They thrive on autonomy that allows them independence to handle their jobs as they see fit; thus, they respond poorly to being micromanaged.

Generation Yers

Youngest workforce generation, born between 1981 and 1999.

Generation Yers: born between 1981 and 1999 (15 percent of workforce). Some use the terms Generation Y and Millennials to refer to the same generation; whereas others do not, suggesting that they are similar but not completely overlapping. In this chapter, the terms will be used interchangeably. Generation Yers have been raised in a time of globalism, economic expansion, prosperity, and the Internet. Electronic communication technology—laptops, Blackberries, cell phones, and text messaging—has enabled them to see, learn, and keep in touch more at an early age than any preceding generation.[27]

Generation Zers

Those born after Generation Y.

Generation Zers: Generation Z (Gen Z) or post-millennials are those born after Gen Y. On this experts agree, but on little else. More research will be done as this generation matures to identify consistent characteristics.

Generation Yers are the most diverse, highly educated, and technically literate generation. As the first truly global generation, Generation Yers have some values consistent with traditionalists, including patriotism, valuing family and home, a strong sense of morality, and commitment to volunteer service. They like intellectual challenge and strive to make a difference. Emotionally mature, Generation Yers have lived with strong social stressors ranging from pressures to excel in school to parental divorce to being products of one-parent homes. Of all the generations, one expert says, the Generation Yers are the most willing to "rock the boat."

Because organizations have been run by Traditionalists and Boomers, large corporations' strict rules of engagement especially clash with Generation Yers' values of openness and flexibility. They are accustomed to handling information and getting immediate results, and want freedom rather than rigid controls and standardized ways of doing things. Teachers and parents allowed them to speak their minds freely, so why not ask a supervisor questions such as "Why do I need to do it that way?" Growing up with instant messaging and live views of the Gulf, Iraqi, and Afghanistan wars on their televisions, Generation Yers are the ultimate stimulus junkies. They want instant feedback, rapid results, and jobs that offer excitement as well as a paycheck.[28]

You can see in Exhibit 7-10, some of the specific actions supervisors and organizations can take that may have special impact on individuals of a given generation. For example, traditionalists may be strongly motivated by an opportunity to mentor a younger employee or help train other team members; the opportunity to attend a technology training class might be highly valued by younger Generation X or Y employees. In the next section, you will learn important principles for motivating that cut across all generation types. Peter Sheahan, a most sought-after international speaker on Generation Y, says there are three things all generations, and especially Generation Yers, want in a motivating work environment:

1. Having their supervisor's respect.
2. Feeling like they are making a real contribution—their work must have an impact.
3. Having control—"Gen Yers want to customize their careers just like lattes are customized by coffee shops." This may range from flexible work hours to rotation among job assignments.[29]

Lessons from the Theories: Five Steps to Motivating Employees

11. *Identify five steps to motivating employees.*

Our intent in this chapter has been to explain a number of popular theories of motivation that can help you understand why people act as they do. You have noted the commonalities and close relationships among many of the theories.

Based on these theories, we feel there are a number of things a supervisor can do to help create a motivating environment for employees. Moreover, these five actions apply broadly to supervisors in all types of organizations. These supervisory actions are

1. Help make employees' jobs intrinsically rewarding.
2. Provide clear performance objectives.
3. Support employees' performance efforts.
4. Provide timely performance feedback.
5. Reward employees' performance.

Help Make Employees' Jobs Intrinsically Rewarding

Recall Herzberg's finding that employees believed the most satisfying things about their jobs included feeling a sense of accomplishment, challenge, or responsibility. Also, note the job characteristics model's elements of motivation: task variety, task identity, task significance, autonomy, and feedback. Granted, it is more difficult to make dull, repetitive jobs more rewarding, especially when you cannot alter an assembly line or change the nature of the work being done. However, you can do a number of things to make even dull, unchallenging jobs more rewarding, such as

- *Rotate jobs/tasks.*
- *Assign team members to special projects, giving them a break from the usual grind or enabling them to pick up a new skill.*
- *Have employees train new employees.*
- *Help employees learn skills to prepare them for a more advanced job.*
- *Have employees make a safety presentation at a safety meeting.*
- *Ask for employees' help in resolving problems you face, such as cost or deadline overruns, relationships with other departments, or ways to improve quality.*
- *Have a customer or end-user of your department's product or service speak to your group.*

As a supervisor, it is worth your effort to make employees' work provide opportunities for intrinsic satisfaction.

STOP AND THINK

If you are currently a supervisor, what actions could you take to help make your employees' jobs more intrinsically satisfying? If you are not currently a supervisor, select a job you held that you considered dull and uninteresting. What actions could your supervisor have taken to make the job more rewarding?

Provide Clear Performance Objectives

In line with expectancy and goal-setting theories, make sure employees clearly understand what is expected of them. If possible, set concrete, specific, challenging goals as discussed in goal-setting theory. Moreover, if these are not set by the system itself or by your own manager, try to obtain your employees' assistance in determining these. Employees are more likely to commit to goals they had a hand in setting.

Support Employees' Performance Efforts

View yourself as a coach whose job is to support your team members. Help them through intangibles such as building confidence and encouraging them, but also support them in tangible ways through the resources you provide, through your responsiveness to their needs, by obtaining additional training for them, and so on. Be viewed not only as their best cheerleader, but as someone who delivers tangible support as well.

Provide Timely Performance Feedback

Performance feedback is the fuel employees need to sustain their effort. Although the job itself may provide feedback to them, it is important you acknowledge their progress. Reason would say this is easier to do in favorable situations, but our experiences with managers and employees indicate it is not. Many employees state, they know things must be going well only because they *do not* hear from their supervisor. Managers must give favorable as well as unfavorable performance feedback. Note we are not talking about the feedback that accompanies an employee's 6- or 12-month formal review, but the feedback that occurs on a daily, regular basis. Team or departmental progress should be posted in high-visibility areas where everyone can see it regularly—from the CEO to hourly employees.[30]

Reward Employees' Performance

Be liberal with rewards, making sure they are earned. Reinforce your high performers through the reward system available to you, such as merit increases, praise, recognition, or opportunities to take on a more challenging job. Be creative with rewards, remembering that rewards are valued differently by different individuals.

Mars Embodies the Five Motivational Lessons

Mars Inc. is one organization that continuously practices these five lessons. That's right, the candy maker! Mars is a four-time winner of Gallup's Great Workplace Award and recently tabbed by *Fortune* as one of the best 100 places to work. When people hire on with Mars, they stay, with turnover in the United States at a mere 5 percent. They don't offer basketball hoops, spa treatments, or stress-free commutes, like other companies on *Fortune*'s list (but they do get free candy!), so how do they keep a motivated workforce . . . well, motivated?

You know the answer. They live by the motivational lessons presented in this last section of your chapter.

Mars is a diverse, nonunionized (at least in the United States), global company whose employees across regions, divisions, and levels embrace their products, culture, and principles. Mars is 100 percent family owned and the family used sweat equity to build their candy empire, working right along with the employees, so they have credibility and respect. At Mars, everyone—family, management, employees—are all Martians!

The following five core principles are the foundation of the business: quality, respect, mutuality, efficiency, and freedom. It's not surprising quality is a top priority because even when the company started during the Great Depression the owners were not willing to sacrifice perfection to save money. As Mars grew, it became quite efficient, but it still maintains an entrepreneurial spirit. In fact, it provides autonomy to encourage innovation, while patiently awaiting investment returns. "(T)he freedom principle undergirds all that makes the company exceptional. Freedom means being financially answerable to no one. And for freedom to flourish, the family is requisite: 'Many other companies began as Mars did, but as they grew larger and required new sources of funds, they sold stocks or incurred restrictive debt to fuel their business. . . . We believe growth and prosperity can be achieved another way.'"

Given the importance placed on freedom and autonomy, developing cross-divisional talent by providing employees opportunities to grow within and across divisions is a high priority. "Consider Jim Price, who's now the site-quality and food-safety manager at the chocolate plant in Hackettstown, N.J. Almost 27 years ago, he began his Mars career as a janitor in a boutique chocolate operation in Henderson, Nev. His supervisor urged him to attend community college at night; Mars paid for tuition and books." Mars's commitment to developing its human capital is also evident in its training and mentoring efforts. Employee training assists in developing tacit knowledge while mentoring younger employees satisfies many Gen Y employees' needs. But even executives go through "reverse mentoring" when younger workers teach and coach them on how to use social media.

Mars's emphasis on employee development goes beyond its corporate boundaries. It encourages community involvement through the Mars Volunteers and Mars Ambassadors programs. Those participating as Volunteers (9,600 in 2011) are paid to give back to the community in a variety of ways (37,000 hours in 290 places in 2011), whereas the Ambassador program is more selective. In 2011, only 80 employees were chosen to spend up to six weeks "working with Mars-related partners in remote areas." It could be cocoa bean growers in Ghana or other global suppliers. Regardless, these experiences provide employees a better understanding of the significance of their work, a sense of reward, and an enhanced appreciation for their value to the company.

What a great place to work! It's no wonder multigenerational families choose Mars. Remember, at the beginning of the chapter, we learned on average only 30 percent of employees are actively engaged? Well, take a look at the full list of Gallup's Great Workplace Award winners and find out which companies get an A for employee engagement and satisfaction—visit http://www.gallup.com/events/178865/gallup-great-workplace-award-current-previous-winners.aspx?g_source=great+workplace+award+winners&g_medium=search&g_campaign=tiles.

Sources: David A. Kaplan, "Mars Incorporated: A Pretty Sweet Place to Work," *Fortune* (online), January 17, 2013, http://management.fortune.cnn.com/2013/01/17/best-companies-mars/; "Gallup Great Workplace Award Current and Previous Winners," *Gallup* (online), 2013, http://www.gallup.com/strategicconsulting/157034/gallup-great-workplace-award-current-previous-winners.aspx.Sources: David A. Kaplan, "Mars Incorporated: A Pretty Sweet Place to Work," *Fortune* (online), January 17, 2013, http://management.fortune.cnn.com/2013/01/17/best-companies-mars/; "Gallup Great Workplace Award Current and Previous Winners," *Gallup* (online), 2013, http://www.gallup.com/strategicconsulting/157034/gallup-great-workplace-award-current-previous-winners.aspx.

Chapter Review

1. *Identify the three levels of employee motivation.*

The three levels of employee motivation are (1) the direction of an employee's behavior, (2) the level of effort, and (3) the level of persistence. Direction of behavior relates to those behaviors the individual chooses to perform. Level of effort dictates how hard the individual is willing to work on the behavior. Level of persistence refers to the individual's willingness to pursue the behavior despite obstacles or roadblocks.

2. *Explain the relationship between performance and motivation.*

Motivation is an important contributor to employee performance, but it is not the only one. Also involved are an employee's skill and ability and organizational support in the form of physical resources and assistance. We conclude other things being equal, employees who are more highly motivated will have higher performance records.

3. *Understand and explain Maslow's hierarchy of needs theory and the principle underlying his theory.*

The principle underlying Maslow's theory of a hierarchy of needs is needs are arranged in a hierarchy of importance and that once a need has been satisfied, it is no longer a primary motivator. The lower-level needs include physiological, security, and social needs, and the higher-level needs are esteem and self-fulfillment.

4. *Differentiate between Herzberg's dissatisfiers and motivators.*

Herzberg's research discovered motivators are those factors with an uplifting effect on attitudes or performance, whereas dissatisfier/hygiene factors are those that prevent dissatisfaction but do not motivate by themselves. Motivators are recognition, advancement, achievement, being one's own boss, and the challenge associated with the work itself. Dissatisfiers include pay, benefits, working conditions, job security, and company policy/administration. Motivators relate to the two highest levels of the Maslow hierarchy, self-fulfillment and self-esteem. Dissatisfiers are related to lower-level physiological and security needs.

5. *Understand and explain expectancy theory.*

Expectancy theory views an individual's motivation as a conscious effort involving three variables: (1) expectancy a given effort can achieve a given performance result; (2) probability that achieving the given performance result will lead to a reward; and (3) the value of the reward to the individual. Supervisors can apply expectancy theory by rewarding performance in meaningful ways to employees, by helping employees reach desired performance levels through coaching and training, and delivering rewards as promised to employees.

6. *Explain how supervisors can use goal-setting theory to motivate employees.*

The basic premise of goal-setting theory is that task goals can be highly motivating if properly set and well managed. To maximize their motivational impact, performance goals should be specific and difficult, but achievable. Ideally, employees should participate in the goal-setting process and, if multiple goals are involved, understand their priorities. Performance feedback about progress toward goal attainment should be provided, as well as timely rewards and recognition when goals are achieved.

7. *Define equity theory.*

Equity theory states when people feel they are rewarded inequitably as compared to others, they act in ways to change their circumstances. They may do this by (1) attempting to increase their reward level, (2) decreasing their input level, or (3) seeking to leave the situation by requesting transfer or leaving their employer.

8. *Define and explain reinforcement theory.*

Reinforcement theory uses rewards and punishment following an individual's behavior as a way of shaping future behavior. This theory is based on the law of effect that holds behaviors meeting with pleasant consequences tend to be repeated, whereas behaviors with unpleasant consequences tend not to be repeated.

9. *Explain the job characteristics model.*

The job characteristics model, a form of job design, focuses on five core job elements capable of leading to intrinsic motivation and other positive work outcomes. These five elements are (1) skill variety, (2) task identity, (3) task significance, (4) autonomy, and (5) feedback.

10. *Explain how generational differences affect motivation.*

The five generations are Traditionalists, born before 1945; Baby Boomers, born between 1945 and 1964; Generation Xers, born between 1965 and 1980; Generation Yers, born between 1981 and 1999; and Gen Zers born after 1999. Generalizations based on the common experiences shared during a generation's formative years enable insights into their values, behaviors, and what is likely to motivate them. Traditionalists, the oldest generation, tend to be loyal and hard working, value family, and get satisfaction from jobs well done. Workaholic Baby Boomers are ambitious, driven to succeed, and often materialistic; Generation Xers, raised to fend for themselves, are highly independent, technologically competent, and thrive on autonomy and freedom. Generation Yers, the new workforce entrants, are the Internet generation. Technologically savvy, they are the ultimate networkers, like instant results and feedback and open communications, and value flexibility.

11. *Identify five steps to motivating employees.*

Supervisors, in general, can take five specific steps to motivate employees. They can (1) make employees' jobs more interesting by enabling greater challenge, accomplishment, or responsibility; (2) provide clear performance objectives; (3) support employees' performance efforts through training, coaching, and assistance; (4) provide timely performance feedback to employees; and (5) reward employees generously for performance accomplishment.

Key Terms

motivation, p. 192
intrinsic motivation, p. 195
extrinsic motivation, p. 195
hierarchy of needs, p. 197
physiological or biological needs,
    p. 197
safety or security needs, p. 197
social or belonging needs, p. 198

ego or esteem needs, p. 198
self-fulfillment or self-
    actualization needs, p. 199
dissatisfier or hygiene factors, p. 201
satisfier or motivator factors, p. 201
expectancy theory, p. 203
goal-setting theory, p. 206
equity theory, p. 207

reinforcement theory, p. 208
job characteristics model, p. 209
traditionalists, p. 212
Baby Boomers, p. 212
Generation Xers, p. 213
Generation Yers, p. 213
Generation Zers, p. 213

Discussion Questions

1. Identify and explain the three levels of employee motivation. Give an example of each for one of the situations below:

- *Customer associate at Home Depot*
- *Bagger at grocery chain*
- *Carpenter for construction company*

2. Explain the relationship between motivation and job performance. Can you identify a situation in which a factor other than your skill or motivation level affected your performance?

3. Briefly outline Maslow's theory of the hierarchy of needs. What need levels are addressed by

   - *Being promoted from operator to supervisor*
   - *Setting a new record for individual performance*
   - *Being selected to attend a special training course*

4. In what ways did Frederick Herzberg's research concerning employee motivation correlate with Maslow's hierarchy of needs?

5. In a management seminar taught by one of the authors to supervisors in a large shipyard, one supervisor commented: "We have very little opportunity to 'motivate' employees. All monetary factors—starting pay, yearly merit increases, and bonuses based on the yard's profits—are controlled by upper management, with no input from supervisors. We don't have anything to motivate with." Do you agree or disagree with this supervisor? Why?

6. What are the elements of goal-setting theory? Explain.

7. What relationship, if any, do you see among expectancy theory, goal-setting theory, equity theory, and reinforcement theory? Explain.

8. Identify the five core elements of the job characteristics model.

9. What are some important characteristics of each of the following generations?

   - *Traditionalist*
   - *Baby Boomer*
   - *Generation X*
   - *Generation Y*

10. Identify five important steps to motivating employees.

Skill Builder 7.1

Information

Interpersonal Skill

Career Exercise: What Do You Want from Your Job?

Assume you could create the ideal job for yourself. Examine the 12 items shown below and rank these from most important to least important. In other words, what single item of the 12 is most important to you? Number that item 1. Follow a similar process until you have ranked all items.

YOUR PRIORITY RANK	IDEAL JOB FACTOR
	a. First-class working conditions
	b. Opportunity to achieve wide recognition for job performance
	c. Working in the city/area of your choice
	d. A super-competent boss
	e. Guaranteed job security (lifetime employment)
	f. Exceptional advancement opportunity
	g. Salary 20 percent higher than the industry average
	h. Challenging, interesting job that you really like
	i. Professional, supportive colleagues
	j. Working for a prestigious, nationally known organization
	k. Outstanding fringe benefits
	l. Excellent opportunity to grow and develop job skills

> *Instructions:*
>   1. Now that you have completed the ranking, to what extent, if any, do your results reflect Maslow's needs theory? Herzberg's motivation-hygiene theory?
>   2. Meet with a group of four to six classmates and compare your rankings. To what extent were the rankings similar? Dissimilar? What might account for any different rankings given by your group?
>   3. Present a report to the class summarizing the results of your group's discussion.

Skill Builder 7.2

Information

Interpersonal Skill

Classifying Managerial Rewards

Listed here are 15 actions an organization's managers can take, each of which addresses one or more potential needs on the Maslow hierarchy. Some have been taken from Exhibit 7-8, "Manager's List of Potential Rewards," but others have been added.

Instructions:
  1. For each item, identify the levels on the Maslow hierarchy of needs the action addresses.
  2. Select three items you personally feel would be most important for you at the present time.
  3. In small groups, discuss your results for items 1 and 2. To what extent did your team members agree on the three items? Why were there differences? Be prepared to report your results to the rest of the class.

	ACTION	MASLOW NEED LEVEL(S) ADDRESSED
1.	Day off or time off	_____
2.	Personal call or visit from CEO or senior manager	_____
3.	"Employee of the Month" parking space	_____
4.	Direct oral praise from supervisor	_____
5.	Opportunity to attend special training course	_____
6.	Name in company newsletter	_____
7.	Additional responsibilities	_____
8.	Special task force assignment	_____
9.	Company outing, picnic	_____
10.	Being assigned favorable tasks	_____
11.	Opportunity to attend special seminar	_____
12.	New title, new office, new equipment	_____
13.	Direct praise to individual in presence of others	_____
14.	Receiving bonus for reaching production goal	_____
15.	Being given more responsibility	_____

Skill Builder 7.3

Information

Interpersonal Skill

Technology

The Job Characteristics Survey: Scoring Your Job

In this exercise, you will visit a Web site and complete an online survey called the "Job Diagnostic Survey." Based on the job characteristics model you studied in this chapter, the survey measures the extent to which your job provides intrinsic satisfaction. Score the survey results in the motivation potential score (MPS) of your job. If you are presently employed, use your job when you respond to the questions. If not presently employed, select a job you have once held.

Instructions:

1. Go to http://www.marscafe.com/php/hr2/jds_quiz.php3 and sign in. Click "other" or "college student" for occupation and "other" for your job title.

2. Complete the 15-item assessment.

3. Indicate your score for each of the five job characteristics.

Skill variety	_____
Task identity	_____
Task significance	_____
Autonomy	_____
Feedback	_____

Indicate your job's motivation potential score (MPS) = _____

The maximum score possible = 9,261
The minimum score possible = 27

4. What conclusions can you draw about your job's motivation potential?

5. In groups of four to six students, discuss your scores and possible ways your job's MPS might be improved.

CASE 7-1

THE PACESETTER:

Jean graduated from a two-year college with an associate's degree and landed employment as a national sales representative with a rapidly growing technology firm in a mid-sized southern city. She considered pursuing a four-year degree and possibly a master's, but it was important to her to gain some work experience and save money before making a final decision on school.

She soon found she enjoyed her sales job, which consisted of cultivating and managing a diverse client list. She particularly liked face-to-face time with potential buyers, selling them on the "right" products and services. Jean found communication was the key to helping customers and closing the deal. She regularly came in early and stayed late to make sure she

delivered what she promised and ensured her customers were satisfied.

Jean's sales manager, Jack, took notice of her excellent performance. When Jack hired Jean, he did so based on her potential. She had an unbelievable means of communicating with people, coupled with a high need to achieve and a strong internal desire to continuously learn and grow, but even he could not predict how well she would do her first year. As Jean's skills developed, Jeff offered her new opportunities to learn the business and develop contacts within and outside of the firm. She appreciated it and made the most of them.

At the end of Jean's first full year with the firm, Jack scheduled her performance appraisal session. Jack started off, "I am quite pleased with your performance,

(Continued)

especially because it is your first year on the job. You exceeded expectations and I couldn't be happier." Jean liked what she was hearing and Jack continued, "I want to first go over your global evaluation to show you how I arrived at a score of 9 out of 10. As you can see, the individual performance categories below range from 'Ability to Effectively Generate Sales Leads' to 'Ability to Effectively Close Sales.' You earned outstanding ratings with all your scores falling between 8 and 10 in each performance category. Just so you have a reference point for how well you are doing, the department's average global score was a 6.5, so I consider you to be one of our pacesetters! Your efforts will certainly provide a model for others to follow." Jean was utterly surprised. She knew she worked hard giving 110 percent each day, but she did not anticipate being a pacesetter!

Even though Jack's focus was on Jean's sales productivity, he was actually quite impressed with her willingness to volunteer for projects and take on extra work. He shared, "Jean, I've noticed you are an effective team player, always offering help to other sales representatives even though this can be a competitive environment. I admire that in you. Not only have you been a reliable team player, but you also have demonstrated good leadership." Jack assigned Jean the lead role on several department-level projects to challenge her and see if she had what it took, and she performed admirably building an effective team to accomplish the objectives each time. While these side projects were not financially beneficial in the short term, they provided Jean opportunities to network with higher-ups and those in other departments. If she decided to make a career of it, these experiences would be invaluable to her. Jack knew employees like Jean did not come along often.

Jack shared, "Based on your excellent performance, you have earned a 7 percent base pay increase." Jack made it clear the department average was around 3.5 percent. But that wasn't all. "Based on your leadership potential, I scheduled you to attend two of human resources' leadership training and development programs, one this fall and one in the spring. I know furthering your education is really a top priority for you, and successfully completing these certification programs will provide you an opportunity to be selected for entrance into the firm's continuing education program, where you can complete your four-year degree and possibly your graduate degree as well. If selected, and I have no doubts you will be with strong letters of recommendation coupled with your outstanding performance, the firm will pay your education expenses as long as you maintain at least a 3.0 GPA."

Jean was ecstatic! Her dreams of continuing her education were closer than she imagined. She simply needed to stay motivated and work even harder this next year to qualify for the continuing education program. That would be easy because she loved her job, her boss believed in her, and she couldn't wait to get going.

She enthusiastically returned to her office, where Dan, her coworker, was waiting. Dan knew Jean just came from her performance review and was eager to see how things had gone. Dan and Jean had been hired around the same time, but Dan did not have a degree beyond high school. He opted to start working early, marry his high-school sweetheart, and start a family. While Dan was a committed employee, he was part of a dual-working family and not able to put in the hours Jean could. Jean knew she had to be careful not to share too much because Dan just had his performance evaluation and Jean felt his work efforts would not qualify him to be a pacesetter in the top group. Jean didn't want either one of them to be in an uncomfortable position, so without sharing specifics, she said her evaluation went better than she hoped after just one year with the firm. Dan concurred stating, "I couldn't believe Jack gave me a 7 percent bump on my base, and to top it off, he has scheduled me to attend two of HR's training and development sessions to position me for the firm's continuing education program. I didn't realize I performed so well! This is a great company to work for; they really know how to treat people! If we stay here, Jean, we might just end up running the company some day!"

Dan's words began to trail off as Jean abruptly turned and stormed off. She couldn't believe what she was hearing!

CASE QUESTIONS

1. What were Jean's work attitudes before meeting Dan in the hall? What would you predict about Jean's motivation and performance over the next year if Jean had not learned of Dan's performance evaluation?

2. What were Jean's work attitudes after talking with Dan in the hall? Given your answer, what do you predict about Jean's motivation and performance going forward?

3. What motivation theory in this chapter do you think best applies to explain this situation and predict how Jean might respond?

Source: Case written by Don C. Mosley Jr. The names were changed for privacy reasons.

CASE 7-2

NUCOR, THE SURPRISING PERFORMANCE CULTURE OF STEELMAKER NUCOR:

In the early afternoon, three Nucor electricians got a call from their Hickman, Arkansas, plant colleagues. The Hickman mill's electrical grid had failed, which meant the mini-mill couldn't melt the usual auto parts, appliances, and mobile home parts it uses to produce steel. But why should an outage in Arkansas concern anyone at plants in other Nucor locations? Here's why. At Nucor, steelworker production bonuses are based not only on what their own mill does, but on how others fare also. When a grid goes out, it hurts all. That's why when Hickman's electrician colleagues called for help, people didn't need top management to tell them to go; they responded on their own. Two electricians from the company's South Carolina plant boarded the first plane they could get to Memphis. Arriving at 11:00 P.M., they rented a car and drove two hours directly to the Hickman mill. The third electrician, from the company's Decatur, Alabama, plant, was in Indiana, visiting another Nucor site. He immediately drove to Hickman. Combined with Hickman staff, they camped out on site and worked 20-hour shifts to mobilize the plant in three days—much less than the anticipated week. They received no extra pay for their effort.

Why would they do such a thing? It's because of Nucor's unique way of motivating their workforce and the strong family bond throughout its employment ranks. First, there's pay. Nucor steelworkers make only about $10 hourly, compared to the typical steelworker's $16 to $21 hourly. Managers also earn salaries as much as 20 percent below what competitors pay. But what a difference incentives can make! Based on previous production incentives for their mills, Nucor's steelworkers have averaged $79,000 in pay and incentives. Nucor also has participated in company profit sharing, in which bonuses vary from year to year. In good years, employees earned a $20,000 one-time bonus, bringing the total to $99,000. Workers' incentives are tied not only to quality production in their own mill, but also to that of other mills and overall company profits. They can track their performance each week, so they know exactly where they stand.

However, it's more than just dollars that make Nucor special. The company became the darling of the late 1980s when its unique "pay for performance" system was implemented under then CEO Ken Iverson. Iverson insisted on a culture resulting in employees feeling like owners. In addition to their pay system, Iverson empowered employees to make critical decisions, implement their ideas, and take risks. The rest is history.

Operating in a single North Carolina location then, and in an underdog role to U.S. Steel and other giants, the lean mini-mill company in 2013 had approximately 22,000 employees and was the largest steel producer in the United States, with revenues of $18.91 billion. Between 2002 and 2006 its 387 percent return to shareholders beat almost all companies listed in the Standard and Poor's stock index. However, like most companies, Nucor's market value suffered due to the Great Recession. Successful organizations, like Nucor, take advantage of down times to strategically position themselves for when things improve. Analysts predict as the economy gets stronger, Nucor's sales, revenues, and earnings per share will grow again.

The Nucor culture includes some symbolic actions, like every employee's name being placed on the cover of the annual report. There's something egalitarian in the culture as well, such as present CEO Daniel DeMicco flying commercial jets rather than having his own, finding his own parking space in the headquarters lot like every other employee, or making the coffee when it's his turn. In 2005, when the average CEO pay of big companies averaged 400 times that of the hourly employee, at Nucor, DiMicco's was 24 times that of his steelworkers.

Plant managers' incentives are based on the company's overall return on equity, rather than specific results from their own mill. As one stated, "At Nucor, it's not my plant versus someone else's, as they're all 'our' plants. When one plant has a problem it's everyone's problem."

CASE QUESTIONS

1. What are the most relevant concepts from the chapter reflected at Nucor? Comment specifically about the following:

   Maslow's hierarchy of needs
   Herzberg's motivation-hygiene theory
   Expectancy theory
   Equity theory
   Goal-setting theory

Sources: Nanette Byrnes and Michael Arndt, "What Can You Learn from a Company That Treats Workers Like Owners. Inside the Surprising Performance Culture of Steelmaker Nucor," pp. 56–62. Reprinted from May 1, 2006, issue of *BusinessWeek* by special permission, copyright © 2006 by the McGraw-Hill Companies, Inc.; "Nucor Corporation Key Statistics," Yahoo Finance (online), 2013, http://finance.yahoo.com/q/ks?s=NUE+Key+Statistics; and "Nucor Corporation Analyst Estimates," Yahoo Finance (online), 2013, http://finance.yahoo.com/q/ae?s=NUE+Analyst+Estimates.

Notes

1. "Air Conditioning Market Projected to Reach $167 Billion by 2024." *Journal of Property Management*, November–December 2016, p. 3; "Our History" *One Hour Heating and Air Conditioning* http://www.onehourcomfort. com/about-us/our-history/; (retrieved June 17, 2017 Samantha Sine, "Contracting Success: A True Team Effort," *Air Conditioning Heating & Refrigeration News*, January 30, 2017 , pp. 14–15; Mark Sinatra, "Employee Turnover: Costs and Causes," *Air Conditioning Heating & Refrigeration News*, August 24 2015. Retrieved from http:// www.achrnews.com/articles/130409-employee- turnover-costs-and-causes

2. Holly Dolzeak, "Sick Day or Just Sick and Tired," *Training* 42 (December 2005), p. 8.

3. Matthew Boyle, "Motivating without Money," *BusinessWeek* (online), April 27, 2009, p. 18; Gerald H. Siejts and Dan Crim, "What Engages Workers the Most or the Ten Cs of Employee Engagement," *Ivey Business Journal* (online), March–April 2006, pp. 1–5; "Employee Engagement," *Gallup Business Journal* (online), January 13, 2016. Retrieved from http://www .gallup.com/poll/188144/employee-engagement- stagnant-2015.aspx

4. "Motivation: A Management Challenge," *Training and Development*, November 2006, p. 17.

5. Saul W. Gellerman, *Motivation and Productivity* (New York: American Management Association, 1963), pp. 20-22; Daniel A. Wren, *The Evolution of Management Thought* (New York: Ronald Press Co, 1972), pp. 275–281.

6. Jennifer M. George and Gareth R Jones, *Organizational Behavior*, 3rd ed. (Upper Saddle River, NJ: Prentice-Hall, 2002), p. 182.

7. Reported in Thomas J. Petersand Robert Waterman, *In Search of Excellence: Lessons from America's Best Run Companies* (New York: Harper and Row, 1982), p. xxi.

8. Gareth R. Jones and Jennifer M. George, *Contemporary Management*, 3rd ed. (New York: McGraw-Hill, 2003), p. 411.

9. "Talk about Job Security: Clune," *Crain's Chicago Business* 32 March 2, 2009; Clune Construction Company. Retrieved from http://www.clunegc. com/overview.html

10. William A. Cohen, *The Art of the Leader* (Englewood Cliffs, NJ: Prentice-Hall, 1990), pp. 18–19.

11. Jody G. Hoffer, *The Southwest Airlines Way* (New York: McGraw-Hill, 2005); "Train to Retain," *Incentive*, September 12, 2007.

12. Frederick Herzberg, "One More Time: How Do You Motivate Employees?" *Harvard Business Review* 81 January 2003, pp. 41–47.

13. "Enjoyment is the Top Motivator," *Personnel Today*, April 8, 2003, p. 55.

14. Michael Byrne, "The Implications of Herzberg's Motivation-Hygiene Theory for Management in the Irish Health Care Sector," *The Health Care Manager* 25, January–March 2006, pp. 4–12.

15. Michael Byrne, "The Implications of Herzberg's Motivation-Hygiene Theory for Management in the Irish Health Care Sector," The Health Care Manager 25, January–March, 2006, p. 4–12.

16. Fred Luthans, *Organizational Behavior*, 7th ed. (New York: McGraw Hill, 1995), p. 156.

17. Bob Nelson, "Making the Job Meaningful Down the Line," *BusinessWeek*, May 1, 2006, p. 60.

18. E. A. Locke and G. P. Latham, *A Theory of Goal Setting and Task Performance* (Englewood Cliffs, NJ: Prentice-Hall, 1990).

19. M. Sixel, "Driven by Boss' Challenge," *Houston Chronicle*, May 20, 2006.

20. Condensed from Peters and Waterman, *In Search of Excellence*, p. 68.

21. Samantha Oller, *American Printer*, October 1, 2002.

22. Kevin McManus, "A Simple Thank You," *Industrial Engineer* 37, February 2005, p. 19.

23. Alan Zaremba, *Organizational Communication* (Mason, OH: South-Western, 2003), p. 34.

24. J. R. Hackman and G. R. Oldham, "Motivation through the Design of Work: Test of a Theory," *Organizational Behavior and Human Performance*, August 1976, pp. 250–279; Jennifer M. George and Gareth R. Jones, *Organizational Behavior*, 4th ed. (Upper Saddle River, NJ: Pearson Prentice-Hall, 2005), pp. 208–214.

25. Chuck Williams, *Management*, 4th ed. (Mason, OH: Thomson/South-Western, 2007), p. 287.

26. Susan Eisner, "Managing Generation Y," *SAM Advanced Management Journal* 70, August 2005, p. 4.

27. "Six Steps to Guaranteeing Generation Y Productivity," *Supervision* 68, July 2007, pp. 6–8.

28. Lynn Curry, "Managing the Gen X/Y Employee," *Alaska Business Monthly* 19, November 2003, p. 31.

29. Glenn Bakers, "The Young Ones: So You Want to Attract More Young Talent to Your Business, but Don't Know How? You Need to Understand a Generation before You Can Successfully Recruit and Manage It," *NZ Business* 20, April 2006, pp. 24–30.

30. Dave Hotler, " 21st Century Management and the Quest for Excellence," *Supervision* 63, October 2002, pp. 3–7.

8
Leadership

Leadership is of the spirit, compounded of personality and vision; its practice is an art.

—Sir William Slim

Leadership is action, not position.

—Donald H. McGannon

Pressmaster/Shutterstock.com

Supervisors may adopt different leadership styles in an effort to influence their employees to achieve company goals.

Preview

WAYUP—LEADING MILLENNIALS WayUp was co-founded in 2014 by Liz Wessel and JJ Fleigelman with a mission to "connect students and recent grads with awesome opportunities." What makes this start-up different from others like Monster or LinkedIn's network is its "smart" platform. The applicant data collected are used to match job seekers with the "right" opportunities. Think Netflix for jobs. "Technology offers millennials a personalized approach in almost every other aspect of their lives, and we are here to do that for their careers," Fliegelman said. The startup has over 300,000 employers, including Google and Starbucks, and serves over 3.5 million job seekers. The company's goals include expanding those user and employee bases and becoming "smarter" through "machine learning technology.

Liz Wessel, a recipient of 30 Under 30 in Enterprise Technology, is CEO and responsible for business operations. She manages a team of approximately 50 individuals, mostly recently college graduates. As a leader in this environment, she has several challenges including deciding how to develop a strong team, how best to manage millennials, and how to manage employees that are around her age. With a few exceptions, everyone at the company is under 30. So how does Wessel handle these challenges? She says, "It's less about age and more about years of experience in a relevant role. There are some people brand new to their role [at WayUp] but have four years of experience in another job, but I'm going to treat them exactly the same as someone who just graduated from college and started here [in that role]."

In the beginning, Wessel managed a team of less than 10. That number has grown to over 40 and continues to increase. With a growing team, Wessel says it can be challenging when people have difficulty solving problems. "Sometimes when someone can't figure something out and it's so obvious to me it gets frustrating," she says. "It's one of those situations where we're the same exact age, I know this, you should know this, we have the same kind of experience. I just think overall I have to remind myself that I have two years more of experience at this specific company doing this kind of job than they do."

WayUp is not Wessel's first rodeo. She worked at Google and has been part of three start-ups, so she has experiences from which to draw upon that have helped shape her as a leader. She believes trust is big. "I say to people, in the beginning, you definitely have to gain trust of your manager. I don't want you going off and doing things on your own. Once you gain their trust, then do cool things."

Managing a team comprised primarily of millennials can have advantages as well as blind spots. According to Wessel, "The positives [of managing millennials] are that they aspire to do so many things, they want to achieve, and by 'they' I mean me, too. They want to achieve a ton, they want to learn, they want to grow, they always want to prove that they can accomplish great things." These characteristics are also one of the reasons managing this generational group is so challenging, like a double-edged sword. "It's definitely harder to retain millennials because they want to try out so many things." Some keys to retaining them include "getting content out there about what specific roles entail and having internal mobility opportunities so employees can know where they're headed." Wessel also notes the importance of providing employees feedback so she "implemented several layers of feedback for employees so they have a sense for how they're doing and what they can improve on."

WayUp recently raised $18.5 million in series B funding, bringing its total investment to $27.5 million so far. One challenge for Wessel and Fleigelman will be learning to adapt and manage larger teams as the company grows.[1]

STOP AND THINK

Do you think Wessel can adapt and manage a larger team as WayUp grows? Why or why not?

One thing we need to say about motivation is it cannot take place in a vacuum. For things to happen, effective leadership must be exhibited. This chapter focuses on effective leadership. Today many supervisors and managers use a less effective leadership style than they could be using, often because they don't have the necessary skills or don't even realize the benefits of using other styles. They don't know the most effective style in one situation may not be the most effective in another. Hence, this chapter addresses a number of questions:

1. Why do some leaders use one style and other leaders use another?
2. What effects do different styles have on employee productivity and morale?
3. What style is most appropriate in a particular situation?
4. Should a particular style be used consistently, or should the style be changed as circumstances change?

Such questions are vital for an organization because supervisory leadership is one of the primary determinants of organizational performance and productivity.

leadership

Process of influencing individual and group activities toward goal achievement.

Leadership: What Is It All About?

Leadership is defined as a process of influencing individual and group activities toward goal setting and goal achievement. Leadership is a reciprocal process involving the leader and follower(s). Formal leadership is officially sanctioned by an organization through delegation, while informal leadership is unofficial and accorded someone by organizational members. This chapter provides insights and concepts to assist supervisors in successfully leading their work groups.

Factors Affecting Leadership Style

1. Describe factors that affect the leadership style used.

Three factors, or variables, have a major impact on the choice of leadership style: (1) Theory X or Theory Y management philosophy, (2) the followers' readiness level, and (3) the situation faced by the supervisor. As Exhibit 8-1 shows, these factors are interrelated.

Theory X or Theory Y Management Philosophy   A supervisor's management philosophy is basically determined by his or her assumptions about the nature of people. Whether they are aware of it or not, most supervisors have a philosophy influencing their style in working with and through people. This philosophy is affected by several factors. Four critical factors interact to influence a supervisor's view of the nature of people and consequently shape his or her philosophy:

1. The supervisor's personality characteristics;
2. The supervisor's family and early school environment;
3. The supervisor's experience and training in the area of leadership; and
4. The supervisor's present work environment, including the type of work and the general management system.

Let's take a look at Jimmy Burckhartt, a Jimmy John's franchise owner, and his personal characteristics. We'll reflect on Burckhartt and his Jimmy John's franchise throughout the chapter to highlight different concepts.

> *For Jimmy, work has never been about the paycheck. It has always been about helping others and the work itself. He is an ambitious person who enjoys a challenge. His high need for achievement comes naturally and is why "failure" is not in his vocabulary! Coupled with his high need for achievement, Jimmy is also an intuitive personality type that enables him to be a visionary, seeing all sorts of possibilities, as evidenced by his diverse career interests. He is able to see how the different parts of a business fit together to create a positive service scape for the customer. As such, Jimmy understands how important each individual employee is to Jimmy & Company's success, but his main focus is coaching people to help them reach their full potential. He has a knack for sizing people up, identifying their strengths, and putting them in positions to succeed.[2]*

EXHIBIT 8-1
Factors Affecting
Choice of Leadership
Style

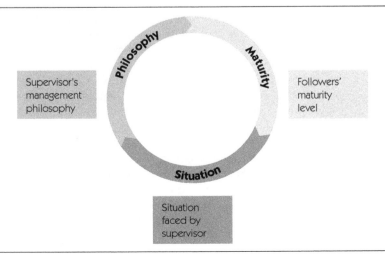

One of the most widely publicized approaches to the study of management philosophy is Douglas McGregor's concept of Theory X and Theory Y.[3] Based on his consulting and research work in industry, McGregor outlined two contrasting sets of assumptions about the nature of people. A manager's leadership style is influenced by the set of assumptions to which he or she subscribes.

Following are the most significant assumptions of **Theory X**:

Theory X

The average person has an inherent dislike of work and wishes to avoid responsibility.

1. The average human being has an inherent dislike of work and will avoid it if possible.
2. Because of this human characteristic—dislike of work—most people must be coerced, controlled, directed, or threatened with punishment to get them to put forth adequate effort toward the achievement of organizational objectives.
3. The average human being prefers to be directed, wishes to avoid responsibility, has relatively little ambition, and, above all, seeks security.
4. The average human being cannot be trusted.

Supervisors who accept Theory X assumptions are inclined to prefer a structured, autocratic leadership style.

The basic assumptions of **Theory Y** are as follows:

Theory Y

Work is as natural as play or rest.

1. The expenditure of physical and mental effort in work is as natural as play or rest.
2. External control and the threat of punishment are not the only means of bringing about effort toward organizational objectives. People exercise self-direction and self-control in the service of objectives to which they are committed.
3. Commitment to objectives is a function of the rewards associated with their achievement.
4. The average human being learns, under proper conditions, not only to accept but also to actively seek greater responsibility.
5. The capacity to exercise a relatively high degree of imagination, ingenuity, and creativity in the solution of organizational problems is widely, not narrowly, distributed in the population.
6. Under the conditions of modern industrial life, the intellectual potential of the average human being is only partially utilized.
7. The average human being believes she or he is a winner, so treat her or him like a winner.

Supervisors who hold Theory Y assumptions are inclined to prefer a supportive, participative leadership style when the situation calls for it. This last point is important because some people misconstrue Theory Y by assuming it always dictates a supportive, participative approach. Although a leader holding Theory Y assumptions about people might prefer a participative approach, the theory does not preclude a tough-minded approach or decisions. For example, Henri Fayol, one of the pioneers of management thinking, used the term "commanding" for what we now call "leading." One of Fayol's principles of command (leadership) is to eliminate the incompetent. However, he indicates before you take that step, you attempt to develop competence in the employee through training, coaching, counseling, and so on. If these strategies do not work, you eliminate the individual through firing and everyone knows the action was fair and warranted. This illustration reflects a Theory Y set of assumptions, and the outcome reflects a tough-minded decision.

Edgar Schein, an international expert on organization culture and process consultation, stated, "Show me an organization that has a key leader with Theory X assumptions about people, and I predict they will eventually screw things up."[4] The authors agree with Schein.

STOP AND THINK

Which of these Theory X or Y assumptions do you think Wessel holds concerning her people? Why?

---

readiness level

The state of a person's drive or need for achievement.

The Followers' Readiness Level   **Readiness level** is the state of a person's drive and need for achievement. It results from his or her experience, education, attitudes, and willingness and ability to accept responsibility. These readiness variables should be considered only in relation to a specific task to be performed.

The readiness concept is expressed by the following formula:

$$\text{Readiness} = \text{Ability} + \text{Willingness}$$

If followers are less ready, the leader should use a different style than if followers are more ready. Unfortunately, some supervisors fail to take into consideration the readiness level of their employees.

Let's look at Jimmy Burckhartt again to see what type of followers work at his Jimmy John's franchise (doing business as Jimmy & Company).

The majority of Jimmy & Company's employees are under the age of 25. Many never worked in the restaurant business before, and even if they have, they have not worked for someone with such high expectations. Jimmy is not content with just being good; he wants to be the best restaurant—period. For individuals in their late teens or earlier twenties working part time to pay for their school and social activities, such high-performance expectations can be difficult to grasp. Therefore, Jimmy typically has a one-on-one conversation with his new hires soon after they come on board to ensure they have the right attitude and reason for working at Jimmy & Company. You see, Jimmy's philosophy is simple: What you do now, today, ultimately influences what you do in the future. He imparts to his new employees they need to have pride in what they do, perform their jobs well no matter what, and come to the store every day with a sense of urgency to create the most awesome store in the community. Over time, these actions influence the employees' sense of self-worth, which spills over into other areas of their lives and creates positive career opportunities down the road. As Jimmy states, "If people are not happy and excited about working here, why spend four to eight hours a day doing something they don't like? Those people need to find something else they enjoy doing." This straightforward approach has been effective in terms of employee self-selection decisions—those truly committed to Jimmy's vision are the ones who ultimately stay.[5]

The Situation Faced by the Supervisor   Common sense dictates the situation faced by supervisors should have a major influence on their leadership style. A platoon leader directing troops in combat, an airline pilot who suddenly has engine trouble, or a supervisor faced with an immediate safety crisis would certainly not call for a group meeting and get people involved to deal with the emergency.

The nature of the work and the types of assignments must be considered in assessing a situation. Research scientists who perform creative and complex jobs, for example, require more freedom to operate than workers who perform repetitive, assembly-line work. Finally, leaders' choice of style is influenced by how their unit progresses. For example, a football team with outstanding potential that loses the first three games would get a different leadership response from its coach than a team that won its first three games.

2. *Discuss and explain two frequently used leadership models.*

Leadership Grid

Categorizes leadership styles according to concern for people and concern for production results.

authority compliance

The leader has a high concern for production results and uses a directive approach.

country club management

High concern for people.

middle-of-the-road management

Places equal emphasis on people and production.

impoverished management

Management with little concern for people or production.

team management

High concern for both people and production.

3. *Determine which leadership style is most appropriate in different situations.*

Two Leadership Models

Of the many theories and theoretical models regarding leadership, we selected two especially applicable for supervisors. These are (1) Robert Blake and Anne Adams McCanse's well-known Leadership Grid® and (2) Paul Hersey and Kenneth Blanchard's Situational Leadership® Model. Probably more supervisors have been trained using these models than any others. More than a million people have trained in both the Situational Leadership and Leadership Grid models in 40 countries worldwide.[6] Clearly businesses see these two models as more practical than the theory-based models.

Leadership Grid   The **Leadership Grid** in Exhibit 8-2 (originally published as the Managerial Grid by Robert Blake and Jane S. Mouton) shows a leader has two concerns: production and people.[7] Concern for Results is plotted on the horizontal axis of the grid, while "Concern for People" is plotted on the vertical axis. Although the exhibit identifies seven basic leadership styles, theoretically, 81 combinations of "concerns" can be plotted by using the nine-point system in the grid.

If a supervisor is primarily concerned with production and shows little concern for people, he or she is a 9,1 leader (9 in concern for production results and 1 in concern for people). The 9,1 leader is one who structures the work, delegates as little as possible, and usually is an autocrat in getting work accomplished. This style is called **authority compliance** or *task management*.

Conversely, the supervisor who shows primary concern for people and little concern for production is a 1,9 leader. The 1,9 leader is supportive and somewhat permissive, emphasizing the need to keep employees happy and satisfied. Leaders of this type tend to avoid pressure in getting the work done. This style is called **country club management**.

The 5,5 leader uses a **middle-of-the-road management** style, placing emphasis on production and on people. Usually the unstated agreement in this style is "If you give me reasonable production, I will be reasonable in my demands on you."

The 1,1 leader reflects the poorest of all styles, called **impoverished management**. Supervisors using this type of leadership have completely abdicated the leadership role. If any significant work is done, it is due to the initiative of people working for this leader. In actuality, the leader has retired on the job!

The 9,9 leader believes the heart of directing work lies in mutual understanding and agreement about what organizational and unit objectives are and the proper means of attaining them. This type of leader has a high concern for both people and production and uses a participative approach called **team management** to get the work done.

STOP AND THINK

Which style do you think Blake and associates advocate as the style that works best?

If your answer was the 9,9 style, then you are correct. Blake and associates strongly believe that the 9,9 style is the way to manage in leadership situations. They cite the many managers and supervisors with whom they have worked, regardless of political, religious, or business practices, who concluded a 9,9 (team management) leader is using the ideal style.

EXHIBIT 8-2

The Leadership Grid Figure

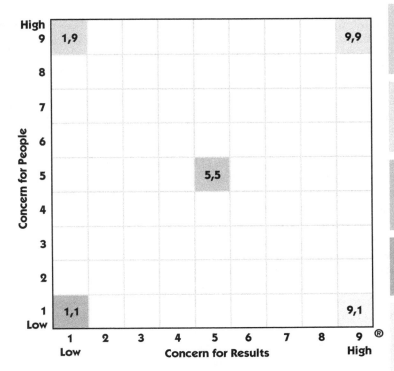

1,9 Country Club Management: Thoughtful attention to the needs of the people for satisfying relationships leads to a comfortable, friendly organization atmosphere, and work tempo.

9,9 Team Management: Work accomplishment is from committed people; interdependence through a "common stake" in organization purpose leads to relationships of trust and respect.

5,5 Middle-of-the-Road Management: Adequate organization performance is possible through balancing the necessity to get work out while maintaining morale of people at a satisfactory level.

1,1 Impoverished Management: Exertion of minimum effort to get required work done is appropriate to sustain organization membership.

9,1 Authority-Compliance Management: Efficiency in operations results from arranging conditions of work in such a way that human elements interfere to a minimum degree.

In Opportunistic Management, people adapt and shift to any grid style needed to gain the maximum advantage. Performance occurs according to a system of selfish gain. Effort is given only for an advantage for personal gain.

9+9: Paternalism/Maternalism Management: Reward and approval are bestowed to people in return for loyalty and obedience; failure to comply leads to punishment.

Source: Adapted from the Leadership Grid® Figure, Paternalism Figure, and Opportunism Figure from Leadership Dilemmas—Grid Solutions, by Robert R. Blake and Anne Adams McCanse (Formerly The Managerial Grid by Robert R. Blake and Jane S. Mouton). Houston: Gulf Publishing Company, 1991 (Grid Figure: p. 29, Paternalism Figure: p. 30, Opportunism Figure: p. 31).

**life-cycle theory
of leadership**

Leadership behaviors
should be based on
the readiness level of
employees.

task behaviors

Clarifying a job, telling
people what to do and
how and when to do
it, providing follow-up,
and taking corrective
action.

**relationship
behaviors**

Providing people with
support and asking for
their opinions.

**Situational
Leadership® Model**

Shows the relationship
between the readiness
of followers and the
leadership style.

Hersey and Blanchard's Situational Leadership   It sounds as if we have leadership licked, doesn't it? You may conclude the best approach is a high concern for both production and people. But not so fast—a number of people disagree, saying there is *no one best approach for every situation*, but only a best approach for a given situation.

One of the most popular situational approaches is called the **life-cycle theory of leadership**. It draws heavily on leadership research conducted at The Ohio State University. In these studies, leadership behaviors and strategies in a number of different organizations were examined. The researchers concluded many leadership behaviors fall into one of two areas: task behaviors or relationship behaviors. **Task behaviors** involve clarifying the job; telling people what to do, how to do it, and when to do it; providing follow-up; and taking corrective action. **Relationship behaviors** involve providing people with support, giving them positive feedback, and asking for their opinions and ideas.

These two concepts, along with the concept of the readiness level of followers, are central to understanding the Hersey-Blanchard model.[8] Recall the readiness level of followers is assessed in relation to their ability to do a *specific* job or task. It encompasses their desire for achievement, experience, education, attitudes, and willingness to accept responsibility. Now that we have a few building blocks, let's examine Hersey and Blanchard's situational leadership model, as shown in Exhibit 8-3.[9]

The Hersey-Blanchard **Situational Leadership® Model** shows the relationship between the readiness of followers and the leadership style based on task and relationship behaviors of leaders. The model consists of four labeled blocks, or quadrants, with a curved line running through each quadrant. At the bottom of the model is a scale showing various ranges of readiness: high, moderate, and low. The direction of the arrow on the readiness scale and the direction of the arrow on the task behavior axis indicate the higher the degree of readiness, the lower the degree of task behavior required.

To use this model, first identify the readiness level of the members of your work group (high, moderate, or low) on the readiness scale. Keep in mind this point represents your assessment only as to their ability to carry out a specific task or assignment. Then draw a vertical line. The point where it intersects the curved line will fall within one of the four quadrants, and the label on that quadrant gives the most effective leadership style for the particular situation.

Hersey and Blanchard use the model to explain not only leadership in dealing with adults, but also parents' leadership in raising children. Let's first illustrate the model using a family situation.

STOP AND THINK

Assume a four-year-old boy is to walk to a birthday party. Although the party is in the neighborhood, it is two blocks away and there are two busy streets to cross. Diagnose the leadership style the child's mother would use to get her son to the party.

**structuring and
telling style**

Used with individuals
or groups relatively
less ready for a given
task.

If you responded a high-task and low-relationship style is appropriate, then you are correct. The task involves some danger (crossing busy streets), and the follower is less ready. Hence, the mother should use a structured, high-task approach, accompanying the child and perhaps even holding his hand as they cross the streets.

The four quadrants in the top portion of Exhibit 8-3 can be translated into four basic leadership styles: (1) structuring and telling, (2) coaching and selling, (3) participating and supporting, and (4) delegating and empowering. The **structuring and telling style**

EXHIBIT 8-3

The Hersey-Blanchard Situational Leadership® Model

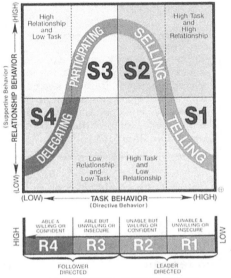

(S1: high task and low relationship) usually works best with new or less-ready employees and individuals or groups whose performance is slipping. For example, if a department's costs increased considerably beyond the standard, then a highly structured, close leadership style is called for to correct the situation. Thus, the structuring and telling style would be used with an individual or a group that is relatively low in readiness with respect to a given task.

The **coaching and selling style** (S2: high task and high relationship) is best used with individuals or groups with potential but haven't completely mastered their assignments. For example, a high school football coach with young but talented players should probably use this approach. The coach has a high concern for both task accomplishment (coaching) and convincing the players through positive reinforcement they have the ability to win (selling).

An appropriate style to use as individuals or groups mature is the **participating and supporting style** (S3: high relationship and low task). The leader should use more participative management in getting ideas and should involve the followers in setting objectives and solving problems. Think of Maslow's hierarchy of needs theory: As employees gain experience and competence, they have a need for more support for and involvement in their work.

The **delegating and empowering style** (S4: low relationship and low task) is one of the more difficult styles for a supervisor to use even when individuals or groups working under the supervisor are exceptionally ready and capable. A primary reason is supervisors are held accountable for results and therefore are reluctant to involve employees in their work. Perhaps you have heard the expression "If it ain't broke, don't fix it." This saying sums up

---

coaching and selling style

Used with individuals or groups with potential but haven't realized it fully.

participating and supporting style

Best used with ready individuals or groups.

delegating and empowering style

Used with exceptionally ready and capable individuals and groups.

why the wise supervisor leaves well enough alone as long as results are satisfactory. But what happens when conditions change?

STOP AND THINK

Suppose you are a supervisor and have a skilled, capable worker who has never caused you any difficulties. For three years, she has been a productive person in your department. Because she has proved to be a capable person, you would probably be using a delegating style in regard to her work. However, in the past two weeks, her work has steadily deteriorated. Projects are late and the work, when completed, is of poor quality. As her supervisor, what leadership style would you use in this situation?

You certainly would not continue to delegate, would you? Most supervisors would shift all the way to a coaching and selling style or even to a structuring and telling style. Depending on the problem, either style could be appropriate. This situation shows how a leader might use a different style with an individual or a group, depending on the situation.

Continuum of Leadership Behavior

The full range of leadership behaviors in terms of the relationship between a supervisor's use of authority and employees' freedom.

Tannenbaum and Schmidt's Leadership Continuum

Robert Tannenbaum and Warren Schmidt are two writers who take a situational viewpoint toward leadership.[10] Their **Continuum of Leadership Behavior**, shown in Exhibit 8-4, is especially useful when a supervisor is considering the degree to which employees should be involved in decision making. The figure is a rectangular block representing a continuum of power that is divided by a diagonal line into two distinct parts: (1) use of authority by the supervisor and (2) the area of freedom for employees. The more authority the supervisor

---

EXHIBIT 8-4
Continuum of Leadership Behavior

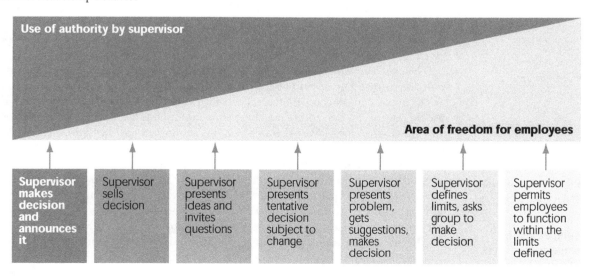

Source: Modified and reprinted by permission of *Harvard Business Review*. An exhibit from "How to Choose a Leadership Pattern" by Robert Tannenbaum and Warren H. Schmidt (May–June 1973). Copyright © 1973 by the Harvard Business School Publishing Corp. All rights reserved.

has, the less freedom there is for employees. Conversely, the more freedom employees are given, the less authority the supervisor uses. The continuum also indicates the range of available behaviors from which the supervisor can draw.

Tannenbaum and Schmidt maintain that each situation calling for a decision may require a different approach. The path the leader chooses to follow should be based on a consideration of the following three types of forces:

1. *Forces in the leader.* These include the leader's value system, confidence in employees, leadership inclinations, and feelings of security or insecurity.
2. *Forces in the employees.* These include the employees' need for independence and increased responsibility, knowledge of the problem, attitude toward and interest in tackling the problem, and expectations with respect to sharing in decision making.
3. *Forces in the situation.* These include the type of organization, the group's effectiveness, the pressure of time, and the nature of the problem itself.

These three types of forces can be compared to the three factors affecting leadership (discussed at the beginning of the chapter and shown in Exhibit 8-1). For example, a supervisor's management philosophy is greatly influenced by his or her value system.

The key point to remember is the successful supervisor is skilled in assessing the appropriate behavior to use in a given situation. Using this approach, how would you deal with the following stop and think question?

STOP AND THINK

As the result of a dramatic upward shift in sales, the XYZ firm has to rearrange vacation schedules. The previous supervisor consulted individually with employees and, when possible, gave them their first or second choice of vacation time. Because of time pressure, this approach would take too long now. Donna Douglas, the current supervisor, has confidence in her group of employees. They have a good work record. Drawing from the continuum of leadership behavior, what approach would you recommend she use in rearranging vacation schedules?

Is One Leadership Style Best?

As we indicated, research supports the thesis there is no single-best style for all situations. However, Hersey and Blanchard and others recognize, in most situations, the appropriate style is either coaching and selling or participating and supporting. We can learn much from the Blake and associates' thesis regarding the payoffs from utilizing a participative, team approach to managing.

The long-run trend in U.S. industry is for supervisory managers to use more participative styles, although they initially resist the move toward more participation.[11] An explanation for this trend is employees are becoming better educated and their lower-level needs are relatively satisfied. It is only through tapping their higher-level needs that significant motivation occurs. We believe the leadership approaches discussed next (developmental leadership, transformational leadership, adaptive leadership, and servant leadership) are the most affirming of supervisors who hold a Theory Y set of assumptions regarding people. We also believe these approaches are the most rewarding for the employees, the organization, and the supervisors in arriving at win-win outcomes. Although there is some overlap, enough differences exist among the approaches that we present them individually.

Developmental Leadership

4. Contrast heroic supervisors with developmental supervisors.

developmental leadership

An approach that helps groups evolve effectively and achieve highly supportive, open, creative, committed, high-performing membership.

heroic managers

Managers who have a great need for control or influence and who want to run things.

Earlier in the chapter we noted no single leadership approach is effective in all situations and a contingency approach is called for to achieve effective results. In many environments with educated personnel, however, a contingency diagnosis calls more and more for an approach known as *developmental leadership* as especially effective in managing groups.

Developmental leadership is an approach that helps groups evolve effectively and achieve highly supportive, open, creative, committed, high-performing membership. To understand developmental leadership better, let us first examine what David Bradford and Allen Cohen called "heroic management."

Heroic Managers

Heroic managers are those with a great need for control or influence and want to run things. If they are dynamic and capable, they may do an effective job and produce good results, particularly in the short run. However, it is critical they do not over-control and stymie the development of subordinates. Heroic managers are depicted heroically in films, especially those dealing with the Wild West. Some examples are the trail boss who gets the wagon train through to its destination and the sheriff who takes care of the bad guys. From interviews with managers providing their views of what a good leader is like, Bradford and Cohen developed the following list of characteristics of heroic managers:

1. The manager should know at all times what is going on in the department. (In westerns, when asked for information, the trail boss always seems to know what is going on.)
2. The manager should have enough technical expertise to supervise subordinates. (The really good trail boss not only can outdraw and outshoot anyone around but also can handle troublemakers quite effectively with his bare fists.)
3. The manager should be able to solve any problem that arises or at least solve it before the subordinate does. (If the trail boss cannot handle any problem, he loses face and his leadership position is undermined.)
4. The manager should be the primary (if not the only) person responsible for how the department is working. (The trail boss has total responsibility for the welfare of the group, so shared leadership is out of the question.)

As desirable as these characteristics are, if carried to extremes, they lead to over-control and lack of development of subordinates, as shown in Exhibit 8-5. Therefore, what is needed is an orientation focusing on *building heroes* rather than *being a hero.*

Developmental Managers

Building heroes is the goal of developmental leaders. Bradford and Cohen's model of the manager as a developer has three interrelated components: (1) building a shared responsibility team, (2) continuously developing individual skills, and (3) determining and building a common department vision.[12]

Building a Shared-Responsibility Team In talking about building a shared-responsibility team, we are really talking about shared leadership. Instead of using meetings primarily for reporting and providing information to the group, developmental leaders deal with real issues and actual problem solving.

EXHIBIT 8-5

The Self-Fulfilling Consequences of Using the Heroic Management Approach

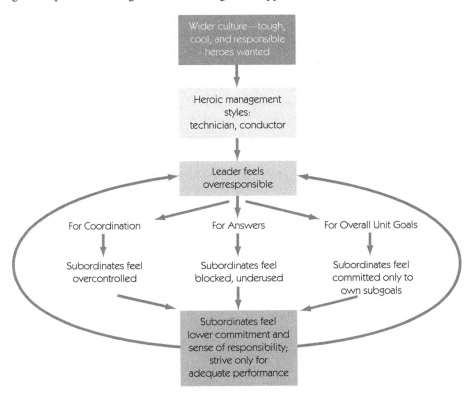

Source: Adapted from David L. Bradford and Allen R. Cohen, *Managing for Excellence.* Copyright © 1984, John Wiley & Sons, reprinted by permission of John Wiley & Sons, Inc.

STOP AND THINK

Refer to the continuum of leadership behaviors shown in Exhibit 8-4. What behaviors support building a shared-responsibility team?

Developing Individual Skills   The second component of developmental leadership, continuous development of individual skills, is closely interconnected with the first. One of the best opportunities for individual development is offered by an effective team dealing with real issues. It is no secret many effective top executives derived considerable development from serving on committees or task forces tackling tough issues. In addition, developmental leaders encourage and seek out opportunities for their people to attend various developmental courses of either a technical or a managerial nature and to increase both knowledge and skills continually.

Shaping a Common Vision   Many times, the final component, determining and building a common group vision, is the first step in a manager's movement toward developmental leadership. Bradford and Cohen refer to this as developing the work group's *overarching goal*, which is supportive of the mission and overall goals of the organization. They go on to say creating a tangible vision makes group members excited about where they are going.

When Jimmy Burckhartt decided to buy his first Jimmy John's franchise (DBA Jimmy & Company), he had a clear vision of the culture he wanted.

Jimmy created a culture centered on the following vision: Have pride in what you do, perform your job well no matter what, understand what you do today impacts your future, and come to the store every day with a sense of urgency to create an awesome store environment. But as the developmental leadership approach suggests, a common vision is only part of the equation. Fortunately for Jimmy, he is also an effective coach.

Dale Roberts began working for Jimmy as a delivery driver shortly after the store opened to have something to do while he was between jobs. The job itself was not difficult and the tips were good, so he thought it would be a good fit for a few months. Dale could not have foreseen that 19 months later, he would be the general manager! Jimmy developed Dale slowly during down periods, teaching him how to prep the store in the mornings and close in the evenings. The transition was probably easier because Dale liked the store's "be yourself" environment and has been passionate about cooking and food. Before long, Dale was promoted to PIC (person in charge), and his responsibilities gradually increased as he learned how to manage schedules, deliveries, time cards, and reports. One reason he was motivated to change from an hourly position with tips to a salaried employee working

Jack Hollingsworth/Digital Vision/Jupiter Images

In developmental leadership, the manager needs to have the ability to share a common vision or overarching goal for the group.

40 to 50 hours a week was the respect and admiration he had for both Jimmy and Sherry. As Dale states, "They're just good people that treat us with respect. If something is on my mind, I know I can go to them and we can talk about it." Dale became quite confident in performing most of his managerial tasks. The fact that he developed to a point where he can completely run the store has been a confidence builder. However, he admitted managing time and people were still challenges for him. Getting everyone to "live the vision" each day can be tricky. Jimmy continues to assist Dale in developing his people skills so even when he is in the store and a customer or employee has a question or concern, Jimmy just tells them, "Hey, I'm just the owner. Dale is the manager in charge." This approach not only forces Dale to learn through direct experience, but it is also a source of pride and motivation to know Jimmy has complete confidence in his new General Manager![13]

Transformational and Transactional Leadership

5. *Contrast transformational leadership with transactional leadership.*

Transformational leadership is one influential theory and way of looking at leadership that emerged in more recent years; it is closely related to team leadership.

John MacGregor Burns[14] and Bernard Bass[15] were the first to identify and explore the differences between transactional and transformational leadership. Both authors make the case transformational leadership is a paradigm shift to a more visionary and empowering leadership style, particularly needed in a world of rapid and turbulent change. As Burns states, "the result of transforming leadership is a relationship of mutual stimulation and elevation that converts followers into leaders and may convert leaders into moral agents."

transformational leadership

Converts followers into leaders and may convert leaders into moral agents.

transactional leadership

Leaders identify desired performance standards and recognize what types of rewards employees want from their work.

Transactional leadership is a more traditional leadership approach and similar to an exchange process. For example, a supervisor may implicitly or explicitly get this message across: "If you give me reasonable production, I will keep higher management off your back." Let us first examine transformational leadership and then transactional leadership.

Transformational Leadership

Bass and others have taken Burns' general framework and applied the concepts to the field of management. Their research resulted in identifying a number of past and current transformational leaders. A recent study found three factors that were an integral part of being a transformational leader: charismatic leadership, individualized consideration, and intellectual stimulation.

The most important factor of transformational leadership is charismatic leadership. To receive a high score on this factor, a leader needs to instill pride, respect, and esprit de corps and have a gift of focusing on what is important, as well as a true sense of mission. The second factor, individualized consideration, indicates the leader uses delegated assignments to provide learning and development and gives personal attention to individuals. The third factor, intellectual stimulation, indicates the leader has vision and presents ideas that require rethinking of past methods of operation and allows for development of new ways of thinking.

Even more recently, Rafferty and Griffin tested and found a five-factor model best represents transformational leadership: vision, inspirational communication, supportive leadership, intellectual stimulation, and personal recognition.[16]

Regardless of these different views, some common themes exist among the research findings. First, it is important for the leader to instill pride, respect, and esprit de corps as well as focus on what is important and have a true sense of mission. Second, the leader delegates, supports, and empowers followers so they may grow to reach their full potential. Third, the leader provides followers personal attention and support to nurture their development. Fourth, a leader intellectually challenges followers to change past practices and paradigms and stretch their limits to create and innovate. Lastly, the leader must meaningfully communicate with followers to ensure these four practices are successful.

STOP AND THINK

Based on the aforementioned research results, who would you consider to be a transformational leader?

Some leaders considered to be exceptionally high on the charismatic leadership factor are R. David Thomas (founder of Wendy's), John F. Kennedy, Margaret Thatcher, Dr. Martin Luther King Jr., Ronald Reagan, Oprah Winfrey, Sam Walton (founder of Walmart), Anne Mulcahy, and Jack Welch (former CEO of General Electric). Although charisma is important for effective leadership, it may be exercised to meet objectives that do not benefit society—Adolf Hitler and Saddam Hussein are cases in point.[17]

Research today reveals transformational leaders are not limited to only world-class leaders. In the chapter preview, you see many of the characteristics of this type of leader.

Transactional Leadership

Of course, not everyone can be a transformational leader; many leaders fall into the category of transactional leaders. These leaders identify desired performance standards and recognize what types of rewards employees want from their work. They then take actions that make receiving these rewards contingent on achieving performance standards. In essence, this exemplifies an exchange process, a quid pro quo or "I'll do this if you'll do that." The transactional leader operates within the existing culture and employs traditional management strategies to get the job done. Transactional leadership is based on the premise the leader can positively reward or reinforce employees for their completion of the bargain. For example, if a leader used a management-by-objectives system and was able to reward employees who met or exceeded their objectives, this approach would work quite well.

A number of effective leaders demonstrate both transformational and transactional leadership behaviors. One example is Franklin D. Roosevelt, who "illustrated a balance with respect to transformational and transactional leadership. . . . Roosevelt played the consummate transformational leader with his inspiring addresses, encouragement of intellectual solutions, and fireside chats. He also played the consummate transactional politician in the give-and-take of the balance of powers among executive, legislative, and judicial functions."[18]

Comparison of Transactional and Transformational Leadership   One who believes some people have the ability to grow and develop through levels of leadership and become transformational leaders is George McAleer, former air force pilot and now on the faculty of the National Defense University's Industrial College of the Armed Forces. McAleer agrees with Bass's thesis that transactional leadership can result in lower-order improvements, but if one wants higher-order improvements, transformational leadership is needed. This is the challenge that faces select military officers chosen to spend a year at a senior service college such as the Industrial College in Washington, D.C. This year is critical in one's military career: Out of this select group, approximately one in five becomes a general or an admiral in the next 5 to 10 years.

In McAleer's words:

"What made them successful up to this point in their careers may not necessarily be the best avenue for them to proceed over the next several years. That's the formidable task my colleagues and I have at the Industrial College. Part of the challenge is encompassed in a course entitled 'Strategic Decision Making.'"[19]

6. *Discuss and explain the benefits and side effects of adaptive leadership.*

adaptive leadership

Organizational members take a hard look at the past to identify what to hold on to, while deciding what needs to go. Employee participation in the change process is the key.

The challenge is to convince these officers the leadership style that will serve them best in the future as strategic decision makers is transformational. One way to convince them is to contrast the two leadership styles, as shown in Exhibit 8-6.

Adaptive Leadership

Ronald Heifetz's book *Leadership Without Easy Answers* was so well received he has since coauthored two follow-ups: *Leadership on the Line: Staying Alive through the Dangers of Leading*, with Marty Linsky, and *The Practice of Adaptive Leadership: Tools and Practices for Changing Your Organization and the World*, with Marty Linsky and Alexander Grashow.[20] As these books point out, not all situations require transformational change. **Adaptive leadership** is about organizational members taking a hard look at the past to

EXHIBIT 8-6
Contrasting Leadership Approaches

TRANSACTIONAL	TRANSFORMATIONAL
Characteristics	
Exchange Process	Relations Orientation
Evolutionary Ideas	Revolutionary Ideas
Within Existing Structure	Emerges in Crisis
Reactive	Proactive
Motivation	
Contingent Reward (Extrinsic)	Inspiration; Recognition (Intrinsic)
Power	
Traditional	Charismatic
Focus	
Outcomes	Vision
Leader	
Specifies Talk	Consultant, Coach, Teacher
Clarifies Roles	Emphasis on Empowering the Individual
Recognizes Needs	Gives Autonomy; Good Listener; Informal
Manages by Exception	Accessible; Model of Integrity
Employees	
Seek Security; Needs Fulfilled	Transcend Self-Interests for the Organization
Separate Organization from Individual	Do More Than They Are Expected to Do
Outcomes	
Expected Performance	Quantum Leaps in Performance

Source: George McAleer's presentation at Association for Psychological Type, Special Topic Symposium, Type and Leadership, Crystal City, VA, March 5–7, 1993.

identify what to hold on to, while deciding what needs to go. Employee participation in the change process is the key because with adaptive problems, many times the employees themselves are the source. If your people are empowered to evaluate the past and explore new ideas and ways of operating, they will be more motivated to implement the changes. "[A]daptive Leadership requires an experimental mindset approach, not an 'I've got the answer' mindset. It's not enough to have a vision for the future and identify a critical path for moving forward. Adaptive leaders have to understand today's plan is simply today's best guess. They must be able to deviate from the plan when they discover realities they hadn't anticipated."[21]

STOP AND THINK

Based on what you know about Jimmy Burckhartt, who we have followed throughout the chapter, would you consider him an adaptive leader? Why or why not?

Amanda Kohn has a unique perspective regarding Jimmy & Company because she is one of the few employees who has worked in the store since the beginning. She is a family friend of Jimmy's wife Sherry and grew up baby-sitting their children, so when she took the job, she knew what she was signing up for. Her work ethic, people skills, and effervescent personality contribute to her success, so as soon as she turned 18, Amanda was promoted to PIC (person in charge), providing additional managerial support. When asked about the store's development, Amanda replied, "It takes trial and error to get a sense of what works and what needs to change. We continuously improve." Before, Jimmy worked seven days a week and never got any time off. "It made a big difference when Jimmy and Sherry decided to promote Dale to General Manager and me to PIC," she shares. "We've created a solid team and the flow of people we have makes the store feel different." In fact, during one of the in-store interviews, a grandmother, mother, and two children came in to eat lunch and commented on how different Jimmy & Company was from other sandwich shops—upbeat, hip, friendly, alive! As Amanda notes, "Every person has the same goal/vision for the store; each day it is about being the best at what we do!" The key has been continuous learning and adaptation to find what works.[22]

STOP AND THINK

Which would be more challenging for you, changing leadership roles as owner of a construction company to a restaurant or vice versa? Why?

One important issue to be aware of regarding this topic is many times, adaptive leaders who present tough questions become marginalized within the organization because their views and opinions are not consistent with the current paradigm. Let's face it: People seek comfort in what they know—the familiar. Signals of this resistance include being let go or possibly promoted to a job with no direct impact on an organization's outcomes.[23] Consider the Historical Insight story of the fall and rise of John Lasseter.

HISTORICAL INSIGHT

Power and Politics in the Fall and Rise of John Lasseter

John Lasseter grew up in a family heavily involved in artistic expression. Lasseter was drawn to cartoons as a youngster. As a freshman in high school, he read a book titled *The Art of Animation*. The book, about the making of the Disney animated film *Sleeping Beauty*, proved to be a revelation for Lasseter. He discovered people could earn a living by developing cartoons. Lasseter started writing letters to The Walt Disney Company Studios regarding his interest in creating cartoons. Studio representatives who corresponded with Lasseter many times told him to get a great art education, after which they would teach him animation.

When Disney started a Character Animation Program at the California Institute of Arts film school, Disney Studios contacted Lasseter, and he enrolled in the program. Classes were taught by extremely talented Disney animators, who also shared stories about working with Walt Disney. During summer breaks from Cal Art classes, jobs at Disneyland further fueled Lasseter's passion for working as an animator for Disney Studios. Full of excitement, Lasseter joined the Disney animation staff in 1979 after graduation from the California Institute of Arts, but he met with disappointment. According to Lasseter, "[t]he animation studio wasn't being run by these great Disney artists like our teachers at Cal Arts, but by lesser artists and businesspeople who rose through attrition as the grand old men retired." Lasseter was told, "You put in your time for 20 years and do what you're told, and then you can be in charge." He continues, "I didn't realize it then, but I was beginning to be perceived as a loose cannon. All I was trying to do was make things great, but I was beginning to make some enemies."

In the early 1980s, Lasseter became enthralled with the potential of using computer graphics technology for animation but found little interest among Disney Studios executives for the concept. Nonetheless, a young Disney executive, Tom Willhite, eventually allowed Lasseter and a colleague to develop a 30-second test film that combined "hand-drawn, two-dimensional Disney-style character animation with three-dimensional computer-generated backgrounds." Lasseter found a story that would fit the test and could be developed into a full movie. When Lasseter presented the test clip and feature movie idea to the Disney Studios head, the only question the studio head asked concerned the cost of production. Lasseter told him the cost of production with computer animation would be about the same as a regular animated feature, and the studio head informed Lasseter, "I'm only interested in computer animation if it saves money or time."

Lasseter subsequently discovered his idea was doomed before he ever presented it to the studio head. Says Lasseter, "[w]e found out later that others poked holes in my idea before I had even pitched it. In our enthusiasm, we had gone around some of my direct superiors, and I didn't realize how much of an enemy I had made of one of them. I mean, the studio head had made up his mind before we walked in. We could have shown him anything and he would have said the same thing." Shortly after the studio head left the room, Lasseter received a call from the superior who didn't like him, informing Lasseter his employment at Disney was being terminated immediately.

Despite being fired, Lasseter did not speak negatively of the Disney organization, nor did he let others know anything other than the project he was working on ended. His personal admiration and respect for Walt Disney and animation were too great to allow him to do otherwise.

Lasseter was recruited to Lucasfilm by Ed Catmull to work on a project that "turned out to be the very first character-animation cartoon done with a computer." Not too long afterward, Steve Jobs bought the animation business from George Lucas for $10 million and Pixar Animation Studios was born. Lasseter became the chief creative genius behind Pixar's subsequent animated feature film successes like *Toy Story, Toy Story 2, A Bug's Life*, and *The Incredibles*, among others.

In 2006, Disney CEO Robert Iger and Pixar CEO Steve Jobs consummated a deal for Pixar to become a wholly owned subsidiary of Disney. Iger wanted to reinvigorate animation at Disney, and as the top creative executive at Pixar, John Lasseter was viewed as a key figure in achieving this objective. "Lasseter . . . is regarded by Hollywood executives as the modern Walt [Disney] himself [with capabilities] . . . that have made Pixar a sure thing in the high stakes animated world." Former Disney Studios head Peter Schneider says Lasseter "is a kid who has never grown up and continues to show the wonder and joy that you need in this business." Current Disney Studios chief Dick Cook says that Lasseter is like the famous professional basketball player Michael Jordan: "He makes all the players around him better."

Lasseter now oversees development of movies at both Pixar's and Disney's animation studios. Says Lasseter, "I can't tell you how thrilled I am to have all these new roles. I do what I do in life because of Walt Disney—his films and his theme park and his characters and his joy in entertaining. The emotional feeling that his creations gave me is something that I want to turn around and give to others."

Source: From "Case: Power and Politics in the Rise and Fall of John Lasseter," in Instructor's Resource CD-ROM for Debra L. Nelson and James Campbell Quick, *Organizational Behavior: Science, The Real World, and You*, 2008 ed. © 2009 South-Western, a part of Cengage Learning, Inc. Reproduced by permission. www.cengage.com/permissions.

STOP AND THINK

Steve Jobs bought the animation business from George Lucas for $10 million and Pixar Animation Studios was born. How much did Iger and Disney pay to consummate the deal with Steve Jobs to bring Lasseter back? Google "Disney buys Pixar" to find out!

Adaptive leaders can survive and provide meaningful guidance and direction within traditional command-and-control environments, but it simply requires an understanding of yourself, the situation, and the people you manage. See the end-of-chapter case about Kenny, the effective supervisor.

Servant Leadership

servant leadership

Defines success as giving and measures achievement by devotion to serving and leading. Winning becomes the creation of community through collaboration and team building.

Although the concept of **servant leadership** has been around for centuries, only recently has it been seriously taught in management and leadership courses. In fact, few supervisory books even mention the concept. Today, however, it is once again recognized as a powerful and useful concept and philosophy.

The Paradox of Servant Leadership

Bennett J. Sims, Bishop Emeritus of the Episcopal Diocese of Atlanta and president of the Institute for Servant Leadership, provides a beautiful description of the nature of this paradox:

The idea of paradox in the abstract is murky, but in a person it can shine like moonlight on tranquil water. Paradox will always need incarnation—embodiment—in order to be real. Logic falls short as a persuader.

Consider the paradox of servant leadership. A servant is one who stands below and behind, while a leader's position is above and ahead. Logically then, it is impossible to make these two positions fit a single point in space or in the make-up of one person. But paradox, like servant leadership, is not bound by logic. When paradox is understood as a formula for great truth, then the opposite of a great truth becomes another great truth. Servant and leader combine to form an ideal blend of personal attributes in toughness and tenderness.[24]

When one of the authors first read this passage by Sims, he immediately thought of an officer he served under in the army. Captain Paul J. Padgent won a battlefield commission in Korea and was the most highly decorated officer or enlisted man in the 82nd Airborne Division. He carried a pearl-handled revolver, was tough, and had exceptionally high expectations and standards for members of the infantry rifle company he commanded. His troops believed they were the best and would follow him anywhere. An example from a three-month, peacetime, simulated battle in southern Louisiana swamps and forests gives us a clue to his troops' devotion and loyalty. Most of the company commanders had small tents where officers were served individually on plates. Their troops went through a long mess line being served on their mess kits. But in our company, the officers were at the end of the line and followed the troops, and if any item was short, the officers missed it, not the troops. Incidentally, at the end of this three-month field exercise, Captain Padgent's company was singled out as the top-performing company by the umpires.[25]

The U.S. Marine Corps has a history of training its troops, officers, and noncommissioned officers by placing the well-being of the group before the individual. This notion is an important part of servant leadership and is expounded on in an excerpt from a leadership autobiography by a former student (Exhibit 8-7).

Servant leaders are often empathetic listeners who are committed to the growth of the people they lead.

EXHIBIT 8-7 A Distant Drum	Joining the United States Marine Corps at age 17 was the single most important choice I have made for my life. I graduated from boot camp, then from technical school with honors. I was meritoriously promoted and given my choice of duty stations. This was the first real accomplishment I had achieved on my own, and I knew that I didn't even really put forth much effort. It was then that I realized there was a whole world of opportunity available for me, and I was determined to go after a better way of life. I chose El Toro, California, as my duty station. I was proud to be a Marine, and I worked hard in my assigned unit. I learned innumerable lessons throughout my military service, but the main ones were ingrained during boot camp (the dreaded "Parris Island"), and I live by them still:

1. Tell the truth.
2. Do your best, no matter how trivial the task.
3. Choose the difficult right over the easy wrong.
4. Look out for the group before you look out for yourself.
5. Don't whine or make excuses.
6. Judge others by their actions, not their race, culture, religion, or sexual orientation.

I cannot think of even one important situation in life, which cannot be made better by applying these six creeds. I have tried to instill these lessons into my own child, and I am proud to say I believe he lives by them as well.

The exceptional men and women I met and worked with during my military service are still an inspiration to me. I feel a special kinship with each and every Marine I meet.

Source: Cheryl Templet, "My Leadership Autobiography," March 1, 1999. A requirement in an MBA Leadership course taught by Donald C. Mosley, Spring Semester 1999, University of South Alabama, Mobile, Alabama.

Characteristics of Servant Leadership

The person to whom we owe the greatest debt for providing us with insights into servant leadership is retired AT&T executive Robert K. Greenleaf. Prior to his retirement, he served seven years as director of management research and led an internal consulting group concerned with the values and growth of people. After his retirement, he worked as a consultant for businesses, foundations, professional societies, church organizations, and universities.[26] Greenleaf makes the important point that the servant leader wants to serve first and then lead. The servant leader focuses on meeting the needs of others and responding to problems first by listening. Greenleaf believes leaders who empathize with others provide a climate in which followers have the ability to grow and develop. Greenleaf also makes the point leaders "who empathize and who fully accept those who go with them on this basis are more likely to be trusted."[27]

Larry Spears is a scholar who studied Greenleaf's original writings for a number of years. He is also CEO of the Greenleaf Center for Servant Leadership. He has identified 10 characteristics of servant leadership, shown in Exhibit 8-8.

EXHIBIT 8-8 Ten Characteristics of Servant Leadership	1. **Listening.** Leaders have traditionally been valued for their communication and decision-making skills. Servant-leaders reinforce these important skills with a focus on listening intently and reflectively to others to identify and clarify the will of a group of people. 2. **Empathy.** Servant-leaders strive to understand and empathize with others. They accept and recognize others for their unique gifts and spirits. One assumes the good intentions of coworkers and does not reject them as people. 3. **Healing.** Learning how to help heal difficult situations is a powerful force for transforming organizations. Servant-leaders recognize they have an opportunity to help make whole those people and institutions with whom they come in contact. 4. **Persuasion.** Another characteristic of servant-leaders is a reliance on persuasion, rather than using one's positional authority, to make organizational decisions. Servant-leaders seek to convince others, rather than coerce compliance. They are effective at building consensus with groups. 5. **Awareness.** General awareness, and especially self-awareness strengthen the servant-leader. Awareness aids one in understanding issues involving ethics and values, and enables one to approach situations from a more integrated, holistic position. 6. **Foresight.** The ability to foresee the likely outcome of a given situation is a characteristic that enables the servant-leader to understand the lessons from the past, the realities of the present and likely consequences of a decision for the future. It is deeply rooted within the intuitive mind. 7. **Conceptualization.** Servant-leaders seek to nurture their abilities to dream great dreams. This means one must be able to think beyond day-to-day management realities. 8. **Commitment to the growth of people.** Servant-leaders believe people have an intrinsic value beyond their tangible contributions as workers. As such, servant-leaders are deeply committed to the personal, professional, and spiritual growth of everyone within an organization. 9. **Stewardship.** Greenleaf's view of organizations is one that CEOs, staff members, and trustees all play significant roles in holding their institutions in trust for the greater good of society. In effect, everyone has a responsibility for being a good steward within an organization. 10. **Building community.** Servant-leaders seek to build a sense of community among those within an organization. **Source:** Larry C. Spears, "Creating Caring Leadership for the 21st Century," *The Not-For-Profit CEO Monthly Letter*, 5, no. 9, (July 1998) (The Robert K. Greenleaf Center for Servant Leadership, 921 East 86th Street, Suite 2000, Indianapolis, IN 46240).

STOP AND THINK

Do you think training in servant leadership would be useful for business organizations? Why or why not?

Core Leadership Functions

7. *Discuss how to inspire self-confidence, develop people, and increase productivity.*

The best of the contemporary leadership studies and books support the value of working toward developmental, transformational, adaptive, and servant leadership. Seven leadership functions reinforcing these macro-level approaches are valuing, visioning, coaching, empowering, team building, promoting quality, and listening with empathy. The effective leader is value driven and able to implement these functions (see the following Leadership Profile). Brief descriptions of the core leadership functions are as follows:

Valuing Having a good grasp of the organization's values and being able to translate these values into practice and elevate them to higher levels.

Visioning Having a clear mental picture of a desired future for the organization or organizational unit.

Coaching Helping others develop the knowledge and skills needed for achieving the vision.

Empowering Enabling others to move toward the vision.

Team building Developing a coalition of people who will commit themselves to achieving the vision.

Promoting quality Achieving a reputation for always meeting or exceeding customer expectations.

Listening with empathy Clarifying where others are coming from and acceptance of others even with imperfections. Anyone can lead perfect people if perfect people are to be found.[28]

LEADERSHIP PROFILE

Maureen McNamara: A Profile of an Effective Leader

One who effectively demonstrates the core leadership functions is Maureen McNamara, hospital administrator extraordinaire. Being a hospital administrator is a difficult job today. The industry, in the eyes of one experienced observer, is 10 years behind other industries in employing enlightened leadership and management practices.[29] Maureen attended the Katherine Gibbs secretarial school. The skills she mastered there proved invaluable in her early career, her first job being administrative assistant with the American Mathematical Society. While there, she developed and improved processes and systems for the society. Maureen went on to earn a B.S. in business from the University of Rhode Island and an M.B.A. from Bryant College.

Maureen took a position at Brown University and worked her way through a number of positions in the medical school and at the affiliated hospital. She progressed from management assistant in the department of microbiology and molecular basic science to the dean's office in charge of faculty affairs to assistant administrator for the department of medicine. She was then promoted to associate vice president of operations for the hospital, then to senior vice president of operations, and finally to chief operating officer of the Medical College and hospital. The hospital at that time had 1,500 employees and a budget of $125 million.

Through these positions, Maureen gained insights regarding organization politics and organization inertia and noticed organizations did not leverage their resources. Each move around the medical school and hospital system gave her increased responsibility, and no matter where she was, she felt she could improve the system and bring people on board.

Her greatest opportunity and challenge came when she was made chief operating officer. She states she was fortunate to have a CEO involved in community and statewide affairs who allowed her to run the operation. Throughout her career, she confronted issues and problems and took the responsibility for initiating action to solve them.

When going into positions of greater responsibility, it is important for a leader to know his or her strengths and to be aware of areas needing help and improvement. Maureen believed her strengths and the reasons for her success were

- her ability to see the big picture, make connections, and create a vision and mobilize resources to achieve it;
- her ability to inspire others to achieve and grow to an extent they never thought possible;
- her integrity, as well as her direct, candid, straightforward manner; and
- her commitment to always challenge individuals and the organization.

The areas where she perceived she needed help and needed to improve were

- asking for help (early in her career, she was reluctant to bring others in when she needed help; later this weakness was turned into a strength when she brought in an outside facilitator in organization development [to be discussed later]); and
- listening empathetically and being overly impatient when things did not move or change as fast as she would like.

Her goal and vision were to develop a team approach in delivering health care. In the process of doing so, she wanted to shift the management system to a participative culture and eliminate the undesirable aspects of bureaucracy. Shortly after being made chief operating officer, Maureen faced a major challenge. The union tried to organize the maintenance and engineering department employees. Maureen had no anti-union feelings; rather, she felt most unions came into existence to protect employees against poor and arbitrary management practices. She wanted a chance

to talk with the 35 employees who made up the department. Prior to meeting with them, she studied the files and backgrounds of each employee. At the meeting, she played primarily an active and empathetic listening role. Based on the relationships she built and the approach she took, the union was unsuccessful in two organizing attempts.

Over time, Maureen developed a close relationship with the employees and used their input and participation in an organization development (OD) change program she initiated early in her 10-year stay in senior management. In developing a strategy for the OD change program, she worked closely with Cynthia Bielecki, an excellent and bright internal staff person in human resources. They decided to bring in an outside consultant to assist them in formulating a shared-leadership approach to improving and managing the organization. They brought in Keith Krewson, who worked in organization development all of his life and was then in his early 70s. He assisted them throughout the change effort and became a trusted mentor for Maureen.

Some of the innovative steps initiated in the change effort included changing the organization from within by giving employees ownership of the change process; communicating early the expectations and goals through oral and written communication and ongoing communication throughout the process; inviting people to apply for two teams—the clinical redesign team and the administrative redesign team; putting on a big party to launch the program and making clear the ground rules and the need to bring in the various stakeholders; going on a retreat into the mountains for team building and action planning; and making herself (Maureen) available to answer questions and having weekly sessions to communicate what was happening.

The outcome was a revitalized organization that became more efficient and effective in delivering patient health care. Leadership expert Joan Goldsmith says it is important for leaders to link commitment with action. She elaborates, "Committed action is sustained over time . . . and [is] focused on achievement. To encourage committed action, linking leaders radically expand participation and the range of options for organizational direction."[30] Goldsmith's words summarize the success of Maureen McNamara as a leader and team builder. Today, she has her own firm named Bridgework, whose slogan is "Connecting businesses and their leaders to a better future."[31]

Throughout this chapter, we emphasize the importance of values, visioning, empowering, promoting quality, listening with empathy, coaching, and team building. Note the commonality between the core functions and the contemporary approaches to leadership. Also, as we have seen throughout the chapter with Jimmy Burckhartt, leadership of this nature is not restricted to the highest levels of corporate management, but can occur at any level in any size organization.

Like many other managers, Jimmy Burckhartt strove to achieve the appropriate balance between "driving sales" (task orientation) and "managing employees" (people orientation), in his franchise. His values and vision for the store have always been the foundation for the business, but it took time to attract, train, and coach a group of individuals into a cohesive team that bought into his business philosophy. In the meantime, he worked 80-plus hours, seven days every week, for over a year and a half. The secret is to set goals each day that concern your people and your task and take it one step at a time—be patient—which is hard for achievement-oriented people! But over time, this approach enables you to shift from an 80/20 balance between sales and people to a 20/80 split.[32]

STOP AND THINK

Because most of Jimmy's experience has been in health care, construction, and restaurant management, do you think he would be successful if he chose to pursue an opportunity in another industry such as hotel management, banking, or ship building? Why or why not?

Emotional Intelligence

8. *Explain why emotional intelligence is so important for effective leadership.*

An important foundation of successful leaders is a concept called emotional intelligence. **Emotional intelligence (EI)** refers to an assortment of skills and characteristics that influence a person's ability to succeed as a leader. During the 1990s, a healthy dialogue began regarding the true essence of EI. Daniel Goleman, a leading EI researcher, stated, "I.Q. and technical skills are important, but emotional intelligence is the sine qua non of leadership." Goleman and others are proponents of what is referred to as a mixed model of EI that includes the following dimensions: self-awareness, self-regulation, motivation, empathy, and social skill. Goleman suggests EI not only pinpoints outstanding leaders, but also can be linked to strong performance.[33]

emotional intelligence (EI)

The capacity to recognize and accurately perceive one's own and others' emotions, to understand the significance of these emotions, and influence one's actions based on this analysis; an assortment of skills and characteristics that influence a person's ability to succeed as a leader.

John Mayer and Peter Salovey offer an alternative EI perspective referred to as the four-branch ability model. Their model is a direct response to mixed-model proponents, such as Goleman, who suggest EI is a "catch all" meant to include every human capacity except intelligence quotient (IQ). Mayer and Salovey believe EI is four distinct skill areas that can be developed in people to enhance their abilities to perceive, process, and manage emotions and behaviors.[34] Exhibit 8-9 provides the four dimensions associated with the four-branch ability model. We will briefly summarize each of these.

1. *Perceiving emotion.* The most basic dimension of EI involves accurately perceiving others' emotions through verbal and nonverbal forms of communication. This is the starting point from which one can process the other dimensions.
2. *Using emotions to facilitate thought.* The second dimension is the capacity of the emotions to initiate thinking. When an individual responds emotionally to something, he or she is then cognitively focused. In addition, emotions facilitate as well as hinder creativity and innovation.
3. *Understanding emotions.* "Emotions convey information: Happiness usually indicates a desire to join with other people; anger indicates a desire to attack or harm others; fear indicates a desire to escape, and so forth. Each emotion conveys its own pattern of possible messages, and actions associated with those messages."[35]
4. *Managing emotions.* The last dimension deals with managing emotions. If the information provided by the emotion is understood, then one can "regulate and manage one's own and others' emotions to promote one's own and others' personal and social goals."[36]

EXHIBIT 8-9

Mayer and Salovey's
Four-Branch Model of
Emotional Intelligence

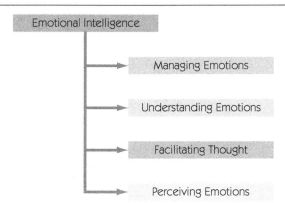

Source: John D. Mayer, "Emotional Intelligence Information: The Four Branch Model of Emotional Intelligence" (Durham, NH: University of New Hampshire, July 31, 2009), from http://www.unh.edu/emotional_intelligence/ ei%20What%20is%20EI/ei%20fourbranch.htm. Reprinted by permission of the author.

Emotional intelligence was a major factor in Abraham Lincoln's political success. Lincoln was able to work with people who opposed him. His cabinet included all three of the men he defeated for the Republican nomination.

STOP AND THINK

Can you identify three to five emotionally intelligent leaders based on the above four dimensions? Using a 1 to 10 scale, where 1 = low emotional intelligence and 10 = high emotional intelligence, how emotionally intelligent are you? Why did you give yourself this rating? Assuming you want to and have room to, in what ways can you enhance your EI?

EI is having a large impact in assessing and evaluating leadership and leaders by researchers, historians, and practicing managers. Take a look at how Roadway Express uses EI to influence effective outcomes.

The Influence of Emotional Intelligence at Roadway Express—A Trucking Company

Current researchers and consultants are publishing important work showing how to change the culture using EI. Ellen Van Oosten of Case Western Reserve and Richard Boyatzis, an early collaborator with Daniel Goleman, give us the story of Roadway Express:

> *Frank Sims was standing on Roadway Express's shipping dock, watching one of the company's trucks drive away with goods for Specialty Glassware (a pseudonym), one of Roadway's large customers. Frank was worried. The damage problems had been mounting and he was worried about how this might be affecting Roadway's customers. As he walked to his office, Frank began to recall a workshop on emotional intelligence (EI) he had attended recently. Simply recalling the workshop immediately put Frank in a better state of mind: Instead of worrying about the damage and an angry customer, he started to ask himself how he could use what he learned in the workshop to do something constructive and important. As he watched another truck being loaded, an idea began to take shape. What, he wondered, if Roadway's dock-workers and drivers understood how important loading the trucks was for their company? Immediately, he started thinking about how he could engage people in solving the customer's problems.*
>
> *The dock crew was surprised that the customer's top management would put so much effort into helping them understand the glassware business. He felt good knowing how their efforts fit into the big picture, how important the glassware products were, and how well Specialty Glassware served its own customers' needs. It made them want to be more careful and find ways to help Specialty Glassware succeed. Later on, workers would describe these meetings to new hires as an example of why Roadway was a great place to work.*
>
> *Leaders like Frank Sims are among the many who can raise the human spirit and make their organizations better. They do so by using their emotional intelligence to create an atmosphere in which people want to do and be their best . . . we describe how emotionally intelligent leaders ignite organizations and people to perform better. The article also provides the not insignificant hope that, though EI-based leadership may be rare, it can be developed.[37]*

Roadway is a trucking company with more than 20,000 employees and 379 terminals in the United States and Canada. It had a traditional structure that was hierarchical and primarily command and control in the competitive trucking industry. Inspired by Frank Sims's experience, higher management began to look for ways to improve its financial performance, developing a partnership with Case Western Reserve University and designing a tailored program. The leadership program focuses on helping supervisors identify areas for behavioral change and gives them opportunities to apply new habits on the job.[38]

The culture has changed dramatically, right down to the drivers and mechanics. An example cited in the article noted how a mechanic and driver teamed up to save Roadway $130,000 on one route. Applied to 379 terminals and many routes, it does not take long to see the impact of this one change.

In conclusion, Roadway feels like a new company in an old business. Its people are excited about being leaders and expanded the ways they can make a personal impact. Inspiration and energy have become contagious. A new culture emerged, one in which people are motivated and innovative. The new Roadway surpasses many of its competitors in revenue and net profit growth through savvy acquisitions and cost savings during a period that has not been kind to the industry. Roadway's experience is a powerful example of how EI ignites excitement and inspires better performances from everyone in an organization.[39]

Chapter Review

1. *Describe factors that affect the leadership style used.*

Leading is a process of influencing individual and group activities toward goal setting and goal achievement. How well this process is carried out has a major impact on both performance and morale.

Three interrelated variables have an impact on the choice of leadership style. These are (1) the supervisor's management philosophy, (2) the followers' readiness level, and (3) the situation faced by the supervisor. The followers' readiness level must be evaluated only with regard to carrying out a specific task or assignment.

2. *Discuss and explain two frequently used leadership models.*

Two leadership models widely used in leadership training programs are Blake and associates' Leadership Grid® and Hersey and Blanchard's Situational Leadership® Model. The Leadership Grid® plots five basic leadership styles. The one Blake and associates recommend as the ideal leadership style is the team management style.

3. *Determine which leadership style is most appropriate in different situations.*

Hersey and Blanchard highlight four basic leadership styles: structuring and telling, coaching and selling, participating and supporting, and delegating. They make a strong case that the ideal style to use depends on the maturity level of employees and the situation faced by the supervisor.

Research tends to support the Hersey and Blanchard position that there is no one best style for all situations. However, with the increasing readiness and education of employees today, the trend in U.S. industry is toward using both the coaching and selling style and the participating and supporting style in influencing individual employees and groups.

Tannenbaum and Schmidt maintain each situation calling for a decision may require choosing a solution that balances the three forces found in the leader, the employees, and the situation.

4. *Contrast heroic supervisors with developmental supervisors.*
Heroic supervision often leads to over-control and lack of group development. By contrast, developmental supervision involves the group by using the three interrelated components of (1) building a shared-responsibility team, (2) continuously developing individual skills, and (3) determining a department vision in the form of an overarching goal.

5. *Contrast transformational leadership with transactional leadership.*
While research supports the thesis no one leadership style is best for all situations, transformational and transactional leadership styles emerged as two influential theories. Three important factors of transformational leadership are charismatic leadership (instilling pride, respect, and esprit de corps), individualized consideration (delegating assignments and giving personal attention), and intellectual stimulation (requiring rethinking of past methods and developing new solutions).

Transactional leadership is a more traditional approach. The transactional leader operates within the existing culture, positively rewarding and reinforcing employees for jobs well done.

6. *Discuss and explain the benefits and side effects of adaptive leadership.*
Adaptive leadership is about organizational members taking a hard look at the past to identify what to hold on to, while deciding what needs to go. Employee participation in the change process is key because with adaptive problems, many times the employees themselves are the source. However, adaptive leaders are often marginalized because their views and opinions challenge the status quo.

7. *Discuss how to inspire self-confidence, develop people, and increase productivity.*
No one single leadership style or model provides a magic formula for inspiring self-confidence, developing people, and increasing productivity. However, by being familiar with all styles, using good common sense, and developing a contingency/situational leadership approach, one can become an effective leader who realizes the preceding objectives. Servant leadership is particularly valuable in inspiring self-confidence, tapping higher-level needs, and developing people.

8. *Explain why emotional intelligence is so important for effective leadership.*
Research shows emotional intelligence is a foundation for successful performance as a leader. There is clearly an assortment of skills and characteristics that influence a person's ability to succeed over the long term. These skills were shown in Exhibit 8-9 and demonstrated in the leaders profiled in this chapter.

Key Terms

leadership, p. 228
Theory X, p. 230
Theory Y, p. 230
readiness level, p. 231
Leadership Grid, p. 232
authority compliance, p. 232
country club management, p. 232
middle-of-the-road management,
    p. 232
impoverished management,
    p. 232

team management, p. 232
life-cycle theory of leadership,
    p. 234
task behaviors, p. 234
relationship behaviors, p. 234
Situational Leadership® Model,
    p. 234
structuring and telling style, p. 234
coaching and selling style, p. 235
participating and supporting style,
    p. 235

delegating and empowering style,
    p. 235
Continuum of Leadership
    Behavior, p. 236
developmental leadership, p. 238
heroic managers, p. 238
transformational leadership, p. 241
transactional leadership, p. 241
adaptive leadership, p. 243
servant leadership, p. 246
emotional intelligence (EI), p. 251

Discussion Questions

1. What is meant by leadership?
2. Briefly discuss the major factors that may influence the choice of an individual's leadership style. Correlate these factors with different leadership styles.
3. Discuss how a supervisor would determine the readiness level of an employee.
4. What leadership actions fall under the category of task behaviors, and what actions fall under the category of relationship behaviors?
5. Do you agree or disagree with Blake and associates there is one best leadership style? Support your position.
6. Can you identify any transformational leaders from your own experience or reading? Please list the reasons why you placed them in the category of transformational leader. If you cannot identify someone, do you agree with the leaders identified in this chapter—R. David Thomas (founder of Wendy's), John F. Kennedy, Margaret Thatcher, Dr. Martin Luther King Jr., Ronald Reagan, Oprah Winfrey, Sam Walton (founder of Walmart), Anne Mulcahy, and Jack Welch (former CEO of General Electric)? Why or why not?

7. Can you identify any adaptive leaders based on your experiences or other readings? Under what circumstances will an adaptive leader be most effective? Why?
8. What traits or characteristics regarding servant leadership appeal to you the most?
9. Of the various leadership approaches discussed in the chapter, which one would you most prefer your boss to use in working with you and your group? Explain your reasons.
10. How does transactional leadership differ from the telling and structuring style of Hersey and Blanchard?
11. What are the components of emotional intelligence, and why is emotional intelligence important for effective leadership?
12. Can emotional intelligence be taught to aspiring leaders and integrated into their philosophy and approach? Why or why not?
13. Given what you have learned about Jimmy & Company, how would you describe Jimmy's solution to his situation? Was there a silver bullet?

Skill Builder 8.1

Information

Theory X and Theory Y Attitudes
For each pair of statements, distribute 5 points based on how characteristic each statement is of your attitude or belief system. If the first statement totally reflects your attitude and the second does not, give 5 points to the first and 0 to the second. If the opposite is true, use 0 and 5. If the statement usually reflects your attitude, then the distribution can be 4 and 1, or 1 and 4. If both statements reflect your attitude, the distribution should be 3 and 2, or 2 and 3. Again, the combined score for each pair of statements must equal 5.

Here are the scoring distributions for each pair of statements:

0–5 or 5–0   One of the statements is totally like you, the other is not like you at all.
1–4 or 4–1   One statement is usually like you, the other is not.
2–3 or 3–2   Both statements are like you, although one is slightly more like you.

1. ____   People enjoy working.
____   People do not like to work.
2. ____   Employees don't have to be closely supervised to do their job well.
____   Employees will not do a good job unless you closely supervise them.
3. ____   Employees will do a task well for you if you ask them to.
____   If you want something done right, you need to do it yourself.
4. ____   Employees want to be involved in making decisions.
____   Employees want the managers to make the decisions.
5. ____   Employees will do their best work if you allow them to do the job their own way.
____   Employees will do their best work if they are taught how to do it the one best way.
6. ____   Managers should let employees have full access to information that is not confidential.
____   Managers should give employees only the information they need to know to do their job.
7. ____   If the manager is not around, the employees will work just as hard.
____   If the manager is not around, the employees will take it easier than when being watched.
8. ____   Managers should share the management responsibilities with group members.
____   Managers should perform the management functions for the group.

To determine your attitude or belief system about people at work, add up the numbers (0–5) for the first statement in each pair; don't bother adding the numbers for the second statements. The total should be between 0 and 40. Place your score on the continuum below.

Theory X 0—5—10—15—20—25—30—35—40 Theory Y

Generally, the higher your score, the greater your Theory Y beliefs, and the lower the score, the greater your Theory X beliefs. Leaders with Theory Y beliefs find it easier to implement participative and empowerment strategies.

Source: From Robert N. Lussier and Christopher F. Achua, *Leadership: Theory, Application, and Skill Development*, 2nd ed. © 2004 South-Western, a part of Cengage Learning, Inc. Reproduced by permission. www.cengage.com/permissions.

Skill Builder 8.2

Information

Diagnosing and Selecting the Appropriate Leadership Style
In each of the following situations, choose the appropriate leadership style. Afterward, your instructor will give you the best and worst answer for each situation.

1. The interdepartmental task force you manage has been working hard to complete its division-wide report. One of your task force members has been late for the last five meetings. He has offered no excuses or apologies. Furthermore, he is far

(Continued)

Systems

behind in completing the cost figures for his department. It is imperative he present these figures to the task force within the next three days.

a. Tell him exactly what you expect, and closely supervise his work on this report.

b. Discuss with him why he has been late and support his efforts to complete the task.

c. Emphasize when the cost figures are due and support his efforts.

d. Assume he will be prepared to present the cost figures to the task force.

2. In the past, you had a great deal of trouble with one of the people you supervise. She has been lackadaisical, and only your constant prodding brought about task completion. However, you recently noticed a change. Her performance improved, and you had to remind her of meeting deadlines less and less. She even initiated several suggestions for improving her performance.

a. Continue to direct and closely supervise her efforts.

b. Continue to supervise her work, but listen to her suggestions and implement those that seem reasonable.

c. Implement her suggestions and support her ideas.

d. Let her take responsibility for her work.

3. Because of budget restrictions imposed on your department, it is necessary to consolidate. You asked a highly experienced member of your department to take charge of the consolidation. This person worked in all areas of your department. In the past, she has usually been eager to help. Although you believe she has the ability to perform this assignment, she seems indifferent to the importance of the task.

a. Take charge of the consolidation yourself, but make sure you hear her suggestions.

b. Assign the project to her, and let her determine how to accomplish it.

c. Discuss the situation with her. Encourage her to accept the assignment in view of her skills and experience.

d. Take charge of the consolidation and indicate to her precisely what to do. Supervise her work closely.

4. Your staff members asked you to consider a change in the work schedule. In the past, you encouraged and supported their suggestions. In this case, your staff members are well aware of the need for change and are ready to suggest and try an alternative schedule. Members are competent and work well together as a group.

a. Allow staff involvement in developing the new schedule, and support the suggestions of group members.

b. Design and implement the new schedule yourself, but incorporate staff recommendations.

c. Allow the staff to formulate and implement the new schedule on their own.

d. Design the new schedule yourself, and closely direct its implementation.

Source: W. Alan Randolph, *Understanding and Managing Organizational Behavior* (Homewood, IL: Richard D. Irwin, 1985), pp. 255–257. A complete 20-item Leader Behavior Analysis II questionnaire is available from the Ken Blanchard Companies at 1-800-728-6000.

Skill Builder 8.3

Information

Leadership Characteristics and Skill Assessment

This survey is designed to provide feedback and self-assessment regarding your servant leadership characteristics and your emotional intelligence at work. Read each item listed and decide to what extent you exhibit each characteristic using the following five-point scale:

| 1—very weak | 2—fair | 3—average | 4—very good | 5—excellent |

_____ 1. At work I strive to build community within my group.

_____ 2. I do a good job in understanding the personalities of other people, and usually understand where they are coming from in discussions and problem solving.

_____ 3. I accept the good intentions of others and recognize their unique gifts.

_____ 4. In working with other people, I am trustworthy and have integrity.

_____ 5. In general, I place the interests of my group and customers ahead of my own self-interest unless there is an ethical conflict.

_____ 6. I am confident in the work I am doing and have a self-deprecating sense of humor.

_____ 7. I try to listen intently and reflectively to determine where a person is coming from and/or the will of the group.

_____ 8. I tend to pursue goals with optimism, energy, and persistence.

_____ 9. I am committed to the growth and development of people.

_____ 10. I have developed the skills and feel confident in building and leading teams.

_____ 11. I rely on persuasion and discussion rather than coercion in team building.

_____ 12. I am committed and dedicated to providing service to clients and customers.

Instructions: Add your individual scores and divide by 12 to obtain your average.

Scoring scale interpretation

4.5–5.0	A	Excellent
4.0–4.4	B	Moderately high
3.5–3.9	C	Average
3.0–3.4	D	Below average
2.9	E	Very weak

It would be valuable to have members of your group evaluate you and to compare your self-evaluation with the evaluation from your group.

CASE 8-1

THE NEW LUMBER YARD EMPLOYEE:

Terance graduated from high school and his plan was to work and save enough money to start college in a couple of years. His high school football coach helped him land a job at the local lumber company. He started in the lumber and sheetrock sheds and was progressing nicely but was soon moved to the plywood and siding shed due to personnel shortages. Terance was a hard worker, picking up things quickly. His primary responsibilities included working with the other shed employees to bundle ticket orders for truck deliveries as well as assisting walk-in customers with their individual orders. The

(Continued)

work was honest and there was a sense of camaraderie among the guys such that they had each other's backs and had fun joking around, but when it was time to get to work, everyone pitched in to get it done. Terance learned how to handle customers, bundle deliveries, and operate the equipment, such as the forklifts.

Cliff was Terance's foreman and he noticed the young man had potential when he was hired; he just lacked experience. So, Cliff brought him along slowly, at first helping him learn the different products and their uses and then putting his limited knowledge to use pulling together and bundling orders several times each day for truck deliveries. As Terance gained product knowledge, he was given more responsibility for truck orders and additional interaction time with walk-in customers.

Cliff believed Terance was really getting the hang of it. He noticed of all the employees, Terance received the most positive customer comments.

Terance felt more confident in his job and showed a willingness to continue to learn. Because Terance's knowledge and skills were quickly improving, Cliff believed it was time for him to take the next step. By far the most difficult skill to learn was how to handle the plywood and siding using the forklift without damaging the product. Cliff taught him how to use the lift to pull and load small orders. In order to prepare a large order, Terance would have to deal with several challenges: (1) Expertly maneuver the forks between the pieces of plywood so as not to crimp or splinter the sides; (2) effectively balance various siding (some slippery and flexible like lap siding as well as firmer Hardie board siding, etc.) on the forks when moving around the yard; (3) properly lift, balance, and load the large trucks while also knowing which products to place where for optimum hauling; and (4) efficiently manage time and personnel to move orders quickly.

Cliff began teaching Terance the skills necessary to become an effective forklift driver during slow periods on the job. Terance's willingness and smarts enabled him to progress nicely. Cliff felt like he advanced beyond the skills of a novice so he could be counted on to pull and load small to medium jobs, but he was not ready to proceed without supervision on the large jobs just yet. Cliff let Terance manage large loads under his watchful eye and believed after another month or so he could handle most types of jobs on his own.

One late Friday afternoon just before the yard was closing, a "rush" ticket was sent over for a large truck delivery that had to go out immediately so it would be on the job first thing in the morning. The yard

superintendent sent the order to the yard supervisor to be filled, but he was already in the middle of another large order for an important customer. The yard supervisor was concerned because they were shorthanded since Cliff left to go to the doctor at 3:00 P.M. That left three available employees in the shed: Calvin, Kenny, and Terance. Calvin was blind in his right eye and recently injured his leg so he wasn't the best person to put on the lift. Calvin would need to assist the walk-ins until closing time. That left the two new hires and Terance had received the most training from Cliff on operating the lift so it was decided Terance would drive the lift and Kenny would assist him.

The order was coming along fine. Terance made few mistakes, and when he got in a little trouble, Kenny was there to assist, demonstrating good teamwork. So far, they had loaded the lower level of the truck bed and now it was time to load the top. This was going to be the hardest part of the order because several bundles of lap siding had to be placed on the top because they would be crushed on the bottom. Terance was a little anxious because he had less training with the lap siding and this product tended to be harder to handle, but he was determined to give it his best. Kenny and Terance loaded all the siding for the job on the lift and proceeded toward the open yard to load the truck. Terance pulled the lift up to the right side of the truck as he and Kenny discussed the best location to place the siding. They decided Terance would lift the siding all the way up and lean it forward so it rested on the top of the plywood and lumber bundles. Kenny would then maneuver each siding bundle separately into its proper position. Afterward, they would be ready to tie the load down for delivery. Sounded like a good plan.

The driver was becoming impatient and urging Terance to hurry. He had to get to the job site before dusk and had plans for later that evening. Time was of the essence, so Terance began inching the lift upward and slightly forward; Kenny waited. As the lift reached its maximum height, Terance could feel "it" before Kenny saw "it"—the siding began sliding, coming off the lift and crashing to the ground. The driver started cussing at Terance, "You idiot, I'll have to make another trip in the morning just because of your dumb***!" He angrily jumped in the cab, gunned the engine, and headed out of the yard. As the driver left the gate, the yard supervisor headed around the corner and saw thousands of dollars of lap siding busted in the middle of the yard. He told Terance, "This isn't good. That load is for one of our best and biggest customers. Son, the best thing for you to do is go ahead and clock out and when your

(Continued)

foreman is back in the morning, we'll discuss how to handle this situation."

Terance felt sick to his stomach. He didn't know how Cliff was going to react. Terance knew he screwed up, but he tried his best; he didn't mean to mess up. The worst thing about it was he knew he let Cliff down.

CASE QUESTIONS

1. How would you describe Cliff's approach to developing Terance using Hersey and Blanchard's Situational Theory? What styles were evident in the case and what job readiness levels did Terance exhibit? Do you think Cliff did a good job matching the right leadership style(s) with Terance's job maturity level(s)? Discuss.

2. Using Hersey and Blanchard's Situational Theory, what type of leadership style did the yard supervisor use with Terance? What style should he have used?

3. Put yourself in Cliff's shoes; how do you handle the situation with Terance tomorrow morning? What approach would you take? Why?

CASE 8-2

KENNY: AN EFFECTIVE SUPERVISOR

The most effective supervisor encountered by one of the authors of this textbook was Kenny, and he was maintenance supervisor in a chemical plant of an international corporation.* The author was called in as a consultant because the plant was suffering from the results of the ineffective, autocratic leadership of a former plant manager. Such leadership at the top adversely affected all levels, resulting in low morale and losses from plant operations. In gathering data about the plant through interviews, questionnaires, and observations, the consultant discovered one maintenance crew, unlike the rest of the departments in the plant, had very high morale and productivity. Kenny was its supervisor.

In the interview with Kenny, the consultant discovered Kenny was a young man in his early thirties who had a two-year associate's degree from a community college. The consultant was impressed with his positive attitude, especially in view of the overall low plant morale and productivity. Kenny said the plant was one of the finest places he'd ever worked and the maintenance people had more know-how than any other group with which he had been associated. Kenny's perception of his crew was they did twice as much work as other crews, everyone worked together, and participative management did work with them.

The consultant was curious about why pressure and criticism from the old, autocratic manager seemed not to have had any effect on Kenny's crew. The crew gave the consultant the answer. They explained Kenny had the ability to act as a buffer between upper management and the crew. He would get higher management's primary objectives and points across without upsetting his people. As one crew member described it:

> The maintenance supervisors will come back from a "donkey barbecue" session with higher management where they are raising hell about shoddy work, taking too long at coffee breaks, etc. Other supervisors are shook up for a week and give their staff hell. But Kenny is cool, calm, and collected. He will call us together and report that nine items were discussed at the meeting, including shoddy work, but that doesn't apply to our crew. Then he will cover the two or three items that are relevant to our getting the job done.

Unfortunately, Kenny did have a real concern at the time of the consultant's interview. He was being transferred from the highest-producing crew to the lowest-producing one. In fact, the latter was known as the "Hell's Angels" crew. The crew members were a renegade group who constantly fought with production people as well as with one another. The previous supervisor had been terminated because he could not cope with them.

After Kenny was assigned to the new crew, he had to make a decision on the leadership strategies he would use in dealing with them. His initial diagnosis was the crew had the ability to do the work but lacked the willingness because of a poor attitude.

* The company would not permit use of its name.

(Continued)

Through discussion with members of the "Hell's Angels" crew, the consultant learned that on the first day on the job, Kenny called a meeting, shut the door, and conducted a "bull session" that lasted over two hours. Among other things, he told them about his philosophy and the way he liked to operate. He especially stressed he was going to be fair and treat everyone equally. The crew members were allowed to gripe and complain as long as they talked about matters in the plant, while Kenny played a listening role without arguing with them. In the course of the session, Kenny expressed his expectations of the crew. They, in turn, told him they would do it his way for two weeks to see if he "practiced what he preached."

As you may have surmised by now, Kenny's leadership made the difference. Before the year was out, his new crew was the most productive in the plant. Clues to his success may be found in the following comments made about him by his old crew, his new crew (the former "Hell's Angels" group), the plant's production manager, and Kenny's boss, the plant's maintenance manager.** It should be noted that both the production manager and the maintenance manager are relatively new to their positions and are not part of the former "autocratic management system." As you read these comments, review what you have learned in the preceding chapters and summarize the principles, points, and concepts from the text that Kenny puts into practice as a leader.

MAINTENANCE MANAGER, KENNY'S BOSS

- He's very knowledgeable in the maintenance area.
- He has considerable self-confidence.
- He interacts with people in the plant more than other supervisors do and works well with people from other departments.
- He has the ability to motivate his crew and gets along well with them.
- He functions well as a leader in one-on-one situations and in conducting crew meetings. For example, in both cases he lets people know how they stand and provides them with feedback, and together they discuss ways of improving performance.

** Except for minor editing, the comments are presented as they were made to Donald Mosley.

- He is better organized than most supervisors, and there is less confusion in his department than elsewhere in the company.

PRODUCTION MANAGER

- He doesn't give the production people any hassle. He doesn't ask a lot of questions about why production wants it done. Instead, he tells the production people what needs to be done and why.
- He's a team player, and he wants to get the job done.
- He's good with people—a great leader—and his crew work well together.
- He's conscientious—he does his job, does it right, and wants others to do the same.
- He goes out into the plant with his people, and he's there with them when they need help and advice.
- His crew doesn't give planners and coordinators a lot of static about what they put into a memo.

KENNY'S OLD CREW

- He's fair.
- He has a good attitude and a positive outlook.
- He's concerned about and looks out for the welfare of his people.
- He keeps crew problems within the crew and doesn't run to upper management with every little detail.
- He has a broad-based knowledge of our work; people feel confident about his decisions.
- He's a good intermediary between upper management and the crew.
- He gets points across without getting the crew upset.
- When things are tight, he doesn't mind helping his men with the actual work.
- He has a level personality—he doesn't show much emotion.
- He's very supportive of his crew.

KENNY'S NEW CREW (THE FORMER "HELL'S ANGELS")

- He treats us fairly and equally.
- He takes up for the crew and his men.
- He doesn't threaten you and doesn't come back after a bad job and nitpick and tell you what you

(Continued)

did wrong. He takes a positive approach to solving problems.

- He can be trusted.
- He helps you with your personal problems.
- He's competent at what he does and relates the competency to us.
- He places his employees really well. We're not all like oranges—some are like apples—but he places us where we can do our best.
- He lets us work at our own pace—actually makes us want to work harder.
- He never appears to get angry; he's always the same—cool, calm, and collected.
- He's helpful on the job. He's there, but he's not there—doesn't hang over you, telling you what to do and how to do it. Instead, he wants results but lets us get them our own way.

- He seems to enjoy work and being around us.
- He listens to anything we have to say.

CASE QUESTIONS

1. How do you explain Kenny's acceptance by so many other people and the respect they have for him?

2. Can all supervisors operate the way Kenny does and be effective? Explain your answer.

3. Given Kenny's effectiveness in his present job, would you recommend promoting him into high levels of management? Explain.

4. Review the characteristics of transformational leadership (Exhibit 8-6), adaptive leadership, and servant leadership (Exhibit 8-9). Which characteristics apply to Kenny?

Notes

1. WayUp, https://www.wayup.com/; Natalie Sportelli, "How a 25-Year-Old CEO Leads a Workplace Full of 20-Somethings," *Forbes*, 2016, https://www.forbes.com/sites/nataliesportelli/2016/05/18/how-a-25-year-old-ceo-leads-a-workplace-full-of-20-somethings/#4593ced06c10; Valentina Zarya, "This Startup Wants to Be the Netflix for Jobs," *Fortune*, March 23, 2017, http://fortune.com/2017/03/23/female-founder-machine-learning/.

2. Interview with Jimmy Burckhartt by Don C. Mosley Jr., July 2009.

3. Douglas McGregor, *The Human Side of Enterprise* (New York: McGraw-Hill Book Co., 1960), pp. 33–42.

4. Notes from Workshop on Process Consultation conducted by Edgar Schein, Albert Einstein Institute, Cape Cod, August 1991.

5. Interview with Jimmy Burckhartt by Don C. Mosley Jr., July 2009.

6. Interview with Dr. Paul Hersey, Trainer's Bookshelf (San Diego, CA: Learning Resources Corporation, 1982).

7. Robert R. Blake and Jane S. Mouton, *The Managerial Grid III: The Key to Leadership Excellence* (Houston, TX: Gulf Publishing, p. 1985).

8. Paul Hersey and Kenneth H. Blanchard, *Management of Organizational Behavior: Utilizing Human Resources*, 3rd ed. (Englewood Cliffs, NJ: Prentice-Hall, 1977), pp. 161–162.

9. Hersey and Blanchard acknowledge that they were strongly influenced by William J. Reddins, "3-D Management Style Theory," found in William J. Reddins, *Management Effectiveness* (New York: McGraw-Hill, 1970). We use Hersey and Blanchard's model because it is better known.

10. Robert Tannenbaum and Warren Schmidt, "How to Choose a Leadership Pattern," *Harvard Business Review* 51 (May–June 1973), pp. 162–180.

11. Leonard M. Apcar, "Middle Managers and Supervisors Resist Moves to More Participatory Management," *The Wall Street Journal*, September 16, 1985, p. 25.

12. David L. Bradford and Allen R. Cohen, *Managing for Excellence* (New York: John Wiley & Sons, 1984), pp. 71–98.

13. Interviews with Dale Roberts and Jimmy Burckhartt by Don C. Mosley Jr., July 2009.

14. John MacGregor Burns, *Leadership* (New York: Harper and Row, 1978).

15. Bernard Bass, *Leadership and Performance beyond Expectations* (New York: The Free Press, 1985).

16. A. E. Rafferty and M. A. Griffin, "Dimensions of Transformational Leadership: Conceptual and Empirical Extensions," *The Leadership Quarterly* 15, no. 3 (2004), pp. 329–354.

17. B. M. Bass, B. J. Avolio, and L. Goodheim, "Bibliography and the Assessment of Transformational Leadership at the World Class Level," *Journal of Management* 13 (Spring 1987), p. 7.

18. Ibid., p. 16.

19. George R. McAleer, "Leadership in the Military Environment," Association for Psychological Type, Special Topic Symposium, Type and Leadership, Crystal City, VA, March 5–7, 1993.

20. Ronald A. Heifetz, *Leadership Without Easy Answers* (Cambridge, MA: Belknap Press of Harvard University Press, 1994); Martin Linsky and Ronald A. Heifetz, *Leadership on the Line: Staying Alive through the Dangers of Leading* (Cambridge, MA: Belknap Press of Harvard University Press, 2002); Ronald A. Heifetz, Martin Linsky, and Alexander Grashow, *The Practice of Adaptive Leadership: Tools and Practices for Changing Your Organization and the World* (Cambridge, MA: Belknap Press of Harvard University Press, 2009).

21. Loren Gary, "Thought Leadership; Ronald Heifetz—The Challenge of Adaptive Leadership," *New Zealand Management* 52, no. 7 (August 1, 2005), pp. 46–48, http://findarticles.com/p/articles/mi_qn5305/is_20050801/ai_n24914910/?tag=content;col1 (retrieved July 25, 2009).

22. Interview with Amanda Kohn by Don C. Mosley Jr., July 2009.

23. Gary, "Thought Leadership; Ronald Heifetz."

24. Bennett J. Sims, *Servanthood—Leadership for the Third Millennium* (Boston: Cowley Publications, 1997).

25. Operation Sagebrush, Fall 1955.

26. Robert K. Greenleaf, *Servant Leadership* (Mahwah, NJ: Paulist Press, 1991), p. 3.

27. Ibid., p. 21.

28. William D. Hitt, "The Model Leader: A Fully Functioning Person," *Leadership and Organization Development Journal* 14, no. 7 (December 1993), p. 10.

29. Interview with Bill Donaldson, hospital middle-level manager, by Donald C. Mosley Sr., Cape Cod Institute's Leadership Course, July 1–4, 2003.

30. Kenneth Cloke and Joan Goldsmith, *The End of Management and the Rise of Organizational Democracy* (San Francisco: Jossey-Bass/John Wiley & Sons, 2002), p. 179; Interview with Maureen McNamara by Donald C. Mosley Sr., Cape Cod Institute's Leadership Course, July 1–4, 2003.

31. Interview with Maureen McNamara by Donald C. Mosley Sr., Cape Cod Institute's Leadership Course, July 1–4, 2003.

32. Interviews with Dale Roberts, Amanda Kohn, and Jimmy Burckhartt by Don C. Mosley Jr., July 2009.

33. Daniel Goleman, "What Makes a Leader?," *Harvard Business Review*, November–December 1998, pp. 93–94.

34. J. D. Mayer and P. Salovey, "What Is Emotional Intelligence?," in *Emotional Development and Emotional Intelligence: Implications for Educators*, ed. P. Salovey and D. Sluyter (New York: Basic Books, 1997), pp. 3–31.

35. John D. Mayer, "Emotional Intelligence Information: The Four Branch Model of Emotional Intelligence" (Durham, NH: University of New Hampshire, July 31, 2009), http://www.unh.edu/emotional_intelligence/ei%20What%20is%20EI/ei%20fourbranch.htm (Retrieved July 31, 2009).

36. Ibid.

37. Richard E. Boyatzis and Ellen van Oosten, "A Leadership Imperative: Building the Emotionally Intelligent Organization," *Ivey Business Journal*, January–February 2003, pp. 1–5.

38. Ibid., p. 2.

39. Ibid., p. 5.

9

Group Development and Team Building

LEARNING OBJECTIVES

After reading and studying this chapter, you should be able to:

1. *Identify the types of formal groups used in organizations.*

2. *Identify the stages of group development.*

3. *Compare the advantages and limitations of groups.*

4. *Describe the variables that determine a group's effectiveness.*

5. *Discuss the strengths of the four team player styles.*

6. *Determine what is involved in team building.*

7. *Describe what makes team building successful at SEI.*

The essence of [collaboration] is working with people rather than over people or under people.

—Mary Parker Follett

There is nothing permanent except change.

—Heraclitus

B2M Productions/Photodisc/Jupiter Images

Teamwork is a critical factor for success in many work environments, especially in a retail environment such as Family Dollar.

Preview

FAMILY DOLLAR "In 1958, a 21-year-old entrepreneur with an interest in merchandising became intrigued with the idea of operating a low-overhead, self-service retail store. Leon Levine believed he could offer his customers a variety of high-quality, good-value merchandise for less than $2. Because he grew up in his family's retail store, he understood value, quality, and customer satisfaction.

In November 1959, Leon Levine opened the first Family Dollar store in Charlotte, North Carolina, and was on his way to becoming a retailing legend. Right from the start, he had a well-developed philosophy of what Family Dollar would be and how it would operate, a philosophy from which he and his management team have never strayed. The concept is a simple one: 'The customers are the boss, and you need to keep them happy.'

He created a general floor plan he used in each of his stores that allowed customers to easily shop for their favorite products in any Family Dollar store. With the stores uniformly laid out and stocked, store managers were able to focus on providing good customer service. This concept for a self-serve, cash-and-carry neighborhood discount store in low- to middle-income neighborhoods proved successful."[1]

In 2015, Dollar Tree finalized its acquisition of Family Dollar.[2] The acquisition involves downsizing certain stores and transforming underperforming units. Margaret Gibson has a knack for turning unprofitable stores around. Known affectionately as the "turnaround lady," Margaret has worked in retail since she was 17 years old. She has been with Family Dollar for over 25 years, and during that time she has held a variety of jobs ranging from a frontline employee to district manager. Because of her expertise, she currently floats where needed.

According to Margaret, "There are two keys to turning a store: increasing sales and reducing shrink" (inventory losses). Her most recent "project" involves turning around a store that had over $240,000 in shrinkage. The former store manager and all employees were fired by the company, enabling Margaret to start from scratch. She began by hiring nine employees; five had previous dealings with her, and that was important in terms of creating a high-performance team. They understood what they were getting into when they signed on for the job. Margaret openly admits, "I have very high expectations, and I am extremely picky. I don't tell anybody my schedule because I want to drop in on my days off and see how things are running without me there!" In the beginning, she watched them closer than she does now, but that was part of building an effective team. Initially, morning meetings typically involved Margaret "laying down the law," but she always followed up with some form of positive reinforcement, like pizza for lunch. She used other positive reinforcement, such as a monthly employee covered dish lunch. As Margaret says, "It is important for me to get on their levels and speak to them in a relaxed environment" and vice versa. Such bonding is an important part of team functioning.

A key member of her team is a young man by the name of Vernon Mason, who worked for Margaret before. She was able to persuade him to come on board by promising him she would be flexible with his schedule while he worked on his bachelor's degree in business administration. According to Margaret, "Vernon cares about his job and works extremely hard. He is a self-starter and very dependable. To him, it is more than just a paycheck. Not everyone is cut out to work in retail; it takes a special person, but Vernon has retail in his blood." Margaret learned during their previous stint together he had a special gift for merchandising, so her goal was to make him assistant manager and teach him the administrative side of the business, especially loss prevention.

Once Vernon mastered the paperwork, he was able to perform every job in the store. In fact, all nine employees are cross-trained to perform all of the store functions except the paperwork. One advantage is if anyone is ever out for personal reasons, it does not have a negative impact on the team; other employees are able to fill that void. Margaret also assigns each person a specific section of the store based on his or her skills and abilities. Thus, team members feel confident in their abilities to perform their jobs well. This approach to team management pays dividends, especially when the delivery truck arrives; it takes Margaret's store only half the time to get the stock on the floor compared to other stores within the district.

The team culture is a big reason Margaret has been successful in increasing sales to help turn around this "project" store. Vernon readily admits, "Our store is really a family environment. We do things for the employees to let them know they are doing a good job, like celebrating birthdays. Some have to work two jobs just to make it, but everybody likes their jobs here and is motivated to do well. The employees, in turn, interact with our customers in the same manner. We treat our customers with respect, and we say hello and ask how they are doing. We try to help them find what they need." This family-friendly approach actually attracts the types of customers who respond to those forms of reinforcement, and they continue to come back. In fact, Vernon notes, "Some customers stop to say hello even when they are not shopping!" In addition to heightening sales, Margaret's team has been able to curb shrinkage as well. Family Dollar's average shrinkage is approximately 2:5, whereas, Margaret's store average is 1:91. Such success is motivating for her team because raises are partially based on inventory management.[3]

As the chapter preview indicates, creating and maintaining an efficient and effective team can be challenging but quite rewarding. Throughout this chapter, we cover group and team-related topics ranging from group formation to team development and change. In addition, we approach team building from several vantage points to assess commonalities as well as differences, but first, the forces that necessitate team functioning are presented.

Forces Causing Change

Numerous factors affect an organization. Continuously changing forces leading to or causing change originate both outside and within the organization, as shown in Exhibit 9-1. You might compare this situation to yourself. You must respond to such external stimuli as the condition of the weather, the requirements of your daily work schedule, and the different needs arising each day. Also requiring responses are the internal stimuli, such as your

EXHIBIT 9-1
External and Internal
Change Forces

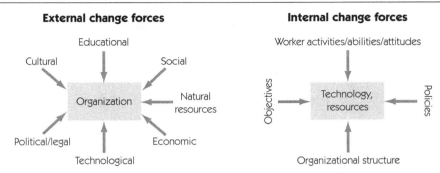

Source: Donald C. Mosley, Paul Pietri, and Leon Megginson, *Management:Leadership in Action*, 5th ed. (New York: HarperCollins, 1996), p. 425.

hunger level, the state of your health, or your attitude. A similar situation exists when we substitute an organization for the individual.

External Change Forces

external change forces

Forces outside the organization that have a great impact on organizational change. Management has little control over these numerous external forces.

Management has little control over the strong impact of numerous **external change forces**. Yet an organization depends on and must interact with its external environment if it is to survive. Specifically, resources, profits, and customers for products and services are all from the outside. Therefore, any force that impacts or changes the environment affects the organization's operations and brings about pressures requiring a change response. External forces—from technological advancements to consumers' changing requirements—cause an organization to alter its goals, structure, and methods of conducting business.

STOP AND THINK

Suppose you were the director and owner of a 30-bed nursing home. What kinds of external change factors might have an impact on your organization?

Internal Change Forces

internal change forces

Pressures for change within the organization such as cultures and objectives.

Change forces also come from within. **Internal change forces** may result from different organization goals or new challenges, as in the case of Family Dollar, or they may be caused by new quality initiatives, changing technologies, or employee attitudes. For example, shifting the goal from short-run profit to long-term growth directly impacts the daily work of most departments and may lead to a reorganization that streamlines overall operations. Changing to automated equipment and robotics to perform work previously done by people causes changes in work routines and just-in-time supplies. Altering incentive programs and personnel policies and procedures may result in different hiring and selection procedures. Employee attitudes about child and/or parent care, insurance needs, or flexible working hours may change daily business practices.

External and internal forces for change are often interrelated, not isolated from one another. At times, this linkage results from the changes in values and attitudes affecting people within the system. Some of these changes from within are from people who have entered the organization. For example, many of the changes now occurring in organizations are the result of the increasing availability of a highly trained workforce, including the need for increased flexibility and responsiveness of the organization to employees' and customers' needs and a flattened hierarchy allowing greater responsibility to be placed with frontline workers.

Planned Change

For management to plan for change, it must decide what needs to be changed in the organization. In general, management seeks to change things that prevent greater organizational effectiveness. **Organizational effectiveness** results from activities that improve the organization's structure, technology, and people so it can achieve its objectives.

The nature of the problem causing the organization to be less than ideally effective determines the choice of the particular technique used to achieve change. From a choice of alternatives, management determines which one is most likely to produce the desired outcome. Diagnosing the problem includes defining the outcome desired from the change. In general, the desired outcome is either improved employee behavior or activities that result in improved performance. This can be achieved by changing the organization's structure, technology, and/or people (Exhibit 9-2).

This classification of organizational elements in no way implies a distinct division among elements. According to the systems concept, a change in one element is likely to affect other elements. In general, the more change that is required, the more likely it is management will change all three elements.

Management must decide the desired outcomes and the type of change programs to use to modify the specific organizational element—including those activities needed to get the work done effectively (Exhibit 9-2). Changing the organization's *structure* involves modifying and rearranging internal relationships. This includes such variables as authority–responsibility relationships, communications systems, work flows, and size and composition of work groups.

Changing the organization's *technology* may require modifying such factors as tools, equipment, and machinery; research direction and techniques; engineering processes; and production system, including layout, methods, and procedures. Changing technology may result from or contribute to altering tasks to be performed. Products and other inputs may be revised. For example, mechanization changes the nature of work performed.

organizational effectiveness

The result of activities that improve the organization's structure, technology, and people.

EXHIBIT 9-2
Organizational Effectiveness Results from Changing Structure, Technology, and/or People

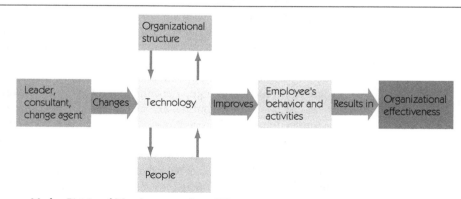

Source: Mosley, Pietri, and Megginson, op. cit., p. 429.

EXHIBIT 9-3
Different Responses to
Change

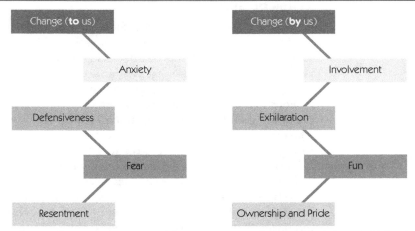

Source: William Walker, management consultant, presentation to the North Mississippi Health Services Board of Directors and staff, May 1, 1999. The Wynfrey Hotel, Birmingham, Alabama.

Changing the organization's *people* may include revising recruiting and selection policies and procedures, training and development activities, reward systems, and/or managerial leadership and communication.

Supervisors and employees are likely to support change if they perceive the change is directed at the real cause of the problem, such as being an effective solution, and not affecting them adversely. Most importantly, those who participate in a change process respond entirely differently than those merely affected by it. Exhibit 9-3 shows these different responses to change.

Next, we turn to the study of group dynamics that provides greater insight into creating a climate of positive change.

Importance of Work Groups

synergy

The concept that two or more people working together in a cooperative, coordinated way can accomplish more than the sum of their independent efforts.

To achieve synergy and gain the most from employees, organizations require groups. **Synergy** means the whole is greater than the sum of the parts. This is especially applicable when using teams and ad hoc task forces. Assume a five-person ad hoc task force is given the opportunity to solve a problem that has an impact on the entire organization. If the team reaches a synergistic solution to the problem, then synergy can be mathematically defined as $1 + 1 + 1 + 1 + 1 =$ more than 5. It is important for supervisors to understand the basic concepts of group or team development because work groups or teams produce the synergistic effect needed for management to reach its goals.

What Are Groups?

groups

Two or more people who communicate and work together regularly in pursuit of one or more common objectives.

Groups have been defined in various ways. The definition we prefer is a group is two or more people who communicate and work together regularly in pursuit of one or more common objectives. This highlights that at least two individuals must work together to constitute a group. If a group becomes too large, interaction among all members is difficult. This leads to the evolution of smaller groups. Remember, one finding of the Hawthorne studies was groups could be either supportive of organizational goals or opposed to them overall.

Types of Groups

Groups in organizations are either formal or informal. Formal groups are those created by the organization. The most common example is the group formed by a manager and his or her immediate team members. Informal groups evolve out of the formal organization but are not formed by management. Neither are they shown in the organization's structure. An example would be a friendship group that enjoys discussing sports during lunch.

formal groups

Group prescribed and/or established by the organization.

Formal groups are deliberately formed by management and are often shown on the organizational chart. For example, command groups are formal groups composed of staff who report to a designated manager, such as a group of vice presidents for worldwide marketing. Committees and task forces are additional examples of formal groups. Exhibit 9-4 illustrates how one manager can be a member of several different groups while employed by one organization. Next, we discuss several formal organizational groups in more detail.

Network groups are dispersed and require collaboration and coordination across different projects and sometimes from groups outside the organization. The members' roles and responsibilities are based on connections, collaboration, and a targeted expertise. The idea that groups need to be viewed as part of a network working within an organization is taking on greater prominence. The reasons for this are (1) many groups are formed and disbanded

EXHIBIT 9-4

A Manager's Membership in Different Groups

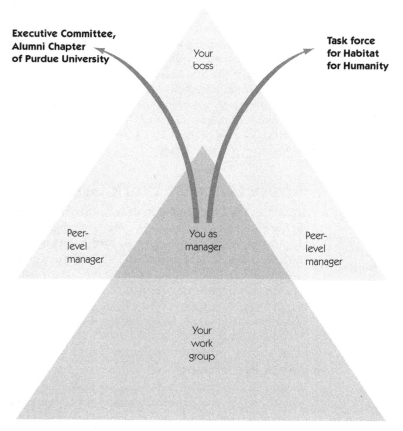

Source: Adapted from W. Alan Randolph, *Understanding and Managing Organizational Behavior* (Homewood, IL: Richard D. Irwin, 1985), p 385.

network groups

Network groups are dispersed and require collaboration and coordination across different projects and sometimes from groups outside the organization. The members' roles and responsibilities are based on connections, collaboration, and a targeted expertise.

virtuoso groups

Groups composed of top performers who excel in their respective specialties and are usually focused on important performance issues.

Virtual groups or teams

Group that is dislocated—and mostly, if not exclusively, meets online and can face the added challenges of different time zones, less frequent verbal communications, the lack of a physical presence, and any informal interactions that lead to social ties among more co-located groups.

self-managing work groups

Groups that tend to operate by member consensus rather than management direction.

quickly, not allowing for normal group dynamics to emerge; (2) teams are dislocated across cities and countries and composed of members who work on multiple projects within many different teams; and (3) these groups frequently require collaboration and coordination across different projects and sometimes from groups outside the organization. When groups are viewed as a network, the roles and responsibilities of group members are based on connections, collaboration, and a targeted expertise. The leader and follower roles and responsibilities shift as necessary away from a hierarchical structure to one where natural leaders may emerge, decision making is decentralized, and relationships, both within and outside of the organization, are cultivated.

Virtuoso groups are composed of top performers who excel in their respective specialties and are usually focused on important performance issues. Whereas most groups celebrate diversity of thought and background, virtuoso groups attempt to put together only people who excel in their respective specialties while disregarding possible managerial skills, diversity of thought, or other relational considerations. While this sounds like a great idea, and it sometimes is, it also presents unique challenges. For instance, just because someone is an expert at a particular task does not mean he or she works well with others. In fact, finding a team leader able to manage a group of prima donnas who know they are the best can be the most difficult aspect of managing a virtuoso group. Virtuoso groups differ from traditional ones in most dimensions. They bring in members only for their top skills, celebrate the individual egos of team members, force members into physical proximity, and focus on creativity over efficiency.[4]

A **Virtual groups or teams** is dislocated—and mostly, if not exclusively, meet online. While all groups are dislocated to some extent (different floors and offices prevent some communication and cohesion), virtual groups can face the added challenges of different time zones, less frequent verbal communications, the lack of a physical presence, and any informal interactions that lead to social ties among more co-located groups. These challenges make it more difficult for collaboration, but virtual groups provide some advantages such as the ability to tap into more diverse and talented members, and better cost advantages. Thus, if companies emphasize and provide teamwork opportunities within these groups, promote leadership within these groups, and allow for periodic face-to-face meetings through direct meetings or web teleconferences, virtual groups can be just as productive as co-located groups.[5]

Self-managing work groups have become more common today, partly because of management's efforts to sustain competitive advantages through downsizing, increased efficiencies, enhanced technologies, etc. Europe was in the forefront of experimenting with self-managing work teams, but managers in Canada and the United States quickly followed, using these types of groups/teams as building blocks of a corporate renaissance in productivity. In Exhibit 9-5, strategies for implementing self-managing work groups successfully are presented. Illustrated here is the experience of a small southern plant.

A small parts plant is owned by a large corporation and employs 320 workers. Most of the self-managed work teams consist of eight to 12 members who select their own leader. At the next level are coordinators, who work with several teams. The coordinators report to an upper-management group called the support team and operate primarily as developmental leaders. Their basic leadership practice is to encourage the teams to do things themselves—to be self-managing. Under this structure, there are productivity gains of significantly more than 20 percent.[6]

Even companies that rely on an appointed leader make use of some forms of empowerment, a key concept of self-managed work groups and teams. Michael Lloyd Odom, who received IBM's Global Project Manager of the Year award, is a prime example.

EXHIBIT 9-5

How to Succeed with
Self-Directed Work
Teams

The self-directed work team is usually thought of as a "leaderless" group of workers who take the place of supervisors and fulfill many management functions.

However, many of the attempts to install self-directed work teams have failed because the teams have neither the skill nor the experience to ensure their successful outcome.

There are some guidelines, if followed, which can increase the success of self-directed teams. Some of the guidelines are not simple and do take some work but they can decrease the mistakes management often makes in trying to develop teams.

1. Have a well thought-out vision of how these teams will fit into the scheme of the entire organization. A common vision of the leadership must be in place and supported by everyone in management with a complete understanding of the concept of teams.

2. With this vision, the entire organization must be prepared to change the culture to support the teams. Teams may be radically counter to what the organization has been doing, so the preparation must be thorough. The change must be a result of incremental steps so everyone will understand the vision and philosophy behind the change. Employee attitudes are sometimes difficult to change, so they will have to have a good idea as to what the teams will do for them and what's in it for them. Management must have a complete understanding of the culture of the organization and how to change it.

3. The organization must have the resources necessary to commit to this type of change in time, money, and people. A large upfront investment will be needed and the time frame will be long-term. People to train and develop the teams will be needed. Either in-house personnel (if they have the skills) or consultants can initially be used, but in the long-term, facilitators and supervisors must be available to help the team. Management must be certain that they have assessed the resources accurately and are willing to commit them to the endeavor.

4. Training is an extremely significant part of developing the teams. Team members must be trained in skills to allow them to function together: conflict management (probably the most difficult skill for team members to learn), assertiveness, communication (listening in particular), problem solving and decision making, and other skills that will enable people to work together effectively. At the same time, facilitators and supervisors must be trained to work with teams. There are new skills supervisors will need to help the teams be successful. It is important they get these skills. Coaching and counseling are skills a supervisor must learn to help the work teams.

5. After the training takes place, it will take time for the teams to get used to one another and develop their new-found skills. When the training is over, the development begins and the development is just as important as the training. Many organizations believe that once the training is over, the teams are ready to function, and this is not necessarily the case. Some teams will take longer to develop than others. Management must have the patience and people available to help this development. In fact, development is an ongoing process and if done correctly, will never end.

6. Performance expectations of the teams must be developed so they will know what is expected of them. The performance standards must be attainable and not "pie-in-the-sky" type standards no one really understands or will be able to achieve. Not only must expectations be developed but also a method to measure these expectations so management can actually see what the teams are accomplishing. Many organizations never measure team performance, and this is a very disastrous mistake.

7. A feedback method to teams must be developed so they can also see what they are doing and make corrections where necessary. The only way there can be continuous improvement in performance is for them to know where they are in relation to the developed standards. If they know, they can and will improve.

8. Boundaries must be set in which the teams will be allowed to operate. This is different from performance expectations in that the teams have to know and understand the limits of their empowerment. Many organizations start right off wanting teams to make

(Continued)

"all" the decisions. The problem is the organization doesn't really understand what "all" means and they have problems because the teams are making decisions they should not be making. When management corrects the decision, it causes a setback in team development and long-term effectiveness. Teams should start with narrow boundaries, maybe only simple decisions until they begin to understand and become more comfortable with the decision-making process. As the teams become more sophisticated, they can expand their boundaries and take on more complex decision making. However, teams should only make decisions which affect their immediate team.

9. Do not develop the thinking that self-directed work teams are "leaderless" or never need management intervention. These teams may be able to take over some of the functions of management, but to think they will never need "coaching" or guidance and they will survive on their own will lead to failure of the teams. Supervisors will not be completely replaced, but they will develop a new roll [sic] of coaches and advisors to teams. These advisors, having been trained to work with teams, can help the teams be very successful, or they can cause a serious problem. If they offer the kind of facilitation needed, they can make the difference between success and failure.

These are guidelines to help develop successful self-directed work teams. There are no overnight successes that have been documented as of yet. I doubt there will ever be, but if these guidelines are followed, there can and will be long-term success.

Source: T. Capozzoli, "How to Succeed with Self-Directed Work Teams," *Supervision* 67, no. 2 (February 2006), pp. 25–26. Reprinted by permission of National Research Bureau.

One of Mike's projects ran into some difficulty, and he received a lot of negative feedback about one of the team members. Although this team member had good technical skills, he was insecure, and with the layoffs he feared he would lose his job. If there was a problem on the project, he pointed a finger and accused other team members of being at fault. As a consequence, a lot of defensive behavior took place within the team.

Mike called the problem employee in, held up the mirror, and gave him the feedback Mike received from other team members. He also urged the employee to bring any issue or problem to the team as a whole and not criticize individual members. He emphasized winning or losing *as a team*. He also called in other team members, one at a time, and asked for support in changing this employee's attitude to help him become a team player. The problem employee turned his behavior around, and the project was successful at meeting or exceeding objectives.[7]

From his experiences, Mike Odom learned valuable lessons about how to manage a group effectively that he shares with us and can be applied to true self-managed groups or hybrids.

1. "IBM values its people as a key asset. It places a high priority on development of its people. I share the strong belief that people are your greatest asset."
2. "You need to understand the principles of managing a project."
3. "To be successful you have to build a good team; picking a good team is the first step."
4. "You need to be a good coach and work with people to help them understand what it takes to be successful."
5. "A key thing is to understand you are not alone. We are a lot smarter as a team than we are as individuals."
6. "Attitude can make all the difference in the world, not only from the standpoint of the team leader, but from the standpoint of all team contributors."

7. "A team leader's management style can make the difference between a high-performing team and a team that just gets the job done."
8. "I think having good coaching skills is even more important than good technical skills in project management."

STOP AND THINK

In what type of business environments do you think self-managed teams would be most effective? Easier to implement and manage?

---

informal groups

A group that evolves out of the formal organization but is not formed by management or shown in the organization's structure.

Informal groups evolve out of the employees' need for social interaction, friendship, communication, and status. Although not a part of the formal organization, an informal group can sometimes be the same as a formal work team. The group members might give more allegiance to the informal leader than to the formal manager.

Other types of informal groups cross formal work team boundaries and are based on common interests. An informal interest group may come together to seek increased fringe benefits or attempt to solve a particularly broad-based software problem. Another type of informal group is a friendship group. Its members also have common interests, but they are more social in nature. Such groups could include a running team, a band, or the people who gather to chat during a break.

In general, informal groups provide a valuable service by helping members meet affiliation and social needs. Ideally, management tries to create an environment in which the needs and objectives of informal groups are similar to the needs and objectives of the formal organization.

Franz Pfluegl/Shutterstock.com

In a team environment, the leader functions like a coach, picking the right members, helping them develop their skills, and recognizing their individual and team achievements.

How Groups Develop

2. *Identify the stages of group development.*

B. W. Tuckman developed a model of small-group development that encompasses four stages of growth.[8] A desirable feature of this classical model—that basically has been followed by later researchers[9]—is it examines the stages in terms of task functions and interpersonal relations, both essential concerns of any group.

Stages of Group Development   The stages of group development defined by Tuckman are (1) forming, (2) storming, (3) norming, and (4) performing. There is some overlap between the stages, and the length of time spent in each stage can vary. However, the central concept is a group usually remains in a stage until key issues are resolved before moving to the next stage. Sometimes a group appears to resolve key issues but really has not. In this case, after moving to the next stage, the group shifts back to the earlier stage to resolve the unsettled issue. The characteristics of each stage follow.

Stage 1: Forming   This is the stage in which members first come together and form initial impressions. Among other things, they try to determine the task of the group and their role expectations of one another. In this stage, members depend on a leader to provide considerable structure in establishing an agenda and guidelines because they tend to be unsure of what is expected of them.

Stage 2: Storming   The storming stage is typically a period of conflict and—ideally—organization. Conflicts arise over goals, task behaviors (that is, who is responsible for what), and leadership roles. Relationship behaviors emerge because people have strong feelings and express them, sometimes in a hostile manner.

It is a mistake to suppress conflict; the key is to manage it. If a group gets through stage 2 successfully, it becomes organized and begins developing norms, rules, and standards.

Stage 3: Norming   This is a stage of developing teamwork and group cohesion and creating openness of communications with information sharing. Members feel good about one another and give each other positive feedback, and the level of trust and cooperation is usually quite high. These desirable characteristics of team development result from establishing agreed-on goals and finalizing the processes, standards, and rules by which the group will operate.

If the issues of the earlier stages have not been resolved, the group can regress. Later in this chapter, we will discuss norms in more detail.

Stage 4: Performing   This is the stage at which the group shows how efficiently and effectively it can operate to achieve its goals. Information exchange develops to the point of joint problem solving, and there is shared leadership.

As one organizational behavior text points out, "Some groups continue to learn and develop from their experiences and new inputs. . . . Other groups—especially those that have developed norms not fully supportive of efficiency and effectiveness—may perform only at the level needed for their survival."[10] Thus, group development, like individual development, is a continuing process.

Evaluating Groups

3. *Compare the advantages and limitations of groups.*

Groups, whether formal or informal, are a fact of organizational life. In this section, we discuss important advantages and limitations of groups.

Advantages of Groups   Among the major advantages of groups are they (1) provide members with opportunities for need satisfaction and (2) may function more effectively than individuals.

Provide Opportunities for Need Satisfaction   Group membership provides an opportunity for members to satisfy security and relationship needs as well as higher-level esteem and self-actualization needs. Group membership can be highly satisfying. For example, being viewed as a member of a high-performing problem-solving task force brings out feelings of pride. At times, a task you perceive as drudgery may actually turn out to be less distasteful when you are working together in a group.

May Function More Effectively Than Individuals   Synergy is the concept that two plus two can equal five. This is one of the major potential advantages of groups. The combination of members possessing different perspectives, experiences, and job skills can often work in a team's favor. Moreover, individuals operating as a group may feel a collective responsibility that often leads to higher motivation and commitment.

Limitations of Groups   Among the general limitations of groups are they may (1) encourage social loafing, (2) diffuse responsibility, and (3) be less effective than individuals.

Encourage Social Loafing   *Social loafing* is the term used to describe "taking a free ride" when working with others as a team. We have all known team members who did not pull their weight as part of a team writing a group term paper or putting together a classroom presentation. Generally, social loafing occurs because some members genuinely believe their contributions to the group are not significant or they hope for a free ride. Free riders are reinforced when they receive rewards or recognition on an equal basis with those who have carried the greater load.

Diffuse Responsibility   The diffusion of responsibility among members of a group is somewhat related to social loafing and is also one of its major causes. Because each person may be expected to do only a part of a project, no one person may feel totally responsible.

Manfred Rutz/The Image Bank/Getty Images

Employees who work in groups often find they are able to accomplish more than they can by working alone. In addition, working in a group can be a satisfying social experience.

Diffused responsibility may result in groups assuming positions individual members would not take if held individually accountable. The "Oh, what the heck" attitude, as well as the idea "they" will handle it, leads to more liberal risk taking. This also means the more mundane, routine, and undesirable group tasks may be neglected by individual members in the hope someone else will complete them.

May Be Less Effective Than Individuals   Although the concept of synergy is an attractive argument in favor of group effort, the sad fact is sometimes two plus two equals three. One classic study showed this effect dramatically. One would expect a group of three pulling on a rope to exert three times the pulling power each could attain separately. Such was not the case: Groups exerted a force only two and a half times the average of individual performance.[11]

Thus, as a result of social loafing, diffusion of responsibility, and other factors, groups may not necessarily be more productive and effective than individuals.

Determining Group Effectiveness

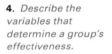

4. *Describe the variables that determine a group's effectiveness.*

What are the key factors determining the effectiveness of groups? Exhibit 9-6 highlights the essential variables affecting group satisfaction, goal accomplishment, and productivity. As the model demonstrates, there is a cause-and-effect relationship between leadership (the causal variable), group characteristics (the intervening variables), and the end result variables. Variables affecting group effectiveness are (1) group size, (2) member composition and roles, (3) norms, and (4) group cohesiveness.

Group Size   Without question, the size of the work group has an impact on a group's effectiveness. The size of a group depends to a large extent on its purpose. Organizations can take a contingency approach to determining a manager's span of control, which influences the size of the natural group. With the increasing use of committees, task forces, quality circles, and self-managing work teams, we need additional guidelines for determining the size of these types of groups. Exhibit 9-7 provides guidelines on the effects of size on group leadership, members, and group processes. It has been our experience the ideal size for a problem-solving group is five to seven members. As Exhibit 9-7 highlights, with this size, there is less chance for differences to arise between the leader and members, less chance of domination by a few members, and less time required for reaching decisions.

In company and project workshops, we usually use ad hoc task forces of five to seven to study an issue and report back to the larger group with a recommended plan of action. Almost invariably, the action plan is accepted with only minor modifications. The one time we ran into difficulty was when we used a larger group—14 people—to develop an action plan. In that instance, the reported agreement was later sabotaged by a subgroup of the original group of 14. Their complaint was the agreement had been rushed through by

---

EXHIBIT 9-6
Model of Group
Effectiveness

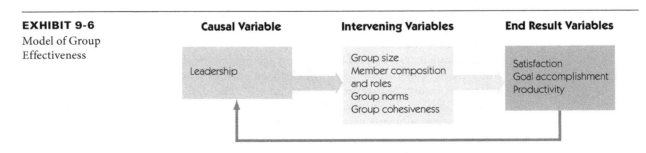

Causal Variable	Intervening Variables	End Result Variables
Leadership	Group size Member composition and roles Group norms Group cohesiveness	Satisfaction Goal accomplishment Productivity

EXHIBIT 9-7

Possible Effects of Size on Groups

CATEGORY/DIMENSIONS	GROUP SIZE		
	2-7 MEMBERS	8-12 MEMBERS	13-16 MEMBERS
Leadership			
1. Demands on leader	Low	Moderate	High
2. Differences between leaders and members	Low	Low to moderate	Moderate to high
3. Direction by leader	Low	Low to moderate	Moderate to high
Members			
4. Tolerance of direction from leader	Low to high	Moderate to high	High
5. Domination of group interaction by a few members	Low	Moderate to high	High
6. Inhibition in participation by ordinary members	Low	Moderate	High
Group Process			
7. Formalization of rules and procedures	Low	Low to moderate	Moderate to high
8. Time required for reaching judgment decisions	Low to moderate	Moderate	Moderate to high
9. Tendency for subgroups to form within group	Low	Moderate to high	High

Source: Adapted from Don Hellriegel, John W. Slocum Jr., and Richard Woodman, *Organizational Behavior*, 10th ed. © 2004 South-Western, a part of Cengage Learning, Inc. Reproduced by permission. www.cengage.com/permissions.

two of the more dominating members. On the other hand, one study has found a group of 14 members is the ideal size for a fact-finding group.[12] This shows once again the ideal size depends on the group's purpose.

Member Composition and Roles   The composition of a group has considerable impact on productivity. At the minimum, the ability of members to carry out the mission is a major factor. The more alike members are in age, background, value systems, education, personality type, and so forth, the more similarly they see things. The literature suggests for tasks that are relatively simple and require maximum cooperation, homogeneous groups are superior.[13] Conversely, for complex tasks, groups composed of members with widely differing backgrounds are superior because a greater number of different ideas would be generated, increasing the probability of creativity.

Whatever the group's composition, key task and maintenance roles must be carried out if the group is to be effective (Exhibit 9-8). In carrying out the group's activities, members tend to shift back and forth between these roles naturally. This is especially true in problem-solving groups and regular work teams where the formal leader is skillful in getting everyone to participate.

Many members in a problem-solving group play several task or maintenance roles. Unfortunately, ineffective roles or behaviors, such as dominating, can have a negative impact on group effectiveness (see Exhibit 9-8). The skill is for the leader to operate so members share the leadership role and ineffective behaviors are minimized. Exhibit 9-9 is a questionnaire allowing individual members of a group to assess how well they function in helping the group achieve its goals and in minimizing ineffective behaviors.

EXHIBIT 9-8

Task and Maintenance Roles in Groups

EFFECTIVE ROLES		INEFFECTIVE ROLES
WORK OR TASK* FUNCTIONS	**MAINTENANCE* FUNCTIONS**	
Initiating. Proposing tasks or goals; defining need for action; suggesting a procedure or an idea for a course of action.	*Consensus testing.* Checking with the group to see how much agreement has been reached, or how near it is to a united conclusion.	*Displays of aggression.* Deflating others' status; attacking the group or its values; joking in a barbed or semiconcealed way.
Information giving. Offering facts; providing relevant information; giving an opinion.	*Harmonizing.* Attempting to reconcile disagreements; reducing tensions; getting people to explore differences.	*Blocking.* Disagreeing/opposing beyond "reason"; stubbornly resisting group wishes for personal reasons; using hidden agenda to thwart the movement of a group.
Information seeking. Requesting facts; seeking relevant information; checking on meaning; asking for suggestions or ideas.	*Gate keeping.* Helping to keep communication channels open; facilitating the participation of others; suggesting procedures that permit sharing remarks.	*Dominating.* Asserting authority or superiority to manipulate group or some of its members; hindering others' contributions; controlling through flattery or other forms of patronization.
Clarifying. Interpreting ideas or suggestions; defining terms; clarifying issues before group; clearing up confusions.	*Encouraging.* Being friendly, warm, and responsive to others; indicating by facial expression or remark the acceptance of others' contributions; giving others opportunity for recognition.	*Playboy behavior.* Making a display, "playboy" fashion, of one's lack of involvement, "abandoning" the group while still physically in it; seeking recognition in ways not relevant to group task.
Summarizing. Pulling together related ideas; restating suggestions after group has discussed them; offering a decision or conclusion for group to consider.	*Compromising.* When one's own idea or status is involved in a conflict, yielding status; admitting error; disciplining oneself to maintain group cohesion.	*Avoidance behavior.* Pursuing special interests not related to task; staying off subject to avoid commitment, preventing group from facing up to controversy; filibustering.
Reality testing. Making a critical analysis of an idea; testing an idea; testing an idea against some data to see if the idea would work.	*Sharing feelings.* Sensing feelings, moods, relationships within the group; sharing feelings with other members; sharing observations on group processes.	*Sniping.* Ridiculing opinions and ideas of others by word or action; personal criticism.

*The distinction between "task" and "maintenance" roles is somewhat arbitrary. Some of these terms could be classified in either column.

---

5. *Discuss the strengths of the four team player styles.*

Another way to approach member composition and roles is from a team player or follower style perspective. Becoming a team player and a good follower may be as important as, if not more important than, having or being a good leader. Being a good follower starts with understanding your own team player style and finding a way to match that style with what the leader and the team need. There are four types or styles: contributors, collaborators, communicators, and challengers. Any style can be effective, but each style contributes differently.[14]

contributors

Help keep the group or team focused on the *task*.

Contributors.   These are task-oriented, dependable team members who provide good technical data, do their homework when requested, push the team to set a high bar for performance, and use team resources wisely. Basically, contributors help keep the group or team focused on the task.

EXHIBIT 9-9

Assessing Your Behavior as a Team Member

Instructions:

Select a team you are currently working with or have worked with in the recent past. Assess your behavior on each item for the team you selected by using the following scale.

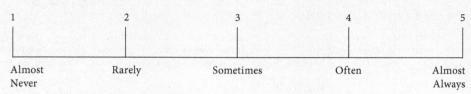

1	2	3	4	5
Almost Never	Rarely	Sometimes	Often	Almost Always

Place the appropriate number value next to each item.

Task-oriented behaviors: In this team, I . . .

_____ 1. initiate ideas or actions

_____ 2. facilitate the introduction of facts and information

_____ 3. summarize and pull together various ideas

_____ 4. keep the team working on the task

_____ 5. ask whether the team is near a decision (determine consensus)

Relation-oriented behaviors: In this team, I . . .

_____ 6. support and encourage others

_____ 7. harmonize (keep the peace)

_____ 8. try to find common ground

_____ 9. encourage participation

_____ 10. actively listen

Self-oriented behaviors: In this team, I . . .

_____ 11. express hostility

_____ 12. avoid involvement

_____ 13. dominate the team

_____ 14. free ride on others

_____ 15. take personal credit for team results

Total scores of 20–25 on task-oriented behaviors, 20–25 on relations-oriented behaviors, and 5–10 on self-oriented behaviors would indicate you are probably an effective team player.

Source: Adapted from Don Hellriegel, John W. Slocum Jr., and Richard Woodman, *Organizational Behavior*, 10th ed. © 2004 South-Western, a part of Cengage Learning, Inc. Reproduced by permission. www.cengage.com/permissions.

---

collaborators

Keep the members focused on the team's actual *goal(s)* or purpose.

Collaborators.   These are goal-directed, big-picture team members who see the ultimate goal as overriding but are flexible and open to new ideas, pitch in when and where necessary, and share the limelight with other team members. Collaborators' main role is to keep the members focused on the team's actual purpose.

Communicators.   These are process-oriented, positive-people team members who are effective listeners and facilitators of any conflict among team members. They build consensus, provide feedback, and keep the group relaxed through informal relations. These roles of the communicators fill the social and emotional needs of the group or team.

communicators

Fill the *social and emotional needs* of the group or team.

challengers

Are *questioning*, playing the role of devil's advocate when necessary and pushing the team to move out of its comfort zone.

norms

Rules of behavior developed by group members to provide guidance for group activities.

group cohesiveness

The mutual liking and team feeling in a group.

team

A collection of people who must rely on group cooperation.

6. *Determine what is involved in team building.*

Challengers.   These are questioning, open, and candid team members who are willing to disagree, banter, contest assumptions, and encourage the team to take calculated risks when appropriate. Challengers play the role of devil's advocate when necessary and push the team to move out of its comfort zone.

These roles are not exclusive, meaning group members can have more than one role and, in fact, similar to the MBTI, most members share characteristics and preferences of several of these team player responsibilities. You also may note each role has a primary style associated with it—that is, the style of the challenger is to question. Teams need all four roles to be successful, so small teams need players to assume the role of multiple styles while larger teams may have members assume one primary role.

Norms   **Norms** are generally thought of as rules of behavior developed by group members to provide guidance for group activities. Norms, standards, and action plans in an effective team are highly interrelated and supportive of the organization's goals. However, if a group is not well led, negative norms result, working against the organization's goals. An example of a negative norm is an informal leader in a construction team sending the message, "Don't rush the work—they'll just give you more to do."

The critical role of leadership is especially important in influencing positive norms. An example of a positive norm is the informal leader in a marketing group sending the message, "Make sure it looks nice—we want to be proud of our work." Business ethics are similar to norms because they provide guides to behavior. The top leadership of an organization has significant influence on ethical normative values of groups as well as individuals.

Group Cohesiveness   **Group cohesiveness** is the mutual liking and team feeling in a group. As we have already seen, size plays a major part in the cohesiveness of a group. Another major factor is the frequency of communication.

In the partnering workshops we conducted, communications were frequently issue-oriented. This led to the development of group cohesiveness. Agreement on overall goals, with the processes and plans to achieve those goals, also enhances group cohesiveness.

Conversely, the major factors preventing group cohesiveness are dysfunctional conflicts, internal power struggles, and failure to achieve goals. However, sometimes a group will be congenial, agree on goals, and feel like a team, yet fail in its mission.

Three other concepts that play a key role in healthy group development are listening, supporting, and differing. How many times have you been in a group discussion and been cut off in midsentence? How many times have you thought about the point you want to make next rather than listening to the other person? Sometimes we find ourselves responding to another person's idea or suggestion with the thought, "That's a great idea—I would never have come up with that." At those moments, it is important to give positive feedback in support of the suggestion if we want to create a supportive group environment for generating ideas. Finally, and perhaps most important for creativity in groups, is establishing an environment in which people can disagree without being disagreeable. In several of the end-of-chapter activities, you have an opportunity to solve an unfamiliar problem first on your own and then in a small group. While working in the small group, make a conscious effort to carry out the concepts of listening, supporting, and differing.

Different Approaches to Team Building

Now that you have insight into groups and group dynamics, we focus on teams and team building. Many supervisors are now shifting to the role of team leader, so we use that term throughout the remainder of this chapter. A **team** is a collection of people who must rely on group cooperation if the team is to experience the most success possible and thereby achieve its goals.[15] Experience has demonstrated successful teams are empowered to establish some or all of a team's goals, make decisions about how to achieve those goals, undertake the tasks required to meet them, and be mutually accountable for their results.[16]

Unfortunately, a number of teams do not achieve their optimum success and potential. This is often caused by the team leader's leadership style being too autocratic or permissive in managing the group. Consequently, several of the characteristics of an effective team are lacking. These characteristics are shown in Exhibit 9-10. The following sections illustrate how the characteristics of an effective team are implemented through the use of organizational team building.

Teams and organizations may not be successful because they fail at one or more of the following concepts, first identified by the renowned leadership expert John W. Gardner:

1. effective leadership at the top of the team and/or organization;
2. effective recruitment of good and talented people; and
3. the creation of an environment so good and talented people grow and develop.

EXHIBIT 9-10

Characteristics of an Effective Team

Clear Purpose	The vision, mission, goal, or task of the team has been defined and is now accepted by everyone. There is an action plan.
Informality	The climate tends to be informal, comfortable, and relaxed. There are no obvious tensions or signs of boredom.
Participation	There is much discussion, and everyone is encouraged to participate.
Listening	The members use effective listening techniques such as questioning, paraphrasing, and summarizing to get out ideas.
Civilized Disagreement	There is disagreement, but the team is comfortable with this and shows no signs of avoiding, smoothing over, or suppressing conflict.
Consensus Decisions	For important decisions, the goal is substantial but not necessarily unanimous agreement through open discussion of everyone's ideas, avoidance of formal voting, or easy compromises.
Open Communication	Team members feel free to express their feelings on the tasks as well as on the group's operation. There are few hidden agendas. Communication takes place outside of meetings.
Clear Roles and Work	There are clear expectations about the roles played by each team member.
Assignments	When action is taken, clear assignments are made, accepted, and carried out. Work is fairly distributed among team members.
Shared Leadership	While the team has a formal leader, leadership functions shift from time to time depending on the circumstances, the needs of the group, and the skills of the members. The formal leader models the appropriate behavior and helps establish positive norms.
External Relations	The team spends time developing key outside relationships, mobilizing resources, and building credibility with important players in other parts of the organization.
Style Diversity	The team has a broad spectrum of team-player types, including members who emphasize attention to task, goal setting, focus on process, and questions about how the team is functioning.
Self-Assessment	Periodically, the team stops to examine how well it is functioning and what may be interfering with its effectiveness.

Source: Glenn M. Parker, *Team Players and Teamwork*, p. 33. Copyright © 1991 Jossey-Bass. Reproduced with permission of John Wiley & Sons, Inc.

To gain insight into how effective these concepts and characteristics are, we examine team building in the financial industry.

Team Building in the Financial Sector

SEI (NASDAQ: SEIC) is an international provider of asset management, investment processing, and investment operations software for institutional and wealth management funds. The company's clients include banks, investment advisors and managers, institutional investors, and affluent individuals.[17]

7. Describe what makes team building successful at SEI.

As one would imagine, SEI's stock, like most other finance-related businesses, did not perform well during the economic meltdown of 2008–2009. However, SEI had the potential for strong growth as it emerged from the downturn.[18] Workplace design was one reason for the optimism. Consider the following description of team structures at SEI.

When a new employee joins SEI, it is an unusual experience. The new hire is given a map and sent down to a storeroom on the lower floor of the main building. There, the employee is issued a chair and desk, both on wheels, with a computer and phone on the desktop. The map shows where in the complex of nine barnlike buildings on the corporate campus in Oaks, Pennsylvania, the new hire will initially be located. The employee then rolls the desk through the buildings, into the oversized elevators designed for this purpose, and past hallways filled with a provocative (and sometimes shocking) collection of contemporary art.

In a large, open room (filled with similar desks on wheels), the employee finds the spot on the map, nudges neighboring desks aside and pulls down a thick, red wire that snakes down from the ceiling, containing computer, phone, and electrical connections. Once this "python" is plugged in, the company computer recognizes the new employee and routes calls or visitors to the location. Welcome to work.

The message from Day One is clear. This is an organization that is flexible, creative, and ready for constant transformation. The company is open and not hierarchical. The atmosphere and dress code is [sic] business casual. There are no corner offices—or offices at all. There is no need for an open-door policy because there are no doors. Employees are empowered. They can pick up their entire "office" and move to another location to join another team. On average, with the exception of a few anchored departments, they relocate about twice a year. This may sound unsettling—but that is the point. In a world in which the business environment can change overnight, particularly in financial services, this design gives SEI the flexibility and the mind-set to transform itself just as quickly.

While this might not work for every organization, the buildings and artwork at SEI are designed to reflect the culture of the organization. This environment has helped make SEI a perennial member of Fortune's list of "Best Companies to Work for in America."[19]

STOP AND THINK

Would SEI's approach work for furniture manufacturers? Shipbuilders? Resort hotel chains? What type of organizations would be best suited for SEI's model?

● Chapter Review

1. *Identify the types of formal groups used in organizations.*

A network group is a contemporary formal group whose members' roles and responsibilities are based on connections, collaboration, and a targeted expertise. Within these types of groups, natural leaders may emerge; decision making is decentralized; and relationships, both within and outside of the organization, are cultivated. A virtuoso group is a formal group composed of only top performers based on their respective specialties while disregarding possible managerial skills, diversity of thought, or other relational considerations. A virtual group is one that is dislocated—and mostly, if not exclusively, meets online. Virtual groups face the added challenges of different time zones, less frequent verbal communications, the lack of a physical presence, and any informal interactions, but virtual groups provide some advantages such as the ability to tap into more diverse and talented members and better cost advantages. Self-managing work groups are increasingly used, partly because of management's efforts to sustain competitive advantages through downsizing, increased efficiencies, enhanced technologies, etc. Using these types of groups as building blocks, managers have achieved a corporate renaissance in productivity in many countries.

2. *Identify the stages of group development.*

The focus turns to the development of work groups and the types—formal and informal—and stages of development. Formal groups are those formed by management. Informal groups are those not part of the official organizational structure and evolve out of employees' affiliation needs. An examination of synergy tells us two or more people working together in a cooperative way can accomplish more than the sum of their independent efforts, and to achieve synergy, it is important for a group to move through all four stages of group development: forming, storming, norming, and performing.

3. *Compare the advantages and limitations of groups.*

The primary advantages of groups are that they (1) give members an opportunity for needs satisfaction and (2) may function more effectively than individuals.

Some limitations are they may (1) encourage social loafing, (2) diffuse responsibility, and (3) be less effective than individuals.

4. *Describe the variables that determine a group's effectiveness.*

Group effectiveness is determined by (1) group size, (2) member composition and roles, (3) norms, and (4) group cohesiveness.

5. *Discuss the strengths of the four team player styles.*

Contributors are task-oriented, dependable team members who provide good technical data, do their homework when requested, push the team to set a high bar for performance, and use team resources wisely. Basically, contributors help keep the group or team focused on the task. Collaborators are goal-directed, big-picture team members who see the ultimate goal as overriding but are flexible and open to new ideas, pitch in when and where necessary, and share the limelight with other team members. Communicators are process-oriented, positive-people team members who are effective listeners and facilitators of any conflict among team members. They build consensus, provide feedback, and keep the group relaxed through informal relations. Challengers are questioning, open, and candid team members who are willing to disagree, banter, contest assumptions, and encourage the team to take calculated risks when appropriate.

6. *Determine what is involved in team building.*
Teams are successful if they have effective leadership at the top, effective recruitment of talented people, and an environment permitting good people to grow. The supervisor relies on group cooperation to establish the team's goals and make decisions to achieve these goals.

7. *Describe what makes team building successful at SEI.*
The open workplace design makes SEI successful. The workplace design facilitates open communication, egalitarianism, and creativity.

Key Terms

external change forces, p. 269
internal change forces, p. 269
organizational effectiveness, p. 270
synergy, p. 271
groups, p. 271
formal groups, p. 272

network groups, p. 272
virtuoso groups, p. 273
virtual groups, p. 273
self-managing work groups, p. 273
informal groups, p. 276
contributors, p. 281

collaborators, p. 282
communicators, p. 282
challengers, p. 283
norms, p. 283
group cohesiveness, p. 283
team, p. 283

Discussion Questions

1. Is change as pervasive as the authors claim? Explain.
2. What are some of the primary reasons people resist change? What are some of the ways a team leader can ensure that change is accepted or at least not resisted?
3. What major changes in the last 10 years have had considerable impact on organizations? Do these changes provide support for or make a case against the use of team building in organizations? Defend your position.
4. Compare and contrast formal groups and informal groups. Explain the importance of leadership in both types of groups.

5. Identify conditions and organizations where self-managing work teams would not be the way to organize. Then identify conditions and organizations where self-managing work teams would be the way to organize.
6. If groups have so many limitations, why are they so popular?
7. Of the factors affecting group effectiveness, do you think there is any order of importance? If so, rank the factors 1 through 4, and explain why you chose to rank them in that order.
8. How would you deal with an informal leader in a task force who seemed to be totally opposed to the group's objectives?

Skill Builder 9.1

Resources

Interpersonal Skill

Team Scavenger Hunt

Introduction Think about what it means to be a part of a team—a successful team. What makes one team more successful than another? What does each team member need to do for his or her team to be successful? What are the characteristics of an effective team?

Procedure
1. Form teams as assigned by your instructor. Locate the items on the list below while following these important rules:
   a. Your team *must stay together at all times*—that is, you cannot go in separate directions.
   b. Your team must return to the classroom in the time allotted by the instructor.

(Continued)

Information

Systems

Technology

The team with the most items on the list will be declared the most successful team.

2. Next, reflect on your team's experience. What did each team member do? What was your team's strategy? What made your team effective? Make a list of the most important things your team did to be successful. Nominate a spokesperson to summarize your team's experiences? That is, what helped each team to be effective?

Source: Adapted from Michael R. Manning and Paula J. Schmidt, "Building Effective Work Teams: A Quick Exercise Based on a Scavenger Hunt," *Journal of Management Education* 19, no. 3 (Thousand Oaks, CA: Sage Publications, August 1995), pp. 39–398. Used by permission. Reference for list of items for scavenger hunt from C. E. Larson and F. M. Lafas, *Team Work: What Must Go Right/What Can Go Wrong* (Newbury Park, CA: Sage Publications, 1989).

Items for Scavenger Hunt Each item is to be identified and brought back to the classroom.

1. A book with the word "team" in the title.
2. A joke about teams that you share with the class.
3. A blade of grass from the university football field.
4. A souvenir from the state.
5. A picture of a team or group.
6. A newspaper article about a team.
7. A team song your group composes and performs for the class.
8. A leaf from an oak tree.
9. Stationery from the Dean's office.
10. A cup of sand.
11. A pine cone.
12. A live reptile.
13. A definition of group "cohesion" that you share with the class.
14. A set of chopsticks.
15. Three cans of vegetables.
16. A branch of an elm tree.
17. Three unusual items that you share with the class.
18. A ball of cotton.
19. The ear from a prickly pear cactus.
20. A group name.

(*Note:* Items may be substituted as appropriate for your locale.)

Skill Builder 9.2

Resources

Information

Synergy and Social Loafing

Let's take a look at what logically would be the perfect sized team, a baseball battery. A battery in baseball is a pitcher and a catcher, a team of two. During practice, each person is expected to throw the ball 45 feet, 30 times. Imagine how long it would take if there was only one person on the team. Have you ever practiced tennis by yourself? There is a great deal of wasted effort. A two-person team is synergistic. That is to say, two working together can do more than twice what two can do individually. If two are good, three must be better. Right? What about social loafing? Could it be that adding a third person when he/she is not needed creates or encourages loafing? So, in this case,

Systems

two is perfect. Adding or subtracting just one might cause inefficiencies. Can you think of other situations where you should have close to a certain number of people on the team? How about over-the-road truck drivers? Could you make an argument for a certain number being preferable? How about members of a band? Is there an upper limit to how many would work well?

Skill Builder 9.3

Information

Virtual Groups

Have you ever worked or played online with someone to accomplish a goal? What was the goal? Did you ever meet that person? If so, how did that go? If not, would you want to meet the online person? What changes after you have actually met and interacted personally with that person? Now let's fast forward into your management career. Should you, as a manager, encourage the personal interaction of team members? Specifically, should two people who share a job (each works 20 hours a week) get to know each other? Why or why not?

Skill Builder 9.4

Interpersonal Skill

"Win as Much as You Can" Tally Sheet

The detailed instructions for completing this exercise will be provided by your instructor. Basically, for 10 successive rounds, you and your partner choose either an X or a Y on the scorecard. The payoff for each round depends on the pattern of choices made in your group. The payoff schedule is given at the bottom of the scorecard provided.

You are to confer with your partner in each round and make a joint decision. In rounds 5, 8, and 10, you and your partner may first confer with the other partnerships in your group before making your joint decision.

Information

Systems

	ROUND	YOUR CHOICE (CIRCLE)	CLUSTER'S PATTERN OF CHOICES	PAYOFF	BALANCE
	1	X Y	_X _Y		
	2	X Y	_X _Y		
	3	X Y	_X _Y		
	4	X Y	_X _Y		
Bonus Round Payoff × 3	5	X Y	_X _Y		
	6	X Y	_X _Y		
	7	X Y	_X _Y		
Bonus Round Payoff × 5	8	X Y	_X _Y		
	9	X Y	_X _Y		
Bonus Round Payoff × 10	10	X Y	_X _Y		

PAYOFF SCHEDULE

4 Xs:	Lose $1.00 each
3 Xs:	Win $1.00 each
1 Y:	Lose $3.00 each
2 Xs:	Win $2.00 each
2 Ys:	Lose $2.00 each
1 X:	Win $3.00
3 Ys:	Lose $1.00 each
4 Ys:	Win $1.00 each

Source: Adapted from an exercise by William Gellermann, Ph.D., in J. Pfeiffer and J. Jones, *Structured Experiences for Human Relations Training*, Vol. II (Tucson, AZ: University Associates, 1974).

CASE 9-1

THE SHIFT TO TEAM LEADERSHIP (GROUP ACTIVITY):

You work for a company interested in initiating a team leadership training program, and your plant manager has appointed you to an ad hoc task force to study the feasibility of implementing such a program in your plant. In one of the company's other plants, however, supervisors resisted team leadership, giving the following reasons:

1. Lack of time
2. Leader mind-set ("It's the leader's job to make the major decisions.")
3. Lack of trust in employees
4. Lack of confidence in employees' abilities or judgment
5. Potential for major negative consequences ("too risky," "too costly")
6. Leader's belief that the leader knows best
7. Leader's concern that developed employees will erode leader's base of power ("They're not dependent anymore.")
8. Leader's perception that employees don't desire development ("They don't really care; they only want to do the minimum required.")

INSTRUCTIONS

1. Divide the class into teams of three to six students.
2. Each team should brainstorm ways to overcome supervisors' predicted resistance to developmental leadership.
3. Each team is to outline an initial training agenda for the developmental leadership program to present to the plant manager.
4. The teams are to present their analysis and recommendations to the plant manager (represented by the instructor or a designated class member).
5. Vote with your class to determine which program appears to have the best chance of success.

(*Note:* Students may not vote for their own team's program.)

CASE 9-2

THE AFS STUDENT ORGANIZATION (GROUP ACTIVITY):

The AFS (All for Students) student organization was created in the mid-1970s and quickly became a popular, co-ed, undergraduate student group. AFS is a multipurpose organization focused on providing good fellowship and friendship among its members, encouraging its members to grow and develop academically, assisting members with career planning and development through seminars, promoting social interest and activities, and participating in charitable and benevolent events within the community.

AFS has historically been one of the top 10 most popular student organizations on campus, continuing to grow and achieve prominence within the university community. Four years ago, AFS actually won the coveted "Challenge Award," awarded to the top student organization each year by the university. Winning the Challenge Award is based on several criteria, including community service hours, university event participation, and head-to-head competition with other student organizations.

AFS's popularity has declined for the past three years. This is evident in the low attendance at regular meetings, the apathy displayed by the current members, and the overall decline in the number of active members on the roster. One potential reason for the situation is the worsening economy has led many students to take on additional work hours. However, to continue to provide the type and quality of activities and events the membership expects, the AFS Leadership Council was forced to raise dues. Unfortunately, this decision only led to additional defections. The officers on the leadership council disagreed as to the best remedy for the current situation and have at times been in conflict with one another. They attempted to initiate several strategies to turn things around, including lowering dues, cutting back programs and events, and stopping the harassment of delinquent members. However, even with an improving economy, nothing has really worked. Many individuals appear to be waiting for the end of the term so changes at the top can be made during elections.

You joined AFS during the current year based on the recommendation of your professor. She said it would be a great leadership opportunity from which you could learn and grow; at the very least, it would serve as a line item on your resume. Several of your friends joined at the same time for similar reasons.

You and your friends recognize the potential of AFS within the university community, but the right leadership and teamwork are needed to restore AFS as a prominent member of the community. Obviously, many of the other members agree because you and two of your friends, Jen and Terrance, were selected to run for president, vice president, and treasurer, respectively. On election night, the membership voted resoundingly for you, Jen, and Terrance to lead AFS for the next school year.

INSTRUCTIONS

1. Divide the class into teams of three to six students.
2. Each team should brainstorm ways to create an effective team environment in AFS.
3. Each team is to outline an initial plan of action.
4. The teams are to present their analysis and recommendations to the class members.
5. Vote with your class to determine which plan appears to have the best chance of success.

(*Note:* Students may not vote for their own team's program.)

Notes

1. Family Dollar History, http://familydollar.com/history.aspx (retrieved August 1, 2009).

2. Jennifer Thomas, "Dollar Tree Completes Acquisition of Matthews-Based Family Dollar," *Charlotte Business Journal*, July 6, 2015, http://www.bizjournals.com/charlotte/news/2015/07/06/dollar-tree-completes-acquisition-of-matthews.html.

3. Interviews with Margaret Gibson and Vernon Mason by Don C. Mosley Jr., July 2009.

4. Bill Fischer and Andy Boynton, "Virtuoso Teams," *Harvard Business Review*, July–August 2005, pp. 117–123.

5. Frank Siebdrat, Martin Hoegl and Holger Ernst, "How to Manage Virtual Teams," *MIT Sloan Management Review* 50, no. 4 (Summer 2009), pp. 63–68.

6. Charles C. Manz and Henry P. Sims Jr., "Superleadership: Leading Others to Lead Themselves to Excellence," in *The Manager's Bookshelf*, ed. Jan L. Pierce and John W. Newstrom (New York: Harper & Row, 1988), p. 328.

7. Interviews with Mike Odom, Kay Montgomery, and others, by Donald C. Mosley Sr., November 2002.

8. B. W. Tuckman, "Developmental Sequence in Small Groups," *Psychological Bulletin*, May 1965, pp. 384–399.

9. See, for example, F. Steven Heinen and Eugene Jacobson, "A Model of Task Group Development in Complex Organizations and Strategy of Implementation," *Academy of Management Review* 1 (October 1976), pp. 98–111.

10. Don Hellreigel, John W. Slocum Jr., and Richard Woodman, *Organizational Behavior*, 5th ed. (Mason, OH: South-Western Publishing, 1989), p. 210.

11. R. Bruce McAfee and Paul J. Champage, *Organizational Behavior: A Manager's View* (Mason, OH: South-Western Publishing, 1987), p. 250.

12. Don Hellriegel and John W. Slocum Jr., *Management* (Reading, MA: Addison-Wesley, 1986), pp. 539–542.

13. W. Allen Randolph, *Understanding and Managing Organizational Behavior* (Homewood, IL: Richard D. Irwin, 1985), p. 399.

14. Glenn M. Parker, *Team Players and Teamwork* (San Francisco: Jossey-Bass Publishers, 1990), pp. 63–87.

15. William C. Dyer, *Team Building: Issues and Alternatives* (Reading, MA: Addison-Wesley, 1977), p. 4.

16. Don Hellriegel and John W. Slocum Jr., *Management*, 7th ed. (Mason, OH: South-Western, 1995), p. 52.

17. About SEI, http://www.seic.com/enUS/about.htm (retrieved August 3, 2009).

18. Google Finance, http://www.google.com/finance?q=NASD AQ: SEIC (retrieved August 3, 2009).

19. Alfred P. West Jr. and Yoram Wind, "Putting the Organization on Wheels: Workplace Design at SEI," *California Management Review* 49, no. 2 (Winter 2007), pp. 138–153.

10
Meetings and Facilitation Skills

LEARNING OBJECTIVES

After reading and studying this chapter, you should be able to:

1. Explain how technology is enhancing meetings.

2. Explain the four basic purposes of meetings.

3. Differentiate between the leader-controlled approach and the group-centered approach used in meetings.

4. Identify the advantages and disadvantages of meetings.

5. Describe the actions a supervisor can take before, during, and after a meeting to make it effective.

6. Explain the process of consensus decision making in meetings.

7. Define group facilitation.

8. Explain the role of group facilitator.

9. Differentiate between process consultation and other models of consultation.

10. Specifically identify what can be done to make teleconferencing more effective.

Meetings are places where minutes are taken, but hours often wasted.

—Anonymous

You know you're in a bad meeting when you look out the window on a sunny summer day wishing you were the person sitting on the mower.

—Anonymous

Monkey Business Images/Shutterstock.com

Expert facilitation can help any organization be more successful, whether profit or non-profit.

Preview

TERESSA RAMSEY, EXTRAORDINARY LEADER AND FACILITATOR Supervisors and managers are increasingly being called on to demonstrate effective meeting and facilitation skills with their employee teams. As companies continue to downsize in efforts to operate more efficiently, meetings are the chosen method to facilitate employee engagement in decentralized organizations. Teressa Ramsey, the former Executive Director of Family Promise of Coastal Alabama, is a leader who possesses outstanding meeting and facilitation skills. Teressa led her Family Promise affiliate during a very challenging time and we want to highlight her leadership because her affiliate was recognized by the national office as one of the best in the entire nation!

Family Promise of Coastal Alabama's mission is "To provide temporary shelter, related services, and nurturing support to families as they work to achieve and sustain independence." In many communities, homeless families do not have social support options that keep families together. Most assume organizations like the Salvation Army fill this need, but they are not able to accommodate families. Homeless children have no control over their situation and no one outside their family they can turn to for help. During a time when they need their parents most, they are faced with not only being homeless but of their family being separated. The average age of the homeless population in the United States is 9.

Families with children are the fastest-growing segment of the homeless population with 25 percent under the age of 5. That is why Family Promise's mission to serve families in need and help them regain their independence is so critical.

Teressa Ramsey knew she was going to face many challenges when she decided to become the executive director, but with only one full-time case manager and several part-time employees, it was evident one of her first priorities would be expanding the staff to serve the increasing number of families in need. Teressa has a true passion for helping others, which is a good thing because she worked tirelessly coordinating a multitude of activities. Teressa's responsibilities included overseeing the screening of families for the program, coordinating with the volunteers to provide support, working with the Board of Directors to manage operations and raise money to keep the doors open, and also working with city and county agencies that receive homeless funding, as well as the public schools that teach and care for over 5,000 homeless children.

As you can imagine, Teressa spent much of her time in meetings with various stake-holders! Weekly staff meetings were generally informational, but when the office manager was out sick, they became a means to adjust the work schedule and continue operations with limited staff. The monthly board meetings allowed for give and take of information, whereas the board's committee structure facilitated fact-finding and problem solving efforts. Teressa also interacted with community partners such as Sybil Smith Family Village (a Dumas Wesley program) to co-sponsor the annual fund-raiser, Cardboard City. With so much to be done, Teressa learned to manage her time preplanning her days, weeks, and months as much as possible.

She also knew the appropriate roles to play in different situations, which was a real strength. One of the more challenging roles was that of the process consultant, which involved bringing key stakeholders together to solve problems and in doing so, enhancing the group's overall skills. Teressa's ability to act as a process consultant during a challenging time for her organization is the reason Family Promise of Coastal Alabama still serves those in need today.

The Great Recession hit nonprofits quite hard and Family Promise was no exception. In one quarter, their budget decreased by $55,000 (an 18.3 percent drop) because of city and county cutbacks and continued to decline as individuals and corporations gave less. At the same time, the numbers of homeless families significantly rose because people lost their jobs. During this turbulent period, many nonprofits closed their doors because they simply ran out of money, but not Family Promise of Coastal Alabama. Teressa put on her facilitator hat and coordinated joint problem solving among board members, staff, volunteers, and the community, which proved to be the difference.

While it is challenging for diverse groups to reach consensus, Teresa is a skilled facilitator. She always made sure the purpose of the meeting was clear and saw to it all participants got a chance to contribute and be heard. She intuitively knew when to push forward to keep momentum and when to stop and summarize the group's position. She knew participants would commit and follow through to implement strategies if they helped create them. Through their combined efforts, the stakeholders identified several key goals and developed action plans.

Some of those plans included the timing of fund-raisers, transitioning from relying on government funding to private donors, and branding Family Promise to increase visibility. In the short term to improve cash flow, the group spaced the fund-raisers quarterly throughout the year to coincide with months when cash flow was a problem. This stabilized cash fluctuations that resulted in less reactive and more proactive management. The group also began an aggressive "branding" campaign to increase community awareness and private funding sources. The five-year goal was to reduce government support from more than 80 percent to less than 50 percent by increasing private giving that would stabilize year-to-year funding. The three-year goal was to bring in enough private funds to hire three part-time positions: a fund-raising manager, a grant writer, and another case manager. The burnout rate for directors of nonprofits is quite high so with a larger staff Teressa could delegate many of her duties and responsibilities. This was important because it enabled Teressa to focus strategically—to help Family Promise reach its potential—rather than on the day-to-day operations. The two-year goal was to obtain enough private support to actually have a "cushion" in the bank to offset unexpected events.

The stakeholders worked diligently and achieved their two- and three-year goals, then continued to strive for the longer-term goal of 100 percent private funding. They achieved all of this during an extremely difficult economic period due to Teressa's leadership. Family Promise of Coastal Alabama grew its staff and maintained an 80 to 85 percent success rate, so more than 80 percent of the families were able to attain and sustain their housing. In addition, more than 40 percent of the families increased their incomes while working to attain their independence. These productivity levels would be desirable in any industry, but to achieve these outcomes with a budget of less than $400,000 is quite impressive!

Given Teressa's success leading a local affiliate, it is probably not a surprise that she was promoted to a regional director position with Family Promise, the position she currently holds.

Sources: Personal interviews and experiences with Teressa Ramsey between 2009 and 2013 and 2017 by Don C. Mosley Jr.; Steven G. Rogelberg, Cliff Scott, and John Kello, "Opinion & Analysis: The Science and Fiction of Meetings," *Sloan Review* (Online), January 1, 2007, http://sloanreview.mit.edu/article/the-science-and-fiction-of-meetings/.

Today's supervisors are increasingly being called on to function effectively in meetings, as both leaders and participants. This requires a supervisor to understand certain fundamentals about small group behavior and have certain facilitation skills. The first part of this chapter addresses important information about meetings, including the purpose, approaches, advantages, disadvantages, and important principles of conducting effective meetings. The second part of the chapter addresses specifics of group facilitation.

The Changing Technology of Meetings

1. *Explain how technology is enhancing meetings.*

There is no question advances in technology are altering the meeting landscape for many organizations and supervisors. As greater numbers of employees work at remote sites some distance from their supervisor, whether in an office or perhaps at home, electronic meetings have become a necessary and valuable communication tool. Computers (including laptops and computer software), smartphones, and videoconference equipment have broadened available communication media. Meetings conducted through e-mail or web-based computer software are becoming standard for many organizations and will increase as these tools become simple and cost effective.

Technology changes also serve as support tools for face-to-face meetings. PowerPoint software enables high-quality visual presentation; other packages support participation through voting, immediate electronic tabulation, and display of results. Still other technology enables electronic display of a working agenda and can record the disposition of each agenda item discussed, including action taken, names of people responsible for action, dates for completion, and so on. These are visually displayed for everyone at the meeting to see. McKinsey and Company and Allstate use software packages at their meetings to allow participants' spoken comments at a meeting to be instantly displayed on a computer connected to a large overhead projector. Resulting discussion/comments can be identified, linked, or edited onscreen and serve as an immediate basis for meeting minutes.[1]

Jon Feingersh/Blend Images/Getty Images

New technologies enable team members at distant locations to meet more easily without the time or expense of travel.

Mentor Graphics uses software to create an information hub that allows individuals to keep track of documents, procedures, and policies. Chris Sholler, a former general manager at Mentor, states, "We created a wiki using the software to help us track meeting notes, especially for regularly recurring meetings. It stores any documents, meeting minutes, and assigns/tracks action items by sending e-mail reminders to meeting attendees. You can configure it to do a lot of things actually (e.g., track program decisions, identify key stakeholders and their roles for the meeting, create agendas—great for project or program management). It's accessible over the web, but usually through an intranet so only company personnel can reach it."[2] High-tech support tools will continue to impact meeting effectiveness, for all types of meetings, whether all members are physically present in the same room or electronically linked.

For many managers and supervisors, the face-to-face meeting remains the setting most utilized. Although this is the setting that forms the backdrop of this chapter, most principles presented also apply to electronically linked settings.

Purposes of Meetings

2. *Explain the four basic purposes of meetings.*

Meetings in today's organizations are a fact of organizational life. Estimates of time spent in meetings ranges from several hours to several days weekly, depending on the organization and position, with supervisors spending more time than nonsupervisory personnel.[3] According to a recent CBS news story, one unfortunate employee analyzed her work calendar and found before the month even began she was scheduled for 100 meeting hours. Based on a 40-hour workweek, she already had 100 out of 160 hours planned for meetings, leaving little room for much else. When she shared this information with her manager and colleagues, they were appalled, so the department eliminated several standing obligations, freeing up 30 hours a month. Even so, with 70 out of 160 hours planned for standing meetings, the need to manage and facilitate efficient and effective meetings becomes critical.[4] So much time is devoted to meetings some organizations, including Nestlé USA, have established a policy of scheduling one day weekly when no meetings are held to allow personnel time to "get their work done."[5] Indeed, we have all experienced meetings that are unproductive because irrelevant information is presented, key people are missing, meeting leadership is poor, and nothing meaningful is achieved. To supervisors and most organization members, though, meetings are indeed a fact of organizational life. At Intel, meetings are considered so important every employee completes an in-house course on effective meetings. In fact, former CEO Andy Grove was himself a course instructor.[6]

Meetings generally are called to achieve one or more of the following purposes (see Exhibit 10-1): (1) give information, (2) exchange information, (3) obtain facts about a particular situation, and (4) solve a problem.

Information Giving

information-giving meeting

Held to announce new programs and policies or to update present ones.

The **information-giving meeting** is held to make announcements of new programs and policies or update information on the present ones. Generally, the meeting is closely controlled by the leader or those who are called on to provide information to the group, frequently by means of committee reports. There tends to be little feedback from group members unless they have questions to ask or points to clarify about the information presented. Normally this is the easiest type of meeting to conduct because its format is highly structured and lends itself well to large groups.

Information Exchange

information-exchange meeting

Held to obtain information from group members.

The **information-exchange meeting** is called to obtain information from group members and allow them to provide information to one another.

At Family Promise, weekly staff meetings are held to present a status report on the number of families in the program and their stage in the process. This weekly exchange ensures the staff is knowledgeable about issues that might affect them during the week and helps them better serve those in need.[7]

EXHIBIT 10-1
Purposes of Meetings

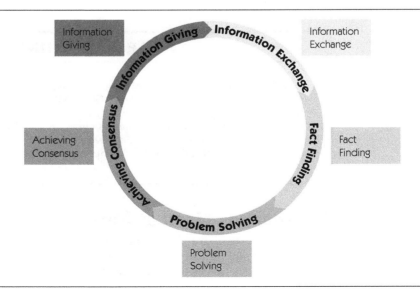

Fact Finding

Only relevant facts about a problem or situation should be sought in a **fact-finding meeting**. The meeting leader focuses not on finding solutions but rather on understanding the problem or situation. A supervisor might begin such a meeting as follows: "I called this meeting to discuss the high cost overruns we've been experiencing during the past month. I want to find out as much as I can about your perspective on the causes of this situation. Later, we can consider some steps we can take to reduce these costs." Once the facts have been uncovered, the supervisor has a better understanding of the situation.

Problem Solving

Typically, the **problem-solving meeting** combines the other purposes of information giving, information exchange, and fact finding. Considered the most challenging of the meeting types, this type of meeting is held to identify the major elements of a problem, discuss and evaluate alternative solutions, and ultimately make a decision as to the proper action to take. Topics of problem-solving meetings might include any of the following:

1. improving customer service;
2. reducing absenteeism;
3. determining production schedules or job assignments;
4. finding and remedying the causes of project delays; or
5. implementing a new policy in the best way.

> When Meg Whitman took over as CEO of Hewlett-Packard, the world's largest tech company, she had the herculean task of figuring out how to fix the company. She enlisted the support of her employees to help solve problems. Her job was to facilitate the process and she did so by asking relevant and probing questions "until the path ahead is obvious." Meg's approach to problem solving was to figure out what she did well and bring people on board that were good at what she was not. She reviewed her to-do-list weekly so she was always focused on the most important issues. She was not afraid to walk away from gridlock, and in fact believed walking away provided perspective. She believed in keeping meetings under control to best manage everyone's time. It was imperative to spend time asking, "What are the things we need to measure? . . . If you start to see things going south, then you can get in front of them."[8]

STOP AND THINK

Lois Kelly, founder and principal of Meaning Maker, a major marketing consulting firm, and former senior vice president of one of the largest public relations firms in the world, says, "Meetings have become 'let me show you my PowerPoint presentation.' The best thing that can happen in corporate America is there is a ban on PowerPoint. To me a meeting is a place where there is interaction and something gets decided and learned. I have sat through so many meetings where people just go through their slides."[9] What do you think about Kelly's assertion?

Approaches Used at Meetings

The interactions that take place at meetings vary greatly. Much depends on the purpose of the meeting and the meeting leader's personal style. One of two approaches is generally used in conducting meetings: (1) a leader-controlled approach or (2) a group-centered approach.

Leader-Controlled Approach

leader-controlled approach

Used at meetings of large groups when the leader clearly runs the show and the open flow of information is impeded.

The **leader-controlled approach** is when the leader clearly runs the show, and is often used at information-giving meetings or when the large size of the group prohibits an open flow of information among members. The leader opens the meeting, makes announcements, or calls on those who have information to present. If anyone in the group has questions or comments to make, he or she addresses them to the leader. The leader may answer the questions or bounce them to someone else. Exhibit 10-2 illustrates this approach. Should a stranger walk in after the meeting has begun, she or he would have no difficulty identifying who is in charge.

One advantage of this approach is it is generally easier on the leader because the fairly rigid structure means there are few surprises. Another advantage is this approach allows a large amount of material to be covered quickly. It also lends itself to larger groups.

William Pagonis, chief of operations for Sears, requires attendees to stand during his regular briefings. Pagonis boasts he can cover more material in a 15-minute stand-up meeting than he could in a two-hour seated version.[10]

An obvious disadvantage of the leader-controlled approach is it discourages a free flow of information. The fact that comments from the group must go through the leader means spontaneous, direct remarks may go unmade. The creativity that results from the "piggy-backing" of ideas is stifled. Another disadvantage is members have no real opportunity to get sensitive and emotional issues out in the open and blow off steam.

Group-Centered Approach

group-centered approach

Used at meetings when group members interact freely and address and question one another.

In a **group-centered approach**, group members interact more freely with one another, as shown in Exhibit 10-3. The meeting leader does not dominate the discussions; neither does he or she simply sit back and allow the group to formulate its own direction. Quite the contrary; the leader uses facilitation skills to keep the meeting moving by directing/redirecting focus, asking for clarification, making sure everyone speaks, summarizing the group's position, testing for consensus, moving the group to the next issue, and so on.

The advantages of the group-centered approach stem from the greater interaction that occurs at the meeting. First, it results in a better understanding of members' viewpoints. Second, if the purpose of the meeting is to solve a problem, the free flow of information

EXHIBIT 10-2
Interaction in the Leader-Controlled Approach

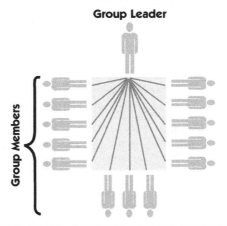

Group Leader

Group Members

EXHIBIT 10-3
Interaction in the
Group-Centered
Approach

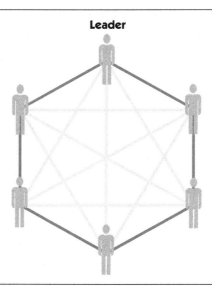

Leader

may contribute to a better decision. Third, when people can express their emotions or disagreements, they feel better.

One disadvantage of the group-centered approach is the meeting takes up a great deal more time than does the leader-controlled approach. Another disadvantage is the increased interaction among members means the leader's skills are tested more severely. The leader must determine when to move the discussion of a topic along. He or she must make sure everyone gets a chance to speak and discussions stay close to the subject. Also, because the leader must deal with diverse personalities, he or she must know how to handle emotions that may arise. A third disadvantage is this approach is not well suited to large groups because of its interpersonal nature.

Which Approach Should You Use?

Which approach is better for you, as a supervisor, to use? There is no best answer to this question. The answer depends on such factors as the meeting's purpose, the size of the group, the abilities of the group members, the amount of time allowed for the meeting, your skills, and the subjects to be discussed. Remember, you can shift from one approach to the other at a single meeting, depending on the nature of the items on your agenda.

Yoshi Tanabe's approach at meetings suits his purposes. Take Wednesday's meeting, for instance. The first item on his agenda was the new vacation scheduling procedure. At this point Tanabe was the expert in the room. He made a three- to four-minute presentation on the new procedure and then fielded questions from the group.

The next topic on the agenda was the need to develop and submit to higher management a plan for the department's participation in the company's 10-year anniversary open house for members of the community. Tanabe used a more open approach for the discussion of this topic. It took up about 20 minutes, with much interaction among the group. Within this time, Tanabe and the group came up with a plan for the department's role during the open house.

4. Identify the advantages and disadvantages of meetings.

Advantages and Disadvantages of Meetings

Some supervisors despise attending and conducting meetings. They prefer to communicate on a one-on-one basis. Because meetings are a fact of life for supervisors, it is appropriate at this point to consider the advantages and disadvantages of meetings. Then, in the remainder of the chapter, we provide pointers on how to make meetings more effective.

Advantages of Meetings

Meetings save time, ensure the supervisor's communications are consistent, and permit a formal exchange of important information and ideas. Let's explore how these advantages work.

Save Time   Suppose you, as a supervisor, have a group of employees whose jobs are *not* performed in the same work area (as is the case with outside sales, delivery services, maintenance, or patient care). To communicate on a one-on-one basis, you would have to move from one location to another during the work period. By having a meeting, you can save a great deal of your personal time that would otherwise be spent tracking down each of your employees.

Moreover, when minutes of the meeting are distributed to members, they serve as a permanent record of what occurred or was agreed on. In this way, they save time that might otherwise be needed to clarify or repeat what was said.

Ensure Consistency of Information   Meetings provide an opportunity for all present to hear the same message. If you communicate separately with each of your team members, you may present the information more effectively to some than to others. Also, some of your team members may ask questions or make comments that help clarify the communication or add a slightly different flavor to it. With one-on-one contacts, the grapevine goes to work, especially if there is a long lapse of time between when you talk with the first team member and when you speak with the last team member.

Permit Formal Exchange of Information   Sometimes individual members of a work group have information that *must* be shared with all the other group members. This is particularly true when a problem confronts the work group. In a meeting, a comment made by one member frequently triggers an important idea in another member. This exchange can lead to solutions that might not have been thought of by any one member.

The degree of formality inherent in a meeting can be used to advantage by a supervisor. For example, suppose that you, a supervisor, have been told by the plant manager that production must be increased by 15 percent over the next year or the plant will be closed. Presenting this information to your work group in a meeting conveys the seriousness of the situation and dramatizes the impact of the message.

Disadvantages of Meetings

Meetings may result in watered-down decisions, may not be cost effective, and may be too impersonal. Let's see how these disadvantages arise.

Many Are Unnecessary   Many supervisors claim they waste too much time in unnecessary meetings. Yet they themselves hold many meetings perceived by their members as unnecessary. Meetings interrupt members' work day, may take them away from higher priority tasks and compete with other activities such as deadline-driven tasks, and can add significantly to job stress. Is the structure provided by a meeting essential to achieving

EXHIBIT 10-4
Meetings Cost!

Many managers overlook the cost of meetings. The following table approximates hourly costs for employees at four salary levels. The hourly rates include only salary and normal benefits. They do not include costs of meeting planning and preparation time, travel time/costs, follow-up costs, and the like.

SALARY/BENEFIT HOURLY MEETING COSTS

	NUMBER OF PARTICIPANTS				
SALARY	25	10	8	6	4
$100,000	$1,825	$730	$584	$438	$292
80,000	1,460	584	467	350	234
60,000	1,095	438	350	263	175
40,000	730	292	234	175	117

your purpose? Could it be achieved as effectively through other means, such as by telephone, e-mail, or memo? Do all members of your group need the information or just a few? At Intel, most conference rooms are lined with posters reminding those present to adhere to guidelines for effective meetings. Among the posters, one asks, "Is This Meeting Necessary?"[11]

May Not Be Cost Effective Meetings are more expensive than most people realize. When employees attend meetings, they are not doing their normal jobs. Suppose 10 people, with an average annual salary of $60,000, attend a one-hour meeting. The cost of the meeting includes not only their salaries for that hour, but also costs for vacations, holidays, sick leave, medical insurance, Social Security, travel time, and so on. As shown in Exhibit 10-4, the cost of the meeting is $438. The meeting must therefore provide information important enough to justify the cost associated with it. Exhibit 10-4 does not include the costs associated with time spent planning for the meeting or traveling.

May Water Down Decisions Unless a meeting is properly conducted and its members are committed to effectiveness, the decisions made at the meeting may simply reflect the average input of members, rather than the ideas of the best members. Sometimes opinions voiced by the group's brightest or best-informed members may not be accepted by the majority. At other times, knowledgeable members may suppress their own disagreements simply for the sake of harmony.

May Become Too Impersonal Meetings may not allow the personal interaction required for many sensitive issues. On a person-to-person basis, employees may communicate readily to their supervisor. Because a meeting involves a more formal setting with many people present, some employees will be reluctant to speak up.

Making Meetings Effective

5. *Describe the actions that a supervisor can take before, during, and after a meeting to make it effective.*

This section presents some ideas that should help you conduct more effective meetings. Some of the actions discussed are performed *before* the meeting, some *during* the meeting, and some *after* the meeting. As a prelude to this section, we invite you to complete Exhibit 10-5.

EXHIBIT 10-5
Scoring Your Meeting
Leadership

How would you rate yourself as a meeting leader? For each of the 12 items below, circle the response that comes closest to how you view your own meeting conduct. If you do not conduct meetings, assess the meeting leadership of your own boss or another leader of meetings that you normally attend.

		STRONGLY AGREE	AGREE	DISAGREE	STRONGLY DISAGREE
1.	I assess whether a meeting is the most effective use of everyone's time before calling it.	1	2	3	4
2.	I have in mind a specific objective for each meeting that I call.	1	2	3	4
3.	I plan in advance the details of my meetings, such as who should attend, materials to distribute, meeting place, etc.	1	2	3	4
4.	Where time allows, I plan and distribute an agenda in advance of my meetings.	1	2	3	4
5.	My meetings stick to the published agenda without too much straying.	1	2	3	4
6.	I do not monopolize discussion in meetings.	1	2	3	4
7.	I maintain balanced participation among all meeting members.	1	2	3	4
8.	I encourage discussion of all sides of issues without showing my bias.	1	2	3	4
9.	Participants would say that I keep a meeting moving toward its objectives.	1	2	3	4
10.	At the end of a meeting, I summarize the key ideas presented/actions taken.	1	2	3	4
11.	I maintain and circulate meeting minutes.	1	2	3	4
12.	I follow up in a timely manner on actions taken during meetings.	1	2	3	4

Scoring: Sum your circled responses.

Score of 12 − 15 = Excellent

16 − 19 = Very Good

20 − 24 = Good

25 − 29 = Average

30 − 48 = Below Average

Factors to Consider Before the Meeting

Two important premeeting steps ensure an effective meeting: (1) have a clear purpose and (2) preplan the meeting.

Have a Clear Purpose   Assuming a meeting is necessary, you should have a clear purpose for it; otherwise, you waste everyone's time, including your own. Earlier, we noted meetings can serve any of several purposes: (1) give information, (2) exchange information, (3) obtain facts, and (4) solve a problem.

Having a clear purpose responds to the question participants ask themselves: "Why are we here?" Having a clear purpose also enables other premeeting plans to be developed to support the purpose.

STOP AND THINK

What are the pros and cons of having regular weekly meetings at an established time?

Preplan the Meeting   Many meetings are doomed from the start because of poor initial planning. Perhaps another group reserved the conference room or the bulbs in the overhead projector are burned out. Maybe the people present at the meeting weren't notified they should bring certain needed information or the leader simply hasn't done his or her homework! Proper planning requires you to do some work before the meeting begins. Such work might include the following:

1. Make sure the people who are to attend the meeting have adequate advance notice (unless it's an emergency meeting).
2. Make sure key people will be able to attend.
3. Develop and distribute copies of the meeting agenda in advance. This enables people to bring essential documents with them or gather information that may prove helpful. See Exhibit 10-6 for agenda planning insights.
4. Let people know in advance if they are expected to provide information or make a report.
5. Check to see the meeting room is arranged as you desire and the visual aids you intend to use function properly.
6. Form a general idea of how long the meeting should last. You may want to indicate this to those who will attend. It is easier to predict the length of information-giving and information-exchange meetings, however, than meetings held for fact finding or problem solving.

Factors to Consider During the Meeting

When the meeting time arrives, you can take a number of steps to help ensure the meeting's success. Among these are (1) starting the meeting on time, (2) designating someone to take minutes, (3) clarifying your objectives and expectations, (4) keeping the meeting on the desired topic, (5) encouraging participation, and (6) making sure there is closure.

Start on Time   Eli Mina, author of *The Complete Handbook of Business Meetings*, says starting on time is a cardinal meeting principle.[12] There may be occasions when one or two employees do not arrive on time for a meeting. To avoid unnecessary delays, the supervisor should begin the meeting as scheduled. If a supervisor consistently waits for late arrivals, attendees may get the message it's okay to be late, and successive meetings will start later and later. Such delays waste the time of those who arrive promptly.

minutes

A written record of the important points discussed and agreed on at a meeting.

Designate Someone to Take Minutes   Especially for information exchange, fact-finding, and problem-solving meetings, it is helpful to have someone record the important points discussed and agreed on at the meeting. These points are then outlined in a document called the **minutes** of the meeting and copies are distributed after the meeting. If no one takes minutes, those attending the meeting would be well advised to take notes on their own.

EXHIBIT 10-6

Agenda Planning

Having a well-planned agenda is a critical starting point toward effective meetings. Many organizations have provided meeting "templates," which serve as guides for creating effective agendas. The template may reflect the components of a well-planned agenda and provide an actual physical design that can be used. The sample agenda below illustrates the details of a well-planned agenda for a fact-finding and decision-making meeting.

SAMPLE AGENDA

Date:	March 5, 2018	Location:	3rd floor conference room
Meeting called by:	Beth Shapiro	Attendees:	See distribution list
Facilitator:	Beth Shapiro, Alice Chang	Please read:	Attached memo from Beth on expectations, deadlines, etc.
Note taker:	Bill Smith	Please bring:	Memo, So. Am. Strategy Plan

Objectives

- Review past efforts at launching products in South America
- Identify problems or obstacles to product introduction
- Determine possible approaches to overcoming problems
- Assign tasks and establish deadlines

Agenda

Time	Topic	Responsibility
8:30–8:40	• Introductions and review of agenda	Beth Shapiro
8:40–9:00	• Review of past launches in So. America (presentation)	Mario Cisneros
9:00–9:45	• Potential problems and solutions (brainstorming)	Alice Chang
9:45–10:00	• Assignment of action items	Beth Shapiro

Additional Information: This meeting will be the first of two. For this one, the goal is to surface all ideas, so each person should come prepared to contribute. At the end of the brainstorming session, we will decide as a group which solutions to pursue and will assign tasks to the appropriate team members.

Note that the agenda indicates three specific people other than the meeting leader who will have a formal role in the meeting: (1) a note taker (the basis for meeting minutes), (2) a presenter other than the leader, and (3) a resource person who will serve as facilitator for the brainstorming session. Here are some other helpful agenda planning insights:

1. If possible, distribute an agenda several days before a meeting.
2. Allow an opportunity for members to add topics to the agenda.
3. Indicate the time allotted for agenda topics. This will help time management during the meeting.
4. Where the list of agenda topics is long, begin with routine items.
5. In longer meetings, controversial topics should be addressed sufficiently early in the agenda while group energy is high. Placing controversial items at the end of an agenda when discussion time is limited may give the impression that you are manipulating the group.
6. Build a break into meetings that last longer than 90 minutes. This will allow members to network, address other work-related items, and use the restroom as needed.

Source: Sample Agenda adapted from Deborah J. Barrett, *Leadership Communication* (New York: McGraw Hill/Irwin, 2006), p. 216. Other information from http://www.3com/meetingnetwork/reaing-room/meetingguide_anatomy.html.

Prior to a meeting, check to see if the visual aids you intend to use function properly.

Clarify Your Expectations   Earlier in this chapter, we stated a meeting was generally called to serve one or more of the following purposes: to give information, exchange information, obtain facts or solve a problem, and make a decision. As the leader of the meeting, make sure you introduce each item on the agenda by stating your purpose for including it. For example:

1. "I'd like to *give you some information* about . . . ." [information giving]
2. "Attached to the agenda I sent each of you was the memo from Human Resources regarding the new benefits. I'd like to get your reactions to these new benefits." [information exchange]
3. "The purpose of this meeting is to review the recent changes in our billing policy and their impact on collections. Your input will give me an idea of the success or failure of our new billing policy. In your experience, what has been the effect of the billing policy?" [fact finding]
4. "I'd like to get your ideas on what we can do to show our department in its best light during our open house. After hearing your ideas, I'll put together our plan." [problem solving and decision making]
5. "The branch manager wants to know our department's position on switching to a week of four 10-hour days, as we discussed in our meeting last week. I can go any way you want to on this. *What do we want to do?*" [decision making]

In each example, the supervisor spelled out and clarified his or her expectations regarding an item on the agenda. Take special notice of examples 4 and 5, where the supervisor carefully outlined the role of the group in the decision-making process.

Provide Leadership   Ineffective leadership ruins many well-prepared meetings. The supervisor must be prepared to demonstrate leadership in the following ways:

1. Keep the meeting moving. *Don't allow a meeting to drag on and on, and don't stray too far from the topic being discussed. If people wander from the topic, you might say, "We seem to have drifted from our major issue. Let's go back. . . ."*

2. See to it most or all members contribute to the discussion. *Don't allow one or two people to dominate the meeting. If this happens, call on others first for their comments or reactions.*
3. Summarize the apparent position of the group from time to time. *You might say, "Do I read the group properly? You seem to be saying...."*
4. Address various problems related to participant behavior. Exhibit 10-7 *shows how to deal with some inappropriate behaviors.*

Encourage Two-Way Communication   In most meetings, the leader's job is to facilitate openness and interaction among group members. This is particularly important when the leader uses the group-centered approach. The leader must be an alert listener and skilled in helping individuals in the group to express themselves. A key skill is the ability to use questions to involve individual members or the entire group in the communication process. Exhibit 10-8 shows some questioning techniques used by the meeting leaders.

Work to Achieve Consensus Decisions

6. *Explain the process of consensus decision making in meetings.*

consensus

The acceptance by all members of the decision reached.

Given the current trend toward participative management, a particularly important concept is that of consensus decision making.

Consensus is frequently misunderstood. It does not mean members agree with the decision; it means they agree to *accept* it, even though they may not personally favor it. The following example illustrates consensus.

Charles Evans couldn't win support from other team members regarding his position on the team's recommendation about a company parking lot policy. Evans favored a process that allocated preferred parking places for key personnel in the company—some by seniority, some by position. Most other team members favored a process that had no preferred parking. The team leader stressed the need for a consensus decision that all members could accept.

Charles spoke openly about why he felt his approach was best, responded to questions raised by other team members about his position, and raised many questions about their position. The team leader had given him extra time to survey how other companies in the community handled the situation. Finally, after all issues seemed to have been fully discussed, the team leader said, "I sense that after our full examination of the issue, while not unanimous, the group favors a system that will operate as an open, first-come, first-served system. Is this correct?" No one dissented. She continued, "That, then, is what we will send to the president. Charles, thank you for helping us to more fully explore all aspects of the system that we're recommending. Can you accept the team decision?" Evans reflected, "It was a fair process. I presented my views; they just think differently on this one." He said, "Yes, I can support it, even though I disagree with it." "Good," said the team leader, "We have reached consensus."

Consensus is more difficult when members have personal stakes in decision outcomes and when there is much member diversity. Such is often the case with cross-functional teams. Consensus is not always achievable; some members openly state their intent not to support the group's decision. Perhaps they feel others do not listen meaningfully to dissenting views or attacks are made on personality rather than position. At times, the team decision is hurried, or the dissenter feels too strongly pressured or takes the position, "If it's not my way, I won't support it, period." Sometimes members appear to accept the group's decision but work to sabotage it or divorce themselves from it once the group leaves the meeting room.

EXHIBIT 10-7

Suggestions for Handling Disruptive and Inappropriate Behaviors at Meetings

TYPE	BEHAVIOR	SUGGESTED RESPONSE
Hostile	"It'll never work." "That's a typical engineering viewpoint."	"How do others feel about this?" "You may be right, but let's review the facts and evidence." "It seems we have a different perspective on the details, but we agree on the principles."
Know-It-All	"I have worked on this project more than anyone else in this room...." "I have a Ph.D. in economics, and...."	"Let's review the facts." (Avoid theory and speculation.) "Another noted authority on this subject has said...."
Loudmouth	Constantly blurts out ideas and questions. Tries to dominate the meeting.	Interrupt: "Can you summarize your main point/question for us?" "I appreciate your comments, but we should also hear from others." "Interesting point. Help us understand how it relates to our subject."
Interrupter	Starts talking before others are finished.	"Wait a minute, Jim. Let's let Jane finish what she was saying."
Interpreter	"What John is really trying to say is...." "John would respond to that question by saying...."	"Let's let John speak for himself. Go ahead, John, finish what you were saying." "John, how would you respond?" "John, do you think Jim correctly understood what you said?"
Gossiper	"Isn't there a regulation that you can't...?" "I thought I heard the V.P. of Finance say...."	"Can anyone here verify this?" "Let's not take the time of the group until we can verify the accuracy of this information."
Whisperer	Carries on irritating side conversation.	Walk up close to the guilty parties and make eye contact. Stop talking and establish dead silence. Politely ask the whisperers to wait until the meeting is over to finish their conversation.
Silent Distractor	Reads newspapers, rolls eyes, shakes head, fidgets.	Ask questions to determine the distractor's level of interest, support, and expertise. Try to build an alliance by drawing him or her into the discussion. If that doesn't work, discuss your concerns with the individual during a break.
Busy-Busy	Ducks in and out of the meeting repeatedly, taking messages, dealing with crises.	Schedule the presentation away from the office. Check with common offenders before the meeting to make sure interruptions during the planned time will be minimal.
Latecomer	Comes late and interrupts the meeting.	Announce an odd time (8:46) for the meeting to emphasize the necessity for promptness. Make it inconvenient for latecomers to find a seat, and stop talking until they do. Establish a "latecomers' kitty" for refreshments.
Early Leave	Announces, with regret, the need to leave for another important activity.	Before starting, announce the ending time and ask if anyone has a scheduling conflict.

Source: "Ten Deadly Sins of Poor Presentation," from *Presentation Plus* by David Peoples, pp. 52-54. Copyright © 1988 John Wiley & Sons, Inc., New York. Reproduced with permission of John Wiley & Sons, Inc.

EXHIBIT 10-8

Questioning Techniques for Leaders of Meetings

- *Clarifying or elaborating on a point made by someone.*
  Example: "Are you saying that . . . ?" or "Alice, would you mind giving us a little more detail about the situation? When did it happen?"

- *Calling on someone who is reluctant to talk.*
  Example: "Pete, you've been through more maintenance shutdowns than most of us. What do you think about all of this?"

- *Getting specific facts.*
  Example: "Exactly what were our production figures last month? Can someone give us those figures?"

- *Examining possible alternatives.*
  Example: "What are the pros and cons of converting to the new system?" or "Would we be able to keep up our quality under the new system?" or "What would happen if . . . ?"

- *Initiating group discussion.*
  Example: "What is your reaction to this new vacation policy?" or "Does this new policy affect anyone here?"

- *Obtaining more participation from the group.*
  Example: "We've heard two alternatives. Are there any more?"

- *Guiding the meeting tactfully in certain directions.*
  Example: "We seem to have already discussed this issue pretty thoroughly and agreed on a course of action. Is everyone ready to move on?"

- *"Testing the water" as to the group's feeling.*
  Example: "What would be your reaction if we went to the system we've been discussing? Would you support it?"

Consensus is more likely when a group's members

1. Openly state their true feelings, ideas, and disagreements.
2. Examine their different views fully.
3. Try to understand underlying reasons behind their differences on an issue.
4. Actively listen to and seek to understand other members' positions.
5. Focus on issues rather than on personalities.
6. Avoid actions that polarize members or lock them into positions. This may be the case with voting or taking sides, especially in early stages of discussion.

Following discussion of alternatives (or causes), it is sometimes helpful in gaining consensus to determine a group's priorities, especially when several alternatives are available. One approach is the "dot plan." Alternatives are recorded on a flip chart or board. Each team member is given the same number of adhesive dots—say five—in three colors. One color represents high priority, another medium priority, and another low priority. Members then post their assigned dots to the different items. Some teams allow only one dot from one person on any one item; others may allow more passionate advocates to assign more than one. Following posting, a team can easily visualize how its members feel about alternatives. A variant is the "10-4" method used by teams at Bowater Carolina, the large newsprint manufacturer. Under this option, instead of colors, each member may assign a total of 10 points to items but no more than four to a single item. This achieves the same purpose as the dot listings. An example is shown in Exhibit 10-9.

EXHIBIT 10-9 Eleven Team Members' Scoring of Six Alternatives Using the 10-4 System	**Item for 10-4 Team Scoring: "Possible Ways to Increase Teamwork in Our Department"** a) Change incentive system so that it reflects part individual, part department results 3, 1, 2, 1 = 7 b) Include teamwork as an item on performance evaluation system 2, 3, 1, 3, 4, 4, 3, 4, 3, 4 = 31 c) Develop system for recognizing when someone has been a good team player 4, 4, 4, 4, 3, 4, 4, 4, 2, 4, 3 = 40 d) Include teamwork-related behaviors as part of everyone's job description 2, 2, 2, 3, 1, 1, 2, 2 = 15 e) Cross-train members so that they better understand all jobs in the department 4, 1, 2, 3, 2, 2, 1, 1 = 16 f) Rotate positions occasionally so that members perform each other's jobs 2 = 2 *Key:* letter = alternative; numbers = each member's allocation of 10 points; a maximum of 4 points can be awarded to a single alternative.

Get Closure on Items Discussed   At many meetings the authors observed, an item will be discussed, but then the leader goes on to the next item on the agenda, leaving everyone to wonder what has been concluded.

closure

Successfully accomplishing the objective for a given item on the agenda.

Achieving **closure** means reaching a conclusion with respect to a given agenda item that has been discussed. In the following example, notice how a department head achieves closure for a particular agenda item.

Martha Briem, a department head, presented comparative information showing her department had a quality-rejection rate 10 percent higher than that of other departments in the company. She asked for her supervisors' input about possible actions. The discussion lasted about 25 minutes. Then she asked each supervisor to come up with a plan for improving product quality in his or her area and to make a five-minute presentation at a meeting to be scheduled in two weeks.

Factors to Consider After the Meeting

Even though the meeting is over, your work isn't finished. Follow up by making sure the minutes (if any) are distributed and any important decisions or responsibilities assigned to specific individuals are carried out.

Distribute Copies of the Minutes   Distributing copies of the minutes of the meeting is important for the following reasons:

1. The minutes serve as a permanent record of what has been agreed on and committed to at the meeting.
2. The minutes identify topics on the agenda that have not been dealt with completely or have been suggested for a future meeting.
3. The minutes permit a smooth transition, allowing you to take up where you left off at the next meeting.

Follow Up on Decisions Made   It is crucial the supervisor follow up on any actions agreed on and any decisions made during the meeting. The follow-up may consist

ColorBlind Images/The Image Bank/Getty Images

Ideally, meetings will conclude with consensus and closure.

of personal observations or visits. It also may involve reports that keep the supervisor informed of progress regarding the agreed-on commitments.

"Oh, I make it a point to follow up on my meetings," stated Luis Santos. "We have a pretty active crowd who say what they think. If I feel that someone has really gotten ticked off or hurt by what was brought up at the meeting, I'll make it a point to try to smooth things out on a one-on-one basis. I also go one-on-one with somebody who said something I wanted to follow up on if I didn't feel the meeting was the place to do it."

More and more organizations are using facilitators to help make their meetings more effective, and they are training team leaders in group facilitation. We examine this important area next.

7. *Define group facilitation.*

Group facilitation

The process of intervening to help a group improve goal setting, action planning, problem solving, conflict management, and decision making in order to increase the group's effectiveness.

What Is Group Facilitation?

Group facilitation is a process of intervening to help a group improve goal setting, action planning, problem solving, conflict management, and decision making in order to increase the group's effectiveness. Although an outside facilitator can be helpful, as we saw in the chapter preview, the ideal is for managers and supervisors to gain facilitation skills and use shared leadership in carrying out the process.

As organizations cope with the world of increasingly rapid change, the need for facilitation to improve their effectiveness increases. Examples run the gamut from empowering employees, developing shared visions, and creating self-managing work teams to changing to a more participative organizational culture. It is hard to imagine successful change efforts in the areas of total quality management, reengineering, partnering, mergers, or downsizing without some form of facilitation.

Role of the Facilitator

8. *Explain the role of group facilitator.*

In our discussion of group dynamics and conducting meetings, you were introduced to facilitation challenges and suggestions for handling inappropriate behavior at meetings. A good foundation for being an effective facilitator requires experience and knowledge, not only of dynamics of the group but also of decision making, problem solving, communications, motivation, and leadership. In addition, the core skills shown in Exhibit 10-10 are essential.

Process Consultation

9. *Differentiate between process consultation and other models of consultation.*

Among the many roles facilitators must play is that of process consultant. In fact, process consultation skills are identified as being among the core skills of an effective facilitator. This role involves sitting in on team or task force meetings, observing the group's process, and intervening, if needed, to help the group function more effectively. Skill Builder 10.4 is designed to help you better understand when and how to intervene. Increasingly, facilitators are used in major change efforts of total quality management, reengineering, and partnering. In essence, a facilitator becomes a consultant. The following sections describe three consultation models; we draw extensively from author/consultant Edgar Schein in comparing them.

It is important to keep in mind the effective facilitator is primarily a helper and wants the group to achieve long-term development and continuous process improvement. Exhibit 10-11 highlights this emphasis by showing the distinction between basic facilitation and developmental facilitation.

An effective facilitator is primarily a helper.

EXHIBIT 10-10

Core Skills for the
Effective Facilitator

- Communication skills—listening and asking the right questions.
- Leadership skills—participative management and developmental leadership.
- Problem-solving skills.
- Group dynamics skills.
- Conceptual and analytical skills.
- Conflict management skills—principled negotiation.
- Process consultation skills—intervention and diagnostic insights.

EXHIBIT 10-11

Basic and Developmental Facilitation

CHARACTERISTIC	BASIC FACILITATION	DEVELOPMENTAL FACILITATION
Group objective	Solve a substantive problem or problems.	Achieve group goals along with solving substantive problems while learning to improve processes.
Facilitator role	Help group temporarily improve its processes.	Help group permanently improve its processes.
	Take primary responsibility for managing the group's processes.	Help group assume primary responsibility for achieving goals and managing processes.
Outcome for group	Emphasize dependence on facilitator for solving future problems.	Reduce dependence on facilitator for solving future problems.

Source: Roger M. Schwartz, *The Skilled Facilitator: Practical Wisdom for Developing Effective Groups*, Table 1.1, p. 7, adapted as submitted. Copyright © 1994 Jossey-Bass Inc. Reproduced with permission of John Wiley & Sons, Inc.

Purchase-of-Expertise Model   The most widely used form of consultation is the purchase-of-expert-information model. The organization, or someone within the organization, decides there is a need to call on an expert to help solve a problem or add a service. For example, someone to initiate an organizational attitude survey or introduce a performance evaluation system may be called. An individual who specializes in conducting marketing surveys or initiating total quality improvement programs also may be needed. Schein points out this model frequently produces a low rate of implementation of the consultant's recommendations. Further, this model is based on many assumptions that must be met for it to succeed, and therein lies its weakness. The assumptions are

1. The manager correctly diagnosed the organization's needs.
2. The manager correctly communicated those needs to the consultant.
3. The manager accurately assessed the capabilities of the consultant to provide the information or the service.
4. The manager considered the consequences of having the consultant gather such information and is willing to implement changes that may be recommended by the consultant.

Another weakness is the fact the model is based on a "tell and sell" method by the expert and there is no "ownership" or commitment by the client.

Doctor-Patient Model   A relationship between a consultant and an organization can be likened to that of a doctor and a patient. When an organization suffers symptoms such as declining sales or profits, low morale, or high turnover, a consultant may be brought in to check these problems. After the "checkup," the consultant prescribes what the organization needs to do to "get well" again. As Schein points out, this model places a great deal of power in the hands of the consultant in that he or she makes a diagnosis and also prescribes a treatment. The success of the model then depends on whether

1. The initial client accurately identified which person, group, or department is "sick."
2. The "patient" revealed accurate information.
3. The "patient" accepts the prescription, that is, does what the doctor recommends.[13]

process consultation

A consultation model that involves others in making a joint diagnosis of the problem and eventually provides others with the skills and tools to make their own diagnoses.

Process Consultation Model   In contrast to the other models, **process consultation** involves others in making a joint diagnosis and eventually provides others with the skills and tools to make their own diagnoses. Also, even though the consultant may be an expert in the area of consultation, he or she refrains from solving the problem for the client. The emphasis is on facilitating the process so the client learns problem-solving skills. Although the facilitator may make suggestions or raise questions that broaden the diagnosis or develop more alternatives, the client makes the ultimate decision and develops the action plan or remedy. The underlying assumptions of the process consultation model follow.

1. Clients/managers often do not know what is wrong and need special help in diagnosing what their problems actually are.
2. Clients/managers often do not know what types of help consultants can give to them; they need to be informed of the kind of help to seek.
3. Most clients/managers have a constructive intent to improve things but need help to identify what to improve and how to improve it.
4. Most organizations can be more effective if they learn to diagnose and manage their own strengths and weaknesses.
5. A consultant probably cannot, without exhaustive and time-consuming study or actual participation in the client organization, learn enough about the culture of the organization to suggest reliable new courses of action. Therefore, unless remedies are worked out jointly with members of the organization, who know what will and will not work in their culture, such remedies are likely to be either wrong or resisted because they come from an outsider.
6. Unless the client/manager learns to see the problem for him- or herself and thinks through the remedy, he or she will not be willing or able to implement the solution. More important, he or she will not learn how to fix such problems should they recur. The process consultant can provide alternatives, but decision making about such alternatives must remain in the hands of the client.
7. The essential function of process consultation, or PC, is to teach the skills of how to diagnose and fix organizational problems. In this way, the client is able to continue on his or her own to improve the organization.[14]

How do facilitators determine whether they are being effective? One group that facilitates partnering workshops always asks the participants to evaluate the effectiveness of both the workshop and the facilitator(s). The following comments demonstrate the facilitator provided good process consultation skills.

"The facilitators did an excellent job in serving as catalysts for dialogue."

"The facilitator took the time to help each person or group with problem solving and with staying focused."

"The techniques of the workshop leader improved communications and helped us to solve our problems in a collaborative manner."

"The facilitator provided good, constructive, visionary thinking and identified personal and group blind spots."

"The facilitator was collaborative, but firm enough to keep things focused and keep things moving."

"The facilitator's people skills were exceptional. He was genuinely interested in the individual and group needs, which made the workshop most effective."

"The facilitator achieved the goal of allowing us to solve our problems."

"The facilitator kept us focused without inhibiting the interaction of the participants."[15]

In two of the skill builders at the end of the chapter, you will have an opportunity to develop your process consultation and facilitation skills. Increasingly, team leaders (supervisors) are asked to play facilitator roles that previously were the domain of outside consultants.

Facilitating Teleconferencing

10. *Specifically identify what can be done to make teleconferencing more effective.*

Sometimes because of the expense of bringing people from distant locations to a meeting, a facilitator needs to set up or make arrangements for a teleconference. Susan Fox, executive director of the Society of American Archivists, developed excellent tips for facilitators in both for-profit and nonprofit organizations. They are presented in Exhibit 10-12.

STOP AND THINK

Would Ms. Fox's tips apply or need any modifications to accommodate a hybrid tele/web conference using software that enabled your participants to simultaneously see and interact with a common desktop? Discuss.

Leadership Strategies

As a young child, were you ever entertained by blowing bubbles? If so, you might recall playing a game with friends to see whose bubble could last the longest, and thus be the winner! Facilitation can be likened to gently guiding and protecting a bubble to ensure it stays intact and does not pop! Learning effective facilitation skills can be quite challenging because of the complex blend of art and science. Fortunately, to become an expert facilitator, you simply need the proper training and experience.

Effective facilitation requires the supervisor to learn how to balance three key dimensions: process, relationships, and outcomes. The process must be open, achieve desirable results, ensure participants feel safe, and guide—not lead—the group. With regard to maintaining effective relationships, participants must feel as if tension is managed appropriately, everyone has the opportunity to participate and contribute, and individuals listen respectfully. Ultimately, the facilitator's goal is for the group to accomplish its task or achieve its desired outcome.[16]

The authors' experience in working with organizations in strategic planning, partnering, team building, and organization development is that having effective internal facilitators is critical for success. Effective facilitators, in most instances, come from the supervisor/team leader ranks and are closest to where the real work of the organization

EXHIBIT 10-12

Tips for Facilitating Teleconferencing

Preparation

1. *Decide who will be in on the call.* The first thing you need to consider is who should participate in the call. Usually conference calls address a specific issue that requires discussion leading to consensus. Think about including members who hold information relevant to the topic at hand. This may or may not include the obvious participants. You will also want to include key representatives from constituencies potentially affected by the outcomes resulting from the call.
2. *Establish a clear set of desired outcomes.* Ask yourself these kinds of questions:
    - *Is this call necessary?*
    - *Can the issue wait?*
    - *If not, what needs to occur as a result of our discussion?*
    - *How quickly?*
    - *Who should be involved?*
    - *What will be the chief result?*
3. *Create and distribute an agenda.* Once you have the rationale and desired outcome firmly established, develop an agenda and distribute it to participants well in advance of the call, if at all possible. Remember to include clear instructions about how to dial into the call.

    All meetings, regardless of how they are convened, require an agenda. Don't try to cover too much ground. Keep the topic tightly focused, communicate your desired outcomes, and give each major agenda item a time limit. Cover minor items up front so that you can quickly move to items of substance. Conclude the agenda with next steps, which can be agreed on at the conclusion of the call.

Facilitation

Remember that a conference call is a cross between a face-to-face meeting and a telephone conversation. You will therefore need to draw on a number of skills. For example, similar to a face-to-face meeting, greet participants as they "check in," and engage those who are waiting for the quorum in small talk. Hold logistical and substantive topics until everyone is on line.

1. *Designate a timekeeper and note taker.* Once you have a quorum, ask one participant to be the timekeeper and another to take notes. You will, of course, take notes yourself, but having additional help will keep you focused on facilitation rather than dictation.
2. *Ask members to identify themselves each time they speak.* Because participants can't actually see one another, self-identification ultimately makes the discussion flow more easily. If a member forgets to identify him or herself, take it upon yourself to make the identification as quickly and as unobtrusively as possible.
3. *Call on the silent.* Lack of visual clues can easily result in people stepping in on each other's conversation or, more likely, in one or two members dominating the discussion. It's up to you to provide balance and to call on those who remain quiet. You will need to ascertain whether their silence is the result of agreement, disagreement, or shyness.
4. *Poll each member.* It's up to you to solicit full participation. If you take a vote, register each participant. In fact, poll each member each time you reach a decision point. Bottom line, never assume.
5. *Watch the clock.* As in any meeting, work with your timekeeper. Groups naturally gravitate toward less difficult issues, which can quickly waste valuable time. Keep the discussion moving toward substantive issues and outcomes.
6. *Consider alternatives for difficult issues.* You may discover that the more difficult issues cannot be resolved on the telephone. If the group cannot reach consensus or engages in a heated disagreement, it may well be that a conference call is not the best communication mechanism for that particular issue. Acknowledge that fact and either give members time to reflect and eventually convene a second call or, if necessary, find another way to meet and work things out.
7. *Review assignments and close positively.* End the call on a positive note, then reiterate the tasks and deadlines and the individuals assigned to carry them out. Congratulate your colleagues on their fine work, and thank them for their time.

Follow-Up

As soon as the call is complete, prepare the to-do list with the deadlines and designees and send it out immediately. Within the week, if not sooner, gather your notes from the call and summarize the proceedings for all participants. Most of us tend to quickly forget what we say and promise to do, so this point can't be emphasized strongly enough.

It also helps to solicit feedback about how participants viewed the usefulness of the call. Did it accomplish its aims? Are there areas in which you can improve your facilitation skills? Most of us are unaware of our own telephone habits, and this kind of feedback can be enormously helpful.

Source: "Tips for Facilitating Teleconferencing." Copyright © 1999. Reprinted with permission of Gale, division of Cengage Learning, www.cengage.com/permissions.

takes place, whether it is constructing a building, making a product, or providing a service. Thus, there are a number of firms that either provide training for facilitators who then return to their own organizations or provide facilitator consultants who work with organizations in-house. The International Association of Facilitators (IAF), a nonprofit organization, provides opportunities for members (facilitators) to meet and exchange ideas to improve competencies in helping groups and organizations.

● Chapter Review

1. *Explain how technology is enhancing meetings.*
Electronic technology is enhancing meetings dramatically. As greater numbers of employees work at sites distant from their supervisor, electronic technologies such as cell phones, videoconferences, and the computer have become valuable meeting tools. Moreover, face-to-face meetings are being enhanced through various computer software meeting-support programs, which include on-the-scene display of discussion points made, voting by members, actions taken, and on-the-scene meeting minutes.

2. *Explain the four basic purposes of meetings.*
Meetings can serve four general purposes: (1) give information, (2) exchange information, (3) find facts, and (4) solve problems. Group consensus is an important process in many meetings, especially in problem-solving meetings where decisions are made by the group.

3. *Differentiate between the leader-controlled approach and the group-centered approach used in meetings.*
With a leader-controlled approach to a meeting, the leader clearly runs the show and conducts a structured meeting. The advantages of this approach are it lends itself better to established timeframes, has more predictable outcomes, and is more appropriate for large groups. With a group-centered approach, more interaction occurs among members. This approach permits greater understanding, and the exchange of ideas is more apt to generate creative solutions.

4. *Identify the advantages and disadvantages of meetings.*
The typical supervisor frequently must conduct meetings with his or her work group. Meetings have the following advantages over one-on-one contacts: they (1) save time, (2) allow all present to hear exactly the same message, and (3) lend a degree of formality. The disadvantages of meetings are they (1) may result in watered-down decisions, (2) may not be cost effective, and (3) may become too impersonal.

5. *Describe the actions a supervisor can take before, during, and after a meeting to make it effective.*
A number of actions can help make meetings more effective. *Before* the meeting, the supervisor should determine whether a meeting is necessary, establish a clear purpose for the meeting, and plan it. *During* the meeting, the supervisor should start promptly, designate someone to take minutes, clarify his or her expectations, provide leadership, encourage two-way communication, and see to it closure is achieved on the items discussed. *After* the meeting, minutes of the meeting should be distributed and agreed-on commitments should be followed up.

6. *Explain the process of consensus decision making in meetings.*

Group consensus means members agree to accept the decision made by the group, even though not all of them may agree with it.

7. *Define group facilitation.*

Group facilitation is a process of intervening to help a group improve in goal setting, action planning, problem solving, conflict management, and decision making to increase the group's effectiveness.

8. *Explain the role of group facilitator.*

Among the many roles facilitators play is that of process consultant. In carrying out that role, the effective facilitator is primarily a helper and wants the group to achieve long-term development and continuous process improvement.

9. *Differentiate between process consultation and other models of consultation.*

In contrast to other approaches, process consultation involves others and eventually provides others with the skills to diagnose and solve their own problems.

10. *Specifically identify what can be done to make teleconferencing more effective.*

Teleconferencing can be made more effective by following these guidelines:

1. Include as participants those with information concerning the topic of the call and those affected by the outcome.
2. Establish desired outcomes and keep the call short.
3. Because the participants cannot see each other, involve all members and ask each to identify him- or herself before speaking; poll each member to ensure full participation.
4. Consider alternative solutions for difficult issues and the possibility of another call or another way to meet.
5. Review the tasks and deadlines and the individuals responsible for working on them.
6. Finally, close on a positive note.

Key Terms

information-giving meeting, p. 299
information exchange meeting, p. 299
fact-finding meeting, p. 300

problem-solving meeting, p. 300
leader-controlled approach, p. 301
group-centered approach, p. 301
minutes, p. 306

consensus, p. 309
closure, p. 312
group facilitation, p. 313
process consultation, p. 316

Discussion Questions

1. Explain some of the ways technology is impacting meetings.
2. Name the four basic purposes of meetings. Of these, which generally requires the most skill on the part of the leader?
3. Differentiate between the leader-controlled approach and the group-centered approach used in meetings.

4. What are the advantages and disadvantages of meetings?
5. Describe the actions a supervisor can take before, during, and after a meeting to make it effective.
6. Discuss the purpose of group facilitation and the role of the facilitator.
7. How does process consultation differ from other models of consultation?

Skill Builder 10.1

Resources

Interpersonal Skill

Information

Systems

Achieving Group Consensus (Group Activity)

The table below lists the qualities most valued in a leader. These qualities appear in no special order and do not represent an all-inclusive listing. You will be asked to rank these according to your personal view of what is most important to what is least important.

	QUALITY	RANK
a.	intelligent	____
b.	caring	____
c.	dependable	____
d.	inspiring	____
e.	mature	____
f.	forward-looking	____
g.	courageous	____
h.	honest	____
i.	fair-minded	____
j.	competent	____

Instructions:

1. Complete your personal ranking of the 10 qualities listed. Rate as "1" your most important, "2" your second most important, and so on, with "10" being the least important.
2. Break into groups of seven to nine persons. The group will select a leader and two observers, who will follow additional instructions outlined below.
3. As a group, reread the discussion on the consensus process.
4. The allotted time for this instruction is 30 minutes. *As a group, your leader will conduct a team meeting in which the team uses a consensus approach that results in a team ranking of the items. Make sure you fully explore differences of opinion among your members about the way your team will proceed to develop its ranking, as well as selection of what the team feels is #1, #2, and so on. Try to avoid voting, which tends to restrict discussion of an issue. Make sure all members "buy into" decisions of the group. It is not necessary you complete the ranking in the time permitted for the task. It is more important you reach consensus on what you achieve rather than totally completing the ranking of items. If you complete half or more of the items in the time allowed, the likelihood is you have sacrificed consensus to do so.*

Instructions to the leader:

Your team will have 30 minutes to work on the task. Remember, do not forge ahead without full discussion of all relevant issues. The consensus process takes time; make sure differences are fully explored and consensus achieved before moving along to the next issue. Your effectiveness as a leader and as a team is not based on how many items you rank, but rather the extent you effectively lead your group toward consensus.

(Continued)

Instructions to observers:

1. Your task is to observe the meeting, taking notes. Evaluate (a) the effectiveness of the leader's behavior in conducting the meeting and (b) the extent to which consensus was actually achieved by the group. Complete the leader assessment scale below.

		GOOD	FAIR	WEAK
a.	Clearly established the objective of the meeting.	___	___	___
b.	Kept discussion relevant.	___	___	___
c.	Made sure everyone participated.	___	___	___
d.	Used questioning techniques effectively.	___	___	___
e.	Kept the meeting moving along.	___	___	___
f.	Helped the group fully examine issues.	___	___	___
g.	Summarized key points thoroughly.	___	___	___
h.	Achieved closure for each item on the agenda.	___	___	___
i.	Maintained "consensus" approach within the group.	___	___	___

2. After the instructor calls time, or when the meeting is complete, whichever comes first, report your observations to the group. (Keep the report to five minutes.)

Skill Builder 10.2

Interpersonal Skill

Information

Systems

Effective/Ineffective Meetings Survey (Group Activity)

Likely you have been a participant in numerous meetings, perhaps in your job or as a member of a social group or student organization. Some of these have been effective and others less so.

Instructions:

1. Identify a specific meeting in which you have participated that you would consider highly effective. Make a written list of the reasons why you considered the meeting "highly effective."
2. Identify a specific meeting in which you participated that you would consider "highly ineffective." Make a written list of the reasons why you considered the meeting "highly ineffective."
3. Form teams of three to five persons, compare your lists with those of other members, and discuss the two lists.
4. Select a spokesperson to present to the class a summary of your team's lists to discuss.

Skill Builder 10.3

Technology

Resources

Interpersonal Skill

Information

Systems

Meeting Facilitation Challenges (Group Activity)

Assume you are the supervisor leading your work team in addressing an important issue. Each situation below represents an incident that crops up during the meeting.

1. Two of your team members, Jean Morton and Taylor Lester, are hard-nosed people who often compete for attention. They often argue with each other as a way to get the spotlight. This meeting you're conducting is no exception. After stating the problem and requesting alternatives from the group, you have a good idea who the first two to make comments will be. Morton gives the first alternative. Lester gives his alternative, which is, of course, quite different from Morton's. Morton mounts a counterattack by defending her own proposal. As she speaks, you can see by Lester's body language he is preparing his own counteroffensive.

2. One of your team members, Ernie Statler, is especially long winded. He always stretches what could be said in 10 seconds to a minute or more. The meeting has now lasted about 10 minutes and Statler has already spoken four or five times. You can see the boredom on everyone's face as he interrupts another member and gets set to talk again. You must intervene.

3. As your meeting moves along, Ann Stiles and Harry Curran have become distracting. They have whispered a few comments to each other, and you have noted some other team members' raised eyebrows and glances cast in their direction. Harold Rodriguez, one of your quiet, soft-spoken members, has the floor as Stiles and Curran continue their private conversation. It's time you intervened.

4. It's now about 35 minutes into the meeting, and someone in the group makes a comment about the upcoming big football game tomorrow between the state's two large college archrivals. Several members chime in with comments. Your group has some strong fans pulling for each school; several members are going as a group to see the game. They would obviously rather talk football than the subject at hand. You need to have them refocus.

5. At the start of the meeting, you told the group you could live with any decision they made. It's now about 45 minutes into the meeting and your team has fully discussed four workable alternatives. You feel one alternative is the best, but you can truly live with any of the alternatives offered. You say, "Well, we seem to have done a good job discussing the alternatives; let's see if we can now make a decision." At that point, one of the members asks which of the alternatives you favor.

6. Based on the team's responses, considerable time has been spent discussing the pros and cons and the best choice of the four. It appears seven of your nine members favor alternative 3. The other two members favor alternatives 2 and 4. You feel everyone has had a chance to speak up and hear each other out. You say, "It appears having heard from everyone on this issue, this group strongly favors alternative 3. Is this alternative workable with everyone?" Rasheed Khan, one of the dissenting members, states, "No, it's not okay with me. I'm firmly convinced it's not workable. I refuse to vote for something I don't think is best."

Instructions:

1. Indicate how you would handle each situation by writing down the exact words you would say.
2. In groups of four to six students, compare your responses to each situation. Select one for each situation that your group feels is best and read it to the rest of the class.

Skill Builder 10.4

Interpersonal
Skill

Developing Skills as a Facilitator/Consultant (Group Activity)

In preparation for this exercise, reread the section on process consultation. Keep in mind the primary role of the facilitator/consultant is that of helper to an individual, group, or organization.

Instructions:

1. Each member of the class is to identify a problem or issue with which he or she needs help. It may be you need help improving your study habits and grades. It may be you are having a problem at work with your boss or with someone who works with you or for you. The guideline is it must be a real problem or issue and you "own" the problem.
2. The class is to be divided into groups of three. Each member of the trio will take turns being the client and receiving help from the other two members. The client will start the process by stating the issue or problem and will have 20 minutes to receive help.
3. The other two members will ask questions to clarify, expand on, and sharpen the diagnosis. In carrying out the questioning, the facilitators will play an active listening role and ask questions that not only help them in understanding the problem, but also aid the individual being helped to better understand. Examples of such questions would be: "When did you first start having this problem? Can you expand on the history of your relationship with this coworker?"
4. Ask the client what steps, if any, have been initiated to solve the problem.
5. Move into a joint problem-solving framework where all three of you engage in brainstorming ideas on how to deal with the problem.
6. Put together an action plan using the best ideas on specific actions the client can take to solve the problem.

Skill Builder 10.5

Information

Systems

Resources

Interpersonal
Skill

Facilitator Training (Group Activity)

Assume you are in training to become an external facilitator/consultant and are faced with the following situations:

Your Task First you are to choose the correct answer from the three alternatives and write the letter (a, b, c) that corresponds to the answer provided under the heading "Your Answer." You will have 10 minutes to complete the task.

Team Task You will be assigned to a small team of trainees to develop a team answer. Although the team will arrive at its answer through consensus, remember consensus does not always mean unanimity. It means everyone has an opportunity to have his or her views considered before a choice is made. You will have 30 minutes to complete the team task.

How would you handle the following situations if you were the facilitator?

1. You are the facilitator at a workshop with 35 participants. The participants have agreed on a common set of goals, and they identified five issues they need to deal with to achieve their goals. Five ad hoc subgroups of seven participants have been assigned to develop a plan to solve one of the top issues. The first step in the problem-solving process is to clearly state the problem. The members of one of the subgroups approach you as facilitator and state they are having difficulty defining the problem and need your help.

   a. Tell them to do the best they can. (Your logic is that people learn from experience—success as well as failures.)

Information

Systems

   b. Ask a few questions, and then write your version of the problem on the flipchart.

   c. Suggest each person write a statement of the problem and then record all of them on the flipchart to see if one stands out or if there is a central theme.

Your Answer   Team's Answer   Expert's Answer

_____   _____   _____

2. You are facilitating a two-day workshop between the Navy and a contractor regarding the environmental clean-up progress of a Pacific island. Several former Navy personnel now work for the contractor. Toward the end of the first day, during a break, a public works civilian from the Navy approaches you and expresses a concern that a former Navy captain, who now works for the contractor, always begins a suggestion or recommendation with the following comment: "When I was Captain of XYZ installation and we were faced with this situation, we did so and so."

   a. Do nothing.

   b. As facilitator, talk with the former captain and level with him about the concern of a member of the Navy's group. Suggest he make recommendations without mentioning his former leadership positions in the Navy.

   c. As facilitator, mention the problem to the former captain's boss with the contractor. Leave it to him to decide whether or not he wants to say anything to the former captain.

Your Answer   Team's Answer   Expert's Answer

_____   _____   _____

3. You are facilitator for a group of 25 participants of two organizations who must work together to complete a major task such as building a dam. The two groups are having difficulties. As facilitator, you have taken them through a process where the group has identified and prioritized five issues they need to work on to ensure they achieve their goals. After this task is completed, the group takes a short break before they start work on the priority issues. During the break, a key manager of one of the organizations comes to you and says that unless the lack of trust issue is addressed, very little progress will be made in resolving the other issues.

   a. Tell the key manager to trust the process and by working on the five prioritized issues, team building will occur and trust will develop.

   b. Prior to reconvening, have a short meeting between four of the leaders, two from each organization, to gain their opinion on adding the trust issue to the list. Have the key manager present his case to them, and you, as facilitator, point out that developing trust is an important factor in successful teamwork and task accomplishment.

   c. When the group reconvenes, you, as facilitator, add the trust issue to the list to be worked on.

Your Answer   Team's Answer   Expert's Answer

_____   _____   _____

4. Assume you are facilitating a quarterly improvement meeting between representatives from the production and maintenance departments of a chemical plant. There are seven participants: four from production and three from maintenance. The meeting has become bogged down and is not making progress because of the strong views of two participants—one from production and one from maintenance. It appears to you although both views have merit, neither participant is hearing what the other is saying, and each is strictly focusing on his or her own viewpoint.

   a. Intervene and remind the participants of the time constraints and suggest they move on to something else.

(Continued)

b. Intervene and request to hear the views of the other participants.

c. Intervene by asking the production representative to summarize the maintenance representative's viewpoint to be sure the viewpoint was understood correctly by the production representative; then reverse the process.

Your Answer   *Team's Answer*   *Expert's Answer*

_____   _____   _____

5. Assume you are the facilitator/consultant for two medical firms located in a U.S. city with a population of 300,000 people. The firms are considering a merger; there are a number of win-win outcomes from such a merger (lower costs, better offices and facilities, more complete medical coverage, etc.). You are facilitating an initial exploratory meeting with eight doctors (four from each firm). After three hours, the meeting runs into difficulties, despite several interventions by you to get things on track. The problem is one of the doctors in the first firm is, from a leadership standpoint, very Theory X oriented and is strongly against the merger. It is obvious he basically does not trust the other doctors, and by voice tone and verbal and nonverbal actions, he is behaving in an autocratic manner.

a. Take a long break and have each group meet for an hour to decide if they really want to pursue the merger.

b. Intervene by giving a short theory input on Theory X and Theory Y management philosophies, and for this discussion, suggest that a participative shared leadership style should prevail.

c. Intervene by having all eight members respond on a 3 x 5 card to the following instructions:

   • Evaluate on a five-point scale how well we've done in focusing on substantive issues and ways to achieve our joint goals of better patient care, service, and profits.

   • Evaluate on a five-point scale how well we have done in carrying out good group dynamics of listening, supporting good ideas, sharing leadership, and differing without being disagreeable.

   • Post the results and use them as a basis for the group to discuss how to improve the group's functioning and progress.

Your Answer   *Team's Answer*   *Expert's Answer*

_____   _____   _____

6. Assume you are the facilitator for a national sales organization changing its culture to a team approach from an individual entrepreneurial approach. The theme of the two-day workshop is "working together to grow stronger."

   After the national sales director reviews the overall company objectives and history, each regional team prioritizes issues, problems, and opportunities they need to address to achieve overall company objectives. Next, each regional team works on an action plan involving the top-ranked item.

   As facilitator, you visit the four regional breakout rooms and are quite pleased three of the four regional teams are progressing well and demonstrating most of the characteristics of an effective team—shared leadership, good participation and listening, and so on. Unfortunately, the last regional team is having difficulty. After observing for some time, it is apparent the problem lies with the regional manager. He is doing 80 percent of the talking, cutting people off in midsentence who offer suggestions, and forcing his own viewpoint.

a. As facilitator, suggest the team members brainstorm ideas and write them on the flipchart before evaluating them.

   b. As facilitator, take over the leadership of the group by "playing traffic cop" and directing the flow of who talks when.

   c. Privately provide some coaching to the regional manager on how the session could be more productive.

   Your Answer   Team's Answer   Expert's Answer
   _____   _____   _____

7. This situation is a bonus question and provides an opportunity to find an answer comparable to, or even better than, the expert's answer. The instructor, with class input, will decide if a bonus is deserved.

   You have been asked as an outside facilitator to assist the chairperson of an appointed task force involving a department of the federal government. This department is moving into a new federal building under design and construction. The task force has been charged to determine such interior design questions as size and type of offices, paint color, size and number of conference rooms, and so forth.

   The task force consists of 10 government employees and has had two meetings. There was no progress made in the meetings, however, primarily because of two disruptive task force members. One of the disruptive individuals is very skeptical about any new, innovative ideas and is playing the role of devil's advocate (challenger), to the point of causing frustration and unproductive meeting progress. The other individual obviously has no interest in being on the committee and has done paperwork during both meetings. What advice would you give the meeting chairperson regarding how to handle this situation?

   Your Answer   Team's Answer   Expert's Answer
   _____   _____   _____

Source: This skill builder was developed by the Synergistic Group, Mobile, AL.

CASE 10.1

THE QUIET MEETING:

Debbie Ronson, sales supervisor, was just opening a meeting she had called for members of her department. Debbie did most of the talking for the first five minutes, recounting her group's performance over the past week. Then she asked, "Are there any questions?" No one responded.

Debbie then changed subjects. "As you know, in two weeks we'll be going to a new format for scheduling our calls. This was outlined in the memo from the vice president, copies of which I sent to each of you. This is going to alter your calling schedules and significantly change the way we've been doing things. I have some ideas on how we can best work into this new system. But before getting into that, I'd like to see if anyone here has any ideas . . . [pause]. Anyone care to contribute anything?" No one in the group responded.

Debbie continued, "Well, here's what I think we should do. . ." She then spent eight minutes outlining her plan. After the meeting was over, Debbie discussed it with one of her fellow supervisors. "I don't know what it is," she said, "but I can never get my people to say much at meetings. I try to give them a chance, but I always end up doing most of the talking. It seems they're either shy or disinterested, but I really don't know if that's the reason or not. I just wish they'd contribute their ideas."

INSTRUCTIONS

1. What might be some reasons for participants not saying much at Debbie's meetings?

2. Assume you are a facilitation consultant. What advice would you give Debbie for encouraging participation in future meetings?

Notes

1. Kitty Locker and Stephen Kyo Kaczamarek, *Business Communication*, 3rd ed. (New York: McGraw-Hill/Irwin, 2007), p. 323.

2. Interviews with Chris Sholler by Don C. Mosley Jr., July and August 2009.

3. Daniel L. Plung and Tracy Montgomery, *Professional Communication: The Corporate Insider's Approach* (Mason, OH: South-Western, 2004), p. 237; Steven G. Rogelberg, Cliff Scott, and John Kello, "Opinion & Analysis: The Science and Fiction of Meetings," *Sloan Review* (online), January 1, 2007, http://sloanreview.mit.edu /article/the-science-and-fiction-of-meetings/.

4. Laura Vanderkam, "Are Many Meetings Wasting Your Employees' Time?," *CBS News Moneywatch* (online), January 3, 2012, http://www.cbsnews.com /8301-505125_162-57351156/are-many-meetings-wasting-your-employees-time/.

5. Daniel McGinn, "Mired in Meetings," *Newsweek*, October 16, 2000, p. 152.

6. Heera Singh, "Ensuring Effective Meetings," *Asia African Intelligence Wire*, November 12, 2005.

7. Personal interviews and experiences with Teressa Ramsey by Don C. Mosley Jr., between 2009 and 2013.

8. George Anders, "The Reluctant Savior of Hewlett-Packard," *Forbes*, June 10, 2013, pp. 64–76.

9. Ibid.

10. Daniel McGinn, "Mired in Meetings," *Newsweek*, October 16, 2000, p. 152.

11. Ibid.

12. Cited in Robyn D. Clarke, "Whipping Up a Great Meeting," *Black Enterprise* 31 (December 2000), p. 82.

13. Edgar H. Schein, *Process Consultation*, vol. 1, 2nd ed. (Reading, MA: Addison-Wesley, 1988), p. 6.

14. Ibid., p. 9.

15. Client evaluation feedback to the Synergistic Group, Mobile, Alabama.

16. *Journal of Extension*, http://www.joe.org/joe /2006april/tt5.php (retrieved August 22, 2009).

11
Coaching for Higher Performance

We grow because we struggle; we learn and overcome.

—R. C. Allen

The mediocre teacher tells; the good teacher explains; the superior teacher demonstrates. The great teacher inspires.

—William A. Ward

My ultimate goal for every player is performance at the highest possible level.

—Don Shula, Coauthor, *Everyone's a Coach*

Ian Dagnall/Alamy Stock Photo

Effective managers, like those at Google, are able to coach their employees and help them reach their full potential.

Preview

GOOGLE: EIGHT BEHAVIORS OF EFFECTIVE MANAGERS Google's culture is unconventional, quirky, empowering, and performance driven. Its engineers are techno-savvy and eschew being managed or having to manage. Instead, they prefer focusing on tasks and achieving goals. In the early days, founders Larry Page and Sergey Brin even wondered if managers were necessary. But as the company grew, managers became a necessary evil. Think of the challenge. Since its inception, the company has focused on selecting individuals that "fit" the Google culture—individuals who are intelligent, are ambitious, think outside the box, work well within a team, and are self-directing with little to no need to be managed. Now, you have to convince them that being managed and managing others is good, not evil. How do you do it?

Google's answer was Project Oxygen, a research project that applied analytics in innovative ways to figure out what makes a great manager. Prasad Setty, one of the program's architects focused on analyzing management data, such as performance reviews and feedback surveys. The data were content analyzed, correlating words and phrases, resulting in eight characteristics or behaviors Google's best managers exhibited. The results were simple, yet powerful. In order of priority, an effective manager

1. Is a good coach.
2. Empowers the team and does not micromanage.
3. Expresses interest in and concern for team members' success and personal well-being.
4. Is productive and results-oriented.
5. Is a good communicator—listens and shares information.
6. Helps with career development.
7. Has a clear vision and strategy for the team.
8. Has key technical skills that help him or her advise the team.

These findings are significant for several reasons. First, coaching trumps technical skills, which came as a surprise to many at Google. Second, the results validated what academics and practitioners had been preaching for years—that coaching matters. Third, coaching principles are generalizable to different environments. Google—along with General Electric, Cargill, Eli Lilly, Adobe, and Accenture—has been highlighted as a "cutting edge" performance management organization. The one thing they all have in common is they make coaching a top priority. Lastly, these behaviors are the basis for Google's management training programs. The behaviors are general enough so training can be tailored to address individual manager's needs.

To illustrate, an employee recounts, "My manager was able to see my potential and gave me opportunities that allowed me to shine and grow. For example, early on in my role, she asked me to pull together a cross-functional team to develop a goal-setting process. I was new to the role, so she figured it would be a great way for me to get to know the team and also to create accountability and transparency. Once it was developed, she sent me to one of our Europe offices—on my own!—to deliver the training to people managers there."

Also, Lazlo Bock, former Senior VP of People Operations, "tells the story of one manager whose employees seemed to despise him. He was driving them too hard. They found him bossy, arrogant, political, secretive. They wanted to quit his team. 'He's brilliant, but he did everything wrong when it came to leading a team,' Mr. Bock recalls. Because of that heavy hand, this manager was denied a promotion he wanted, and was told that his style was the reason. But Google gave him one-on-one coaching—the company has coaches on staff, rather than hiring from the outside. Six months later, team members were grudgingly acknowledging in surveys that the manager had improved."

In part due to their concerted efforts to develop great managers, Google retained the top spot on *Fortune*'s list of "the country's Best Companies to Work For" for the sixth straight year. Ninety-six percent of employees surveyed indicated they worked for a great boss. In a decentralized culture with over 60,000 employees, effective coaching is a key ingredient.

Sources: "Great Place to Work: Google Inc.," *Fortune*, September 19, 2016, http://reviews.greatplacetowork.com/google-inc?utm_source=fortune&utm_medium=referral&utm_content=reviews-link&utm_campaign=2017-fortune100-list; "100 Best," *Fortune*, 2017, http://fortune.com/best-companies/google/ (retrieved July 2, 2017); David Garvin, "How Google Sold Its Engineers on Management," *Harvard Business Review*, December 2013, https://hbr.org/2013/12/how-google-sold-its-engineers-on-management; Kris Duggan, "Six Companies that are Redefining Performance Management," *Fast Company*, December 2015, https://www.fastcompany.com/3054547/six-companies-that-are-redefining-performance-management; Adam Bryant, "Google's Quest to Build a Better Boss," *New York Times*, March 12, 2011, http://www.nytimes.com/2011/03/13/business/13hire.html?mcubz=0.

What Is Coaching?

1. *Explain the concept of coaching.*

Did you ever play an organized sport, such as football, basketball, soccer, or volleyball, or take individual lessons in piano, karate, or math? In each case, you had a coach whose goal was to improve your performance. Tenor Andrea Bocelli had a coach. So do many top managers, who employ professional coaches to help them with anything from better managing their time to softening an abrasive personality.[1] In fact, coaching has become a $2 billion industry.[2] The essence of supervisory coaching—just as in those situations—is helping individuals become more effective performers. In the chapter preview, much of Google's culture is based on employee growth and development. Managers focus on helping team members learn, grow, and be the best they can be. That is the objective of this chapter—to help you learn more about coaching and the skills required to perform it effectively.

coaching

Helping individuals reach their highest levels of performance.

Think of **coaching** as the interpersonal process supervisors and managers use to help individuals continually reach their highest levels of performance.[3] It is a personal activity, a one-to-one relationship that starts when a new employee joins the team and continues throughout his or her tenure in your work unit. It may seem new employees would be the primary focus of supervisory coaching. However, this is not true, given today's goals of *continuous* performance improvement. Supervisors continually coach individuals to help them achieve increasingly higher performance levels throughout their careers. As one well-known coaching expert puts it:

Coaching is the process by which managers stay in touch with subordinates. All the walking around in the world will not help managers get the best from their employees unless they are walking around as coaches. Coaching is "eyeball to eyeball" management. Every conversation between managers and employees is potentially a coaching conversation. It is a chance to clarify goals, priorities, and standards of performance. It is a chance to reaffirm and reinforce the group's core values. It is a chance to hear ideas and involve employees in the processes of planning and problem solving.[4]

In the popular book *Managing for Excellence*, Bradford and Cohen advocate the days of the heroic leader who makes all key decisions and resolves all important problems are numbered. Given today's changing work environments, employees' greater competencies, and the need for employee "commitment" to excellence, the leader might be best served by using a "developer" leader style. The central orientation shifts from leader as primary decision maker to "how can each problem be solved in a way that further develops my subordinates' commitment and capabilities?"[5]

Coaching Is Performance Linked

The focus of coaching conversations is employee performance. The underlying assumption is through effective coaching, a supervisor can help an employee become an increasingly effective performer, as shown in Exhibit 11-1. If a topic has a present or future impact on an employee's performance, then it should be considered suitable for a coaching situation. Some situations, such as helping an employee learn a new skill or addressing a problem of substandard work, are more obviously performance linked. Others are less directly performance related, such as helping an employee to prepare for advancement or to better understand and overcome insecurities. Notice the wide-reaching range of coaching situations shown in Exhibit 11-2 and how each is in some way performance linked. Quite a broad list, isn't it?

EXHIBIT 11-1
Performance-Linked
Coaching

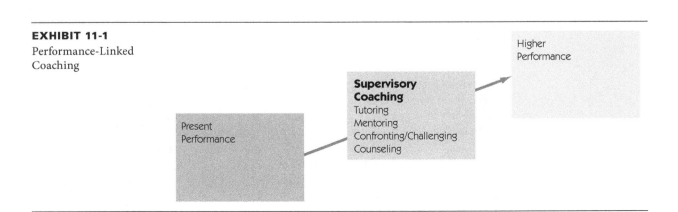

EXHIBIT 11-2

Examples of Coaching Situations

- Assigning a new challenging task; reviewing results.
- Determining with an employee his/her training needs.
- Following up with an employee after his/her training events.
- Showing an employee how to perform a task.
- Discussing a plan for employee career advancement.
- Listening to an employee's fears of job cutbacks.
- Providing an employee insight into company politics.
- Helping an employee adapt psychologically to job changes.
- Discussing poor employee performance.
- Helping an employee manage stress.
- Discussing how a long-term, excellent employee can reach an even higher performance level.
- Conducting a disciplinary interview.
- Discussing a problem of poor work or failure to follow organization rules/policy.
- Conducting a performance appraisal.
- Allowing an employee to "blow off" some emotional "steam."

In the middle of the last century, a number of large organizations experimented by employing professionals to serve as organization-wide counselors. Their job was not to give advice, but essentially to become the organization's primary vehicle to listen to employees' job-related, personal, and emotional problems. Granted, it helped employees to vent their feelings about job frustrations and conflicts as well as personal problems, but the success of these programs was limited because the counselors worked outside of the formal chain of command. Today, although a number of large organizations employ full-time counselors, the individual supervisor often is considered the "first line" of counseling. She or he is best able to help an employee adjust to working conditions, work load and assignments, and employee–supervisor relationships.

STOP AND THINK

Note in the chapter preview when a Google manager helps her employee adjust to her new role. She saw her potential and gave her appropriate opportunities to grow. Can you think of a manager or teacher that noticed your potential and helped you develop?

A team member's problems—be they job or personal—often affect his or her work performance (as well as the performance of others), but they also affect attendance, relationships with colleagues, and so on. Therefore, the supervisor has an immediate concern in these matters and assumes the legitimate role to address such employee problems. Supervisors cannot resolve personal problems such as poor health, substance abuse, or financial matters. However, they must at least understand the problem and urge the employee to seek adequate help if the problem has the potential to impact the employee's job performance negatively. The supervisor's role in these types of situations is discussed later in the chapter.

Current Emphasis on Coaching

Coaching gained momentum in the quality-driven 1990s and today is increasingly becoming the trademark in "best of class" organizations, such as Google, highlighted in the chapter preview.[6] As the supervisor's role has evolved into one of being a developer of people and a facilitator whose job is to help team members maximize their potential, effective coaching is recognized as a powerful supervisory skill. At pension and investment company Skandia, a program has been installed that helps its managers learn how to have in-depth conversations with employees to identify what they both want. Following this, the conversation shifts to what support, coaching, and development the employee needs to commit to the goals. Skandia top managers attribute a large increase in employee motivation directly to these coaching conversations and their follow-up.[7]

Organizations and work units are diverse, so managers and supervisors must understand their people as individuals, considering their needs, competencies, goals, attitudes, insecurities, and concerns. Coaching becomes an important vehicle by which a supervisor understands team members; that in turn allows the supervisor to target his or her coaching efforts. Organizations recognize coaching efforts should be tailored to the individual being coached. Coaching directed toward the younger, more insecure employee, who must learn many job essentials, differs dramatically from coaching directed toward the senior employee, who values advancement to the next level. And note, while coaching may have been primarily directed toward "B" and "C" level employees 10 years ago, today coaching also is directed to employees transitioning from one role to another, demonstrating great potential, and managing their careers.[8]

Why Supervisors Reject Coaching

Coaching appears to be a natural activity; however, in actual practice, many supervisors neglect their coaching role. First, many lack confidence. They may feel uncomfortable counseling employees and embarrassed to discuss problems of substandard performance.[9] There is always the risk confronting a performance problem with an employee creates more problems than it resolves. Supervisors may have to deal with an employee's excuses, anger, or hurt feelings; the quality of a good relationship may be jeopardized. Ignoring a performance problem in the hope it will resolve itself is often seen as a more desirable alternative.

Second, many supervisors view coaching as a passive process. They are more inclined through experience, and perhaps the expectation of their own managers, to have ready answers for everyone's problems and to deal with performance matters expeditiously. As one supervisor related in one of our coaching seminars:

> *When people are not doing a job, you get on their case and they had better shape up. There's no way I can see myself sitting around saying "Oh, really, tell me more about that." My own boss would think I've lost it. I've always been direct with people—you tell them exactly what they're to do, see that they do it, and get on them when they don't. This is the best way to handle it.*

We are all products of our past. Our parents told us what to do when we were young, as did our teachers or athletic coaches. If we had military experience, platoon leaders took over the telling. Then, when we went to work, our bosses told us what to do. When we become supervisors, it is only natural we tend to become "tellers," which is an active, expeditious way to handle things. However, today's supervisory environment has changed considerably. The supportive relationship required for effective coaching involves open, two-way communication and greater emphasis on the supervisor's listening skills. As you see throughout this chapter, coaching behavior always distinctly addresses continually improving performance.

Third, supervisors reject coaching because it takes considerable time. Faced by many pressures, supervisors are not prepared to abandon their heroic fire-fighting pace. Many are so immersed in managing "details" they cannot effectively spare the time coaching on a personal one-to-one level requires.

The Coaching Functions

2. *Identify the four major coaching functions.*

There are different ways to understand effective coaching. One is to examine *why* someone conducts a coaching session—that is, the *function* coaching is intended to serve. Another is to examine what *skills* a coach uses during a coaching session. We will examine the functions first and then the skills. Coaching serves four fundamental functions: (1) tutoring, (2) mentoring, (3) confronting/challenging, and (4) counseling.[10]

Tutoring

tutoring

Helping team members gain knowledge, skill, and competency.

Tutoring involves a large range of coaching situations that help a team member gain knowledge, skill, and competency. Tutoring encourages team members to learn, grow, and develop. The goal is to avoid complacency with present skill levels and develop a commitment to continuous learning. It also encourages members to put into practice those skills that are learned.

Mentoring

mentoring

Helping others develop careers.

Mentoring is the coaching activity that helps develop careers in others. Mentoring may teach political savvy, understanding of the organization's culture, and ways to advance one's career. It also may mean

1. Helping an employee see the potentially negative impact of behavior he or she is considering.
2. Understanding how to approach and gain influence with powerful organization members.
3. Learning who key players are in given circumstances.
4. Understanding how relevant past or current events should influence the team member's actions and behavior.

An important coaching function, tutoring is the guidance offered by a supervisor to help employees master the skills necessary to perform their jobs.

Michael Newman/PhotoEdit

Successful supervisory coaches help team members make key organizational contacts and develop their own networks. They aid in giving good career guidance and keep a watchful eye for effective development of their team members' careers.

It is estimated supervisors perform formal mentoring in about 75 percent of the companies listed as *Computerworld*'s "Top 100 Best Places to Work." At companies such as Quicken Loans, Aflac, Southern Co., Ultimate Software, and Axxess, employees receive heavy doses of training to keep them challenged, satisfied, and employed. Mentoring comes into play by being more personal, practical, and job specific than training. It shows people shortcuts to using the skills learned in formal training. Or, as one manager puts it, mentoring shows people where the rocks and land mines are—how to avoid the mines and step on the rocks in moving toward career goals.[11]

Confronting/Challenging

confronting/ challenging

Establishing clear performance standards, comparing actual performance against those standards, and addressing performance that doesn't meet those standards.

The **confronting/challenging** coaching function is most directly performance related. Supervisory coaches establish clear performance standards, compare actual team member performance against those standards, and address performance not meeting those standards. Through confronting/challenging, successful coaches help less-than-successful performers become successful and challenge successful ones to reach even higher levels.

STOP AND THINK

Note in the chapter preview the Google manager who was disliked by his employees. He was highly intelligent but lacked interpersonal skills necessary to relate well to others and lead his team. By confronting and challenging him, his coach was able to develop him such that his team acknowledged he had gotten better. What are some specific confronting or challenging tactics that could have led to this type of behavioral change?

Often, supervisors who are good, sensitive listeners and effective tutors and mentors experience difficulty in confronting and challenging team members regarding performance issues. They may find it uncomfortable to establish clear, concrete performance standards and talk directly about performance. They may not be willing to address performance problems when a team member's behavior falls below standard. Confronting/challenging sessions, when finally held, may be superficial and apologetic and skirt the poor performance problem. This issue is so important we discuss confronting/challenging in greater detail later in the chapter.

Counseling

counseling

Helping an individual recognize, talk about, and solve either real or perceived problems that affect performance.

Counseling is the coaching function whereby the supervisor helps an individual recognize, talk about, gain insight into, and solve either real or perceived problems that affect performance. The manager's role is essentially to help the individual determine his or her own course of action. Many supervisors feel inept and poorly trained to deal with employees' personal problems. Perhaps the most common mistake is the tendency to give advice rather than to help an employee think through, understand, and develop alternatives to problems.

In conducting counseling, it is especially important to show sensitivity and help a team member understand how personal problems affect, or potentially affect, job performance. It is also important to help a team member gain confidence in his or her ability to handle problems. In serious cases—such as drug abuse, financial problems, or health issues—this means recommending the individual seek help through the company's employee assistance program or an outside professional.

You can gain more insight into the four coaching functions by examining the different outcomes associated with each function, as shown in Exhibit 11-3.

STOP AND THINK

Which functions—tutoring, mentoring, confronting/challenging, and counseling— are reflected by each of the following coaching situations?

1. Helping an employee understand the political implications of his or her behavior.
2. Meeting with an employee to address his or her increased absenteeism.
3. Conducting an annual performance review with your top-rated employee.
4. Discussing with an employee her upcoming attendance at an advanced training course for which you nominated her.

All four functions have much in common and are often combined in a single coaching session. For example, when a new employee is struggling to perform, a single coaching session may involve confronting/challenging, counseling, and tutoring. Many of the skills and processes involved in all four functions are similar—the need for sensitivity, listening, and movement toward some form of closure.

EXHIBIT 11-3

Outcomes of the Four Coaching Functions

TUTORING	MENTORING
1. Increased technical know-how	1. Developing political understanding/savvy
2. Increased understanding of processes and systems	2. Sensitivity to the organization's culture
3. Increased pace of learning	3. Expanded personal networks
4. Movement to expert status	4. Increased sensitivity to key players' likes/ dislikes
5. Commitment to continual learning	5. Greater proaction in managing own career

CONFRONTING/CHALLENGING	COUNSELING
1. Clarification of performance expectations	1. Accurate descriptions of problems and their causes
2. Identification of performance shortcomings	2. Technical and organizational insight
3. Acceptance of more-difficult tasks	3. Ventilation of strong feelings
4. Strategies to improve future performance	4. Commitment to self-sufficiency
5. Commitment to continual performance improvement	5. Deeper personal insight about own feeling and behavior
	6. Changes in point of view

Source: Adapted from Dennis C. Kinlaw, *Coaching for Commitment* (San Diego, CA: Pfeiffer & Company, 1993), pp. 22–23.

Coaching and Understanding Diversity

Today's organizations reflect considerably more employee uniqueness and diversity than in past years. Perhaps in no other supervisory activity is recognition of individual differences as important to success as in coaching. Because coaching requires a highly personal, one-on-one relationship, a supervisor's ability to relate to and understand an employee's needs, sensitivities, and uniqueness and to reflect these concerns in his or her interactions is crucial to successful coaching.[12]

> *Sharon Olds, marketing supervisor at AutoFin, supervises 12 associates. Her department reflects the wide diversity of employees found in organizations today. There are seven men and five women; seven Caucasians, three African Americans, one Asian, and one Hispanic. Their ages range from 23 to 59; three are single, never married; four are single and divorced or widowed. Half are college graduates, three never attended college, and three have completed some college or are presently attending college part time. Five different religions are represented, not to mention the differences in individual values, needs, interpersonal styles, and cultures. Sharon states, "I always thought a correct saying was you treat people the same way you would like to be treated, or you treat people the same. I've learned that's not true. Some people are so different. I have to be consistent and fair, but a key to being a good supervisor is being able to relate differently to the individual needs of my people."*

Recall our earlier discussion in Chapter 7 about differences in motivating employees from the four generations. Coaching of Traditionalists will be quite different from coaching of younger Generation Yers. The differences in age, qualities, strengths, values, and style make coaching a highly personal, tailored activity rather than "one approach for all."[13]

The Coaching Skills

3. *Describe the important skills used in coaching.*

When a supervisor initiates a formal coaching session, he or she should have an objective to achieve and establish a basic framework for the session, adapted to the coaching function and the circumstances. However, the coaching process largely involves a number of spontaneous interactions that occur in a relaxed, personal setting. Many coaching interactions are initiated by the team member rather than the supervisor. These may include requests for help, advice, or informal discussion of a work-related matter. In some cases, such as those of a personal nature, work may not be directly involved.

A supervisor must create a supportive atmosphere that encourages contact. He or she must maintain a climate that makes people feel welcome, respects their views and feelings, and shows patience when communicating with them. A supportive climate exists when a supervisor understands what team members want to accomplish and when members are encouraged to try new approaches without fear of reprisal. It is difficult for many individuals to approach their supervisor for advice or acknowledge job-related or personal problems that affect their job. Supervisors must establish an open, receptive communication climate, and effective listening is a critical coaching skill.

Coaching: The Core Skills

The core coaching skills are discussed in the following sections. A given coaching session may involve several or perhaps even most of these skills. As you read these skills, note the importance of an atmosphere of respect and understanding and the clear need for an outcome of the coaching effort.

acknowledging

Showing by nonevaluative verbal responses that you listened to what the employee has stated.

attending

Showing through nonverbal behavior you are listening in an open, nonjudgmental manner.

affirming

Communicating to an employee his or her value, strengths, and contributions.

confirming

Ensuring an employee understands what has been said or agreed upon.

pinpointing

Providing specific, tangible information about performance to an employee.

probing

Asking questions to obtain additional information.

reflecting

Stating your interpretation of what the employee has said.

resourcing

Providing information, assistance, and advice to employees.

Acknowledging is showing, through a range of nonevaluative verbal responses, that you listened to what the employee has stated. These comments may range from a brief "uh-huh," "oh," "hmmm," or "I see," to longer phrases like "I can understand that" or "So that's how it happened." The acknowledging skill is designed to bounce the communication ball back to the employee and allow him or her to develop the information further.

Attending is showing through nonverbal behavior you are listening in an open, nonjudgmental manner. In attending, your body language, such as alert posture, head nods, eye contact, and facial expressions, conveys full interest and attention. Nonattending behavior includes blank stares, nodding off, being distracted, glancing at your watch, or exhibiting other body language that displays uneasiness or disagreement with the topic being discussed. Effective attending behavior clearly communicates "I am interested and I am listening." A forest supervisor for a paper company offered one of the authors an interesting perspective on his attending environment: "When I have something personal I want to discuss with an operator, I can wait till the end of the day when I am in an office setting. But I often prefer handling sensitive things directly in the field, which is less formal and likely more comfortable for my crew members. We might sit on a recently cut tree trunk, just the two of us, and I'll handle things right there, if possible."

Affirming is communicating to an employee his or her value, strengths, and contributions or other positive factors. An example might be "You have made excellent progress learning the new system" or "It always amazes me how quickly you catch on" or "I've always valued your willingness to share your feelings with me about things."

Confirming is making sure an employee understands what has been said or agreed upon. The coach can do this by summarizing and repeating the key points or by requesting the person being coached to do so. The coach might ask, "How about going over these steps in your own words and telling me how you would proceed?" Confirming also may occur with an eye to the future: "How about modifying your estimates as we've discussed, using the highest quality materials available, and let's take a look at this at 3:00 P.M. tomorrow."

Pinpointing is providing specific, tangible information. For instance, "You did a poor job on the write-up" is a vague, general statement that covers wide territory. It is not as helpful as "The write-up used figures that were three years old, contained over 20 spelling and typographical errors, and lacked a specific recommendation." We will cover pinpointing in more detail in the next section.

Probing asks questions to obtain additional information or exploring a topic at greater length, such as the following: "So you feel your group is ready to take on more responsibility? In what ways have they signaled this?" or "So you would do it differently next time, given what you now know. What would you do differently?"

Reflecting is stating in your own words your interpretation of what the employee has said or feels, such as "So you feel you should have received more help from your teammates on this?" or "It seems like you're really upset with them for not helping out."

Coaches should act as resources for their team members. **Resourcing** can be done by providing information, assistance, and advice: "I really wouldn't recommend bypassing Mason on this. It cost someone his job about five years ago when he did it." or "Talk to the human resources people. They should be able to answer your question." or "Let me show you how to do that."

At the end of a coaching session, reinforcing key points to ensure common understanding is the skill of **reviewing**. This can be done by the coach as follows: "Let's pull this together. It seems we've identified three things you'll do with the survey data. First,

reviewing

Reinforcing key points at the end of a coaching session to ensure common understanding.

summarizing

Pausing in the coaching conversation to summarize key points.

you'll send your supervisors their individual results and the overall company results. Then you'll conduct one-on-one meetings with them to discuss their results. Following this, your supervisors will develop a written plan, accepted by you, as to what they'll do to improve." Another example is, "Let's make sure we're together on this. How about summarizing what you'll do with the survey results?"

Summarizing is pausing in the coaching conversation to summarize key points: "Let's see if I understand you. You believe two factors have hurt your sales performance: one, our promotion strategy was changed; and two, extra committee work has taken time away from your sales calls."

Note that some skills such as acknowledging and attending relate to the *atmosphere* or environment of the coaching session—its openness and the fact the coach is interested and is listening. Other skills such as pinpointing, probing, and resourcing are more directly tied to the *content* of the session, or the issue(s) involved.

STOP AND THINK

All 10 coaching skills are necessary and useful, but employees are different in age, qualities, strengths, values, and styles, making coaching a highly personal, tailored activity. Given what you have learned about the differences in employees from the four generations, how would you approach coaching Traditionalists, Baby Boomers, Gen Xers, and Generation Yers? Be sure to note key differences as well as similarities in your approaches.

Fancy/Jupiter Images

Coaching involves several core communication skills, such as acknowledging, affirming, pinpointing, probing, and summarizing.

Coaching for Improved Performance: Confronting and Challenging

4. *Differentiate between general and pinpointed coaching statements.*

One of the things supervisors must do, but often do poorly, is address performance problems. Many managers do it in a blunt, threatening way that may cause resentment. Too often, they blame, lecture, put down, warn, or coerce a person in attempting to make that person improve. It is questionable whether a good chewing-out is the best way to do this. Supervisors are not mind readers, and until you understand the reason for poor performance, you cannot adequately coach someone to improve. It simply is not coaching to call someone in, read the riot act, and send that person away. Often, the result is no change, a half-hearted change, or resentment at having been "called on the carpet." By contrast, some supervisors dislike discussing poor performance and are reluctant to bring it up. They avoid confronting a poor performer only to find the poor performance escalates, making the inevitable coaching meeting involve more serious stakes than if it had occurred earlier. An employee's poor performance can relate not only to actual on-the-job work performance, but to other types of behavior as well, such as attendance, safety, attitude, and adherence to various company rules and policies.

While individual situations may differ, the suggestions for dealing with substandard performance contained in Exhibit 11-4 are often effective.

It is essential the issue of poor performance be addressed by the supervisor early in the meeting. Your comments should pinpoint the issue(s) specifically. For example, instead of telling an employee, "Your job performance is poor," it is more informative to say, "You reached only 75 percent of your work goal" or "You have been absent three times in the past two weeks." In this way, the employee is given something concrete. Here are some further examples:

General	Pinpointed
1. Your attendance is poor.	**1.** You have missed a day in each of the past four pay periods.
2. You need to cooperate better with department heads.	**2.** Company policy is to give department heads the cost information when they request it.
3. You need to follow our safety rules	**3.** This morning I saw you performing the job without wearing your safety goggles.
4. You haven't made the progress that you'd agreed to.	**4.** You and I agreed that you would complete the first draft by today, but you tell me you need two more days.

STOP AND THINK

How might you better pinpoint the following statement about an employee's performance? General statement: "You have a bad attitude."

Your pinpointed statement: _____

Note a number of steps shown in Exhibit 11-4 require you to listen and/or to actively involve the team member in the discussion, especially step 2: Seek and listen to the team member's point of view; step 3: Get agreement on the problem; step 4: Try to get the employee's involvement in determining a solution; and step 5: Agree on a plan of action to improve performance.

Exhibit 11-5 illustrates a supervisor conducting a confronting/challenging coaching session. Note the supervisor's use of the steps involved in confronting poor performance, as well as many of the skills of pinpointing, acknowledging, reflecting, resourcing, and summarizing. The exchange also illustrates how, even while willing to listen to Bob's views, the supervisor remains focused on the performance issue.

EXHIBIT 11-4 Suggestions for Confronting Poor Performance	**1.** Describe the performance situation in specific detail. **2.** Seek and listen to the team member's point of view. **3.** Get agreement on the problem. **4.** Try to get the employee's involvement in determining a solution. **5.** Agree on a plan of action to improve performance. **6.** Summarize the agreement and reinforce the changed behavior. **7.** Plan for follow-up, if needed.

EXHIBIT 11-5
Script of Confronting/Challenging Coaching Session

Sup 1	Bob, I wanted to talk with you because I have a problem. I'd thought after we last talked about quitting time that you understood our policy and that you intended to stick to it. So I was surprised yesterday to see you'd left a little after 5:00 and not 5:30. I'm upset about it.
Bob 1	I've been trying hard not to leave before 5:30. I hadn't left early in about 2 months until this emergency.
Sup 2	You've had a good record recently. So yesterday was something special?
Bob 2	I had a call in the middle of the afternoon from the guy I ride with in my neighborhood. Said he had to leave a little before 5:30, and if I wasn't out on the street, he'd have to leave me.
Sup 3	Put you in a bind, huh?
Bob 3	You're right about that. Once when he was sick I took the bus, and it took me an hour and a half to get home.
Sup 4	So you hated to use that alternative, huh?
Bob 4	Yep. It only takes about 30 minutes driving with him.
Sup 5	So you were torn between losing time getting home and sticking with our rule.
Bob 5	Yeah, I looked around for you in the afternoon; you can ask Art. You were out of the office and I couldn't find you. Fifteen minutes didn't seem like such a big deal since I'd had a good record recently.
Sup 6	So you hoped I'd approve, if you could ask me?
Bob 6	I was sure of it.
Sup 7	Apparently, you felt it was very important for you to go home and not miss your ride, even to the point of breaking a rule and our agreement.
Bob 7	Well, it was a rare emergency that happens from time to time. Seems like a few minutes don't matter that much. I'm here working sometimes 20 minutes early in the morning.
Sup 8	I understand that. You're always here on time, and I appreciate that. But we have two policies—one for getting here on time and one for staying until 5:30—and both must be kept.
Bob 8	I wouldn't expect this to happen again, at least only very rarely.
Sup 9	I felt that [way] after we had our last talk, Bob, but then something came up and it's happened again.
Bob 9	I told him then that I have to stay until 5:30, so he usually waits, except for yesterday. At least he called me.

(Continued)

EXHIBIT 11-5 continued	Sup 10	Can you think of something you might do to avoid this happening in the future? Because this rule is not to be broken unless there is an emergency more serious than this. I don't consider this to be the type of emergency that would warrant your leaving early. Can you think of anything you could do to keep it from happening again?
	Bob 10	I could make sure that you know I'm leaving early, if he ever needs to leave again.
	Sup 11	That solution doesn't satisfy me—I don't think I could agree. I don't think I could give my permission for this.
	Bob 11	Not even for 10 or 15 minutes?
	Sup 12	Not for that. We need a solution that will satisfy you and satisfy me and the company policy.
	Bob 12	Maybe I'd have to ride a bus on those days.
	Sup 13	In other words, you can take a bus if you have to.
	Bob 13	Yeah, but it seems to me that the hour and a half it takes is a long time for just 10 or 15 minutes. Seems unreasonable to me, the policy, that is.
	Sup 14	Seems to you like, if you keep the policy most of the time, it's all right to break it once in a while.
	Bob 14	It seems that way to me.
	Sup 15	If the 20 people working in our department took the same approach, almost every night someone would be leaving early. I wouldn't feel that would be fair. Would you?
	Bob 15	Well, no. Maybe I could find someone right here who could drive me home on those days. I wouldn't even mind catching the bus and then walking a little way.
	Sup 16	Think that would solve it, huh?
	Bob 16	Yes, but how would I go about finding someone?
	Sup 17	Why don't you stop by the administrative office and post a request on the announcement board?
	Bob 17	O.K., I'll drop over there today.
	Sup 18	Bob, it's important that I can count on you to keep the rules by working through until 5:30. Thanks for discussing this with me, and I appreciate your working it out.

Source: Adapted from Thomas Gordon, *Leader Effectiveness Training (L.E.T.)* Copyright © 1977, 2001 Penguin Putnam. Reprinted by permission of the author.

5. *Describe an "I" message.*

"I" message

Attempt to change an employee's behavior by indicating the specific behavior, how it makes you feel as a supervisor, and the effect of the behavior.

Tom Gordon, a well-known writer on leadership and interpersonal issues, advocates the use of what he calls "I" messages when we want to effectively alter someone's behavior.[14] He says there are three major parts of an **"I" message**:

- *Feelings:* Indicate how you feel about the effects of the behavior (angry, embarrassed, frustrated, concerned, etc.).
- *Behavior:* Identify the specific behavior (absenteeism, not keeping appointments, not meeting quota, etc.).
- *Effect:* Spell out the end result of the behavior (poor example for others, making the work unit look unproductive, inconvenience to others in the unit, etc.).

When you send an "I" message, you appeal rather than demand the other person change. Note in the following examples the focus is the *behavior*, its *effect*, and how it makes you *feel*. Although no one likes being told his or her behavior is causing a problem, framing your displeasure in an "I" message addresses the problem more openly and tactfully and is more likely to pave the way toward a resolution in an objective, supportive manner.

"You" Message	"I" Message
1. You neglected to proofread that report; you should know better than to let a report go out like that.	1. When I noticed the many typos in the report, I was really upset. It makes our unit look careless and unprofessional.
2. You know I expect you to attend our regular meetings. You need to attend them from now on.	2. When you don't attend our regular meetings, I'm concerned we miss your expertise and insight.

In using the "I" message, it is important to keep in mind the coaching skills from the previous section. Your goal as a supervisor is to correct the inadequate performance in a way that shields the employee's ego *and* maintains a positive relationship between you and the employee. Thus, the session should focus on the employee's *performance* rather than personality—in other words, the problem and not the person. Your use of "I" messages can be an important tool in focusing on the employee's behavior rather than on the employee's ego.

STOP AND THINK

Refer to Exhibit 11-5. Can you identify the supervisor's use of an "I" message?

Coaching: The Counseling Function

6. *Explain the extent to which a supervisor should counsel an employee about personal problems.*

Counseling, one of the four coaching functions, involves a broad range of emotional areas, ranging from an employee's frustrations, insecurities, anger, and resentment to his or her lack of commitment. The problem can be attributed to real or perceived factors and can be work related or personal. The objective of counseling is to help an employee better understand him- or herself and, when needed, develop a plan of action to resolve the issue. The coach's job is to help the individual more fully discuss and understand the problem being experienced. Feelings, emotions, and attitudes may be exchanged. As shown in Exhibit 11-6, counseling attempts to identify and help both supervisor and team member

EXHIBIT 11-6
Iceberg Model of Counseling

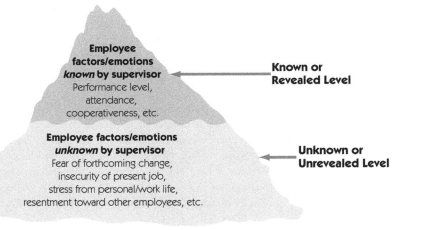

Employee factors/emotions *known* by supervisor
Performance level, attendance, cooperativeness, etc.

Known or Revealed Level

Employee factors/emotions *unknown* by supervisor
Fear of forthcoming change, insecurity of present job, stress from personal/work life, resentment toward other employees, etc.

Unknown or Unrevealed Level

understand those "below-the-surface" factors that are influencing or may potentially influence the team member's performance. In counseling, the listening-related skills of attending, acknowledging, reflecting, and probing are especially essential.

A coach often has no advance notice when counseling is needed; these coaching opportunities are usually initiated by the team member. On other occasions, a team leader will plan to perform one of the other coaching functions, for instance, tutoring or confronting/challenging, when the need for counseling arises. The leader must be sufficiently flexible to shift gears and address counseling, as pointed out below.

What started as a routine tutoring session for supervisor Rosa Bender turned out quite differently when she learned Rudy, a new technician, felt ignored by senior people in the department. Bender temporarily dropped her tutoring agenda and devoted about 10 minutes to reflecting and probing why Rudy, the youngest and newest member of the team, felt this way. Learning he felt slighted because senior employees offered him little help, Bender helped him understand senior employees, while likely supportive, were independent performers who thoroughly immersed themselves in their own work. Although perhaps they hadn't offered help, they would gladly help if asked.

Rudy agreed to ask senior employees for help when he needed it and communicate to Bender his degree of success. Satisfied this addressed the immediate counseling issue, Bender then shifted back to the tutoring session she originally planned.

Areas of Employee Counseling

Counseling is involved in virtually all aspects of the supervisor–employee relationship. It begins with the hiring phase and does not end until the employee leaves the company. Certain areas, though, are more likely to necessitate counseling than others.

Job Performance   We already indicated counseling is often used in combination with the other four coaching functions. It is especially important in the area of job performance. Numerous factors, many the supervisor is unaware of, influence employees' job performance. A good rule of thumb is always be prepared to engage in counseling when addressing below-standard employee performance, especially for employees without performance difficulties in the past or who only recently engaged in negative job behavior. This includes performance changes in quality and quantity of work, absenteeism, adherence to policy and rules, and changes in cooperativeness and relationships with others, including the supervisor.

Physical and Emotional Illness   Another common need for counseling arises because of physical and emotional illness. In some cases, these issues are initially addressed by the supervisor as performance problems, but in many cases, they may be initiated by the employee. Although the team leader must play a supportive, listening role in counseling, it is imperative the employee clearly see the impact or potential impact of such problems upon performance.

When Avery Williard showed up late, his supervisor coincidentally happened to be present at Williard's work area. While Williard appeared quite uncomfortable and embarrassed, his supervisor expressed surprise because Williard was never late. It was then the supervisor smelled alcohol. He asked Williard to join him in his office. Williard acknowledged he had been drinking a lot lately because of "problems at home" but pledged he would not do it again. His supervisor listened patiently, noting Williard didn't volunteer particulars. He praised Williard for his excellent work and dependability over the years but reminded him should it happen again, he would have no choice but to formally discipline him. Seeing Williard was in no condition to work, his supervisor sent him home after setting a meeting for the next day. This meeting was to reinforce (1) his support for Williard and (2) the fact that Williard's behavior could not be tolerated again on the job. He also planned to strongly suggest Williard consider referral to the company EAP (Employee Assistance Program) as a source of help.

Often it is difficult for a supervisor to diagnose an employee's substance abuse, especially when it is not accompanied by performance slippage. Behavior that differs from the norm may be the telltale sign. Note in Exhibit 11-7 that many behaviors, such as increased accidents, need for increased rest breaks, frequent off-the-job emergencies, deteriorating personal appearance, and overreaction to criticism, are indicators substance abuse may be involved.

As in the preceding situation, supervisors are increasingly called on to counsel employees with many forms of physical and emotional problems. These problems range from substance abuse and job stress to debilitating physical illnesses, such as cancer, heart disease, and acquired immunodeficiency syndrome (AIDS). Moreover, the rash of corporate downsizings, mergers, and financial and ethical mismanagement has created unparalleled emotional anxiety, as reflected by present and former employees who commit acts of physical violence against employers.

Personal Problem To what extent should a supervisor counsel an employee with personal problems, such as financial, health, or marital issues? The answer depends largely on the extent to which the problem impacts present or future job performance. If it affects job performance, it is essential the supervisor use counseling to understand the nature of the problem, if for nothing more than to help the employee appreciate the need for professional assistance. However, a supervisor should tread carefully before becoming entwined in personal problems, for several reasons:

EXHIBIT 11-7
Profile of Typical Substance Abusers

Here are some characteristics of typical substance abusers.

- Four times more likely to have on-the-job accidents than nonabusers.
- Four to six times more likely to have off-the-job accidents than nonabusers.
- Five times the number of workers' compensation claims as nonabusers.
- Five times the number of medical claims as nonabusers.
- Two-and-a-half times more absenteeism/tardiness than nonabusers, especially on Mondays and Fridays and before and after holidays.
- Take extended breaks and lunch hours.
- Have numerous restroom breaks.
- Experience frequent off-job emergencies.
- Experience frequent colds, flu, upset stomach, headaches, etc.
- Dramatic change in personality or work performance during the day, especially after breaks.
- Deteriorating personal appearance and ability to get along with others.
- Tendency to overreact to real or imagined criticism.
- Experience difficulty handling instructions.
- Depressed or anxious disposition.
- Work at 67 percent of potential.

Sources: Chris O'Neill and Joel Bennett, "New Approaches to Drug Free Workplace Programs," *The Journal of Employee Assistance* 38 (October 2008), pp. 20–22; Janet Gemignani, "Substance Abusers: Terminate or Treat?," *Business & Health* 17, no. 6 (June 1999), pp. 32–37; Laura A. Lyons and Brian H. Kleiner, "Managing the Problem of Substance Abuse . . . Without Abusing Employees," *HR Focus* 69, no. 4 (April 1992), p. 9; Peter Ellis, "Substance Abuse and Work," *Occupational Safety & Health* 30, no. 13 (March 2000), pp. 38–41; Substance Abuse and Mental Health Services Administration, *Results from the 2010 National Survey on Drug Use and Health: Summary of National Findings*, NSDUH Series H-41, HHS Publication No. (SMA) 11-4658 (Rockville, MD: Substance Abuse and Mental Health Services Administration, 2011).

Brand X Pictures/Alamy Stock Photo

Sometimes superiors must counsel employees who have an emotional or physical illness or personal problems.

STOP AND THINK

Note in Exhibit 11-5 to fully address the performance issue (employee leaving work early), the supervisor helped the employee address his personal problem (transportation after work).

---

1. Employees may feel resentful or embarrassed after "opening up" and disclosing highly personal matters. This may jeopardize their future job relationship with their supervisor.
2. If the supervisor makes too concerted an effort to probe into more than an employee cares to divulge, the employee may be resentful.
3. If the supervisor gives advice on personal problems—such as marital difficulties, problems with children, or buying and selling property—and the results turn out unsatisfactorily, the supervisor will be blamed. In addition, the supervisor and/or the company may be open to legal liability.

In general, supervisory counseling should be restricted to factors that affect job performance. Supervisors work hard to develop trusting, supportive relationships and are often placed in a position of counseling team members in problem areas only peripherally related to job performance. To reject the counseling opportunity outright may be perceived as lack of interest. The supervisor can always listen sufficiently to determine the nature of the employee's problem and then steer the individual toward a professional or other source of help. That is where an Employee Assistance Program enters the picture.

Role of Employee Assistance Programs in Counseling

Employee Assistance Programs (EAPs) have emerged to extend professional counseling and other services to employees confronted by unresolved personal or work-related problems.[15] These may include counseling for substance abuse, emotional illnesses, marital issues, divorce, or stress. Many companies have broadened the counseling services available through their EAPS. At Comcast, employees and their families may receive counseling assistance in such wide-ranging areas as help with weight loss, smoking, budgeting, taxes, estate planning, legal matters, and even buying a car or house.[16] In cases where an EAP does not exist, a supervisor may refer an employee to counseling services provided within the community; most have public mental health or social service professional counseling available. However, most larger organizations offer EAP support of some kind, and a Society of Human Resource Management survey of small firms with fewer than 100 employees showed 70 percent provided EAP services.[17] Exhibit 11-8 gives you a good idea of the counseling services offered by one company's EAP.

Employee Assistance Programs (EAPs)

Professional counseling and other services for employees with unresolved personal or work-related problems.

EXHIBIT 11-8
Example of an Employee Assistance Program (EAP)

Most of the time, we like to think we are in control of our lives. All of us, however, occasionally experience personal crises that may cause us to feel out of control. These crises may be due to health problems, financial or legal difficulties, or emotional problems. Because we care about our employees, an Employee Assistance Program (EAP) has been implemented. The EAP will provide confidential, professional counseling and referral to employees who seek assistance with personal problems. Realizing that an employee may be affected by a family member's personal problem, the EAP is also available to the families of our employees.

What the EAP is:
- *Voluntary:* Employees or family members can contact the program directly. Participation in the program is always voluntary.
- *Independent:* The EAP is administered by Human Affairs Inc., a national company that provides assistance programs to many companies across the country.
- *Confidential:* Because of the two components mentioned above, EAP participants are assured that any information revealed to EAP staff will be held in the strictest professional confidence.
- *Professional:* All EAP staff are licensed Master's-level therapists and counselors.
- *Free:* All counseling and referral services provided by the EAP are free to employees and their families. If an EAP counselor does recommend that employees consult a special outside resource, the counselor can let employees know what part of that service may be covered by their other medical benefits.
- *Accessible:* EAP counselors are available for emergency situations 24 hours a day, 7 days a week. Appointments are made for non-emergency situations during day or evening hours.
- *A Valuable Resource:* The EAP can serve as a resource concerning counseling, information, and management consultation to employees, supervisors, and family members.

(Continued)

EXHIBIT 11-8
continued

What the EAP is NOT:
- *A Branch of Human Resources:* The EAP is not designed to replace any personnel or management procedures.
- *A Refuge for Poor Job Performance:* Participation in the EAP will not protect employees from disciplinary action.

Procedures
- *Self-Referral:* An employee or an immediate family member may use the service by contacting Human Affairs Inc. directly in complete privacy whenever they would like to consult with the counselor. Self-referrals are both anonymous and completely confidential. Self-referrals will not affect job security or promotional opportunity.
- *Supervisor/Management Referral:* A supervisor may recommend that an employee contact Human Affairs Inc. when there is a job performance or conduct problem which has not responded to ordinary supervisorial techniques. Whether or not the employee decides to contact Human Affairs Inc., it is the employee's responsibility to perform satisfactorily on the job; and if problems go unresolved and performance continues to deteriorate, disciplinary action up to and including discharge may result. Participation in the EAP is not a guarantee that these actions will not continue to occur, but improved performance often results from problem resolution.

The Company sincerely hopes that all staff and their dependents who might benefit from this service will take advantage of it.

Source: "Purpose of Company E.A.P.," *Personnel Policy Briefs*, Sample Issue, n.d., p. 2, as found in Leon C. Megginson, Geralyn McLure Franklin, and M. Jane Byrd, *Human Resource Management* (Houston, TX: Dame Publications, Inc., 1995), p. 296.

Where present, the EAP can be a big help to supervisors by handling referred cases at a professional level. Studies of EAP programs at Abbott Labs and McDonnell Douglas show employees who participated had fewer absentee days and fewer terminations than other company employees in general.[18] Thus, it is in the supervisor's best interest to encourage employees to participate when necessary. Supervisors typically are given training and policy guidance in how and under what conditions to refer employees to a company's EAP, should one exist. Skill Builder 11-5 gives you insight into how the University of Maine provides a monthly newsletter to assist supervisors and managers in resolving EAP issues.

● Chapter Review

1. *Explain the concept of coaching.*

Coaching is the interpersonal process used by supervisors and managers to help individuals continually reach their highest levels of performance. Coaching is performance oriented, whether it helps a new employee gain new skills or accept challenges, or helps a seasoned employee reach even higher levels of performance. The current emphasis on coaching reflects the changing role of supervisors as facilitators and developers of people.

Despite its importance, supervisors tend to experience difficulty in practicing effective coaching. Many lack the confidence in their communication skills, especially listening, to be an effective coach. Others see it as too passive and prefer to provide answers to employees rather than work jointly with them to develop their own answers to problems. Still others are uncomfortable in spending the large amount of time effective coaching requires.

2. *Identify the four major coaching functions.*

There are four coaching functions. Tutoring helps a team member gain knowledge, skill, and competency. Mentoring develops political savvy, an understanding of key players, and the way to advance one's career. Confronting/challenging focuses directly upon performance itself—from setting clear objectives to follow-up meetings that discuss results. It can address performance problems and inspire top performers to continue to grow and improve. Counseling helps an individual recognize, talk about, and thereby gain insight into his or her real or perceived problems that may affect performance.

3. *Describe the important skills used in coaching.*

Coaching is a one-on-one relationship that utilizes such skills as acknowledging, attending, affirming, confirming, pinpointing, probing, reflecting, resourcing, reviewing, and summarizing.

4. *Differentiate between general and pinpointed coaching statements.*

In coaching designed to confront/challenge an employee with a performance problem, supervisors should pinpoint, in specific, concrete language, the employee's performance level, rather than using general terms.

5. *Describe an "I" message.*

"I" messages, which indicate the problem behavior, its effect, and the supervisor's feelings, can be an effective way to focus on the performance problem. For example, "Your lunch break was in excess of an hour and a half. I was embarrassed when the plant manager came by looking for you on two occasions and found other people covering your work area."

6. *Explain the extent to which a supervisor should counsel an employee about personal problems.*

In general, supervisors should restrict their counseling to factors that affect an employee's job performance. However, many personal problems, such as physical and emotional health, substance abuse, and financial and family problems, actually affect or may affect future performance. The supervisor should focus counseling on the performance-related aspects of the problem. Many firms today have an Employee Assistance Program (EAP) to which supervisors can refer troubled employees.

Key Terms

coaching, p. 333
tutoring, p. 336
mentoring, p. 336
confronting/challenging, p. 337
counseling, p. 337
acknowledging, p. 340

attending, p. 340
affirming, p. 340
confirming, p. 340
pinpointing, p. 340
probing, p. 340
reflecting, p. 340

resourcing, p. 340
reviewing, p. 340
summarizing, p. 341
"I" message, p. 344
Employee Assistance Programs
   (EAPs), p. 349

Discussion Questions

1. What is meant by coaching?
2. Of the four major coaching functions— tutoring, mentoring, confronting/challenging, and counseling—which do you feel is most difficult? Why?

3. Describe the following coaching skills and give an example of each:
   a. attending
   b. affirming
   c. resourcing
   d. reviewing

4. Give an example of a "general" coaching statement as contrasted to a "pinpointed" coaching statement. Which is more effective and why?

5. What is an "I" message? Why is it an effective way to confront someone's behavior? Give an example.

6. To what extent should a supervisor counsel an employee about the employee's personal problems?

7. What is an EAP?

Skill Builder 11.1

Information

Interpersonal Skill

The Personal Trainer and Coaching

Given everyone's addiction to good health, physical fitness has experienced much popularity. One of the fastest growing professions is that of personal fitness trainer. Consider the fitness trainer's job: Listen to the client's goals, outline a program of activities to achieve the client's goals, and then, through coaching, help the client achieve them. Once the client learns the basics, the trainer's job essentially becomes one of encouraging, supporting, and giving feedback. You know the language: "That's it"; "All the way down, now"; "Tighten up a bit"; "Way to go"; "You can do it"; "That's great"; "Terrific"; "That's the way to push yourself"; "Hold that form. Come through for me"; "That's OK. You showed improvement. We'll get it next time"; and so on.

Instructions:

Break into teams of four to six members. Select a spokesperson and discuss the following questions:

1. In what way are the roles of personal trainer and manager/supervisor similar? Dissimilar?
2. In what types of circumstances can all or most of the coaching behavior of personal trainers be applied to the manager/employee relationship? Give examples.
3. Have any team members worked for a manager/supervisor who functioned much like a personal trainer? In what ways?
4. Following discussion, the spokesperson will present to the class the results of the team's discussion.

Skill Builder 11.2

Information

Interpersonal Skill

Practicing "I" Messages

In reading this chapter, you learned an "I" message consists of (1) how someone's behavior makes you feel, (2) what the specific behavior is, and (3) the effect of the behavior. The following three situations show a need for an "I" message.

1. Four of your employees share a single telephone line. You are aware that one of them, Harry R., is especially long-winded on the phone and talks for as long as 15 minutes. This prevents others from placing outgoing calls and ties up the line, preventing customers from getting through.
2. It is a requirement that waiters at the upscale restaurant you manage wear white shirts and ties. One waiter has been loosening his tie, dropping the knot about two inches, and unbuttoning his shirt collar.
3. Coffee breaks for your office staff are normally 15 minutes. When someone occasionally takes a few minutes longer, it's not a big deal. Lately, however, one staff member has had three consecutive days when the break exceeded 20 minutes.

Instructions:

1. Write a hypothetical "I" message for each of the three situations.
2. Gather in groups of three to five students and share answers.
3. From your answers, select some good examples and present them to the rest of the class.

Skill Builder 11.3

Information

Interpersonal Skill

Practicing Coaching Responses

Assume the role of shipping supervisor at Apex Company. One of your employees, Jason, has been an excellent performer for the past five years. However, during the past two weeks, Jason has not seemed himself. He operated a forklift when a careless accident caused about $2,000 in damages. Moreover, Jason punched in late twice. When you discussed these incidents, he apologized, attributing his tardiness to car trouble. Normally outgoing and energetic, he appears tired and edgy. Usually one of the liveliest contributors at meetings of your group, he said nothing at yesterday's safety meeting. During afternoon break on the loading dock today, Spud, another employee, made a joking comment about Jason's favorite college football team, which had been beaten handily by its cross-state rival this past weekend. Jason responded angrily with an expletive, then got up and left the area. Another employee commented, "What's been eating Jason, anyway?" Everyone shrugged their shoulders. You decide to have a coaching meeting with Jason.

It is about two hours later. Jason just walked into your office. You stand, acknowledge him, and close the door behind him. Jason takes a seat, and as you move to sit down, he says, "So you wanted to see me about something."

a. **In the space below, write the opening statement you will make to Jason that pinpoints the reason for the meeting.**

Assume following your statement, a discussion with Jason lasts for several minutes. He is soft-spoken and avoids eye contact. Then he looks you in the eye and says, "I'm glad I have this chance to talk with you. I feel like so much is going on with me lately. I guess I've just taken on more than I should . . . and I don't know what to do about it."

b. **In the space below, write the statement you will make to Jason that demonstrates reflecting.**

Assume the discussion continues. Jason is quite talkative now, volunteering information about financial problems brought on by a house addition, his son's college expenses, and a recent auto accident that cost him $750 to cover the deductible on his policy. To meet his financial needs, Jason tells you he has been moonlighting for 30 hours weekly as a security guard at a local hotel. He has gotten little sleep the past two weeks. He now worries he can't sustain the pace because his job performance at Apex is being affected. He says, "I know I haven't been much of a contributor around here lately."

c. **In the space below, write the statement you will make to Jason that demonstrates affirming, but also reinforces the need for him to improve performance.**

During the remaining discussion, Jason commits to making his present job performance his number one priority, despite his short-term financial needs. You discuss several alternatives that would allow him to do both, two he proposed: (1) reduce his hotel hours, with most of them being worked on weekends, and (2) getting a loan from the company credit union or a bank. A third idea—taking his two-week vacation now, would allow him to work his full hotel hours for two weeks—was one you suggested he consider. You tell him you will look into waiving the normal two-week vacation notice. You also suggest he consider making an appointment with the company's EAP office, and arrange for financial counseling. Jason expresses interest in this.

(Continued)

You agree to let Jason know tomorrow about the vacation matter and to be available as needed to discuss things further should Jason need to talk. You note Jason picks up his hard hat that was placed on the floor and says: "Well, I feel much better having talked with you about this. It's taken a lot off my mind, and it's helped me think some things through. Thanks for being so patient."

   d. **In the space below, write the statement you will make to Jason that demonstrates confirming/summarizing and closes the meeting.**

   e. **Meet with other students and compare your responses.**

Skill Builder 11.4

Conducting a Coaching Meeting: Role Plays
In this exercise, you will break into small groups as determined by your instructor. The entire group should read the role for the manager/supervisor and the employee. One person should be designated to perform each role, with the others being observers. Several minutes of planning time should be allowed for players and observers to study their roles before beginning the actual coaching meeting.

General Instructions for Observers
Following each role play, you will lead a discussion of the manager's effectiveness in handling the performance coaching meeting. Use the pre–role play planning time to review some of the important coaching principles presented in the chapter to help evaluate the manager's performance. The following questions give insight into your critique of the meeting:

   1. What do you feel was the objective of the meeting?
   2. Were the steps in Exhibit 11-4, "Suggestions for Confronting Poor Performance," followed? Were any done especially well? Which might have been improved?
   3. Which of the "Core Coaching Skills"—such as acknowledging, attending, affirming, and so on—did the manager use in the meeting?
   4. To what extent do you feel the manager achieved the objective of the meeting?

Coaching Meeting 1: Assistant Principal and Teacher
(a) Role for Assistant Principal (to be read by all)
You are assistant principal at an elementary school. Twelve teachers report to you. One is Jan Wilson, who has been with you for three years. Jan teaches fourth grade. She has an excellent record as a teacher and is well liked by her students' parents.

   A well-known rule at your school deals with teacher absences—when a teacher will miss classes because of illness or emergency, your office should be notified so a substitute teacher can be employed. Earlier in the year, Jan failed to show up for class and did not notify you until later in the day. You scurried to cover Jan's class, and when Jan returned the following day, you reminded her of the notification policy. You learned her absence was related to a family emergency with one of her elderly parents.

   Yesterday, it happened again. A teacher from an adjacent classroom notified you Jan's class was unattended. Again, you exerted much energy finding a temporary replacement for the rest of the day. Jan did leave a short voicemail at 10:30 A.M. yesterday for you in which she apologized for the inconvenience and said she would be back in class today. No reason for her absence or late notification was offered.

Today, you made it a point to pass Jan's classroom shortly before class began. You asked if everything was okay, and Jan responded, "Yes, thank you." You then asked Jan to drop by your office at 3:15 P.M. following dismissal of classes.

Instruction: In a few minutes, you will conduct a performance coaching session with Jan.

(b) Role for Teacher Jan (to be read by all)

Background facts for your role are presented in the "Role for Assistant Principal" as outlined in "a" above. In a few minutes, you will meet with your assistant principal. You expect the subject will relate to your class absence yesterday. To develop your role, take a few minutes to determine a reason why you may have missed class and why you didn't notify the assistant principal earlier. Remember, you are a talented, conscientious teacher who has a good relationship with other teachers and your assistant principal. During the role play, you may have to adapt your role as the discussion ensues.

Coaching Meeting 2: Restaurant Manager and Server

(a) Role for Manager (to be read by all)

You are manager of a well-known national casual dining restaurant in your area. You are reviewing customer comment cards mailed by customers to your regional office, tabulated, and then forwarded to you each month. Results are compared to goals set for such important criteria as quality of service, food quality, and other factors. About 200 comment cards were returned to you from the past month. Your goal for server ratings is to average 85/100; during the past month, your restaurant's customers rated your 15 servers an average of 81/100. These scores ranged from a high of 95 to a low of 68.

Kelly's score of 68 is clearly poor! A new server like Kelly (presently in her second month) sometimes scores lower than more seasoned servers, but Kelly's is the lowest you have seen in the past year. Most customers rated her as "excellent" or "good." But Kelly bombed on five of 17 customers' cards, being rated as "unacceptable." Four of these found fault with Kelly's language—one labeling it as "foul mouthed," another as "profane." One mentioned some four-letter words attributed to Kelly: "hell," "damn," and "crap." This troubles you. Kelly's training emphasized how important courtesy, pleasantness, and most assuredly nonoffensive language by servers is as part of a "quality" experience for your customers.

Much business is with Sunday and Wednesday churchgoers and families with small children, so four-letter language is totally inappropriate. In her interview with you, Kelly displayed excellent interpersonal and rapport-building skills. Presently majoring in leisure services at the local university, she saw the server position as an excellent opportunity to help understand customer service.

Although you are clearly disappointed in the comment cards from Kelly's customers and with its impact on your restaurant's goals, Kelly has promise of becoming an excellent server. Clearly, however, she must clean up her language. You will conduct a coaching meeting with Kelly when she shows up for work this evening.

(b) Role for Server Kelly (to be read by all)

Read the background facts for your role as a server as presented in the "Role for Manager" outlined in "a" above. In a few minutes, you will meet with your manager, who has asked to see you. Take a few minutes to decide how you will respond in the role play to the likely things your manager will bring up in the meeting. During the role play, you may have to adapt your role as the discussion proceeds.

CASE 11-1

CRITIQUING A COACHING MEETING:

The following exchange took place between Charlene Rowe, human resources manager, and one of her senior team members, Leonard Busche.

Rowe 1: Come in, Leonard, have a seat. [Leonard sits down.] I suppose you're wondering why I wanted us to get together.

Busche 1: Yes, I guess I am, Charlene.

Rowe 2: Leonard, yesterday something happened that I want to know your feelings about. It's about the quality steering report I asked you to put together for my committee meeting yesterday afternoon.

Busche 2: [Somewhat defensively] What about it?

Rowe 3: To be quite frank, Leonard, I was too embarrassed to distribute it at the meeting. It just wasn't up to your usual standards. For one thing, it seemed superficial in that it described only a few of the programs we'd benchmarked, rather than all seven. Because this will be the major document the committee will use as a reference, we needed coverage of all the visits we've made. Also, some of the most important processes were not included—like J&J's 360-degree feedback system and Motorola's team incentives.

Busche 3: [only half joking] Gee, it seems as if I may need a union steward in here with me. [Leonard is a salaried, nonunion employee.]

Rowe 4: No, Leonard, I don't mean to give that impression. It's just that this job isn't like you at all, and that concerned me. You've always done exceptional work in putting together material like this for me. For all I know, it might have been my own fault, a misunderstanding between us. I wanted to meet and get your perspective on the situation.

Busche 4: Well, there isn't much to say. I guess I should have figured it wouldn't be of much help. [Getting a little emotional] I wasn't tickled about it either.

Rowe 5: You weren't pleased with it yourself?

Busche 5: No, I wasn't. Charlene, that report would have taken about 8 to 10 hours for me to do it up right. Do you know how long I had? About four hours, that's all. I couldn't do much in four hours.

Rowe 6: So you didn't get to put in the time on the report.

Busche 6: No, I didn't. In fact, you weren't the only one embarrassed by it. But I can't promise it'll be the last lousy job. . . . I just can't handle everything that

comes my way. I know we're a service department [human resources], but we're not the little outfit we were five years ago. I just can't keep up.

Rowe 7: It sounds as if the quality report is only part of the problem.

Busche 7: That's exactly what I'm saying. I'm expected to do everybody's odds and ends besides my regular job in training and safety. I've got the two accidents we're investigating from two weeks ago and all that paperwork. We're approaching our deadlines on the new training manuals. I'm heading up the newsletter committee that puts out our first edition next month. Then, you gave me the quality report with one week's notice. I would have gotten it done, but last week Bushman [vice president and general manager] asked me to be his facilitator. I had to put in some eight hours observing his meetings with the budget committee. So the quality report was lousy, I know. But if things continue as they are, it won't be the last. I hate it more than you do.

Rowe 8: Leonard, you know how we've all come to expect so much from you. Granted, we are a service department, but in retrospect, I wish you'd confided in me about this. I could have simply pushed back my quality committee meeting, which is what I essentially did, anyway. What can we do to help you?

Busche 8: How can we help? [Flippant] Oh, give me an assistant.

Rowe 9: Is additional help the answer?

Busche 9: I don't know the answer to that. I think what's really got me upset is Bushman. He didn't ask me to facilitate; he told me to. I should have turned him down, but I guess I haven't got the guts to say "no" to a vice president. But then, I didn't want to let you down, either.

Rowe 10: I think it's terrific that Bushman values your abilities. Politically, it's in both of our interests for you to act as Bushman's facilitator. That is, if you want to do it.

Busche 10: Oh, I don't mind facilitating for Bushman. He needs a lot of help and he knows it. It would normally be a real compliment for me; it was just the timing that was bad.

Rowe 11: Leonard, you have a lot of things going on that I didn't know about. Maybe I'm the one who has to do some changing. I can see why, given your schedule the past two weeks, taking on that quality project was too much. It wasn't fair to you. Leonard, I need to feel confident that your work for me from now on will be what I can count on. What can we do to prevent this from happening again?

Busche 11: I could probably do a better job of letting you know what I've got going on. I could also be more honest with you. I just hate saying I can't do something, especially to my boss. You probably didn't know the newsletter was eating up my time last week, as were the safety problems. I guess I could keep you more up to date. I could also be more direct and tell you if I honestly don't have the time to take something on and do a good job. But it's hard for me to say no.

Rowe 12: Okay, let's give this a try. You'll give me a brief typed report on projects other than your normal training and safety activities. If you're skeptical about a commitment request from outside the department, you'll discuss it with me before taking it on. You're also agreeing to level with me about whether you have time to commit to special projects that I throw your way. We'll try this process for a month and see what happens. Is that acceptable?

Busche 12: Yep, that sounds acceptable. Hopefully, I'll not get caught up in a bind like this again.

INSTRUCTIONS

1. What type of coaching function was reflected in Rowe's meeting with Busche?
2. In terms of effectiveness on a 1–10 scale, with 1 being "poor" and 10 being "excellent," what score would you assign to Rowe's handling of the session? Why?
3. Identify specific transcript comments by Rowe that reflect the following coaching skills: (a) reflecting, (b) pinpointing, (c) probing, (d) affirming, and (e) confirming.
4. To what extent did the meeting reflect the seven suggestions for confronting poor performance (Exhibit 11-4)?
5. Meet with a group of three to five other students, discuss your answers, and be prepared to report these to the rest of the class.

CASE 11-2

COACHING CHALLENGE: OVER-IDENTIFYING WITH AN EMPLOYEE:

Kara thinks she has a problem. She is worried that she may be over-identifying with an employee, meaning she is too much like him to be able to coach him effectively. Ken is an affable person who is achievement oriented, driven, and goal directed. He thinks creatively when confronted with challenges and is a visionary. However, he gets frustrated with others when they do not pick up on things quickly or seem to be slow to see opportunities. He also has a tendency to push people too hard because success is important to him. As such, he is unrealistic at times about project schedules and the amount of work others can handle. Kara notes, "I believe we possess similar characteristics and I have some of the same challenges. I am not sure I am the right coach for Ken. He says he is getting something out of our sessions, but I believe he might be able to make more progress with someone less like him."

INSTRUCTIONS

1. What do you think? Do you agree with Kara's assessment of the situation?
2. Based on the situation, what would you recommend?

Source: Gladeana McMahon, "A Question of Coaching," *Training Journal*, February 2012, p. 63.

Notes

1. JoAnn Greco, "Hey Coach," *Journal of Business Strategy* 22, no. 2 (March 2001), p. 28.
2. "2016 ICF Global Coaching Study: Executive Summary," *International Coach Federation*, 2016, pp. 1–21.
3. D. T. Hall, K. L. Otrazo, and G. P. Hollenbeck, "Behind Closed Doors: What Really Happens in Executive Coaching," *Organizational Dynamics* 27, no. 3 (1999).
4. Dennis Kinlaw, *Coaching for Commitment* (San Diego, CA: Pfeiffer & Co., 1993), p. 19.
5. David L. Bradford and Allan R Cohen, *Managing for Excellence* (New York: John Wiley & Sons, 1984), pp. 62–63.
6. Kris Duggan, "Six Companies That Are Redefining Performance Management," *Fast Company*, December 2015, https://www.fastcompany.com/3054547/six-companies-that-are-redefining-performance-management.
7. "Use these 10 Tips to Brush Up Your Coaching Skills," *Pay for Performance Report*, January 2002, p. 10.
8. Duggan, "Six Companies That Are Redefining Performance Management"; Jie-Tsuen Huanga and Hui-Hsien Hsieh, "Supervisors as Good Coaches: Influences of Coaching on Employees' In-Role Behaviors and Proactive Career Behaviors, *The International Journal of Human Resource Management* 26, no. 1 (2015), pp. 42–58, http://dx.doi.org/10.1080/09585192.2014.940993; Diane Coutu and Carol Kauffman, "HBR Research Report: What Can Coaches Do for You?," *Harvard Business Review*, January 2009, pp. 91–97; Julie Barker, "Too Good to Ignore: Getting More Out of Top Producers: That's Right, 'A' Players Need Coaching, Too," *Sales and Marketing Management* 157 (March 2005), pp. 38–41.
9. K. R. Phillips, "The Achilles Heel of Coaching," *Training and Development* 52, no. 3 (March 1998), pp. 41–46.
10. Dennis C. Kinlaw, *Coaching Skills Inventory* (San Diego, CA: Pfeiffer & Co., 1993), pp. 1–13.
11. "Computerworld Recognizes the 2017 Best Places to Work in IT," *Computerworld*, June 2017, http://www.marketwired.com/press-release/computerworld-recognizes-the-2017-best-places-to-work-in-it-2221306.htm; David Bicknell, "Keep It Personal and Keep Your Staff," *Computer Weekly*, July 8, 1999, p. 2.
12. See Marcus Buckingham, "What Great Managers Do," *Harvard Business Review* 83 (March 2005), pp. 70–79.
13. Tip Fallon, "Retain and Motivate the Next Generation: 7 Ways to Get the Most Out of Your Millennial Workers," *Supervision* 70 (May 2009), pp. 5–7.
14. Thomas Gordon, *Leader Effectiveness Training* (New York: Wyden Books, 1977), pp. 92–107.
15. George Bohlander and Scott George, *Managing Human Resources*, 15th ed. (Mason, OH: South-Western Cengage Learning, 2010), p. 551.
16. "2012 Corporate Social Responsibility Report," *Comcast/NBC Universal*, http://corporate.comcast.com/csr2012/supporting-our-employees-and-their-families.
17. "Small Companies Fuel Rising Use of EAPs," *HR Magazine* 24 (September 2007), p. 1.
18. "It's Your Problem Too," *BusinessWeek* 3670 (February 29, 2000), p. 26.

12
Managing Conflict, Stress, and Time

LEARNING OBJECTIVES

After reading and studying this chapter, you should be able to:

1. *Identify the causes of conflict.*

2. *Discuss conflict management styles and identify when each would be appropriate.*

3. *Describe principled negotiation.*

4. *Explain why modern life makes us particularly vulnerable to stress.*

5. *Describe both the costs and the benefits of stress.*

6. *Explain the major causes of stress.*

7. *Compare and contrast Type A behavior and Type B behavior.*

8. *Elaborate on personal ways to cope with stress.*

9. *Discuss some ways to effectively manage time.*

Nothing in life is to be feared. It is only to be understood.

—Marie Curie

Everything that irritates us about others can lead us to an understanding of ourselves.

—Carl Jung

Difficulties are meant to rouse, not discourage. The human spirit is to grow strong by conflict.

—William Emery Channing

Monkey Business Images/Shutterstock.com

As many management consultants will tell you, it can be challenging to establish trust and communicate clearly among project stakeholders, but it is vital to the long-term health and viability of the project.

Preview

THE FACILITATOR: DEALING WITH STAKEHOLDER CONFLICT John Duncan*
works for TSI Consultants* facilitating partnering workshops for large-scale
construction projects. His job involves coordinating pre-meetings with the key
stakeholders, who typically include the owner(s), architect(s), prime contractor(s),
and key subcontractors, to determine the main issues and establish an agenda for
the partnering meeting. John's task during the one- to three-day partnering retreat
is to provide facilitation to the group so they are able create a project management
culture with a common vision, mission, and values and focused on joint problem
solving.

The project John was assigned was a large federally funded, state construction project,
unique for that region of the country. In his pre-meeting conversations with the key stakeholders (owner's representative, architectural firm, general contractor, and key subcontractors), John did not detect any noticeable tension or conflict. He proceeded to develop a
one-day agenda focused on establishing common goals, creating a project mission statement,
identifying potential issues, and developing action plans to address each issue. Although
preliminary staging for the project had been underway for several weeks, the actual on-site
work was just beginning. The one-day session started well, with the stakeholders getting to

*The names have been changed for privacy reasons.

know each other better. However, during the early afternoon session, John detected undercurrents of tension among some of the participants. In particular, Bill, the general contractor's project manager, was agitated with the process so far. He did not believe Jim, whose firm represented the owner (in this case, the federal and state funding agencies), was being fully transparent and forthcoming about what he wanted, how their team "really" planned to operate, and the critical issues facing the project. Bill shared with his younger, assistant project manager, "I have worked with these types before. The contract specifications are clear, but these guys always want something else. They tell you one thing and then change their minds. It just ends up costing us money because they won't agree to the change order." John could tell Bill was influencing the younger members on his team such that they were beginning to second-guess the intentions of the other stakeholders.

John learned early in his career "if trust is an issue, it needs to be dealt with and the sooner the better." So he had to do something. Before the afternoon break, John approached Bill and Jim separately and asked them if he could talk to them during the break. When it was time, he asked both men to step into one of the side rooms. John started by saying, "I just wanted to touch base with both of you to get your thoughts and feedback on the sessions so far." Bill responded, "I know this partnering session is part of our contract on this job, but I don't think it is helping us to build a project team." John asked Bill why he felt that way and he responded truthfully, "I have been in this business a long time. Owners and architects think the low bidder makes money on changes to the contract, but in reality, most changes are because of them. We try to make them happy, but they blame us for change orders and cost increases and don't want to pay."

Jim's firm represented the owner's interest on this project. He was an engineer by trade but a seasoned veteran, having managed other large-scale projects. He responded, "Bill, I get it. If I hear what you are saying, we need to earn your trust. We say, 'we are going to do things differently,' but you have to see us walk the talk. Right? Well, we want to be a good partner. We will try and earn your trust each and every day. What can I do to show you we are serious?" Bill said, "PROVE it, but for now, I'm good if we shake on it. I'll wait and see how things play out in the field." It appeared this tactic worked, as everyone was able to refocus on the project's goals and develop actions plans to implement over the next six months, at which time a follow-up partnering session would be held to pivot as needed.

After six months, while preparing for the follow-up partnering session, John was not surprised to learn that Bill's trust issues were not fully resolved. Bill's perceptions and behaviors were clouding his team's view of the owner's group and negatively affecting the project. John decided the best approach for the follow-up meeting would be to implement a negotiation technique referred to as role negotiation. Role negotiation helps a group assess relationships and determine what changes are necessary. The process involves diagnosing issues and negotiating and agreeing to changes. He modified the technique for this particular project.

John suggested the project team be separated into two main groups for the activity: (1) general and subcontractors and (2) owner representatives and architects. John checked with everyone, and they agreed this was the best approach due to natural alliances. John proceeded asking each group to privately discuss and record their answers to the following questions:

1. What is the other stakeholder group doing really well that enhances our performance? In other words, what would you like them to keep doing and not change? (Keep doing, not change)
2. What is the other stakeholder group doing that you would like to see them do more of or do better? (Do more of or do better)
3. What is the other stakeholder group doing that you would like to see them do less of or stop doing? (Do less of or stop doing)

When the activity was complete, John asked them to share their answers, question by question. John knew this was a critical step in the process because it could easily lead to increased anxiety, anger, and conflict.

Because this was a federally funded, state construction project, the contractor with the lowest, best bid was selected. Based on what he saw when the groups were processing, John felt he had a good idea why Bill was so negative, sometimes displaying outright anger. Bill believed Jim's management firm and the owner had wanted a different contractor and were unhappy with the selection. Bill did not want people to think his company was inferior or underhanded. His insecurities or maybe his pride had gotten the best of him and he was acting like a petulant child. John had had conversations with Jim and seen the groups' answers to the questions, so he knew Bill's views were unfounded. His intuition told him the owner representatives and architects needed to present their answers first. He felt this was the key to breaking the tension.

Jim began presenting his group's answers to the first question. They listed over 25 things Bill's company was doing to positively impact the project and they wanted them to keep doing. About halfway through the list, John could see Bill's demeanor change. When it was Bill's turn to present, he projected a totally different attitude that changed the mood in the room. It was evident to John that Bill realized he had been wrong. This fortuitous turn of events led to a meaningful discussion and negotiation on the remaining items, "what to do more or better" and "what to do less or stop." It was also the start of a strong partnership between Bill and Jim that remained for the life of the project.

Source: Consulting experiences, The Synergistic Group, Mobile, AL.

As we have seen in the chapter preview, handling tension effectively leads to positive outcomes, and why it is so important for a supervisor/team leader to possess a variety of skills. Two of the most critical are conflict and stress management. When stress is excessive, one's behavior can become dysfunctional. However, we must keep in mind a certain amount of conflict and stress is healthy because it can lead to more effective decision making.

For example, intrapersonal stress can motivate an individual to proactively make life changes for the better. When a certain amount of conflict is present, the status quo is examined. Individuals grapple with various solutions through their analysis of the situation. In many cases, this evaluation leads to better decisions.

Causes of Conflict

1. *Identify the causes of conflict.*

A supervisor/team leader must have a basic understanding of the causes of conflict before he or she can determine what is functional or dysfunctional. This section looks at some of those causes.

1. **Different goals or objectives**. If departments or individuals within an organization are working toward different goals, then conflict is almost always dysfunctional. It is important to develop a common set of goals everyone supports.
2. **Communication**. Misunderstandings due to semantics, unfamiliar language, or ambiguous or incomplete information will surely lead to conflict.
3. **Structure**. Competition for scarce resources, power struggles between departments with conflicting objectives or reward systems, or interdependence of two or more groups to achieve their goals occur with organizational changes such as downsizing.
4. **Personal**. Incompatibility of personal goals or social values of employees with the role behavior required by their jobs will lead to conflict, as will certain personality characteristics, such as authoritarianism or dogmatism. Individual stress also can be a source of intrapersonal and interpersonal conflict.

5. **Change**. Fears associated with having to accomplish a task differently, job security, or the loss of personal power and prestige can cause abnormal behavior. Change can be threatening. Even change perceived to be positive can cause conflict when individuals are responsible for new duties and tasks.

HISTORICAL INSIGHT

Mary Parker Follett's Integration Process

One of the first to focus on conflict in organizations from a research/consultant standpoint was sociologist Mary Parker Follett (1869–1933). Ignored for a time, her ideas are found in many management and psychology textbooks today. One of her contributions was her analysis of how to deal with conflict. She believed any conflict of interest could be resolved by (1) voluntary submission of one side, (2) struggle and victory of one side over the other, (3) compromise, or (4) integration (today, we call it joint problem solving).

Her preferred solution was the **integration process**, whereby everyone wins, as opposed to a win-lose situation or a watered-down compromise so neither side gets what it wants. An example Follett gave to illustrate the concept of integration was an incident that occurred when she was working in a small room in the Harvard library. The other person in the room wanted the window open, while Follett wanted it closed. After discussion, integration was achieved when they opened a window in the next room. This solution was not a compromise because both got what they wanted: The other person got fresh air, and Follett did not have a cold draft on her back.

Follett also believed the essence of collaboration and teamwork was creating the feeling of working with someone rather than over or under someone—the notion of "power with" rather than "power over."

Source: Oliver Sheldon, *The Philosophy of Management* (New York: Pitman, 1939; originally published in 1923), p. 2.

---

integration process

A conflict resolution strategy in which everyone wins.

STOP AND THINK

How many of the previous causes of conflict were operative in the chapter preview?

Conflict Management Styles

2. Discuss conflict management styles and identify when each would be appropriate.

Individuals must cope with all forms of interpersonal and intergroup conflict. It is important to properly diagnose the conflict situation so it can be dealt with in the most effective manner. Exhibit 12-1 is a diagram of five conflict-handling styles based on the concern an individual has for oneself and for others. The five styles, influenced by Mary Parker Follett's original model, are as follows:

- **Avoiding**. It is an unassertive, uncooperative style in which the individual's concern for self and others is low. It is a useful style when dealing with trivial issues or when the negative consequences of confrontation outweigh the need for resolution.
- **Accommodating**. It is an unassertive, cooperative style in which the individual's concern for self is low while the concern for others is high. The accommodating approach downplays the parties' differences. It is an appropriate style to use when the issue is more important to the other party or the other party is right.
- **Forcing**. It is an assertive, uncooperative style in which the individual's concern for self is high while the concern for others is low. This approach uses power to resolve conflict. A forcing style is useful in an emergency, where quick decisions are necessary. It is also useful for correcting unethical behavior.

EXHIBIT 12-1
Interpersonal Conflict
Management Styles

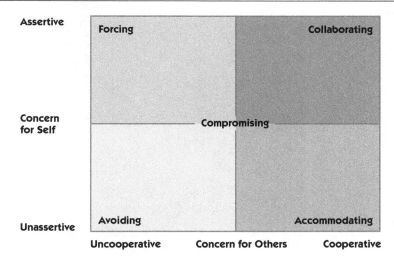

Source: Adapted from Thomas Ruble and Kenneth Thomas, "Support for a Two-Dimensional Model of Conflict Behavior," *Organizational Behavior and Human Performance* 16 (1976), p. 145. Reprinted with permission from Elsevier.

- **Compromising**. It is a somewhat assertive, cooperative style in which the individual has a moderate amount of concern for both self and others. The objective is to find a middle ground. The compromising style is appropriate when the parties have reached an impasse due to mutually exclusive goals.
- **Collaborating**. It is an assertive, cooperative approach in which the individual has a high concern for self and others. Collaboration is a problem-solving style. It is effective when dealing with conflict "head on," trying to surface all of the pertinent issues, and attempting to interpret differing points of view.

Conflict management theory today supports collaboration as the appropriate approach to resolve conflict. Because collaboration in many cases leads to win-win outcomes, it is easy to discern why collaboration advocates support this approach as "the model" for handling conflict.

During the latter part of the last century, the contingency movement gained momentum. Proponents of this theory maintained collaboration in all situations is unrealistic. For example, a management student, who is a member of a local emergency response team, made these observations when conflict management styles were covered in class:

The student's emergency response unit was activated shortly after a tragic train wreck occurred. The emergency response team prepares for these types of situations regularly. However, unanticipated problems arise that must be dealt with effectively as quickly as possible to save lives. Although the team members may utilize the collaborative approach during the planning stages, they do not have time to rely on this method while in the field. She indicated that the approach most often used by the team in the field was the forcing style because it was the most effective.

Conflict management styles must be adapted to fit the situation at hand. The avoiding, accommodating, forcing, and compromising conflict management styles are usually best used when dealing with tactical, day-to-day, short-term problems, whereas collaboration (and compromising, to a limited extent) is a conflict management style more appropriate for ad hoc task forces and long-term strategic problems.

Zastolskiy Victor/Shutterstock.com

Conflict management styles must be adapted to fit the situation at hand.

STOP AND THINK

In the chapter preview, what primary conflict management style(s) was/were used? Explain.

Using Principled Negotiation to Resolve Conflict

3. *Describe principled negotiation.*

A real breakthrough in conflict management and resolution is found in the concepts proposed by Roger Fisher and William Ury of the Harvard negotiation project. They emphasize, whether negotiation involves a peace settlement among nations or a business contract, people often engage in positional bargaining. This common form of negotiation involves proposing and then giving up a sequence of positions. The idea is to give up things that are not important. Hence, proposals are "padded" initially. For this form of negotiation to succeed, it must meet three criteria of fair negotiation: "It should produce a wise agreement if agreement is possible; it should be efficient; and it should improve, or at least not damage, the relationship between the parties."[1]

principled negotiation

Negotiation on the merits by separating the people from the problem; focusing on interests, not positions; generating a variety of possibilities before deciding what to do; and insisting the result be based on some objective standard.

When people bargain over positions, they tend to back themselves into corners defending their positions, resulting in a number of either win-lose or lose-lose outcomes. Moreover, arguing over positions often endangers an ongoing relationship by straining and sometimes shattering relationships. In a marriage, this results in divorce; in business, the result can be the breakup of an otherwise successful operation. Many negotiations involve more than two parties, and in these cases, positional bargaining compounds the problem of negotiating an agreement.

In their work with the Harvard negotiation project, Fisher and Ury developed an alternative to positional bargaining they call **principled negotiation**, or negotiation on the merits. The four basic components of principled negotiation are as follows:

1. Separating the people from the problem.
2. Focusing on interests, not positions.

EXHIBIT 12-2
Contrast of Positional Bargaining and Principled Negotiation

PROBLEM: POSITIONAL BARGAINING: WHICH GAME SHOULD YOU PLAY?		SOLUTION: CHANGE THE GAME—NEGOTIATE ON THE MERITS
SOFTBALL	HARDBALL	PRINCIPLED
Participants are friends.	Participants are adversaries.	Participants are problem solvers.
The goal is agreement.	The goal is victory.	The goal is a wise outcome reached efficiently and amicably.
Make concessions to cultivate relationship.	Demand concessions as a condition of the relationship.	**Separate the people from the problem.**
Be soft on the people and the problem.	Be hard on the problem and the people.	Be soft on the people, hard on the problem.
Trust others.	Distrust others.	Proceed independent of trust.
Change your position easily.	Dig in to your position.	*Focus on interests, not positions.*
Make offers.	Make threats.	Explore interests.
Disclose your bottom line.	Mislead as to your bottom line.	Avoid having a bottom line.
Accept one-sided losses to reach agreement.	Demand one-sided gains as the price of agreement.	**Invent options for mutual gain.**
Search for the single answer: the one they will accept.	Search for the single answer: the one you will accept.	Develop multiple options to choose from; decide later.
Insist on agreement.	Insist on your position.	**Insist on using objective criteria.**
Try to avoid a contest of will.	Try to win a contest of will.	Try to reach a result based on standards independent of will.
Yield to pressure.	Apply pressure.	Reason and be open to reason; yield to principle, not pressure.

Source: "Positional Bargaining: Which Game Should You Play?" chart from *Getting to Yes*, 2nd ed., by Roger Fisher, William Ury, and Bruce Patton. Copyright © 1981, 1991 by Roger Fisher and William Ury. Reprinted by permission of Houghton Mifflin Harcourt Publishing Company. All rights reserved.

3. Generating a variety of possibilities before deciding what to do.
4. Insisting the result be based on some objective standard.

Consultant facilitators for a number of joint ventures and partnerships involving multiple parties noted that educating the joint venture parties in the concepts of principled negotiation resulted in a high percentage of win-win resolutions in dispute settlements. Exhibit 12-2 illustrates the difference between positional bargaining and principled negotiation. Notice in positional bargaining, one can play either "hardball" or "softball."

Overcoming Interpersonal Conflicts

The authors are convinced principled negotiation is an excellent approach for dealing with conflicts among departments within an organization or resolving conflicts in joint ventures or partnerships. Perhaps a more pervasive challenge is managing interpersonal conflicts. This challenge has accelerated because of fears of downsizing, mergers, and unknown organizational futures. Job insecurity fueled by these fears produces fertile ground for conflict. Dysfunctional interpersonal conflict can lead to a variety of negative outcomes, including poor morale, low productivity, increased absenteeism, and higher turnover. In fact, in exit interviews, 50 percent of individuals list unresolved conflict as their primary reason for leaving.[2]

Industrial psychologist and trainer Dr. Jack Singer makes a strong case that human resource professionals and supervisors must learn conflict resolution strategies and teach them to other employees. He recommends a three-step program for assessing and implementing a conflict resolution strategy, as shown in Exhibit 12-3. As evidenced by the following example, conflict assessment and training can be quite effective.

EXHIBIT 12-3

Three-Step Program for Conflict Resolution

STEP 1. EVALUATING CONFLICT STYLE
Several self-assessment questionnaires have been developed over the years geared toward offering participants insight into how they react in typical conflict situations. Consider using them. The insight they provide allows you to understand what "buttons" get pushed when a person is provoked, and becomes useful as a tool to reevaluate and enhance one's behavior.

STEP 2. IDENTIFYING CONFLICT BEHAVIORS
Nonproductive Behaviors. Confronting, dominating, defending, using sarcasm and hostile humor, repressing emotions, insisting on being right, stonewalling, blaming.
Neutral Behaviors. Avoiding, cooling off, apologizing, giving in, backing off to avoid confrontation.
Positive Behaviors. Active listening, empathizing, disarming, inquiring, using "I feel" statements, recognizing how internal dialogue impacts emotional reactions. The goal is to eliminate negative and neutral behaviors and practice positive confrontation reduction skills until they become new habits.

STEP 3. LEARNING POWERFUL CONFRONTATION REDUCTION SKILLS
Active Listening. The key to all interpersonal communications is genuine listening, as opposed to defensive listening, where you plan your retort *while* the other person is talking to you. To begin to really listen, set up a role-playing environment.
   First, paraphrase what the other person says in your own words, without judging, agreeing, or disagreeing. Listen to and reflect upon the content, needs, and feelings of the other person.
   Second, ask for feedback to determine whether you interpreted correctly. If you have not, ask for clarification.
   Third, once you are sure you grasp the message and feelings of the other person, respond.
   Fourth, the other person then should listen and paraphrase for you. This process continues until you have both clarified your positions.
Empathizing. This involves putting yourself in the other person's shoes and trying to see the world through his or her eyes, taking into account cultural, racial, gender, and experiential differences.
Disarming. The fastest way to defuse an argument is to find some truth in what the other person is saying, even if you do not agree with the basic criticism or complaint. For example, saying, "*I can understand* how you'd feel angry with me since you believed I started the rumor" acknowledges and validates the angry person's feelings without actually agreeing with what was said. This opens the door to clarification.
Inquiring. By asking for clarification of ideas, needs, and feelings *you* signal a feeling of working toward mutual understanding and compromise.
"I Feel" Statements. Expressing yourself with such statements as "I feel angry because you seem to be avoiding me" is much more productive than the accusatory "*You* made me angry and it's *your* fault that I've had a bad day at work today." In the first scenario, *you* take responsibility for your own feelings and share them; in the second, you escalate the confrontation by blaming and putting the person on the defensive.

Source: Resources, Aberdeen Woods Conference Center, 201 Aberdeen Parkway, Peachtree City, GA 30269–1422; Jack N. Singer, *Personality Collisions* 3, no. 3 (November 1997), pp. 5–6.

When Fernando Costa became divisional manufacturing manager at MM Kembla Products in Kembla, Australia, relationships between management, supervisory, and shop floor personnel had broken down, and interactions often resulted in confrontation. "Dialogues were nonexistent and threats were the acceptable way of putting a position forward. Any issue—no matter how trivial—would be addressed through union representatives," says Costa. The company decided to offer conflict resolution training, and, two years later, the benefits are evident. "There is a total change in the way people talk to each other today," Costa says. Union representatives no longer use abusive language to intimidate management, and management addresses problems more effectively, using the conflict resolution techniques they learned. Employees can resolve some issues without involving senior management, and without increasing tensions on the floor."[3]

Many interpersonal conflicts occur when one person finds another person's behavior uncomfortable, bullying, or irritating. Robert Bramson identified basic types of difficult behavior, three of which are particularly troublesome when trying to resolve conflicts. Exhibit 12-4 identifies these three types and gives suggestions for coping with them.

EXHIBIT 12-4
Coping with Difficult Behavior

Hostile-Aggressives: Hostile-aggressive behavior occurs when individuals bully other people by bombarding them with cutting remarks, or by throwing a tantrum when things do not go their way. Their focus is on attacking the other party in a conflict. Openly emotional, they use these displays to create discomfort or surprise in their adversaries. Underlying their behavior is a strong sense of "shoulds," internal rules about the way things ought to be. A key to dealing with hostile-aggressive behavior is to recognize the behavior and not to be drawn into it yourself.

HOSTILE-AGGRESSIVES:

- Stand up for yourself.
- Give them time to run down.
- Use self-assertive language.
- Avoid a direct confrontation.

Complainers: Complainers gripe constantly but never take action about what they complain about, usually because they feel powerless or they do not want to take responsibility. You may want to hear complainers out and let them know you understand their feelings, but do not get drawn into pitying them. Use a problem-solving stance. For instance, a manager might say, "Joan, what do you want the outcome of our meeting to be? What action needs to be taken?" This focuses the complainer on solutions, not complaints.

COMPLAINERS:

- Listen attentively.
- Acknowledge their feelings.
- Avoid complaining with them.
- State the facts without apology.
- Use a problem-solving mode.

Clams: Clams are silent and unresponsive when asked for opinions. They react to conflict by closing up (like their namesakes) and refusing to discuss problems. The challenge in coping with clams is getting them to open up and talk. Open-ended questions are invaluable, as is patience in allowing them their silence for a reasonable time.

CLAMS:

- Ask open-ended questions.
- Be patient in waiting for a response.
- Ask more open-ended questions.
- If no response occurs, tell clams what you plan to do because no discussion has taken place.

Source: Adapted from *Coping with Difficult People* by Robert M. Bramson, copyright © 1981 by Robert Bramson. Used by permission of Doubleday, a division of Random House, Inc.

What Is Stress?

4. *Explain why modern life makes us particularly vulnerable to stress.*

A number of concepts presented earlier in this chapter lend insight into how to manage stress. Organizations and supervisors can suffer serious consequences if stress is not understood and managed. We now examine the topic in more depth.

Definition of Stress

For many years, the medical community failed to take stress seriously. One of the reasons for this failure was the lack of an adequate definition of stress and of research into its effects. **Stress** can be defined as any external stimulus that causes wear and tear on one's psychological or physical well-being.[4]

stress

Any external stimulus that causes wear and tear on one's psychological or physical well-being.

Stress researchers point out modern men and women sometimes react to the strains of work and everyday life the same way our primitive ancestors did. In the days of the caveman, when there was danger, a chemical reaction in the body geared our ancestors to either fight or flee. The problem for some modern men and women is their bodies still react the same way to external stimuli, causing them to maintain a constant fight-or-flight readiness. The anxiety is similar to soldiers in combat, and it causes wear and tear on our bodies.

Jane Coleman was driving to work during the morning rush hour. An irresponsible driver nearly caused an accident by cutting into her lane. By the time Jane arrived at work, she was already tense; the problem was compounded when she discovered that one of her key employees was out with the flu. Two emergencies during the day caused her to end the day anxious and exhausted.

Many of us face situations similar to Jane's. Note stress can be caused by an external stimulus, such as driving on the freeway, or by conditions on the job. An excellent definition of job stress is "a condition arising from the interaction of people and their jobs and characterized by changes within people that force them to deviate from their normal functioning."[5] Under normal conditions, our bodies and minds are in a state of equilibrium. As a result of occurrences on or off the job, however, our equilibrium may be disrupted. In attempting to recover from this imbalance, we function differently and sometimes generate a fight-or-flight chemical reaction. Obviously, Jane, as a supervisor, cannot leave her job or pick a fight with someone, but the chemical reaction in her body occurs anyway.

The Costs of Stress

5. *Describe both the costs and the benefits of stress.*

It has been estimated two-thirds of all visits to physicians can be traced to stress-related symptoms. It is, for example, a major contributor to heart disease, cancer, lung problems, accidents, cirrhosis of the liver, and suicide. Even the common cold and skin rashes are sometimes related to a person's experiencing prolonged and severe stress. Industry leaders are aware such symptoms play a major role in absenteeism, accidents, and lost productivity.

Certainly a person under severe and/or prolonged stressful conditions cannot function as effectively as a person leading a more balanced life. Almost 70 percent of employees report work is a major source of stress and 51 percent indicate they are less productive because of stress.[6] However, we are not implying stress is all negative, because a certain amount adds zest to life.

The Positive Aspects of Stress

Some amount of stress is necessary to accomplish anything meaningful. The teams that play in the Super Bowl are certainly in a stressful situation. Anyone who has played a sport or spoken in front of a large group has been in a stressful situation. Without question, moderate amounts of stress improve performance. For example, difficult but attainable

Traffic is an external stimulus that can act as a common stressor. What is one example of an internal stimulus?

objectives motivate better than easy objectives. People who seek types of work and leisure that engage their skills find life zestful and interesting. The secret is to involve yourself in challenging work and active leisure accompanied by sufficient rest and retreat. Life is full of stressors that stimulate, energize, and aid in such positive outcomes as individual health and high productivity. We call the constructive dimensions of positive stress *eustress*, which can be a powerful motivator. Examples of eustress include going to an athletic event or participating in sports.

Major Causes of Stress

6. *Explain the major causes of stress.*

A number of factors contribute to individual stress. Among these are (1) life events, (2) personal psychological makeup, and (3) organizational and work-related factors. Especially in the case of organizational and work-related factors, the result is likely to be burnout.

Life Events

Stress occurs whenever we face situations that require changes in behavior and a higher level of activity. It would be impossible to list all of the situations that place stress on human beings because the mere fact of living does so. However, researchers have identified major life events, both positive and negative, that require drastic changes in a person's behavior. If many of these events occur within a year's time, a person becomes particularly susceptible to unpleasant physical or psychological consequences of excessive stress.

life event

Anything that causes a person to deviate from normal functioning.

Exhibit 12-5 lists a number of stress-provoking life events. A major **life event** is anything that causes a person to deviate from normal functioning. The events listed below are ranked in order of impact on a person's life. The death of a spouse has the most impact; change in

EXHIBIT 12-5

Sources of Stress

LIFE EVENT	POINTS
Death of a spouse	99
Divorce	91
Marriage	85
Death of close family member	84
Fired at work	83
Pregnancy	78
Marital separation	78
Jail term	72
Personal injury or illness	68
Death of close friend	68
Retirement	68
Change of financial state	61
Spouse begins or stops work	58
Marital reconciliation	57
Christmas	56
Change in health of family member	56
Foreclosure of mortgage or loan	55
Sex difficulties	53
Addition of new family member	51
Change to different line of work	51
Business readjustment	50
Mortgage over $10,000 (Present-day amount of $80,000)	48
Change in residence	47
Change in number of arguments with spouse	46
Change in responsibilities at work	46
Begin or end school	45
Trouble with boss	45
Revision of personal habits	44
Trouble with in-laws	43
Vacation	43
Change in living conditions	42
Son or daughter leaving home	41
Outstanding personal achievement	38

Change in work hours or conditions	36
Change in school	36
Minor violations of law	30
Change in eating habits	29
Mortgage or loan less than $10,000 (Present-day amount of $80,000)	27
Change in sleeping habits	27
Change in recreation	26
Change in church activities	26
Change in number of family get-togethers	15

Source: From "The 1990s Stress Scale," *Albuquerque Journal*, December 16, 1991, p. B1. © McClatchy-Tribune Information Services. All Rights Reserved. Reprinted with permission.

the number of family get-togethers causes the least stress. To obtain your score, record the points for each event you experienced in the past year. Add the events' points to get your total; anything above 300 points is the change level. Steps and action plans can be initiated to offset a high score and thus avoid adverse consequences. We discuss this later in the chapter.

Patrick Hogan, a 34-year-old supervisor, seemed to have it all. He had a good job, was happily married, had two children, and was on top of the world. At work, he was highly productive and outgoing and considered a leading candidate for advancement.

In the course of a year, several events occurred in Patrick's life that disrupted his patterns of living. A long-time friend enticed him to invest in a steakhouse the friend would operate. The restaurant lost money and the friend left town, leaving Patrick responsible for the bank note. To save his investment, he started moonlighting at the restaurant, not getting home until 1:00 A.M. most nights.

While Patrick struggled with the restaurant, his mother died after a lingering illness. Two weeks after the funeral, his wife had an accident and was confined to bed with a slipped disk. For the first time in his life, Patrick prepared meals, washed clothes, and cared for the children while at the same time carrying on his regular job and struggling with the restaurant. At work, Patrick's behavior changed drastically. He showed impatience with his employees and lost his temper quickly. He became depressed and found it difficult to reach decisions about matters he previously handled decisively.

STOP AND THINK

Based on the description of what happened in Patrick Hogan's life within the past year, calculate his score from the life event table. Assume you are his supervisor, and Patrick comes to you to talk about his situation. What advice would you give him?

Personal Psychological Makeup

7. Compare and contrast Type A behavior and Type B behavior.

Americans have long been noted for their emphasis on work. The United States has a justifiable reputation as a country where individuals, through hard work, can achieve considerable economic success. Some people, however, have become so caught up in the work ethic that work becomes the end itself rather than the means to an end. New Zealanders say,

Any major life event, even a positive one, can provoke stress because it causes an individual to deviate from normal functioning.

Type A behavior

Behavior pattern characterized by (a) trying to accomplish too much in a short time and (b) lacking patience and struggling against time and other people to accomplish one's ends.

Type B behavior

Behavior pattern characterized by (a) tending to be calmer than someone with Type A behavior, (b) devoting more time to exercise, and (c) being more realistic in estimating the time it takes to complete an assignment.

"Americans live to work and New Zealanders work to live." Our point is some Americans have become workaholics, and this excessiveness has behavioral consequences that take a toll over a period of time. Researchers have identified two basic types of behavior characterizing people in our society: Type A and Type B.

Type A Behavior. Cardiologists Meyer Friedman and Roy Rosenman first defined the term **Type A behavior**. Individuals who exhibit Type A behavior tend to accomplish too many things in a short time. Lacking patience, they struggle against time and other people to accomplish their ends. As a consequence, they become irritated by trivial things. Type A people also tend to be workaholics. Because of their psychological makeup, they may be subject to stress over prolonged periods. For this reason, Type A people have a much higher risk of heart disease than Type B people.[7]

Type B Behavior. People exhibiting **Type B behavior** tend to be calmer, to take more time to exercise, and to be more realistic than Type A's in estimating the amount of time needed to complete an assignment. Type B's also worry less and, in general, desire more satisfaction from their work.

Studies of Type A and B behaviors indicate 60 percent of managers and supervisors fall into the category of Type A people (see Exhibit 12-6). Many supervisors respond to all events as if they were emergencies or life-threatening situations. Managers and supervisors who exhibit extreme Type A behavior patterns tend to practice close supervision and find it difficult to delegate. They are concerned errors might reflect on past achievements, so they become excessively task oriented.[8]

EXHIBIT 12-6
Behavior-Type Quiz

To find out which behavior type you are, circle the number on the scale below for each trait that best characterizes your behavior.

Casual about appointments	1	2	3	4	5	6	7	8	Never late
Not competitive	1	2	3	4	5	6	7	8	Very competitive
Never feel rushed even under pressure	1	2	3	4	5	6	7	8	Always rushed
Take things one at a time	1	2	3	4	5	6	7	8	Try to do many things at once; think about what I'm going to do next
Slow doing things	1	2	3	4	5	6	7	8	Fast (eating, walking, etc.)
Express feelings	1	2	3	4	5	6	7	8	"Sit on" feelings
Many interests	1	2	3	4	5	6	7	8	Few interests outside work

Total score: _____ Total score multiplied by 3: _____

The interpretation is as follows:

NUMBER OF POINTS	TYPE OF PERSONALITY
Less than 90	B
90 to 99	B1
100 to 105	A2
106 to 119	A
120 or more	A1

Source: A. P. Brief, R. S. Schuler, and M. V. Sell, *Managing Job Stress* (Boston: Little, Brown & Co., 1981), p. 87. Reprinted by permission of Arthur P. Brief.

STOP AND THINK

Complete the Behavior Type Quiz in Exhibit 12-6. What type of personality are you? What are the strengths and weaknesses of your personality? Can you acquire balance in your life? If so, how?

Organizational and Work-Related Factors

We discussed many organizational and work-related factors that may cause excessive stress. As shown in Exhibit 12-7, these range from having poorly defined job descriptions to autocratic or permissive leadership. If these factors exist in an organization over a period of time, they will cause extensive damage in the form of dissatisfaction, high turnover, low productivity, incomplete goal accomplishment, and job burnout. As the following example shows, stress can even create an opportunity for union activity.

A union organizer approached several employees from the home office of XYZ Life & Casualty Insurance Company. He was quickly told they were not interested in joining a union because they had excellent pay, good working conditions, and a high regard for their supervisors.

EXHIBIT 12-7

Organizational and Work-Related Factors That Cause Excessive Stress

- A highly centralized organization with decision making concentrated at the top.
- Many levels and narrow spans of control.
- Excessive and continuous pressure from higher levels.
- Conflicting demands on lower levels.
- Lack of clarity with respect to organizational and work objectives.
- Widespread autocratic leadership and close supervision.
- Little or no participation in decision making by supervisor and workers.
- Inconsistent application of company policies.
- Favoritism in decisions regarding layoffs, salary increases, promotions, and the like.
- Poor working conditions.
- Poor communication.
- Lack of structure and job descriptions.
- Widespread permissive leadership.
- Technical glitches with computer interfaces.

Six months later, a supervisor retired from the claims department. The new supervisor, after being on the job a month, called two long-time employees into the office and gave them dismissal notices without a reason for doing so. That night, five employees drove 90 miles to a meeting in another city with the union organizer. Upon their return, they obtained enough employee signatures to force an election to determine whether the union would represent employees in the XYZ home office.

Burnout

burnout

A malady caused by excessive stress in the setting where people invest most of their time and energy.

One of the most common results of excessive stress is burnout. **Burnout** is a stress-related malady that generally originates in the setting where people invest most of their time and energy. This setting is usually the work environment, but it could just as well be the home or the golf course.

Early research by Robert Golembiewski and Robert Munzenrider highlighted the seriousness of the problem. Using an adapted version of the Maslach Burnout Inventory (MBI), they discovered 40 percent of more than 12,000 respondents in 33 organizations suffered from advanced phases of burnout. A more recent longitudinal study found burnout predicted both depression and life dissatisfaction across temporal stages.[9] Exhibit 12-8 explains the subscales used in the MBI and charts the eight phases of burnout. A person scoring in phase I would be highly energized and motivated by the positive aspects of stress. In Maslow's terms, such a person would be operating at the esteem and self-fulfillment level of the need hierarchy. To a lesser extent, the same would be true of a person in phases II, III, IV, and V. Difficulties occur when a person reaches phases VI, VII, and VIII, the advanced stages of burnout.

Candidates for job burnout have three distinguishing characteristics. First, they experience stress caused predominantly by job-related stressors. Second, they tend to be idealistic and/or self-motivated achievers. Third, they tend to seek unattainable goals.

Although over the long term the ideal way to deal with burnout is to address the factors causing it, in the short term, burnout can be managed through use of any of a variety of strategies for coping with stress. Some of the ways companies are preventing or attacking burnout are by providing an on-site fitness center or a subsidy program. Others, like Apple, Yahoo!, and Google, offer increasingly popular on-site massage therapies and meditation classes. It is estimated job stress and related problems cost U.S. companies between $190 and $300 billion a year.[10]

EXHIBIT 12-8

MBI Subclass and
Phases of Burnout

The adapted Maslach Burnout Inventory, or MBI, consists of 25 items, rated on a scale of 1 (very much *unlike* me) to 7 (very much *like* me). There are three subscales.

Depersonalization: Individuals with high scores on this subscale tend to view people as objects and to distance themselves from others. Example: "I worry that this job is hardening me emotionally."

Personal Accomplishment (reversed): Respondents with high scores on this subscale see themselves as not performing well on a task that they perceive as not being particularly worthwhile. Example: "I have accomplished few worthwhile things on this job."

Emotional Exhaustion: Individuals with high scores on this subscale see themselves as operating beyond comfortable coping limits and as approaching "the end of the rope" in psychological and emotional senses. Example: "I feel fatigued when I get up in the morning and have to face another day on the job."

Emotional exhaustion is considered most characteristic of advanced phases of burnout, and depersonalization is considered least virulent. Ratings of high or low on the three subscales determine the progressive phases of burnout, generating an eight-phase model of burnout:

	PROGRESSIVE PHASES OF BURNOUT							
	I	II	III	IV	V	VI	VII	VIII
Depersonalization	Low	High	Low	High	Low	High	Low	High
Personal accomplishment	Low	Low	High	High	Low	Low	High	High
Emotional exhaustion	Low	Low	Low	Low	High	High	High	High

Source: Adapted from Robert T. Golembiewski and Robert F. Munzenrider, *Phases of Burnout*, Copyright © 1988, pp. 19–28. Reproduced with permission of Greenwood Publishing Group, Inc. Westport, CT.

Ways to Cope with Personal Stress

8. *Elaborate on personal ways to cope with stress.*

Four methods that helped many supervisors cope with stress are (1) engaging in physical exercise, (2) practicing relaxation techniques, (3) gaining a sense of control, and (4) developing and maintaining good interpersonal relationships.

Physical Exercise

People who exercise a minimum of two or three times a week are less prone to the adverse symptoms of stress than those who do not. The exercise should be vigorous to the point of inducing perspiration. A person's muscles and circulatory system are not designed for a life of inactivity. People who revitalize their bodies are much less likely to worry and become upset over events and problems. Exercise can take many forms: tennis, handball, jogging, walking, swimming, gardening, or workouts at a health and exercise spa.

Earlier in the chapter, we highlighted the problems Patrick Hogan faced and saw how the stress of dealing with these problems drastically changed his behavior. Patrick's manager noticed the change and counseled him regarding the situation. After Patrick discussed his circumstances, the manager asked him if he engaged in regular exercise. Patrick answered he simply did not have the time as a result of having to moonlight at the restaurant.

Patrick's manager persuaded him to work out three times a week in the company exercise room. Within two weeks, Patrick's on-the-job behavior was back to normal, and he began developing a plan to cope with some of the problems outside of work.

Relaxation Techniques

Exhibit 12-9 summarizes several of the relaxation techniques that are easy to use and effective. These techniques are particularly useful to supervisors/team leaders because they are neither time-consuming nor costly. Research shows when practiced on a regular basis, these techniques enable one to deal more effectively with stress, may lower blood pressure, and, in general, improve physical and emotional health.

A Sense of Control

Supervisors having a sense of control over their own lives handle stress much better than those who feel they are manipulated by life's events or by other people. If they have other interests, supervisors are better able to look at work as only one aspect of life. Many of them also have a deep faith in religion that allows them to cope with adversity. Some ways to gain control are as follows:

1. Plan. Look ahead, identifying both long- and short-term goals. Also, identify causes of stress and ways to alleviate them.
2. Get to know and like yourself. Identify your strengths and interests and pursue activities that capitalize on your strengths.
3. Perceive situations as challenges rather than as problems.
4. Take a long vacation rather than a series of short vacations.
5. Do things for others, either through a religious group or by becoming involved in some kind of volunteer work or youth activities such as Boy or Girl Scouts, Big Brother or Big Sister, or Junior Achievement.
6. Provide yourself with positive reinforcement when you do a task well. Treat yourself to a reward when you accomplish something worthwhile.

Pete Saloutos/Shutterstock.com

Yoga is one option for both relaxation and physical exercise.

EXHIBIT 12-9
Relaxation Techniques

Relaxation Response. One of the best studied stress-relievers is the relaxation response, first described by Harvard's Herbert Benson, M.D., more than 20 years ago. Its great advantage is it requires no special posture or place. Say you're stuck in traffic when you're expected at a meeting, or you're having trouble falling asleep because your mind keeps replaying some awkward situation.

- Sit or recline comfortably. Close your eyes if you can, and relax your muscles.
- Breathe deeply. To make sure you are breathing deeply, place one hand on your abdomen, the other on your chest. Breathe in slowly through your nose, and as you do you should feel your abdomen (not your chest) rise.
- Slowly exhale. As you do, focus on your breathing. Some people do better if they silently repeat the word "om" as they exhale; it helps clear the mind.
- If thoughts intrude, do not dwell on them; allow them to pass on and refocusing on your breathing.

Although you can turn to this exercise any time you feel stressed, doing it regularly for 10 to 20 minutes each day can put you in a relaxed mode to see you through otherwise stressful situations.

Cleansing Breath. Epstein, who searched the world literature for techniques people claimed valuable for coping, focuses on those that are simple and powerful. He calls them "gems," devices that work through differing means; can be learned in minutes and be done anytime, anywhere; and have a pronounced physiologic effect. At the top of his list is the quickest of all—a cleansing breath.

Take a huge breath in. Hold it for three to four seconds. Then let it out v-e-r-y s-l-o-w-l-y. As you blow out, blow out all the tension in your body.

Relaxing Postures. "The research literature demonstrates that sitting in certain positions, all by itself, has a pronounced effect," says Epstein. Sit anywhere. Relax your shoulders so they are comfortably rounded. Allow your arms to drop by your sides. Rest your hands, palm side up, on top of your thighs. With your knees comfortably bent, extend your legs and allow your feet, supported on the heels, to fall gently outward. Let your jaw drop. Close your eyes and breathe deeply for a minute or two.

Passive Stretches. It's possible to relax muscles without effort; gravity can do it all. Start with your neck and let your head fall forward to the right. Breathe in and out normally. With every breath out, allow your head to fall more. Do the same for shoulders, arms, back.

Imagery. Find a comfortable posture and close your eyes. Imagine the most relaxed place you've ever been. We all have a place like this and can call it to mind anywhere, any time. For everyone it is different. It may be a lake. It may be a mountain. It may be a cottage at the beach. Are you there?

Five—Count 'Em, Five—Tricks. Because you can never have too many tricks in your little bag, here are some "proven stress-busters" from Paul Rosch, M.D., president of the American Institute of Stress:

- Curl your toes against the soles of your feet as hard as you can for 15 seconds, then relax them. Progressively tense and relax the muscles in your legs, stomach, back, shoulders, neck.
- Visualize lying on a beach, listening to waves coming in, and feeling the warm sun and gentle breezes on your back. Or, if you prefer, imagine floating, with your eyes closed while waves gently rock you back and forth.
- Set aside 20 to 30 minutes a day to do anything you want—even nothing.
- Take a brisk walk.
- Keep an iPod handy and loaded with relaxing, enjoyable music.

"Beating stress is a matter of removing yourself from the situation and taking a few breaths," says Rosch. "If I find myself getting stressed, I ask myself, 'is this going to matter to me in five years?' Usually the answer is no. If so, why get worked up over it?"

Source: Adapted from John Carpi, "A Smorgasbord of Stress-Stoppers," *Psychology Today* 29, no. 1 (January/February 1996), p. 39. Reprinted with permission from *Psychology Today* Magazine, Copyright © 1996 Sussex Publishers, LLC.

EXHIBIT 12-10
Strategies That Make
You Feel Great

- Savor the moment. "Happiness," said Benjamin Franklin, "is produced not so much by great pieces of good fortune that seldom happen as by the little advantages that occur each day."
- Take control of your time. There is nevertheless a place for setting goals and managing time. Compared to those who've learned a sense of helplessness, those with an "internal locus of control" do better in school, cope better with stress, and live with greater well-being.
- Act happy. Study after study reveals three traits that mark happy people's lives: (1) They like themselves, (2) they are positive thinkers, and (3) they are outgoing. In experiments, people who feign high self-esteem begin feeling better about themselves.
- Seek work and leisure that engage your skills. Even if we make a lower but livable wage, it pays to seek work that we find interesting and challenging.
- Join the movement. A slew of recent studies reveal that aerobic exercise is an antidote for mild depression.
- Get rest. Happy people live active, vigorous lives, yet they reserve time for renewing sleep and solitude.
- Give priority to close relationships. People who can name several close, supportive friends—friends with whom they freely share their ups and downs—live with greater health and happiness.
- Take care of your soul. Actively religious people are much less likely than others to become delinquent, abuse drugs and alcohol, divorce, or commit suicide. They're even physically healthier.

Source: Adapted from David G. Meyers, "Pursuing Happiness," *Psychology Today* 26 (July–August 1993), pp. 32–35 and 66–67.

Developing and Maintaining Good Interpersonal Relationships

It is most important for one's mental health and happiness to give priority to close relationships—family and friends. These relationships provide a base of mutual support where one can discuss success, opportunities, issues, and problems.

According to psychologist Alex Michalos, good interpersonal relationships are more important to one's happiness and well-being than either income or looks. When one is facing a major challenge or problem, it is helpful to be able to discuss it with a spouse or friend. It is also important to maintain relationships and confront problems between yourself and loved ones and friends through discussion rather than through avoidance. Exhibit 12-10 provides a summary of strategies that help make you feel great. The second strategy, "take control of your time," is discussed next.

Managing Your Time

Organizations have three types of resources: human, physical, and financial. Some management experts include time as a fourth resource. Make no mistake about it—time is one of the greatest resources a supervisor has. Therefore, effective time management is essential for effective supervision. **Time management** is the ability to use one's time to get things done when they should be done. Another definition, which reflects planning and prioritizing, is "arranging to accomplish the things you choose to get done within the time available." Without this ability, all of your other management skills are for naught. Even if you have excellent human relations skills, poor time management can leave you too distracted to effectively listen to an employee's problems, or pressures can keep you from thinking clearly enough to use your conceptual skills fully. You may not even be able to take the time to display your technical skills by showing a new employee the ropes. To be effective as a supervisor, then, you must make effective use of your time.

time management

Ability to use one's time to get things done when they should be done.

The Time Log: Where Your Time Goes

Time management experts say the first step in making effective use of your time is to determine how your time is actually being spent. Conscientiously filling in a time log like the one shown in Exhibit 12-11 is an excellent way to get this information.

EXHIBIT 12-11

Daily Time Log

DAILY TIME LOG						
Name _____						
Date _____ March 1, 2018 _____						
On this log record each activity that you performed during the workday. Make sure that you include every activity performed such as telephone calls, conversations, rest breaks, reading, and so on. Do this for a period of time long enough to reflect normal "workdays." A week should normally be sufficient.						
From – To	Minutes	Type of Activity	People Involved	Priority A	B	C
8:00 – 8:05	5	Talked in hall	Dan, Patsy			
8:05 – 8:15	10	Read status report on work progress				
8:15 – 8:20	5	Checked progress on slow job	Ronald			
8:20 – 8:30	10	Prepared for supt. meeting				
8:30 – 9:30	60	Attended supt. meeting	Dept. heads & Supt.			
9:30 – 9:45	15	Coffee	Al, Peter, Karen			
9:45 – 9:50	5	returned to eight texts				
9:50 – 10:02	12	Completed questionnaire from Personnel Dept				
10:02 – 10:06	4	Checked facebook				
10:06 – 10:20	14	read and respond to e-mails				
10:20 – 10:23	3	Called Purchasing Dept to check status of order	Kawahara			
10:23 – 10:50	27	Discussion with Supt. about objectives for dept.	McWilliams			
10:50 – 11:00	10	Visited Personnel office to check status of applicants	Alice			
11:00 – 11:55	55	Met with United Way Committee	too many!			
11:55 – 12:10	15	Began work on dept. budget proposal				
12:10 – 12:50	40	Lunch	Dan, Patsy, Al			
—						
—						

Setting Priorities: A "Must"

Once you know where your time is going, you can analyze whether it is going in the proper direction. Not everyone can do all he or she wants to do. The secret, then, is to spend time on those activities that are most important and urgent and contribute most significantly to your doing a top-notch job.

> *Hoi Mon Sol, whose time log is shown in Exhibit 12-11, said he could not find enough time to do everything he wanted to do because he was so busy. Yet, when he got home, he looked back at his day and called his activities "wheel spinning." He didn't feel good about what he accomplished. Sol, like many supervisors, typically spent his day handling many low-priority activities rather than the high-priority ones!*

To use a time log most effectively, one must establish a rating system for classifying the priority of activities to be performed in a given day, such as the following:

1. A activities are the most important—they are critical to your job.
2. B activities are medium priority—important, but less so than A activities.
3. C activities are low priority—routine and/or relatively unimportant.

The more efficient supervisor spends a greater percentage of his or her time performing A activities.

Many of the "brush fires" supervisors devote a large percentage of their time to are B or perhaps even C priority items. In the next section, we hope to help you learn to spend more of your time on your A activities!

Handling the Common Time Wasters

9. *Discuss some ways to effectively manage time.*

Many activities you carry out during a typical day are time wasters—inefficient uses of your time (Exhibit 12-12). These may include doing routine work someone else could handle, socializing excessively, or fighting a losing battle against paperwork.

STOP AND THINK

Examine the list of activities shown in Exhibit 12-11. Identify an A activity and a C activity. On what types of activities did Sol spend most of his time?

Supervisory jobs vary a great deal in terms of the demands on the supervisor's time. That's why maintaining a time log (Exhibit 12-11) is an important first step in diagnosing your time management habits. Exhibit 12-13 is a broad list of "do's" that may help you to use your time more effectively.

EXHIBIT 12-12

Eight Common Supervisory Time Wasters

- Distractions and interruptions
- Failure to set priorities
- Procrastination
- Doing routine work subordinates could handle
- Indecision
- Personal disorganization
- Failure to delegate
- Excessive or unnecessary paperwork

EXHIBIT 12-13

How to Use Your
Time More Effectively

1. *Set priorities.*
   a. Establish A, B, and C priorities.
   b. Determine daily priorities.
   c. Focus effort on high-priority items.

2. *Do not procrastinate.*
   a. Break big jobs into smaller parts.
   b. Get started, even if on a minor part of a job.
   c. Do the more unpleasant parts of a job first.
   d. Reward yourself for doing things on schedule.

3. *Manage e-mails effectively.*
   a. Handle all return e-mails at set times of the day.
   b. Prioritize e-mails based on importance and urgency.

4. *Manage the telephone effectively.*
   a. Have someone else take your calls and handle them if possible.
   b. Handle all return calls at set times of the day.

5. *Make your meetings effective.*
   a. Prepare and announce an agenda before the meeting.
   b. Begin meetings on time.
   c. Stick to the topics on the agenda.
   d. Make decisions or come to conclusions.

6. *Learn to delegate.*
   a. Delegate time-consuming details.
   b. Delegate jobs that help employees' development.
   c. Delegate jobs employees can perform better than you.

7. *Handle people who drop in.*
   a. Close your door for periods of time.
   b. Stand up and remain standing until the visitor leaves.
   c. Meet long-winded persons at their work area so you can leave when you are ready.
   d. Train your boss and work group to respect your time.

8. *Be decisive.*
   a. Set a personal deadline for making a decision.
   b. Once you have the facts, make the decision.

9. *Get organized.*
   a. Use a daily time planner.
   b. Implement a filing system.
   c. See 1b above.

10. *Stay on top of paperwork.*
    a. Handle papers only once!
    b. Handwrite short notes directly on original documents and forward them to the persons concerned.
    c. Have someone classify papers according to importance and route them for you.

11. *Avoid distractions and interruptions.*
    a. Keep a neat desk; work and papers piled on a desk are distracting.
    b. Try to set aside uninterrupted blocks of time.
    c. Face your desk away from the view of others.

● **Chapter Review**

1. *Identify the causes of conflict.*
A key skill needed by supervisors is conflict management. Two of the causes of conflict are having unclear or different objectives and communication breakdowns.

2. *Discuss conflict management styles and identify when each would be appropriate.*
The five conflict management styles are avoiding, accommodating, forcing, compromising, and collaborating or joint problem solving. Two of the most widely used styles are forcing and collaborating. Collaborating seems to be most successful in dealing with conflicts caused by communication difficulties, whereas forcing is sometimes necessary when dealing with conflicts of personal values and personality.

3. *Describe principled negotiation.*
Principled negotiation holds promise in keeping personalities out of conflict by focusing on the problem rather than the person.

4. *Explain why modern life makes us particularly vulnerable to stress.*
Stress is any external stimulus that causes wear and tear on a person's psychological or physical well-being. Modern men and women react to stress as our primitive ancestors did, with a chemical reaction designed to ready the body for fight or flight. This chemical reaction is not helpful in normal situations today, so we need to develop ways to cope with and manage stress.

5. *Describe both the costs and the benefits of stress.*
When we are unsuccessful in coping with stress, the costs are enormous. Stress is a major cause of many illnesses, from the common cold to heart disease. It plays a role in absenteeism, accidents, and lost productivity. Not all stress is negative, however. Small and great achievements occur as a result of moderate amounts of stress.

6. *Explain the major causes of stress.*
Major causes of stress are life events, personal psychological makeup, and organizational and work-related factors. The death of a spouse or a divorce places tremendous stress on most individuals. Similarly, working in an extremely high-pressure environment under prolonged autocratic leadership can cause stress and job burnout.

7. *Compare and contrast Type A behavior and Type B behavior.*
A person's psychological makeup influences how that person handles stress. Type A people try to accomplish too many things in a short time and tend to lack patience when dealing with people. Type B people tend to be calmer and more realistic in their assessment of the length of time needed to complete an assignment.

8. *Elaborate on personal ways to cope with stress.*
Fortunately, many of us can do a better job of managing stress if we develop certain strategies and behaviors. On a personal level, we can (1) exercise, (2) practice relaxation techniques, (3) gain a sense of control over our lives, and (4) develop and maintain good interpersonal relationships. On the job, a supervisor can apply many of the concepts discussed throughout this book. Techniques particularly helpful in reducing stress in a work unit are to practice the concept of balance through participative management, when appropriate; to delegate effectively without losing control; and to control our time.

9. *Discuss some ways to effectively manage time.*

One of a supervisor's greatest resources is time. However, activities performed by supervisors vary in importance and urgency. The effective supervisor concentrates on the important and urgent activities. Maintaining a time log is a necessary first step toward becoming a more efficient time manager. Such a log enables a supervisor to see exactly where his or her time is spent. More effective supervisors spend a greater proportion of their time on A priorities—activities ranked number one in terms of importance to the effective performance of their jobs. The following time-saving tips can help you make better use of your time: (1) Set priorities, (2) do not procrastinate, (3) manage the telephone effectively, (4) make meetings effective, (5) delegate to others, (6) handle people who drop in, (7) be decisive, (8) get organized, (9) stay on top of paperwork, and (10) avoid distractions and interruptions.

Key Terms

integration process, p. 364
principled negotiation, p. 366
stress, p. 370

life event, p. 371
Type A behavior, p. 374
Type B behavior, p. 374

burnout, p. 376
time management, p. 380

Discussion Questions

1. Identify the five conflict management styles and describe when each one would be appropriate.
2. Discuss what is involved in principled negotiation. How does it differ from hard or soft negotiation?
3. Compare and contrast Type A behavior and Type B behavior.

4. What are the major causes of stress on the job? Off the job?
5. Explain why exercise and relaxation techniques are helpful for coping with stress.
6. What can a supervisor do to prevent stress in his or her unit?
7. Why and how can time management help with stress and the achievement of effective results?

Skill Builder 12.1

Information

Systems

Up in Smoke—Are You Burned Out?
Answer each question on a scale of 1 to 5 (1 = never; 2 = rarely; 3 = sometimes; 4 = often; 5 = always).

Do you
- Feel less competent or effective than you used to feel in your work?
- Consider yourself unappreciated or "used"?
- Dread going to work?
- Feel overwhelmed in your work?
- Feel your work is pointless or unimportant?
- Watch the clock?
- Avoid conversations with others (coworkers, customers, and supervisors in work setting; family members in the home)?

(Continued)

- Rigidly apply rules without considering creative solutions?
- Get frustrated by your work?
- Miss work often?
- Feel unchallenged by your work?

Does your work

- Overload you?
- Deny you rest periods—breaks, lunch time, sick leave, or vacation?
- Pay too little?
- Depend on uncertain funding sources?
- Provide inadequate support to accomplish the job (budget, equipment, too few people, etc.)?
- Lack clear guidelines?
- Entail so many different tasks that you feel fragmented?
- Require you to deal with major or rapid changes?
- Lack access to a social or professional support group?
- Demand coping with a negative job image or angry people?
- Depress you?

Add up your scores for the test and record your total:

SCORES	CATEGORY
94–110	Burnout
76–93	Flame
58–75	Smoke
40–57	Sparks
22–39	No fire

The categories are interpreted as follows:

- **Burnout.** If your score is between 94 and 110, you are experiencing a very high level of stress in your work. Without some changes in yourself or your situation, your potential for stress-related illness is high. Consider seeking professional help for stress reduction and burnout prevention. Coping with stress at this level may also require help from others—supervisors, coworkers, and other associates at work and spouse and other family members at home.

- **Flame.** If you scored between 76 and 93, you have a high amount of work-related stress and may have begun to burn out. Mark each question that you scored 4 or above, and rank them in order of their effect on you, beginning with the ones that bother you the most. For at least your top three, evaluate what you can do to reduce the stresses involved, and act to improve your attitude or situation. If your body is reflecting the stress, get a medical checkup.

- **Smoke.** Scores between 58 and 75 represent a certain amount of stress in your work and are a sign you have a fair chance of burning out unless you take corrective measures. For each question you scored 4 or above, consider ways you can reduce the stresses involved. As soon as possible, take action to improve your attitude or the situation surrounding those things that trouble you most.

- **Sparks.** If your score is between 40 and 57, you have a low amount of work-related stress and are unlikely to burn out. Look over those questions you scored 3 or above, and think about what you can do to reduce the stresses involved.

- **No fire.** People with scores of 22 through 39 are mellow in their work, with almost no job-related stress. As long as they continue at this level, they are practically burnout-proof.

For many people, both the job and the home have the potential to produce high stress and burnout. For this reason, having at least one "port in a storm" is important. Ideally, if things are going badly on the job, rest and comfort can be found in the home. Similarly, if home conditions involve pressure, conflict, and frustration, having a satisfying work life helps. The person who faces problems on the job and problems in the home at the same time is fighting a war on two fronts and is a prime candidate for stress overload and burnout.

Source: From *Stress Without Distress: Rx for Burnout*, 1st edition, by George Manning and Kent Curtis. 1988. SouthWestern, 1988. Copyright © 1988 by George Manning. Reprinted by permission of the author.

Skill Builder 12.2

Systems

A Planning Strategy to Cope with Stress

List the things that cause stress in your life at the present time. Determine which factors are causing positive stress and which are potentially negative and harmful.

Develop an action plan to enable you to cope with the negative factors more effectively. A good action plan looks ahead and deals with what, when, where, and how to solve the problem.

Skill Builder 12.3

Resources

Information

Systems

A Personal Time Survey

List the things that cause stress in your life at the present time. Determine which factors are causing positive stress and which are potentially negative and harmful.

To begin managing your time, you first need a clearer idea of how you use your time. The Personal Time Survey will help you estimate how much time you currently spend in typical activities. To get an accurate estimate, you might keep track of how you spend your time for a week. This will help you determine how much time you need to prepare for each subject. It also will identify your time wasters. But for now, complete the Personal Time Survey to get an estimate.

The following survey shows the amount of time you spend on various activities. When taking the survey, estimate the amount of time spent on each item. Once you have this amount, multiply it by seven. This will give you the total time spent on the activity in one week. After each item's weekly time has been calculated, add all these times for the grand total. Subtract this from 168, the total possible hours per week. Here we go:

1. Number of hours of sleep each night   __ × 7 = __
2. Number of grooming hours per day   __ × 7 = __
3. Number of hours for meals/snacks per day time   __ × 7 = __
   (include preparation time)
4a. Total travel time weekdays   __ × 7 = __
4b. Total travel time weekends   __ × 7 = __

(Continued)

5.   Number of hours per week for regularly scheduled __
      functions (clubs, religious services, get-togethers, etc.)

6.   Number of hours per day for chores, errands, extra __ × 7 = __
      grooming, etc.

7.   Number of hours of work per week   __

8.   Number of hours in class per week   __

9.   Number of average hours per week socializing, __
      dates, etc. Be honest!

      Now add up the totals:_

Subtract the above number from 168.   168 − X = __

The remaining hours are the hours you have allowed yourself to study.

Study Hour Formula To determine how many hours you need to study each week to get A's, use the following rule of thumb. Study two hours per hour in class for an easy class, three hours per hour in class for an average class, and four hours per hour in class for a difficult class. For example, basket weaving 101 is a relatively easy three-hour course. Usually, a person would not do more than six hours of work outside of class per week. Advanced calculus is usually considered a difficult course, so it might be best to study the proposed 12 hours a week. If more hours are needed, take away some hours from easier courses, that is, basket weaving. Figure out the time you need to study by using the previous formula for each of your classes.

Easy class credit hours   __ × 2 = __

Average class credit hours   __ × 3 = __

Difficult class credit hours   __ × 4 = __

Total   __

Compare this number to your time left from the survey. Now is the time when many students might find themselves a bit stressed. Just a note to ease your anxieties: It is not only the quantity of study time but also its quality. This formula is a general guideline. Try it for a week, and make adjustments as needed.

Source: Prepared by the Self-Development Center, a service of the Counseling and Student Development Center at George Mason University. Reprinted by permission.

Skill Builder 12.4

Stuart Diamond's *Getting More*: How to Negotiate to Achieve Your Goals
Stuart Diamond is an American Pulitzer Prize–winning author and professor emeritus at the University of Pennsylvania's Wharton School of Business, where he has taught negotiation for more than 20 years. He has published *Getting More*, which describes an alternate approach to negotiation. It is a *New York Times* best-seller and has sold over a million copies. The *Getting More* model has been adopted for negotiation training by leading organizations, such as Google and U.S. Special Operations (e.g., Green Berets and Navy SEALs).

To expose you to the *Getting More* principles of negotiation, follow the link to view Stuart Diamond's talk at Google (https://www.youtube.com/watch?v=2QtZ-vObJrk).

What are your takeaways from Dr. Diamond's talk? What did you learn that can be applied to future negotiation opportunities? Create a list. The challenge is to apply these principles, so are you currently facing a situation in which you could apply the *Getting More* model? If so, think through how you would accomplish this goal. If not, what can you do to become, as Dr. Diamond notes, an expert when you look at future situations?

CASE 12-1

THE ENTREPRENEUR:

Sam Hinton Construction (SHC) is a small, entrepreneurial firm in a midsized city situated in the southeastern United States. SHC is run by Sam, the owner. Sam began the remodeling and repair business out of necessity when he couldn't find anyone to perform the needed work on his own home. External environmental changes, specifically the real estate and housing boom occurring across the nation due to monies being shifted from the stock markets to better investment opportunities in real estate, were impacting many communities just like Sam's. Add to this trend the impact of several years of active hurricane seasons in the southeastern region of the country, and it is no surprise that construction supplies—skilled labor, materials, equipment, and management—were harder and harder to obtain for reasonable prices. Based on this and other data, Sam saw an opportunity for a planned career change, and after talking the situation over with his wife, Ellen, he decided to make the transition and start his own business. Sam's initial vision for his small company was to make money to support his family while meeting the needs of his customers in a cost-effective way. Sam lacked significant up-front capital, relying on his family's savings to start operations, so marketing efforts were limited to advertising in the local Yellow Pages. Once under way, he relied heavily on word-of-mouth to grow his small firm. He was a one-man show determined to make the venture successful.

He was not as experienced as his competitors, so he took every opportunity to read, observe, learn, and acquire the competencies necessary for his new profession. Initially, Sam chose work opportunities based on his personal experiences with his own home. Thus, he was confident in the accuracy of his materials and labor estimates and his ability to complete a quality job on time. Sam's initial strategy paid off because other contractors did not seem to want to fool with the small-sized jobs. Those that did were not reputable. However, as his business grew, he found himself bidding for work he was not as familiar or comfortable with. More and more of Sam's training occurred on the job. Sam won a bid to remodel an older home built prior to 1950 that included extensive plumbing and structural work. Unfortunately, he underestimated the types of work, amount of time, and supplies needed to complete the job and was forced to use a significant amount of his savings to finish the job.

Sam soon began building this "learning cost" into future bids to ensure he stayed afloat and remained in a positive-cash-flow position. His estimates for more complex projects were more like guesstimates and tended to be higher than competitors' proposals. Sam decided to strategically reposition his small firm to survive. To justify the dollar difference to potential customers, Sam sold his firm as a quality renovating and remodeling operation—"You can go with the low bid, but you get what you pay for. My price is higher because I pay attention to the details."

He really liked getting new work and prided himself on his ability to interact and communicate with his potential clients. Sam also believed he was quite adept at seeing the "vision" for a given project. For example, he could take a customer's rough ideas and create a detailed drawing of what the completed work would look like. Even if the clients were not sure what they wanted, Sam found through dialogue and listening to his customers he could understand their wants and needs.

Sam committed to providing his customers with the best service possible. As he generated additional work, he worked more hours to complete projects. Sam would routinely rise at 4:30 A.M. to begin his day. The first order of business was making sure he had the proper materials and equipment for the job each day. Over time he was much better at planning so that he rarely had to stop and leave the site for additional supplies. Because of his improved planning and efficiency, he found he finished jobs much quicker than before, but he still felt he was always one step behind where he needed to be. Sam typically knocked off around 4:30 P.M. so he could visit with potential clients. The early evening hours were spent providing bids to secure future work. Once he arrived home, it was time for a quick bite before doing paperwork, tracking costs, and preparing estimates.

Although Sam felt he had learned quite a bit during the past year and believed he had an effective strategy in place, he often found he was stretched too thin with managing the work and finances and filling the pipeline with new jobs to manage the schedule, produce quality work, handle customers, and continuously develop his knowledge. As the months passed, Sam's wife, Ellen, noticed he was not as easygoing as he once was, and she rarely got a chance to visit with him on the weekends, much less during the week. Ellen was becoming concerned about his health. He rarely slept through the

(Continued)

night anymore, often getting up several times. She was shocked one night when she woke to find him at his desk at 2:00 A.M. buried in receipts and bills. In addition to problems sleeping, Sam developed bad eating habits. Ellen knew he often worked through lunch to complete various stages of his projects, but now he rarely had time for evening meals. Ellen believed Sam's sleep deprivation and poor eating habits were partly to blame for his increasingly short temper. Uncharacteristically, Sam was more on edge, flying off the handle at the smallest incidents. Ellen's feelings were confirmed when she got off the phone with one of Sam's clients. The client called quite unhappy with the way the project was going. The seams in the crown molding were unacceptable, the paint runs were unsightly, and when the client approached Sam about the imperfections, he got gruff

and defensive. As the customer complaints mounted, Ellen realized Sam was overwhelmed.

CASE QUESTIONS

1. Divide into teams of three to five people. Each group is to assume the role of a consulting team asked to help Sam Hinton get control of his company and his life.
2. Drawing from your own experiences and from what you learned in this chapter, develop some alternatives for Sam.
3. Select the best alternative and present your recommendations to the rest of the class. Each class member will then vote for the team (excluding his or her own team) he or she thinks had the best plan for SHC.

CASE 12-2

THE MISSED PROMOTION:

Susan Williamson was worried. For the past six months, her husband, Paul, was a different person from the man she married. Until that time, Paul had been a cheerful and caring husband and father. He took an interest in their children, was active in church, and had a zest for day-to-day living. In recent months, he turned moody, abrupt, and withdrawn. He spent his time at home watching television and drinking beer. He never talked about his job as maintenance supervisor at the ABC Company as he once had. Recently Susan asked if something at work was bothering him and, if so, whether he would discuss it with her. His reply was, "No, there's nothing bothering me! You take care of the house and the children, and I'll take care of the job and making a living!"

Actually, the job had been bothering Paul for about a year. Before that, he was considered one of the outstanding maintenance supervisors. In those days, his two immediate supervisors, the maintenance superintendent and the maintenance manager, called on him frequently for advice and used him as a troubleshooter within the plant. Although Paul did not have a college degree in engineering, the maintenance manager strongly hinted when the maintenance superintendent retired, Paul would be promoted to his position. The maintenance manager told Paul that, despite having

three engineering graduates in the supervision group, he considered Paul the best in the department.

A year ago, the maintenance manager was transferred to another plant. A new maintenance manager came aboard and, from the start, favored college graduates. Gradually Paul was used less and less for troubleshooting assignments, and his advice was rarely sought. Then, six months ago, the maintenance superintendent retired and a young engineering graduate named Bobbi, whom Paul trained, was promoted to the superintendent's job. That was when Paul's personality changed. He began sleeping longer each night, often falling asleep in front of the television set. He also developed a tightness in his stomach that created a burning sensation.

Bobbi, the engineer promoted to maintenance superintendent, was worried. For several months, she had concerns about the performance and health of one of her maintenance supervisors, Paul Williamson. Paul had been Bobbi's boss at one time and she always admired his ability as a supervisor and his knowledge of the maintenance area.

Recently, while attending a regional meeting of maintenance managers from different plants of the ABC Company, Bobbi ran into the former maintenance manager at her plant, who was now at another plant. He asked how Paul was doing. Bobbi, glad to share her concern with someone, said she was worried about him. "His performance has slipped, for one thing. Also, he used to have perfect attendance, but lately he's been calling in sick a lot."

The maintenance manager replied, "I wonder if disappointment over not being promoted to maintenance superintendent has affected his performance. No reflection on you, of course, but before I left, the plant manager and I agreed Paul would be promoted to maintenance superintendent. Then the home office changed its corporate policy so only college graduates could be promoted to superintendent. This made Paul ineligible, and you got the job instead."

Bobbi didn't know Paul had been the first choice for the position she now held. Upon reflection, she decided to have a coaching and counseling session with him when she returned to the plant because she certainly didn't want to lose him.

CASE QUESTIONS

1. How should Bobbi approach Paul about the situation?
2. What do you think Paul's reaction(s) will be?
3. Do you agree with the company's policy of promoting only college graduates to the maintenance superintendent position? Why or why not?

Notes

1. Roger Fisher and William Ury, *Getting to Yes* (New York: Penquin, 1993), pp. 3–4.
2. Kathryn Tyler, "Extending the Olive Branch: Conflict Resolution Training Helps Employees and Managers Defuse Skirmishes," *HR Magazine*, November 2002, p. 47.
3. Ibid.
4. A. P. Brief, R. S. Schuler, and M. W. Sell, *Managing Job Stress* (Boston: Little, Brown, & Co., 1981), p. 2.
5. "The Road to Happiness," *Psychology Today* 27, no. 4 (July–August 1994), p. 34.
6. American Psychological Association Practice Organization, Psychologically Healthy Workplace Program Fact Sheet: By the Numbers (2010), http://www.phwa.org/dl/2010phwp_fact_sheet.pdf.
7. Claudia Wallis, "Stress: Can We Cope?," *Time*, June 6, 1983, p. 52.
8. W. W. Suoganen and Donald R Hudson, "Coping with Stress and Addictive Work Behavior," *Business* (Atlanta, GA: College of Business Administration, Georgia State University) 31 (January–February 1980), p. 11.
9. Robert T. Golembiewski and Robert F. Munzenrider, Phases of Burnout (New York: Praeger, 1988), p. 220; Jari J. Hakanen and Wilmar B. Schaufeli, "Do Burnout and Work Engagement Predict Depressive Symptoms and life'satisfaction" A Three-Wave Seven-Year Prospective Study," *Journal of Affective Disorders* 141 (2012), pp. 415–424.
10. Michael Blanding, "Workplace Stress Responsible for up to $190B in Annual U.S. Healthcare Costs," *Forbes*, January 2015, https://www.forbes.com/sites/hbsworkingknowledge/2015/01/26/workplace-stress-responsible-for-up-to-190-billion-in-annual-u-s-heathcare-costs/#74005a2a235a; American Psychological Association Practice Organization, *Psychologically Healthy Workplace Program Fact Sheet.*

13
Exercising Control

LEARNING OBJECTIVES

After reading and studying this chapter, you should be able to:

1. Define control and explain how it relates to planning.

2. Discuss the characteristics of effective control systems.

3. Discuss the three types of control systems.

4. Discuss the four steps in the control process.

5. Identify the different types of standards.

6. Explain the importance of strategic control points.

7. Discuss management by exception.

8. Discuss the impact of technology on control.

We tried to make some adjustments at halftime. They just didn't pan out.

—Pro Football Coach after His Team Was Beaten in the Playoffs

RosaIreneBetancourt 9/Alamy Stock Photo

As the chapter preview illustrates, it is important for supervisors to get feedback from their employees to build a high performance team.

Preview

THE CITY OF FAIRHOPE IS A RESORT RETIREMENT COMMUNITY with over 16,000 inhabitants situated along the shores of the gulf coast. Many consider this quaint village to be a municipal leader with a progressive recycling program, a state-of-the-art water treatment system, and a comprehensive plan to sustain high-quality living "through controlled growth and development." Fairhope's mission statement is given below.

- The City of Fairhope will continue to economically provide and improve the quality of life for the community through demonstrative, trustworthy leadership.
- The City will embrace, nurture and support open information and the exchange of information through public participation that creates community ownership and implements positive solutions for future needs.
- The City of Fairhope is committed to a sustainable future by promoting environmentally sound conservation, preservation and restoration practices that maintain and improve the ecological integrity of the Fairhope community.

One of the authors had the privilege of working with James Gillespie, a longtime city employee currently serving as an administrative superintendent, to conduct an employee opinion study. James believes the city's top priority is maintaining a high quality of life for everyone. He was born and raised in the community and decided at an early age on a career in public administration. It was this passion for public service that led him to initiate a citywide survey to obtain employee opinions and assess the morale and "health" of those who serve the citizens. As James put it, "The public sector has to deal with expectations that are different from those in the private sector. While employee issues have been widely studied in the private sector, there has been little attention given to the public sector, specifically, municipalities. A municipality must aim to accommodate and assist all citizens, which involves being proactive."

According to James, the city's employees are critical to achieving the mission, and the employees' responses could assist in identifying areas of strength and weakness to improve the city's services and continue to be a pacesetter. James was interested to learn what factors were important in determining the employees' job satisfaction and organizational commitment levels.

The results of the employee survey were interesting. Pay, just like in the private sector, was related to employees' job satisfaction levels, but it was not the most significant factor. The employees' relationships with their supervisors were the most important determinant in whether or not they were satisfied on the job, closely followed by their coworker relationships. The employees' responses regarding the health of their relationships with their supervisors averaged 3.49 on a five-point scale. The average response pertaining to the strength of coworker relationships was 3.91 out of five. As for the employees' commitment to the city, top management support and safe work environments were the most important factors.

The city leaders surmised from the data it would be wise to invest in additional employee support, such as supervisory leadership training, to build strong, lasting relationships with employees, which would ultimately improve employee retention and service. As a result, a leadership training and development program was created and initiated over two years covering important leadership topics, such as performance management, coaching, team building, problem solving, and communication. Through these efforts, the department heads developed a strategic plan and mission statement for the city. They even enacted a job-shadowing program to understand the interconnectedness among the departments to work better together serving the public.

Sources: Personal interviews and experiences with James Gillespie; "City of Fairhope's Mission Statement," http://www.cofairhope.com/about-us/mission-statement (retrieved August 1, 2013); "City of Fairhope History," http://www.cofairhope.com/about-us/history (retrieved August 1, 2013).

When an organization's activities "go according to plan," it is often the result of good planning, but it is just as frequently the result of good control in implementing the plans! In this chapter, we provide you with a broad overview of what is involved in the control function.

What Is Control?

1. *Define control and explain how it relates to planning.*

Have you ever been driving a car on a trip and had one of the dashboard warning lights come on? Perhaps it was the oil pressure or temperature light. Basically, the light indicates something is wrong with the car. Without such a warning system, you would be caught by surprise when the car broke down, perhaps leaving you stranded far from home.

Managers and supervisors are often in a similar dilemma. They go along not knowing whether things are as they should be. Unfortunately, many of them find things are not right only when it is too late to do anything about it. They do not have the advantage of periodic feedback or warning lights to tell them whether they are on track. Thus, you might think of control as consisting of performance markers that tell you whether you and your unit's performance are moving in the right direction.

Controlling is defined as the management function that compares actual performance with planned performance and taking corrective action, if needed, to ensure objectives are achieved. Basically, control has three phases: (1) anticipating the things that could go wrong and taking preventive measures to see they don't, (2) monitoring or measuring performance in some way to compare what is actually happening with what is supposed to be happening, and (3) correcting performance problems that occur. This last step is the therapeutic aspect of control.

Control's Close Links to Planning

Planning and controlling are closely related. Planning "sets the ship's course," and controlling "keeps it on course." When a ship begins to veer off course, the navigator notices it and recommends a new heading designed to return the ship to its proper course. Essentially, supervisory control works the same way. You set goals and seek information on whether they are reached as planned. If not, you make the adjustments necessary to achieve your goals. Thus, controlling may be thought of as the process supervisors use to help carry out their plans.

EXHIBIT 13-1 Murphy's Laws	• Left to themselves, things always go from bad to worse. • There's never time to do it right, but always time to do it over. • If anything can go wrong, it will. • Of the things that can go wrong, the one that will is capable of the most possible damage. • If you think nothing can go wrong, you have obviously overlooked something. • Of those things that "cannot" go wrong, the most unlikely one will. • Inside every large problem are many small problems struggling to get out. • Any object will fall so that it lands in the one spot where it is capable of doing the most damage.

EXHIBIT 13-2 Some Common Examples of Supervisory Control	• At the end of the workday, a production supervisor spends 30 minutes examining a printout showing each employee's output, quality, and scrap. The supervisor notes those employees whose performance is below par and makes plans to discuss their performance with them the next day. • A nursing supervisor studies a survey completed by all patients who were housed in her ward in the past six months. The survey lists items such as nurses' friendliness, professionalism, appearance, and a number of other factors related to job performance. • A maintenance supervisor tours the building, examining the progress of each worker or work team. • After a college football game, the head defensive coach views the game films several times, assigning performance grades to each defensive player. Grades below 60 reflect areas to which the coach must devote special attention during upcoming practices.

Importance of Controls

Perhaps you have heard the old saying: "Things never go as planned." That truth is a primary reason supervisors need to perform the control function effectively. Control is important in view of the many variables that can put things off track. Murphy's laws (some of which are listed in Exhibit 13-1) seem to operate everywhere. Because anything involving humans is imperfect, supervisors must use control to monitor progress and to make intelligent adjustments as required.

Examples of Controls

We live in a world of controls. Circuit breakers in our homes and offices are examples of controls. When an electrical overload occurs, the system adjusts by shutting itself down. Security alarm systems send out signals when a protected area is violated. As mentioned earlier, the dashboard in your car contains numerous control signals to warn you when something is not the way it is supposed to be—low oil pressure, overheated engine, alternator malfunction, keys left in car, seat belt not on, and so on. Exhibit 13-2 illustrates a number of other common examples of control.

Characteristics of Effective Control Systems

2. Discuss the characteristics of effective control systems.

To be effective, a control system must have certain characteristics. Among them, these are the most important:

1. Controls need to focus on appropriate activities. Effective controls must focus on critical factors that affect both the individual's and the organization's abilities to achieve objectives. These critical objectives should include the essential areas of production and personnel activities, as well as related costs.

2. Controls should be timely. Information needed for comparisons and control purposes needs to be in a supervisor's hands for him or her to take effective corrective action. Therefore, delays in generating, gathering, or disseminating information can prolong the occurrence—and extent—of deviations.

3. Controls must be cost-effective. The benefits of using appropriate controls should be worth the cost of their installation and operation. Too much control can be worse than too little. Controls should be appropriate for the situation and provide savings greater than the costs involved.

4. Controls should be accurate and concise. Controls must provide information about operations and people in sufficient quality and quantity to enable managers to make meaningful comparisons to operations standards. As with control, too much information can be as bad as too little.

5. Controls should be accepted by the people they affect. Controls and their applicability to specific situations should be communicated clearly to those responsible for implementing them and to those who will be governed by them.

Although all of these characteristics are important, a given control system need not have all of them in order to do the job for which it is designed.

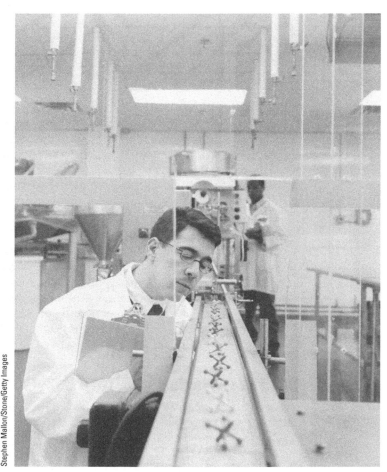

Stephen Mallon/Stone/Getty Images

Quality control inspection is one type of control system that provides timely and accurate feedback to the production line.

Types of Control Systems

3. *Discuss the three types of control systems.*

There are essentially three types of control systems: (1) feedforward controls, (2) concurrent controls, and (3) feedback controls.

feedforward controls

Preventive controls that try to anticipate problems and take corrective action before they occur.

concurrent controls

Sometimes called screening controls; these controls are used while an activity takes place.

feedback controls

Controls that measure completed activities and then take corrective action if needed.

Feedforward controls are preventive controls that try to anticipate problems and take corrective action before they occur. This type of control allows corrective action before a real problem develops. For example, Hart Schaffner Marx, a leading producer of quality clothing, inspects every bolt of cloth it plans to use in its tailored men's clothing before starting to cut pieces.

See Exhibit 13-3 for tips on establishing preventive controls. Notice the first step is to focus on your goals or plans. Again, you can see how closely linked the planning and controlling processes are.

Concurrent controls (sometimes called screening controls) occur while an activity is taking place. Thus, an inspector or an inspection system can check items on the assembly line to see if they meet standards. Production systems today are capable of providing operators with a wealth of information.

Carotek ECS offers a visual inspection system that can be used to trigger a shutdown of the production line if something looks amiss. First, "good" images are uploaded onto the system. Then, the cameras are trained on different points in the production line. The new images are automatically compared to the good images stored in the computer. If the images do not match, the system will either alert an operator or shut the system down entirely.[1]

Feedback controls measure activities already completed. Thus, corrections can take place after performance is over. Organizations evaluate their managers' performance levels in a variety of ways. For example, Marriott hotel managers' promotions and pay increases are dependent on more than just hotel profitability. Guest satisfaction scores and staff ratings are factored in to a manager's overall performance score, thus providing a broader means of assessment. This evaluation process is critical for developing and coaching managerial talent because most managers start as hourly workers. Even most of the executive team was promoted internally.[2]

STOP AND THINK

What type(s) of control were used in the chapter preview? Explain.

Steps in the Control Process

4. *Discuss the four steps in the control process.*

The steps in the control process are illustrated in Exhibit 13-4. Note that step 4 may require going back to any of the previous three steps. It may consist of modifying the original standard, changing the frequency and manner of measuring performance, or achieving

EXHIBIT 13-3
Tips for Establishing Preventive Controls

1. Identify your department's major goals.
2. Identify those factors most crucial to accomplishing your department's major goals. These may be items such as properly running machinery and equipment, availability of raw materials, availability of key personnel, or a balanced demand for your department's services.
3. Determine the most likely problems or circumstances that could prevent the items in (2) from occurring. These could be factors such as machine breakdown or absence of key personnel.
4. Develop a plan for preventing the problems listed in (3). You might consider input from employees, staff personnel, your immediate supervisor, peers, and others in arriving at your preventive control plans.

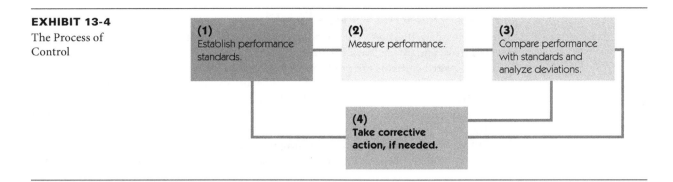

more insight into the possible cause of the problem. Let us examine the details of each of these steps.

Step 1: Establishing Performance Standards

The first step of the controlling process is really a part of the planning step. You set your sights on something you want to accomplish. As a supervisor, you exercise control by comparing performance to some standard or goal. A **standard** is a unit of measurement that serves as a reference point for evaluating results. Properly communicated and accepted by mployees, standards become the bases for the supervisor's control activities.

Types of Standards   Standards can be either tangible or intangible. **Tangible standards** are quite clear, concrete, specific, and generally measurable. For instance, when you say, "I want the machine online by 3:00 P.M.," the goal is specific and concrete. Either the machine is online at 3:00 P.M. or it is not.

Tangible standards can be further categorized as numerical, monetary, physical, or time related. **Numerical standards** are expressed in numbers, such as number of items produced, number of absences, percentage of successful sales calls, or number of personnel who successfully complete training. **Monetary standards** are expressed in dollars and cents. Examples of monetary standards are predetermined profit margins, payroll costs, scrap costs, and maintenance costs. **Physical standards** refer to quality, durability, size, weight, and other factors related to physical composition.

Time standards refer to the speed with which the job should be done. Examples of time standards include printing deadlines, scheduled project completion dates, and rates of production.

Note there may be some overlap among the types of tangible standards. For instance, when you say, "I want the machine online by 3:00 P.M.," you obviously communicated a time standard, but the standard is expressed numerically. Monetary standards also are expressed numerically.

In contrast to tangible standards, **intangible standards** are not expressed in terms of numbers, money, physical qualities, or time because they relate to human characteristics that are difficult to measure. Examples of intangible standards are a desirable attitude, high morale, ethics, and cooperation. Intangible standards pose special challenges to the supervisor, as the example illustrates.

Supervisor Maude Leyden of the State Employment Office overheard one of her newer employment counselors, David Hoffman, berating a job applicant. The tone of his voice was domineering, as though he was scolding a child, although the applicant was perhaps 30 years his senior. Maude heard David conclude the interview with the words, "Now don't come back here and bother us again until you've had someone fill this form out properly. That's not what I'm paid to do!"

After the applicant left, Maude listened to David's explanation of what just happened. He said he'd been under a lot of pressure that day and grown impatient, and he acknowledged his rudeness toward the applicant. Maude told him that he had not handled himself in a professional manner and discussed what he should have done differently. Later in the day, David was to call the applicant, apologize, and offer to be of further help.

He did call and apologize.

It is much more difficult to clearly explain an intangible standard, such as "interviewers must observe standards of professional conduct with clients," than to tell someone the standard is "to service six malfunctioning computer systems each day." Just what is professional conduct? Is it patience, friendliness, courtesy, or keeping a level head? Certainly it is less specific than "servicing six computers daily." As difficult as it may be, every supervisor has to establish, communicate, and control some types of intangible job standards.

STOP AND THINK

Employee cooperation, desirable employee attitude, appropriate employee personal hygiene, and mature employee behavior are intangible standards organizations and supervisors typically must control. Can you think of others?

How Standards Are Set   Standards can be set in many ways. A supervisor frequently sets standards based on familiarity with the jobs being performed by his or her employees. The supervisor is generally knowledgeable about the time required to perform tasks, the quality necessary, and the expected employee behavior. This is especially true of supervisors promoted through the ranks. If you are not technically knowledgeable about the work performed in your department, there are a number of ways to become familiar with standards. You can gain insights from past records of performance, if available, and from fellow supervisors, employees, and your own boss. Exhibit 13-5 presents some types of standards for a variety of positions.

For many jobs, various staff departments strongly influence the standards set. The industrial engineering department, for example, may utilize systematic studies of movements and speed to set quantity and time standards. The quality control department may establish standards for finish, luster, or precision. Cost accounting may develop standards for material costs or scrap. Thus, many standards already may be established for the people you supervise.

Staff departments also may have a hand in setting standards for supervisors. For example, the budget department may help determine standards regarding material and payroll costs. Personnel may establish standards regarding the quantity and quality of grievances and turnover in a department. The ability to meet your departmental standards, in turn, determines the amount of control your own boss exercises over your activities.

Step 2: Measuring Performance

Setting standards is an essential first step in control, but by itself, it doesn't go far enough. A supervisor must monitor performance to ensure it complies with the established standards. Two issues the supervisor must deal with are (1) how often to measure performance and (2) how to measure performance.

EXHIBIT 13-5

Types of Standards for Various Positions

POSITION	TYPE OF STANDARD
Bank teller	Monetary (balance), time (speed of teller line), physical (orderliness of work area)
Postal letter carrier	Time (hours taken to complete run)
Server in a large restaurant	Physical (appearance), time (speed), intangible (courtesy and friendliness)
Real estate salesperson	Monetary (volume), numerical (number of listings and closings)
Offensive-line football coach	Numerical (yards per game rushing), intangible (leadership of players)
Upholsterer in a manufacturing plant	Numerical (number of units completed), physical (quality of units)
Third-grade teacher	Intangible (appearance, classroom behavior), physical (quality of lesson plans)

6. *Explain the importance of strategic control points.*

How Often to Measure Performance   Determining how often to measure performance is an important control decision supervisors make. Sometimes this decision has already been made by the system, as shown in the examples:

> *Kay Davis, sales manager of City Motors, need only look at the sales chart prominently displayed on the sales floor outside her office to see how her sales personnel are doing. The chart lists the number of new and used cars sold by each salesperson for the week and the month, as well as total sales volume for the entire company.*

> *The production control system at DAVO Company provides a constant reading of activity on each of the production floor's operating machines. At any time, a production supervisor can view the work performed by any of the operators up to that time.*

Notice in each of the preceding examples, performance is constantly monitored. This does not mean supervisors should spend the entire day monitoring performance. Instead, they should establish strategic control points. As shown in Exhibit 13-6, a **strategic control point** is a performance measurement point located sufficiently early in an activity to allow any necessary corrective actions to be taken to accomplish the objective. For each job, ask yourself: Considering the importance of this job, at what point do I need to know the progress being made so I can make any required adjustments and still complete the job as planned?

Certain types of jobs, such as maintenance, personnel, and sales, don't lend themselves to frequent measurement of progress. Measurement takes time, unless an automated system is in place. On the other hand, effective monitoring is crucial for some jobs. For example, the work of an emergency room nurse requires more careful monitoring than does the work of a sales representative or a clerical worker.

strategic control point

A performance measurement point located early in an activity to allow any corrective action to be taken.

How to Measure   A supervisor can measure performance in several basic ways:

1. Personal observation.
2. Written or oral reports by or about employees.
3. Automatic methods.
4. Inspections, tests, or samples.

SHERWIN CRASTO/RTR/Newscom

Customer service representatives are monitored against time standards such as how quickly they answer the telephone and how long it takes them to help each customer.

Exhibit 13-7 is an example of the second method that could be used frequently at little cost. Notice how precisely the information requested is stated.

STOP AND THINK

Can you suggest instances or situations when each of these ways of measuring performance might be used?

In some jobs, supervisors and their employees work in the same area. The supervisor can easily move among the workers, observing their performance. In other departments,

EXHIBIT 13-6
Setting Strategic
Control Points in the
Control Process

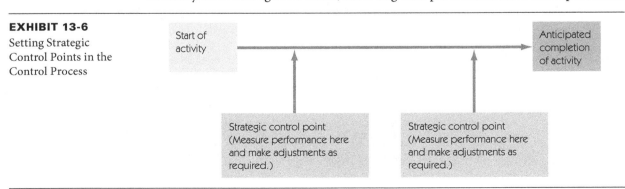

however, the supervisor may have workers spread out in various locations, making direct observation impractical. Consider a sanitation supervisor whose eight work crews collect garbage on various routes throughout the city. Such a supervisor must depend on written or oral reports or occasional inspections as the primary means of measurement. Here is what one sanitation supervisor said:

How do I know if my crews are doing the job properly? Mainly by the complaints I get from customers. Complaints range from garbage that isn't picked up on schedule to overturned trash cans, surrounded with litter. That's how I know what's going on in the field. Sometimes I will drive around and make a visual inspection. We also survey residents annually to see if our people are considered timely, friendly, and efficient.

Sales supervisors may seldom see their employees if the sales work takes them outside the office. As a result, salespersons are required to complete reports about number of calls made, sales results, travel expenses, customer comments, and numerous other matters.

EXHIBIT 13-7

Example of a Written Report about an Employee

Management Encourages Your Comments

Date **5/15/2018**

Waiter or waitress **Phyllis**

Please circle meal   Breakfast   (Lunch)   Dinner

	Yes	No
1. Were you greeted by host or hostess promptly and courteously?	✓	
2. Was your server prompt, courteous, and helpful?	✓	
3. Was the quality of food to your expectations?		✓
4. Was the table setting and condition of overall restaurant appearance pleasing and in good taste?	✓	
5. Will you return to our restaurant?		✓
6. Will you recommend our restaurant to your friends and associates?		✓

Comments

Food was overcooked. Potatoes were leftovers. Meat was tough. This was my second visit and I brought a friend with me. We were both very disappointed.

Name and address
(if you desire)

Please drop this in our quality improvement box located near the exit.

Thank you and have a good day.

These reports are received by supervisors or the home office staff. Many salespersons, in fact, complain that they are required to do too much administrative work!

Supervisors without frequent contact with their employees must come up with some meaningful, valid ways to measure results. They need to find some manner of making sure the measurements are reliable. Because of pressures to conform to standards, employees may attempt to falsify reports to make themselves appear better.

Several years ago, a nationally respected youth organization set very high membership goals for its local offices. The results appeared spectacular until it was discovered a number of local chapters considerably inflated the number of new members enrolled to avoid looking bad.

In other words, you have to be careful about attempts to "beat" the control system. People may extort money, falsify documents, and distort oral reports to make themselves look good. For example, if you ask an employee to give you an oral report on a job's progress, he or she may tell you, "Everything's just fine, boss," when, in fact, it is not.

Step 3: Comparing Performance with Standards and Analyzing Deviations

Unfortunately, many supervisors receive information that demonstrates a serious departure from standards but make little effort to understand what caused the difference between planned and actual performance. Failure to meet standards may result from a variety of causes. A supervisor needs to understand the reasons for below-average performance. Many supervisors jump to conclusions about the causes of problems, and, as a result, the corrective action they take is ineffective.

Suppose the quality control standard for producing a certain part is 99/100. This means there should be no more than one defective product per hundred units produced by a worker. You find out that of the last 200 units produced by employee Kevin Rae, almost 13 percent were defective. What could cause this problem? Could it have been poor materials? Could Rae's equipment be the cause? Is this like Rae's previous performance? What will you do about it? These are some questions you have to ask yourself. Simply giving Rae an oral or a written warning may be highly inappropriate and may not correct the problem!

It is also important to compare results that are substantially above standard to determine why they varied from standard. The supervisor should check to see if all operating procedures are followed correctly, or if there is an improvement in operations that should be included in new standards.

It is important to find out the opinions of those close to a particular problem to determine why standards are not being met. For example, an employee's explanation or those of other employees or fellow supervisors might be obtained. Frequently, people in other departments can add insight. Here is what one supervisor said:

I was all set to really chew Emily out. She had an important job to complete for me this morning and didn't show up as scheduled. Fortunately, before I made a fool of myself, I learned from one of her friends that she'd gotten here early and the plant manager asked her to do an even more important job. I checked this out with the plant manager, and, sure enough, that was the case. She was supposed to notify me but just forgot.

Step 4: Taking Corrective Action if Necessary

The final step in the control process is to take corrective action if needed. You have undoubtedly seen many athletic contests turn completely around after halftime. This change is often due to corrective action taken by the coach—the modifications, adjustments, and fine-tuning done in response to problems encountered earlier.

The supervisor's job is much like that of a coach. Adjustments, fine-tuning, and perhaps even drastic actions may be necessary to pull off important tasks or maintain standards. Examples of corrective actions a supervisor might take include the following:

1. Making a decision to retrain a new operator whose performance has not progressed as expected.
2. Shifting several employees from their normal jobs to help meet a deadline on another job.
3. Counseling an employee whose performance has recently been below standard.
4. Reprimanding an employee for failure to adhere to safety rules.
5. Shutting down a piece of equipment for maintenance after defective output is traced to it.

Management by Exception

7. Discuss management by exception.

Even under the best of circumstances, deviations from performance standards are bound to occur. Given the broad range of areas over which supervisors exert control, it is essential to distinguish between critical and less-critical deviations. The fact that many performance deviations are due to normal operating variances means supervisors must exercise some discretion in distinguishing between relevant variations and those that are less so.

management by exception

A supervisor focuses on critical control needs and allows employees to handle most routine deviations from the standard.

Under **management by exception**, a supervisor focuses on critical control needs and allows employees to handle most routine deviations from the standards. Exhibit 13-8 shows the key issue is whether a deviation is exceptional.

The idea is to set priorities for activities, depending on their importance, and focus your efforts on top-priority items. Management by exception works essentially the same way. Your attention should be focused on exceptional rather than routine problems.

STOP AND THINK

Suppose you are a sales supervisor and your departmental sales goal is 800 units weekly (or 3,200 units monthly). Each of your eight sales representatives, then, has a goal of 100 units weekly (or 400 units monthly). At the end of the first week, your sales results show the following:

SALESPERSON	WEEKLY GOAL	UNITS SOLD
A	100	105
B	100	95
C	100	90
D	100	102
E	100	102
F	100	88
G	100	98
H	100	115
	Total = 800	795

What corrective action will you take?

Managers who practice management by exception might do absolutely nothing about the previous situation. "But wait!" you say. "Look at Salesperson C, who performed 10 percent below standard, and Salesperson F, who was 12 percent below standard. Shouldn't a supervisor do something about these two employees?" Of course, a supervisor should be

DIRK WAEM/AFP/Getty Images

When a quality control standard has not been met, a supervisor must investigate for possible causes.

aware of these deviations. However, recall that only the first week has gone by. It is probably normal to find such variances in a single week; the more pertinent information is how performance compares to the monthly benchmark of 3;200 units. With three weeks to go, the supervisor who gets too upset after week one may be overreacting. Naturally, the supervisor should keep an eye on sales data in the upcoming weeks to see whether Salespersons C and F improve their performances. In this situation, the assumption of management by exception is that Salespersons B, C, F, and G realize they are below standard and will work to improve.

STOP AND THINK

Suppose at the end of the second week, sales results are as shown:

SALESPERSON	WEEKLY GOAL	WEEK 1	WEEK 2
A	100	105	107
B	100	95	101
C	100	90	97
D	100	102	101
E	100	102	101
F	100	88	84
G	100	98	99
H	100	115	126
	Total = 800	795	816

What will you do now?

EXHIBIT 13-8
Management by
Exception

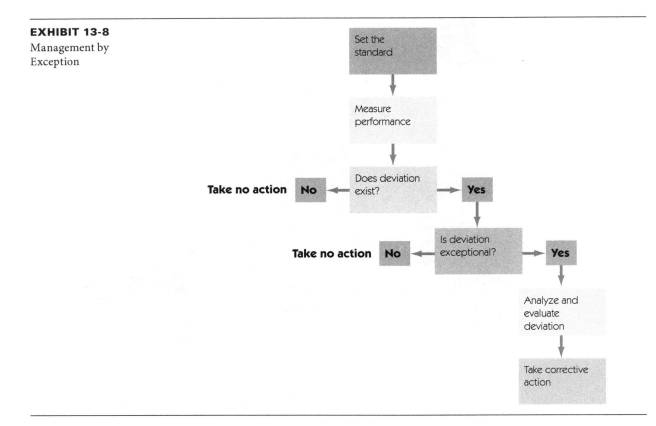

Sales perked up, and, with the exception of Salesperson F, everyone is in reasonable shape. As supervisor, you'd be justified in entering the control process with Salesperson F because the "red flag" is still up on this one. You may want to discuss this person's results, identify actions that produce below-standard results, and develop a plan of corrective action.

Note Salesperson H has been setting the standards on fire, averaging more than 20 percent above standard the first two weeks. This performance is also an exceptional departure from standard. What is behind these results? Is Salesperson H using some techniques that will work for others? Is this person's territory so choice it becomes easy to make the standard? Should you modify the standard for Salesperson H? Management by exception can be applied to both favorable and unfavorable deviations from standard.

The Impact of Technology on Control

8. *Discuss the impact of technology on control.*

As the world's economies—and their environments—continue to become more dynamic and complex, managers—including supervisors—must obtain, organize, and use huge amounts of information to make decisions and exercise control over them. Progressive managers realize that a high-speed information infrastructure is needed to cope with the rapid pace of operations in all types of economic activities.

One result of this "information revolution" is the redistribution of power in today's advanced organizations. For example, decision making and control have been shifted downward to lower levels of management, including the supervisory level. With practically unlimited types and sources of information at their fingertips, even operative employees

UPS uses technology that allows the employee and supervisor to monitor and control desired results for their deliveries.

no longer have to rely on others for facts and figures to make decisions. Organizations now have information and monitoring systems that permit supervisors to give instructions and control operations from a distance away from those activities.

> *For example, at the start of his workday at 8:30 each morning, Washington R., a delivery person for United Parcel Service (UPS), picks up a hand held computer he carries all day as he makes his deliveries and returns to home base at night. On his personal hand held computer, he can view all the day's tasks, each one timed to the minute. As he makes his deliveries, Washington keys the details into the computer, which electronically transmits the data to his home depot. His supervisor can determine where he is at any time and if he is on schedule. At the end of the day, Washington hooks up to the UPS computer, and all the information he accumulated during the day is automatically transferred.*
>
> *During the night, the computer downloads Washington's next day's itinerary and individual tasks into his box.*[3]

Today's information technology makes possible—for better or worse—this form of digital monitoring and control.

● Chapter Review

1. *Define control and explain how it relates to planning.*
Controlling is the supervisory process of making plans and following through on them. Because of the many variables involved in executing and carrying out plans, supervisory control is an essential part of the management process.

2. *Discuss the characteristics of effective control systems.*
For control systems to be effective, they should (1) focus on appropriate activities, (2) be timely, (3) be cost-effective, (4) be accurate and concise, and (5) be accepted by people who will be controlled by them.

3. *Discuss the three types of control systems.*
The three types of control systems are (1) feedforward controls, which try to anticipate problems and take corrective action before they occur; (2) concurrent controls, used while an activity is taking place; and (3) feedback controls, measuring activities that are completed and then take corrective action if needed.

4. *Discuss the four steps in the control process.*
The four steps in the control process are (1) establish performance standards, (2) measure performance, (3) compare performance with standards and analyze deviations, and (4) take corrective action if needed.

5. *Identify the different types of standards.*
Standards can be tangible (numerical, monetary, physical, and time) or intangible (attitudes, ethics, and morals). They can be set by supervisors or staff departments.

6. *Explain the importance of strategic control points.*
It is important the supervisor establish strategic control points. These points measure performance early enough in the process to permit sufficient adjustments or corrective actions to be made in order to achieve the goal. Supervisors measure performance through direct observation; by written or oral reports by or about employees; through automatic methods; and by inspections, samples, or tests.

7. *Discuss management by exception.*
Management by exception focuses supervisory attention on exceptional departures from standard rather than routine variances.

8. *Discuss the impact of technology on control.*
The growth of information technology redistributed power in organizations, thus enhancing the position of supervisors.

Key Terms

feedforward controls, p. 397
concurrent controls, p. 397
feedback controls, p. 397
standard, p. 398

tangible standards, p. 398
numerical standards, p. 398
monetary standards, p. 398
physical standards, p. 398

time standards, p. 398
intangible standards, p. 398
strategic control point, p. 400
management by exception, p. 404

Discussion Questions

1. In what ways are planning and controlling related?
2. Discuss the following statement made by a supervisor: "I don't have to worry much about controlling. My view is, if you plan a job properly, things will go right; so you don't have to worry about control."
3. Name the primary characteristics of effective control systems.
4. Identify and explain each of the four steps in controlling.
5. Give an example of each type of standard:
   a. Numerical standard
   b. Monetary standard
   c. Physical standard
   d. Time standard
   e. Intangible standard
6. Name and explain the three types of control systems.
7. In management by exception, the supervisor focuses on exceptional deviations from the standard rather than every deviation. Will employees grow lax when they realize they can perform below standard as long as they are not too far below? Discuss.
8. Explain the impact technology has on control.

Skill Builder 13.1

The Overcontrolling Supervisor

As a new operations supervisor, Clarise Rogers was conscientious about wanting to do a good job and pleasing her boss. She spent a large part of the day watching her employees perform their jobs, moving from one workstation to another. She inquired how things were going and tried to engage in friendly small talk. One day a senior operator asked to see Clarise in her office. The operator said, "We know you mean well, but there's no need for you to be constantly checking up on everybody. We had one of the best departments in this company under Morgan [the previous supervisor], and she stayed off our backs. We're professionals and we don't need somebody constantly looking over our shoulders. We're going to do a good job for you. Just give us some breathing space."

Answer the following questions:
1. What should Clarise do?
2. Suppose Clarise had just taken over one of the poorest performing departments in the company. Would this make a difference in the control techniques she should use? How?

Skill Builder 13.2

Systems

Interpersonal Skill

Setting Standards and Measuring Performance (Group Activity)

Instructions: Form small groups to discuss each of the jobs listed below. Assume each group member directly supervises that position. In each case, indicate the major type(s) of standard(s) that would be used (physical, monetary, time, or intangible) and the frequency and manner of measuring performance for each job. Discuss with group members your ideas about how to handle each situation.
1. Bank teller
2. Postal letter carrier
3. Server in a large restaurant
4. Real estate salesperson
5. Offensive-line football coach
6. Upholsterer in a furniture manufacturing plant
7. Third-grade teacher in an elementary school

Skill Builder 13.3

Systems

Competitor Assessment (Group Activity)

Assemble teams of three to five members. Choose two well-known direct competitors (e.g., Jimmy Johns and Firehouse, Walgreens and CVS, and Walmart and Target); then, using the Internet, find information (articles, blogs, company Web sites, etc.) about each organization.

Instructions:
1. Specifically, your team should identify and classify (feedforward, concurrent, and feedback) the different types of control systems each competitor utilizes.
2. Pick one form of control for each company and evaluate its effectiveness based on the characteristics of effective control systems presented in this chapter. What improvements could each company make?
3. Prepare and give a 10-minute PowerPoint presentation of your overall findings to the class.

CASE 13-1

CONTROLLING ABSENTEEISM:

Anna McIntyre had been named head nurse of the university hospital pediatrics department the previous day. She would officially begin her new job in one week, when Carla Smith, the present head nurse, would move to a new department. Anna reflected on the conversation she had with Gail Sutherland, director of nursing, when Gail offered her the position. "Anna," Gail said, "you'll be taking over a department that has 8 percent absenteeism compared to 2 percent for other nursing units in the hospital. This has always been a problem and Carla never could handle it—that's a major reason she was transferred. I want you to make it your number 1 priority."

Anna reflected on Carla's performance as head nurse. Carla was a skilled, competent nurse, but since

being promoted to head nurse in pediatrics, she had been too soft. Many nurses took advantage of her good nature—Carla found it impossible to discipline—and the situation in pediatrics began to deteriorate. Anna knew from her own experience absenteeism was high in the department. This was especially true of weekend work. Carla never took action, even when it was obvious that personnel were making petty excuses.

CASE QUESTIONS

1. What additional information should Anna attempt to obtain regarding the absenteeism problem?
2. Advise Anna on the steps she should take to control absenteeism.
3. What types of standards should she use?
4. What strategic control points should she establish?

CASE 13-2

AN EMPLOYEE OPINION STUDY IN AN URBAN HOSPITAL:

The health care industry is in a state of flux due to an aging population, increasing costs, and environmental uncertainty. However, Jean,* the administrator of an urban hospital, believes each day offers an opportunity to make a difference. She is aware of the daily challenges and her responsibility for ensuring quality care is provided and costs are managed so that the hospital remains viable long term. To assist in accomplishing this goal, Jean hired outside consultants to conduct an employee opinion study. Employees in different departments and working different shifts completed questionnaires over a period of several months. The results were quite telling.

Overall, the employees enjoyed their jobs and felt committed to the hospital's mission. They really believed key services, such as the burn and trauma units, provided unique assistance to those in the community.

However, they also perceived they were overworked and underpaid, and communications were inadequate. When asked whether their departments were adequately staffed, the employees' responses averaged a 2.2 on a five-point scale. They perceived increased work demands were contributing to nonattendance issues. However, one of the more significant findings was that most of the respondents didn't believe that the hospital administration would act on the results.

CASE QUESTIONS

1. Given the results of the employee survey, identify a list of alternatives to address the employees' concerns. Consider the costs and benefits of each one.
2. Which alternatives would you recommend Jean implement and in what priority?

_____
*Name changed for privacy purposes.

Notes

1. Andres Kaplan, "Mission Control: Systems for Monitoring Beverage Production Can Keep Lines Running as Smoothly as Possible, While Trimming Excess Costs at the Same Time," *Beverage World* 122 (July 15, 2003).

2. Marc Gunther, "Marriott Gets a Wake-Up Call," *Fortune*, July 6, 2009, pp. 62–66.
3. Simon Head, "Big Brother in a Black Box," *Civilization* 6, no. 4 (August–September 1999), pp. 52–55.

14
Controlling Productivity, Quality, and Safety

You can never inspect quality into products. You can only build it into them.

—Akio Morita, Co-founder, Sony Corporation

kali9/E+/Getty Images

Don Chalmer's emphasis on employee training and development is a key reason they are a Malcom Baldrige Award winner.

Preview

DON CHALMERS FORD: REAL VALUE, REAL PEOPLE, REAL SIMPLE

In 1987, in an effort to encourage quality initiatives, the U.S. Congress established the Malcolm Baldrige National Quality Award (see Exhibit 14-10) at the urging of business leaders. It has symbolized America's best in quality and is named for the much-admired former U.S. Secretary of Commerce Malcolm Baldrige. Applications are scored by examination teams drawn from senior ranks of business, consultants, and academics. The highest scoring applicants move on to stage two—a site visit by four to six examiners who verify the facts in the application and probe more deeply into organizational processes. They report back to a nine-judge panel, which recommends winners to the Secretary of Commerce. The White House makes the formal announcements and this award is "the nation's only Presidential award for performance excellence."

Don Chalmers Ford, an independent Ford Motor Company franchise, was the 2016 Malcolm Baldrige National Quality Award recipient in the small business category. Gary Housley is the general manager and principal dealer. The company's motto is "Real Value, Real People, Real Simple" and their vision is "To be the premier Ford dealership in New Mexico." They intend to accomplish this vision by surpassing their customers' expectations, being innovative, and providing "consistent high quality products and services." Don Chalmers Ford has been recognized nationally for "customer satisfaction and market share available to Ford dealerships 13 times over the last 17 years. This feat has only been accomplished by 4 percent of domestic Ford dealerships." In 2015, the company employed 182 people and grossed $126 million in sales.

To continuously achieve peak performance, Don Chalmers Ford relies on its human capital. It provides training and growth opportunities to employees focused on "customers, operations, compliance, and leadership." For example, new employees receive orientation training, "followed by role-specific sales or technician training." Also, seasoned leaders mentor new members using the "How I Connect" program to demonstrate how their roles align with "the company's core values and how they are to deliver the 'DCF Experience.'" The result has been increased retention rates that are significantly higher than the national averages. Recently, the company surpassed its training goal and achieved on average 71 hours of training for each team member. Its commitment to training differentiates it among other dealers.

Don Chalmers Ford's approach to strategic planning creates annual performance goals, metrics, and plans that are strategically mapped throughout the organization so that analysis and communication among first-line supervisors, technicians, and sales associates is daily, weekly, and monthly, ensuring the organization continues to focus on its mission and vision. Don Chalmers Ford employs a diverse set of performance management strategies to engage team members. Managers at all levels of the company track key performance data at all stages of the sales and service processes to ensure quality and find ways to continuously improve. Over 70 percent of the performance goals "are at or above benchmark levels." This is due in part to having an open-door policy that enables managers to informally coach their employees, but it also has more formal programs such as the "Consumer Experience Movement, a program to increase employee engagement," as well as weekly and monthly reviews to address any issues and opportunities. Team members "submit ideas for improvement to the senior leadership team, which then reviews, discusses, and prioritizes them."

Sources: "2016 Malcolm Baldrige National Quality Award Application," Don Chalmers Ford, 2016, http://patapsco.nist.gov/Award_Recipients/PDF_Files/2017_Don_Chalmers_%20Ford_Application_Summary.pdf (retrieved July 16, 2017); NIST, Department of Commerce, "Don Chalmers Ford, Malcolm Baldrige National Quality Award 2016 Award Recipient, Small Business," 2016, https://www.nist.gov/baldrige/don-chalmers-ford; and http://www.donchalmersford.com/.

The chapter preview highlights the importance of quality and performance. The remainder of the chapter provides the supervisor with the knowledge needed to improve productivity, reduce costs, improve quality, and promote safety. Mastering these central areas requires learning about regulations, business policies, reporting requirements, management concepts, and various calculations. Management counts on the supervisor to ensure organizational plans are executed properly and objectives met.

Defining Productivity

1. *Explain the concept of productivity.*

productivity

Measure of efficiency (inputs to outputs).

Productivity is a measure that compares outputs to inputs. It tells you how efficiently a system is performing. For example, your car's gas mileage is a productivity measure of energy performance. For a certain input, say 1 gallon of gas, your car achieves a certain output, say 22 miles of travel. The figure of 22 miles per gallon (MPG) is the productivity measure of your car's energy performance. How is this figure useful? You now have a basis for comparing (1) your car's performance to that of other cars and (2) your car's present performance to its previous performance. For example, if your MPG were to fall to 15, you would know your car's performance had fallen, and you would try to determine the reasons—assuming, of course, such an energy loss was important to you! Productivity is expressed as a ratio; that is, output is divided by input. In our example of the car's gas mileage, the ratio might look like this:

$$\frac{\text{Total miles (220)}}{\text{Number of gallons (10)}} = 22 \text{ MPG}$$

EXHIBIT 14-1
Factory Workers in
Bottling Plant

Monty Rakusen/Cultura/Jupiter Images

STOP AND THINK

What would be some meaningful input–output relationships for the following service organizations: restaurants, community colleges, beauty salons, insurance companies, and department stores? What inputs do these service organizations have in common?

The official productivity measure of the United States, as shown in Exhibit 14-2, is based on labor output and input per hour. This is the productivity announced each quarter by the government and discussed in the media. Basically, it is the ratio of the total output of the nation's goods and services to the total hours of labor that went into producing those goods and services. Business organizations use numerous input–output performance measures; some are shown in Exhibit 14-2. Generally, when people in business discuss improved productivity, they are talking about total costs and total goods or services produced. Assume a department has a mandate from upper management to increase productivity by 15 percent in the next year or it will be shut down. Upper management's goal is by the end of the next 12-month period, the department's productivity ratio would look like this:

$$\frac{\text{Total output goods/service}}{\text{Total costs}} = 15 \text{ percent more than previously accomplished}$$

EXHIBIT 14-2

Examples of
Productivity
Measurements

INPUT	OUTPUT
Salesperson labor hours	Sales volume per salesperson
Energy used, in BTUs*	Number of pounds fabricated
Training hours for customer service personnel	Percent of error-free written orders
Number of hours of plantwide safety meetings	Number of accident-free days
Labor hours spent on preventive maintenance	Number of hours without a machine breakdown
Cost of raw materials	Quantity of finished goods produced
Total labor hours of service personnel	Total quantity of services produced
Total labor hours of production workforce	Total quantity of goods produced
Total costs	Total number (or value) of goods or services produced

*BTU, British thermal unit.

Basically, there are three ways to accomplish the 15 percent productivity increase:

1. *Increase* the total output without changing the total costs.
2. *Decrease* the total input costs without changing the total output.
3. *Increase* the output and decrease the input costs.

Assume the department produced 48,000 units (output) at a cost of $24,000 for raw materials, energy, and labor. The productivity ratio is

$$\frac{48,000 \text{ units (output)}}{\$24,000 \text{ input}} = 2.0 \text{ units/dollar}$$

To achieve a 15 percent increase in productivity, the department needs to raise the final ratio by 0.3 (i.e., $2.0 \times 15\%$). In other words, the department needs to produce 2.3 units per dollar to achieve a 15 percent productivity increase. There are three basic ways to achieve this, as discussed next.

Example 1: Increasing Output   One approach to attaining the productivity increase is to hold the line on costs while increasing output. How much additional output would be needed to reach the new productivity rate of 2.3? This can be calculated by the following steps:

(a) $\dfrac{\text{Total units}}{\$24,000} = 2.3 \text{ units per dollar}$

(b) Total units $= 2.3$ units per dollar $\times$ \$24,000

(c) Total units $= 55,200$

Because the department is presently producing 48,000 units, it would have to produce 7,200 additional units without increasing costs to attain the 15 percent productivity increase.

Example 2: Decreasing Input   Another approach is to maintain present output while reducing costs. By how much would the department need to reduce costs to attain the 15 percent increase? This can be calculated by the following steps:

(a) $\dfrac{48,000 \text{ units}}{\text{Costs}} = 2.3 \text{ units per dollar}$

(b) $\text{Costs} = \dfrac{48{,}000 \text{ units}}{2.3 \text{ units per dollar}}$

(c) Costs $= \$20{,}870$

Producing the 48,000 units at a cost of $20,870 would provide the 15 percent productivity ratio improvement. The department would have to maintain production of 48,000 units while reducing costs by $3,130 (i.e., $24,000 − $20,870).

Example 3: Increasing Output and Decreasing Input   Suppose the department could reduce costs by only $1,000. By how much would the department have to increase output to achieve the 15 percent productivity increase?

(a) $\dfrac{\text{Total units}}{\$24{,}000 - \$1{,}000} = 2.3 \text{ units per dollar}$

(b) $\dfrac{\text{Total units}}{\$23{,}000} = 2.3 \text{ units per dollar}$

(c) Total units $= 2.3 \text{ units per dollar} \times \$23{,}000$

(d) Total units $= 52{,}900$

Thus, reducing costs by $1,000 and increasing output by 4,900 units (52,900 − 48,000) also would provide the 15 percent productivity increase.

Why Productivity Is Important

Productivity is important for several reasons. From an individual company's standpoint, increased productivity translates into lower prices, larger market share, and greater profits. The firm's stronger financial position enables it to invest in research and development, utilize new advanced technology, increase wages and benefits, improve working conditions, and so on. Let us examine the following service-oriented business example:

Assume you manage a steakhouse restaurant that uses seven waiters/waitresses. Their pay (including benefits but excluding tips) averages $10:00/hour. The maximum number of tables they can serve effectively is five per hour. Thus, the labor cost for serving each table is $10/5, or $2 per table. Assume business picked up recently. The kitchen can handle the extra business, and, by rearranging tables, five new tables could be added. Because the current waiter/waitress maximum of five tables served per hour has already been reached, a new waiter/waitress must be hired to handle the extra workload. Before hiring another waiter/waitress, though, you pose the problem to your waitstaff and they devise a plan.

"We could each handle an extra table an hour if we didn't have to set each table," they say. "Couldn't the hostess who seats the party distribute the silverware and menus? Also, might we arrange each waiter's tables in a more compact area? This would reduce walking time among tables. The time saved with these two changes might allow us to effectively serve another table hourly (which, by the way, would mean an additional tip)."

So you try it out, and, behold, it works. Your waiters/waitresses handle the extra table per hour effectively. Let's calculate the effect on productivity—it increased by one-fifth, or 20 percent. Moreover, your labor costs decreased from $2.00 per table to $1.67 per table ($10.00 ÷ 6 tables = $1.67 per table). Because labor costs typically account for 30 to 60 percent of a company's expenses, increasing the efficiency of labor is important to an organization's success.

David Woolley/Taxi/Getty Images

Productivity is important for restaurants and other service-minded businesses.

On a larger scale, increased productivity greatly enhances the economic growth and health of the United States. In the international market, companies from the United States compete with firms from other nations. Increased productivity in the United States enhances the success of U.S. companies in international markets, keeps prices down, reduces inflation, and improves our standard of living.

Groups Influencing Productivity

2. Identify and explain the ways in which management, government, unions, and employees affect productivity.

Basically, four groups play important roles influencing productivity, as shown in Exhibit 14-3.

1. **Management.** A major force in determining productivity is management. Supervisors can play an important role in supporting management's plans and vision for productivity improvement. The supervisor needs to take the time and effort needed to learn and understand management's decisions to build more modern plants, upgrade equipment, improve processes, and train employees. In what ways do the managers at Don Chalmers Ford in the chapter preview influence productivity?

2. **Government.** Another important productivity player is government. For example, tax incentives encourage business investment in new facilities and technology; government regulations also play an important role. When businesses spend huge amounts on the costs of compliance to satisfy, for instance, pollution and environmental controls, consumer protection requirements, and employee safety and health, this not only diverts expenditures from more efficient labor-saving technology, equipment, and plants, but it also requires many new positions. These personnel do not contribute directly to output. Although government regulation of business is necessary, the amount of regulation is a constant source of debate in this country as well as in others. Supervisors are expected to comply with government regulations.

EXHIBIT 14-3

Groups Influencing
Productivity

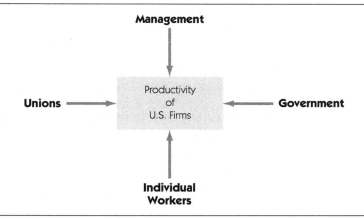

EXHIBIT 14-4

Toyota's Production
System

Toyota's Philosophy and Framework of Organizing Manufacturing Facilities Efficiently
The global company with the strongest reputation for efficiency is unquestionably Toyota
Motors. The "Toyota Production System" (TPS) has been admired, studied, and copied by most
large manufacturers, including competitors. In fact, in Erlanger, Ohio, Toyota has created a
training center to teach outside firms its TPS. The "system" refers to Toyota's philosophy and
framework of organizing manufacturing facilities and having them interact with suppliers and
customers in the most efficient way. TPS's goal is the elimination of waste—be it through defective materials, overproduction, inefficient logistics, or inventory buildup. The TPS requires a
strong top management commitment and what for many companies is a dramatic change from
their current ways of doing things.

One of the best-known aspects of Toyota's approach to efficiency is its effort to continuously improve, called *kaizen*. Another is an *Andan*, part of every Toyota plant, which is a cord
that any employee can pull to stop the production line when a problem or defect is spotted.
The story is told of an American supervisor in Toyota's Georgetown, Kentucky, plant who
feared for his job after one of his crew pulled the Andan, shutting the line down for four hours
to trace and remedy the problem. Afterward, he was called to the desk of the Japanese plant
executive, where he nervously explained the problem and the solution. Only then did he learn
he was summoned not to explain the problem and shutdown, but to receive recognition for
his team having done it.

Source: Jingshan Li and Dennis Blumenfield, "Qualitative Analysis of a Transfer Production Line with
Andan," *IIE Transactions* 38 (October 2006), pp. 837–847; Dan Monk, "Productivity Machine," *Business
Courier Serving Cincinnati–Northern Kentucky* 16 (June 25, 1999), pp. 1–2.

3. **Individual workers.** Another important productivity player is the individual worker.
   Employees' ability, motivation, and commitment strongly affect individual and team
   performance. The age and education of employees impact their skills. Less-experienced
   employees are less productive initially. As the chapter preview noted, Don Chalmers
   Ford invested 71 hours on average for training employees to operate at peak performance. It also paired new employees with mentors to increase retention, reducing
   turnover costs.
4. **Unions.** Unions also play a role in productivity by their posture toward technology
   enhancements, new work methods, and displacement of inefficient jobs. While union
   activity in certain industries has been on the decline in recent years, some movement
   has been seen in the service sector.

In summary, then, all of these groups play a role in productivity. However, management that directly controls decisions about facilities, technology, research, and the company "productivity climate" is most responsible because it strongly impacts relationships with its union and sets the stage in numerous ways for the productivity of individual employees. Toyota is considered to be one of the most productive companies in its industry. A historical insight about the Toyota Production System (TPS) is provided in Exhibit 14-4.

The Supervisor's Role in Improving Productivity

3. *Describe some steps supervisors can take to increase productivity.*

Supervisors often have little control over spending for technology and equipment, but as the persons in direct contact with operating employees, they are important players in the productivity issue. The supervisor needs to learn the new technology and train employees to use it. The employees may doubt their ability to learn the new technology or may believe it is a threat to their jobs. The supervisor must be prepared to address these concerns. How do you go about it? Ideas for improving employee productivity are listed in Exhibit 14-5.

The supervisor is responsible for his/her employees' overall performance. Therefore, it is important the supervisor learns how to track the productivity of his/her employee team. A bowler tracks pins, baseball teams track home runs, the golfer tracks strokes, and the dieter tracks pounds. These groups, although involved in different activities, have something in common. They all keep score and see the value in measuring performance. Measuring provides the opportunity to control and improve.

The Supervisor's Role in Cost Control

As we pointed out earlier, the productivity of a department is based on its total outputs and inputs. Upper management is cost conscious because costs represent major inputs. Supervisors direct the operating work of an organization; thus, they have a key role in

---

EXHIBIT 14-5
How Supervisors Can Improve Employee Productivity

- Train employees. Can their abilities be upgraded?
- Clearly communicate the need for high standards so workers understand what is expected of them.
- Use motivation techniques to inspire workers to increase output. Pride, ego, and security are several important motivators available.
- Provide feedback to your employees. Recognize good work when it occurs.
- Coach employees to learn from their mistakes so errors will not be repeated.
- Eliminate idleness, extended breaks, and early quitting time.
- Build in quality the first time work is done. Productivity is lost when items are scrapped or need to be reworked to be salvaged.
- Work on improving attendance and turnover in your work group.
- Reduce accidents. Accidents normally result in time lost to investigations, meetings, and reports—even if the employee does not suffer a lost-work-time injury.
- Seek to improve production measures. Will process or work-flow improvements help?
- Try to eliminate or reduce equipment or machinery breakdowns. Preventive maintenance is important.
- Exercise good control techniques. Follow up on performance and take corrective action promptly.
- Learn to calculate your team's productivity. Share the results with your team.
- Involve your employees in the process of improvement. Select their ideas and suggestions for improvement. Form special productivity improvement teams.
- Celebrate productivity improvements.

controlling a firm's cost in labor hours and efficiency, maintenance of machinery and equipment, supplies, energy, and other matters.

Budgets are one aid that can help supervisors control costs. Different budgets are normally prepared for sales, production, scrap, equipment, grievances, lost-work-time accidents, and the like. Moreover, they may be set for different time periods such as a week, a month, a quarter, or a year. Because a budget reflects expected performance, it becomes a basis for evaluating a department's actual performance (see Exhibit 14-6).

STOP AND THINK

Assume that you are supervisor of the fabrication department in Exhibit 14-6. If you were really trying to tighten up costs, which activities in your department would you focus on? Why?

Note in Exhibit 14-6 the supervisor's department performed well in some cost areas and not so well in others. Output is off by 473 pounds, overtime is 50 percent higher than budgeted, and maintenance and repairs are also over budget. On the plus side, the department has been efficient in using raw materials.

Budgets are not carved in stone; there will always be unusual occurrences that affect performance. An investigation of the unfavorable variances in Exhibit 14-6 may reveal the supervisor or team member could have done little to avoid them. For example, perhaps a crucial piece of equipment had faulty parts, causing the high repair costs; or the high overtime may have resulted from an unexpected weekend job thrust upon the supervisor. A budget does, however, serve as an important supervisory tool by signaling areas that need attention. Such attention might take the form of combining certain jobs, reducing scrap, achieving better-quality production, or focusing on large-cost items rather than numerous smaller ones. When unfavorable variances occur, the supervisor looks for opportunities to generate offsetting favorable variances. The supervisor can challenge his/her team to look for ways to cut costs in other areas.

EXHIBIT 14-6
Performance Report

Name of department	Fabrication	Performance period	November 2006
Budgeted output	15,700 lbs	Budgeted scrap	152 lbs
Actual output	15,227 lbs	Actual scrap	120 lbs
Variance	−473 lbs		+32 lbs

ITEM	ACTUAL	BUDGETED	VARIANCE
Direct labor	$32,000	$32,000	$0
Overtime	1,500	1,000	−500
Supplies	500	385	−115
Maintenance and repairs	4,250	3,000	−1,250
Utilities	1,300	1,200	−100
Scrapped material	1,200	1,520	+320
Total	$40,750	$39,105	−$1,645

Recently, advanced software technology proved especially helpful to supervisors in achieving effective cost control. It is now possible for supervisors in some circumstances to have up-to-the-minute cost data on payroll, raw materials, utilities, and other costs as nearby as a computer monitor or printer. The supervisor should share and explain these reports to his/her teams.

Productivity Improvement Methods for Controlling Quality

In an effort to improve productivity, three productivity improvement measures have been introduced in manufacturing firms. These improvements, which are due to advances in computer and machinery technology, are (1) robotics, (2) radio frequency identification (RFID), and (3) computer-assisted manufacturing (CAM).

robot

A machine controlled by a computer that can be programmed to perform a number of repetitive manipulations of tools or materials.

Robotics   A **robot** is a machine, controlled by a computer, programmed to perform a number of repetitive manipulations of tools or materials. The International Federation of Robotics estimates in its *2016 World Robotics Report* that "[t]he number of industrial robots deployed worldwide will increase to around 2.6 million units by 2019. That's about one million units more than in the record-breaking year of 2015. Broken down according to sectors, around 70 percent of industrial robots are currently at work in the automotive, electrical/electronics and metal and machinery industry segments."[1] Industrial robots are typically used to perform hazardous, monotonous tasks or tasks needing high speed or precision. Exhibit 14-7 shows a robot spray painting cars. The ability of the industrial robot to handle these tasks demonstrates the advantages of industrial robotics. There are, however, disadvantages such as high costs, space requirements, and the need for high skills to operate and repair the robots. In addition to the industrial uses, robots also are used in services. Service robots are used to milk cows, fight fires, pick fruits, and clean houses.

STOP AND THINK

What are the advantages of using robots for services? Disadvantages?

RFID

Radio frequency identification technology uses radio waves to identify inventory and other objects.

computer-assisted manufacturing (CAM)

Special computers assist equipment in performing processes.

Radio Frequency Identification (RFID)   RFID tags (Exhibit 14-8) have many uses. A common use is tracking and controlling inventory. As the RFID technology improves and the cost decreases, many new applications are developed. Pet owners can use the tags to track their dogs. The tags offer quick payment for gasoline, tolls, buses, and trains. Access to buildings, power plants, hospitals, and other sensitive areas can be controlled by including the tags in employee identification badges. The use of these tags has raised security and privacy issues. The tags can be misused to track people and their property. However, these tags offer businesses several advantages not offered by bar code technology. RFID tags hold more information than bar codes and, unlike bar codes, they can be reused. Although the costs are decreasing, RFID tags remain more costly than bar codes.

Computer-Assisted Manufacturing   In **computer-assisted manufacturing (CAM)**, special computers assist automated equipment in performing the processes necessary for production. These computers can be reprogrammed to permit machinery to easily produce a product or part to different specifications. Whereas proper planning and coordination normally take hours, CAM equipment can be programmed to make adjustments

EXHIBIT 14-7
Robots Used to Spray
Paint Cars

Kim Steele/Digital Vision/Jupiter Images

EXHIBIT 14-8
Close Up of an
RFID Tag

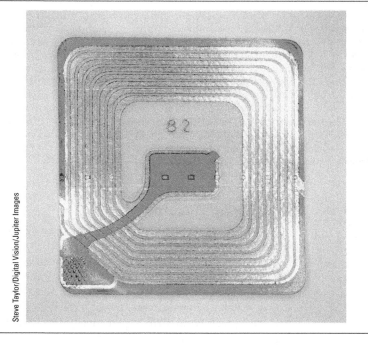

Steve Taylor/Digital Vision/Jupiter Images

within seconds. CAM is especially useful when small orders of customized products must be filled. Once the computer is programmed, the electronic signals control the machine processor, resulting in the correct sequence of steps to properly complete the task. The supervisor working in an area using CAM needs the operational and technical knowledge required to effectively supervise in an automated environment. For example, at carpet manufacturers, computer software programs control patterns, weaves, and the size of carpets being produced. At apparel manufacturers, such as Hart Schaffner and Marx, computer software programs determine optimum cutting of patterns and sizes to minimize waste and ensure perfect cuts.

HISTORICAL INSIGHT

Evolution of the Quality Explosion in the United States

The background of today's surging quality movement in the United States can be traced to Japan. Following World War II, the words "Made in Japan" connoted cheap, inferior quality. As part of General MacArthur's program to rebuild the country, 50-year-old W. Edwards Deming, a U.S. statistical quality control advocate, was brought to Japan to teach statistical quality control concepts. Deming addressed 21 top Japanese executives who were eager to learn and represented the industrial leaders of the country. His theories formed the basis of **Deming's 85-15 rule**. This rule assumes when things go wrong, 85 percent of the time the cause is attributed to elements controlled by management, such as machinery, materials, or processes, whereas only 15 percent of the time employees are at fault. Thus, Deming believed management rather than the employee is to blame for most poor quality. The Japanese embraced Deming's message and transformed their industries by using his techniques. His "14 points for quality," shown in Exhibit 14-9, are the actions he believed necessary for an organization to successfully make the quality "transformation."

Deming's contributions were recognized early by the Japanese. In 1951, the Deming Application Prize was instituted by the Union of Japanese Scientists and Engineers, and Deming was awarded the nation's highest honor, the Royal Order of the Sacred Treasure, from the Emperor of Japan. By the mid-1970s, the quality of Japan's products exceeded that of Western manufacturers, and Japanese companies made significant U.S. and global market penetration in areas such as autos, steel, computers, and electronics.

The United States' quality problem was first highlighted in a 1980 NBC program titled *If Japan Can . . . Why Can't We?* The program introduced the 80-year-old Deming, who, although an American, was virtually unknown in this country. This program ignited a spark that awakened American executives and helped fuel a quality turnaround. Major companies, especially those threatened, embarked on extensive programs to improve quality. Ford Motors was among the first to invite Deming to help transform its operations. Within a few years, Ford's results improved dramatically; its profits became the highest for any company in automotive history. By 1992, its Ford Taurus unseated the Honda Accord as the best-selling domestic model.

In 1987, in an effort to encourage quality initiatives, the U.S. Congress established the Malcolm Baldrige National Quality Award (see Exhibit 14-10), which continues to generate remarkable interest in quality by American organizations.

The American quality story has been a successful one. Since the 1990s, the quality of U.S. goods and services has achieved a stunning turnaround, making "Made in the USA" again a symbol of world-class quality.

Deming's 85-15 rule

Assumes when things go wrong, 85 percent of the time the cause is from elements controlled by management.

Controlling Quality

In recent years, perhaps no other aspect of management has received as much attention of organizations as the effort to improve quality. As you learned from the previous section, quality of an organization's products and services and the organization's productivity are intricately linked. That is one reason why organizations are so quality-oriented today. Quality expert Dr. Philip Crosby estimates nonconformance—products and services that do not match up to requirements—cost the typical manufacturer about 20 percent of sales and the typical service firm 35 percent of sales. This includes the cost of scrapped materials, wasted time, costs of rework, and customers' exercise of warranties. Thus, quality directly affects the bottom line.

A second reason for quality consciousness is global competition (see Historical Insight). Many U.S. firms, such as Citigroup, 3M, Coca-Cola, Exxon, and others, earn over half of their revenues from foreign markets. Moreover, high-quality foreign firms, such as Michelin, Toyota, Seiko, Nokia, Nestlé, and others, compete vigorously, and that requires

EXHIBIT 14-9

Deming's 14 Points for Quality

1. Top management should establish and publish a statement of the organization's purpose and commitment to quality products and services and continuous improvement.
2. Everyone throughout the organization should learn the new philosophy.
3. Dependence on "inspecting" quality into products should be shifted to an attitude of "expecting" quality by having it built into the system.
4. There must be a systematic way to select quality suppliers, rather than simply on the basis of cost.
5. The organization must be devoted to continuous improvement.
6. All employees should be trained in the most modern quality and problem-solving techniques.
7. Leadership techniques consistent with getting the most commitment from employees should be practiced throughout the entire organization.
8. Fear should be eliminated from the work environment.
9. Teams and work groups must work smoothly together; barriers between functional departments must be eliminated.
10. Exhortations, posters, and slogans asking for new levels of workforce productivity must be backed by providing the methods to achieve these.
11. Numerical production quotas should be eliminated. Constant improvement should be sought instead.
12. Barriers that deprive employees from pride in their work must be removed.
13. A vigorous program of education, retraining, and self-improvement for all employees must be instituted.
14. A structure in top management that will push the thirteen points above to achieve the transformation must be created.

Source: From W. Edwards Deming, *Out of the Crisis* (Cambridge, MA: MIT Press, 2000), pp. 23–24.

EXHIBIT 14-10

The Malcolm Baldrige National Quality Award

The prize is only a gold-plated medal encased in a crystal column 14 inches tall. But since 1987, when Congress created the Malcolm Baldrige National Quality Award at the urging of business leaders, it has symbolized America's best in quality. Named for the much-admired former U.S. Secretary of Commerce Malcolm Baldrige, who died in 1987, the award is administered by the National Institute of Standards and Technology, with endowments covering costs of administration and judging of applicants.

Applications are scored by examination teams drawn from senior ranks of business, consultants, and academics. The highest-scoring applicants move on to stage two—a site visit by four to six examiners who verify the facts in the application and probe more deeply into organizational processes. They report back to a nine-judge panel, which recommends winners to the Secretary of Commerce. The White House makes the formal announcements.

Winning a Baldrige has proved tough. Organizations must observe eight essentials to win:

1. Establish a plan to seek improvement continuously in all phases of operations—not just manufacturing, but purchasing, sales, human relations, and other areas.
2. Put in place a system that accurately tracks and measures performance in those areas.
3. Establish a long-term strategic plan based on performance targets that compare with the world's best in that particular industry.
4. Link closely in a partnership with suppliers and customers in a way that provides needed feedback for continuous improvement.
5. Demonstrate a deep understanding of customers in order to convert their wants into products.
6. Establish and maintain long-lasting customer relationships, going beyond product manufacture and delivery to include sales, service, and ease of maintenance.

(Continued)

EXHIBIT 14-10
continued

7. Focus on preventing mistakes instead of developing efficient ways to correct them; that is, feedforward control is a must.
8. Perhaps most difficult, but imperative, is to make a commitment to quality improvement throughout all levels of the organization, including top, middle, and bottom.

Winners for 2012–2016 are

2016	Winners
Small Business	Don Chalmers Ford
	Momentum Group
Health Care	Kindred Nursing and Rehabilitation–Mountain Valley
	Memorial Hermann Sugar Land Hospital
2015	Winners
Small Business	MidwayUSA
Education	Charter School of San Diego
Health Care	Charleston Area Medical Center Health System
Nonprofit	Mid-America Transplant
2014	Winners
Service	PricewaterhouseCoopers Public Sector Practice
Health Care	Hill Country Memorial
	St. David's HealthCare
Nonprofit	Elevations Credit Union
2013	Winners
Education	Pewaukee School District
Health Care	Sutter Davis Hospital
2012	Winners
Health Care	North Mississippi Health Services
Manufacturing	Lockheed Martin Missiles and Fire Control
Small Business	MESA Products Inc.
Nonprofit	City of Irving, Irving, Texas

U.S. firms to keep up or lose market share. In another reflection of globalization, many organizations require all supplier firms to achieve ISO 9000 certification—an assurance they meet international quality standards in such areas as product design, manufacturing processes, testing, inspection, and service.

A third reason for greater quality emphasis is the increased information available to the public regarding product and service quality. Media coverage quickly informs potential consumers about safety problems, such as the abrupt tilting of a Princess Cruise ship that injured 240 passengers, contaminated beef from ConAgra Foods, or Dell Computers' recall of 6 million notebook computers that contained potentially hazardous Sony lithium batteries.[2] Additionally, independent quality ratings given by such organizations as JD Power and Associates (auto quality), AAA and Mobil (hotels and restaurants), and Consumer Reports (consumer products) significantly affect consumer behavior.

4. *Differentiate between total quality and quality control.*

total quality

Refers to an organization's overall effort to achieve customer satisfaction through continuous improvement of products or services.

Total Quality and Quality Control

Sometimes the terms *total quality* and *quality control* are used interchangeably. However, they are not the same. **Total quality** refers to an organization's overall quality effort that strives to achieve customer satisfaction through continuous improvement of the organization's products, services, and processes. The "father" of the total quality management

EXHIBIT 14-11
The Total Quality
Chain

movement is considered to be W. Edwards Deming (see Exhibit 14-9). It was this approach to quality that empowered Japanese firms to become so successful in the 1980s and such intense competitors today. In 1987, in an effort to encourage quality initiatives, the U.S. Congress established the Malcolm Baldrige National Quality Award (see Exhibit 14-10). The term *total quality* indicates its comprehensiveness, involving all management levels, employees, suppliers, and customers. It is based on the quality chain shown in Exhibit 14-11: Increased quality leads to more customers and increased market share, which enable greater profitability.

STOP AND THINK

Think of a service that performed to your satisfaction. Note how the service used a total quality approach.

---

quality control

Defined measurements designed to check whether the desired quality standards are being met.

5. *Describe the role of variance in controlling quality.*

Quality control, on the other hand, is a narrower process, consisting of the measurement and analysis of quality performance and actions taken to correct quality problems. It occurs during or after performance and may include inspection, testing, sampling, and statistical analysis.

Understanding Variance in Controlling Quality

Every product, as well as every service, is the output or result of a process. You might consider a process to be a set of related activities designed to accomplish a goal.

The nature of processes is to exhibit variation; for example, items produced in a machining or manufacturing process are not all exactly alike. Some measurable dimensions, such as length, diameter, or weight, will vary. These variations may be quite small and not perceivable by the naked eye, but sophisticated gauges or test equipment reveals them. Similarly, service processes also are subject to variation. Fast-food customers wait different periods of time before being served. Some luggage checked on a commercial airline will not arrive with its owner. At a steakhouse, steaks prepared as "rare" may vary considerably.

Two types of variation exist: common cause and special cause. Let's use a classic example to illustrate process variation: writing. Note the variations of handwritten letters below, although each one was carefully written by the same author.

$$p \quad p \quad p \quad p \quad p \quad p \quad p \quad p$$
$$a \quad a \quad a \quad a \quad a \quad a \quad a \quad a$$

You don't need to use a magnifying glass to note that differences exist. The differences in each "p" are normal and to be expected. This we call *common cause variation*. Now look at each "a." Note that the middle one is clearly different from the others. Perhaps the writer was bumped, or the paper quality in that one spot was different, or a different pen was used. (Actually, it was made by the same writer but using the other hand.) The variation is not routine or expected; clearly, there was excessive variation, or *special cause variation*. Common cause variation is a general, routine variation built into the system. Special cause variation occurs intermittently and is associated with a specific event.

Effective control of quality can have two focuses: (1) reducing common cause variation and (2) reducing special cause variation. As Deming and other quality experts note, special causes can sometimes be addressed by individual workers, but common causes ordinarily can be corrected only through management action to improve the process. This might include such things as upgrading raw materials, using more sophisticated equipment, providing additional training, and so on. Adjustments made to a system experiencing common cause variation in an attempt to improve quality are unnecessary and unwise. The employee observing natural variation may believe he or she should intervene by changing machine settings or making other adjustments. The supervisor with the knowledge to differentiate common cause from special cause variation can coach the employee when and when not to take corrective action. Much of the effort by organizations to seek continuous quality improvement is aimed at reducing common cause variation by improving processes.

Reducing special cause variation entails identifying the problem, isolating it, examining the cause, and remedying it. This might mean, for instance, replacing an erratic piece of equipment, reassigning an employee who cannot keep pace with job demands, or reassigning personnel to handle peak customer demand periods.

Six Sigma is a specific type of quality control technique developed at smaller companies and perfected at two large ones, Motorola and Allied Signal; Six Sigma is a specific methodology designed to slash the number of defects in a company's end-to-end process of producing, improving, selling, distributing, and servicing its products.[3]

As a supervisor, it is important to understand variation and the extent different levels of quality performance can be attributed to normal or special cause variables. Statistical sampling is one useful tool for doing so but is beyond our scope here. However, we will examine other important tools.

Some Tools for Controlling Quality

6. *Identify some important tools for controlling quality.*

A number of tools are available to assist in effective control of quality. Often, these are used by individuals who are part of special problem-solving or quality-improvement teams. Among the tools discussed here are check sheets, flowcharts, histograms, run charts, Pareto charts, control charts, and fishbone diagrams. Several, such as check sheets, histograms, run charts, and control charts, represent displays of the actual performance data that must be addressed. Keep in mind these tools apply not just to the quality of manufacturing processes (although this is perhaps the most common application), but to service processes as well.

The supervisor can view these quality improvement measures like tools in a mechanic's toolbox. It takes practice and experience for the mechanic to be able to select and use the proper tool or tools to accomplish a successful repair. Some of the mechanic's tools are easy to use, like the screwdriver, and others are more difficult, such as a feeler gauge. A mechanic using a new tool will practice using the tool and ask experienced mechanics for tips and help.

Just like the mechanic's tools, some of the quality tools are simple and others complex. For example, the check sheet is a rather simple quality tool. A check sheet can be done with paper and pencil. The control chart is more complex. A computer and knowledge of basic statistics are required to use this tool effectively. With practice and determination, the supervisor, like the successful mechanic, develops the skills needed to select and use the proper quality tool.

check sheets

A tool used to collect and organize data.

Check sheets   The **check sheets** does not require the use of a computer. An effective check sheet can be developed using a pencil and paper. Sometimes the simplest of tools can be the most powerful. Exhibit 14-12 is a check sheet collecting information regarding the frequency and types of power failures. Check sheets can be used to collect data on a variety of situations such as reasons for shipment rejections, equipment failures, and tallies of weights, to name a few.

flowchart

Visual representation of the sequence of steps needed to complete a process.

Flowchart   A **flowchart** is a visual representation of the sequence of steps needed to complete a process. Its purpose is to help individuals understand the process they are attempting to control. Flowcharts are frequently used by problem-solving teams to address quality issues involving processes with a number of sequential steps to complete (see Exhibit 14-13). Often such processes cut across departmental lines. The visual representation of the process enables team members to examine the relevant steps and note where improvements can be made, as reflected in the following example.

> *Boise Cascade's Timber and Wood Products Division formed a team of 11 people from diverse backgrounds in administration, marketing, and operations to improve customer claims processing. The group first created a flowchart of the process and discovered over 70 steps needed to process each claim within each division; combined division steps for the same customer claim often took hundreds of steps, taking months to resolve the claim. By studying systematically the steps involved in processing claims and addressing the concerns within each division, the team eliminated 70 percent of the steps in most claims.[4]*

EXHIBIT 14-12
Check Sheet: Type of Power Failures

Date	A	B	C	D	E	F	Comments	Location
12/6/17	X						Crew delay	P21
1/2/18			X				6 hr. service	P3
2/15/18				X			3 hr. service	P22
3/7/18				X			Snowstorm	P21
4/29/18			X				3 hr. service	P3
5/15/18						X	Flooding	R40
6/7/18			X				Crew delay	P5
7/29/18		X					R40/no service	P21–R40
8/21/18			X				Road delays	B2
9/30/18			X				Crew delay	R40
11/2/18				X			Partial crew	P3
12/14/18		X					Flat tire	P5
Total	1	2	4	3	1	1		

EXHIBIT 14-13

Flowchart of a Fast-Food Drive-Through Process

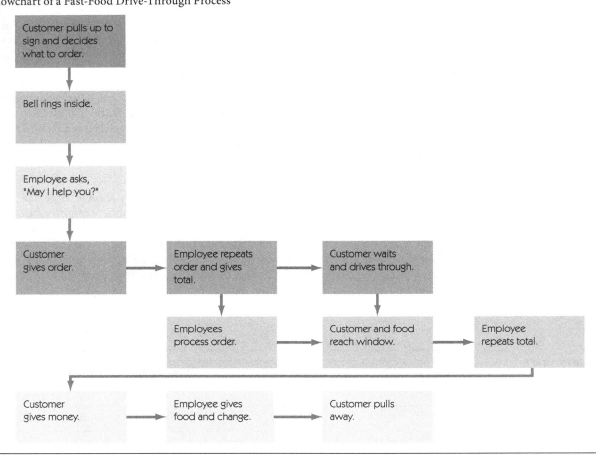

histogram

Graphical representation of the variation found in a set of data.

run chart

Data presentation showing results of a process plotted over time.

Pareto charts

Problem-analysis charts that use a histogram to illustrate sources of problems.

Histogram   A **histogram** is a graphical representation of the variation found in a set of performance data. It can provide clues about the population's characteristics. The visual presentation reflects how the process's output varies and what proportion of output falls outside of the performance targets. The histogram in Exhibit 14-14 represents data on the length of time it took a bank to process loan requests. Note how easy it is to see how the output of the process varies and what proportion falls outside of any specification limits.

Run Chart   A process sometimes performs differently over a period of time. A **run chart** is a data presentation that shows the results of a process plotted over a period of time. It might be used to show the number of hotel checkouts per hour, the number of employee absentees per day, or the percentage of customers waiting in excess of one minute to be seated. Note in Exhibit 14-15 how the run chart points out specific patterns of behavior in the process. The percentage of patrons who have to wait falls into a definite pattern. A much larger percentage waits early in the week, with the percentage decreasing throughout the week.

Pareto Charts   **Pareto charts** are problem-analysis charts that use a histogram to graphically illustrate the sources of problems. They typically list problem causes from left to right in descending order of seriousness. Named after Vilfredo Pareto, the economist who originated the use of such analyses, the Pareto chart helps problem solvers zero in on the

EXHIBIT 14-14

Histogram Showing Frequency and Length of Time Taken by Home Office to Process Loan Request

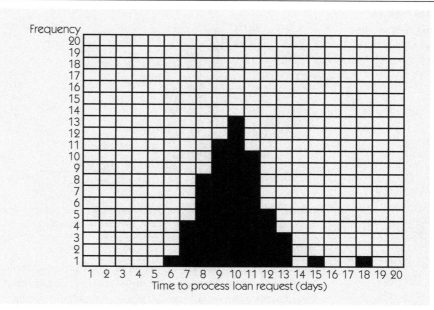

EXHIBIT 14-15

Run Chart of Percentage of Restaurant Customers Waiting in Excess of One Minute to Be Seated

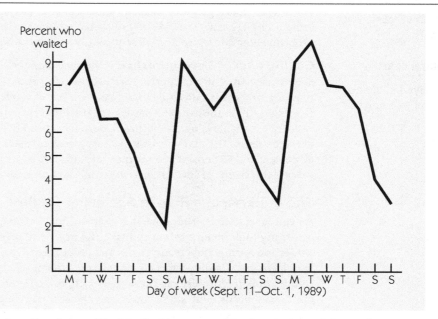

EXHIBIT 14-16
Pareto Chart of Customers' Complaints about Restaurants

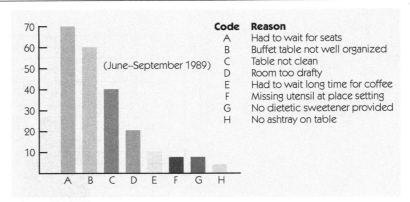

Code	Reason
A	Had to wait for seats
B	Buffet table not well organized
C	Table not clean
D	Room too drafty
E	Had to wait long time for coffee
F	Missing utensil at place setting
G	No dietetic sweetener provided
H	No ashtray on table

(June–September 1989)

Source: From *Foundations of Total Quality Management: A Readings Book*, 1st ed., by Joseph Van Matre, p. 146. 0030078660. Copyright © 1995 by Joseph Van Matre. Reprinted with permission of the author.

dominant rather than trivial problem. For example, Exhibit 14-16 shows the results of an extensive survey of customer complaints in a restaurant over an extended period of time. The chart is a consistent reminder to the problem-solving team its time would be best used by focusing on the complaints of customers waiting for seats and dealing with a poorly organized buffet table. The supervisor challenged to solve a problem can find this to be overwhelming. By finding and focusing on the top two or three problem causes, the majority of the problem can be addressed.

cause-and-effect diagram

A graphical display of a chain of causes and effects.

Cause-and-Effect Diagram   A useful tool for understanding and identifying the causes of performance problems is the **cause-and-effect diagram**. This is also called a fishbone or Ishikawa diagram, named for the Japanese quality expert who popularized it. The diagram represents a graphical display of a chain of causes and effects. The result, shown in Exhibit 14-17, resembles the skeletal system of a fish, with the horizontal line representing the problem being addressed and subsequent lines representing major causes and sub-causes.

control chart

Displays the "state of control" of a process.

Control Chart   The **control chart** is the "backbone" of statistical process control (SPC) and displays the "state of control" of a process. If a process is free from special cause variation, the process is said to be under control. An example of a control chart is shown in Exhibit 14-18. In the exhibit, time is measured in terms of days on the horizontal axis; the value of a variable is on the vertical axis. The central horizontal line corresponds to the average value of the characteristic measured. In this case, as long as the values fall between 97 percent and 89 percent and no unusual pattern exists (such as a succession of decreasing values), it is likely no special cause variation is present and the process is "under control."

The Supervisor's Role in Achieving Quality

As you have noted throughout this chapter, upper management lays the foundation for achieving high quality by committing the organization's resources, communicating its values and norms, and creating rules and procedures. On a daily basis, though, lower-level managers and first-line supervisors have the critical role because it is operating-level personnel who directly perform the activities of producing the goods or services that address customers' needs. One study confirmed the crucial role played by first-line supervisors. Written surveys of 3,500 employees in a food service company found the quality of service they felt they delivered was strongly impacted by the extent their first-line supervisor (1) emphasized the importance of high quality, (2) provided information and support to help employees achieve it, and (3) provided meaningful feedback.[5]

EXHIBIT 14-17

Cause-and-Effect Diagram for "Why Tables Are Not Cleared Quickly"

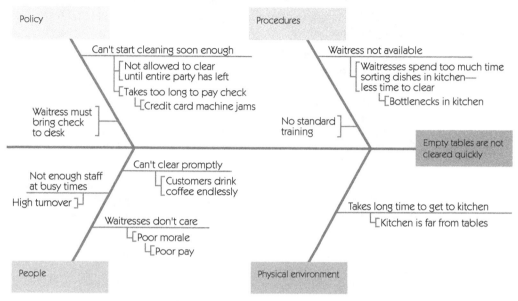

Source: From *Foundations of Total Quality Management: A Readings Book*, 1st ed., by Joseph Van Matre, p. 146. 0030078660. Copyright © 1995 by Joseph Van Matre. Reprinted with permission of the author.

EXHIBIT 14-18

Example of a Control Chart

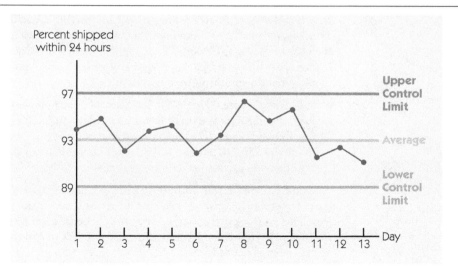

Source: From James W. Dean and James R. Evans, *Total Quality, Management, Organization, and Strategy*, 4th ed. Copyright © 2005 South-Western, a part of Cengage Learning, Inc. Reproduced by permission. www .cengage.com/permissions.

Motivating workers to perform high-quality work consistently is one of the most challenging jobs a supervisor faces. Two ways to do this are to (1) let employees know you expect quality performance and (2) involve workers in achieving quality.

Let Employees Know You Expect Quality Performance   Many firms could be said to try to inspect quality into their product or service rather than make it right the first time. Fortunately, some companies and supervisors emphasize the right way from the start. They do this by stating their quality expectations for a job and include these expectations in training new personnel.

A large bank trains new tellers not only in the technical aspects of the job, but also how to interact with customers. In a number of trial runs, a "customer" walks up to the teller to complete a hypothetical transaction. The teller's actions are observed by a number of trainees and the trainer, and a critique is given of the way the customer was handled. Frequently, an experienced teller demonstrates how the situation should have been handled. Included are such actions as smiling, looking directly at the customer, calling the customer by name, and efficiently handling the transaction. As a result, the bank's quality expectations are instilled in new tellers.

The best place to make an impact regarding your quality expectations is with the new employee. Yet many current employees may have spotty quality records. What can you do about this? We can tell you one thing not to do! Ignoring poor-quality performance results in

1. The existing employee getting the message you do not expect any better or that mediocre quality is acceptable to you.
2. Other employees also assuming mediocre performance is acceptable.

Assuming workers know the quality standards, you must exercise supervisory control over quality. Sometimes a quality control specialist will help a line supervisor determine the quality of workers' performance by presenting run charts, histograms, or other statistical tools. In many departments, however, the supervisor plays the only role.

Involve Workers in Achieving and Controlling Quality   As Peter Coors, of Coors Brewing, puts it, "We're moving from an environment where the supervisor says, 'This is the way it is going to be done,' to an environment where the supervisor can grow with the changes, get his [or her] group together and say 'Look, you guys are operating the equipment. What do you think we ought to do?'"[6]

SSM Health Care (SSMHC), a St. Louis, Missouri, not-for-profit health system that won the first Baldrige given in the health care category (2002), makes extensive use of employee involvement teams. The company addresses such issues as developing standardized ways to care for SSMHC patients at its 24 hospitals and nursing homes in four states to improving outcomes of patients with congestive heart failure.[7]

Quality teams are an important part of the quality scene. These may include special cross-functional teams, self-directed teams, or teams from within individual work groups. Problems (and opportunities) can be brought up by team members, team leaders, or higher management. Many companies allow these teams to call in staff experts for information or expertise as needed.

At Pella Windows, a standard team kaizen session—the Japanese term for continuous improvement—meets anywhere from one to five days to address important quality issues. Over a thousand such yearly sessions have been the norm for Pella's kaizen teams. A typical five-day schedule works like this: Get everyone thinking about the problem and how to attack it on Monday, come up with tentative solutions on Tuesday, and, if it's a production problem, move the machinery that night. Start working the new arrangement on Wednesday, tweaking as necessary. On Thursday, prove that it works, and on Friday show it off to everyone.[8]

EXHIBIT 14-19
Characteristics of
Effective Employee
Involvement Teams

- Managers at all levels, especially at the top, should be committed to the concept and give it their unqualified support.
- Projects undertaken should relate directly—or at least indirectly—to participants' work.
- Projects should be team efforts, not individual activities.
- Participants should be trained in quality-control, decision-making, and problem-solving techniques.
- Team leaders also should be trained in group dynamics and leadership of a group.
- Teams should be given feedback—in the form of results—regarding their recommendations and solutions.

Exhibit 14-19 presents the overall characteristics of effective employee involvement teams. The kinds of teams we have discussed are implemented formally and require top management's approval and commitment. *Individual supervisors may, however, capture the spirit of employee involvement on their own.* The following comments from the manager of a hotel convention center, show what can be achieved by encouraging employees to become involved:

The best quality ideas come from the people directly involved in the work. Frequently, poor quality is not caused by something they directly control. We noted many clients show up for a meeting and say the room arrangement is not what they requested. This often required hurriedly rearranging a stage, tables, and chairs for as many as 700 people. The clients would get flustered, as did our people.

The problem was our meeting coordinator would talk with the client, usually by phone, and take instructions as to how the meeting room should be set up. There was much room for interpretation as to exactly what the client wanted and the last-minute changes drove everyone nuts.

We presented this problem to a team of four of our workers who met, studied the process used by our meeting coordinator, and learned she usually took instructions by phone. This left much room for interpreting what the client wanted. They also learned that often the person who called in to make the booking wasn't the one who had responsibility for the event, but was perhaps a secretary or an assistant. This person's choice of room arrangement would then get overridden when the group arrived. Our team developed a form that graphically illustrates alternatives for arranging our rooms and audiovisual equipment we provide. The client now selects the desired alternative, signs the form, and returns it to our coordinator. We now have something specific to go by, and our client is more committed to it. We'll still meet their last-minute needs or make adjustments if needed, but we've only had two such major cases all year.

7. *Describe the supervisor's role in supporting lean concepts.*

The lesson here is to seek out workers' advice on how to improve the quality of their work. Because they are so directly involved in the work, they frequently have excellent suggestions.

Lean Approach

The lean organization is interested in increasing value for the customer while using fewer resources.

Learning and Applying Some Lean Concepts

The **Lean Approach** consists of techniques and approaches aimed at eliminating waste. Lean concepts can be applied to all types of business, not just manufacturing. The supervisor can support managements' efforts in building a lean organization by focusing on eliminating waste, using just-in-time inventory control, and adopting five S (5S) practices.

Eliminating Waste

Eliminating waste is often considered by its narrowest definition—when material is misused and must be discarded. A lean operation thinks more broadly about the elimination of waste. Lean operations view waste as anything that does not add value. The lean organization takes the customer's viewpoint of value. In a lean organization, there are **seven types of waste**: overproduction, movement, transportation, waiting, extra processing, defects, and inventory. Each of these will be discussed below.

seven types of waste

In a lean organization, there are seven types of waste: overproduction, movement, transportation, waiting, extra processing, defects, and inventory.

1. Overproducing is making too much too soon. Materials are purchased before they are needed to serve the customer. Labor to produce the product is scheduled before it is needed. Space is wasted storing the product until the customer needs it.
2. Movement is another form of waste. If employees are walking from area to area without adding value to the product, this is wasteful. The manager needs to carefully observe the work area to determine if poor layout, work design, or product design is the cause of the movement. Tools and materials needed for production should be conveniently located and thereby eliminate the need for unnecessary travel.
3. Transportation within the same facility or from facility to facility can be wasteful. Management focusing on lean should carefully consider the location of production, warehouses, and supplier locations. The lean organization attempts to locate production, warehousing, and supplier facilities as close together as possible.
4. Waiting is a form of waste due to inactivity. Machinery that stopped operating is inactive. The employee who stopped working is inactive. Perhaps the machinery and employee are idle because they are waiting for a material delivery. The machinery may be idle due to a breakdown or lack of sufficient maintenance resources. The employee may be idle due to a lack of the proper tool or insufficient work instructions. It is the role of the manager to investigate the cause of inactivity and initiate corrective action.
5. Examples of waste due to overprocessing include unnecessary inspections, unnecessary steps or time added to production, or outdated product designs. The supervisor should work closely with product development and engineering personnel to eliminate extra processing waste.
6. Defects result in rework or scrap. The customer determines if the quality of the product or service is acceptable. The product or service either meets the customers' expectations or falls short of expectations. Shortfalls are defective. Rework requires additional resources in order to correct the product. The resources can include materials, labor, energy, and machine capacity. The poor-quality product evaluated as scrap will likely end up in a landfill.
7. Reducing or eliminating the need for inventories is a challenging goal, but lean organizations seek to produce only the products needed by the customer, when they are needed. This is a challenging endeavor. Holding excess inventory is costly. Some of the costs associated with excess inventory are space, insurance, theft, obsolescence, and scrap due to damage.

Just-in-Time (JIT) Inventory Control

JIT

A system whereby materials (inputs) arrive as close as feasible to the time they are needed in the production or service process.

Pioneered by Toyota, **JIT** is a system whereby materials (inputs) arrive as close as feasible to the time they are needed in the production or service process. Through enhanced technologies, companies link with their suppliers to keep them informed about their up-to-the-minute needs. JIT enhances an organization's flexibility and profitability by minimizing or, in some cases, completely eliminating inventory holdings and storage costs. Toyota Motors is a well-known inventory manager, such that its Georgetown (KY) plant has only

2.8 hours of inventory on hand. The majority of the plant's suppliers are located within 200 miles and parts are delivered up to 16 times each day, but the plant saves millions.[9] Other companies like Walmart, Home Depot, and Trader Joe's also practice JIT from their hundreds of suppliers.

Implementing 5S Practices

5S practices

The 5S's are sort, straighten, shine, standardize, and sustain.

Promoting good housekeeping is essential in a variety of production environments. For the lean organization, adopting **5S practices** is a key tool. The 5S's are sort, straighten, shine, standardize, and sustain.

Sort, the first of the 5S's, guides the supervisor to remove unneeded materials from the work area. The supervisor works with the employees to keep only what is needed. Once the work team succeeds in removing the unneeded items, the employees are ready for *straighten*, the second of the 5S's. There is a place for everything and everything is put in its place. The end result is a neatly arranged and organized work area. The employees are ready to *shine* and clean the work area. The cleaning needs to be thorough and complete. This is why it is called shine. Clean until the area shines. The cleaning process needs to be formalized and *standardized*. Standard procedures for cleaning need to be written. Checklists can be used to make sure nothing is forgotten. The employees can be involved in writing procedures and checklists. The supervisor needs to make sure the employees are trained to follow the procedures. In order to *sustain* the first four practices, the supervisor needs to periodically review and evaluate the team's performance. To motivate employees, the supervisor may choose to use rewards and incentives to encourage sustaining good housekeeping.

STOP AND THINK

Read this article about Trader Joe's by following the link: http://money.cnn .com/2010/08/20/news/companies/inside_trader_joes_full_version.fortune/index .htm.

Are TQM and the Lean Approach part of the reason Trader Joe's is so successful? What aspects of TQM and the Lean Approach does Trader Joe's utilize?

Promoting Employee Safety

The final aspect of supervisory control we discuss in this chapter is employee safety. This subject has been in the business limelight since 1970, primarily as a result of the government's passage of the Occupational Safety and Health Act (OSHA). Management has had an interest in employee safety for over a century because safety, efficiency, and productivity are closely related.

The results of poor safety are documented, and even though safety performance in the United States has improved in recent years, the costs of poor safety have gone in the opposite direction. According to the *2017 Liberty Mutual Workplace Safety Index*, the most disabling workplace injuries and illnesses in 2014 (most recent data) "cost U.S. employers $59.9 billion" (see Exhibit 14-20). "The top three causes—which collectively represent almost half of the cost of the leading accidents—are overexertion ($13.8 billion, 23 percent), falls on same level ($10.6 billion, 17.7 percent) and falls to lower level ($5.5 billion, 9.2 percent)."[10]

EXHIBIT 14-20

Top 10 Causes of
Disabling Injuries in
2009 ($ in billions)

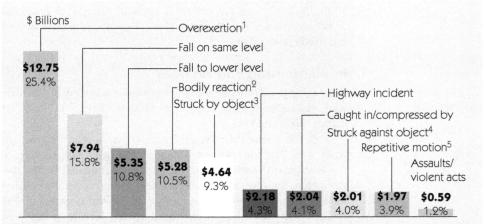

1 Overexertion—Injuries from excessive lifting, pushing, pulling, holding, carrying, throwing
2 Bodily reaction—Injuries from bending, climbing, reachimg, standing, sitting, slipping, or tripping without falling
3 Struck by object—Such as a tool falling on a worker from above
4 Struck against object—Such as a worker walking into a door
5 Repetitive motion—Injuries due to repeated stress or strain

Source: Liberty Mutual Research Institute for Safety, *Scientific Update* 14, no. 3 (2011), p. 7. Reproduced with permission from the Liberty Mutual Research Institute for Safety.

STOP AND THINK

Do such organizations as banks, supermarkets, and department stores really need to be concerned about occupational safety and health?

---

8. *Explain what the Occupational Safety and Health Administration (OSHA) does.*

Occupational Safety and Health Administration (OSHA)

The federal Occupational Safety and Health Administration was created by the Occupational Safety and Health Act in 1970 to ensure safe working conditions for employees.

What the Occupational Safety and Health Administration Does

The **Occupational Safety and Health Administration (OSHA)** is a federal agency created by the Occupational Safety and Health Act in 1970 and went into operation in April 1971. Previously, different states had different emphases on occupational health and safety. To ensure uniformity and enforcement, the federal government stepped into the picture. OSHA ensures state governments, labor unions, and management provide consistently safer and healthier working conditions for employees.

OSHA requires organizations to keep safety logs and records of illnesses and injuries incurred on the job (see Exhibit 14-21). OSHA also has the right to develop standards, conduct inspections to see that standards are met, and enforce compliance by issuing citations and penalties against organizations that fail to comply. In addition, OSHA provides help by performing pre-investigations upon invitation from the organization.

Factors Influencing Safety

Several factors affect job safety. Among these are (1) the size of the organization, (2) the type of industry, and (3) the people.

Size of Organization   The safest places to work are the smallest and largest organizations. Companies with fewer than 20 employees or more than 1,000 employees have better safety statistics than medium-sized organizations.

EXHIBIT 14-21

Record Keeping Required by OSHA

OSHA's *Form 301*
Injury and Illness Incident Report

This *Injury and Illness Incident Report* is one of the first forms you must fill out when a recordable work-related injury or illness has occurred. Together with the *Log of Work-Related Injuries and Illnesses* and the accompanying *Summary*, these forms help the employer and OSHA develop a picture of the extent and severity of work-related incidents.

Within 7 calendar days after you receive information that a recordable work-related injury or illness has occurred, you must fill out this form or an equivalent. Some state workers' compensation, insurance, or other reports may be acceptable substitutes. To be considered an equivalent form, any substitute must contain all the information asked for on this form.

According to Public Law 91-596 and 29 CFR 1904, OSHA's recordkeeping rule, you must keep this form on file for 5 years following the year to which it pertains.

If you need additional copies of this form, you may photocopy and use as many as you need.

Completed by ___JOSEPH DIXON___

Title ___SUPERVISOR___

Phone ___903_465_1996___ Date ___6/23/2018___

Attention: This form contains information relating to employee health and must be used in a manner that protects the confidentiality of employees to the extent possible while the information is being used for occupational safety and health purposes.

U.S. Department of Labor
Occupational Safety and Health Administration

Form approved OMB no. 1218-0176

Information about the employee

1) Full name ___Robert L. Whitehead___
2) Street ___707 Eighth St.___
   City ___Sherman___ State ___TX___ ZIP ___75059___
3) Date of birth ___12/01/68___
4) Date hired ___3/14/99___
5) ☑ Male ☐ Female

Information about the physician or other health care professional

6) Name of physician or other health care professional ___RITA SORENSON, RN___
7) If treatment was given away from the worksite, where was it given?
   Facility ___N/A___
   Street ___
   City ___ State ___ ZIP ___
8) Was employee treated in an emergency room?
   ☐ Yes ☐ No
9) Was employee hospitalized overnight as an in-patient?
   ☐ Yes ☑ No

Information about the case

10) Case number from the *Log* ___31___
11) Date of injury or illness ___6/21/18___
12) Time employee began work ___7:30___ AM ☑ PM
13) Time of event ___2:09___ AM ☑ PM ☐ Check if time cannot be determined
14) What was the employee doing just before the incident occurred? ___CLEANING POLES IN PREPARATION FOR PAINTING. WAS STANDING ON STEPLADDER.___
15) What happened? ___As he put splatter down, sodium hypochlorite drifted inside face shield and entered right eye___
16) What was the injury or illness? ___CHEMICAL BURN in RIGHT EYE___
17) What object or substance directly harmed the employee? ___SODIUM HYPOCHLORATE___
18) If the employee died, when did death occur? Date of death ___N/A___

Public reporting burden for this collection of information is estimated to average 22 minutes per response, including time for reviewing instructions, searching existing data sources, gathering and maintaining the data needed, and completing and reviewing the collection of information. Persons are not required to respond to the collection of information unless it displays a current valid OMB control number. If you have any comments about this estimate or any other aspects of this data collection, including suggestions for reducing this burden, contact: US Department of Labor, OSHA Office of Statistical Analysis, Room N-3644, 200 Constitution Avenue, NW, Washington, DC 20210. Do not send the completed forms to this office.

STOP AND THINK

What do you think accounts for the fact that large companies of, say, *10,000* employees have better safety performance than those with *100* employees?

In a small firm, the owner or manager is more personally involved with employees and tends to take on the role of safety officer. Large firms have more resources available, such as safety departments, whose sole mission is to improve employee safety. Medium-sized firms have neither the direct personal involvement of the top manager nor the resources to create full-fledged safety departments. Often, the person assigned to oversee the safety function has additional job responsibilities. The safety focus therefore may be diluted by other important assignments.

Type of Industry   Some types of industry are safer than others. Exhibit 14-22 shows rates of occupational injury and illness for various industries. Note the rates are highest for general medical and surgical hospitals, general merchandise stores, administrative and support services, and ambulatory health care services. But also consider safety issues affect a wide spectrum of service industries, such as limited-service and full-service restaurants, as well as supermarkets and grocery stores.

Despite increased safety emphasis, some industries still suffer from a high incidence of employee lost workdays due to job-related injuries/illnesses.

EXHIBIT 14-22

Rates of Occupational Injuries and Illnesses for Various Industries, 2010

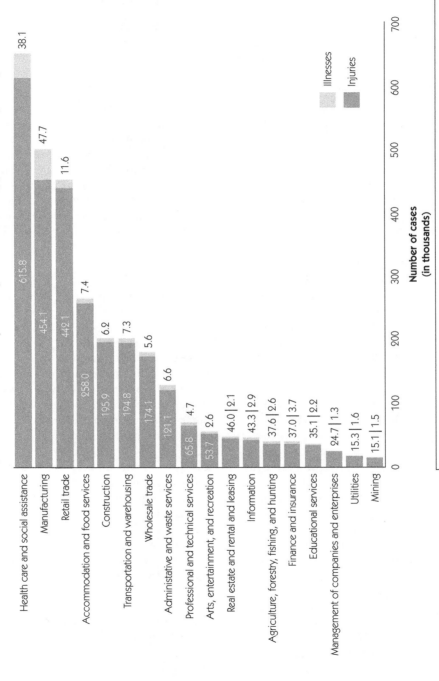

Distribution of nonfatal occupational injuries and illnesses by private industry sector, 2010

Similar to the distribution of injuries and illnesses reported among all private industry establishments in 2010, injuries accounted for most cases reported among individual industry sectors—illnesses accounted for only a fraction of cases reported in each industry sector.

Source: Bureau of Labor Statistics.

Additionally, look at the seriousness of cases of the industries listed. General medical and surgical hospitals may have more serious accidents, resulting in a greater number of lost work days per incident.

Despite increased safety emphasis, some industries still suffer from a high incidence of employee lost workdays due to job-related injuries/illnesses.

People   The attitudes of managers and supervisors strongly influence the safety of work performance. Moreover, employees' attitudinal, emotional, and physical factors definitely impact their safety performance.

Causes of Accidents

What causes on-the-job accidents? Basically, job-related accidents are caused by three types of factors: human, technical, and environmental. *Human factors* include carelessness, horseplay, fighting, drug use, poor understanding of equipment or processes, risk taking, poor attitudes, and fatigue. Human factors account for most work-related injuries. *Technical factors* include unsafe mechanical, chemical, and physical conditions, such as those caused by defective tools and equipment, poor mechanical construction or design, or improper personal protective equipment (safety shoes, glasses, or mechanical guards or shields). *Environmental factors* are agents that surround the job, such as poor housekeeping, inadequate lighting and ventilation, or management pressure to increase output.

The Supervisor's Role in Promoting Safety

9. Describe the supervisor's role in promoting safety.

Good safety practices among employees help the supervisor in many ways. For one thing, on-the-job injuries can take up much of a supervisor's time because he or she may have to fill out accident reports, attend meetings to investigate the injury, and make recommendations (see Exhibit 14-23). Furthermore, safety is linked to productivity. The work group's productivity suffers when an injured employee is treated for or is recovering from an accident. Temporary or full-time replacements must be recruited, selected, and trained, and an inexperienced worker is unlikely to be as productive as the more experienced employee being replaced. This drop in productivity also is experienced by other employees. The human resources employees must devote time to the hiring process. The accounting employees must make arrangements for the replacement employees' pay.

The injured employee may be hesitant to report an accident. There can be several reasons why the employee would choose not to report. The experienced employee may feel embarrassed if the accident was due to an unsafe act or lapse in judgment. The inexperienced employees may believe reporting the accident would threaten their job. Perhaps the work team has a longstanding accident-free record. The injured employee may not report the accident to avoid disappointing the team by ending their accident-free record. The work team also can exert their influence on an employee to not report an accident if an accident would result in the loss of a safety contest, safety-related incentive, or reward.

Under certain circumstances, an employee may report an accident that did not occur, intentionally cause an accident, or report an injury that occurred outside of the workplace. These situations are serious and need to be brought to the attention of management. Because human factors are the major cause of work-related injuries, the supervisor, as top management's link with operating employees, plays a crucial role in employee safety.

EXHIBIT 14-23
Personal Injury
Investigation

Injured:	Fred Hanna
Position:	Lab Assistant
Presiding:	L. C. Smithson, Technical Supt.
Date of meeting:	4/15/2018
Time of meeting:	2:34 P.M.
Place of meeting:	Plant Conference Room
Present:	L. C. Smithson (Technical Supt.), Fred Hanna (injured), Jim Berry (Housekeeping), Tom Ahens (Safety Director), Kim Jernigan (Supervisor)
Nature of injury:	Fractured distal end of radius, right arm
Lost time:	42 days (estimated)
Accident time and date:	4/13/2018 at 7:15 A.M.
Cause of injury:	Floor was wet—appeared to be water. Investigation revealed that bags of Seperan (a synthetic polymer) had been rearranged during the 11:00 P.M.–7:00 A.M. shift. One bag was torn, and its contents trickled onto the floor, causing it to be exceptionally slippery when washed at the end of the shift. Janitor noticed but did not flag it or attempt to remove hazard, as he noted at the end of his shift.

Corrective steps/recommendations:

1. Apply grit to slippery areas; mark with appropriate warning signs.
2. Remind incoming shift personnel of hazardous conditions.
3. Communicate to incoming shift personnel any job priorities.
4. Store Seperan in a more remote area of the plant.

He or she is accountable for safety, just as for output or quality. Good safety control by the supervisor begins with a positive attitude.

"Safety is very important at the company and especially in my work unit," said Vera Edwards, a machine tender for Supreme Manufacturing. "When you drive into the parking lot, a large sign shows our company's safety record for the week and the year. Our supervisor is always talking safety, we have safety meetings monthly, and there are posters and signs throughout the work area. Our supervisor also makes us toe the line in following safety rules. He can really be tough on you when he catches you bending a rule such as not using your goggles or failing to put on your machine guard."

Exhibit 14-24 shows a number of steps supervisors can take to improve safety performance in their departments. Even though supervisors play a critical role in controlling safety, they cannot do it alone. Top management must be committed to such factors as proper plant layout and design, safe machinery and equipment, and good physical working conditions. Note how recognition by management plays a major role in reinforcing safety for UPS, with over 2,400 nonmanagement employee Comprehensive Health and Safety Committees at its locations throughout the United States.

EXHIBIT 14-24

What Supervisors Can
Do to Improve Safety

- Push for upgraded safety equipment and safer work methods.
- Establish and communicate safety goals for the department.
- Clearly communicate safety requirements to all employees.
- Listen to employee job complaints about safety-related matters, including noise, fatigue, and working conditions.
- Make sure new employees thoroughly understand equipment and safety rules.
- Make sure safety rules are kept up to date.
- Prohibit use of unsafe or damaged equipment.
- Encourage safety suggestions from your workers.
- Post safety bulletins, slogans, and posters to reinforce the need for safety.
- Refuse to let rush jobs cause relaxed safety standards.
- Set a proper example. Don't bend safety rules yourself.
- Conduct periodic safety meetings, with demonstrations by employee safety specialists or insurance representatives.
- Refuse to tolerate horseplay.
- Compete with other departments in safety contests.
- Report to employees any accidents that occur elsewhere in the company.
- Review past accident records for trends and insights.
- Encourage reporting of unsafe conditions.
- Make regular safety inspections of all major equipment.
- Include your employees in periodic safety tours and inspections.
- Enforce the rules when they are broken—take appropriate disciplinary action to demonstrate your safety commitment.
- Look for signs of fatigue in employees, such as massaging shoulders, rubbing eyes, and stretching or shifting position to relieve pain or fatigue. In such a case, relief for the employee may be warranted.
- Thoroughly investigate all accidents and attempt to remedy the causes.
- Develop a system for rewarding or acknowledging excellent safety conduct.

At UPS, drivers travel a million miles yearly with less than one avoidable accident! This performance is no coincidence; UPS strongly emphasizes driver safety. At 5-year intervals, drivers with no avoidable accidents are feted with ceremonies at the local level. Drivers with a 25-year unblemished record are inducted into the company's Circle of Honor at a national celebration dinner where they receive a camel-hair blazer and special plaque. Each year UPS publishes the names of its 2,700-plus Circle of Honor members in The Wall Street Journal *and in* USA Today.[11]

Chapter Review

1. *Explain the concept of productivity.*

This chapter examined three aspects of control important to supervisors: productivity, quality, and safety. Productivity is a measure of outputs compared to inputs. Company-wide, it refers to the total value of the units or services a company produced as compared to the total cost of producing them. Productivity can be increased by raising output with the same input, decreasing input and maintaining the same output, or increasing output while decreasing input.

2. *Identify and explain the ways in which management, government, unions, and employees affect productivity.*

Four groups influence the productivity of U.S. firms. Management is considered by most experts to be the most influential group because it controls spending for new or upgraded facilities and technology. Government also plays a role through its policies that require financial outlays by companies to meet federal laws for air and water pollution, energy, safety, and other regulatory requirements. Unions play a role in that, while management's job is to increase efficiency through new labor-saving technology and work methods, the role of unions is to protect the jobs of their members. Finally, employees play a role through their skill levels, motivation, and job commitment.

3. *Describe steps supervisors can take to increase productivity.*

Actions supervisors can take to increase productivity include upgrading workers' skills through training, improving worker motivation, using machinery and equipment better, improving quality, and preventing accidents.

Cost control is an important measure of a supervisor's productivity. One helpful device is a budget, which shows expected outcome for a given period expressed in numbers. Robotics, RFID, and computer-assisted manufacturing (CAM) are three recent productivity enhancement measures.

4. *Differentiate between total quality and quality control.*

A second major area discussed in this chapter was quality. Total quality is the entire system of policies, procedures, and guidelines an organization institutes to attain and maintain quality. Quality control, on the other hand, consists of after-the-fact measurements to see if quality standards are actually being met.

Quality control consists of actions taken during or after production to measure, analyze, and, if necessary, correct quality problems. It is a much narrower concept than total quality, which is an organizationwide commitment to quality and includes such factors as top management commitment, employee training, relationships with customers and suppliers, continuous quality improvement, and employee involvement in the quality process.

5. *Describe the role of variance in controlling quality.*

An understanding of variance is important in controlling quality. Common cause variance is built into organizational processes and considered normal. Common causes normally can be corrected only through management action to improve a process through such things as upgrading raw materials, using more sophisticated equipment, or providing additional training. The supervisor needs to coach the employee experiencing common cause variation not to make unnecessary adjustments to machinery or processes. On the other hand, special cause variance is nonroutine and entails identifying the problem, isolating it, examining the cause, and remedying it. It might involve an erratic piece of equipment, damaged raw materials, or an employee who is not performing properly. The supervisor needs the ability to recognize special cause variation and work with employee teams to take the appropriate corrective action.

6. *Identify some important tools for controlling quality.*

A number of tools are available to help in controlling quality. Often these tools are used by individuals who are part of special problem-solving or quality-improvement teams.

These include such tools as check sheets, flowcharts, histograms, run charts, Pareto charts, cause-and-effect diagrams, and control charts. These tools are applicable to a broad range of manufacturing and service-related situations.

7. *Describe the supervisor's role in promoting lean concepts.*
The supervisor plays a key role in eliminating waste and implementing 5S practices. The supervisor needs to learn the seven types of waste, not just discarded materials.

8. *Explain what the Occupational Safety and Health Administration (OSHA) does.*
Employee safety has become important to organizations in recent years, especially since the passage of the Occupational Safety and Health Act in 1970. The Occupational Safety and Health Administration (OSHA) is charged with enforcing compliance with the law. It sets standards and regulations, requires organizations to maintain safety logs and records, conducts inspections, and has the authority to issue citations and penalties for violations found.

9. *Describe the supervisor's role in promoting safety.*
Supervisors play an important role in promoting safety. Because supervisors are the primary management link with operating employees, supervisory behavior greatly impacts employee safety performance. Supervisors do this in many ways, such as in setting departmental safety goals, ensuring employees understand safety requirements and procedures, conducting safety meetings, encouraging safety suggestions from employees, investigating accidents thoroughly, and enforcing rules when they are broken.

Key Terms

productivity, p. 414
robot, p. 422
radio frequency identification (RFID), p. 422
computer-assisted manufacturing (CAM), p. 422
Deming's 85-15 rule, p. 424
total quality, p. 426

quality control, p. 427
check sheets, p. 429
flowchart, p. 429
histogram, p. 430
run chart, p. 430
Pareto charts, p. 430
cause-and-effect diagram, p. 432
control chart, p. 432

Lean Approach, p. 435
seven types of waste, p. 436
just-in-time (JIT) inventory control, p. 436
5S practices, p. 437
Occupational Safety and Health Administration (OSHA), p. 438

Discussion Questions

1. Explain what happened to U.S. productivity in 2007.
2. Do you believe management and unions must always be on opposite sides of the productivity issue? Why or why not?
3. Identify some of the steps supervisors can take to improve their department's productivity.
4. How does quality control differ from total quality? Explain. Describe the role of variance in controlling quality.
5. Identify each of the following tools for controlling quality: Pareto chart, run chart, and flowchart.
6. Explain the supervisor's role in supporting lean concepts.
7. What does OSHA do?
8. Describe some ways supervisors impact safety performance.

Skill Builder 14.1

Information

Interpersonal Skill

Determining Productivity Measurements

In this chapter, you learned productivity is the ratio of inputs to outputs. Consider each of the following organizations:

(a) bank
(b) community college
(c) large laundry/dry cleaners
(d) hospital
(e) restaurant

Instructions:

1. For each of the organizations shown, identify several important productivity measures managers could use to measure the efficiency of their organization. (Hint: Think broadly, including measures that go beyond profitability or cost measures.)
2. Meet with groups of four to six other students and discuss your items.
3. Present your results to the whole class.

Skill Builder 14.2

Resources

Information

Systems

Quality Survey

Visit a local fast-food restaurant, such as McDonald's, Burger King, or Wendy's, and order a meal.

Instructions:

1. During your visit, perform a quality analysis of the store, including but not limited to:
   (a) external store appearance, including shrubbery, cleanliness, and upkeep of outer building and parking lot
   (b) drive-through, including ease, speed, and accuracy of service
   (c) cleanliness of inner store, including tables, floors, and restrooms
   (d) employee factors, including appearance, friendliness, and efficiency
   (e) service factors, including speed and accuracy
   (f) food quality, including taste, freshness, temperature, and portion size.

2. Assume you are the store manager and want to improve the areas you found to be weak. Outline the corrective actions you would take.
3. Meet with other students in groups of five to six to discuss your findings.

Skill Builder 14.3

Resources

Interpersonal Skill

Implementing Lean 5S Practices

One of the cornerstones of lean organizations is the effective implementation of 5S practices. The first three of these are sort, straighten, and shine. To accomplish sort, the employees need to discard unneeded items, and the straighten practice requires organizing the needed items. The third practice, shine, is cleaning the work area until it shines. After the employees accomplish the first three practices, they need to recognize this is not a one-time effort. Lacking a plan to sustain these practices, in time unneeded items will creep back into the work area. The work area will revert to a disorganized condition. It will be dirty and need cleaning.

(Continued)

Information

Systems

After the employees complete the first three practices, the supervisor needs to focus on accomplishing the fourth and fifth practices: standardize and sustain. In implementing the practices of standardize and sustain, the supervisor is on a path to build a permanent 5S practice. The practice of standardize requires the supervisor to write standard operating procedures and checklists for the first three practices. For the fifth practice, sustain, the supervisor formulates a method to evaluate employee performance and provide incentives to encourage employee success. These practices need to be formalized and structured so they become part of the employees' work routine.

1. Meet with groups of students to discuss strategies for assigning the first three practices to employees. Will you assign the work by area, by task, or by employee preference? Will you rotate assignments?

2. How will you motivate the employees to continue to sort, straighten, and shine?

3. How will you evaluate employee performance?

Skill Builder 14.4

Resources

Interpersonal Skill

Information

Systems

Increasing Safety Performance

Assume the role of a newly appointed store manager of a regional food chain superstore. All stores in the chain have been pressured to turn a profit in this highly competitive industry. While the former store manager achieved his profit goal, he fell far short in another: the store's safety performance. You are expected to do much better.

Last year the store accident rate was twice that of other stores in the chain: 16 reportable incidents per 100 employees, 9 of which involved lost workdays. The lost days involved cuts, burns, slips, and falls. Many cuts occurred in the meat and deli areas; two burns occurred in the bakery area. One bagger sustained a fall in the parking lot while riding an empty grocery cart, a clear violation of policy. But the most serious fall resulted when a janitor left puddles of wax in an aisle and failed to put up warning cones when his work was interrupted to clean up a spill in another area. Another employee slipped on the wax and fell, injuring his left leg and head. This injury resulted in nine months (and counting) of disability costs, nearly $200,000 in medical costs, and a reserve of about $150,000 for future rehabilitation payments. Analysis of the injury-causing incidents showed all were caused by human error.

As the new store manager, you are expected to immediately address the safety issues with your employees.

Instructions:

1. Outline a plan for bringing your employees' safety performance next year up to the average of other stores in the chain. You may assume your boss has approved a one-time $1,000 safety budget allocation to spend as needed to help you achieve this goal.

2. Meet with a group of other students to share your ideas. Your instructor may ask you to select a spokesperson to summarize the ideas of your team members.

Skill Builder 14.5

Interpersonal Skill

Information

Resources

Clarence, an Ally in Improving Labor Productivity

Sarah Nelson was the receiving department supervisor for a Fortune 500 manufacturer. One of the tasks in the receiving department was weighing products by placing them on a floor scale. The weight was written on paper that was stapled to the product box. New technology, a scale mounted on a lift truck, eliminated the need for the floor scale and the job of floor scale operator. Sarah's boss asked her to implement this new technology and do away with the floor scale operator job.

Clarence was the floor scale operator. Although his job was to be eliminated, he would be reassigned to another job. Fortunately, the business was growing and other work was available. Clarence was the department's senior employee. This was one of the highest paid and easiest jobs in the department. He performed these duties well and had one of the best attendance and safety records. Many employees quietly joked this monotonous and simple job was ideally suited to Clarence. Before joining the company, Clarence was a boxer and an alcoholic. These activities exacted their toll on him. He walked slowly, was quiet, and sat alone during lunch and breaks. Employees and managers rarely talked to Clarence. They avoided him. They knew him only as a former boxer and recovering alcoholic. As his supervisor, Sarah planned to involve Clarence in implementing this new technology. It was her goal to turn Clarence into an ally and champion for this labor productivity project.

Instructions:

1. How can Sarah gain Clarence's support to eliminate his job? Develop a plan of action to gain Clarence's support.
2. Team up with another student and share your plans with each other.
3. Based on what you both have shared, come to a consensus on how best to approach Clarence and prepare a role play to perform in front of the class to demonstrate how Sarah can be successful.

CASE 14-1

USING QUALITY TOOLS:

Welz Business Machines sells and services a variety of copiers, computers, and other office equipment. The company receives many calls daily for service, sales, accounting, and other departments. All calls are handled centrally by customer service representatives and routed to other individuals as appropriate.

A number of customers complained about long waits when calling for service. A market research study found customers became irritated if the call was not answered within five rings. Scott Welz, the company president, authorized the customer service department manager, Tim Nagy, to study the problem and find a method to shorten the call-waiting time. Tim met with his service representatives who answered calls (Robin Coder, Raul Venegas, LaMarr Jones, Mark Staley, and Nancy Shipe)

to attempt to determine the reasons for long waiting times. The following conversation ensued:

Nagy: This is a serious problem. How a customer phone inquiry is answered is the first impression the customer receives from us. As you know, this company was founded on efficient and friendly service to all our customers. It's obvious why customers have to wait: You're on the phone with another customer. Can you think of any reasons that keep you on the phone for an unnecessarily long time?

Coder: I've noticed quite often the person I need to route the call to is not present. It takes time to transfer the call and see if it is answered. If the person is not there, I end up apologizing and transferring the call to another extension.

(Continued)

Nagy: You're right, Robin. Sales personnel often are out of the office on sales calls, away on trips to preview new products, or away from their desks for a variety of reasons. What else might cause this problem?

Venegas: I get irritated at customers who spend a great deal of time complaining about a problem I cannot do anything about except refer to someone else. Of course, I listen and sympathize with them, but this eats up a lot of time.

Jones: Some customers call so often, they think we're long-lost friends and strike up a personal conversation.

Nagy: That's not always a bad thing, you realize.

Jones: Sure, but it delays my answering other calls.

Shipe: It's not always the customer's fault. During lunch, we're not all available to answer the phone.

Venegas: Right after we open at 9 A.M., we get a rush of calls. I think many of the delays are caused by these peak periods.

Coder: I've noticed the same thing between 4 and 5 P.M.

Nagy: I've had a few comments from department managers who received calls that didn't fall in their areas of responsibility and had to be transferred again.

Staley: But that doesn't cause delays at our end.

Shipe: That's right, Mark, but I just realized sometimes I simply don't understand what the customer's problem really is. I spend a lot of time trying to get him or her to explain it better. Often, I have to route it to someone because other calls are waiting.

Venegas: Perhaps we need to have more knowledge of our products.

Nagy: Well, I think we've covered most of the major reasons why many customers have to wait. It seems to me we have four major reasons: the phones are short-staffed, the receiving party is not present, the

customer dominates the conversation, and you may not understand the customer's problem. Next, we need to collect some information about these possible causes. Raul, can you and Mark set up a data collection sheet we can use to track some of these things?

The next day, Venegas and Staley produced a sheet that enabled the staff to record the data. Over the next two weeks, the staff collected data on the frequency of reasons why some callers had to wait. The results are summarized as follows:

REASON	TOTAL NUMBER
A. Operators short-staffed	172
B. Receiving party not present	73
C. Customer dominates conversation	19
D. Lack of operator understanding	61
E. Other reasons	10

INSTRUCTIONS

Form groups of three to five students and, based on the conversation between Nagy and his staff,

1. Draw a cause-and-effect diagram.
2. Perform a Pareto analysis of the data collected.
3. Develop some possible actions that the company might take to improve the situation.

Source: Adapted from "The Quest for Higher Quality: *The Deming Prize and Quality Control*," by RICOH of America, Inc., and presented in James W. Dean and James R. Evans, *Total Quality: Management, Organization, and Strategy* (Mason, OH: South-Western, 1994), pp. 96–98. Reprinted with permission of South-Western, a division of Thomson Learning: www.thomsonrights.com.

CASE 14-2

ELIMINATING WASTE:

The Healthy Beverage Company (HBC) processes and bottles organic juices for the health conscious consumer. It uses only certified organic fruits and recycled packaging in the manufacture of its products. It recently experienced increased competition from large beverage companies. The large companies have access

to a variety of organic farmers and can negotiate better prices. These companies use similar packaging for their nonorganic carbonated beverages. Therefore, their packaging costs are lower due to the large quantities they purchase. Although its customers value products from small local organic businesses and realize organic products are more expensive than nonorganic, there is a limit to the premium they are willing to pay. HBC needs to lower its costs.

The president and founder of HBC hired a consultant to help her. The consultant recommended she implement lean concepts in her operations. They agreed to meet.

President: The employees of the Healthy Beverage Company are dedicated and hard working. Unfortunately, our best is no longer good enough. In order to compete, we must lower our costs.

Consultant: I recommend HBC implement lean concepts. The lean organization is interested in increasing value for the customer while using fewer resources. Taking a Lean Approach will result in lower costs.

President: This approach sounds like a good fit for our customers and our company culture. How do I start?

Consultant: Start by eliminating waste.

President: The employees are careful and dedicated. It is difficult to believe they are wasting materials.

Consultant: First, it is important to understand your customer views waste as anything that does not contribute to the value of your product.

President: That makes sense. Can you be more specific?

Consultant: Using the Lean Approach to eliminating waste considers seven types of waste, not simply materials tossed in the dumpster.

President: What are the seven types of waste?

Consultant: The seven types of waste are overproducing, movement, transportation, waiting, extra processing, defects, and inventory.

President: Do you recommend the supervisors focus on all seven?

Consultant: I recommend the supervisors begin by focusing on eliminating wasted movement and waiting. These two types of waste are often overlooked.

CASE QUESTIONS

1. Assume you are a supervisor working for the Healthy Beverage Company. How will you go about explaining the seven wastes to your employees?
2. Form groups of three to five students and brainstorm ways to reduce movement. Wasted movement occurs when an employee is walking without purpose. The employee is not adding value to the product. Why would this occur and how can it be corrected?
3. Form groups of three to five students and brainstorm ways to reduce waiting. What are some of the possible causes for employee waiting?

Notes

1. International Federation of Robotics, "World Robotics Report 2016," press release, September 29, 2016, https://ifr.org/ifr-press-releases/news/world-robotics-report-2016.
2. Machingo Nakamoto, "Battery Trouble Hinders Sony Bid for Global Brand Supremacy," *The Financial Times*, August 26, 2006, p. 19.
3. James W. Robinson, *Jack Welch and Leadership* (Roseville, CA: Prima Publishing Co., 2001), pp. 129–130.
4. James R. Evans and William Lindsay, *The Management and Control of Quality*, 5th ed. (Mason, OH: South-Western, 2002), pp. 604–605.
5. Deanne N. Den Hartog and Robert M. Verburg, "Service Excellence from the Employees' Point of View: The Role of First Line Supervisors," *Managing Service Quality* 12, no. 3 (2002), pp. 159–164.
6. Quoted in Evans and Lindsay, *The Management and Control of Quality*, p. 301.
7. Malcolm Baldrige National Quality Award Profile, http://www.nist.gov/public_affairs/releases/ssmhealth.htm (accessed November 22, 2002).
8. Philip Seikman, "Glass Act: How a Window Maker Rebuilt Itself; Not Waiting for Perfect Answers, Pella Conducted Thousands of Kaizen, or Continuous Improvement, Sessions," *Fortune* 142, no. 11 (November 13, 2000), p. 384.
9. Norihiko Shirouzu, "Why Toyota Wins Such High Marks on Quality Surveys," *The Wall Street Journal*, March 15, 2001, p. A1.
10. "The Most Serious Workplace Injuries Cost U.S. Companies $59.9 Billion Per Year," *2017 Liberty Mutual Workplace Safety Index*, https://www.libertymutualgroup.com/about-liberty-mutual-site/news-site/Pages/2017-Liberty-Mutual-Workplace-Safety-Index.aspx (retrieved July 16, 2017).
11. "National Safety Council Lauds UPS Safety Program," U.S. Newswire, June 24, 2002, p. 1008175.

15

Selecting, Appraising, and Disciplining Employees

LEARNING OBJECTIVES

After reading and studying this chapter, you should be able to:

1. *Explain who is responsible for selecting, appraising, and disciplining employees.*

2. *Describe the steps in the employee selection procedure, including the proper orientation of new employees.*

3. *Explain the importance of training and developing employees.*

4. *Explain what an employee performance appraisal is and who performs it.*

5. *State why performance-appraisal interviews are difficult for both the employee and the supervisor.*

6. *Define discipline and explain why it is necessary.*

7. *Describe how discipline is imposed under due process.*

8. *Explain the supervisor's disciplinary role.*

Here lies a man who knew how to enlist in his service better men than himself.

—Andrew Carnegie's Epitaph

No one is free who cannot command himself.

—Pythagoras

Dmitriy Shironosov/Alamy Stock Photo

Recruiting and mentoring the way Adrian Grubb has done for his employees can be an effective way to help develop and manage human resources.

Preview

ADRIAN GRUBB: GETTING THE MOST FROM EMPLOYEES When hiring someone for a job, it is important to achieve good person–job fit, which is when the individual's knowledge, skills, abilities, and experiences (KSA + Es) fit with the requirements of the job. But what do you do if you can't find a person with the requisite KSA + Es? They may have a great attitude but no skills or experiences. Let's hear from Adrian Grubb and see how he dealt with these issues.

Originally from New Orleans, LA, Adrian has over 18 years' management experience in the hospitality industry, manufacturing sector, and port management. Earlier in his career, he specialized in new restaurant openings for a Fortune 500 "casualesque restaurant chain." According to Adrian, "When we opened a new restaurant, it was protocol to hire individuals with experience for each job. If we needed a grill cook, we looked for someone that had been a grill cook before. For a dishwasher, we wanted someone with experience. But one time we were opening a store in a smaller college town, and the applicants applying for the jobs were college students and fast-food workers that didn't have the skills and experiences we were looking for. In order to find the right spot on the bus (a reference to the book *Good to Great*) for the new employees, we rotated them around throughout the course of training until we found the best spot for that employee."

Adrian's team got feedback from upper management to stick with the protocol and force feed the system, but he decided it was not in the company's best interest to follow this rule. He bucked the system. As Adrian puts it, "Rotating employees during training to find the right fit for the employee was the best way and it worked well"—so well, in fact, the new restaurant retained 80 percent of its employees, which is considerably above the industry's average of 40 percent for new restaurant openings. Adrian states, "It was so successful it became the blueprint for future store openings when faced with this problem."

Adrian also understands employees have a great amount of potential, "even though you may not recognize it at first. Sometimes you might hire for potential because you believe in them." He recounts a story when he was a manger with a different Fortune 500 restaurant group and an applicant he thought had potential was written off by the other managers. "This gentleman (we will call him Willie) had a great attitude and sometimes I truly believe we should hire for attitude; we don't just hire for skills. I can teach skills, but I can't teach attitude."

After several discussions with the other managers about whether to hire Willie, Adrian "put his foot down" and said, "I believe in him, and I'll take care of him; he's mine." Willie was hired, but he struggled trying to get his feet wet learning the system. According to Adrian, "On one particular shift when I was not there, the regional manager asked Willie to make a particular dish called the Enormous Nachos. There is really nothing enormous about it. It is a big plate, but it's for one person, so it really isn't ENORMOUS. But Willie took it literally and built this huge mound of an appetizer that seemed like it would feed a small village and presented it to the regional manager." The regional manager turned beet red; he was thinking about everything from food costs to how he had not even wanted to hire Willie in the first place. He said, "WHAT IS THIS?!!" Willie responded, "Well, sir, you told me to make an enormous nacho."

According to Adrian, "Willie turned out to be one of the best employees I ever had. He showed up every day and did a great job. He learned every single position in the kitchen because he cared about the organization, the job, and the opportunity that we gave him. You are not going to experience immediate dividends off an employee, but if you believe in them, take your time to nurture them, and help them grow, they will."

Source: Interviews with Adrian Grubb by Don C. Mosley Jr., July 25, 2013.

In this chapter, we look at the processes of staffing, developing, appraising, and disciplining employees. When Art Linkletter, owner of over 75 companies, was asked the secret of his success, his answer was "I bet on people!" As Tom Collins emphasizes in his book *Good to Great*, you have to make sure you have the right people on the bus (his analogy of the company) before you decide where you are going. Thus, a key supervisory challenge, as noted in the chapter's opening vignette, is properly selecting and developing people. Management must emphasize putting the right employees in the right jobs and then motivating them to perform well.

Candidates for a given job can be obtained from inside or outside the organization, but there must be some method of selection to find capable people. The organization must improve employees' performance through training and developing their abilities adequately, then compensate them. Selecting, appraising, training, and disciplining employees are covered in this chapter.

We believe supervisors need to "see the big picture" of the staffing process. Certainly not all supervisors are involved in the activities presented in this chapter, but, if they understand the total process of staffing, they will be in a better position to perform their part of this process.

Responsibility for Selecting, Appraising, and Disciplining Employees

1. Explain who is responsible for selecting, appraising, and disciplining employees.

An organization can be successful only if it has the right number and types of people to do the required work. Therefore, a primary duty of all supervisors is the proper selection, placement, employee training and development, compensation, and utilization of competent employees. How well—or poorly—supervisors perform these functions is a major factor in their success or failure.

A Shared Responsibility

Like almost all aspects of supervision, selecting, appraising, and disciplining employees are shared tasks, though the primary responsibility should be left to supervisors. In general, the responsibilities are divided as follows:

1. *Top managers* set human resource objectives, establish policies, and do long-range planning and organizing.
2. *Middle managers* control the operating procedures needed to achieve these objectives and carry out personnel policies.
3. *Supervisors* interpret policies for employees and carry out the organization's wishes for selecting and training employees. Also, they interpret and transmit workers' interests to higher management.

With today's emphasis on *empowerment*, teams are often used at all three of these levels. At a minimum, it is especially important to have potential fellow employees involved in an advisory role.

The Supervisor's Role

Operative employees usually have little contact with high-level managers. Therefore, they tend to think of their supervisor as being "management" or "the organization." Because employees interpret their supervisor's actions, attitudes, and methods as representing those of all managers, supervisors are probably the most important people in achieving an organization's human resources objectives. Supervisors usually have the final word in selecting, appraising, and disciplining employees. They supervise and control the employees' daily activities.

STOP AND THINK

In many large department stores, sales positions are filled directly by human resources. When a selection decision is made, the sales department supervisor is notified, and the new employee reports to her or him for a job assignment. Typically, the new employee first meets his or her supervisor on the first day of work. What are the pros and cons of this system?

Selecting Employees for Specific Jobs

2. Describe the steps in the employee selection procedure, including the proper orientation of new employees.

A suggested procedure for selecting employees is shown in Exhibit 15-1. Individual employers may find it desirable to modify this procedure—or depart from it—under certain conditions. In this section, each of the steps listed in the exhibit is briefly explained.

Requisition

Selection really begins with a requisition from the supervisor to the human resource department. This requisition, based on the previously prepared job description and specification, is the authorization the department needs to recruit applicants for the position(s)

EXHIBIT 15-1

Flowchart of a Suggested Selection Procedure

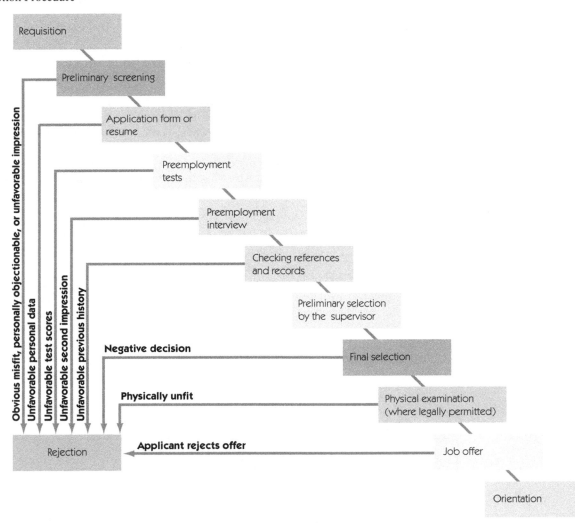

Source: From Figure 9-4, "Techniques for Gathering Information About Potential Employees," by Leon C. Megginson, Mary Jane Byrd, and William L. Megginson, published in a 2003 issue of *Small Business Management: An Entrepreneur's Guidebook*, 4th ed., p. 228. Reprinted by permission, uschamber.com, Sept. 2009. Copyright 2003, U.S. Chamber of Commerce and McGraw-Hill Companies.

available. In many small- and medium-sized firms, the supervisor makes an informal visit or phone call to the senior officer who is authorized to make the final job offer.

A reminder is needed at this point! If you, as a supervisor, are involved in recruiting and selecting job applicants, all aspects of your procedures must conform to the Equal Employment Opportunity Commission's (EEOC) *Uniform Guidelines on Employee Selection Procedures*. The guidelines cover *all selection procedures*, not just testing. Your procedures also should comply with your Affirmative Action Program (AAP) for hiring people from various groups. The human resource officer, in particular, should be certain the selection procedure conforms to national and local laws and customs.

When Bryan Seibt accepted the position of Human Resources Director for the City of Fairhope, Alabama, personal referral was the primary recruiting source used to match individuals with vacant jobs throughout the city's various departments. He worked for several years with the department heads to proactively broaden the applicant pool. A multisource strategy using the city's Web site, local and regional newspapers, the state's league of municipalities' network, and a variety of association groups generated more diverse applicants. The result is more diversity within the city's departments.[1]

Preliminary Screening

Whether formal or informal, some type of preliminary screening weeds out those persons who do not seem to meet the employer's needs—thus saving their time and yours. This step deals with such obvious factors as educational background, training, experience, physical appearance, grooming, and speech—if these are relevant to job performance. Also, the applicant should know something about the organization and the job being sought.

Mike, a bright, young college student, applied at a local hotel for employment while home on summer break. He was rejected at the preliminary interview because his hair was below his collar—even though it was neatly pulled back. He was told that even the groundskeepers and dry cleaning plant workers had to have their hair above their collars. The next year, he was rejected by a grocery chain because he had a beard. Finally, he did find a lucrative job waiting tables at an English pub—with great tips and free meals.

STOP AND THINK

Should employers make selection decisions based on an applicant's hair length or whether he has facial hair?

Application Form or Résumé

After passing the preliminary screening, the job applicant usually completes an application form. (Some applications are submitted online, by e-mail or snail mail, or in person before preliminary screening.) The applicant usually lists information such as former employers, titles of jobs held, and length of employment with each one. Background, education, military status, and other useful data are listed. The form should be carefully designed to provide the information needed about the applicant's potential performance; it should not be a hodgepodge of irrelevant data.

The manager of a tire store once told one of the authors he requires all applicants to fill out an application in person on the premises. "When they ask to take it home," he said, "I can be almost sure they cannot read and need help filling it out."

The EEOC and many states have restrictions concerning the kinds of questions included on an application form. Therefore, you should check any laws your state may have on such practices. See Exhibit 15-2 for a list of topics to avoid on application forms and during interviews.

EXHIBIT 15-2

Topics to Avoid when Interviewing Applicants

Here is a summary of 10 of the most dangerous questions or topics you might raise during an interview.

1. *Children.* Do not ask applicants whether they have children, or plan to have children, or have child care.
2. *Age.* Do not ask an applicant's age.
3. *Disabilities.* Do not ask whether the candidate has a physical or mental disability that would interfere with doing the job.
4. *Physical Characteristics.* Do not ask for such identifying characteristics as height or weight on an application.
5. *Name.* Do not ask a female candidate for her maiden name.
6. *Citizenship.* Do not ask applicants about their citizenship. However, the Immigration Reform and Control Act does require business operators to determine that their employees have a legal right to work in the United States.
7. *Lawsuits.* Do not ask a job candidate whether he or she has ever filed a suit or a claim against a former employer.
8. *Arrest Records.* Do not ask applicants about their arrest records.
9. *Smoking.* Do not ask whether a candidate smokes. Although smokers are not protected under the Americans with Disabilities Act (ADA), asking applicants whether they smoke might lead to legal difficulties if an applicant is turned down because of fear that smoking would drive up the employer's health care costs.
10. *AIDS and HIV.* Never ask job candidates whether they have AIDS or are HIV-positive because these questions violate the ADA and could violate state and federal civil rights laws.

Source: Originally published July 1992 in *Nation's Business*. Reprinted by permission, uschamber.com, November 2009. Copyright © 1992, U.S. Chamber of Commerce.

Chris Whitehead/Jupiter Images

Workers' emotional adjustment and attitude will have a strong impact on work performance, especially those tasks requiring interpersonal skills.

Preemployment Testing

Various tests can be used to assess an applicant's intelligence quotient (IQ), skills, aptitudes, vocational interests, personality, and performance. Preemployment testing, especially "personality" or psychological testing, is growing in use by industry. These tests can minimize turnover because companies are now trying to hire for "fit" between the workers and employees, and testing can help them ensure that "fit." However, the tests must be approved by the EEOC, valid, and reliable. Only the most popular tests are discussed here.

Types of Tests   **IQ tests** are designed to measure the applicant's capacity to learn, solve problems, and understand relationships. They are particularly useful in selecting employees for supervisory and managerial positions. **Aptitude tests** are used to predict how a person might perform on a given job and are most applicable to operative jobs. **Vocational interest tests** are designed to determine the applicant's areas of major work interest. Although interest does not guarantee competence, it can result in the employee working and trying harder. **Personality tests** are supposed to measure the applicant's emotional adjustment and attitude. These tests are often used to evaluate interpersonal relationships and see how the person might fit into an organization.

Probably the most effective tests the supervisor can use in selecting operative employees are **achievement, proficiency, or skill tests**. These tests measure fairly accurately the applicant's knowledge of and ability to do a given job. They can also spot *trade bluffers*— people who claim job knowledge, skills, and experience they don't really have. One type of proficiency test is **work sampling** or **work preview**, when the prospective employee is asked to do a task that is representative of the work usually done on the job. In addition to showing whether the person can actually do the job, the test gives the applicant more realistic expectations about the job.

Finally, some organizations now test for drug use, especially where the use of drugs by employees poses a serious safety risk, as in the case of machine operators or airplane pilots. Although such tests are controversial, they are legal in most states.[2]

Validity of Tests   If tests are used in making the selection decision, employers must be prepared to demonstrate their validity. **Validity** is demonstrated by a high positive correlation between the applicant's test scores and an identifiable measure of performance on the job. Furthermore, the tests must be designed, administered, and interpreted by a professional (usually a licensed psychologist); be culturally neutral so they don't discriminate against any ethnic group; and be in complete conformity with EEOC guidelines.[3] Tests also must have **reliability**; that is, the results will be the same if the test is given to the same person by different testers or by the same tester at different times. Care should be exercised in interpreting test results because some persons are adept at faking answers. Because of these and other problems, many firms are dropping testing in favor of other selection techniques.

It should be reemphasized at this point that all selection techniques are subject to scrutiny by the EEOC. It also should be mentioned that the most frequently used selection criteria are supervisory ratings and job performance.

Preemployment Interviewing

In preparing for the employment interview—that is, the only two-way part of the selection procedure—you should use the information on the application form and test results to learn as much as you can about the applicant. A list of questions prepared before the interview can help you avoid missing information that might be significant in judging the applicant. Compare your list of questions with the job specification to ensure you match

---

IQ tests

Measure the applicant's capacity to learn, solve problems, and understand relationships.

aptitude tests

Used to predict how a person might perform on a given job.

vocational interest tests

Determine the applicant's areas of major work interest.

personality tests

Measure the applicant's emotional adjustment and attitude.

achievement, proficiency, or skill tests

Measure the applicant's knowledge of and ability to do a given job.

work sampling *or* **work preview**

A test the prospective employee must perform that is representative of the job.

validity

A high positive correlation between the applicant's test scores and an objective measure of job performance.

reliability

The probability that test results won't change if the test is given to the same person by different individuals.

the individual's personal qualifications with the job requirements. Some specific questions you might ask are

1. What did you do on your last job?
2. How did you do it?
3. Why did you do it?
4. Of the jobs you have had, which did you like best? Which the least?
5. Why did you leave your last job?
6. What do you consider your strong and weak points?
7. Why do you want to work for us?

If you are observant and perceptive during the interview, you can obtain several impressions about the candidate's abilities, personality, appearance, speech, and attitudes toward work. You also should provide the applicant with information about the company and the job. Remember, the applicant needs facts to decide whether to accept or reject the job, just as you need information to decide whether to offer it.

The interview may be carried out individually by the supervisor or in cooperation with someone else—a team member, the human resource manager, or another senior manager. It may be structured or unstructured. **Structured interviews** are standardized and controlled with regard to questions asked, sequence of questions, interpretation of replies, and weight given to factors considered in making the value judgment as to whether or not to hire the person. In unstructured interviews, the pattern of questions asked, the conditions under which they are asked, and the basis for evaluating results are determined by the interviewer.

Not long ago, a former student started a new division within the family business. As part of the hiring process, she conducted numerous interviews to staff both clerical and production positions. At first, there wasn't a set structure to the interviews. She preferred for the interaction to unfold naturally. However, she quickly realized how difficult it was to make a decision by comparing the knowledge, skills, and abilities across applicants for a particular job using this approach. As a result, she structured her interviews, developing a list of questions to guide her actions. The structured interview setting helped her better differentiate among applicants.

structured interviews

Standardized and controlled with regard to questions asked, sequence of questions, interpretation of replies, and weight given to factors considered in making the hiring decision.

Checking References and Records

The importance of carefully checking applicants' references cannot be overemphasized.

Reference checks provide answers to questions concerning a candidate's performance on previous jobs. They are helpful in verifying information on the application form and other records, as well as statements made during the interviews. They are also useful in checking on possible omissions of information and in clarifying specific points. However, many potential employers find former employers, fearing lawsuits, tend to say nothing—or only nice things—about past employees. In fact, most former employers will only give dates of employment and position(s) held.

Reference checks made in person or by telephone are greatly preferable to written ones because past employers are sometimes reluctant to commit to writing any uncomplimentary remarks about a former employee. Be sure to ask specific questions about the candidate's performance. The type of information you are allowed to seek is restricted by laws such as the Fair Credit Reporting Act and the Privacy Act. But you can check on dates and terms of employment, salary, whether termination was voluntary, and whether this employer would rehire the candidate. Many organizations are now using credit checks to obtain information about prospective employees. If this source is used and is the basis for rejecting a candidate, he or she has the right to see the report.

Preliminary Selection by the Supervisor

By this point in the selection process, you—the supervisor—have narrowed the number of candidates to one or a very few. If there is only one, the applicant can be hired on a trial basis. If you have more than one qualified candidate, a review of the information collected should reveal the best choice. Although your preliminary selection may be subject to approval by the human resource department or some higher authority, usually the person will be offered the job.

Final Selection

Human resource officers are usually brought in on the final hiring decision because of their expertise. They ensure that all laws and regulations, as well as company policies, are followed. Also, they have a voice in such questions as the salary and employee benefits to be offered to the applicant.

Physical Examination

The final step in the selection procedure may be a physical examination to see if the applicant can do the job. However, the Americans with Disabilities Act (ADA) and the Genetic Information Non-Discrimination Act have limited this part of the process.

> *Employers may not require an exam before a preliminary job offer is made or ask an applicant if he/she has a disability (or the nature of an obvious disability). Employers can ask the applicant if he/she can perform the job and if so how, with or without reasonable accommodations. After making a job offer, an employer may "condition the offer on the applicant answering certain medical questions or successfully passing a medical exam, but only if all new employees in the same type of job have to answer the questions or take the exam."*[4]

Job Offer

Job offers to applicants for hourly positions are usually made by the human resource office. They are often in writing and contain the terms and conditions of employment. At this point, the offer is either accepted or rejected. If it is rejected, an offer may be made to the next most qualified applicant. If there are no other qualified candidates, the selection procedure must start all over again.

After a candidate accepts the job offer, those not hired should still be kept in mind for possible future openings. It is common courtesy to notify applicants that someone else has been selected, and a diplomatic rejection will maintain their goodwill.

STOP AND THINK

Have you ever applied for a job and been told, "We'll let you know within a week if we want you?" Even when the week was up, were you still hoping you might get a call, if only to say definitely that you had not been hired? How did this uncertainty make you feel toward the employer?

---

orientation

Procedures of familiarizing a new employee with the company surroundings, policies, and job responsibilities.

Orientation

The first day on a new job is confusing for anyone. Therefore, new employees should be given a proper **orientation**. A job description should be given to them and explained in detail. Proper instructions, training, and observation starts employees off on the right foot. A tour of the facilities and a look at the firm's product or service help new employees understand

Properly socializing employees who are new to an organization through orientation and other means can have a positive impact on employee retention.

where they fit into the scheme of things. New employees need to know the firm's objectives, policies, rules, and performance expectations. Frequent discussions should be held with them during the orientation program to answer questions and ensure proper progress.

A formal interview with the new employee may be appropriate at some point during the first week. Other interviews can be held during the probationary period, which is usually from three to six months long. The purpose of these interviews should be to correct any mistaken ideas the employee may have about the job and to determine whether he or she feels you and your people are fulfilling your commitments.

After orientation is completed, a checklist is generally reviewed with the new employee. Then, the employee and a representative of the employer sign it, and it is placed in the employee's file as proof of knowledge of rules. If done properly by the supervisor, orientation accelerates the building of a positive working relationship with the new employee.

A manufacturing company one of the authors worked with had employee retention problems. Even though turnover is relatively high in this particular industry, this firm seemed to have a higher-than-average rate of turnover. Examination of the problem identified a lack of proper socialization of new employees as one contributing factor. The company developed and implemented a detailed employee orientation program that includes an initial orientation day when information about the company—policies, procedures, benefits, and so on—is communicated to all new employees. Each employee is given a "developmental book" during orientation used in conjunction with the supervisor to track the development of key task and performance objectives. The supervisor and the newly hired employee meet regularly each week during the first month to evaluate the employee's development and address any concerns. In addition, each person is informally paired with a tenured employee within the work department who can be relied upon to answer questions and provide guidance. By implementing a multifaceted socialization process, the manufacturer cut its turnover in half.

Huntstock/Getty Images

Employee Training and Development

3. *Explain the importance of training and developing employees.*

training

The process by which employees are educated to improve their capabilities, competencies, productivity, and/or performance.

Employee training and development are important for both the organization and the employee—so much so that companies spent over $156 billion in 2011 to develop a "ready" workforce.[5]

Training is the process by which employees are educated to improve their capabilities, competencies, productivity, and/or performance. There are needs for training such as safety training, legal compliance, new technology adoption, and new product knowledge, but, regardless of the type of training, the ultimate goal is for knowledge to transfer to the job.

Supervisors tend to perform a significant amount of on-the-job training, especially for newer employees, but employees also are provided with many off-the-job training opportunities. Regardless of the location, for training to be effective and learning to take place, the employees need to be motivated to learn. Keller's ARCS Model offers a motivationally centered approach to instruction and training. The ARCS model contains four motivational categories: attention (A), relevance (R), confidence (C), and satisfaction (S). These four categories represent sets of conditions that are necessary for a person to be fully motivated, and each of these four categories has component parts, or subcategories.[6]

Gaining your employees' attention so they are "plugged in" is critical. This can be accomplished in a variety of ways, including presenting a problem to be solved, a troubling statistic, or an unexpected action or image, or simply varying your approach to training.

Making the training relevant to your employees also can be challenging. Adrian Grubb, highlighted in the opening vignette, had an experience when he was responsible for designing and delivering a safety training program with little support across the organization. Instead of taking a top-down approach and telling the employees they were required to be trained on "Emergency Action Planning," he took a personal approach. "We care about each of you as a person and believe the training on 'Emergency Action Planning' will pay dividends for you and your family, as well as the company. The odds are quite good your family will encounter some form of natural disaster in the next two years. Are you as prepared as you should be? Do you have young children? Does your family have a rendezvous point? Do you know what you need if you are evacuating or have to live without city services for an extended period?" Adrian's ability to develop an employee-centered training program ensured the individuals were prepared for natural disasters on the job as well as at home.

The third aspect of motivating trainees is building their confidence levels. The key is to set training objectives appropriate for the employee given the subject or skill to be learned. Human beings are goal-oriented, and, as such, we tend to learn better if we set SMART training goals (Specific, Measurable, Attainable, Rewarding, and Time defined). SMART goals motivate us to learn new skills and competencies because we have something to shoot for. The level and types of goals vary depending on the type of skill or subject as well as the employee's current level of knowledge, skills, abilities, competencies, and experiences. If the employee is learning how to operate a machine on which they have no prior training or experience, the learning goals are simpler to start, becoming more challenging as the employee demonstrates acquisition of certain knowledge, skills, and competencies. It is important during the training process to coach your employees, providing the right mix of support and feedback to increase their confidence as they strive to achieve more challenging goals. Track and review their progress often, and remember—failure is part of learning. They need to know getting it right the first time shouldn't be their goal; rather, giving their all and continuing to develop should be.

Satisfaction, the fourth category, is necessary to sustain your employee's motivation to perform the new task. Employees need to be recognized for their success. Recognition might take the form of verbal praise, certificate of completion, grade, monetary incentive, promotion, or additional responsibility to demonstrate their acquired skill.

STOP AND THINK

Consider training you have had, either on or off the job. What types of rewards or recognition were used that reflect satisfaction, the fourth category of motivation? Based on what you learned in the motivation chapter, what might be effective for employees participating in Adrian's Emergency Action Planning sessions?

The Role of Performance Appraisals in Supervisory Management

Because performance appraisal is such an important part of the management process, enlightened managers are now upgrading their appraisal programs. Most employers already have developed some kind of formal program for improving employee performance, growth, and development.

It should be strongly emphasized that performance appraisals—when properly designed, conducted, and discussed with the person being appraised—are beneficial to the employee as well as the organization. In other words, reviews can be positive and motivational if they are conducted with an attitude designed to improve performance and help each employee move toward maximizing his or her potential. Regardless of the appraisal method used, however, *the appraisal should be constructive* and future oriented.

4. *Explain what an employee perfor-mance appraisal is and who performs it.*

performance appraisal *or* merit rating *or* efficiency rating *or* service rating *or* employee evaluation

Determines to what extent an employee performs a job the way it was intended.

What Is a Performance Appraisal?

A **performance appraisal** is the process used to determine to what extent an employee performs a job in the way it was intended to be done. Other frequently used terms for this process are **merit rating**, **efficiency rating**, **service rating**, and **employee evaluation**. Regardless of the term used, the process always has the purpose of seeing how actual employee performance compares to the ideal or standard.[7]

How a Performance Appraisal Operates

If employees' output can be physically measured, then their rewards can be based on their actual output and there is little need to formally appraise them. However, many jobs today do not lend themselves to physical measurement. Therefore, the supervisor determines what personal characteristics employees have that lead them to have satisfactory performance. As you can see from Exhibit 15-3, the process works as follows: An employee's personal qualities (1) lead to job behaviors (2) that result in work performance (3), which the manager appraises (4), and that appraisal results in some kind of personnel action (5).

An *employee's qualities are* his or her abilities, attitudes, interests, skills, knowledge, and values. These qualities lead the employee to take certain actions that result in output or productivity. The manager appraises the employee's performance and then may reward the employee through a pay increase, transfer, promotion, employee training and development, or career progress.

Most human resource departments now have computerized files on all employees. *These management staffing and development programs* should include appraisal criteria

EXHIBIT 15-3

How Performance
Appraisals Operate

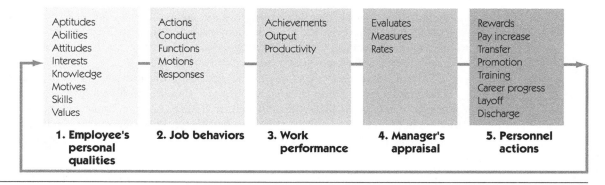

1. Employee's personal qualities	2. Job behaviors	3. Work performance	4. Manager's appraisal	5. Personnel actions
Aptitudes Abilities Attitudes Interests Knowledge Motives Skills Values	Actions Conduct Functions Motions Responses	Achievements Output Productivity	Evaluates Measures Rates	Rewards Pay increase Transfer Promotion Training Career progress Layoff Discharge

and ratings, along with consistent definitions of skills, level of experience, and development activity.[8]

Purposes of the Performance Appraisal

Specific reasons for appraising employee performance are to (1) recognize "good" performance; (2) point out areas that need improvement, especially if the employee hopes to progress in the organization; (3) validate selection techniques to meet EEOC/AAP requirements; and (4) provide a basis for administrative actions such as wage increases, promotions, transfers, layoffs, and/or discharges. Appraisal for these purposes is usually done by comparing the performance of one employee to that of others. Administrative action sometimes takes the form of dealing with managers who have problems, as well. A well-developed appraisal system can detect "problem managers" in time to take appropriate action.[9]

STOP AND THINK

Notice in Case 15-1 how Robert Trent manipulates the appraisal of Jane Smith to get her transferred. Although we do not condone the method he used, the case does show how a performance appraisal can be used as a basis for administrative action.

Performance appraisals also can be used for communications and motivational purposes, such as to provide a basis for giving advice, coaching, or counseling so employees have better expectations on the job or as a basis for career planning and development. When used for these purposes, performance appraisal is usually done by comparing employees' actual performance to some previously determined work standard(s). In such cases, the role of the supervisor is that of a counselor, mentor, or instructor, and the appraisal serves to motivate employees by giving them a better understanding of their job responsibilities, of what is expected of them, and of their training needs.

The Role of the Appraisal Interview

Most organizations cannot afford poor performance and workers cannot afford poor reviews. One way to satisfy both these requirements is for the supervisor to conduct an **appraisal interview** to communicate the results of a given performance appraisal to an

5. *State why performance-appraisal interviews are difficult for both the employee and the supervisor.*

appraisal interview

Supervisor communicates the results of a performance appraisal to an employee.

employee. This method is compatible with the objective of providing feedback on workers' progress and encouraging improvement on the job. However, conducting the appraisal interview is the job aspect supervisors like least. This dislike, together with the poor way the appraisal interview often is handled, has caused this interview to be criticized heavily for damaging relationships between supervisors and employees. One of the main problems with such interviews is that too much is expected of them. The interview alone cannot improve performance; uncover training needs; and serve as the basis for pay increases, promotions, and so forth—but it can certainly help!

The appraisal interview is one of the most difficult duties required of a supervisor. Such an interview used to be along the lines of "Call Joe in and tell him what needs to be straightened out and what's expected of him." Today, however, interviewers are expected to aim for cooperation, constructiveness, and greater understanding.[10] Let us look at what tends to happen during the typical interview, even though it is conducted according to the rules of good performance-appraisal interviewing.

Once a year, Gloria Rogers calls her employees in one at a time for the appraisal interview. Both parties tend to "psych up" for this event. Rogers plans what she's going to say, and the employee tends to be apprehensive about what he or she is going to hear. At the beginning, Rogers tries to put the employee at ease by talking about the weather, the latest major league baseball game, or the employee's family. The employee knows this is just the prelude to getting down to serious business—and tends to resent the delay.

Then Rogers explains her overall appraisal in broad terms. Initially, she'll mention a few good aspects of the employee's performance and give the employee a chance to express his or her views. Next, she enumerates the employee's weaknesses and past failures. She allows the employee to explain these. Then, she explains what steps are needed to improve the employee's performance. At this point, she may ask for the employee's ideas on improvement. One variation of the procedure allows the employee to give his or her own self-evaluation and compare it with Rogers' evaluation after it is given.

The conventional approach to the appraisal interview is emotionally upsetting for both the supervisor and the employee. There is no doubt in the employee's mind he or she is in the hot seat and that there's little point in disagreeing with the supervisor about her judgments. It's best simply to remain submissive and accept the criticism, even if the employee disagrees with it. Supervisors likewise tend to feel anxiety over performance appraisal because, as management theorist Douglas McGregor points out,

Managers are uncomfortable when they are put in the position of "playing God." . . . [We become] distressed when we must take responsibility for judging the personal worth of a fellow man. Yet the conventional approach to performance appraisal forces us not only to make such judgments and to see them acted upon, but also to communicate them to those we have judged. Small wonder we resist.[11]

It is fairly common practice for employers to require managers to discuss their appraisals with employees. The authors of this textbook have talked with numerous supervisors who suffer the double-barreled discomforts of performance appraisal. These supervisors dislike being appraised by their own bosses, and they dislike appraising their employees—or at least telling them the results. All this may lead to appraisal inflation. For example, in one company, when a policy was adopted requiring supervisors to give their appraisals to their employees, their appraisals of their employees suddenly jumped remarkably.[12] Another important aspect of performance appraisals is that they should contain aspects of

EXHIBIT 15-4
Hints for the
Appraisal Interview

DO	DON'T
• Prepare in advance.	• Lecture the employee
• Focus on performance and development.	• Mix performance appraisal and salary or promotion issues.
• Be specific about reasons for ratings.	• Concentrate only on the negative.
• Decide about specific steps to be taken for improvement.	• Do all the talking.
• Consider your role in the employee's performance.	• Be overcritical or "harp on" a failing.
• Reinforce the behavior you want.	• Feel it is necessary that both of you agree on all areas.
• Focus on future performance.	• Compare the employee with others.

Source: From Robert L. Mathis and John H. Jackson, *Human Resource Management*, 12th ed., p. 318. © 2008 South-Western, a part of Cengage Learning, Inc. Reproduced by permission. www.cengage.com/permissions.

career planning for the employee. In other words, the appraisal should help the employee plan for the future.

In summary, the appraisal interview presents both an opportunity and a potential danger for the supervisor because both praise and constructive criticism must be communicated. A major effort should be made to emphasize the positive aspects of the employee's performance while also discussing ways to make needed improvements. One classic study showed a group of employees, who took some form of constructive action as a result of performance appraisals, did so because of the way their supervisor conducted the appraisal interview and discussion.[13] Exhibit 15-4 provides some helpful hints for conducting a more effective interview.

The Need for Discipline

6. *Define discipline and explain why it is necessary.*

Effective job performance requires both managerial and hourly employees to maintain discipline. Most employees would rather work with a group that is well organized, trained, and disciplined than with one that is not. Employees benefit from discipline and suffer from disorder. An early study found that, although workers do not necessarily want to be personally punished, they do want to be supervised "not too much—but also not too little."[14] Successful supervisors know how to find the "middle road" that allows their employees to know exactly what they may and may not do. These generalizations may lead to confusion unless the question "What is discipline?" is answered.

What Is Discipline?

discipline

Training that corrects and molds knowledge, attitudes, and behavior.

To start out, let us emphasize that good discipline is based on good leadership. On that assumption, the term *discipline* is used in this chapter to refer to any of three concepts: (1) self-control, (2) conditions leading to orderly behavior in a work environment, or (3) punishment for improper behavior. Many companies say in their discipline policy **discipline** is training that corrects, molds, or perfects knowledge, attitudes, behavior, or conduct. We agree with this overall definition.

Discipline as Due Process

The Fourteenth Amendment to the U.S. Constitution guarantees every citizen due process under the law. Essentially, the following conditions ensure an individual receives justice in the form of **due process**:

due process

Guarantees the individual accused of violating an established rule a hearing to determine the extent of guilt.

1. Rules or laws exist.
2. There are specific, fixed penalties for violating those rules, with progressive degrees in the severity of penalties.
3. Penalties are imposed only after a hearing has been conducted for the accused, at which time the extent of guilt is determined after considering the circumstances of the situation.

Unions insisted this same process be used within organizations in disciplining employees; even nonunion employers now use it. Today, most arbitrators uphold a disciplinary action if it can be shown that (1) the rules are reasonable, (2) the penalty is related to the severity of the offense, and (3) the worker was given a fair hearing. Underlying the due process concept is the assumption the employer has the right to maintain a well-disciplined work environment and administer discipline when rules are violated. Of course, where there's a union, its representative wants to be present when a member is disciplined. At this point, we want to emphasize that employers can avoid employee grievance proceedings by developing equitable and objective disciplinary procedures.[15]

How Disciplinary Due Process Operates

7. *Describe how discipline is imposed under due process.*

As indicated earlier, disciplinary due process involves three steps. First, rules are established. Second, fixed penalties are set for each infraction of a rule (the penalties usually vary according to the degree of severity of the offense and how many times the rule is broken). Third, the penalty is imposed only after the employee has been given a fair hearing.

Establishing Rules of Conduct　If employees are to maintain self-discipline, they must know what they can and cannot do, and they must know it in advance. Therefore, most progressive organizations publish rules, usually in their employee handbook.

Determining Penalties　The types of penalties, as well as the ways they are used, are determined in consultation with the union. What usually results is termed **progressive discipline** because it involves a graduated scale of penalties. If there is no union, the penalties stem from management's philosophy of how to treat employees, as well as from its fear of the entry of a union or government action. The normal steps in a progressive-discipline policy are

progressive discipline

Discipline that uses a graduated scale of penalties.

1. *Oral warning* that does not go into the employee's record.
2. *Oral warning* that goes into the employee's record.
3. *Written reprimand,* which usually comes from some level above the supervisor.
4. *Suspension,* which usually consists of a layoff lasting from a day to a number of months.
5. *Discharge,* the ultimate penalty, which constitutes a break in service and wipes out the employee's seniority. Most supervisors are reluctant to use it because it is the economic equivalent of the death penalty and affects the worker's family as well as the worker. Justification must be strictly established because discharge is almost always subject to the grievance procedure and arbitration.

graduated scale of penalties

Penalties become progressively more severe each time the violation is repeated.

Several other infrequently used penalties are demotions, transfers, and the withholding of benefits such as promotions, raises, or bonuses.

Unions, personnel managers, and most supervisors favor using a **graduated scale of penalties**, under which punishment for a given violation becomes progressively more severe each time the violation is repeated. The penalty may be, first, an oral warning; second, a written warning; third, suspension; and fourth, discharge. However, when the disciplinary problems are of such a drastic, dangerous, or illegal nature they severely strain or endanger employment relationships, they are called **intolerable offenses**, and the first time one is committed, the employee is discharged.

intolerable offenses

Disciplinary problems of a drastic, dangerous, or illegal nature.

Imposing the Penalty Only after a Fair Hearing   Supervisors must follow the correct procedure in taking any action against an employee. In other words, discipline must be properly administered in accordance with previously established and announced rules and procedures. Penalties should be based on specific charges, with notice given to the employee and the union, if there is one, in advance of management's attempt to take corrective action. The charges and their underlying reasons should be definite and provable. There should be provisions for a prompt hearing, witnesses, protests, and appeals. Finally, adequate remedies should be available to employees whose punishment has failed to meet the requirement of "fair play."

In summary, the main requirements for a proper disciplinary procedure are to (1) make definite charges; (2) notify the employee (and union), in writing, of the offense; and (3) have some provision for the employee to answer the charges either by protest or by appeal.

The Supervisor and Discipline

8. *Explain the supervisor's disciplinary role.*

Regardless of whether supervisors work in unionized firms, they must exercise discretion when recommending or imposing penalties on employees. In dealing with mistakes, supervisors must consider what the mistakes were and under what circumstances they were made. Mistakes resulting from continued carelessness call for disciplinary action. Honest mistakes should be corrected by counseling and positive discipline, not by punishment. These should be corrected in a way that helps the employee learn from the mistakes and become a more proficient and valuable worker.

Martin Jenkinson/Alamy Stock Photo

Employees who understand exactly what is and is not expected of them are better equipped to avoid unpleasant disciplinary measures.

In light of recent incidences of violence in the workplace, supervisors need to be proactive in establishing boundaries, identifying problems, counseling employees, and taking corrective actions. Violent behaviors at work are not random acts. These types of behaviors are caused by a series of events that occur over time and come to a head. In most cases, coworkers and supervisors were aware that it was just a matter of time before the person "snapped." First-line supervisors are the key to preventing workplace violence. How they choose to deal with issues and handle employees can have an impact.[16]

The Supervisor's Disciplinary Role

One of the primary duties of present-day supervisors is to maintain discipline. Top managers expect—and depend on—their supervisors not only to set disciplinary limits but also to enforce them. Only then does an organization operate effectively.

To achieve this goal, supervisors must instill a desire for self-discipline in employees. If employees are not required to face up to the realities of their jobs, goals, resources, and their potential, then they are in a poor position to function properly and make their best contribution to the organization. It's surprising how quickly organizational problems melt away when interpersonal forthrightness is applied.

When applying discipline, a supervisor must consider these points:

1. Every job should carry with it a certain margin for error.
2. Being overly concerned with avoiding errors stifles initiative and encourages employees to postpone decisions or avoid making them altogether.
3. A different way of doing something should not be mistaken for the wrong way of doing it.

Supervisors are more likely than higher-level managers to avoid administering severe disciplinary action because of the likelihood of generating undesirable effects. Other managers, including some personnel managers, take a stronger—perhaps more punitive—position on matters of discipline. A possible explanation is that supervisory managers are inclined to give stronger consideration to individual circumstances and behavior than are top managers. Also, supervisors are somewhat reluctant to follow rules strictly for fear they'll lose the cooperation of their employees if they're too severe.

Principles of Effective Discipline: The Hot-Stove Rule

hot-stove rule

Compares a good disciplinary system to a hot stove.

Four important principles of effective discipline are discussed in this section. These principles are often referred to as the **hot-stove rule** because they draw a comparison between touching a hot stove and experiencing discipline.[17] Here are the four principles:

1. You know what will happen if you touch a hot stove (it carries a clear warning).
2. If you touch a hot stove, it burns you right away (it is immediate).
3. A hot stove always burns you if you touch it (it is consistent).
4. A hot stove doesn't care whom it burns (it is impersonal).

Discipline Carries a Clear Advance Warning   Employees should know what is and is not expected of them. This means there must be clear warning that a given offense leads to discipline, and there must be clear warning of the amount of discipline imposed for an offense.

Supervisor C. D. Yates (name has been changed) had long ignored a safety rule that employees wear short-sleeved shirts while operating their machines. In fact, for over a year, several employees routinely worn long-sleeved shirts in the department. After learning of an injury in another department when an employee's long-sleeved shirt got caught in a conveyor belt, Yates immediately wrote up warnings to five employees in his department who wore long-sleeved shirts that day.

STOP AND THINK

If you were one of the five employees, would you consider Yates's action fair? Probably not. Because the safety rule was so openly ignored, it was the equivalent of no rule at all. For adequate warning to take place, Yates needed to communicate to his employees that, although the rule had been ignored in the past, it would now be enforced in the department. If you were an outside arbitrator, how would you rule? Why?

Discipline Is Immediate   The supervisor should begin the disciplinary process as soon as possible after he or she notices a violation. This is important for several reasons:

1. An employee may feel he or she is "putting one over" on the supervisor and try to violate other rules.
2. An employee may assume the supervisor is too weak to enforce the rules.
3. An employee may believe the supervisor doesn't consider the rule important enough to be enforced. Thus, all the other employees may be encouraged to break or stretch the rule as well. It is not surprising to find an employee responding, "Well, I've been doing this for several days (or weeks) and nobody said anything about it to me before."

Discipline Is Consistent   This principle means for similar circumstances, similar discipline should be administered. If two people commit the same offense under the same circumstances, they should receive the same punishment.

Helen had a high absenteeism record. Recently she missed work for two days without a legitimate excuse. Considering her past record, this offense justified an immediate one-week suspension. However, her skills were badly needed by the supervisor because the department was snowed under by a tremendous backlog of work. Helen was given only an oral warning.

What will Helen's supervisor do when another worker misses work for two days without a legitimate excuse? If supervisors are inconsistent, then they will develop a reputation for playing favorites and losing credibility with employees. Does this mean a supervisor always has to dish out identical penalties for similar offenses? Note: we said the supervisor must be consistent as long as circumstances are similar. An employee's past record is a major factor to consider.

Two employees were caught drinking an alcoholic beverage on the job. The rules clearly prohibited this. For one employee, it was the first such offense; for the second worker, it was his third in the past year. Would the supervisor be justified in giving the second employee a more serious penalty than the first? You better believe it!

STOP AND THINK

What are the pros and cons of giving an employee a "break" regarding discipline?

Discipline Is Impersonal   As a supervisor, you shouldn't get into personalities when administering discipline. You need to be as objective as possible. Moreover, after administering discipline to an employee, try to retain a normal relationship with that person. Two common mistakes supervisors make in imposing discipline are apologizing to employees and chastising employees. Discipline the act, not the person. Your focus should be *on getting the employee's work behavior consistent with the rules.*

Applying Discipline

Two of the more unpleasant aspects of the supervisor's job are (1) laying off a worker for disciplinary reasons and (2) discharging an unsatisfactory employee.

disciplinary layoff
***or* suspension**
***

Time off without pay.

Disciplinary Layoff   If an employee repeatedly commits major offenses and previous warnings have been ineffective, a **disciplinary layoff**, or **suspension**, is probably inevitable. Such a layoff involves a loss of time—and pay—for several days. This form of discipline usually comes as a rude shock to workers. It gets their attention! Generally, it impresses on the employee the need to comply with the organization's rules.

Because this form of discipline is quite serious and involves a substantial penalty—loss of pay—most organizations limit the power to use it to managers who have attained at least the second level of management; often the human resources manager is involved as well. Yet supervisors have the right to recommend such action.

Not all managers believe the layoff is effective, and some seldom apply it as a disciplinary measure. First, they may need the worker to continue production. Second, they may feel the worker will return with an even more negative attitude. Still, when properly used, it is an effective disciplinary tool.

termination-at-will rule
***

Right of an employer to dismiss an employee for any reason.

Discharge   In 1884, a Tennessee court established the **termination-at-will rule**, whereby an employer could dismiss an employee for any reason—or no reason at all—unless there was an explicit contractual provision preventing such action.[18] The reasoning behind this decision was if an employee can quit work for any reason, then the employer should be able to discharge for any reason.

A supervisor may find it necessary to utilize a disciplinary layoff or suspension as means of redirecting an employee's behavior.

Subsequent legislative enactments and court decisions, as well as union rules and public policy, swung the pendulum of protection away from the employer and toward the employee by limiting the termination-at-will rule.[19] Most union agreements have a clause requiring "just cause" for disciplinary discharge and detailing the order in which employees can be laid off. EEO/AA regulations do essentially the same.

In general, court decisions suggest the safest (legal) grounds for discharge include incompetent performance that does not respond to training or accommodation, gross or repeated insubordination, excessive unexcused absences, repeated and unexcused tardiness, verbal abuse of others, physical violence, falsification of records, drunkenness or drug abuse on the job, and theft.

Because discharge is so severe, supervisors can only recommend it. The discharge must be carried out by top management—usually with the advice and consent of the human resources manager.

Unions are quite involved in discipline when they represent the employees. Even many nonunionized organizations now follow the union's disciplinary procedure.

Supervisors' Personal Liability for Disciplining Employees

Recent court decisions holding supervisors personally liable for discharging disabled employees are making some supervisors reluctant to exercise their judgment in hiring, promoting, and firing employees. They are unwilling to take the punitive action indicated for unsatisfactory actions of employees if their personal assets, such as their houses or cars, can become subject to steep jury awards.

Supervisors have been held individually liable in some blatant and serious sex and race harassment cases.

● Chapter Review

1. *Explain who is responsible for selecting, appraising, and disciplining employees.*

This chapter presented ways to select, appraise, and discipline employees. In general, the human resource department is responsible for overall planning, recruiting, and handling the details of staffing. The role of supervisors is to requisition needed workers, interview applicants, orient new employees, and appraise and discipline current employees.

2. *Describe the steps in the employee selection procedure, including the proper orientation of new employees.*

The procedure for selecting employees for specific jobs includes (1) a requisition from the supervisor; (2) a preliminary screening-out of the obvious misfits; (3) the applicant's completion of an application form; (4) preemployment tests; (5) various interviews by the supervisor and human resource officer; (6) checking of records and references; (7) a preliminary selection by the supervisor; (8) physical exam, if legal; and (9) a job offer. If the offer is accepted, the new employee is given a job orientation by the supervisor.

3. *Explain the importance of training and developing employees.*

Employee training and development are important for both the organization and the employee. For training to be effective and learning to take place, the employees need to be motivated to learn. Keller's ARCS model offers a motivationally centered approach to instruction and training. The ARCS model contains four motivational categories: attention (A), relevance (R), confidence (C), and satisfaction (S).

4. *Explain what an employee performance appraisal is and who performs it.*

An employee's performance is always being appraised, either formally or informally. The purpose of formal performance appraisals, however, is to compare employee performance to a standard or ideal—a sort of personnel quality control. Appraisal is more critical for employees whose output cannot be easily measured. Specific reasons for appraising employee performance are to provide a basis for some administrative action (such as a pay increase, promotion, transfer, layoff, discharge, or recommendation for training or development), to justify these actions for EEO/AA purposes, and to improve supervisor–employee relationships. Performance appraisals can be done by employees rating themselves, by employees rating supervisors, or by employees rating one another, but the immediate supervisors ultimately should be responsible because they are most familiar with their employees' work.

5. *State why performance-appraisal interviews are difficult for both the employee and the supervisor.*

One of the jobs supervisors like least is conducting the appraisal interview, which is used to communicate the results of the appraisal to the concerned employee. A supervisor's reluctance to criticize employees may lead to appraisal inflation.

6. *Define discipline and explain why it is necessary.*

Another important supervisory activity is applying discipline. Because discipline is necessary for supervisory success, higher-level managers expect supervisors to set and enforce disciplinary limits. The three types of discipline are (1) self-control, (2) conditions for orderly behavior, and (3) punishment. Employee discipline is a process of control, either internally or externally imposed. As such, it is a method of maintaining management's authority—authority necessary to keep an organization operating effectively.

7. *Describe how discipline is imposed under due process.*

Although the right to discipline is still management's responsibility, today supervisors must be sure they follow due process, which requires (1) stated rules, (2) specific penalties, and (3) an orderly procedure for assessing guilt and punishment. The rules usually classify offenses as (1) minor infractions, (2) major violations, or (3) intolerable offenses. Penalties can include (1) oral warnings, (2) oral warnings with a written record, (3) written reprimands, (4) suspension, and (5) discharge. Usually a graduated scale of penalties is imposed, with the penalty increasing with the frequency and severity of violations.

8. *Explain the supervisor's disciplinary role.*

To be effective, discipline must be enforced. The manner of enforcement, in turn, affects the morale of the organization. One of the most difficult supervisory tasks is to strike an acceptable balance between severity and leniency in administering discipline. Four principles of effective discipline, collectively referred to as the "hot-stove rule," are that discipline should (1) carry a clear warning, (2) be immediate, (3) be consistent, and (4) be impersonal.

When lesser forms of discipline imposed by the supervisor are ineffective, it may be necessary to resort to layoff or discharge of the employee. Usually such action is carried out by higher levels of management. In any case, it is important to be sure due process has been observed and there is just cause for such action.

Key Terms

IQ tests, p. 459
aptitude tests, p. 459
vocational interest tests, p. 459

personality tests, p. 459
achievement, proficiency, or skill tests, p. 459

work sampling *or* work preview, p. 459
validity, p. 459

Discussion Questions

1. What is performance appraisal, and what are some of the other names for it?
2. Explain why performance appraisal is such an important part of the management process.
3. What are some of the purposes of performance appraisal? Explain.
4. Name and explain the steps in the suggested procedure for selecting workers for specific jobs.
5. What is discipline?
6. Why is discipline so important in organizations?
7. What is the due process of discipline, and why is it so important?
8. What is the union's role in the disciplinary process?
9. Why should disciplinary layoff and discharge decisions be restricted to higher levels of management?

Skill Builder 15.1

Resources

What Would You Do?
Three people applied to you for an opening as a lathe operator. One is totally unqualified. One is experienced but has a poor attitude. The third lacks experience but seems especially eager for the job; you think she would be a good worker if she had more experience, but you're not sure.

    You have some rush work you need to get out. Which of the following courses would you choose?

1. If the eager applicant has good references, hire her for a probationary period. But keep looking for a more qualified person in case she doesn't work out.
2. Pass up the three applicants. Keep looking.
3. Hire the experienced person, ignoring his attitude—you've got work to get out!

Skill Builder 15.2

Information

Resources

What Do You Want from Your Job?
Rank the employment factors in the following chart in order of their importance to you at three points in your career. In the first column, assume you are about to graduate and looking for your first full-time job. In the second column, assume you have been gainfully employed for 5 to 10 years and are presently working for a reputable firm at the prevailing salary for the type of job and industry in which you work. In the third column, try to assume 25 to 30 years from now you have found your niche in life and have been working for a reputable employer for several years. (Rank your first choice as "1," second as "2," and so forth, through "9.")

(Continued)

| | YOUR RANKING | | |
EMPLOYMENT FACTOR	AS YOU SEEK YOUR FIRST FULL-TIME JOB	5–10 YEARS LATER	15–20 YEARS LATER
Employee benefits	____	____	____
Fair adjustment of grievances	____	____	____
Good job instruction and training	____	____	____
Effective job supervision by your supervisor	____	____	____
Promotion possibilities	____	____	____
Job safety	____	____	____
Job security (no threat of being dismissed or laid off)	____	____	____
Good salary	____	____	____
Good working conditions (nice office surroundings, good hours, and so on)	____	____	____

Answer the following questions:
1. What does your ranking tell you about your motivation now?
2. Is there any change in the second and third periods?
3. What changes are there, and why did you make them?

Source: Donald Mosley, Paul H. Pietri, and Leon Megginson, *Management: Leadership in Action*, 5th ed., p. 386. Copyright © 1996, Addison Wesley Longman, Inc. Reprinted by permission of Addison Wesley Longman.

Skill Builder 15.3

Information

Resources

Gloria Rogers Appraises Her Employees
Review the example of how Gloria Rogers conducts her performance appraisal interviews. Notice they are "conducted according to the rules of good performance appraisal interviewing."

Instructions:
Assume you are Gloria's supervisor (manager). How would you advise her to improve her performance appraisals?

CASE 15-1

WHEN THE TRANSFER BACKFIRES:

Jane Smith abruptly rose and stormed out of the office of Robert Trent, the director of purchasing at a major eastern university. As she made her hasty exit, Trent wondered what had gone wrong with a seemingly perfect play—one that would have rid his department of a "problem" employee. How could his well-constructed plan, using the university's formal transfer system, have failed so miserably, leaving him with an even more unmanageable situation?

It had all begun in January, when Trent decided something must be done about Smith's performance and attitude. The process was made a little more awkward by the university's not having a formal employee performance-appraisal policy and program. Each department was left with the right to develop and conduct its own employee appraisals. This meant each department could choose whether or not to appraise an employee, as well as choose the format and procedure to be used.

In January, Trent decided to conduct an appraisal of Smith. After writing down some weaknesses in her performance and attitude, he called her in to discuss them. He cited the various weaknesses to her, but, admittedly, most were highly subjective in nature. In only a few instances did he give specific and objective references and did not give Smith a copy of his findings. During the appraisal interview, he hinted possibly that she didn't "fit in" and she "probably would be much happier in some other place." In any event, he was satisfied he began the process for eventually ridding the department of her. He reasoned, if all else failed, this pressure would ultimately force her to quit. At the time, he hardly noticed she was strangely quiet through the whole meeting.

As time went by, Smith's attitude and performance did not improve. In March, Trent was elated to learn an opening existed in another department and Smith was interested in transferring. The university's formal transfer policy required Trent to complete the Employee Transfer Evaluation Form—which he gladly did. As a matter of fact, he rated Smith mostly "outstanding" on the performance and attitude factors. He was so pleased at having the opportunity to use the transfer system he called the other department manager and spoke glowingly of Smith's abilities and performance. Although he had been the purchasing director for only eight months, having been recruited from another college, he even pointed with pride to Smith's five years of experience.

In April, much to Trent's dismay, it was announced that Smith lost the transfer opportunity to a better-qualified candidate. Robert Trent was shocked when Smith's transfer was turned down. To further complicate matters, Trent realized he would have to face Smith in May when it was time to discuss annual pay raises, which included both merit pay considerations and a cost-of-living adjustment. This would be even more difficult because Smith's performance and attitude had not improved since the January appraisal. If anything, they were worse.

Trent just finished the May meeting with Smith by telling her the bad news: Based on both performance and attitude, she should not be recommended for a cost-of-living or merit-pay increase for the new year beginning July 1. Smith, armed with the transfer evaluation forms (completed and given to her in March), threatened to use all internal and external systems for organizational justice due her.

As Trent pondered this dilemma, he fully recognized Smith's unique status within the university community. She was the wife of a distinguished, tenured professor of business, and this situation provided additional pressure. As if this were not enough, he had to contend with the office social process pivoting around a weekly coffee group greatly influenced by Smith. It was not unusual for the former director of purchasing (who retired after 25 years of service) to attend these gatherings. Of course, Smith kept this group fully apprised of her continuing troubles with "this new, young purchasing director who is hardly dry behind the ears."

CASE QUESTIONS

1. What are the facts Trent must consider now?
2. What avenues are now open to Trent? What does this case say to you about the need for supervisors to act morally?
3. Do you believe some supervisors are untruthful where recommendations are concerned? Explain.
4. What three functions are salaries meant to perform?
5. To what extent should employee appraisals be used in salary adjustments? Explain.

Source: Prepared by M. T. Bledsoe, Associate Professor of Business, Meredith College, Raleigh, North Carolina.

Notes

1. Interview with Bryan Seibt by Don C. Mosley Jr., October 2006.
2. "Drug Testing: The Things People Will Say," *American Sales Man*, March 2001, pp. 20–24.
3. See "Adoption by Four Agencies of Uniform Guidelines on Employee Selection Procedures (1978)," 43 *Federal Register* 38,290–38,315 (August 25, 1978).
4. "Disability Discrimination," Equal Employment Opportunity Commission, http://www.eeoc.gov/laws/types/disability.cfm (retrieved August 4, 2013).
5. Laurie Miller, "ASTD 2012 State of the Industry Report: Organizations Continue to Invest in Workplace Learning," November 8, 2012, *ASTD* (Online), http://www.astd.org/Publications/Magazines/TD/TD-Archive/2012/11/ASTD-2012-State-of-the-Industry-Report.
6. John Keller, "How to Integrate Learner Motivation Planning into Lesson Planning: The ARCS Model Approach," February 2000, paper presented at VII Semanario, Santiago, Cuba.
7. Robert Cyr, "Seven Steps to Better Performance Appraisals," *Training and Development* 47, no. 1 (January 1993), pp. 18–19.
8. Ren Nardoni, "Corporatewide Management Staffing," *Personnel Journal* 69 (April 1990), pp. 52–58.
9. Kenneth M. Golden, "Dealing with the Problem Managers," *Personnel* 66 (August 1989), pp. 54–59.
10. Mary Mavis, "Painless Performance Evaluations," *Training and Development* 48, no. 10 (October 1994), pp. 40–44.
11. Douglas McGregor, "An Uneasy Look at Performance Appraisals," *Harvard Business Review* 35 (May–June 1957), p. 90.
12. L. Stockford and W. H. Bissell, "Factors Involved in Establishing a Merit Rating Scale," *Personnel* 26 (September 1949), pp. 97.
13. H. H. Meyer and W. B. Walker, "A Study of Factors Relating to the Effectiveness of a Performance Appraisal Program," *Personnel Psychology* 14 (August 1961), pp. 291–298.
14. For further details, see Irwin H. McMaster, "Universal Aspects of Discipline," *Supervision* 36 (April 1974), p. 19.
15. M. Michael Markowich, "A Positive Approach to Discipline," *Personnel* 66 (August 1989), pp. 60–65.
16. Jennifer Gatewood, "Attacking Violence: Former Hostage Negotiator Warns Workplace Violence Won't Go Away until Managers Take an Aggressive Approach," *Risk & Insurance*, March 14, 2003.
17. Based on concepts in Theo Haimann and Raymond L. Hilgert, Instructor's Manual—Supervision: Concepts and Practices of Management, 6th ed. (Cincinnati, OH: South-Western Publishing Co., 1995). Reprinted with permission of South-Western.
18. Payne v. Western & Atlantic R.R. Co., 81 Tenn. 507 (1884).
19. Youngblood S. A. and G. L. Tidwell, "Termination-at-Will: Some Changes in the Wind," *Personnel* 58 (May–June 1981), p. 24.

16

The Supervisor, Labor Relations, and Legal Issues

Long ago we stated the reason for labor organizations. . . . We said that union was essential to give the laborers opportunity to deal on an equality with their employer.

—U.S. Supreme Court

ADRIAN DENNIS/AFP/Getty Images

An employer has far greater resources than employees have as individuals. For this reason, labor unions unite workers so that they can use their collective power to petition for better benefits and working conditions.

Preview

THE LEGAL LANDSCAPE At one time, employment in the United States was "at-will." Either the employer or the employee could terminate the employment relationship at any time, for any reason, or for no reason at all, so long as there was not a contract or a law prohibiting termination. In the late 1800s and early 1900s there were few contracts of employment and even fewer laws. Today, however, the opposite is true. There are collective bargaining agreements in the union sector, employee handbooks in the union-free sector, and hundreds of laws at the federal, state, and local levels designed to protect employees from unfair employment actions.

Laws influence organizations in important ways, such that today's supervisors need to be knowledgeable about the legal landscape they operate in so they can make informed decisions. For example, take the equal employment opportunity legislation discussed in this chapter. Many may be familiar with the type of employment discrimination referred to as disparate treatment, when the employee believes he or she has been treated differently by the employer because of a protected class such as race, color, religion, sex, or national origin. However, many may not know policies that appear to apply equally to everyone may nevertheless be deemed discriminatory if the application of those policies statistically impacts one group at a significantly higher rate than another. This type of discrimination, known as disparate impact, arises even if the employer did not intend for the policy to affect one group more than another. Employers use a measure known as the four-fifths rule to determine whether an employment practice is discriminatory, such that if there is a 20 percent difference in the employment impact, the practice may be problematic, unless the employer can prove the practice is job-related and consistent with business necessity. For example, a company with a specific height (at least 6'0″) and weight (at least 170 lbs) requirement hires disproportionate numbers of white males relative to members of some protected groups, such as women and individuals with certain ethnic backgrounds.

A recent case illustrates how the disparate impact and disparate treatment theories impact managerial decisions.[1] In 2003, the City of New Haven, Connecticut, administered an exam for firefighters seeking promotion to captain and lieutenant ranks. The test was designed by an outside consultant. Of the 118 firefighters who took the exam, African-American candidates passed at roughly half the rate of white candidates. Forty-one firefighters took the exam for promotion to the rank of captain. Sixteen (64 percent) of the 25 white firefighters passed the exam, three (38 percent) of the eight black firefighters passed, and three (38 percent) of the eight Hispanic firefighters passed. As a result, no blacks qualified for promotion and only the two highest-scoring Hispanics would have made the promotion list for one of the seven captain vacancies. Based on the numbers, the four-fifths rule was triggered. Rather than evaluating the validity of the examination, the City of New Haven invalidated the test results. City officials specified the test results were being thrown out because no black candidates scored high enough for promotion and the City feared a disparate impact lawsuit by African-American firefighters. Instead, 20 white and 2 Hispanic candidates who scored high enough to qualify for promotion sued, alleging disparate treatment.

You make the call. Was the test discriminatory? Did the City of New Haven make the right call by throwing out the test results? You will have an opportunity in one of the end-of-chapter exercises to evaluate the correctness of your response! The chapter's opening preview highlights the fact that today's supervisors must be knowledgeable about a variety of environmental factors to be successful. In this chapter, we focus on two such factors: labor relations and legal issues.

What Are Labor Relations?

1. *Explain what is meant by labor relations.*

At the end of the 19th and beginning of the 20th centuries, many U.S. workers were employed in manufacturing facilities with dangerous working conditions, low wages, and few benefits. Individual employees had little power to pressure employers to improve wages and working conditions. However, if employees worked together collectively to put pressure on an employer, the balance of power shifted. In the early days of the industrial revolution, employees had little protection if they attempted to engage in collective action to better their working lives. Today, times have changed and employees wishing to harness the power of collective action are legally protected. When organizations do not effectively manage their human capital, employees may seek the collective power of a labor union to counter perceived deficiencies in the terms and conditions of the employees' employment—particularly wages, benefits, and job security.

labor union

An organization of workers banded together to achieve economic goals.

A **labor union** is an organization that represents the collective interest of workers in negotiating with the workers' employer to achieve economic goals, especially increased wages and benefits, shorter working hours, improved working conditions, and both personal and job security. It is impossible to cover everything about dealing with unions in one chapter, but we include the most important ideas to help you understand the supervisor's role in labor relations. Even if you are—or expect to be—a supervisor in a nonunion firm, you need to understand how labor relations affect supervisory activities and relationships because they affect nonunion employers as well as unionized ones.

STOP AND THINK

In unionized firms, supervisors are generally required to follow specific procedures before disciplining employees. Even in nonunion firms, supervisors use due process in applying discipline. Do you think this approach by enlightened supervisors improves labor–management relations? Why or why not?

---

labor relations *or* union–management relations *or* industrial relations

The relationship between an employer and unionized employees.

Terms such as **labor relations**, **union–management relations**, and **industrial relations** are often used to refer to the relationships between employers and their unionized employees. In this text, these terms are used interchangeably.

The growth of unionism in the middle of the 20th century forced managers—especially supervisors—to change many of their ways of dealing with employees. Managers in unionized companies are constantly being challenged by union leaders, particularly when managers try to change work rules or policies, or discipline or discharge a represented worker. These challenges force supervisors to consider the rights of workers when developing and applying policies and procedures. Thus, management's freedom of choice has been greatly limited by the emergence of unions. This limitation protects employees from unfair management practices, such as managers rewarding an employee based on favoritism or punishing one without just cause. However, in many unionized companies, it also keeps managers from rewarding individual performance or initiative and requires greater time and effort to rid the organization of unproductive workers.

STOP AND THINK

Think about the last serious strike you can remember. Did it affect you in any way, either directly or indirectly? Even if it didn't affect you, what were the economic, social, political, and cultural effects on your community? On the nation? Did any workers in affected organizations lose jobs or wages? Did any companies lose output or go out of business? Were the sales at retail stores hurt? Were tax receipts reduced? Was there any violence? Did it affect any social or cultural events?

How Unions Developed in the United States

2. *Trace the development of unions in the United States and explain why union membership is declining.*

In general, employees were treated well in the early colonies because of the severe shortage of workers. By the end of the 19th century, however, the situation had changed. The high birthrate, rapid and uncontrolled immigration, concentration of wealth and industry in the hands of a few businessmen, political abuses by some employers, and large numbers of workers in crowded industrial areas led to many abuses against workers.

Early Union Activities

craft unions

Workers in a specific skill, craft, or trade.

Labor unions existed in the United States as early as 1789, but they were small, isolated, and ineffective **craft unions** of skilled, experienced workers. To increase their impact, several of the craft unions joined together in 1869 to form the Knights of Labor. Because the organization was only moderately successful, a more conservative national union was formed in 1881. It was named the American Federation of Labor (AFL). Under the leadership of Samuel Gompers, the AFL grew and had great impact, especially during World War I and World War II.

Period of Rapid Union Growth

During the 1920s and early 1930s, business became so powerful that workers again felt they were being exploited. They were hired, rewarded, punished, and fired at the whim of first-line supervisors, many of whom acted unfeelingly. Therefore, several laws were passed in the 1930s that forced management to recognize unions and protected workers from exploitation.

industrial unions

Unions composed of all the workers in an industry.

Until that time, the AFL and its affiliates were organized on a craft basis. Union growth was thus limited because few craft workers were left to organize. But some workers started organizing **industrial unions**, in which all the workers in a given industry—such as those in iron, coal, and autos—belonged to the same union, whether they were craftsmen, unskilled workers, or clerical employees. These unions broke away from the AFL in 1936 to form the Congress of Industrial Organizations (CIO).

Because of laws and government actions favorable to workers and the demand for workers resulting from World War II, union membership grew rapidly until 1945, when 35.5 percent of the workforce was unionized. After peaking in 1945, union membership declined until 1955, when unions represented 33.2 percent of the workforce. That was the highest point reached in the post-World War II period. Because of this leveling off of union participation by American workers, and in hopes of reversing this trend, the AFL and CIO merged in 1955 into the AFL-CIO. But this move—and other concerted activities—did not stop the decline.

In recent years the trend toward unionization has continued to decline. In 1983, the percentage of U.S. workers represented by unions had declined to 20.1 percent of the U.S. workforce, with 17.7 million unionized workers. By the year 2003, only 13.5 percent of U.S. workers were members of unions, with only 16.3 million unionized workers. In 2016, membership declined even further, with unions representing only 14.6 million workers (10.7 percent of all nonagricultural wage and salary workers). The demographics of modern union membership are interesting. According to the Bureau of Labor Statistics's 2016 Union Member Summary (https://www.bls.gov/news.release/union2.nr0.htm):

- Of the 14.6 million unionized workers, 7.1 million were in the public sector. Government workers were more than five times as likely to belong to a union as private sector employees (34.4 percent of public workers are unionized; only 6.4 percent of private sector employees are represented).
- Teachers, police officers, and firefighters have the highest unionization rates.
- Black workers (13 percent) were more likely to be union members than were white (10.5 percent), Asian (9 percent), or Hispanic (8.8 percent) workers. The unionization rate for men (11.2 percent) was higher than for women (10.2 percent).
- New York had the highest (23.6 percent) and South Carolina had the lowest (1.6 percent) union membership rate. See Exhibit 16-1 for a state-by-state comparison.

EXHIBIT 16-1

Union Membership Rates by State, 2016 Annual Averages (U.S. rate = 10.7 percent)

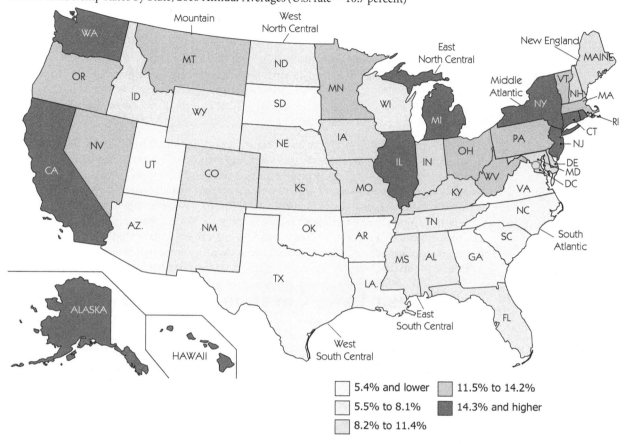

☐ 5.4% and lower	☐ 11.5% to 14.2%
☐ 5.5% to 8.1%	☐ 14.3% and higher
☐ 8.2% to 11.4%	

Source: U.S. Department of Labor, Bureau of Labor Statistics, https://www.bls.gov/opub/ted/2017/union-membership-rates-by-state-in-2016.htm.

STOP AND THINK

Approximately seven out of eight employed workers do not belong to a union. Why do you think this is so? What can unions do to appeal to younger workers who are just entering the workforce?

Some Reasons for Declining Union Membership

There are many reasons for this declining union membership. First, the economy underwent a major shift from manufacturing jobs, which are relatively easy to unionize, to service work, which is more difficult to organize. Second, there is a new kind of service worker—more educated and technologically oriented. These mobile employees are less interested in long-term union contracts, with payments in the distant future, than in such things as portable pensions and employer contributions to retirement plans. They also enjoy "employee involvement" schemes such as quality circles and self-managing teams, which traditional unions tend to oppose. Third, another problem for U.S. unions is the growing global economy. U.S. firms are under pressure to cut costs to compete, so many employers have become more aggressive in opposing union organizing drives. Also, employers feel they cannot compete with foreign competitors if they are bound by the industry-wide bargaining required by many U.S. unions.

Hostess represents a current trend in taking a hard stance against unions, given changing global markets that are competitive.

Hostess, the maker of household staples such as Twinkies and Wonder Bread, closed all of its facilities rather than sign an agreement company officials deemed anticompetitive. In November 2012, a U.S. bankruptcy judge approved the liquidation of the company, resulting in an immediate loss of 15,000 jobs. When the wind-down is complete, 18,500 workers will have lost their jobs.[2]

Fourth, many of today's employees work in environments that make it difficult for them to unionize. For example, there is a growing emphasis on employing part-time and temporary workers and many of these and other full-time and temporary workers telecommute from remote locations. Also, there are now many more small business owners than there are union members, and small firms are difficult for unions to organize.

Finally, unions may have done their jobs too well. Many traditional union issues, such as workplace safety and hours of work, are now the subject of extensive legislation and government regulation. Some states passed laws abrogating employment-at-will and requiring just cause for all discharges—a protection traditionally afforded only to unionized workers.

Some Basic Laws Governing Labor Relations

3. Name and explain some of the basic laws governing labor relations.

The legal basis of union–management relations is provided by the National Labor Relations Act of 1935 (also called the *Wagner Act*), as amended by the Labor–Management Relations Act of 1947 (the Taft–Hartley Act), the Labor–Management Reporting and Disclosure Act of 1959 (the Landrum–Griffin Act), and others. This complex set of laws establishes public policy and controls labor relations. Exhibit 16-2 shows the coverage,

EXHIBIT 16-2
Basic Laws Governing Labor Relations

LAWS	COVERAGE	BASIC PROVISIONS	AGENCIES INVOLVED
National Labor Relations Act (NLRA) as amended (Wagner Act)	Nonmanagerial employees in nonagricultural private firms not covered by the Railway Labor Act; postal employees	Asserts the right of employees to form or join labor organizations (or to refuse to), to bargain collectively through their representatives, and to engage in other concerted activities such as strikes, picketing, and boycotts; establishes unfair labor practices that the employer cannot engage in	National Labor Relations Board (NLRB)
Labor–Management Relations Act (LMRA) as amended (Taft-Hartley Act)	Same as above	Amended NLRA; permits states to pass laws prohibiting compulsory union membership ("right to work laws"); sets up methods to deal with strikes affecting national health and safety; prohibited union unfair labor practices	Federal Mediation and Conciliation Service
Labor–Management Reporting and Disclosure Act (Landrum-Griffin Act)	Same as above	Amended NLRA and LMRA; guarantees individual rights of union members in dealing with their union; requires financial disclosures by unions	U.S. Department of Labor

Source: U.S. Department of Labor publications and the basic laws themselves as mentioned.

unfair labor practices

Specific acts management may not commit against the workers and the union.

closed-shop

All prospective employees must be members of the recognized union before they can be employed.

union-shop

All employees must join the union within a specified period after starting employment.

agency shop

All employees must pay union dues even if they choose not to join the union.

maintenance-of-membership clause

An employee who joined the union must maintain that membership as a condition of employment.

basic provisions, and agencies administering these laws. We'll provide only a few more details about them in the text.

The Most Important Labor Laws

In this section, we examine why basic labor laws were passed. We also point out the important features of these laws and explain how they are administered.

Wagner Act   The National Labor Relations Act (Wagner Act) was passed to protect employees and unions by limiting management's rights. It gave workers the right to form and join unions of their own choosing, protected employees' rights to engage in collective bargaining, and provided both unionized and union-free workers with the right to engage in protected concerted activity for mutual aid and protection. It also established the National Labor Relations Board (NLRB) and gave the NLRB exclusive jurisdiction to enforce the law. The act defined specific **unfair labor practices** management could not commit against the workers and the union, such as interfering with workers' rights to organize, but it had no provision for unfair practices unions might commit against workers and management. As a result, many union abuses arose. One major abuse was unions could impose requirements as to how employees could get or keep a job. This abuse rose to prominence with the rise of union security agreements, particularly closed-shop agreements.

Under a **closed-shop** agreement, all prospective employees must be members of the recognized union before they can be employed, and all current employees must join within a specified time to retain their jobs. Under a **union-shop** agreement, all employees must join the union within a specified period—usually 30 days—after being hired or they can be fired. In an **agency shop**, all employees must pay the union dues even if they choose not to join the union. The **maintenance-of-membership clause** says once an employee joins the union, he or she must maintain membership as a condition of employment.

STOP AND THINK

Do you have trouble seeing the difference between a union shop and a closed shop? In a union shop, management can employ the people it chooses and then these people must become members of the union. In a closed shop, management must hire the workers sent by the union according to each worker's seniority as a member of the union.

---

right-to-work laws

A state statute that prohibits union shops in the state. Protects the right of employees to join or refuse to join a union without being fired.

Taft–Hartley Act   Following World War II, with evidence of abuse of power by some union leaders, Congress passed the Labor–Management Relations Act (Taft–Hartley Act). Enacted in 1947, this act greatly changed the Wagner Act, making it more evenhanded, so unions as well as management could be charged with unfair labor practices.

The Taft–Hartley Act prohibited the closed-shop agreement, except in the construction and shipping industries. Also, Section 14(b) of this act gave states the right to pass laws prohibiting the union shop. By 2012, 24 states had used Section 14(b) to pass **right-to-work laws**, which give workers the right to join or refuse to join a union without being fired. The states with right-to-work laws are highlighted in Exhibit 16-3.

EXHIBIT 16-3

States with Right-to-Work Laws

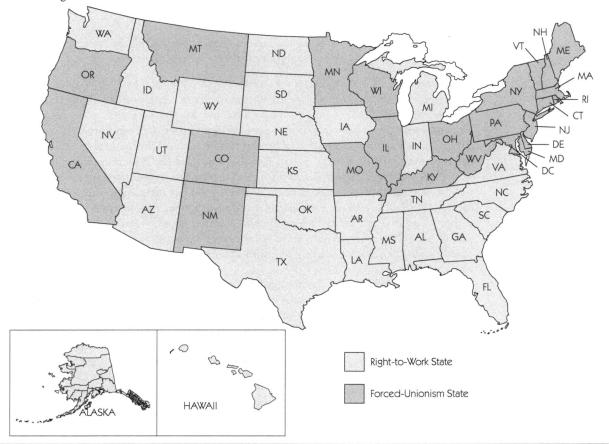

Right-to-Work State

Forced-Unionism State

U.S. Department of Labor, Bureau of Labor Statistics

Landrum–Griffin Act   In 1959, Congress passed the Labor–Management Reporting and Disclosure Act (Landrum–Griffin Act) in an effort to prevent corruption and abuse of employees by union leaders and managers. It provided an **employees' bill of rights**, which protects employees from possible abuse by unscrupulous managers and union leaders.

Exhibit 16-4 contains the rights of employees. Exhibit 16-5 shows what unions may not do and Exhibit 16-6 lists what employers may not do under these laws.

employees' bill of rights

Protects employees from possible abuse by unscrupulous managers and union leaders.

Administration of Labor Laws

The five-person NLRB has the power to enforce the basic labor laws. The functions of the NLRB are (1) to oversee the representation process and certify unions as the exclusive bargaining agent for employees and (2) to see unfair labor practices are either not committed or are punished. Its specific duties are to

- Hold an election to establish the bargaining agent for employees of a given firm.
- Investigate charges of unfair labor practices against the employer or the union.
- Issue complaints against either management or labor.
- Prosecute unfair labor practices and determine guilt.
- Assess fines and prison sentences.
- Ask federal courts to control activities of both management and labor by citing them for contempt.

EXHIBIT 16-4 Rights of Employees	• Form and join unions. • Bargain collectively. • Be free from discrimination on the basis of union affiliation. • Be free from retaliation if they bring charges of unfair labor practices against the employer. • Get a job without first being a member of a union. • Do not have to join a union unless the union and the employer have signed a valid union-shop agreement in one of the states that do not have right-to-work laws. • Cannot be charged exorbitant initiation fees and dues by a union with a valid union-shop agreement. • Receive financial reports from the union.
EXHIBIT 16-5 Unfair Labor Practices of Unions	• Coerce employees into or restrain them from engaging in union activities. • Force management to discriminate against employees on the basis of union membership. • Refuse to bargain in good faith. • Require managers to pay money for work not done. • Engage in a strike or boycott to force management to commit illegal acts. • Charge excessive initiation fees and dues where there is a union shop.
EXHIBIT 16-6 Unfair Labor Practices of Employers	• Interfere with, restrain, or coerce employees who are exercising their rights under the law. • Dominate or interfere with the forming or administering of unions, or contributing support to them. • Discriminate in hiring or in any other terms of employment in such a way as to encourage or discourage membership in a union. • Discharge or otherwise discriminate against employees for filing charges against the employer or testifying under the law. • Refuse to bargain with the union representative.

Union Principles, Objectives, and Methods of Attaining Objectives

4. *Describe union principles and objectives and discuss the methods used to achieve those objectives.*

Samuel Gompers, the AFL's first president, identified the following principles on which unionism is based: (1) strength through unity, (2) equal pay for the same job, and (3) employment practices based on seniority. These principles of unionism lead to the practical goals unions have for their members: (1) higher pay; (2) shorter hours of work on a daily, weekly, or annual basis; (3) improved working conditions, both physical and psychological; and (4) improved security, both of the person and of the job.

How do unions achieve their objectives? The usual methods they use are to (1) organize a firm's employees, (2) become recognized as the employees' exclusive bargaining agent, (3) engage in collective bargaining, (4) go on strike or threaten to strike, and (5) process grievances. Let us look at each of these methods.

union authorization card

Authorizes a particular union to be an employee's collective bargaining representative.

Organizing Employees

First, the union leader must persuade employees of a firm to organize and join the union. The union organizer tries to get the employees to sign a **union authorization card**, stating the employee wants the specified union to be his or her bargaining representative. An example of such a card is shown in Exhibit 16-7. If you are a supervisor in a union-free firm, then it is important you understand employees have a right under the law to form and join unions, and employers have the right to tell their employees why they believe unionization would not be beneficial. As a supervisor in a union-free environment, you should be familiar with the basic steps in the union organizing process, as well as steps taken before a union comes calling.

Samuel Gompers identified the importance of strength through unity, equal pay for equal work, and seniority in relationship to labor unions.

EXHIBIT 16-7

Example of a Union
Authorization Card

COMMUNICATIONS WORKERS of AMERICA, A.F.L.-C.I.O.

Name _____
     (Please Print)   First   Middle   Last

Address _____
             Street

_____
         City   State   Zip Code

Tel. No. _____ Job Title _____

I am an Employee of _____ ,

Department _____ , Section _____ , Shift_____
and I hereby designate the Communications Workers of America, as my collective bargaining representative.

Date _____ Signature _____

FORM O-100   **REPRESENTATION AUTHORIZATION**   150
1-77

EXHIBIT 16-8

Steps in the Union
Organizing Process

1. The union seeks to establish a "showing of interest" from the group of employees the union seeks to represent (the collective bargaining unit), usually through the signing of authorization cards.

2. Once the union obtains signatures from 50 percent or more of the employees in the collective bargaining unit, the union may seek voluntary recognition; that is, it asks the employer to recognize and bargain with the union without an election.

3. If voluntary recognition is not sought or is unsuccessful, the union files a Petition for Election with the National Labor Relations Board and shows that at least 30 percent of the proposed bargaining unit is interested in representation.

4. National Labor Relations Board notifies the employer of the Petition and sets an election date.

5. Employer can file objections to the Petition, seeking to change the scope of the bargaining unit or raise procedural issues with the Petition.

6. The organizing campaign is when both the employer and the union try to persuade employees how they should vote. Employers must maintain the status quo and follow the T.I.P.S. rule—do not Threaten, Interrogate, Promise, or engage in Spying—during the organizing campaign to protect the right of workers to freely and fairly decide whether to vote for or against union representation.

7. On Election Day, the National Labor Relations Board conducts the election. If the union receives a true majority of the vote cast (50% + 1), then the union wins the election and becomes the certified bargaining representative of the employees in the collective bargaining unit. If the union does not achieve a true majority of the votes cast, a one-year election bar prevents any union from seeking to represent the same group of workers for the next 12 months.

The basic steps in the union organization process are shown in Exhibit 16-8.

Appeals Used by Union Organizers   The technique most commonly employed by union organizers to obtain union recognition is to compare the target company's practices to items in contracts the union has with other companies, perhaps in an entirely different industry. If the terms of employment in the target company lag far behind, then the union has a ready-made argument. Of course, the organizer focuses on those parts of the wage-benefit package that make the employer look bad. Union organizers appeal to five main desires of employees:

1. *Job protection.* Unions stress they continually try to ensure employees have a job—or at least an income—for a lifetime. With most employees already enjoying generous benefits, many seem more interested in job security than in higher pay rates. But there are exceptions to this generalization.

2. *Interference running.* Unions assure employees they will act as their agents in grievances and disputes. They will go to bat for employees and they claim to have the know-how to protect employees' interests.

3. *Participation in management.* Unions insist they can and will give employees a greater voice in deciding the policies, procedures, and rules that affect them and the work they do.

4. *Economic gains.* Higher wages, reduced hours, and better benefits are still at the top of an organizer's checklist.

5. *Recognition and participation.* Knowing pro-union workers need and are dependent on attention, sympathy, and support, union organizers promise employees that they'll have greater recognition and participation through union activities.

Union activity in this country has varied considerably, ranging from peaceful negotiations that resolve quickly to strident, impassioned disagreements that take place over a long period of time.

Things to Do Before the Union Calls Knowing the issues commonly used by union organizers to appeal to unorganized workers, supervisors and other managers can do many things to minimize the chances of employees' seeking union representation. The most important ones follow:

1. The company and its higher-level managers must pay close attention to supervisors, for they are the key to successful labor relations. Unhappy supervisors can do tremendous harm to an employer's labor relations. Treat supervisors right, keep them well informed, and make them an integral part of the management team.
2. Make sure no item in the wage-benefit package lags far behind the norm for the area and industry. Ensure workers know and understand what benefits the company offers and how they compare to benefits offered elsewhere in the community.
3. Review jobs frequently to see if they need to be upgraded because responsibilities or working conditions have changed.
4. Make sure employee facilities are adequate, safe, well lighted, well ventilated, and reasonably clean.
5. Keep records of good—and bad—performance by employees and have programs for boosting employee performance, loyalty, and morale.
6. Be firm but fair when imposing discipline.
7. Provide a practical release valve, such as a grievance committee, for employee frustrations and complaints.
8. Be alert for any complaints of abuse or favoritism by employees or supervisors.
9. Establish clear lines for two-way communications with all employees.
10. Provide training for supervisors so they understand how to interact with subordinate employees and the importance of being fair to all workers.

11. Have clear, definite, and well-communicated work rules and ensure supervisors apply those work rules consistently and fairly.

Notice throughout this list the importance of good supervisory practices. It cannot be said too strongly that first-line supervisors play an integral role in making unions unnecessary!

Additional Precautions for Supervisors   In addition, management should make sure that there is nothing in personnel policies and work rules the NLRB can construe as being anti-union. For example, suppose a company has the following sign displayed: "No solicitation at this company." *This prohibition can actually be ruled an unfair labor practice unless it is enforced against all types of solicitation—even by charitable groups—not just union organizing.* A company is obliged to permit solicitation and distribution of literature by union organizers in nonwork areas such as locker rooms and parking lots during nonwork times such as breaks or lunch. Similarly, personnel policies that prohibit employees from discussing their wages have been found to violate the Wagner Act because the policies interfere with the ability of workers to work collectively to better their terms and conditions of employment.

What the Supervisor Should Do—and Not Do—When the Union Enters   A tactic frequently used to gain recognition is for the union organizer to meet with the supervisor and hand over some signed authorization cards. Then the union representative says he or she represents the workers and asks to be recognized as the workers' exclusive bargaining agent to sign or negotiate a contract.

Most labor relations specialists suggest supervisors not touch or examine the cards, for if they do, this action can be construed as acceptance of the union as the workers' agent—a process known as voluntary recognition. Nor should supervisors make any comments to the union representative. If the representative asks, "Are you refusing to recognize the union?" the supervisor should reply, "Any comment concerning the company's position must await full consideration of the matter by higher levels of management" or, using more modern jargon, "the decision whether to recognize or refuse to recognize a union is above my pay grade." If the representative asks, the supervisor should give the name, address, and telephone number of the company's labor relations manager. Of course, as soon as the representative leaves, the supervisor should inform his or her boss about the visit. Supervisors must know that during union organizing, the company is required to maintain the status quo; changes in policy or the way policies are enforced may not occur in response to union organizing. For example, if the company normally does not enforce its no-solicitation or its e-mail policies, now is not the time to start enforcing them.

Exhibit 16-9 contains some suggestions as to what you *may* legally do when a union tries to organize your employees. Some things you should *not* do are listed in Exhibit 16-10. However, because of the fine line between legal and illegal supervisory conduct during union organizing campaigns, most companies hire outside consultants to help guide them through the process and provide detailed training to supervisors on what they can and cannot say and do during the campaign period.

Becoming Recognized as the Employees' Exclusive Bargaining Agent

Once employees sign authorization cards, the union tries to become recognized as the employees' exclusive bargaining agent. An **exclusive bargaining agent** is the employees' representative who has the exclusive right to deal with management over questions of wages, hours, and other terms and conditions of employment. A "certified" union is one that won its representation right through the NLRB election process and has the sole right

exclusive bargaining agent

Person or organization that has the exclusive right to deal with management on behalf of employees over questions of wages, hours, and other terms and conditions of employment.

EXHIBIT 16-9

Things Supervisors
May Do When
a Union Tries to
Organize Their
Company

- Inform employees that signing a union authorization card does not mean they must vote for the union if there is an election, but it may mean they will be required to join the union if the union wins the election.
- Inform employees of the disadvantages of belonging to the union, such as the possibility of strikes, serving on a picket line, dues, fines, assessments, and rule by cliques or one individual. Inform employees the law permits you to hire a new employee to replace any employee who goes on strike for economic reasons.
- Inform employees you prefer to deal with them rather than have the union or any other outsider settle grievances.
- Inform employees about any prior experience you had with unions and whatever you know about the union officials trying to organize them.
- Inform employees that collective bargaining is a give-and-take process and no union can obtain more than you as an employer are able to give.
- Inform employees how their wages and benefits compare with those in unionized or nonunionized concerns in the area or relevant industry.
- Inform employees of any untrue or misleading statements made by the organizer. You may give employees corrections of these statements or suggest the employees get the union to put its promises in writing.
- Inform employees of any known racketeering or other undesirable elements that may be active in the union.
- Reply to union attacks on company policies or practices.
- Administer discipline, layoff, and grievance procedures without regard to union membership or nonmembership of the employees involved.
- Treat both union and nonunion employees alike in making assignments of preferred work or desired overtime.
- Enforce plant rules impartially, regardless of the employee's membership activity in a union.
- Tell employees, if they ask, they are free to join or not to join any organization, so far as their status with the company is concerned.
- Tell employees their personal and job security will be determined by the economic prosperity of the company.

Source: Leon C. Megginson et al., *Successful Small Business Management*, 6th ed., pp. 821–822. Originally published 1991. Reprinted by permission, uschamber.com, Sept. 2009. Copyright 1991, U.S. Chamber of Commerce and McGraw-Hill Companies.

and legal responsibility to represent all of the employees—nonunion members as well as union members—in their dealings with management.

Management may voluntarily recognize the union when presented with authorization cards or some other showing of interest signed by a majority of employees in the proposed bargaining unit. Ordinarily, however, a secret-ballot election is conducted by the NLRB when requested by the union or the company.

For the last several years, unions have lobbied Congress to pass laws to make it easier for unions to organize workers. One proposal is the Employee Free Choice Act, under which a union becomes the certified bargaining representative by simply obtaining signatures from a majority of the employees the union seeks to represent—essentially doing away with secret-ballot elections in most circumstances. Because legislative efforts to change the unionization process have not been successful, the appointed members of the National Labor Relations Board have proposed modifying its election rules to accomplish through agency rule-making what the elected legislature has been unable to accomplish through changes to statutory law.

EXHIBIT 16-10

Things Supervisors May Not Do When a Union Tries to Organize Their Company

- Engage in surveillance of employees to determine who is and who is not participating in the union program, attend union meetings, or engage in any undercover activities for this purpose.
- Threaten, intimidate, or punish employees who engage in union activity.
- Request information from employees about union matters, meetings, etc. Employees may, of their own volition, give such information without prompting. You may listen but not ask questions.
- Prevent employee union representatives from soliciting memberships during nonworking time in nonwork areas.
- Grant wage increases, special concessions, or promises of any kind to keep the union out.
- Question employees or prospective employees about their affiliation with a labor organization, including whether they signed an authorization card or are union members.
- Threaten to close up or move the plant, curtail operations, or reduce employee benefits.
- Engage in any discriminatory practices, such as work assignments, overtime, layoffs, promotions, wage increases, or any other actions that could be regarded as preferential treatment for certain employees.
- Discriminate against union people when disciplining employees for a specific action, while permitting nonunion employees to go unpunished for the same action.
- Transfer workers on the basis of teaming up nonunion employees to separate them from union employees.
- Deviate in any way from company policies for the primary purpose of eliminating a union employee or quashing union organizing activities.
- Intimate, advise, or indicate in any way that unionization will force the company to lay off employees, take away company benefits or privileges enjoyed, or make any other changes that could be regarded as a curtailment of privileges.
- Make statements to the effect you will not deal with a union.
- Give any financial support or other assistance to employees who support or oppose the union.
- Visit the homes of employees to urge them to oppose or reject the union in its campaign.
- Be a party to any petition or circular against the union or encourage employees to circulate such a petition.
- Make any promises of promotions, benefits, wage increases, or any other items that would induce employees to oppose the union.
- Use a third party to threaten or coerce a union member or attempt to influence any employee's vote.
- Use the word *never* in any predictions or attitudes about unions or their promises or demands.
- Talk about tomorrow. When you give examples or reasons, you can talk about yesterday or today instead of tomorrow, to avoid making a prediction or conviction that may be interpreted as a threat or promise by the union or the NLRB.

Source: Leon C. Megginson et al., *Successful Small Business Management*, 6th ed., pp. 823–824. Originally published 1991. Reprinted by permission, uschamber.com, Sept. 2009. Copyright 1991, U.S. Chamber of Commerce and McGraw-Hill Companies.

collective bargaining

Conferring in good faith over wages, hours, and other terms and conditions of employment.

Engaging in Collective Bargaining

Once the union has been recognized as the employees' bargaining agent, it starts negotiating with management. Legally, **collective bargaining** is the process by which (1) representatives of the employer and the employees (2) meet at reasonable times and places (3) to confer in good faith (4) over wages, hours, and other terms and conditions of employment. Note the representatives of the two parties must negotiate "in good faith" by making valid

mediator

Tries to bring the parties together when collective bargaining reaches an impasse.

arbitrator

Makes a binding decision when collective bargaining reaches an impasse.

strike

When employees withhold their services from an employer.

picketing

Walking back and forth outside the place of employment, usually carrying a sign.

lockout

A closing of a company's premises to the employees and refusing to let the employees work.

collective bargaining agreement or contract

The document prepared when an accord has been reached to bind the company, union, and workers to specific clauses in it.

offers and counteroffers about any question involving wages, hours, and other "terms and conditions of employment." Simply put, both sides must show they are *trying* to reach an agreement.

It is a "must" that supervisors be consulted at each step of this bargaining procedure. They should carefully examine every union proposal—and management counterproposal—to see how the proposals affect the supervisors' relationships with the employees.

If no agreement is reached, an impasse develops. At this point, there are three alternatives: (1) to call in an outside **mediator**, provided by the Federal Mediation and Conciliation Service, who brings the parties together and tries to help them reach an agreement; (2) to agree to bring the issue to an outside **arbitrator**, who will make a decision binding on both parties; or (3) for the union to go on strike or for management to stage a lockout.

Conducting a Strike or Lockout

The ultimate strategy used by unions to achieve their objectives is the strike. A **strike** occurs when employees withhold their services from an employer to achieve a goal. The employees tell the public why they are striking by means of **picketing**—walking back and forth outside the place of employment, usually carrying signs.

It cannot be emphasized too strongly that most union leaders *do not like to use the strike*. In fact, only a small percentage of the thousands of contract negotiations conducted annually result in strikes. Although the strike itself is the ultimate device in collective bargaining and is the technique resorted to when all other methods of resolving differences fail, *the threat of a strike* is a continuing factor in almost all negotiations. Both the union and the employer frequently act as if one could occur.

Just as the union can call a strike if it isn't satisfied with the progress of negotiations, so can management stage a lockout. A **lockout** closes company premises to the employees and refuses to let employees enter to resume work. In both strikes and lockouts, the company can legally hire replacement workers to keep the company running while the union workers are not working.

Reaching an Agreement

When an accord is reached, a document is prepared that becomes the **collective bargaining agreement or contract** among the company, the union, and the workers. It usually contains clauses covering at least the following areas:

1. Union recognition
2. Wages and benefits
3. Vacation and holidays
4. Working conditions
5. Layoffs and rehiring
6. Management prerogatives or "rights"
7. Hours of work
8. Seniority
9. Grievance and arbitration procedures
10. Renewal clause

Specifics are set forth in each of these areas, and rules are established that should be obeyed by management and the union. The management rights clause defines the areas in which supervisors have the right to act, free from questioning or joint action by the union.

Living with the Agreement

5. *Name three things that a supervisor must know to live with the union agreement.*

Once the agreement has been signed, managers and supervisors have to live with the contract until it is time to negotiate a new one—usually three or four years later. Therefore, all management personnel—especially first-level supervisors—should be thoroughly briefed on its contents. The meaning and interpretation of each clause should be reviewed, and the wording of the contract should be clearly understood. Supervisors' questions should be answered to prepare them to deal with labor relations matters. Also, it should be impressed on supervisors that their counterpart—the union steward—will probably be well trained, know the contract provisions in great detail, and be skilled in the practice of contract administration.

Supervisors' Rights under the Agreement

Supervisors should view the agreement as the rules of the game because it spells out what they may and may not do. They should take a positive view of what they *may do* rather than a negative one of what they *may not do*. Although agreements differ in detail, most give supervisors the following rights:

1. Decide what work is to be done.
2. Decide how, when, and where the work will be done.
3. Determine how many workers are needed to do the work safely.
4. Decide who will do each job, as long as skill classifications and seniority provisions are observed.
5. Instruct, supervise, correct, and commend employees in the performance of their work.
6. Require that work performance and on-the-job personal behavior meet minimum standards.
7. Recommend promotions and pay increases, as long as they do not violate the union agreement.
8. Administer discipline according to the agreed-upon procedure.

If uncertain as to their authority, then supervisors should check with the firm's human resources or labor relations experts. Supervisors need to have a working knowledge of the agreement's details because the employees and their advocate, the union steward, will be aware of these details.

STOP AND THINK

Would you rather be a supervisor in a unionized or a nonunionized company? Why?

The Supervisor and the Union Steward

union steward

A union member elected by other members to represent their interests in relations with management.

The **union steward**, a union member elected by other members to represent their interests in relations with management, is the supervisor's counterpart. The steward is the link between the workers and their union and between the union and the company, especially in case of controversy. The supervisor represents the company and its interests to workers, who play the dual roles of employees of the company and members of the union. The steward represents the union's position to the workers and the company. The steward is at the same level in the union hierarchy as the supervisor is in the company hierarchy.

The Role of Seniority

seniority

An employee's length of service in a company; provides the basis for promotion and other benefits.

One of the most basic union principles is **seniority**, meaning workers who have been on the job the longest get preferred treatment and better benefits. One of the supervisor's greatest challenges is to maintain high productivity while assigning work, especially preferred jobs and overtime, to the most senior employee, who is not necessarily the most capable worker. Similarly, in unionized companies, promotions within positions covered by the agreement are often awarded to the most senior employee, who may or may not be the best person for the job.

Handling Employee Complaints

In unionized companies, employees' complaints take the form of grievances. Work assignments, promotion decisions, and discipline and discharge decisions lead to most grievances against supervisors.

grievance procedure

A formal way of handling employees' complaints.

The **grievance procedure** is a formal way of handling these complaints. In nonunionized companies, employees may present their complaints to their supervisors and the supervisor and employee try to work through the problem informally.

Grievance Procedures   Exhibit 16-11 shows a typical grievance procedure, such as those usually found in unionized organizations. The form and substance of the grievance procedure depend on several factors:

1. The type of industry (the old-line, "smokestack" industries, such as steel, auto, and transportation, have the most formal and rigid procedures).
2. The size and structure of the organization (the larger, more highly structured organizations have the most formal and inflexible procedures).
3. The type of union (the older, craft-oriented unions tend to have a highly structured procedure).

There are usually five steps in a formal grievance procedure in a unionized organization. However, the *actual* number of steps taken depends on the number of managerial levels in the organization and whether or not the grievance is submitted to arbitration.

EXHIBIT 16-11
Typical Grievance Procedure in a Unionized Organization

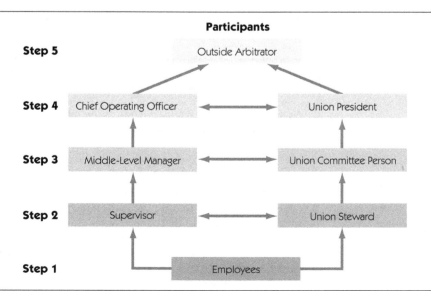

Participants

Step 5 — Outside Arbitrator

Step 4 — Chief Operating Officer ⟷ Union President

Step 3 — Middle-Level Manager ⟷ Union Committee Person

Step 2 — Supervisor ⟷ Union Steward

Step 1 — Employees

1. An employee complains to the supervisor about a presumed wrong. From the employee's viewpoint, the supervisor may be violating the labor agreement or doing something that dissatisfies the employee. If the supervisor straightens out the matter satisfactorily, that's the end of the grievance.
2. Frequently though, the issue is not resolved, so the employee goes to the union steward to present a grievance. The steward then tries to obtain satisfaction from the supervisor. The vast majority of grievances are settled at this stage.
3. The union committee person or business agent tries to resolve the complaint with middle management, such as a department head.
4. The union president and the chief operating officer try to resolve the difference. If they succeed, that ends the grievance.
5. If the chief operating officer and the union president cannot resolve the grievance, it is submitted to outside arbitration. A mutually agreed-upon arbitrator makes the decision.

Complaint Procedures in Nonunionized Organizations

Many nonunion organizations have formal complaint procedures comparable in many ways to the formal union grievance procedures. These procedures permit complaints to go beyond the supervisor to committees composed of higher-level executives, including the human resources manager and sometimes top executives. Historically, these procedures in union-free companies did not provide for arbitration. However, because of the increasing risk of employment-related lawsuits and the rising costs associated with those lawsuits, many union-free companies began including mandatory arbitration provisions in their personnel policies, requiring employees to use alternative dispute resolution procedures, such as arbitration, to settle any disputes arising from the employment relationship.

STOP AND THINK

When disputes arise, many employees are surprised to learn they do not have a right to take their complaints to court because their employer's employee hand-book contains a mandatory arbitration provision. Is it fair to have an employment policy that requires an employee to take employment-related complaints to an arbitrator rather than to a court? Are there any benefits to using arbitration rather than litigation?

As a practical matter, many grievances can be avoided if supervisors are familiar with generational communication techniques; that is, many grievances result from misunderstandings and those misunderstandings can be avoided if the supervisor communicates with the employee in a style to which the employee can relate.

Caution Needed in Terminations

As noted previously, at one time supervisors had the right to terminate, or "fire," employees "at will," that is, without having to show cause or even give a reason. However, federal and state legislation, union agreements, and court decisions largely eliminated the ability of a supervisor to terminate an employee for anything other than "just cause." In other words, today's supervisors must offer a valid, documented reason for discipline and discharge decisions whether they are in a union or union-free workplace.

Labor Law for the Supervisor in a Union-Free Workplace

Concerted Activity   What if you are a supervisor in a nonunion workplace. Do you really need to know about labor law? Surprisingly, the answer is yes. First, as noted above, supervisors are the company's first lines of defense when it comes to union organizing. It is critical for supervisors to know what rights their employees have under the labor laws (e.g., the right to form and join unions) and know what their role is in protecting those rights. Second, the federal labor law does apply to union-free workplaces. In particular, supervisors need to know the Wagner Act provides protection for **concerted activity**. Protected concerted activity involves one or more workers taking action for the mutual aid or protection of the group.

concerted activity

One or more employees take action for mutual aid and protection.

STOP AND THINK

One of your employees posts negative things about you, the supervisor, on Facebook and other workers respond to the posting. Can you fire the employees involved in supervisor-bashing in a public domain like Facebook? What if your workplace is a retail store located in an unsafe neighborhood and the critical posts concerned employee criticism of your decision to keep the store open after dark? What if one employee threatens another employee through social media?

In *Design Technology Group*,[3] the National Labor Relations Board held that Facebook posts constituted protected concerted activity because employees were complaining about terms and conditions of employment and could not be fired for those complaints. When employees get together to talk about wages, hours, or working conditions, the employees are engaged in protected conduct and cannot face discipline or discharge for those discussions. Even negative comments about an employer or supervisor on social media sites are protected if the comments relate to the employees' workplace, working conditions, workplace treatment, or management practices.

Complying with Equal Employment Opportunity (EEO) Laws

6. *State the laws providing equal employment opportunity for protected groups of employees.*

All aspects of employment are affected by federal, state, and local laws, regulations, and court decisions. Most employees in the modern workplace—including men and whites—are protected by one or more laws limiting the ability of a supervisor to terminate an employee "at will." This section examines some of the federal regulations and court decisions, and their effects on recruiting and selection, as well as discipline and discharge. It should be emphasized, however, that EEO laws build on—and enhance—good human resource practices by most employers.

The Most Important EEO Laws

The Civil Rights Act of 1866, the Civil Rights Act of 1964, Executive Order 11246, the Civil Rights Act of 1991, and other legislation prohibit discrimination based on race, color, religion, sex, or national origin in all employment practices. Exhibit 16-12 shows additional laws that protect persons with disabilities, older workers, and veterans. It also shows the laws' basic requirements and the agencies that enforce them.

Supervisors also should be aware that many state and local governments have laws prohibiting discrimination and those laws often create other protected classes such as sexual orientation, gender identity, marital status, and appearance.

EXHIBIT 16-12

Legal Influences on Equal Employment Opportunity and Affirmative Action

LAWS	BASIC REQUIREMENTS	COVERAGE	ENFORCEMENT AGENCIES
Section 1981 of Civil Rights Act of 1866	Prohibits racial discrimination in employment.	All private employers, labor unions, and employment agencies	Judicial system
Title VII of Civil Rights Act of 1964	Prohibits employment discrimination based on race, color, religion sex, or national origin. Requires employers to provide reasonable accommodation for sincerely held religious beliefs.	Private employers engaged in interstate commerce with 15 or more employees, labor unions, employment agencies, federal government workers, and state and local government workers	Equal Employment Opportunity Commission (EEOC)
Executive Order 11246 of 1965, as amended	Prohibits employment discrimination based on race, sex, color, religion, or national origin, and requires contractors employing 50 or more workers to develop affirmative action plans (AAPs) when contracts exceed $50,000 a year.	Federal contractors and subcontractors holding contracts of $10,000 or more	U.S. Department of Labor's Office of Federal Contract Compliance Programs (OFCCP)
Age Discrimination in Employment Act of 1967, as amended	Prohibits employment discrimination against persons over age 40.	Same as those under Title VII, except that private employers with 20 or more employees are covered	EEOC
Vocational Rehabilitation Act of 1973	Prohibits employment discrimination against an otherwise-qualified person with a disability, requires reasonable accommodation, and requires development of AAPs.	Federal contractors and subcontractors holding contracts in excess of $2,500, organizations that receive federal assistance, and federal agencies	OFCCP
Vietnam Era Veterans' Assistance Act of 1974	Requires contractors to develop AAPs to recruit and employ qualified disabled veterans and veterans of the Vietnam War.	Federal contractors and subcontractors holding contracts in excess of $10,000	OFCCP
Pregnancy Discrimination Act of 1978	Prohibits discrimination on the basis of pregnancy, child birth, and related medical conditions.	Same as Title VII	EEOC
Immigration Reform and Control Act of 1986	Prohibits recruiting, hiring, or referring aliens who are not eligible to work in the United States; prohibits employment discrimination based on national origin or citizenship.	Private employers, labor unions, and employment agencies	U.S. Department of Justice's Special Counsel for Unfair Immigration-Related Employment
Americans with Disabilities Act of 1990, as amended by the Americans with Disabilities Act Amendments Act of 2008	Prohibits employment discrimination against qualified individuals with a disability and requires reasonable accommodation. Also prohibits discrimination against those who have a "history of" disability, are "perceived as" disabled, or who are "associated with a person with a disability.	Same as Title VII	EEOC
Civil Rights Act of 1991	Amends Title VII and the Americans with Disabilities Act to allow for punitive and compensatory damages in cases of intentional discrimination and more extensive use of jury trials.	Same as Title VII	EEOC

(Continued)

EXHIBIT 16-12

Continued

LAWS	BASIC REQUIREMENTS	COVERAGE	ENFORCEMENT AGENCIES
The Uniformed Services Employment & Reemployment Rights Act of 1994	Prohibits employment discrimination because of an individual's service in the U.S. armed forces. Generally requires employees returning from active military service to be restored to the position the employee would have attained had the employment relationship continued without disruption.	All employers	U.S. Department of Labor, Veterans Employment & Training Service
Ledbetter Fair Pay Act of 2009	Amends Title VII to virtually eliminate the statute of limitation for pay claims. A pay claim is viable if a "tainted" paycheck was issued during the charge filing period, regardless of when the discriminatory act occurred.	Same as Title VII	EEOC
Genetic Information Nondiscrimination Act of 2008 (GINA)	Prohibits employers from using genetic information, including family medical history, when making employment decisions.	Same as Title VII	EEOC

Source: Various government and private publications.

Enforcement of EEO Laws

The Equal Employment Opportunity Commission (EEOC) is the primary agency enforcing EEO laws. It receives and investigates charges of discrimination, issues orders to stop violations, and may even go to a U.S. district court to enforce its decrees.

One method used to combat the present effects of past discrimination is **affirmative action programs (AAPs)**. Affirmative action may be ordered by the courts, included in settlement agreements or consent degrees, or required by government agencies such as the Office of Federal Contract Compliance Programs (OFCCP) in the U.S. Department of Labor, which enforces Executive Order 11246; by the Vocational Rehabilitation Act; and by the Vietnam Era Veterans' Assistance Act. Employers may voluntarily implement an affirmative action program to eliminate a manifest racial or gender imbalance in a traditionally segregated job category. Voluntary affirmative action plans are only lawful if they are temporary measures designed to remedy the current effects of past discrimination. To determine if a voluntary affirmative action program is lawful, the EEOC and the courts consider whether the affirmative action plan involves a quota or inflexible goal, whether the plan is flexible enough so that each candidate competes against all other qualified candidates, whether the plan unnecessarily trammels the interests of third parties, and whether the action is temporary, for example, not designed to continue after the plan's goal has been met.

In essence, an organization, through an AAP, promises to do the following:

1. Make good-faith efforts to recruit from diverse groups (which include women, African Americans, Hispanics, Vietnam-era veterans, Native Americans, people with disabilities, and older workers) through state employment services.
2. Limit the questions asked of applicants on their application forms or during interviews.
3. Set goals and timetables for hiring the protected groups.
4. Avoid testing applicants unless the test has been statistically evaluated to show the test is valid and job related.

affirmative action programs (AAPs)

Programs to put the principle of equal employment opportunity into practice.

7. *Name and explain the different forms of unlawful discrimination.*

disparate treatment

Form of unlawful discrimination in which a victim suffered an adverse employment action because of the victim's race, color, religion, gender, national origin, or other protected class.

Types of Discrimination   The federal equal employment opportunity laws prohibit covered employers from discriminating with respect to the terms and conditions of employment. Unlawful discrimination generally takes one of two forms: *disparate treatment* and *disparate impact.*

Disparate treatment requires the complaining person to show he or she suffered an adverse employment action such as a failure to hire or a termination because of his or her protected class (race, color, religion, gender, national origin, age, disability status, veteran's status, military obligations, etc.). The employer's best defense to a disparate treatment case is showing that the employer was motivated by a legitimate, nondiscriminatory business reason. In other words, the employer did what it did for reasons other than the protected class. Frequently, supervisors play a key role in this defense.

STOP AND THINK

In an earlier self-check, you noted in unionized firms that supervisors are generally required to follow specific procedures before disciplining employees and that in nonunion firms supervisors often use due process in applying discipline. How does the use of specific procedures and due process help employers defend themselves against disparate treatment claims? Can deviating from an employer's usual procedures cause problems for employers in discrimination cases?

If involved in the hiring process, supervisors must be able to explain clearly why one candidate was a better fit for a job than another candidate. If involved in discipline or discharge decisions, the supervisor must be able to explain what the person did that resulted in discipline or discharge. Documents created by supervisors such as warning letters and performance evaluations are often important pieces of evidence in disparate treatment cases. A second, though infrequently used, defense to disparate treatment claims is that the protected class constituted a bona fide occupational qualification (B.F.O.Q.); that is, the essence of the business requires the person to be a member of the protected class to successfully fulfill the purpose of the job. For example, when hiring the cast for a new movie, a production company can legally discriminate on the basis of gender to insist, for authenticity purposes, that female characters are played by women and male characters are played by men. The defense is not used often because the employer must admit it has engaged in discrimination, then justify why discrimination was essential to performing the duties of the job. However, under the law, race can never be a B.F.O.Q.

STOP AND THINK

You are the supervisor of two employees who have attendance issues—one is a white male; the other is an Asian female. Both employees have the same number of unexcused absences in the last year. Today, both of the employees are absent and neither follows the company procedure, which requires an absent employee to call his or her supervisor at least an hour before the shift starts. You decide to fire the white male but give the Asian female a final warning. Would firing the white male but not the Asian female have legal risks?

---

disparate impact

Form of unlawful discrimination in which an employer's facially neutral employment policy or practices have a statistically significant adverse effect on a protected group.

As discussed at the beginning of the chapter, the other form of discrimination is **disparate impact** discrimination. This claim arises when an employer's policies or practices are facially neutral—they look like they apply to everyone equally—but when the policies or practices are applied, they statistically impact one group at a statistically higher rate than another. If a policy or practice has a discriminatory effect, then the employer must be able to prove the policy or practice is job related and consistent with business necessity.

To provide an illustration, let's assume a test given to prospective employees to determine eligibility for employment is administered to 100 males and 100 females. If 100 males pass the test, but only 90 females pass the then test, the selection device may escape legal scrutiny. However, if fewer than 80 females pass the test, the selection device is subject to question. What if the employer contends the employment practice is related to the job and justified by business necessity? For example, a company may argue height and weight requirements are necessary because the particular job in question requires a certain amount of strength, that a no-beard policy is required because of health considerations in the food service industry, or that a certain level of knowledge is required about the position to warrant promotion. The Civil Rights Act of 1991 states job relatedness and business necessity may constitute a valid defense to a disparate impact case. However, the employer must be able to prove that the employment practice is actually related to the job and justified by business necessity. A company's assertion, by itself, that the practice is job related and justified by business necessity is not enough to avoid liability. Furthermore, even if the practice is job related and justified by business necessity, it still may be unlawful if another alternative is available that serves the same business purpose but with less impact on a protected class.

Harassment in the Workplace

A particularly perplexing area of concern for supervisors and their managers is how to handle the problem of sexual harassment in the workplace—a problem the courts consider to be a special form of disparate treatment discrimination. At one time, sexually oriented "kidding" between supervisors and their employees was of no concern to management. This is no longer true! Today, such verbal activities would probably be considered sexual harassment and lead to legal issues, regardless of whether the victim is male or female and even if the harasser is of the same gender as the victim.

On June 22, 1999, the U.S. Supreme Court ruled that "victims of workplace sex discrimination can win punitive damages from employers even if the boss's behavior was not 'egregious.'"[4] Federal law now permits victims of such workplace bias to recover punitive damages of up to $300,000 from the employer, in addition to any actual losses such as lost wages. In the 1999 decision, the Court said, "employers can defend themselves against such damages if they can show they made a sincere effort to prevent sex discrimination." Prevention generally includes a policy prohibiting workplace harassment, a specific reporting procedure through which victims can alert management of the workplace issue, and regular training of both managers and employees on acceptable workplace conduct.

sexual harassment

Unwelcome sexual advances that create a hostile, offensive, or intimidating work environment.

The EEOC's *Guidelines on Discrimination Because of Sex* defines **sexual harassment** as unwelcome sexual advances, requests for sexual favors, and other physical *or* verbal conduct, by a member of either sex, when such actions result in one of several consequences. Those consequences are (1) submission to the conduct is made, either implicitly or explicitly, a condition of employment; (2) submission to, or rejection of, the request(s) is used in making employment decisions involving the employee; or (3) the purpose or effect of such conduct is to unreasonably interfere with the employee's work performance or create a hostile, offensive, or intimidating work environment.[5]

Supervisors and their managers should take strong, quick, and positive measures to discourage sexual harassment because *employers are responsible for such harassment by, or of, their employees.* Such measures should include express declarations against sexual harassment that are regularly—and clearly—communicated to all employees, and those statements should be quickly and effectively implemented. Also, internal procedures for

Iofoto/Shutterstock.com

Companies must take measures against sexual harassment and regularly communicate their policies about it.

conducting immediate, thorough, and impartial investigations should be well established and publicized.

Today, sexual harassment litigation is a big business, with thousands of cases filed annually at the EEOC. In fiscal year 2016, the EEOC received a total of 91,503 charges of discrimination, of which 12,860 alleged sexual harassment. Surprising to some, 16.6 percent of those charges were filed by men! The EEOC rigorously explores these sexual harassment charges, and when guilt is determined, assesses steep penalties. In fiscal year 2016, the EEOC collected $40.7 million in monetary benefits on behalf of victims of sexual harassment; collections for 2010 and 2011 were also above the $40 million mark.[6] This example illustrates one of the EEOC s recent enforcement efforts:

> *On May 10, 2013, the Equal Employment Opportunity Commission (EEOC) announced that a jury in Memphis, Tennessee had awarded more than $1.5 million dollars in a sexual harassment lawsuit. The EEOC's lawsuit charged New Breed Logistics with subjecting three female employees to sexual harassment in the form of a supervisor's unwelcome sexual touching and lewd, obscene and vulgar sexual comments. The jury also found that the company retaliated against the three women and a male employee who stood up for them for opposing the harassment in violation of Title VII.[7]*

Managers should be aware that the law not only prohibits sexual harassment, but also harassment on the basis of other protected classes, including race, color, religion, national origin, pregnancy, age, or disability status. In fiscal year 2016, for example, the EEOC reported it received 32,309 charges of racial harassment, 20,857 charges of age harassment, and 28,073 charges of disability-based harassment.[8]

Accommodating Religious Beliefs An often-costly mistake by supervisors is to overlook the employer's duty under Title VII to provide reasonable accommodation for sincerely held religious beliefs. Under Title VII, religion is more than just protection for the traditional organized religion; it also protects and requires accommodations for a variety of other nontraditional religious, ethical, and moral beliefs.

STOP AND THINK

You are the manager of a local retail outlet of a large national chain. One of your employees, Hani, is Muslim and wears a headscarf to work to comply with her religious beliefs. Hani has been working for you for four months when your store is visited by the chain's district manager, who informs you that Hani's religious headscarf violates the company's "Look Policy." He tells you that she either has to work without it or you must fire her. What should you do?[9]

Accommodating Qualified Individuals with Disabilities   Similarly, the Americans with Disabilities Act requires employers to make reasonable accommodations for applicants and employees with physical or mental impairments that substantially limit major life activities. Examples include modified work spaces, special equipment, changes to how a job is performed, removal of nonessential functions from a job, provision of time off for treatment, and transfer of an employee to an open position for which the employee is qualified. Accommodations are not considered reasonable if they place an undue hardship on the employer or would require an employer to violate a collectively bargained seniority system.

Workplace Violence

A Special Report issued by the U.S. Department of Justice in March 2011 reported that in 2009 alone, approximately 572,000 nonfatal violent crimes (rape/sexual assault, robbery, assault) occurred against people while at work. In addition, there were 521 workplace homicides in the same year.[10] According to the Bureau of Labor Statistics, "from 2006 to 2010, an average of 551 workers per year were killed as a result of work-related homicides. . . . Shootings accounted for 78 percent of all workplace homicides in 2010 (405 fatal injuries). More than four-fifths (83 percent) of these workplace homicides from shootings occurred in the private sector, while only 17 percent of such shootings occurred in government."[11] Violence at work may occur for a variety of reasons, including prejudice and discrimination, work-related stress, personality differences, and non-work-related personal problems such as domestic violence. The end-of-the-chapter case (Case 16-1) explores the causes and ramifications of workplace violence and the need for managers to be proactive in addressing issues at work.

STOP AND THINK

The Occupational Safety and Health Administration (OSHA) has taken significant steps in its efforts to combat workplace violence and has a Web site devoted to bringing attention to the problems of workplace violence:

http://www.osha.gov/SLTC/workplaceviolence/. As of June 2013, 20 states had passed some form of legislation allowing workers to bring guns to work. For example, in 2013, Alabama passed a "gun in the parking lot" law that allowed most employees to have guns in their cars parked in their employers' parking lots provided the guns remained locked and out of sight. Are the actions of the federal government and the states consistent in terms of combating workplace violence? If employers comply with state laws that allow workers to possess guns on the worksite, is the employer potentially in violation of its federal duty to provide a safe workplace? Why or why not?

Other Legal Issues

Up to this point, we have discussed several legal issues dealing with labor–management relations, as well as equal opportunity laws. Now, we need to explain other important supervisory responsibilities, including employee benefits, the comparable worth issue, and other factors affecting wage rates.

Legally Required Benefits

8. *Describe the most commonly provided employee benefits.*

Employers are required by law to provide all employees with Social Security and Medicare, workers' compensation, and unemployment insurance. Also, some employers must provide certain employees with family and medical leave. Others will be required to provide health insurance or face penalties under the Patient Protection and Affordable Care Act of 2010.

Social Security and Medicare   The Social Security system is in reality two separate systems. One system provides retirement benefits for workers; the other provides disability, survivors', and Medicare benefits. To be eligible for the program, a worker must have contributed taxes into the system for 10 years (or 40 quarters).

Benefits are financed by a payroll tax paid by both employer and employee. The tax rate, the earnings base on which it is paid, and the benefits are subject to frequent congressional changes. The Social Security tax rate for 2016 was 6.2 percent of the first $127,200 of an employee's earnings, with both the employer and the employee paying that amount. In addition, there is a Medicare tax of 1.45 percent on *all earnings* paid by *both* the employer and the employee.

Workers' Compensation   All states have laws requiring workers' compensation. These laws protect employees and their families from permanent loss of income and high medical payments as a consequence of accidental injury, illness, or death resulting from the job. The amount to be paid for a given condition, such as loss of a hand or an arm, is stipulated in the law.

Workers' compensation funds are provided primarily through employer contributions to a statewide fund. Employers may purchase insurance from private insurance companies

The Family and Medical Leave Act requires an employer to provide up to 12 weeks of unpaid leave for the birth of a child.

to supplement these state funds. In general, employees are able to recover all medical expenses and up to two-thirds of the income lost due to disability or missed work.

Unemployment Insurance   In most states, unemployment insurance laws require that the government provide unemployed workers with benefits from a fund of payroll taxes imposed on employers. The amount paid into the fund by employers varies according to the unemployment rate within the state and the employer's record of unemployment, or **experience rating**. To receive benefits under the law, the unemployed worker is required to register for employment at the state employment office and usually must have worked for a certain length of time before becoming unemployed.

experience rating

Determining, from the record of unemployed workers, the amount the employer must pay into the state's unemployment insurance fund.

Family and Medical Leave   The Family and Medical Leave Act of 1993 requires employers with 50 or more employees employed within a 75-mile radius to offer employees—except *key* employees—up to 12 weeks of unpaid leave during a 12-month period for (1) the birth of a child; (2) placement of a child for adoption or foster care; (3) care of a spouse, child, or parent with a serious health condition; or (4) the employee's serious health condition. The Act was amended in 2008 to add special leave entitlement to permit eligible employees who are the spouse, son, daughter, parent, or next of kin of a service member (National Guard, Reserves, or Regular Armed Forces) with a serious injury or illness incurred in the line of duty to take up to 26 workweeks of FMLA leave during a single 12-month period to care for their family member (military caregiver leave), and to allow eligible employees whose spouse, child, or parent is called up for active duty in a foreign country to take up to 12 workweeks of FMLA leave for "qualifying exigencies" related to the call-up of their family member (qualifying exigency leave). The employer must continue providing health care coverage during the absence and place the employee in the same or a comparable position upon return. In some cases, additional time off for an employee's own serious health condition may be required as a "reasonable accommodation" under the Americans with Disabilities Act.

The Comparable Worth Issue

Despite the Equal Pay Act of 1963, which prohibits unequal pay for men and women doing jobs requiring equal skill, effort, and responsibility, women are often still paid substantially less than men for *similar* jobs. Jobs that have traditionally been held by women, such as nursing and teaching, are generally paid less than jobs traditionally held by men, such as accounting and engineering, even though the amount of training and levels of responsibility are similar. There is much controversy as to the cause of this disparity, particularly as more men enter traditionally female fields and more women enter traditionally male fields. The problem, according to advocates of "pay equity," goes far beyond equal pay for the same job. The real question is this: *Are women being systematically underpaid for work that requires the same skills, knowledge, and responsibility as similar jobs performed by men or are there legitimate, nondiscriminatory reasons for the remaining pay gap?*

comparable worth
***or* pay equity**

Jobs with equal points for the amount of education, effort, skills, and responsibility have equal pay.

Advocates say the solution lies in a system of **comparable worth**, or **pay equity**, in which a formula is used to assign points for the amount of education, effort, skills, and responsibility required for an individual job. These points are then used, along with job evaluation, to set salary rates. Critics say such wage adjustments would destroy the market forces of supply and demand. The arguments of advocates and critics of comparable worth are shown in Exhibit 16-13. In cases involving private sector employers, comparable worth theory has generally been rejected by the courts; however, some public employers are required by state or local law to utilize comparable worth theory in setting pay rates.

EXHIBIT 16-13

Should Jobs of "Comparable Worth" Receive Comparable Pay?

Some women's groups believe the principle of equal pay for work of equal value has been violated in that whole classes of jobs—such as those in the clerical area—are undervalued because they have traditionally been held by women. They want this practice changed so pay for all jobs will be based on their value to the business or community, rather than on who holds the jobs.

The arguments for comparable pay for comparable work are as follows:

1. If one employee contributes as much to the firm as another, the two should be paid the same.
2. It is needed to raise women's pay, which is now only about 65 percent of men's.
3. It will give women greater internal job mobility.
4. It is one way to further women's career ambitions.
5. It would motivate women to be more productive.

The arguments against comparable pay are

1. Federal law only requires equal pay for equal jobs.
2. It violates a firm's structured job evaluation system.
3. Employers must pay salaries competitive with those of other employers, which are based on what employees produce and on the economic value of the work performed.
4. Women receive less than men because two-thirds of new employees are women, and they always receive less than more senior employees.
5. It is practically impossible to determine accurately the real value of a job.

Source: Leon C. Megginson, Geralyn M. Franklin, and M. Jane Byrd, *Human Resource Management* (Houston:Dame Publications, 1995), p. 404.

STOP AND THINK

Do you think jobs of comparable worth should receive comparable pay? Which arguments in Exhibit 16-13 do you accept and why?

Factors Affecting Wage Rates

What most employers think they *should* pay is "competitive wages," but some specific factors affect what they actually pay. Most of these factors relate to what employers *have* to pay, but a final factor is what they are able to pay. Two important factors affecting wage rates are government factors and collective bargaining.

Governmental Factors Governmental laws, rules, and regulations largely determine what an employer *has to pay* workers. Some of these laws are the Fair Labor Standards Act; the Walsh–Healey Act; the Davis–Bacon Act; the Equal Pay Act; and various EEO/AA laws, such as the Civil Rights Act, the Vocational Rehabilitation Act, the Americans with Disabilities Act, and the Vietnam Era Veterans' Assistance Act.

The Fair Labor Standards Act covers all employees working in interstate commerce, all federal employees, and some state employees. The FLSA requires employers to pay at least the minimum wage for all hours worked and to pay most employees at least 1½ times their regular rate for hours worked beyond 40 in the same workweek (better known as overtime). A basic understanding of the FLSA's requirements is critical for supervisors today. In its August 25, 2012, edition, *BusinessWeek* reported wage and hour litigation had reached a 20-year high with 7,064 new federal lawsuits filed between April 2, 2011, and March 31, 2012.

One of the biggest issues in many of the wage and hour cases is whether the complaining employee is even entitled to the protection of the law. For example, on May 9, 2013, the U.S. Department of Labor announced it recovered more than $1 million in back pay for 196 employees an employer mistakenly classified as independent contractors and, as a result, had not ensured payment of minimum wage and overtime.[12]

exempt employees

Employees not covered by the provisions of the Fair Labor Standards Act.

nonexempt employees

Employees covered by the provisions of the Fair Labor Standards Act.

Some employees, referred to as **exempt employees**, including executives, administrators, professional employees, outside sales personnel, and other selected groups, are not covered by all provisions of this law (**nonexempt employees**, however, are covered by the FLSA). To be an exempt employee, however, the employee must meet certain criteria. For example, to be an exempt executive, administrative, or professional employee, the employee must (1) be paid on a salary basis of at least $455 per week *and* (2) have as his or her "primary duty" specific types of job responsibilities. Generally speaking, the job duties of exempt employees are duties that do not neatly fit within a 40-hour workweek and for which it would be difficult to substitute one employee for another at the end of 40 hours of work. For example, when the production manager is in the middle of planning the production and materials schedule for the next quarter when she hits the 40-hour mark, the employer cannot just substitute another production manager to continue that planning process. Planning and scheduling work generally requires continuity—the same person who starts the planning process needs to complete the planning process.

The FLSA also prevents child labor. Age 14 is the minimum working age for most non-farm jobs. On nonhazardous jobs, persons of age 14 and 15 can work no more than three hours on a school day, eight hours on any other day, or 40 hours per week (18 hours per week when school is in session). The times of the day during which a 14- or 15-year-old can work are also significantly restricted. Those who are 16- and 17-years-old can work in nonhazardous jobs for unlimited hours, but supervisors must know that a broad array of job duties, such as a 16-year-old driving, are considered hazardous under the law.

The Davis–Bacon Act and the Walsh–Healey Act impact the wage rates paid by private business that have certain types of contracts with the federal government. Construction firms with government contracts or subcontracts in excess of $2,000 are covered by the Davis–Bacon Act; other employers with government service contracts exceeding $10,000 are covered by the Walsh–Healey Act. These acts differ from the Fair Labor Standards Act in two aspects. First, the actual rate of pay is set by the Secretary of Labor. This rate of pay is called the **prevailing wage rate** in the area and approximates the union wage scale for the area in the given type of work. A second difference is that overtime is paid at time and a half for all hours worked over eight hours in a given day as well as over 40 hours in a given week.

prevailing wage rate

Approximates the union wage scale for the area in the given type of work.

Public policy now prohibits discrimination in pay unless it is based on job-related factors such as performance or experience. For example, the Equal Pay Act prohibits different rates of pay for men and women doing the same type of work. Title VII of the Civil Rights Act prevents discrimination based on race, color, religion, sex, or national origin. The Age Discrimination in Employment Act prohibits discrimination against persons 40 years of age and older. Finally, the Vocational Rehabilitation Act and Americans with Disabilities Act prohibit discrimination against persons with physical or mental impairments.

Collective Bargaining   When unions are involved, basic wages, job differentials, individual rates of pay, and employee benefits tend to be determined through the collective bargaining process. The actual amount of compensation is determined by the relative strength of the union and the employer. Benefits commonly provided in union agreements include health insurance, life insurance, pension or other retirement benefits, disability benefits, sick leave, bereavement leave, and vacation or other paid time off. However, even non-unionized employers are affected by the wage rates and the amounts of benefits paid by unionized firms because to remain competitive in the labor market, union-free employers often offer wages and benefits similar to those required by collective bargaining agreements in the recruiting area.

At this time, it is not completely clear how the various employer-related provisions of the Patient Protection and Affordable Care Act (PPACA) will impact the supervisory function. We do know, however, that under the PPACA, employers are now required to provide breaks to nursing mothers to express breast milk for the first year after the child's birth and provide "a place, other than a bathroom, that is shielded from view and free from intrusion from coworkers and the public, that may be used by an employee to express breast milk."

● Chapter Review

1. *Explain what is meant by labor relations.*

Labor relations, the relationships between employers and their unionized employees, are particularly important to supervisors because supervisors are the managers who must deal with operative employees on a day-to-day basis. An employer usually has good labor relations if the supervisors have good relationships with employees.

2. *Trace the development of unions in the United States and explain why union membership is declining.*

Union activities grew slowly in the United States until the formation of the AFL. Then membership increased steadily until after World War I, when it leveled off. Membership mushroomed during the period from 1935 to 1950, when favorable laws were passed and industrial unions became popular. Since then, union membership has grown more slowly so that now only 11.8 percent of all employees and only 6.9 percent of private employees are members of a union.

Some of the reasons for declining interest in unions among U.S. employees are (1) the economy shifted from manufacturing jobs that are relatively easy to unionize to service work, which is more difficult to organize; (2) today's educated and technologically oriented service workers are more interested in empowerment-type activities; (3) the global economy is forcing U.S. companies to cut costs by resisting organizing drives; (4) the influx of part-time workers resists unionization; (5) the proliferation of small businesses makes organizing more difficult; and (6) the passage of a number of laws at the federal, state, and local levels regulate traditional union issues such as safety and just-cause termination.

3. *Name and explain some of the basic laws governing labor relations.*

The basic law governing labor relations is the Wagner Act, which gives workers the right to freely join unions of their choosing and engage in concerted actions to achieve their goals. The Taft–Hartley Act prohibits the closed shop and provides for states to pass right-to-work laws prohibiting the union shop. The Landrum–Griffin Act provides employees with a bill of rights that protects them from exploitation by unscrupulous management and union leaders. These laws are administered by the NLRB, the Federal Mediation and Conciliation Service (FMCS), and the U.S. Department of Labor. The NLRB tries to prevent both unions and management from engaging in unfair labor practices.

4. *Describe union principles and objectives and discuss the methods used to achieve those objectives.*

Union objectives are higher pay, shorter hours of work, improved working conditions, and improved personal and job security. To achieve those objectives, unions organize (or recruit) an employer's workers into a union, then try to become recognized as the workers' exclusive bargaining agent in dealing with management, usually through an

NLRB-conducted, secret-ballot election. Unions have greater difficulty organizing employees in firms with effective supervisors and good employee relations. Management can try to keep the union out as long as its policies and actions stay within the law. When the union becomes the bargaining agent, it bargains collectively with representatives of management over wages, hours, and other terms and conditions of employment. Supervisors are critical to success at this point, so they should help formulate demands to be made of the union, evaluate proposals made by the union bargaining team, and be kept informed of progress made in the negotiations.

If the two parties cannot agree and reach an impasse, (1) they can call in an outside mediator; (2) they can agree to send the issue to an arbitrator, who will make a binding decision; or (3) the union can conduct a strike or management can stage a lockout. Most negotiations end with an agreement that becomes the contract between management and the employees.

5. *Name three things that a supervisor must know to live with the union agreement.*

Once an agreement is reached, it is up to the supervisor to live with the contract. Disagreements over interpretation of the agreement are settled through the grievance procedure. If agreement is not reached within the company, then the issue goes to an arbitrator for resolution. Supervisors by and large can no longer terminate an employee without a valid, documented reason.

6. *State the laws providing equal employment opportunity for protected groups of employees.*

The Equal Pay Act prohibits pay discrimination between men and women. Title VII of the Civil Rights Act of 1964 prohibits discrimination on the basis of race, color, religion, gender (including pregnancy), and national origin in the terms and conditions of employment, and requires employers to provide reasonable accommodation for religious beliefs. The Age Discrimination in Employment Act prohibits employment-related discrimination against individuals who are 40 and older. The Americans with Disabilities Act prohibits discrimination against qualified individuals with disabilities, as well as individuals who are perceived as disabled, have a history of a disability, or are associated with individuals with disabilities. Employers have to provide reasonable accommodations to individuals with disabilities. The Immigration Reform and Control Act prohibits discrimination on the basis of citizenship. Veterans also receive special protection from discrimination under federal law. The EEOC is the primary agency for enforcing the federal discrimination laws. In addition, many state and local governments have laws prohibiting discrimination on a variety of other grounds, including sexual orientation, gender identity, marital status, and appearance.

7. *Name and explain the different forms of unlawful discrimination.*

The most common form of discrimination is disparate treatment, also known as intentional discrimination. Disparate treatment occurs when an employer takes an adverse employment action against an employee or applicant because of that person's protected class (race, color, religion, gender, national origin, age, disability status, etc.). The second form of discrimination is disparate impact, also known as unintentional discrimination. Disparate impact arises if an employer's facially neutral employment policy or practice has a statistically significant adverse effect on a protected group. A special form of discrimination is called harassment and occurs when an employee is subjected to unwanted conduct because of the employee's protected class and that conduct is so severe or pervasive that it alters the employee's working conditions, creating a hostile working environment. The most common form of harassment is sexual harassment, but harassment based on any protected class is unlawful.

8. *Describe the most commonly provided employee benefits.*
Employee benefits are noncash forms of compensation. Those employers are legally required to provide are (1) Social Security and Medicare, (2) workers' compensation, (3) unemployment insurance, and (4) family and medical leave. Benefits commonly provided by both union and union-free employers include health insurance, life insurance, retirement benefits, disability benefits, sick leave, bereavement leave, and vacation or other paid time off.

Key Terms

labor union, p. 483
labor relations *or* union–
   management relations *or*
   industrial relations, p. 483
craft unions, p. 484
industrial unions, p. 484
unfair labor practices, p. 487
closed-shop, p. 487
union-shop, p. 487
agency shop, p. 487
maintenance-of-membership
   clause, p. 487
right-to-work laws, p. 487

employees' bill of rights, p. 488
union authorization card, p. 489
exclusive bargaining agent, p. 493
collective bargaining, p. 495
mediator, p. 496
arbitrator, p. 496
strike, p. 496
picketing, p. 496
lockout, p. 496
collective bargaining agreement
   or contract, p. 496
union steward, p. 497
seniority, p. 498

grievance procedure, p. 498
concerted activity, p. 500
affirmative action programs
   (AAPs), p. 502
disparate treatment, p. 503
disparate impact, p. 503
sexual harassment, p. 504
experience rating, p. 508
comparable worth *or* pay equity,
   p. 508
exempt employees, p. 510
nonexempt employees, p. 510
prevailing wage rate, p. 510

Discussion Questions

1. Define labor relations.
2. When did unions grow the fastest? Why?
3. Why has union growth slowed? What can unions do to appeal to younger workers entering the workforce?
4. Do you believe union power will increase or decrease in the future? Why?
5. Name the laws that form the legal basis for labor relations, and explain their general provisions.
6. What are the differences among the union shop, the closed shop, and the agency shop? Are these differences really significant? Explain. How do right-to-work laws impact the ability of unions to demand union-shop clauses in collective bargaining agreements?
7. What are "unfair labor practices," and what are some unfair labor practices management sometimes commits?
8. What are some unfair labor practices unions sometimes commit?
9. What are the primary objectives of unions?
10. What are the methods used by unions to achieve their objectives?

11. What provisions are usually included in a labor agreement?
12. Describe the typical grievance procedure.
13. Why have union-free employers begun implementing grievance procedures, including mandatory arbitration, traditionally found only in unionized workplaces?
14. Why has "termination at will" declined as a management tool?
15. What are the protected classes under federal employment discrimination laws? Are white men protected? Why or why not?
16. How do EEO laws affect recruiting and selecting of employees?
17. What is the difference between disparate treatment discrimination and disparate impact discrimination?
18. What is the role of the supervisor in helping the employer defend claims of disparate treatment?
19. What steps should employers take to reduce the risk of sexual harassment in the workplace?
20. Name and describe the four legally required employee benefits.

Skill Builder 16.1

Information

The Legal Landscape
Refer to the chapter preview. Were the City of New Haven's business practices discriminatory?
Using the Internet, follow the links provided:

http://scholars.law.unlv.edu/cgi/viewcontent.cgi?article=1642&context=facpub

— OR —

https://www.dorsey.com/newsresources/publications/2009/07/ricci-v-destefano
--supreme-court-holds-employer-__

Type a one- to three-paragraph summary of the court's decision regarding the City of New Haven case and turn it in to your teacher.

Skill Builder 16.2

Information

Systems

Technology

Social Media in Today's Workplace
You are the manager of XYZ Services Corporation. Today, one of your employees, Janice Smith, brings you a copy of a lengthy Facebook exchange involving a number of your employees. The exchange started when one of the employees posted: "My coworker, Janice Smith, feels we don't help our clients enough at XYZ Corp. I've about had it! My fellow coworkers how do u feel?" A number of employees weighed in on the topic and said a number of unflattering things about Janice, making her feel uncomfortable at work. You know you do not want Janice to be subjected to a hostile working environment, but you have heard that the National Labor Relations Board recently found that social media exchanges can be protected concerted activity. Using the information found in the U.S. Chamber of Commerce's Report "A Survey of Social Media Issues Before the NLRB," http://files.aliaba.org/files/coursebooks/pdf/VCT1017_chapter_02.pdf, answer the following questions:

1. What should you do in this situation?
2. Should your company have a social media policy governing what employees can post on social media sites about the company or its employees? Are there limits on what can be prohibited?

CASE 16-1

UNITED STATES FREIGHT GROUP:

COMPANY BACKGROUND

United States Freight Group (USFG) was founded in the mid-1960s as a small bulk carrier in the transportation industry. Through internal growth, acquisitions, and partnerships, the organization has grown into a diversified transportation company employing over 800 people, 500 of whom are drivers. The company operates internationally in the United States, Canada, and Mexico and is either number one or in the top five of most markets it currently serves. The company is "quality driven" and committed to meeting customer needs 100 percent of the time—providing on-time, contaminant-free deliveries and efficient and accurate billing. The company offers a variety of services ranging from dry bulk transportation to remote silo inventory management. Since 1990, it has been the recipient of eight quality service awards and recently was designated as "supplier of the year." With such a wide range of services and equipment and a focus on quality, USFG has proven it can handle most client needs.

The following situation takes place at one of USFG's remote transloading facilities in the southeastern United States. Operations at this facility entail unloading materials from railcars into trucks and transporting these goods to customers in the surrounding area 24 hours a day, 7 days a week. Because the customer base is "local," the drivers typically travel in a 200-square-mile radius of the transloading facility. This remote location is managed by the regional manager, who is physically located in a different state, but a human resources representative (HRR) is on-site from 8:00 A.M. to 5:00 P.M., Monday through Friday, to handle the daily duties, such as scheduling, paperwork, and employee relations. Thus, the HRR provides staff support without direct line authority. Two shifts (6:00 A.M. to 6:00 P.M. and 6:00 P.M. to 6:00 A.M.) are utilized at the facility, with employees working 12-hour schedules. The HRR sets the schedules on a rotation basis, so the process is considered fair by the employees.

THE MODEL EMPLOYEE

James Redmond enjoyed working at USFG. In fact, he liked it so much he stayed with the company for over eight years—twice as long as the next senior employee. James liked the company for many reasons. Initially, the pay and benefits attracted him. The benefits included medical, dental, and life insurance, as well as a matching 401(k) plan. The safety incentive programs, number of holidays, and paid vacations after time in service also made employment at USFG attractive to James. Another plus was that USFG paid its employees on a multitiered commission basis tied to the number of loads delivered during an employee's schedule. Drivers made $35 per delivery, while loaders made $30. If an employee had the ability, training, and experience to be a loader and a driver, he could earn up to $65 per delivery by doing both jobs. Approximately four to five deliveries could be made during a normal 12-hour shift. Usually, the more senior employees were given the dual designation of "loaders/drivers." Thus, James was motivated early on to obtain additional job and safety training to gain the dual designation and earn the maximum amount possible.

James had been the facility's number one loader/driver in terms of performance, efficiency, and safety for more than six years. He was a model employee whose recent injury had a big impact on the facility's overall performance. James was injured on the job when the hose used to transfer the material from the container to the truck "broke loose" during loading.

The end of the hose hit James in the arm, breaking his arm and causing major nerve damage. The injury was so severe that even after the break healed and he completed physical therapy, he continued to experience "deadness" in his arm due to the nerve damage. As a result, he could no longer load the trucks. He could only drive.

Given that James was such a model employee, USFG welcomed him back in whatever capacity he could perform. James felt equally as blessed to be back, even if it meant only performing part of his old job. It was less money, but he still enjoyed working at USFG. The individual-based work was well suited for his personality. It provided him an opportunity to have time alone, which with a family of five was a precious commodity. Plus, his previous employer, a local shipbuilder, changed to a team-based culture, which James never really felt comfortable with. It was supposed to be a more positive environment with everyone pulling together, but he found it to be just the opposite. The employees tried ways to outshine everyone else to gain favorable recognition, so James found himself always having to watch his back. That was the great thing about USFG: you didn't have to play politics or worry about dealing with complainers, slackers, or brownnosers. Just do your job, perform it well, and get paid, or so James thought.

THE MANAGEMENT PROBLEM

Shortly after James returned to work, USFG lost a local contract that represented a significant amount of work for the transloading facility. Kathy Prunel, the regional manager, was confronted with the challenge of how to keep the employees working when her facility just lost over 25 percent of its business. This remote location was not a top priority for upper management, as evidenced by the lack of marketing efforts for the facility. Without the proper marketing, the facility's client base and production capacity were limited. In the short term, while Kathy explored marketing opportunities with upper management, she decided to change the schedule from 12- to 8-hour shifts (7:00 A.M. to 2:00 P.M., 2:00 P.M. to 10:00 P.M., 10:00 P.M. to 7:00 A.M.) and increase the

(Continued)

amount of "standing time" for each employee on each shift. "Standing time" was time spent in the yard at the facility performing activities such as prepping, cleaning, or maintaining the equipment. Although a certain amount of "standing time" was necessary during every employee's schedule, three to four hours became mandatory. This policy change led to lots of discussion and discord around the yard because "standing time" paid $16 an hour, considerably less than one could make loading or driving.

The workers were told the situation was temporary. "Just get through the next several weeks and things will get back to normal," Kathy told them. After two weeks, all of the equipment was spotless and running smoothly, forcing the workers to spend more time together in the yard. Not everyone was happy about the increased interaction. James felt like the company was doing what it could to avoid layoffs, but some of the newer employees, A. J. Johnson in particular, couldn't seem to see anything but the negative in the situation. James had known others like A. J., always complaining about their situation and what they were going to do if the company didn't do right by them.

After several weeks of hearing A. J. spout off, James finally had enough. "If you hate it here so much, why don't you quit," asked James. "I never quit nothin' in my life, and I ain't startin' now!" replied A. J. "That manager better get her act together and start doing something or she's gonna be hearin' from me! And what's it to you anyway, old man!" barked A. J. The conversation escalated to such a point that James and A. J. had to be restrained by their coworkers. On his way to his car, James could hear A. J. screaming behind him, "You're lucky your buddies were here! You better watch out! Don't let me catch you alone!"

The next day, Cindy Smith, the HRR, was informed of what transpired between James and A. J. the previous night. She was concerned. She suspected that A. J. was the one stealing from the office—supplies, coffee, sugar, and so on. She knew A. J. was trouble, but as long as the facility was operating at full capacity, he didn't have an opportunity to interact much with the other workers. Now, things were different! Cindy immediately contacted Kathy Prunel, who flew down the next day with Mike Ebersol, the safety manager, to meet with Cindy, James, and A. J.

The meeting went as well as could be expected. The regional manager hated to involve Mike, but she saw no other way. Mike was a big man, and he had a way of presenting a situation such that all parties agreed to act responsibly. Basically, Mike threatened James and A. J. that if they couldn't resolve their differences amicably and Kathy had to be brought in again, they would be real sorry! James left the meeting with an uneasy feeling. He didn't think Mike's message had much of an impact on A. J. What was he going to do when A. J. pushed the envelope? How was he going to react? He went to Cindy and asked her not to schedule him and A. J. on the same shift. Cindy knew James was a good person, and she was just as concerned as he was. She agreed.

The next several weeks passed without incident, sort of. Although James and A. J. had no direct contact with each other, thanks to Cindy's scheduling, A. J. attempted to agitate James indirectly. At the end of his schedule, A. J. would "accidentally" spill coffee on the seat of the front-end loader, so when James came on he would sit in it. He tried soiling the equipment (spitting on the steering wheel) because he knew how much pride James took in keeping his machinery clean. A. J. even went as far as to break the front-end loader so James would get blamed. Cindy was well aware of his deliberate antics, and she feared James might eventually be pushed to the breaking point and retaliate. After much deliberation, she called Kathy.

Kathy had not been sure that Mike's approach was going to work, so she was not completely caught off guard by Cindy's call. She thanked Cindy for contacting her and began to develop a plan of action. Kathy realized she didn't have any substantial evidence against A. J. If he and James got into another altercation, then both had to be let go for fighting. She decided to do two things. First, Cindy should continue scheduling the work so James and A. J. didn't come into direct contact. Second, Cindy would begin implementing a "checklist." The "checklist" was a list of safety, maintenance, and cleaning items that had to be performed by each worker on his equipment prior to the end of each scheduled shift. Kathy believed this to be the perfect means of documenting any inappropriate behavior that might be grounds for dismissal. Cindy immediately created and distributed the lists, noting the change in policy with the employees on the next shift.

When Mike Ebersol heard about the checklist being used at the remote transloading facility, he thought to himself, "How is Kathy ever going to learn to be a good manager without confronting these problems head on? She always sidesteps issues. Now is the time to force her to deal with this problem directly." He called Cindy and told her to schedule James and A. J. for the same shift for the upcoming Saturday night. "This will force things to a head! They'll solve their differences one way or the other, and then Kathy can take action," Mike thought to himself.

Cindy was panic stricken! She just knew someone was going to get hurt. A. J. was going to cause trouble for sure, but how was James going to be able to defend himself with his injured arm. She was unable to contact Kathy, who was on vacation for seven days. Without being able to speak with Kathy, she had no choice but to follow Mike's instructions. She scheduled the two for Saturday's night shift.

THE SHOWDOWN

James couldn't believe his eyes when he saw Saturday's schedule. It must be a mistake. He went to talk with Cindy. Cindy was visibly upset and told him what happened. James went into the yard to begin working and planning how he was going to handle the situation. He was adjusting a piece of equipment on the front-end loader when a coworker approached him and said, "James, what you gonna do man? I saw Saturday's schedule, and it ain't good. I heard A. J. flappin' his gums day before yesterday about how he was gonna be packin' some heat. Said if you wuz to get out of line, he'd have to pop you one! You better be real careful James; A. J. is one bad dude!"

EPILOGUE

Trouble began shortly after A. J. and James started their Saturday night shift. A. J. started talking "smack," and James couldn't contain himself. James verbally defended himself and even went as far as telling A. J. he thought A. J. was responsible for most, if not all, of the problems at the yard. This bantering back and forth did not end until A. J. went to his car and returned with a .357 magnum that he fired at James. Fortunately, A. J. missed his intended target—he wasn't as great a marksman as he proclaimed to be! A. J. was immediately fired for leaving his work area and carrying a weapon. USFG is currently trying to replace its lost client (and revenues) but has not been able to find another. A. J.'s position has not been filled. Recently, the employees have been able to return to longer shifts with less "standing time."

CASE QUESTIONS

1. From a management perspective, why did the company allow the initial childish behavior (coffee on the seat, spit on the steering wheel, etc.) to escalate into employee confrontation?
2. When does childish behavior become a harassment issue? At what point does one's practical jokes or intimidating actions toward one employee impact all employees?
3. Visit the Occupational Safety and Health Administration's Web site and review the agency's "Fact Sheet" on workplace violence: http://www.osha.gov/OshDoc/data_General_Facts/factsheet-workplace-violence.pdf. What kind of policy statement and/or plan should the company include in its overall policy and procedures manual to avoid violence in the workplace? What type of training should the company provide all employees on this issue?
4. What additional legal issues does this case's problem raise for USFG?
5. Would USFG face potential liability if it fired A. J. based on the rumored threats of violence?
6. The National Rifle Association is lobbying for states to pass laws that prohibit employers from stopping an employee from bringing a gun to work in the employee's car. As of June 2013, 20 states had enacted "bring your gun to work" laws, including Oklahoma. The Oklahoma statute gives employees the right to keep guns locked in their cars. Other bills are being modeled after the Oklahoma statute. Many employers and business groups oppose the law. Discuss.

Source: Prepared by Don C. Mosley Jr., John S. Bishop Jr., and Kelly Collins Woodford, Mitchell College of Business, University of South Alabama, Mobile, Alabama. The company and individual names are fictitious.

Notes

1. Ricci v. DeStefano, 129 S. Ct. 2658, 2671, 174 L. Ed. 2d 490 (2009).
2. Tiffany Hsu, "Judge Approves Hostess Liquidation, 15,000 Immediate Layoffs," *Los Angeles Times*, November 21, 2012, http://www.latimes.com/business/money/la-fi-mo-hostess-twinkies-liquidation-20121121,0,6123647.story.

3. Design Technology Group LLC d/b/a Bettie Page Clothing, 359 NLRB No. 96 (April 19, 2013).

4. Kolstad v. American Dental Association, 527 U.S. 526 (1999).

5. "Charge Statistics FY 1997 through FY 2016," Equal Employment Opportunity Commission, http://eeoc.gov/eeoc/statistics/enforcement/charges.cfm.

6. "Charges Alleging Sex-Based Harassment (Charges filed with EEOC) FY 2010–FY 2016," Equal Employment Opportunity Commission, https://www.eeoc.gov/eeoc/statistics/enforcement/sexual_harassment_new.cfm.

7. Equal Employment Opportunity Commission, "Jury Awards More Than $1.5 Million in EEOC Sexual Harassment and Retaliation Suit against New Breed Logistics," press release, May 10, 2013, http://www.eeoc.gov/eeoc/newsroom/release/5-10-13a.cfm.

8. Equal Employment Opportunity Commission, "EEOC Releases Fiscal Year 2016 Enforcement and Litigation Data," press release, January 18, 2017, https://www.eeoc.gov/eeoc/newsroom/release/1-18-17a.cfm.

9. Stuart Hunter. "Abercrombie Struggling to Prove Fired Woman's Hijab Hurt Sales: Report," *Huff Post*, July 3, 2013, http://www.huffingtonpost.com/2013/06/19/abercrombie-headscarf-hani-khan-hijab-lawsuit_n_3466226.html.

10. U.S. Department of Justice, Bureau of Justice Statistics, "Special Report: Workplace Violence 1993–2009," March 2011, http://www.bjs.gov/content/pub/pdf/wv09.pdf.

11. U.S. Department of Labor, Bureau of Labor Statistics, "Fact Sheet: Workplace Homicides from Shootings," January 2013, https://www.bls.gov/iif/oshwc/cfoi/osar0016.htm.

12. U.S. Department of Labor, "U.S. Department of Labor Recovers More Than $1 Million in Back Wages and Damages for 196 Employees Misclassified as Independent Contractors," press release, May 9, 2013, http://www.dol.gov/whd/media/press/whdpressVB3.asp?pressdoc=Southeast/20130509xml.

Glossary

Acceptance theory of authority A manager's authority originates only when it has been accepted by the group or individual over whom it is being exercised.

Accountability The obligation that is created when an employee accepts the leader's delegation of authority.

Achievement, proficiency, or skill tests Measure the applicant's knowledge of and ability to do a given job.

Acknowledging Showing by nonevaluative verbal responses that you listened to what the employee has stated.

Active listening A listening technique for understanding others and encouraging open feedback.

Adaptive leadership Organizational members take a hard look at the past to identify what to hold on to, while deciding what needs to go. Employee participation in the change process is the key.

Administrative skills Establishing and following procedures to process paperwork in an orderly manner.

Advisory authority Authority of most staff departments to serve and advise line departments.

Affirmative action programs (AAPs) Programs to put the principle of equal employment opportunity into practice.

Affirming Communicating to an employee his or her value, strengths, and contributions.

Agency shop All employees must pay union dues even if they choose not to join the union.

Alternatives Possible courses of action that can satisfy a need or solve a problem.

Appraisal interview Supervisor communicates the results of a performance appraisal to an employee.

Arbitrator Makes a binding decision when collective bargaining reaches an impasse.

Attending Showing through nonverbal behavior you are listening in an open, nonjudgmental manner.

Attending skills A wide range of actions taken by a listener that facilitate the speaker's freedom of expression, such as eye contact, nods of the head, and eliminating distractions.

Authority Given the right to act in a specified manner in order to reach organizational objectives; the right to tell others how to act to reach objectives.

Authority compliance The leader has a high concern for production results and uses a directive approach.

Baby Boomers Workforce generation born between 1945 and 1964.

Body signals Nonverbal signals communicated by body action.

Brainstorming Freely thinking of ideas without evaluating the ideas as they are generated.

Budget A forecast of expected financial performance over time.

Burnout A malady caused by excessive stress in the setting where people invest most of their time and energy.

Cause-and-effect diagram A graphical display of a chain of causes and effects.

Challengers Challengers are questioning, playing the role of devil's advocate when necessary, and pushing the team to move out of its comfort zone.

Channel The means used to pass a message.

Check sheets A check sheet is used to collect and organize data.

Closed shop All prospective employees must be members of the recognized union before they can be employed.

Closure Successfully accomplishing the objective for a given item on the agenda.

Coaching Helping individuals reach their highest levels of performance.

Coaching and selling style Used with individuals or groups with potential but who haven't realized it fully.

Collaborators Collaborators keep the members focused on the team's actual goal(s) or purpose.

Collective bargaining Conferring in good faith over wages, hours, and other terms and conditions of employment.

Collective bargaining agreement or contract The document prepared when an accord has been reached to bind the company, union, and workers to specific clauses in it.

Communication process model Model of the five components of communication and their relationships.

Communicators Communicators are process-oriented, positive team members who are effective listeners and facilitators of any conflict among team members.

Comparable worth *or* pay equity Jobs with equal points for the amount of education, effort, skills, and responsibility have equal pay.

Computer-assisted manufacturing (CAM) Special computers assist equipment in performing processes.

Conceptual skills Mental ability to become aware of and identify relationships among different pieces of information.

Concerted activity One or more employees take action for mutual aid and protection.

Concurrent controls Sometimes called screening controls; these controls are used while an activity takes place.

Confirming Ensuring an employee understands what has been said or agreed upon.

Confronting/challenging Establishing clear performance standards, comparing actual performance against those standards, and addressing performance that doesn't meet those standards.

Consensus The acceptance by all members of the decision reached.

Contingency planning Thinking in advance about possible problems or changes that might arise and having anticipated solutions available.

Continuum of Leadership Behavior The full range of leadership behaviors in terms of the relationship between a supervisor's use of authority and employees' freedom.

Contributor Contributors help keep the group or team focused on the task.

Control chart   Displays the "state of control" of a process.

Controlling   Comparing actual performance with planned action and taking corrective action if needed.

Cost leadership strategy   Attempts to lower costs below those of competitors by focusing on creating efficiencies within organizational systems.

Cost/benefit analysis   Estimating and comparing the costs and benefits of alternatives.

Counseling   Helping an individual recognize, talk about, and solve either real or perceived problems that affect performance.

Country club management   High concern for people.

Craft unions   Workers in a specific skill, craft, or trade.

Crawford Slip technique   Makes use of two elements that are important in achieving creativity: fluency and flexibility.

Creativity   The process of developing something unique or original.

Critical path   The series of activities that comprise the longest route, in terms of time, to complete the job.

Critical path method   A management scheduling tool that identifies the activities needed to complete a task or project, specifies the time each activity will take, and shows the relationships among the network of activities to determine the total completion time of the task or project.

Decentralization   The extent to which authority is delegated from one unit of the organization to another.

Decision making   Considering and selecting a course of action from among alternatives.

Delegating and empowering style   Used with exceptionally ready and capable individuals and groups.

Delegation of authority   The process by which leaders distribute and entrust activities and related authority to other people in an organization. The three key aspects of organization are (1) granting authority, (2) assigning duties and responsibilities, and (3) requiring accountability.

Deming's 85-15 rule   Assumes that when things go wrong, 85 percent of the time the cause is from elements controlled by management.

Departmentalization   The organizational process of determining how activities are to be grouped.

Developmental leadership   An approach that helps groups evolve effectively and achieve highly supportive, open, creative, committed, high-performing membership.

Differentiation strategy   Used by managers to gain a competitive advantage through goods and/or services that are clearly unique or different from those of the competition.

Disciplinary layoff *or* suspension   Time off without pay.

Discipline   Training that corrects and molds knowledge, attitudes, and behavior.

Disparate impact   Form of unlawful discrimination in which an employer's facially neutral employment policy or practices have a statistically significant adverse effect on a protected group.

Disparate treatment   Form of unlawful discrimination such that a victim suffered an adverse employment action because of the victim's race, color, religion, gender, national origin, or other protected class.

Dissatisfier or hygiene factors   Factors employees said most affected them negatively or dissatisfied them about their job, including low pay, low benefits, and unfavorable working conditions.

Diversity   Refers to the wide range of distinguishing employee characteristics, such as sex, age, race, ethnic origin, and other factors.

Downsizing Eliminating unnecessary levels of management; striving to become leaner and more efficient by reducing the workforce and consolidating departments and work groups.

Downward communication Flows that originate with supervisors and are passed down to employees.

Due process Guarantees the individual accused of violating an established rule a hearing to determine the extent of guilt.

Ego or esteem need The need for self-confidence, independence, appreciation, and status.

e-mail Refers to messages and documents created, transmitted, and usually read entirely on a computer.

Emotional intelligence (EI) The capacity to recognize and accurately perceive one's own and others' emotions, to understand the significance of these emotions, and to influence one's actions based on this analysis; an assortment of skills and characteristics that influence a person's ability to succeed as a leader.

Employee Assistance Programs (EAPs) Professional counseling and other services for employees with unresolved personal or work-related problems.

Employees' bill of rights Protects employees from possible abuse by unscrupulous managers and union leaders.

Empowerment Granting employees authority to make key decisions within their enlarged areas of responsibility.

Equity theory Theory that when people perceive themselves in situations of inequity or unfairness, they are motivated to act in ways to change their circumstances.

Ethical dilemmas Situations in which the supervisor is not certain of the correct behavior.

Ethical organizations Organizations composed of three pillars: ethical individuals, ethical leaders, and sound structures and systems.

Ethics The standards used to judge the "rightness" or the "wrongness" of one person's behavior toward others.

Exclusive bargaining agent Person or organization that has the exclusive right to deal with management on behalf of employees over questions of wages, hours, and other terms and conditions of employment.

Exempt employees Employees not covered by the provisions of the Fair Labor Standards Act.

Expectancy theory Views an individual's motivation as a conscious effort involving the expectancy a reward will be given for a good result.

Experience rating Determining, from the record of unemployed workers, the amount the employer must pay into the state's unemployment insurance fund.

Experiential learning Using an integrated process of experiencing, identifying, analyzing, and generalizing to gain insights into learning.

External change forces Forces outside the organization that have a great impact on organizational change. Management has little control over these numerous external forces.

Extrinsic motivation Behavior performed not for its own sake, but for the consequences associated with it. The consequences can include pay, benefits, job security, and working conditions.

Facial signals Nonverbal messages sent by facial expression.

Fact-finding meeting Held to seek out relevant facts about a problem or situation.

Feedback The response that a communicator receives.

Feedback controls Controls that measure completed activities and then take corrective action if needed.

Feedforward controls Preventive controls that try to anticipate problems and take corrective action before they occur.

Financial resources   The money, capital, and credit an organization requires for operations.

Financing   Providing or using funds to produce and distribute an organization's product or service.

Flexibility   The ability to use free association to generate or classify ideas in categories.

Flowchart   Visual representation of the sequence of steps needed to complete a process.

Fluency   The ability to let ideas flow out of your head like water over a waterfall.

Formal group   Group prescribed and/or established by the organization.

Formal theory of authority   According to the formal theory of authority, authority is conferred; authority exists because someone was granted it.

Functional authority   A staff person's limited line authority over a given function.

Functional departmentalization   A form of departmentalization that groups together common functions or similar activities to form an organizational unit.

Gantt chart   Identifies work stages and scheduled completion dates.

Generation Xers   Workforce generation born between 1965 and 1980.

Generation Yers   Youngest workforce generation, born between 1981 and 1999.

Generation Zers   Generation born after 1999, just starting to enter the workforce.

Glass ceiling   Invisible barrier that limits women from advancing in an organization.

Goal-setting theory   Theory that task goals, properly set and managed, can be an important employee motivator.

Graduated scale of penalties   Penalties become progressively more severe each time the violation is repeated.

Grapevine   Informal flow of communication in organizations.

Grievance procedure   A formal way of handling employees' complaints.

Group   Two or more people who communicate and work together regularly in pursuit of one or more common objectives.

Group-centered approach   Used at meetings where group members interact freely and address and question one another.

Group cohesiveness   The mutual liking and team feeling in a group.

Group facilitation   The process of intervening to help a group improve goal setting, action planning, problem solving, conflict management, and decision making in order to increase the group's effectiveness.

Heroic managers   Managers who have a great need for control or influence and who want to run things. Leaders identify desired performance standards and recognize what types of rewards employees want from their work.

Hierarchy of needs   Arrangement of people's needs in a hierarchy, or ranking of importance.

Hierarchy of objectives   A network with broad goals at the top level of the organization and narrower goals for individual divisions, departments, or employees.

Histogram   Graphical representation of the variation found in a set of data.

Hot-stove rule   Compares a good disciplinary system to a hot stove.

Human relations skills   Understanding other people and interacting effectively.

Human resources   The people an organization requires for operations.

"I" message   Attempt to change an employee's behavior by indicating the specific behavior, how it makes you feel as a supervisor, and the effect of the behavior.

Impoverished management   Management with little concern for people or production.

Industrial unions   Unions composed of all the workers in an industry.

Informal communication   Separate from a formal, established communication system.

Informal group   A group that evolves out of the formal organization but is not formed by management or shown in the organization's structure.

Information-exchange meeting   Held to obtain information from group members.

Information-giving meeting   Held to announce new programs and policies or to update present ones.

Information richness   Amount of verbal and nonverbal information that a channel carries.

Instant message (IM)   Use of intranet or Internet technology that allows people to receive messages in real time.

Intangible standards   Relate to human characteristics and are not expressed in terms of numbers, money, physical qualities, or time.

Integration process   A conflict resolution strategy in which everyone wins.

Internal change forces   Pressures for change within the organization such as cultures and objectives.

Intolerable offenses   Disciplinary problems of a drastic, dangerous, or illegal nature.

Intrinsic motivation   Behavior an individual produces because of the pleasant experiences associated with the behavior itself.

Inverted pyramid   A structure widest at the top and narrowing as it funnels down.

IQ tests   Measure the applicant's capacity to learn, solve problems, and understand relationships.

Job characteristics model   Approach to job design that focuses on five core job elements leading to intrinsic motivation and then positive work outcomes.

Job descriptions   Provide information to employees about the important job-related tasks.

Just-in-time (JIT) inventory control   A system whereby materials (inputs) arrive as close as feasible to the time they are needed in the production or service process.

Labor relations *or* union–management relations *or* industrial relations   The relationship between an employer and unionized employees.

Labor union   An organization of workers banded together to achieve economic goals.

Lateral–diagonal communication   Flows between individuals in the same department or different departments.

Leader-controlled approach   Used at meetings of large groups when the leader clearly runs the show and the open flow of information is impeded.

Leadership   Influencing individual and group activities toward goal achievement.

Leadership Grid   Categorizes leadership styles according to concern for people and concern for production results.

Leading   Guiding, influencing, and motivating employees in the performance of their duties and responsibilities.

Lean Approach   The Lean Approach consists of techniques and approaches aimed at eliminating waste. Lean concepts can be applied to all types of business, not just manufacturing.

Life-cycle theory of leadership   Leadership behaviors should be based on the readiness level of employees.

Life event   Anything that causes a person to deviate from normal functioning.

Line authority   Power to directly command or exact performance from others.

Line organization   An organization concerned with the primary functions of the firm—in this case, production, sales, and office administration/ finance.

Line personnel   Line personnel carry out the primary activities of a business, such as producing or selling products and/or services.

Line-and-staff organization   An organization structure in which staff positions are added to serve the basic line departments and help them accomplish the organization objectives more effectively.

Lockout   A closing of a company's premises to the employees and refusing to let the employees work.

Maintenance-of-membership clause   An employee who joined the union must maintain that membership as a condition of employment.

Management   Working with people to achieve objectives by effective decision making and coordinating available resources.

Management by exception   A supervisor focuses on critical control needs and allows employees to handle most routine deviations from the standard.

Management relations *or* industrial relations   These terms are often used to refer to the relationships between employers and their unionized employees.

Managerial functions   Broad classification of activities that all managers perform.

Marketing   Selling and distributing an organization's product or service.

Matrix departmentalization   A hybrid of form in which personnel from several specialties are brought together to complete limited-life tasks. It usually evolves from one or more of the other types of departmentalization and used in response to demands for unique blends of skill from different specialties in the organization.

Mediator   Tries to bring the parties together when collective bargaining reaches an impasse.

Mentor   An experienced manager who acts as an advocate and teacher for a younger, less experienced manager.

Mentoring   Helping others develop careers.

Messages   Words and/or nonverbal expressions that transmit meaning.

Middle management   Responsible for a substantial part of the organization.

Middle-of-the-road management   Places equal emphasis on people and production.

Minutes   A written record of the important points discussed and agreed on at a meeting.

Mission   Defines the purpose the organization serves and identifies its services, products, and customers.

Monetary standards   Expressed in dollars and cents.

Motivation   Willingness to work to achieve the organization's objectives.

Myers–Briggs Type Indicator® (MBTI®)   The MBTI helps identify an individual's personal style and is based on the work of scholar–physician Carl Gustav Jung. Isabel Myers and her mother, Katherine Briggs, further refined and added to the basic theory.

Network group   Network groups are dispersed and require collaboration and coordination across different projects and sometimes from groups outside the organization. The members' roles and responsibilities are based on connections, collaboration, and a targeted expertise.

Network structure   Sometimes referred to as a modular structure; includes a central business unit, or "hub," linked to a network of external suppliers and contractors.

Nominal grouping technique (NGT)   A structured group technique for generating ideas through round-robin individual responses, group sharing without criticism, and written balloting.

Nonexempt employees   Employees covered by the provisions of the Fair Labor Standards Act.

Nonprogrammed decisions   Decisions that occur infrequently and require a different response each time.

Norms   Rules of behavior developed by group members to provide guidance for group activities.

Numerical standards   Expressed in numbers.

Object signals   Nonverbal messages sent by physical objects.

Objectives   The purposes, goals, and desired results for the organization and its parts.

Occupational Safety and Health Administration (OSHA)   Federal Occupational Safety and Health Administration, created by the Occupational Safety and Health Act in 1970 to ensure safe working conditions for employees.

Operational planning   Consists of intermediate- and short-term planning.

Operations   Producing an organization's product or service.

Opportunity   A chance for development or advancement.

Organization   A group of people working together in a structured situation for a common objective.

Organizational effectiveness   The result of activities that improve the organization's structure, technology, and people.

Organizing   Deciding what activities are needed to reach goals and dividing human resources into work groups to achieve them.

Orientation   Procedures of familiarizing a new employee with the company surroundings, policies, and job responsibilities.

Pareto charts   Problem-analysis charts that use a histogram to illustrate sources of problems.

Participating and supporting style   Best used with ready individuals or groups.

Perception   How one selects, organizes, and gives meaning to his or her world.

Performance appraisal *or* **merit rating** *or* **efficiency rating** *or* **service rating** *or* **employee evaluation**   Determines to what extent an employee performs a job the way it was intended.

Personality tests   Measure the applicant's emotional adjustment and attitude.

Physical resources   Items an organization requires for operations.

Physical standards   Refer to quality, durability, size, and weight.

Physiological or biological need   The need for food, water, air, and other physical necessities.

Picketing   Walking back and forth outside the place of employment, usually carrying a sign.

Pinpointing   Providing specific, tangible information about performance to an employee.

Planning   Selecting future courses of action and deciding how to achieve the desired results.

Policy   Provides consistency among decision makers.

Power   The ability to influence individuals, groups, events, and decisions.

Prevailing wage rate   Approximates the union wage scale for the area in the given type of work.

Principled negotiation   Negotiation on the merits by separating the people from the problem; focusing on interests, not positions; generating a variety of possibilities before deciding what to do; and insisting the result be based on some objective standard.

Probing   Asking questions to obtain additional information.

Problem   An existing unsatisfactory situation causing anxiety or distress.

Problem-solving meeting   Held to identify the problem, discuss alternative solutions, and decide on the proper action to take.

Procedure   Steps to be performed when a particular course of action is taken.

Process consultation   A consultation model that involves others in making a joint diagnosis of the problem and eventually provides others with the skills and tools to make their own diagnoses.

Product departmentalization   A form of departmentalization that groups together all the functions associated with a single product line.

Productivity   Measure of efficiency (inputs to outputs).

Program   A large-scale plan composed of a mix of objectives, policies, rules, and projects.

Programmed decisions   Routine and repetitive decisions.

Progressive discipline   Discipline that uses a graduated scale of penalties.

Project   Individual or group work that is planned, organized, and implemented over a period of time.

Quality control   Defined measurements designed to check whether the desired quality standards are being met.

Radio frequency identification (RFID)   Technology that uses radio waves to identify inventory and other objects.

Readiness level   The state of a person's drive or need for achievement.

Receiver   The ultimate destination of the sender's message.

Reengineering   "It means starting over. . . . It means asking and answering this question: If I were creating this company today, given what I know and given current technology, what would it look like?" Rethinking and redesigning processes to improve dramatically cost, quality, service, and speed.

Reflecting   Stating your interpretation of what the employee has said.

Reflective statement   The listener repeats, in a summarizing way, what the speaker has just said.

Reframing   Examining the situation from multiple vantage points to develop a holistic picture.

Reinforcement theory   Based on the law of effect, holds that behaviors meeting with pleasant consequences tend to be repeated, whereas behaviors with unpleasant consequences tend not to be repeated, and rewards and punishments are used as a way to shape the individual.

Reinventing   Organizations dramatically changing such elements as their size, organizational structure, and markets.

Relationship behaviors   Providing people with support and asking for their opinions.

Relationships network   The major individuals and groups with whom the supervisor interacts.

Reliability   The probability that test results won't change if the test is given to the same person by different individuals.

Resourcing   Providing information, assistance, and advice to employees.

Responsibility   Occurs when key tasks associated with a particular job are specified. The obligation of an employee to accept a manager's delegated authority.

Reviewing   Reinforcing key points at the end of a coaching session to ensure common understanding.

Right-to-work laws   A state statute that prohibits union shops in the state. Protects the right of employees to join or refuse to join a union without being fired.

Risk   The possibility of defeat, disadvantage, injury, or loss.

Robot   A machine controlled by a computer that can be programmed to perform a number of repetitive manipulations of tools or materials.

Roles   Parts played by managers in the performance of their functions.

Rule   A policy that is invariably enforced. Rules are inflexible requirements and are much stronger than guidelines. It is important for supervisors to know when they can be flexible in promoting the objectives of their company and when they have to enforce rules.

Run chart   Data presentation showing results of a process plotted over time.

Safety or security need   The need for protection from danger, threat, or deprivation.

Satisfier or motivator factors   Factors employees said turned them on about their job, such as recognition, advancement, achievement, challenging work, and being one's own boss.

Scenario planning Anticipating alternative future situations and developing courses of action for each alternative.

Schedule A plan of activities to be performed and their timing.

Self-fulfillment or self-actualization need The need concerned with realizing one's potential, self-development, and creativity.

Self-managing work groups Groups that tend to operate by member consensus rather than management direction.

Sender Originates and sends a message.

Seniority An employee's length of service in a company; provides the basis for promotion and other benefits.

Servant leadership Defines success as giving and measures achievement by devotion to serving and leading. Winning becomes the creation of community through collaboration and team building.

Seven Types of Waste In a lean organization there are seven types of waste: overproduction, movement, transportation, waiting, extra processing, defects, and inventory.

Sexual harassment Sexual harassment is a particular type of discrimination in the workplace. A problem the courts consider to be a special form of disparate treatment discrimination.

Single-use plans Developed to accomplish a specific purpose and then discarded after use.

Situational Leadership® Model Shows the relationship between the readiness of followers and the leadership style.

Social or belonging need The need for belonging, acceptance by colleagues, friendship, and love.

Space signals Nonverbal messages sent based on physical distance between people.

Span of control principle States there is a limit to the number of people a person can supervise effectively.

Span of management The number of immediate employees a manager can supervise effectively.

Staff personnel Staff personnel use their expertise to assist the line people and aid top management in various areas of business activities.

Staffing Recruiting, training, promoting, and rewarding people to do the organization's work.

Standard A unit of measurement that serves as a reference point for evaluating results.

Standing plans or repeat-use plans Plans that are used repeatedly over a period of time.

Stereotyping The tendency to put similar things in the same categories to make them easier to deal with.

Strategic control point A performance measurement point located early in an activity to allow any corrective action to be taken.

Strategic planning Has longer time horizons, affects the entire organization, and deals with its interface to its external environment.

Strategies The activities by which the organization adapts to its environment to achieve its objectives.

Stress Any external stimulus that causes wear and tear on one's psychological or physical well-being.

Strike When employees withhold their services from an employer.

Structured interviews Standardized and controlled with regard to questions asked, sequence of questions, interpretation of replies, and weight given to factors considered in making the hiring decision.

Structuring and telling style Used with individuals or groups relatively less ready for a given task.

Summarizing Pausing in the coaching conversation to summarize key points.

Supervisory management Controls operations of smaller organizational units.

Synergy   The concept that two or more people working together in a cooperative, coordinated way can accomplish more than the sum of their independent efforts.

Tangible standards   Clear, concrete, specific, and generally measurable.

Task behaviors   Clarifying a job, telling people what to do and how and when to do it, providing follow-up, and taking corrective action.

Team   A collection of people who must rely on group cooperation.

Team advisors   Share responsibility with team for cost, quality, and prompt delivery of products.

Team management   High concern for both people and production.

Team structure   Utilizes permanent and temporary cross-functional teams to improve horizontal coordination and cooperation.

Technical skills   Understanding and being able to supervise effectively specific processes required.

Termination-at-will rule   Right of an employer to dismiss an employee for any reason.

Text message (TM)   A written message sent by cell phone and that typically uses abbreviations.

Theory X   A leadership style that is based on the assumption that the average person has an inherent dislike of work and wishes to avoid responsibility.

Theory Y   A leadership style that is based on the assumption that the average person exercises self-direction, self-control and a relatively high degree of ingenuity and creativity. Under proper conditions, the average person not only accepts but actively seeks greater responsibility.

Time management   Ability to use one's time to get things done when they should be done.

Time signals   Nonverbal messages sent by time actions.

Time standards   Expressed in terms of time.

Top management   Responsible for the entire or a major segment of the organization.

Total quality   Refers to an organization's overall effort to achieve customer satisfaction through continuous improvement of products or services.

Touching signals   Nonverbal messages sent by body contact.

Traditionalists   Workforce generation born before 1945.

Training   Training is the process by which employees are educated to improve their capabilities, competencies, productivity and/or performance.

Transactional leadership   Leaders identify desired performance standards and recognize what types of rewards employees want from their work.

Transformational leadership   Converts followers into leaders and may convert leaders into moral agents.

Tutoring   Helping team members gain knowledge, skill, and competency.

Type A behavior   Behavior pattern characterized by (a) trying to accomplish too much in a short time and (b) lacking patience and struggling against time and other people to accomplish one's ends.

Type B behavior   Behavior pattern characterized by (a) tending to be calmer than someone with Type A behavior, (b) devoting more time to exercise, and (c) being more realistic in estimating the time it takes to complete an assignment.

Unfair labor practices   Specific acts management may not commit against the workers and the union.

Unified planning   Coordinating departments to ensure harmony rather than conflict or competition.

Union authorization card   Authorizes a particular union to be an employee's collective bargaining representative.

Union shop All employees must join the union within a specified period after starting employment.

Union steward A union member elected by other members to represent their interests in relations with management.

Unity of command principle States that everyone should report to and be accountable to only one boss.

Upward communication Communication that flows from lower to upper organizational levels.

Validity A high positive correlation between the applicant's test scores and an objective measure of job performance.

Virtual group or team It is dislocated—and mostly, if not exclusively, meets online and can face the added challenges of different time zones, less frequent verbal communications, the lack of a physical presence, and any informal interactions that lead to social ties among more co-located groups.

Virtuoso groups Virtuoso groups are composed of top performers who excel in their respective specialties and are usually focused on important performance issues.

Vocational interest tests Determine the applicant's areas of major work interest.

Voice signals Signals sent by placing emphasis on certain words, pauses, or the tone of voice used.

Vroom–Yetton model The Vroom–Yetton model provides guidelines on the extent to which subordinates are involved in decision making or problem solving.

Wagon wheel An organization form with a hub, a series of spokes radiating from the hub, and the outer rim.

Work sampling or work preview A test the prospective employee must perform that is representative of the job.

5s Practices The 5S's are sort, straighten, shine, standardize, and sustain.

Index

A

AAA quality ratings, 426
AAPs. *See* Affirmative Action Programs (AAPs)
acceptance theory of authority, 135
accommodating (conflict management style), 364, 365f
accountability, 133
achievement test, 459
acknowledging (coaching skill), 340
action plan, to improve delegation, 139, 140f
active listening, 181, 368f
Acton, Dahlberg (Sir), 137
ADA. *See* Americans with Disabilities Act (ADA)
adaptive leadership, 243–246
administrative skills, 16
ADT, 161
advisory authority, 112
Affirmative Action Programs (AAPs), 457, 502
affirming (coaching skill), 340
AFL. *See* American Federation of Labor (AFL)
Aflac, 80
AFL-CIO, 484
Age Discrimination in Employment Act, 501t, 510
agency shop, 487
agenda planning, for meeting, 307f
AIG, 26
Allied Signal, 428
Allstate, 297
alternatives, 67, 68, 68f
American Equity Underwriters (AEU), 208
American Federation of Labor (AFL), 484, 489
American Institute of Stress, 379f
Americans with Disabilities Act (ADA), 461, 506, 508–510
Amos, Dan, 80
Andan, 419f
Apple, 60
Apple Computers
    CEO attire, 162

differentiation strategy at, 120
    network structure at, 119
application form, 457–458
appraisal interview, 465–467, 467f
aptitude tests, 459
arbitrator, 496
Argo, 78
Arthur Andersen, 26, 78, 80
Ashley Furniture, 119
A. T. Kearney, 116
ATP Oil and Gas, 207
attending (coaching skill), 340
attending skills, 181
Auburn National Bank, 71
Austin, Nancy, 119
authority
    acceptance theory of, 135
    as communication barrier, 168–169
    defined, 8, 133
    delegation of, 133
    delineating, in line-and-staff organization, 112–114
    formal theory of, 134
    role of, 133–136
    sources of, 134–136
    types of, 112–114
authority compliance, 232
authority-compliance management, 233f
authority–power combination, 137f
autonomy, 209
Average supervisors, 22–23
avoiding (conflict management style), 364, 365f

B

Baby Boomers, 212–213
Baldor Electric Company, 76
Bass, Bernard, 241
behavior
    assessing, as team member, 282f
    conflict, identifying, 368f
    coping with difficult, 369f
    disruptive and inappropriate meeting, 310t

fundamentals of, 192–197
    Type A and B, 374
    See also conduct, rules of
behavior-type quiz, 375f
benefits, legally required, 507–508
Benson, Herbert, 379f
Bernard L. Madoff Investment Securities, 26
Best Buy, reengineering at, 25
Bethlehem Steel, 14
Blake, Robert, 232
Blanchard, Kenneth H., 234
Bloom, Mark, 78
Bocelli, Andrea, 332
Bock, Lazlo, 332
body signals, 162
Boeing, 27, 105
Boise Cascade, 429
bona fide occupational qualification (B.F.O.Q.), 503
Boston Herald, The, 167
Bowater Carolina, 311
Boyatzis, Richard E., 253, 254f
Bradford, David L., 238–240
brainstorming, 75
Briggs, Katherine, 69
Brin, Sergey, 331
budgets, 50
Bulmahn, T. Paul, 207
Burckhartt, Jimmy, 240–241, 244, 250–251
Bureau of Labor Statistics Union Member Summary (2012), 484
    on workplace violence, 506
burnout, 376, 377f
Burns, John MacGregor, 241

C

CAM. *See* computer-assisted manufacturing (CAM)
Carnegie, Andrew, 140
Castro-Wright, Eduardo, 96
causal variables, 121f, 122
cause-and-effect diagram, 432, 433f